"*Special Revelation and Scripture* is certain to become a classic and standard in the study of the Bible. Its breadth is impressive and its research encyclopedic. Biblically, theologically, and historically, it gives the church what it needs to grasp the marvel and trustworthiness of God's divine revelation. What a gift!"
—**Daniel L. Akin**, president, Southeastern Baptist Theological Seminary

"Holy Scripture is God's great gift to the church, in which he reveals himself to us and tells us what his purposes are in his great works of creation and redemption. That revelation is fundamental to our spiritual life, and *Special Revelation and Scripture* gives us a comprehensive guide to understanding its nature. Pastors, students, and others will learn much from David Dockery and Malcolm Yarnell and will be better equipped to use God's Word for their own spiritual growth and for the upbuilding of the church in truth and love."
—**Gerald Bray**, research professor of divinity, Beeson Divinity School

"The doctrine of revelation in many ways grounds all Christian theological reflection. The triune God's disclosure of himself in the person and work of Jesus Christ and in the inspiration of Holy Scripture are what allow for theology in the first place. David Dockery and Malcolm Yarnell have carefully, ably, and systematically introduced and creatively engaged this fundamental doctrine from a distinctly Baptist perspective and for readers from all Christian traditions. *Special Revelation and Scripture* should be standard reading for those engaging in prolegomena, and especially with respect to the doctrine of Scripture."
—**Matthew Y. Emerson**, dean of theology, arts, and humanities, Oklahoma Baptist University

"Christians do not worship the Bible, but we do worship the God of the Bible. Thus it is imperative that we pay close attention to the doctrine of Holy Scripture, God's Word written. *Special Revelation and Scripture* presents a fulsome study of this critical issue and I commend it to seasoned scholars and young theologians alike. Thank you, David Dockery and Malcolm Yarnell, for this wonderful gift to the Lord's people everywhere!"
—**Timothy George**, distinguished professor, Beeson Divinity School

"David Dockery and Malcolm Yarnell have served faithfully in Christian higher education for decades. This volume contains their mature reflections on the foundational doctrines of special revelation and Scripture. Steeped in and founded on Scripture, each chapter of *Special Revelation and Scripture* interacts with the writings of a wide range of Christian thinkers to present the triune

God revealing himself to humanity—chiefly through Scripture's disclosure of Jesus Christ. The result is a reliable study from trustworthy scholars."

—**Adam Harwood**, McFarland Chair of Theology, New Orleans Baptist Theological Seminary

"When it comes to the doctrine of Scripture, conservative evangelicals face the challenge of needing to write the same book every generation or so, to restate and refresh their confession about the Bible. We are fortunate that David Dockery and Malcolm Yarnell have taken up this noble task today. Their deep curiosity, firm conviction, long memory, lively pastoral instinct, and courageous interdisciplinarity make *Special Revelation and Scripture* a powerful new statement on revelation and Scripture. Its integration of systematic theology and exegesis will make it an especially formative volume for students."

—**Fred Sanders,** professor of theology at the Torrey Honors College, Biola University

"Many Christians today have lost confidence in the Bible to address our contemporary context and our most basic and enduring needs. *Special Revelation and Scripture* shows that knowing God in the fullest sense, and knowing his purposes for the world he created, comes from what he himself has graciously made known and is ultimately grounded in his triune nature and character. This very significant book by David Dockery and Malcolm Yarnell is full of faith, an astonishingly broad scholarship (while remaining resolutely Baptist), deep insight and pastoral wisdom. Highly recommended!"

—**Mark D. Thompson**, principal, Moore Theological College, Sydney, Australia

"David Dockery and Malcolm Yarnell provide an excellent exposition of what Baptists and other evangelical Christians have believed for centuries: that the Bible 'has God for its author, salvation for its end, and truth, without any mixture of error, for its matter.' *Special Revelation and Scripture* also provides a short course in the history of biblical interpretation and another in how Christians should interpret, use, and apply the Bible today. I especially appreciated their concern to add to their grammatical-historical exegesis canonical context, and to canonical context, Rule of Faith, and to Rule of Faith, Christology and theological interpretation. Readers who follow their guidance will become productive in their knowledge of Jesus Christ (2 Pet 1:5–8)."

—**Kevin J. Vanhoozer**, research professor of systematic theology, Trinity Evangelical Divinity School

SPECIAL
REVELATION
AND
SCRIPTURE

SPECIAL REVELATION AND SCRIPTURE

David S. Dockery & Malcolm B. Yarnell III

EDITORS

David S. Dockery | *Nathan A. Finn* | *Christopher W. Morgan*

B&H
ACADEMIC
BRENTWOOD, TENNESSEE

CONTENTS

PREFACE

The doctrine of special revelation and the role of Holy Scripture have been central to the Christian faith for two thousand years. Due to the Bible's importance in providing clarification during the Reformation and in fostering the development of evangelicalism, as well as for its centrality in Baptist life and in our own lives, it is our prayer that this volume will serve this current generation in a helpful way by fostering a love for the Word of God. Following the theological method of our teacher, James Leo Garrett Jr., we have attempted to give serious attention first to the Bible's own teaching about revelation and Scripture and then to the development of thought regarding these matters throughout Christian history. Several of our chapters are significantly informed by Christian thinkers in the universal church.

The Bible is the best-selling book in all human history and has been translated into more languages than any other book. Yet, the nature, authority, and interpretation of the Bible continue to be discussed and debated. Reflecting debates around the truthfulness, authority, and sufficiency of Scripture, strident controversies continue in both church and society. The Christian's views of Scripture, including its inspiration, reliability, and authority, inform and shape the Christian's understanding of many theological doctrines, ethical teachings, and worldview issues. It remains essential for followers of Christ to recognize and use the Bible as the primary source for spiritual formation, strength, nurture, and guidance for faithful living, both as individuals and in community with other believers.

We are honored to contribute this volume to the Theology for the People of God series and are grateful to series editors Chris Morgan and Nathan Finn for their invitation. In addition, we would like to express our gratitude to Madison Trammel, Michael McEwen, Jessi Wallace, and Audrey Greeson at B&H Academic. We join with many others in trusting that the volumes in this series will be used of God in a positive way to equip and build up the church of the Lord Jesus Christ. All the contributors to this series share our commitment to the Bible as the prophetic-apostolic word, God's Word written. Without the Holy Spirit's inspiration of the prophets and the apostles, there would be no Scripture and therefore no certain Word of God available to us today. This calls for a renewed commitment in every generation to the Bible's full truthfulness, sole authority, and supreme sufficiency. With our colleagues and co-contributors to this multivolume series, we gladly affirm the Bible is trustworthy, dependable, infallible, and inerrant.

While this book is designed as a classroom resource, it is our hope that it will also serve pastors, denominational leaders, and those who serve with parachurch organizations. We, moreover, invite faithful church members who serve as Sunday school teachers, small group leaders, and guides for various groups in the churches to read this volume. Of course, we have primarily written with college and seminary students in mind, even as we pray the book will serve the evangelical and Baptist communities who seek to navigate the various challenges found in our twenty-first-century context in a faithful way. We pray the church of Jesus Christ will be edified through this study.

We offer heartfelt gratitude to God for making himself known to us and for giving his self-revelation to his people. We recognize that times and cultures change, but the basic needs shared by all men and women of all ages and ethnicities in all times and cultures remain the same. God's Word is normative, authoritative, and applicable as much for the people of God in the twenty-first century as for people in the first century. We have attempted to note some contemporary applications throughout the book, particularly in the final chapter. The volume builds on some portions of our previous work, but we have attempted to rewrite and reframe each topic in a way that will serve well this series. Each chapter has been co-authored in the sense that each one of us contributed aspects to each chapter and then edited and revised the work of the other.

Our commitments regarding Scripture point to the Bible's authority which speaks to the spiritual needs of women and men, but more importantly, we affirm the Bible reveals the truth of and about God. All Scripture is inspired by him and thus remains the true, reliable Word of God for the community of faith. We ask that as you read this volume you will join with us in renewing your personal trust and confidence in the truthful and authoritative Word of God.

We express our profound gratitude to O. S. Hawkins, Danny Roberts, and the Board of Trustees of Southwestern Baptist Theological Seminary for their support throughout this project, including the sabbatical granted so Malcolm could dedicate time to it. We appreciate the encouragement we have felt from our Southwestern faculty colleagues, particularly Jeff Bingham, Madison Grace, Michael Wilkinson, and Travis Trawick, our colleagues in the School of Theology's department of theology. We are truly thankful for the wonderful assistance provided by Wang Yong Lee and Chris Kim, two of our advanced graduate students, who are both fine theologians in their own rights. Appreciation is also expressed to Lakeside Baptist Church, whose people heard various lessons which made their way into this volume, and to Todd Still and the Truett Seminary of Baylor University for kindly granting the use of a spacious flat at the University of Oxford for Malcolm's research. We are deeply grateful for the support of our families through the months devoted to this project, especially to Lanese Dockery and Karen Yarnell, who have prayed and offered support through yet another writing project.

We trust this volume will be helpful for many and that it will please our gracious, loving, and merciful triune God.

Soli Deo Gloria
David S. Dockery and Malcolm B. Yarnell III

INTRODUCTION

In recent centuries Christians have discussed and debated the nature of Scripture, often in relation to strident controversies in both church and culture, controversies which challenge the place of biblical authority.[1] Hot-item intellectual, ethical, and social questions facing the church today, such as abortion and same-sex marriage, or postmodernism and new age mysticism, point to a wide gap between the teachings of Holy Scripture and opposing beliefs held in society. Struggles over Scripture's message about these matters likewise roil various Christian denominations across the globe and draw in major sectors of the broader culture. To help Christians respond to these and similar crises, it is vitally important that we recover a correct view of divine revelation. We must learn again to relate the Word of God to our day-to-day concerns, not only with regard for pressing cultural issues but just as importantly with regard for the ongoing and vital Christian needs for proper worship of God, affective piety in religious practice, and winsome proclamation of the saving gospel of Jesus Christ.

With these great needs in mind, in this introduction we offer a brief overview of certain key aspects of the doctrine of revelation which require deeper exploration later in this volume for the purpose of addressing contemporary crises. This introduction begins with appreciation for the special nature of Scripture given through its inspiration by the Holy Spirit, proceeds through a summary of various attendant perfections of Scripture, and ends with an affirmation of the need for the Holy Spirit to bring illumination to

---

[1] See D. A. Carson, "Recent Developments in the Doctrine of Scripture," in *Collected Writings on Scripture* (Wheaton: Crossway, 2010), 55–110; also, G. K. Beale, *The Erosion of Inerrancy in Evangelicalism: Responding to New Challenges to Biblical Authority* (Wheaton: Crossway, 2008).

Scripture so that the church may develop its theology and practices. A similar movement of subject matter may be found in the latter half of this book.

However, the trained eye will note the structure of this book first develops the doctrine of divine revelation according to a convictional trinitarian frame: Chapters 1 through 4 delve into the ontology and economy of God's revelation of the truth of himself in the major ways of general revelation and special revelation. Chapter 5 then focuses upon the foundational relationship between the Second Person of the Trinity, our incarnate Lord and Savior Jesus Christ, and Sacred Scripture. We believe the full humanity and full deity of the eternal and personal Word of God, Jesus Christ, provides a helpful analogy for viewing the written Word of God as simultaneously a divine and human book. Next, chapters 6 and 7 consider the work of the Third Person of the Trinity, the Holy Spirit, in the inspiration of the prophetic and apostolic writings and in the preservation of these texts in the biblical canon. The first part of the book thus demonstrates how divine revelation comes by the grace of God the Trinity, discloses the Trinity, and promises the blessed vision of the Trinity. The Bible is properly understood as the revealed Word of the one true God who is the Father and the Son and the Holy Spirit.

After establishing the theological foundation of divine revelation, we then consider various truths which relate divine revelation to its recipients. In chapters 8 and 9 we ponder the biblical text's attributes. The attributes or perfections of Scripture, which are grounded in Scripture's relation to the perfect God through inspiration by the Holy Spirit, include its truthfulness, inerrancy, sufficiency, and authority. Afterwards, as with the original inspiration of the biblical text by the Holy Spirit, we must also rehearse his illumination of the text for its readers. We begin our discussion of the Spirit's illuminating work with an extended survey of the church's historical reception of the sacred writings. Chapters 10 and 11 trace the ways in which Christians throughout the history of the church have developed the reading of Scripture for theology and proclamation. Chapter 12 narrows the focus to our own Baptist tradition's convictions about the Bible. In the concluding chapter, we review how Christians today should interpret Scripture for appropriate understanding of the text's original meaning and contemporary significance, as well as for its practical application.

The general narrative of this book traces the revelation of God the Trinity through history and Scripture to the contemporary church: In ancient times,

God manifested himself through the grace of revelation directly to Israel in specific times and places culminating in the height of his self-revelation in the person of Jesus the Messiah. Since then, God has continued to reveal the person and work of Christ through the special grace of his written revelation of himself by the inspiration of the Holy Spirit. Today, the Holy Spirit's grace of illumination is required for our understanding, appropriation, and application of this revelation of Scripture. In his economy of revelation God directly manifested himself in the historic person of Jesus Christ and continues to reveal him by his Holy Spirit through Scripture to bring about human regeneration. We thus believe it is imperative that God's people apprehend God's special revelation in Christ and Scripture so that through the Holy Spirit human beings may receive the gift of faith for salvation.

I. The Bible Is a Special Book

The Bible describes itself as a special book. Even before the canonization of the sacred texts, importance was attached to the prophetic and apostolic writings. Moses wrote "all the words of the LORD" in the "covenant scroll" (Exod 24:4, 7). Joshua's farewell address was written "in the book of the law of God" (Josh 24:26). Samuel spoke words about the manner of the kingdom and "wrote them on a scroll, which he placed in the presence of the LORD" (1 Sam 10:25). Jesus repeatedly appealed to the authoritative Scriptures (see Matt 5:17–18; 19:4; 22:29). Similarly, Paul and the apostles thought of the scrolls as the "very words of God" (Rom 3:2).

Jesus himself declared that Scripture is the Word of God which cannot be broken (John 10:35). Similarly, the apostles noted it is "the prophetic word strongly confirmed" which the prophets and apostles wrote, because these words were spoken from God as the writers "were carried along by the Holy Spirit" (2 Pet 1:19–21). The Bible itself thus acknowledges that the prophetic-apostolic word is God's Word written. Without the sacred writings there would be no Holy Scripture and therefore no Word of God available to us.[2]

---

[2] Donald G. Bloesch, *Holy Scripture: Revelation, Inspiration & Interpretation* (Downers Grove: IVP, 1994), 49–56.

The Bible affirms God has made himself known in a variety of ways (Ps 19:1; Heb 1:2). Thankfully, God has not abandoned us to our own devices but has manifested himself to us. We know him not due to our seeking him, but because he has made himself known to us. God has acted and spoken in history. The word "revelation" means an uncovering, a removal of the veil, a disclosure of what was previously not known. More specifically, revelation is God's manifestation of himself to humankind in such a way that men and women can know and have fellowship with him.[3] In recognition of the human predicament, God chose from the beginning to make himself known within time and space. He disclosed himself in both acts and works, primarily in a personal way and with a redemptive purpose. Through miracles, the Exodus, and ultimately in Jesus Christ, God has revealed himself in human history. This divine revelation includes not only the Lord's acts in history, but also the prophetic-apostolic interpretation of these events. Thus, we must also say that God's revelation is not merely personal but also propositional, in that it communicates truths about God to his people. While there is tension between these two aspects of revelation, we affirm that revelation is both knowledge about God and knowledge of God. Revelation is knowledge about God which leads us to know God in a personal and salvific way. We give this matter greater attention in the next chapter.

Revelation is also often and properly discussed in two different categories: general revelation and special revelation. General revelation is universal in the sense that it is always God's self-disclosure of himself in a general way to all people in all places. General revelation occurs through nature, through human experience and conscience, and in history. God's general revelation of himself is plain, though it is often misinterpreted because through it sinful and finite humans are trying to understand a perfect and infinite God. General revelation discloses God clearly enough to sinful human beings that they are held accountable for their responses to it. Therefore, no one can be excused for missing God's revelation (Rom 1:20; 3:20).[4] Further elaboration of general revelation and special revelation will occur in chapter 2.

---

[3] Millard J. Erickson, *Christian Theology* (Grand Rapids: Baker, 2013), 153–98. This introductory chapter has adapted several key thoughts from Erickson.

[4] David S. Dockery, *Christian Scripture: An Evangelical Perspective on Inspiration, Authority, and Interpretation* (Nashville: B&H, 1995), 15–36.

The light of nature, including conscience, is not sufficient to import the knowledge of God necessary for salvation. What is needed to understand God's self-disclosure fully is his special revelation. Indeed, special revelation provides the viewpoint through which we can understand and appreciate God's general revelation.[5] Divine truth exists outside special revelation, but it is consistent with and supplemental to, not a substitute for, special revelation. General revelation is consistent with special revelation, yet distinct from it. In contrast to God's general revelation, which is available to all people, God's special revelation is available to particular people at specific times in particular places. Special revelation is not only particular, but progressive, and not only propositional, but personal. The content of special revelation is primarily God himself, his works, and his Word.[6] It is the declaration of truth about God, his character, and his actions and relationship with his creation. God is pleased to reveal himself and his majestic Word to people of faith.[7] God's Word, recorded and interpreted by the prophets and the apostles, calls for us to embrace, with humility and teachable hearts and without finding fault, whatever is taught in Holy Scripture. God is ontologically truth, and his Word is epistemologically true. We will discuss these themes in greater detail in chapters 3 and 4.

II. God and His Purposes

The Bible presents a message about God and his purposes. It describes the creation of the universe, including the direct creation of man and woman in a paradise on earth. The Bible describes the call of Abraham, the giving of the Law, the establishment of the kingdom, the division of the kingdom, and the captivity and restoration of Israel. Scripture sees humankind as fallen from a sinless condition and separated from God. The promise of a coming Messiah who will redeem men and women and reign as King appears throughout the Old Testament. The message of the Word of God promises

[5] John Feinberg, *Light in a Dark Place: The Doctrine of Scripture* (Wheaton: Crossway, 2018), 111–50; Bernard Ramm, *Special Revelation and the Word of God* (Grand Rapids: Eerdmans, 1961).

[6] Carl F. H. Henry, *God, Revelation, and Authority*, 6 vols. (Waco: Word, 1976–83).

[7] Bloesch, *Holy Scripture*, 46–77.

that believers are restored to favor with God through the vicarious sacrifice of Jesus Christ.[8]

The confession of Jesus as Christ the Lord, the Son of the living God and the Savior of the world, is at the heart of the Christian faith. The message about Christ is central to the content of the Christian faith, because it is central to the content of Holy Scripture.[9] Contemporary Christians must not only affirm this message but also affirm the Bible's inspiration, truthfulness, and normative nature, because it is the bearer of this message. Amid the historical challenges to biblical authority, we need to evince our concern for biblical authority by careful biblical interpretation, thoughtful theological reflection, faithful proclamation, genuine repentance, and ongoing prayer. A confession that the Bible is fully inspired and totally truthful is important because it is the foundation which establishes the complete extent of the Scripture's authority. Followers of Jesus Christ must choose to articulate a view of the Bible that is faithful to and in continuity with the consensus of historic positions in the church, and the church has characteristically confessed the Bible to be the written Word of God.[10] Building on these foundational commitments, we can relate to one another in love and humility, fostering truth, fellowship, and community. This will result not only in affirmations of Christian orthodoxy but also in right practice before a watching world. The middle section of this book will address these important aspects of Scripture.

III. Inspired by God

Through the superintending influence of God's Holy Spirit upon the writers of Holy Scripture, the account and interpretation of God's revelation has

---

[8] See John R. W. Stott, *The Incomparable Christ* (Downers Grove: IVP, 2004); Richard Averbeck, *The Old Testament Law for the Life of the Church: Reading the Torah in Light of Christ* (Downers Grove: IVP, 2022); Eric Tully, *Reading the Prophets as Christian Scripture: A Literary, Canonical, and Theological Interpretation* (Grand Rapids: Baker, 2022).

[9] John Wenham, *Christ and the Bible* (Eugene, OR: Wipf & Stock, 2009).

[10] Jason G. Duesing and Nathan A. Finn, *Historical Theology for the Church* (Nashville: B&H, 2021), 71–88, 161–84, 185–206, 251–72.

been recorded as God intended so that the Bible is truly the Word of God.[11] In their sacred writings, the men of God used their own languages and the literary forms which were typical of their day. Yet, within this very human activity, God was at work, conveying his Word through their words. God's inspired Word came to us through human authors. It is even possible to see different personalities, styles, vocabularies, and purposes represented among the various prophets and apostles. Yet, the final product of their writings is equally the inspired Word of God.[12]

In the history of the church, the divine character of Scripture has been the great presupposition for the whole of Christian teaching, preaching, worship, and service.[13] This is readily apparent in the way the New Testament speaks about the Old Testament. As we will see in this volume, that which appears in the Old Testament is cited in the New Testament with formulas like "God said," and "the Holy Spirit says" (Acts 4:24–25; 13:47; 2 Cor 6:16). Scripture and God are so closely joined together in the minds of the New Testament authors that they could speak of Scripture doing what it records God as doing (Gal 3:8; Rom 9:17). The introductory phrase "it stands written" is used as a stamp of authority on both the Old and New Testament writings. Because of the divine origin and content of the prophetic-apostolic writings, Scripture can be described as certain and trustworthy (1 Pet 1:24–25; 2 Pet 1:19). As a result, those who build their lives on Scripture will never be put to shame (1 Pet 2:6). The Word was written for our instruction and encouragement (Rom 15:4), to lead to saving faith (2 Tim 3:15), to guide people toward godliness (2 Tim 3:16b), and to equip believers for good works (2 Tim 3:17).

Second Timothy 3:16–17 focuses primarily on the product of inspiration, the final writing of Scripture, though it also includes secondary aspects of the purpose and process. What is being asserted is the activity of God throughout the entire process, so that the completed, final product ultimately comes from him. As we have previously noted, it is a mistake to think of

---

[11] Dockery, *Christian Scripture*, 61–75.

[12] See Feinberg, *Light in a Dark Place*.

[13] Regarding the recent challenges to this great presupposition, see the sections on critical exegesis, the higher critical method, and critical biblical theology in chapter 11.

inspiration only in terms of the time when the Spirit moved human authors to write. The biblical concept of inspiration allows for the activity of the Spirit in special ways in the process without requiring that we restrict all aspects of the Spirit's working to one and the same way. In the process of the creation and preservation of the universe, God providentially intervened in special ways for special purposes.[14] Likewise, alongside and within his super-intending action of the biblical writings, we can discern a special work of the Spirit in bringing God's revelation to the apostles and prophets. God's Spirit is involved both in revealing specific messages to the prophets (Jer 1:1–9) and in guiding the authors throughout the historical aspects of their research (Luke 1:1–4).

We can assert that inspiration extends to the choice of words even though Scripture's meaning is located at the sentence level and beyond. Thus, our understanding of inspiration affirms the dual nature of Holy Scripture; it is simultaneously a divine book and a human book; it is a divine-human book. This recognition allows us to have a healthy understanding of the diverse literary genres represented in Scripture. The Holy Spirit is the One who, in a profound mystery for which the incarnation of Jesus Christ provides the only analogy, causes the verbal witness of the biblical writers to coincide with God's witness to himself.[15] Sometimes we think of divine action and human action as mutually exclusive. If God did something, humans did not do it. But this is not the case; some actions can be simultaneously fully human and fully divine.

Our approach to inspiration attempts to take seriously the human factors in the composition of the Bible, what we and others have described as "concursive inspiration." This approach avoids any hint that God mechanically dictated the words of Scripture to the human authors, so that they had no real part in the Scripture's composition.[16] A concursive understanding of

---

[14] I. Howard Marshall, *Biblical Inspiration* (Grand Rapids: Eerdmans, 1982).

[15] David S. Dockery, "The Inerrancy and Authority of Scripture: Affirmations and Clarifications," *Theological Educator* 37 (Fall 1988): 15–36.

[16] John R. Rice was perhaps one of the few fundamentalists who seemed to affirm mechanical dictation. See Rice, *Our God-Breathed Book* (Murfreesboro, TN: Sword of the Lord, 1969), 192–287. Otherwise, it is hard to find anyone who advocates for such a position among evangelicals or fundamentalists, even though it is often the caricatured position from some moderate and progressive voices.

inspiration allows for a viewpoint that gladly confesses that God's purpose is accomplished through the human writers, but the emphasis of the Spirit's work remains finally focused on the product of inspiration, the inscripturated Word of God.[17] In the chapters which focus on Jesus Christ and the Bible, the divine-human authorship of Scripture, and the inspiration of the Bible, we will seek to unpack these themes, showing their relationship to one another.

IV. The Perfections of Scripture

Although the cultural background and environment have radically changed since the biblical writings were penned, the human condition has not changed. It is to the human condition—of men and women created in the image of God who have yet fallen—that the unity of the biblical message speaks in a normative manner. The Scriptures are the result of divine inspiration. These prophetic-apostolic writings make known the saving acts of God, to which they are historically proximate. Based on these observations, we conclude in this volume that the inspired Scriptures are normative, truthful, trustworthy, and reliable (Psalm 119). Moreover, we affirm the Bible's total truthfulness or "inerrancy," as well as its coherence, its overall unity, and its clarity made possible by the witness of the Holy Spirit.[18]

The Bible focuses on Christ, is applicable to the church, and is affirmed to us by the testimony of the Spirit of God in our hearts.[19] This understanding of the Bible's inspiration and truthfulness applies to all canonical Scripture and includes the process of its development, the purpose of its construction, and ultimately its final product. We also assert that by the

---

[17] We distinguish the personal Word of God, the Son, who is ontologically God, from the written Word of God, the Bible, whose words communicate truth from God. This distinction is explored more fully in chapters 5 and 6 below. Cf. R. Albert Mohler Jr., "When the Bible Speaks, God Speaks: The Classic Doctrine of Biblical Inerrancy," in *Five Views on Biblical Inerrancy*, ed. J. Merrick and S. M. Garrett (Grand Rapids: Zondervan, 2013), 39.

[18] George J. Zemek, *The Word of God in the Child of God: Exegetical, Theological, and Homiletical Reflections from the 119th Psalm* (Eugene, OR: Wipf & Stock, 2005); D. L. Baker, *Two Testaments, One Bible: The Theological Relationship Between the Old and New Testaments*, rev. ed. (1976; Downers Grove: IVP, 1993).

[19] Bloesch, *Holy Scripture*, 117–30.

concursive action of God the Scriptures are, in their entirety, both the work of the Spirit and the work of human authors.[20] Moreover, we believe that Scripture speaks not only to spiritual matters but to the truth about God and its ramifications affecting all matters related to life and godliness. We have full confidence in the inspired, inerrant, and infallible Scriptures as remaining the trustworthy, dependable, reliable, and authoritative Word of God.[21] Those chapters which engage the topics of inspiration and canonicity, as well as those chapters which address Scripture's attributes of truthfulness, authority, and sufficiency are therefore central to the purpose of the book.

A view of the Bible that affirms its verbal inspiration and total truthfulness is of little value if it is not accompanied by an enthusiastic commitment to the Bible's complete and absolute authority. An approach to the subject of biblical authority must begin with God himself, for in God all authority is finally located. God is his own authority; there is nothing outside him on which his authority is established. When God made his promise to Abraham, he pledged his own name because nothing or no one was greater by whom he could swear (Heb 6:13). God's authority is the authority of who and what God is. Who God is in himself has been made known in his self-manifestation, since God can be known only via his self-revelation.[22] The key to perceiving God's authority must refer to his revelation. In this manner revelation and authority are seen as two sides of the same reality. God declares his authority in his revelation, and he alone is the ultimate source of authority for all other lesser authorities.[23] Therefore, of greatest concern in any discussion of the Bible is its authority, its rightful role to command obedience.

---

[20] Regarding the various theories of inspiration and our advocacy and definition of concursive inspiration, please see chapter 7 below.

[21] Carl F. H. Henry, "The Authority and Inspiration of the Bible," *Expositor's Bible Commentary*, ed. F. E. Gaebelein, 12 vols. (Grand Rapids: Zondervan, 1979), 1:13; Erickson, *Christian Theology*, 215–20.

[22] Our knowledge of God includes only what he wants us to know about him. We see God now as through opaque glass, both reflected and limited (1 Cor 13:12).

[23] D. Jeffrey Bingham, "Biblical Inspiration, Authority, and Canonicity," in *Theology, Church, and Ministry*, ed. David S. Dockery (Nashville: B&H, 2017), 93–114.

Any discussion of biblical authority must also include the doctrines of the clarity of Scripture and the sufficiency of Scripture. The doctrine of the clarity of Scripture affirms that the Bible can be understood, with the Spirit's enablement, by readers who earnestly seek to hear from and follow God. The Bible is clear enough to guide faithfully those who seek its wisdom (Ps 119:105).[24] An affirmation of scriptural clarity should not be understood to mean that all parts are equally clear. Nor does the doctrine suggest there is nothing in the Bible that is difficult to understand. Even the apostle Peter admitted as much when he wrote that some things in Paul's letters present challenges (2 Pet 3:16). Affirming the Bible's clarity does not mean that the Scripture does not need to be studied, interpreted, and taught to others (Acts 17:11; 2 Tim 2:15; 2 Tim 3:15). Maintaining the clarity of Scripture insists on and magnifies the role of the Holy Spirit in interpretation. As Donald Bloesch observes, "Scripture is clear when we submit to its authority and live in the light of its promises."[25]

Illumination is that work of the Holy Spirit, subsequent to the Bible's inspiration, whereby he makes the Bible understandable and applicable to the reader (1 Cor 2:14). Apart from the work of the Spirit, the reader will not grasp the meaning, power, and significance of the biblical text. Robert Plummer notes that "the Spirit brings to the Christian greater cognitive understanding of the biblical text."[26] When followers of Christ approach the Scriptures with the humble desire to listen, learn, and obey, and are willing to work hard to interpret the meaning of the biblical passage, they can obtain sufficient understanding of Scripture by grace.[27] The Spirit impresses upon the conscience of believers that the teachings of Scripture are indeed true, applicable, and incumbent on the reader. Mark Strom insightfully suggests that in and through the reading of Scripture, "the Spirit's presence and ministry assures us of our union with Jesus, or his Father's acceptance of us, and

---

[24] David S. Dockery, "Special Revelation," in *A Theology for the Church*, rev. ed., ed. Daniel L. Akin (Nashville: B&H, 2014), 145–53.

[25] Bloesch, *Holy Scripture*, 193.

[26] Robert L. Plummer, *40 Questions about Interpreting the Bible* (Grand Rapids: Kregel, 2010), 144.

[27] Wayne Grudem, *Systematic Theology* (Grand Rapids: Zondervan, 1994), 105–11; John M. Frame, *The Doctrine of the Word of God* (Phillipsburg: P&R, 2010).

of the reality of the kingdom to which we now belong as he changes us into the image of Jesus (Rom 8:12–27; Gal 5:22)."[28]

The Bible is not only clear and authoritative, but also sufficient for living faithfully before God.[29] The Bible is not only sufficient but is vital and necessary as enabled by God's Spirit to know God, to believe the gospel, and to obey the Lord in all areas of life.[30] The doctrine of the sufficiency of Scripture states that God, who exclusively possesses sufficiency in himself, has endowed his Word with what is needed for believers to accomplish the work and will of God. Wayne Grudem defines the doctrine of sufficiency this way: "The sufficiency of Scripture means that Scripture contained all the words of God he intended his people to have at each stage of redemptive history and that it now contains all the words of God we need for salvation, for trusting him perfectly, and for obeying him perfectly."[31] We agree with Grudem's basic definition but have much more to say in this regard.

In a potent passage, the prophet Isaiah reminds us that from eternity God invests his Word with effective power and sends it to accomplish his own will (Isa 55:11). The apostle John further reveals the profound mystery that Jesus Christ is both "Word" and "God" who became a human being (John 1:1, 14). Both John and the author of Hebrews inform us that the Bible is "the Word of God" in written form (John 10:35; Heb 4:12). As James Leo Garrett Jr. concluded, "the Bible is at the same time the Word of God and the words of human beings."[32] Of course, we must carefully distinguish between the

---

[28] Mark Strom, *The Symphony of Scripture: Making Sense of the Bible's Many Themes* (Downers Grove: IVP, 1990), 212.

[29] Mark D. Thompson, *The Doctrine of Scripture: An Introduction* (Wheaton: Crossway, 2022).

[30] Robert Saucy, *Scripture: Its Power, Authority, and Relevance* (Nashville: Thomas Nelson, 2001).

[31] Grudem, *Systematic Theology*, 127. John Frame observes, "Scripture contains more specific information relevant to theology than to dentistry. But sufficiency in the present context is not sufficiency of specific information but sufficiency of divine words, words that the theologian needs. So, it is just as sufficient for plumbing as it is for theology. And in that sense, it is sufficient for science and ethics as well." Frame, *The Doctrine of the Word of God*, 221.

[32] James Leo Garrett Jr., *Systematic Theology: Biblical, Historical, and Evangelical*, 2nd ed., 2 vols. (Grand Rapids: Eerdmans, 1990), 1:182.

incarnate Word of God and the written Word of God. The incarnate Word is the person of Jesus Christ who was sent from the Father and appeared to the apostles. The written Word is the coordinate testimony of the prophets, apostles, and the Holy Spirit, who was given by Jesus Christ to the apostles. Jesus promised the testimony of the Spirit would inform the testimony of the apostles. The Spirit later reminded them not only of what Jesus previously taught but told them more than they were able to receive before Christ's death and resurrection (John 14:25–26; 15:16–17; 16:12–14).

Because God is sufficient in himself, we know his self-revelation is sufficient to speak through his people and make their words sufficient for that which God designs. Sufficiency is ascribed in the New Testament as a first principle to God. The grace of sufficiency can be detected as it proceeds from God to the church through the apostles' ministry (2 Cor 3:5–6). The ministry of the apostles does not derive from their own competence. As with all Christian ministers, the competence must come from above by divine grace rather than from within by human nature. The sufficiency of the apostolic ministry is a gift of grace from God himself. This grace accompanies the minister's proclamation of the gospel of Jesus Christ through the powerful working of the Holy Spirit. Our confidence in God and his work has nothing whatsoever to do with human abilities. Rather, our confidence results from knowing the grace of God's Spirit accompanies the apostolic words to make them sufficient to accomplish God's will and reveal God's incarnate Word, Jesus Christ.[33]

God's written Word is sufficient to accomplish the task for which God sends it. Regarding the divine purpose and divine power of Holy Scripture, the apostle Paul writes, "And you know that from infancy you have known the sacred Scriptures, which are able to give you wisdom for salvation through faith in Jesus Christ. All Scripture is inspired by God and is profitable for teaching, for rebuking, for correcting, for training in righteousness, so that the man of God may be complete, equipped for every good work" (2 Tim 3:15–17). God inspired Scripture, intending that it would, first, bring "wisdom for salvation" and, second, bring "righteousness" for entire sanctification and good works. Scripture is powerful and profitable

---

[33] Mark D. Thompson, "The Sufficient Word," in *Tend My Sheep: The Word of God and Pastoral Ministry*, ed. Keith G. Condie (London: Latimer Trust, 2016), 27–44.

for the proclamation of salvation and for the completion of holiness, God-honoring communal edification, and human flourishing, being equipped for every good work.

The sufficiency of Scripture is an extremely important, foundational, and necessary doctrine.[34] Still, we are reminded that Scripture does not provide exhaustive teaching. For example, Scripture does not speak to everything about creation. Nor does an affirmation of scriptural sufficiency imply that creeds and confessions are not necessary. Sufficiency reminds us that creeds and confessions must derive from Scripture. The Bible is thereby the primary and sufficient means of God's authoritative self-disclosure for people today. The authority of Jesus Christ is exercised over the church (Eph 1:20–23) and is uniquely expressed through his personal ambassadors, the apostles (Mark 3:14; John 17:18; Acts 1:1–8; 2 Cor 5:20; Gal 1:1–2:9). In this way the apostles serve as the foundation for the church with Christ as the cornerstone (Eph 2:20–3:5; 1 Pet 2:6). In fulfillment of Christ's promises (John 14:26; 16:13), the apostles' authority has been placed permanently in their writings.

Thus, the Holy Spirit of God has inspired the prophetic-apostolic writings, and the Scriptures have become the recognized authority to communicate God's truth. Holy Scripture is to be taught, believed, confessed, and obeyed. The Bible, then, is the book of God's truth. Because the Bible is completely truthful and trustworthy, it is our final authority in all things that pertain to life and godliness. Garrett adds these thoughts: "The authority of the Bible is that of the sovereign God, who commands and persuades but does not coerce human beings and who redeems or liberates but does not enslave human beings."[35]

V. Illumined by God

The Bible is to be seen as the ultimate standard of authority for God's people, because of the Holy Spirit's inspiration of it. The Bible's authority is

---

[34] John MacArthur, "The Sufficiency of the Written Word," in *Sola Scriptura: The Protestant Position on the Bible*, ed. Don Kistler (Morgan, PA: Soli Deo Gloria, 1995), 165.

[35] Garrett, *Systematic Theology*, 1:208.

subsequently and continually perceived through the self-revealing and self-authenticating work of God the Holy Spirit in illumination. Due to the illuminating work of the Holy Spirit, the Bible's authority can and does communicate across cultural, geographical, and temporal differences between the biblical world and our own contexts. Scripture is authoritative as it is rightfully and faithfully interpreted. The Holy Spirit illumines our minds and hearts to understand the biblical message. Likewise, the Spirit leads us to recognize the authority of Scripture and to respond and obey its message today. The Bible calls for obedience to the authority of God revealed in his Word, not in reaction against authority, nor in an authoritarian sense, but from the true freedom which belongs to the children of God.

Highly emotional controversies present in various denominations and across different sectors of society point to the central issues in this book regarding whether God has spoken, and if so, whether this revealed word is still available to us in the Bible. Is there such a thing as revelation, and is it discoverable? Is God's revelation to be believed, and does it have authority for our twenty-first-century context? These questions are prominent in Roman Catholic circles, as well as in Methodist, Presbyterian, Lutheran, and Anglican contexts. These questions receive different responses in progressive contexts than they do in fundamentalist ones. While the differences are not as great, there are still differences between moderates and conservatives. Mainline denominations tend to approach these questions in one way, and evangelicals and free church Christians generally take another approach. While there is much overlap as these differences are expressed and debated, there is still often a denominationally specific aspect to each one.

The Southern Baptist Convention, the community of believers of which we are a part, has been wrestling with these matters in a very public manner for sixty years. Some think it is quite paradoxical that a people who happily refer to themselves as "people of the Book" have argued, debated, and fragmented over these matters our entire adult lives. We write from this context, even though we have both attempted to engage in irenic ways. Our understanding of Baptist life and the implications of these discussions will be explored in the penultimate chapter in this volume. The controversy over the Bible is certainly not unique to Southern Baptist life, though there are distinctive aspects which influence our work. While we write from this context, we nevertheless seek to speak to the broader evangelical community to which we belong and to the church catholic of our Lord Jesus Christ.

Our work throughout this book is shaped and informed by our confessional commitments. Readers will notice that we confess God has truly revealed himself to us. His revelation has been preserved for us in Holy Scripture by the Holy Spirit's work of inspiration. We confess our belief in the divine inspiration, total truthfulness, and complete authority of the Bible. We believe it is important for contemporary churches to choose to articulate a view of the Bible that is faithful to historic evangelical and orthodox positions that have characteristically confessed the Holy Bible is the written Word of God, that it is truthful, infallible, and inerrant, and that it remains the only sufficient, certain, and authoritative rule of all saving knowledge, faith, and obedience.[36]

Even though times and cultures change, the basic needs shared by men and women of all ages and races in all times and cultures remain the same. Thus the written message of God is normative, authoritative, and applicable as much for the church of God in the twenty-first century as it was for the people of God in the first century of our Lord and Savior, and as it was for the ancient Hebrews. We acknowledge that Scripture speaks about the various needs of all men and women, but more importantly we acknowledge that Scripture reveals not only the eternal truth about God and his commands but also the personal saving truth of God in the gospel of Jesus Christ presented by the Word in the Spirit.

We invite you to join us as we now turn our attention to the foundational question of divine revelation. We pray that in the following pages you will come to know God in Christ ever more clearly and treasure his revelation ever more dearly.

---

[36] R. R. Reno, *The End of Interpretation: Reclaiming the Priority of Ecclesial Exegesis* (Grand Rapids: Baker, 2022).

1

The Revelation of God

Holy Scripture is the powerful text by which God personally confronts the human hearer with eternal truth. God thereby reveals himself so as to invite the sinner to consider the certainty of the coming judgment, via the law, along with the offer of his saving mercy, via the gospel. The book of Hebrews employs a famous description for the way revelation works in this divine-human encounter: "For the word of God is living and effective and sharper than any double-edged sword, penetrating as far as the separation of soul and spirit, joints and marrow. It is able to judge the thoughts and intentions of the heart" (Heb 4:12).[1]

---

[1] The identity of the *logos* in Hebrews 4 has elicited various responses among modern commentators. Herschel H. Hobbs treated it as both the voice of God and the person of Jesus Christ without distinguishing the two. Donald Guthrie said it can be used in either the "general sense of the revelation of God" or the "particular sense of Jesus Christ himself in his function as Logos," but he preferred the former. F. F. Bruce said, "If the word of God is personified here, the personification is slight." H. H. Hobbs, *Hebrews: Challenges to Bold Discipleship* (Fincastle, VA: Scripture Truth, 2002), 46–47; Donald Guthrie, *The Letter to the Hebrews: An Introduction and Commentary*, Tyndale New Testament Commentary (Grand Rapids: Eerdmans, 1983), 117; F. F. Bruce, *The Epistle to the Hebrews*, rev. ed., New International Commentary on the New Testament (Grand Rapids: Eerdmans, 1990), 112. Also, see George H. Guthrie, *Hebrews*, The NIV Application Commentary (Grand Rapids: Zondervan, 1998), 155–57; Thomas R. Schreiner, *Hebrews*, Biblical Theology for Proclamation (Nashville: B&H, 2015), 146–47.

Scripture is not an abstract text which speaks distantly, dispassionately, and diffusedly about the divine-human encounter.[2] Rather, in Holy Scripture God powerfully and penetratingly confronts the human being with truth about their eternal state. God truly speaks in biblical revelation. The word of Scripture is the Word of God.

Because God truly speaks in biblical revelation, in their systematic theologies evangelicals rightly begin with God and his revelation. But, as we seek to become specific in our doctrinal analysis, the theologian is faced with a decision: Should we begin with God or his revelation? Systematic theologians must choose where to begin their own personal systems.[3] He or she faces a dilemma when making the traditional early choice between starting with the being of God or with our knowing of God. Some evangelical theologians choose to prioritize the ontological question, "Who is God?" Others have chosen to begin with the epistemological question, "How do we know God?"

Another complicating factor is that theologians necessarily approach the teaching of theology from the abstract perspective. Theology uses abstract definitions in order to try to provide clarity regarding our talk about God with human language. But divine revelation works with language in a concrete and powerful way, with the intent to foster the divine-human confrontation. Systematic theologians deal with the subject matter of God and his creatures primarily through propositions, but the Lord and his prophets and apostles treat God and his creatures in a personal way, though with propositions.

Scripture is a supremely concrete text, while systematic theology necessarily works in an abstract way. In other words, Scripture offers no answer to

---

[2] There are times, however, when God does speak in a temporarily abstract way in order to deliver over to judgment a living rebellious human person or an obstinate human community who has previously been offered God's revelation and rejected it (cf. Isa 6:9–10; Rom 10:18–20).

[3] This book is an exercise in "systematic theology." While we take the dogmas of the churches very seriously and interact with them, as will be seen, we do not intend to explain the *dogmata*, "decrees" or "official teachings," of a church. A "dogmatic theology" is concerned with explaining the teachings of a particular church. A systematic theology is concerned with setting out the author's or authors' own theological perspective. Our source documents and our audience intentionally include numerous churches from numerous traditions.

our question about systematic priority. Scripture assumes the two doctrinal concepts of God and revelation go together. The theologian's doctrine of God (theological ontology) and the theologian's doctrine of the revelation of God (theological epistemology) are, therefore, ultimately inseparable. This can be detected as early as Genesis 1:1, which starts neither with ontology nor epistemology but simply includes the listener in the revealed divine narrative. The theologian's choice concerning systematic priority thereby becomes one of human logic rather than divine revelation.

There are good theological arguments for treating either ontology or epistemology first. From a divine perspective, the ontological reality of God precedes God's epistemological revelation of himself to his creatures. But from a human perspective, our access to the reality of God depends upon the accommodation of God to our knowledge by means of his personal revelation. This revelation comes in the forms which we inhabit such as through sight and hearing. Whichever locus is treated first will, however, immediately require deep interaction with the other locus. Future systematic theologians reading this text, we believe, should feel free to begin with either God or revelation but should avoid failing to engage both adequately.

Manifesting Scripture's continual dialectic of incorporating both divine ontology and divine epistemology, one of the richest New Testament declarations of the deity of Jesus Christ, the preface to the book of Hebrews, also contains one of the thickest descriptions of the activity of divine revelation. This passage from the book of Hebrews serves as the primary whetstone upon which our thoughts about "the revelation of God" shall be sharpened in this chapter. The Holy Bible's correlation of the doctrine of revelation with the doctrine of Christ is no mere coincidence, for God's perfect revelation of himself *is* his only begotten Son. The canonical treatment of theological epistemology is deeply bound together with theological ontology.

In plain language, we may say, "God is the God who speaks." Likewise, "The God who speaks is God." The Word of God speaks of God perfectly, because the Word of God is God himself. God says Jesus Christ is not merely the epistemological way God "has spoken to us," although He is that too. Jesus Christ is also "his Son" in the highest ontological and eternal sense. The inextricable connection between Christian belief in both "Christ as divine revelation" and "Christ as divine person," however, contradicts the preference of the modern guild of biblical theology. That important discipline preferred to discuss the function of Christ for the believer while bypassing the nature of God in Christ.[4] Future theologians reading this text, we believe, should not feel free to ignore either function or ontology but should engage both.

The canonical book of Hebrews has much to say about both divine epistemology and divine ontology, so we shall begin this abstract book about special revelation and Scripture by listening to that concretely personal and passionate scriptural text. Introducing his epistle with a statement about epistemological superiority, the self-effacing author explained the older revelations to the prophets had accelerated and culminated in the Son of God himself.

> Long ago God spoke to our ancestors by the prophets at different times and in different ways. In these last days, he has spoken to us

---

[4] For instance, Oscar Cullmann, a leader in the biblical theology movement, affirmed Christ's role as the mid-point in salvation history but rejected the possibility of making any ontological claims. Marc R. Playoust, "Oscar Cullmann and Salvation History," *Heythrop Journal* 12, no. 1 (1971): 29–43. The penchant of modern biblical scholars to downplay metaphysical ontology began with Baruch Spinoza's misunderstanding of the difference between a Platonic metaphysic and the biblical metaphysic. The Platonic metaphysic treats God as abstract, inert, and generic, and places knowledge before goodness. The biblical metaphysic treats God as personal, active, and unique, and places goodness before knowledge. Edmond La Beaume Cherbonnier, "Is There a Biblical Metaphysic?" *Theology Today* 15, no. 4 (1959): 454–69. After knowledge claims about God were severely limited by Immanuel Kant, theologians shifted away from affirming knowledge of a transcendent God. Seeking a way forward for theology, Friedrich Schleiermacher appealed to human knowledge through the human feeling of dependence upon God, while Albrecht Ritschl prioritized ethics over either knowledge or feeling. Much of Western Christianity has since treated theology from the human perspective—how claims about God and Christ function for the human being. To use Kantian terminology, theologians have come to speak of the positive "value" of God as opposed to the unknowable "fact" of God. Rashkover agrees with this assessment: The "fact-value distinction has functioned as the dominant paradigm for inquiry in the western academy and has been taken for granted by many modern and contemporary Jewish and Christian thinkers." "Taken as a whole, Kant's *Critique of Pure Reason* signals the end of theological efforts to present epistemologically justified claims concerning a supernatural God, leaving believers with little else than the longing or desire for a God whom they cannot know." Randi Rashkover, "Liberalism, Post-Liberalism, and the Fact-Value Divide," *Modern Theology* 33, no. 1 (2017): 140, 142. Later chapters in this volume place these trends in a historical frame.

by his Son. God has appointed him heir of all things and made the universe through him. The Son is the radiance of God's glory and the exact expression of his nature, sustaining all things by his powerful word. After making purification for sins, he sat down at the right hand of the Majesty on high. (Heb 1:1–3)

The prologue concludes in verse 4 by affirming the personal superiority (*kreittōn*) of the Son. The prologue to Hebrews hereby both demonstrates and asserts the superiority of the revelation of God in Christ. The idea of the Son's unparalleled excellence also provides the Letter to the Hebrews with a certain Christological structure.[5] Madison Pierce recently provided detailed evidence that the book of Hebrews also contains a trinitarian structure from the perspective of its doctrine of revelation.[6] With this Christological and trinitarian theme and structure in mind, we shall first consider common biblical terms for revelation in the book of Hebrews and in Scripture more generally before turning to a delineation of the twelve major aspects of divine revelation. To arrive at eleven of these twelve major aspects of divine revelation, we shall interact with modern proponents of both personal revelation and propositional revelation. After explicitly grounding the foremost aspect of divine revelation in theology proper, we shall offer our own considered definition of divine revelation.

---

[5] Our argument for the overarching theme of Christ's superiority was detailed in Malcolm B. Yarnell, "Introduction and Notes to Hebrews," in *CSB Study Bible* (Nashville: Holman, 2017), 1945–62. The notes provided at that time a Christological outline for the book. In the first half, the author of Hebrews showed how Jesus Christ is superior in his person (1:4–2:18), in his faithfulness (chaps. 3–4), in his work (chaps. 5–6), and in his priesthood (chaps. 7–10). In the second half of the letter, the author showed that in and through Christ, we know of the superiority of the Christian faith (chap. 11), the way of the Father (chap. 12), and the church (chap. 13). F. F. Bruce recognized the ubiquity of *kreittōn* and admitted the importance of Christ's superiority but believed the letter intended to establish "the finality of Christianity" by means of Christ's superiority. His structure and argument follow his apologetic religious thrust. Bruce, *The Epistle to the Hebrews*, xi–xii, 29, 50–51.

[6] First, in chapters 1, 5, 7, and 8, God the Father speaks to the Son. Second, in chapters 2 and 10, God the Son responds to the Father. Third, in chapters 3, 4, and 10, God the Holy Spirit speaks to the church. Madison N. Pierce, *Divine Discourse in the Epistle to the Hebrews: The Recontextualization of Spoken Quotations of Scripture* (New York: Cambridge University Press, 2020), 35–174.

I. Biblical Terms for Revelation

Defining "revelation" is no simple matter, for Scripture never provides a formal definition. Rather, Scripture presumes a definition of revelation which becomes apparent only when we pay careful attention to the words of Scripture. The ways in which God reveals himself are so rich, various, and deep that a simple definition will inevitably miss something. Moreover, many "words" must be consulted when seeking a biblical definition of divine revelation, because "there is no single word—in either the Old Testament or the New—that corresponds to our theological idea of revelation."[7] For instance, the book of Hebrews employs numerous terms for the act of revelation. A review of the basic terms used in Hebrews specifically and Scripture more generally will assist us in arriving at a proper definition of "revelation."

First, consider the various terms for divine revelation in Heb 1:1–4. The author's high incarnational Christology repeatedly reinforces the location of revelation in a particular historical person, the Son of God who has assumed to himself our humanity in Jesus the Messianic King. God's prior multiple revelations through the prophets are affirmed yet generalized, while the recent singular revelation of his Son is particularized and emphasized. The personal aspect of revelation of God in Christ's humanity is reinforced with aural, visual, and bodily references alongside human religious experience. As the trivial exception which proves the general rule that revelation is God's concrete personal address to the human located in the history of the world, we should note there is one human sense not included in the biblical activity of divine revelation. "The sense of smell is the only one of the five senses to play no role in divine revelation in Israel and early Christianity."[8]

Personal Terms	Hebrews 1:1–4		
Aural	*laleō*	*rhēma*	
Visual	*apaugasma*	*doxa*	
Bodily	*charaktēr*	*dexios*	*kathizō*

---

[7] Emil Brunner, *Revelation and Reason: The Christian Doctrine of Faith and Knowledge*, trans. Olive Wyon (Philadelphia: Westminster, 1946), 21.

[8] James R. Edwards, *Between the Swastika and the Sickle: The Life, Execution, and Disappearance of Ernst Lohmeyer* (Grand Rapids: Eerdmans, 2019), 51.

Religious	*Theos*	*katharismos*	
Identity	*onoma*		

Aural references to divine revelation come with the common Greek verbs *laleō*, "speak," and *legō*, "say," as well as with the noun *rhēma*, "word" or "saying."[9] The visual references to God's revelation of himself are conveyed through the nouns *apaugasma*, "radiance" or "reflection," and *doxa*, "glory" or "brightness." Bodily references to revelation are indicated with the nouns *charaktēr*, "impression," and *dexios*, "right" or "right hand," and with the verb *kathizō*, "sit." This author's idea of a concrete aural, visual, and bodily revelation of God the Father in the human nature of the person of his divine Son, Jesus Christ, finds an echo in 1 John 1:1–3. John recalled his encounters with the God who became life-giving man in a prologue reminiscent of Genesis 1. "What was from the beginning, what we have heard, what we have seen with our eyes, what we have observed and have touched with our hands, concerning the word of life."

The humanity of the Son is identified as the means of divine revelation through the language of religion applied to him. The religious aspect of the Son's assumed humanity is first affirmed by reference to him as the revelation of *Theos*, "God." The religious dimension of his humanity is reinforced by referring to Christ as the way of reconciliation between God and humanity. Christ brings *katharismos*, "purification," then ascends to the right hand of the Father. We must also note the Greek term *onoma*, "name," which indicates both personal identity and personal authority. It is used to exalt Christ as the superior revelation of God in the conclusion of the prologue to the book of Hebrews.[10]

The aural, visual, and bodily aspects of these terms remind us that revelation comes to human beings who exist in nature and history. The

---

[9] *Legō* does not appear in the prologue but is used of divine speech through the Old Testament throughout the book of Hebrews. Cf. Heb 1:5–7, 13; 2:6, 12; 3:7, 10, 15; 4:4, 7; 5:6; 7:11, 21; 8:9–11, 13; 9:20; 10:7–9, 15–16, 30; 12:26; 13:5–6.

[10] "In most cultures the name is inextricably bound up with the person, whether a human being, a god, or a demon." This is emphatically the case in both the Old and New Testaments. Moisés Silva, ed., *New International Dictionary of New Testament Theology and Exegesis*, 2nd ed., 5 vols. (Grand Rapids: Zondervan, 2014), 3:514–22.

religious nature of these terms reminds us that revelation is for the purpose of restoring human relationships with God. The personal nature of
these terms is sealed through the assignation of "name" to the Son of God.
This Son is simultaneously one with God and the human revelation of
God. Neither the historical and natural dimension nor the eternal and
religious dimension should be forgotten. Both dimensions reinforce our
need to identify the nature of the revelation of God in Jesus Christ as
supremely personal.

Along with these words from the prologue, we should note other important terms conveying the idea of divine revelation. Particularly significant
is the verb, *apokalyptō*, which means "reveal" or "make fully known," and its
related noun *apokalypsis*, "uncovering," "unveiling," or "making fully known."
The verb is derived from *kalyptō*, "cover," "hide," or "conceal," and appears 26
times in the New Testament. The noun is found 18 times and always refers
to some aspect of divine revelation. The noun *apokalypsis*, can also refer to
one of the two comings of Jesus Christ (his first coming in Rom 16:25; his
second coming in Rev 1:1). While neither the noun form nor the verb form
appears therein, the book of Hebrews does employ three important related
verbs: *phaneroō*, which means "reveal" or "disclose" (Heb 9:8); *phanatazō*,
"appear" or "become visible" (12:21); and *dēloō*, "make clear" (9:8). A fifth
common verb for revelation is *gnōrizō*, "make known."

Perhaps the most widely known theological term for revelation, due to
its previous appearance in Greek philosophy and due to its employment to
describe the deity of Jesus Christ in the prologue to the Gospel of John, is
logos.[11] In the book of Hebrews, *logos* may be translated as "word," "reason," or
"reckoning," and is used to describe both Scripture (4:12) and proclamation
(12:19; 13:7). But Hebrews does not, at least on the surface, use this term to
describe Jesus Christ as the eternal Son of God, though *logos* has a close connection to *rhēma*, "word" or "expression" (Heb 1:3; 6:5; 11:3; 12:19), as well as
to *phōnē*, "voice." The noun *rhēma* refers to the Son's work and by implication
his person in Hebrews 1:3. The noun *logos* refers to God's activity through
the biblical text in Heb 4:12.[12] The noun *phōnē* refers to the activity of God

---

[11] George R. Beasley-Murray, *John*, Word Biblical Commentary (Waco: Word,
1987), 1–17.
[12] See note 2 above.

in prophecy throughout the book (3:7; 3:15; 4:7; 12:26). A fourth related noun is *logion*, which may be translated as "saying" or "revelation" (5:12).

Gerald O'Collins lists several terms from the Gospel of John which refer to Christ as the revelation and the revealer of God. These include *doxa*, "glory"; *phōs*, "light"; *alētheia*, "truth"; and *martyria*, "witness," as well as the seven *sēmeion*, "sign," statements and the *egō eimi*, "I am," sayings. O'Collins also develops the Gospel's conceptions of "presence," "experience," and "faith" as indicative of the revelation of God.[13] In addition to the terms mentioned above, B. B. Warfield discusses the Old Testament verbs *galah*, "reveal"; *ra'ah*, "see"; and, *yada'* "know." He also mentions the New Testament terms *epiphaneia*, "appearance"; *deiknumi*, "show"; and, *chrēmatizō*, "impart a divine message." The Old Testament noun *dabar*, "word" was often attached to Yahweh or God to indicate a divine message which came directly to a prophet. The terms related to *torah*, "law" and *graphē*, "writing" or "Scripture" will also prove significant.[14]

From this preliminary New Testament taxonomy of "revelation," we now turn to a personal definition of revelation. The personal definition will be constructed in conversation with a Swiss theologian, Emil Brunner. However, this one-sided approach to revelation requires supplementation, additional clarity, and, as we will see, even correction. A fuller definition of revelation will be prompted through conversation with the American evangelical scholar, Carl F. H. Henry. After Henry's propositional definition is discussed, we shall offer a proposal and definition for special revelation, which will help to frame the themes and issues discussed in the remainder of this volume.

II. The Personal Aspects of Divine Revelation

In his volume *Revelation and Reason*, Emil Brunner attempted to place revelation on a firmer footing than what had been proposed in his mid-twentieth-century European context. After the Enlightenment, both

---

[13] Gerald O'Collins, *Revelation: Towards a Christian Interpretation of God's Self-Revelation in Jesus Christ* (New York: Oxford University Press, 2016), 7–12.

[14] Benjamin Breckinridge Warfield, *Revelation and Inspiration* (New York: Oxford University Press, 1932), 29–33.

divine transcendence and divine revelation had almost disappeared from
the Western worldview. Brunner noted, "a new mentality has gradually
emerged: that of complete preoccupation with the things of this world, and
an immanental philosophy. For the first time in world history there is mass
atheism, and a completely secular culture; hand in hand with this there
goes a kind of religion of 'this world only,' in which the very conception
of revelation has no place."[15] The style of reason used in the natural sciences became dominant, such that any claim to revelation seemed spurious.[16] Rather than submitting revelation to reason, or reducing revelation to
magic, Brunner elevated revelation above reason while rejecting the oppo-
site error of irrationalism.[17]

Brunner provided a six-point outline for the definition of revelation.
While we find his conclusions to be inadequate, requiring supplementation
to present a fully orthodox understanding of revelation, we think his work
offers a good place to begin the discussion related to the personal dimension
of God's revelation. In speaking of the personal nature of divine revelation,
six aspects are highlighted which will require further elaboration in this book.
First, due to his *absolute divine transcendence*, God must choose to reveal himself. God can be known only through his self-revelation. It is God alone who
chooses to reveal himself. "Revelation is the self-manifestation of God."[18]

The second aspect of Brunner's definition of revelation concerns *the
problem of human blindness*. Revelation is necessary not only to overcome
the Creator-creature divide caused by God's absolute transcendence; revelation is also necessary to overcome blindness and bondage on the part of
humanity. "Revelation everywhere includes within itself a negative presupposition; without it man is always in some way or other in a kind of darkness
or bondage."[19] The origin of this bondage is human sin. Our bondage and

---

[15] Brunner, *Revelation and Reason*, 5.

[16] The churches' previous disdain toward science and the clerical use of the
nation-states to advance various theologies did not help matters. Brunner, *Revelation
and Reason*, 5–7.

[17] "Jesus Christ is not the enemy of reason, but only of the irrational arrogance
of those who pride themselves on their intellect, and of the irrational self-sufficiency
of reason." Brunner, *Revelation and Reason*, 16–17.

[18] Brunner, 25.

[19] Brunner, 25.

blindness are due to the choice of humanity during the Fall. "Turning away from God presupposes an original positive relation with God, and thus an original revelation. The sinner is not merely blind; he has become blind; he has been blinded."[20] God is hidden from humanity due to human creatureliness and human fallenness.

The third part of his definition is that revelation entails "the communication of unusual knowledge, of something particular." By *unusual knowledge*, Brunner is making a distinction between natural, ordinary, or secular knowledge on the one side and divine knowledge on the other. Natural knowledge is acquired through human effort, is not necessarily personal, and does not bring transformation. Natural knowledge comes through exposure to and reflection upon this world. Natural knowledge is within the ability of human beings to attain. Divine knowledge, however, comes to humanity only because of God's free love for his creatures. God confronts the human being and invites the sinner to engage him personally. God's revelation "creates community," the possibility of human communion with God.[21]

The fourth component in Brunner's description of divine revelation concerns its redemptive purpose and effect. Revelation is *life-giving*. "Revelation is the communication of life, not merely an intensification of the life that already exists; nor is it merely an enrichment of knowledge, but it is the transformation of that which is evil and destructive into saving, eternal life."[22] In the movement of revealing himself, God is not interested in merely giving "something" but in giving himself to us personally. Through his grace-filled yet confrontational encounter, we are invited to have communion with God in person by faith. Indeed, here is why Scripture remains so important as the necessary means of revelation. "Here we have already approached the decisive point, the heart of the Bible—the justification of the sinner, the forgiveness of guilt."[23] At this point, it should be evident that Brunner is following the traditional Christian theological reading of the biblical narrative, its redemption-history, to construct his definition of

---

[20] Brunner, 26.
[21] Brunner, 26–28.
[22] Brunner, 28.
[23] Brunner, 29.

revelation.[24] The history of salvation includes both the Law and the gospel, the old covenant and the new covenant, Israel and the Messiah of Israel (cf. Heb 2:2–3). God calls humanity to trust and obey God so we might "enter that rest" (4:1, 3, 5, 9–11).

The fifth part of his definition affirms revelation arises from *unexpected grace*. God originally created human life and offers the redemption of life to sinful humanity out of his perfection of love. "The unexpected is that which we cannot fathom. All genuine love is unfathomable; God does not owe love to his creatures. His love is always and everywhere a free gift."[25] Humanity is guilty and requires judgment, but God has chosen to offer forgiveness instead. Human beings deserve nothing but condemnation, but God decided entirely by free election to act with grace toward us. "He does not love the lovable, but he makes the unlovable lovable."[26] The author of Hebrews affirms the Father's throne is "of grace" (Heb 4:16), that the Son "might taste death" for humanity "by God's grace" (2:9), and that his Spirit is likewise characterized by grace (10:29). Hebrews concludes with a prayer that the grace of the trinitarian God would be "with you all" (13:25). The grace of God invites the human heart to embrace him by faith (3:7–8).

The sixth and final aspect of Brunner's definition is that it "has always and everywhere the character of a sudden event." In the sudden event of *the Cross of Christ*, Brunner finds something "unique," "unrepeatable," and "unconditionally personal." This event both transcends time and is rooted in history. The historical root is first and foremost in the cross of Jesus Christ, "the sacrificial death of the Son of God," which remains "the decisive event in history."[27] Brunner centers eternity and history in the cross. "Here, the real revelation takes place, the revelation of the holiness and the mercy of God, of his nature and his will, of his plan for humanity and for the world. Here takes place that which is the fulfillment of all history, and at the same time bursts the framework of all history: the Absolute Event."[28] The

---

[24] Later in the volume, we will discuss redemptive history and its place within the orthodox theological tradition.

[25] Brunner, 29.

[26] Brunner, 30.

[27] Brunner, 30–31.

[28] Brunner, 32.

language of "absolute" closes the circle with the sudden "event" of Christ on the cross. The book of Hebrews closes the distance between the cross of Jesus and the eternal throne of God through the ministry of the Holy Spirit (Heb 9:14, 26).

There are, however, key aspects of an orthodox evangelical doctrine of revelation missing from Brunner's definition. While Brunner retains the doctrine of Scripture, it remains underdeveloped. He affirms the Bible "is itself revelation," but he does not explicitly include the Bible in his six-point definition.[29] Moreover, one important characteristic of the Bible is not merely absented from his definition but often appears repressed in his theological treatment. Brunner periodically argues against the propositional nature of biblical revelation. I. Howard Marshall, in *Biblical Inspiration,* identifies four problems with only representing revelation as personal encounter. Moreover, we recognize the need for clarification or correction from a seemingly unlikely source in the writings of James Barr, a self-identified liberal scholar. In a lengthy reflection, Barr affirmed that the Bible maintains a propositional view of revelation rather than merely personal encounter, acts, or events. He writes:

> In so far as it is good to use the term "revelation" at all, it is entirely as true to say that in the Old Testament revelation is by verbal communication as to say that it is by acts in history. We have verbal communication both in that God speaks directly with men and in that men learn from other and earlier men through the verbal form of tradition. When we speak of the highly "personal" nature of the Old Testament God, it is very largely upon this verbal character of his communication with man that we are relying. The acts of God are meaningful because they are set within this frame of verbal communication. God tells what he is doing or tells what he is going to do. He does nothing, unless he tells his servants the

---

[29] Brunner, 21. See Marshall, *Biblical Inspiration,* 13–15 (see introduction, n. 14); James Barr, *Old and New in Interpretation* (London: SCM, 1966), 77–80; James Barr, "II. Revelation through History in the Old Testament and in Modern Theology," *Interpretation: A Journal of Bible & Theology* 17, no. 2 (April 1963): 193–205; Robert L. Reymond, *A New Systematic Theology of the Christian Faith* (Nashville: Thomas Nelson, 1998), 12–17.

prophets (Amos 3:7). A God who acted in history would be a mysterious and supra-personal fate if the action was not linked with this verbal conversation.[30]

Barr, though not a personal advocate of evangelical theology, has affirmed that those who would maintain God's revelation is limited to personal encounter should admit that their rejection of propositional revelation is based primarily on philosophical and critical grounds rather than on the teaching and example of Scripture. We, therefore, recognize the importance of affirming not only that divine revelation is personal, but that it is also propositional.

III. Revelation Is Both Personal and Propositional

It is undeniable that Scripture conveys truth through words; the words of Scripture convey propositions with ultimate personal meaning. The propositional character of revelation is part and parcel of the means God employs to encounter the human being personally. In this section, we shall review the contributions of several theologians to demonstrate how revelation remains both personal and propositional in nature.

One of many services Carl F. H. Henry performed for twentieth-century evangelicals was to recall the necessity of affirming the propositional and truthful nature of the very words of the biblical text.[31] Henry's primary claim carries the ring of truth, "The loss of revelation as a mental concept has had devastating consequences in modern theology." The tenth of Henry's "Fifteen Theses" regarding divine revelation was important in an age that exalted reason and denigrated revelation. The truth value of Scripture's rational proclamations in the form of words were widely denied or at the least downplayed. Henry contradicted the prevalent view with his claim that "God's revelation is rational

---

[30] Barr, *Old and New in Interpretation*, 77–78.

[31] For an introduction to Henry's theological background and intertwined doctrines of Christ and revelation, see Malcolm B. Yarnell III, "Whose Jesus? Which Revelation?" *Midwestern Journal of Theology* 1, no. 1–2 (Spring 2003): 33–53. Also, see David S. Dockery, "Introduction," in *Architect of Evangelicalism: The Collected Writings of Carl F. H. Henry* (Bellingham, WA: Lexham, 2019).

communication conveyed in intelligible ideas and meaningful words, that is, in conceptual-verbal form."[32]

Like those who stressed personal encounter, Henry deemed the Spirit's illumination of these propositions necessary for them to make sense. However, he was also concerned about those who appealed glibly to a mystical knowledge of God. He observes:

> Yet unless priority is given to the objectively inspired content of Scripture, Spirit-illumination readily gives way to private fantasy and mysticism. The Spirit illumines persons by reiterating the truth of the scriptural revelation and bearing witness to Jesus Christ. Spirit-illumination centers in the interpretation of the literal grammatical sense of Spirit-breathed Scripture. This Scripture the Holy Spirit is alone free to interpret authoritatively in the context of the progressive disclosure of the mind and purpose mediated by the Logos of God.[33]

In no way should the propositional truthfulness of the words of Holy Scripture be dismissed by an appeal to the Spirit.

Abstract human knowledge about certain revealed propositions and intellectual acquiescence to the truthfulness of those propositions are doubtless necessary. But propositional agreement is not the ultimate end, purpose, or goal of Scripture. Propositional concepts about God, Christ, and salvation conveyed by the trustworthy words of the Bible are the necessary means, but they are necessarily not the end. "Knowledge about God" and "knowing God" are two different things altogether. Knowledge about must both precede and follow personal knowledge, but the human being's personally knowing God—knowing God intimately as one's Creator, Savior, and End—is primary, paramount, and ultimate. As the author of Hebrews reminds us, God leads his people via his Word "to enter that rest" with God (Heb 4:1, 5, 11).

Carl Henry learned the importance of propositions from Gordon Clark. But both Clark and Henry have been accused of allowing cognitive

---

[32] Carl F. H. Henry, *God, Revelation and Authority: God Who Speaks and Shows*, 6 vols. (1976, Wheaton: Crossway, 1999), 1:12.

[33] Henry, *God, Revelation and Authority*, 2:15.

propositionalism to diminish the importance of personal encounter with God. Evangelical theologian Donald Bloesch's criticism of Henry reverses Henry's criticism of Brunner.[34] We would prefer to use the term "friendly" to characterize both Bloesch's critique of Henry and Henry's critique of Brunner. On the positive side, we can note that Henry's primary battle was against Karl Barth. Henry often cited Brunner positively, for instance, while starting to defend his own doctrine of revelation and while adopting the latter's definition of biblical terms for revelation.[35] And when Henry adjudicated between Barth and Brunner, he took Brunner's side.[36]

On the other hand, Henry bristled at Brunner's idea of the divine-human encounter. Henry believed propositions were not the problem but the means to fighting undue abstraction. Henry also deemed Brunner's personalism difficult. "The great difficulty with Brunner's doctrine . . . is that it so assimilates the reality of God to internal psychological considerations that it leaves the very existence of the living God in doubt."[37] Still, it is important to recognize that Henry himself affirmed the personal nature of revelation in the sixth of his fifteen theses on revelation, which states, "God's revelation is uniquely personal in both content and form."[38]

In his study of the apostle Paul, the leading Dutch New Testament scholar, Herman Ridderbos, also noted that merely propositional knowledge

---

[34] "Carl Henry has rendered a valuable service in warning of the dangers of capitulating to modernity. All of us should heed his timely admonition against abandoning the conceptual and propositional dimension of revelation for a faith-encounter theology. Yet Henry basically calls for a return to the rationalistic idealism of the early Enlightenment. His indebtedness to Gordon Clark is obvious." Bloesch's remarks about Henry come first in his pivotal critical chapter, "Theology at the Crossroads." Bloesch's remarks about Brunner's participation in the kerygmatic "theology of confrontation" seem, by comparison, quite charitable. Donald G. Bloesch, *A Theology of Word and Spirit: Authority and Method in Theology*, Christian Foundations (Downers Grove: IVP, 1992), 253, 262–64. Avery Dulles summarizes concerns regarding the propositional model of revelation but concludes we still need to speak of propositions. Avery Dulles, *Models of Revelation* (New York: Doubleday, 1983), 48–52.

[35] Henry, *God, Revelation and Authority*, 2:17, 79–80.

[36] Henry's discussion focuses primarily upon natural revelation. Henry, *God, Revelation and Authority*, 2:40–41, 88–91.

[37] Henry, 2:75.

[38] Henry, 2:10.

is insufficient. "The gospel exists, so we may say, for this purpose, to summon man to faith and conversion, not to a religious *gnosis* that informs him concerning the secrets of the universe and of the invisible world inaccessible to him." The revelation of God in Christ and his work in dying and rising again necessarily reorient our understanding of God and the world. But it also calls us into a new personal relation with God, and the noetic effects are transformative. The transformation caused by divine revelation includes teaching the human being "to understand himself in a new way, in respect to God as well as to the world and history surrounding him."[39]

While our understanding of revelation comes much closer to mirroring the work of Carl Henry, we can learn from all these important thinkers. First, Henry reminds us of the necessity to receive the propositional content of Scripture, respecting every single word of it. Second, Herman Ridderbos recalls the Bible's transformative work upon those who hear its gospel. Finally, we affirm Millard Erickson's observations that God does not simply reveal information for the purpose of informing; the knowledge of God is for the purpose of relationship.

These theologians correctly emphasize important truths about revelation. First, we need the inspired propositional words, the unremittingly truthful words, of the Holy Bible. Second, we also need the living and active Word of the gospel of Jesus Christ which the prophets of the Old Testament foretold, and the apostles of the New Testament retold. Finally, we must ultimately receive this knowledge of Jesus Christ personally, entering intimate life with the very One who is the Word of God in flesh.

Before drawing conclusions from our discussion about the dual nature of revelation as propositional and personal, we note two other scholars whose works provide important background information. First, Richard Swinburne, a philosopher of religion at the University of Oxford strongly emphasizes propositional revelation. He recognizes God's personal revelation is Christianity's primary concern, but propositions are inescapable. "It is in any

---

[39] Herman Ridderbos, *Paul: An Outline of His Theology*, trans. John Richard De Witt (Grand Rapids: Eerdmans, 1975), 160. Also, see Millard J. Erickson, "Revelation," in *Foundations for Biblical Interpretation: A Complete Library of Tools and Resources*, ed. David S. Dockery, K. A. Mathews, and Robert B. Sloan (Nashville: B&H, 1994), 3–18.

case very hard to see how God could reveal himself in history without at the same time revealing some propositional truth about himself. For events are not self-interpreting."[40] Swinburne's attempt to define linguistic revelation according to literary context brings clarity to the terminology of revelation. He describes "token sentences" as "truth-bearers," such that propositional statements convey truth.[41] Swinburne works from the "original revelation," which he identifies with the teaching of Jesus,[42] to church, creed, and the Bible. Unexpectedly, this strongly propositional theologian, however, asserts the true propositions of Scripture are mixed with error. Swinburne says the primary message of Scripture regarding Christ and the gospel helps us discern the difference in that mixture of truth and error.[43] His stance demonstrates that propositional revelation and biblical inerrancy are, unfortunately, not always correlative.

Second, Gerald O'Collins is a Roman Catholic Jesuit who traces the concern for propositional revelation among both confessional Protestants and Catholics to the late sixteenth century. Their concern reached its height in the nineteenth and twentieth centuries. "This approach interpreted revelation as the *revelata* (things revealed) rather than as the divine action of self-revelation, and closely associated revelation with doctrine and creed. Logically Vatican I explained the act of faith as assent to truths (plural) or believing 'the things' to be true that God has revealed."[44] O'Collins shows how Jesus taught in propositional form, and that while salvation comes in personal revelation, it is also expressed in propositional statements.[45] "Thus revelation as a person-to-person, I-thou encounter between God and human beings gives rise to true propositions. In their turn they can prompt divine revelation, as when human beings are addressed by the Scripture, preaching, the classic creeds and other doctrinal statements . . ."[46]

---

[40] Richard Swinburne, *Revelation: From Metaphor to Analogy* (New York: Oxford University Press, 1992), 3–4.

[41] Swinburne, *Revelation*, 13.

[42] Swinburne, 101–3.

[43] Swinburne, 196–202.

[44] O'Collins, *Revelation*, 3.

[45] O'Collins, 6–7.

[46] O'Collins continues, "the words and actions which constitute the conferring of the sacraments, various icons and further works of sacred art and music, and

In conclusion, we affirm revelation is both personal and propositional. Its primary nature is the personal revelation of God which invites human beings into personal relationship with God. The secondary nature of revelation, however, is both prior and indispensable, for God reveals himself to people today through the canon of Holy Scripture. The Roman Catholic theologian O'Collins affirms the twofold nature of divine revelation, as did the Baptist theologian James Leo Garrett Jr. Garrett asks, "Must one choose sides completely in this debate?" His answer is unequivocal, "No, for there is some truth on both sides, and these truths need to be correlated. Propositionalism rightly stresses that God has employed human language. Relationalism rightly stresses that divine revelation is not dispensed information about God that does not transform its recipients."[47] O'Collins agrees that the personal and the propositional "imply each other."[48]

In previous reflections on the nature of special revelation, we observed that, "Special revelation is primarily redemptive and personal." And the "ultimate point" of that personal revelation by God "is found in Jesus Christ." We want to assign the first place to personal revelation without losing propositional revelation or diminishing it in any way. "God's self-disclosure is propositional in that it communicates truth about God to his people. Even in mighty acts or personal encounter, there are truths of God and his purposes that could have been learned by the recipients of that revelation." What God reveals is God, but he reveals himself, at least in part, through revealing information about himself. Additionally, it can be said that "The primary purpose of revelation is not necessarily to enlarge the scope of one's knowledge about God but to know God personally." God's revelation has three stages: God's redemptive work in history in Christ; the recording of these events by the apostles in the process of inspiration; and the Spirit's illuminating work in the lives of those who have since read and heard the apostolic writings.[49]

---

other 'accounts' drawn from previous revelatory encounters with God." O'Collins, *Revelation*, 13.

[47] James Leo Garrett Jr., *Systematic Theology: Biblical, Historical, and Evangelical*, 2nd ed., 2 vols. (North Richland Hills, TX: BIBAL, 2000), 1:115.

[48] O'Collins, *Revelation*, 12.

[49] Dockery, "Special Revelation," 105 (see introduction, n. 24); also, David S. Dockery, "The Revelation of God," in *The Holman Illustrated Dictionary of the*

IV. The Propositional Aspects of Divine Revelation

While extolling Brunner's signal contribution to the broader recovery of the doctrine of revelation, we must recognize the shortcomings of his personalist definition. The resulting imbalance requires us to recount the contributions of propositionalists like the Princeton theologians and Carl F. H. Henry. Henry is especially helpful due to his nearly comprehensive corpus alongside his historic commitment to evangelical convictions. As previously noted, Donald Bloesch sought to provide balance by appealing to the necessity of the Holy Spirit.[50] Despite such correction to the emphases in Henry, we should not fail to recognize that Henry accorded the Holy Spirit a place in his system. Henry's doctrine of revelation builds upon the late nineteenth- and early twentieth-century Princeton theologians, especially B. B. Warfield, who played a key role in the development of American evangelicalism's doctrine of revelation.

In one of his most important works, Warfield considered divine transcendence, divine mystery, human sin, the goal of human redemption, and the necessity of grace.[51] Warfield's burden, however, was to highlight the modes of revelation in the construction of the Bible. He quickly worked through the modes of theophany and of dreams and visions to dwell upon how God "put His words in the mouths of His prophets and gave them His commandments to speak."[52] Warfield wanted to preserve the purity of the prophetic message, for "the Divine word delivered through men is the pure word of God, diluted with no human admixture whatever."[53] Warfield then developed a doctrine of "concursive operation." God sovereignly chose to work through the intelligence and morality of the prophets, accommodating his revelation to their minds. Warfield carefully avoided the concept of mechanical dictation.[54]

Bible, ed. Chad Brand, Charles Draper, and Archie England (Nashville: Holman Reference, 2003), 1383–86.

[50] See notes 34 and 35 above and the thoughtful response by Jesse M. Payne, *Carl F. H. Henry on the Holy Spirit* (Bellingham, WA: Lexham, 2021).

[51] Warfield, *Revelation and Inspiration*, 3.

[52] Warfield, 17.

[53] Warfield, 18.

[54] Warfield, 23–27. Warfield does not treat Christ at length, though he does subsequently claim Christ is "the culminating revelation," 28.

On Henry's part, the first eight of his fifteen theses of divine revelation include revelation as "divinely initiated activity," for the benefit of human "communion with our Creator," "God's transcendent mystery," and "the comprehensive unity of divine revelation." These are followed by his affirmations of revelation as due "exclusively" to "divine determination," revelation as "uniquely personal," and the person and work of Jesus Christ as "the climax of God's special revelation."[55] The final three theses in Henry's system concern the proclamation of Scripture and its reception by believers to avoid the coming judgment and to participate in eternal life.[56]

Four major theses, the ninth through the twelfth of his fifteen theses, provide the core of Henry's doctrine of propositional revelation. First, Henry writes, "the Eternal Logos" is the "mediating agent" of all divine revelation. Henry's thesis of *the Eternal Logos* concerns the work of Jesus Christ in the origin and the identification of God's revelation. Christ as Eternal Logos helps keep revelation from being exclusively manifested in the form of Jesus Christ alone and simultaneously from being unmoored from Jesus Christ in content.[57] The Eternal Logos in Henry's propositional proposal joins eternity with history through Christology. John's Gospel makes much of the Christ as the *Logos* who is God and with God (John 1:1), the only begotten God (1:18) who became flesh (1:14). The book of Hebrews exalted Jesus Christ as the eternal one (Heb 13:8, 21), who is the eternally begotten Son of God (1:5–6) that came into the world as a human being (2:6–7).

Henry's second major thesis asserts that revelation to human beings, who are made in the likeness of the Eternal Logos, is *rational and verbal*. "God's revelation is rational communication conveyed in intelligible ideas and meaningful words, that is, in conceptual-verbal form." Where Brunner was concerned to correct the prevalence of secularism's this-worldly orientation, Henry set out to correct the "devastating consequences" of "the loss of revelation as a mental concept" in modern theology. Decrying Karl Barth's proposal in particular, Henry reminded his readers that Jesus Christ

---

[55] Henry explicates the incarnation, death, and resurrection of Christ in one thesis and the person of Christ as the "source and content" of revelation in a separate thesis. Henry, *God, Revelation and Authority*, 2:8–11.

[56] Henry, 2:15–16.

[57] Henry, 2:11–12.

emphasized both "the words" used in revelation (John 14:10) and "the Word" as "written" (Matt 4:4).[58] The book of Hebrews makes much of the very words of the Old Testament, citing numerous texts and explaining their meaning from the perspective of Israel and of the church of Jesus Christ.[59]

Henry's third major thesis recalls contemporary Protestants to maintain the necessity of *the written Word of God*. Maintaining his focus upon divine words as the instrumental conveyors of saving propositions, Henry said, "The Bible is the reservoir and conduit of divine truth." Scripture is particularly necessary for the church today because we do not live in the dispensation of the prophets and the apostles. Henry was sensitive to the progress of divine revelation through several generations. Those who live after the prophets and the apostles must, due to their dislocation from the presence of the prophets and the apostles, look to Scripture as "the authoritative written record and interpretation of God's revelatory deeds, and the ongoing source of reliable objective knowledge concerning God's nature and ways."[60]

Recent scholarship reinforces this aspect of Henry's thesis by noting how the words of the Old Testament are treated as the living Word of God. Ken Schenck argued the biblical texts cited in Hebrews acted as "windows" between the history of Israel and the history of the early Christian community. "In a sense, the text disappears as the interpreter outside the text becomes a part of the world within the text and the world within the text is seen as part of the world outside the text."[61] Myk Habets pictured the phenomenon in living terms, "Hebrews hears the Old Testament as God speaking in the present tense and in the active voice, thus dynamically, and not as a past event and thus statically."[62] Gregory W. Lee detected a collapsing

---

[58] Henry, 2:12–13.

[59] For instance, Dana M. Harris traces the way in which Heb 3:7–11 exposits Psalm 95; Heb 10:15–17 exposits Jer 31:31–34; and Heb 9:6–10 draws from Exodus 25–40. Harris, "'Today If You Hear My Voice': The Spirit Speaking in Hebrews—Implications for Inerrancy," *Presbyterion* 45, no. 1 (2019): 116–23.

[60] Henry, *God, Revelation and Authority*, 2:13.

[61] Ken Schenck, "God Has Spoken: Hebrews' Theology of the Scriptures," in *The Epistle to the Hebrews and Christian Theology*, ed. Richard Bauckham et al. (Grand Rapids: Eerdmans, 2009), 323.

[62] Myk Habets, "That Was Then, This Is Now: Reading Hebrews Retroactively," in *The Voice of God in the Voice of Scripture: Explorations in Constructive Dogmatics*, ed. Oliver D. Crisp and Fred Sanders (Grand Rapids: Zondervan, 2016), 98.

of time, a dynamic address, and the priority of divine intent in Hebrews' treatment of Scripture as "divine address."[63] As noted above, Pierce examined closely how each Person of the Godhead speaks the words of Scripture personally.[64] Harris concludes, "God's words recorded in Scripture are God's words that are still speaking to the audience in Hebrews."[65]

Henry's fourth propositional thesis concerns *the Holy Spirit's superintendence* of biblical revelation. The Spirit "superintends the communication of divine revelation" to the church. There are two parts to the Spirit's superintendence of biblical propositions: inspiration and illumination. By "inspiration," Henry means the Spirit guided the biblical authors such that we may declare their original autographs possess the quality of "inerrancy." The copies of the autographs, which we possess today, are characterized as "infallible" in verbal content for the purpose of bringing human beings to salvation. By "illumination," Henry means the objective writings must have their meaning subjectively opened to human recipients. Henry recalled the necessity of the Holy Spirit's role in biblical revelation and remained emphatic about our constant dependence upon it. "Yet unless priority is given to the objectively inspired content of Scripture, Spirit-illumination readily gives way to private fantasy and mysticism." Hermeneutically, the Spirit leads the church to interpret according to "the literal-grammatical sense."[66]

---

[63] Gregory W. Lee, *Today When You Hear His Voice: Scripture, the Covenants, and the People of God* (Grand Rapids: Eerdmans, 2016), 179–81.

[64] See note 5 above.

[65] Harris, "Today If You Hear My Voice," 113. Harris detected three implications of the Spirit speaking in Hebrews: "First, the Spirit is the source and inspiration of the initial inscripturation phase of Scripture." "Second, the Spirit is the true interpreter of this initial inscripturation (the Old Testament) as it is being applied to a new canonical context." "Third, the Spirit is the source and inspiration of the fulfilled and final inscripturation phase of Scripture (canonically, the New Testament)." Harris, "Today If You Hear My Voice," 124, 126.

[66] Henry, *God, Revelation and Authority*, 2:13–15. While the literal-grammatical sense always requires priority, we agree with proponents of the theological interpretation of Scripture that there is a larger Christological, canonical, and theological meaning that we should not ignore. Gregory Lee examined the way the book of Hebrews interprets the Old Testament and came to a similar conclusion. Figural interpretation must be "indexed to two central facts of redemptive history: the radical newness of the Christ event, and the fidelity of God's promises to Israel." Lee, *Today*

Henry's propositional definition of revelation helped American evangelicals reaffirm the doctrine of biblical inerrancy. At the same time, the propositional nature of revelation became so ascendant that some evangelical theologians have had difficulty finding their way beyond a merely propositional "model of revelation."[67] The appropriation of speech-act theory by Nicholas Wolterstorff and Kevin J. Vanhoozer offers one way for evangelicals to reconnect their propositional emphasis with the personal nature of revelation.[68] Speech-act theory reminds theologians that Scripture includes not merely generic propositions about God and humanity but also divine address, divine command, and divine promise. Anthony C. Thiselton warns that some evangelical thinkers, when discussing the term "revelation," may exclude the personal.[69] We believe it is vital to embrace the personal as well as the propositional nature of revelation.

In summary, to this point, we have affirmed six personal aspects of a doctrine of divine revelation and four propositional aspects. We must now add an important eleventh aspect to a definition of revelation, also drawn from conversation with Carl Henry and others, to assert that *the Spirit empowers the church to proclaim God's saving revelation and to call the world to faith*. The Holy Spirit indwells, enlivens, and guides the church of Jesus Christ to call all human beings to salvation so that they may face the final judgment with confidence that believers in Christ will be saved for

---

When You Hear His Voice, 186. These concepts will be given greater attention in the chapters on "From Biblical Interpretation to Theology."

[67] Avery Dulles is clear that the "models of revelation" he proposed were "simplified," "schematic," "ideal," and "theoretical." The models must not be taken as mutually exclusive, for no model can contain the mystery of God and his revelation: "all theories of revelation are deficient in comparison with revelation itself." Dulles, *Models of Revelation*, 30–32, 35. Dulles saw positive aspects in four of the five models he detected. Dulles, *Models of Revelation*, 26–30.

[68] Nicholas Wolterstorff, *Divine Discourse: Philosophical Reflections on the Claim that God Speaks* (New York: Cambridge University Press, 1995); Kevin J. Vanhoozer, *The Drama of Doctrine: A Canonical-Linguistic Approach to Christian Theology* (Louisville: Westminster John Knox, 2005). Also, see Feinberg, *Light in a Dark Place*, 198–201 (see introduction, n. 5).

[69] Anthony C. Thiselton, "Speech-Act Theory and the Claim that God Speaks: Nicholas Wolterstorff's *Divine Discourse*," *Scottish Journal of Theology* 50, no. 1 (1997): 101.

eternal communion with God but that the lack of saving faith will end in eternal judgment.[70] The author of Hebrews was animated by the desire to see the people saved by true faith in the revelation of the Son. The listener must receive God's revelation into the heart (Heb 3:7–19) and unite with the Word of God and the community of believers by faith (4:1–2).[71] The faith in Christ (11:17–26; 12:2) that comes through the proclamation of God's Word is necessary for justification (11:2, 4–7) and results in our resurrection (11:19).

V. Trinitarian Priority in Divine Revelation

Finally, we are compelled to add a twelfth aspect to our definition of divine revelation, an aspect likely presupposed by the other theologians cited but not always clearly stated. In our opening discussion we noted that the doctrines of God and of revelation are inseparable. We conclude that this aspect really ought to receive first place in any orthodox definition of divine revelation. John Webster reminds us it is God who speaks in the act of divine revelation to the church. "God speaks God's Word through the text of the Bible to the people of God."[72] Webster also notes the God who speaks is triune and that the Trinity is inextricably tied to revelation. Revelation is "the self-presentation of the triune God."[73] Moreover, "the proper doctrinal location for talk of revelation is the Christian doctrine of the Trinity, and, in particular, the outgoing, communicative mercy of the triune God in the economy of salvation."[74] Vanhoozer agrees that "Scripture communicates a share in the triune life,"[75] and that "we must ultimately identify God's speaking as triune

---

[70] Henry, *God, Revelation and Authority*, 2:15–16.

[71] Stephen E. Fowl, "'In Many and Various Ways': Hearing the Voice of God in the Text of Scripture," in *The Voice of God in the Text of Scripture: Explorations in Constructive Dogmatics*, ed. Oliver D. Crisp and Fred Sanders (Grand Rapids: Zondervan, 2016), 53–55.

[72] John Webster, "Hermeneutics in Modern Theology: Some Doctrinal Reflections," *Scottish Journal of Theology* 51, no. 3 (1998): 336.

[73] John Webster, *Holy Scripture: A Dogmatic Sketch* (New York: Cambridge University Press, 2003), 13.

[74] Webster, *Holy Scripture*, 16–17.

[75] Vanhoozer, *The Drama of Doctrine*, 67.

discourse."[76] Vanhoozer went so far as to argue Scripture should not be treated under a standalone locus of revelation but within the locus of the Trinity.[77]

We likewise believe this God who speaks to his church is none other than the One who is eternally the Father and the Son and the Holy Spirit. We rightly call him, "Trinity." During the Enlightenment, the fundamental dogma that God is Trinity became questionable among liberal theologians and was often overlooked by conservative preachers. In the twentieth and twenty-first centuries, systematic theologians began to reconsider the trinitarian approach to theology and revelation. This trinitarian revival began in earnest with Karl Barth in Western Europe, but it was soon joined by theologians in Roman Catholic, Eastern Orthodox, and Mainline Protestant circles. More recently Evangelical Protestants like John Webster, Kevin Vanhoozer, Scott Swain, Robert Letham, and Fred Sanders, among others have exposited the doctrine of the Trinity.

Our prior contribution to the doctrine of the Trinity was designed to help evangelicals in the Believers' Church tradition answer the questions of whether Scripture taught the doctrine of the Trinity and whether it is necessary to believe. After working through eight major biblical texts, it became clear that the doctrine of God the Trinity was both biblical and necessary. "The Trinity is the idiom of Scripture because he inspired his Word as such, and the Spirit illumines him as prominently and inextricably woven into the warp and woof of the text."[78] Once again, we call for a recovery of a "realist conception of Christian revelation," meaning that revelation reveals in a trustworthy manner who God is. "We agree that there is a real correspondence between who God is and how God reveals himself to be. The economic Trinity truly reveals the immanent Trinity."[79]

---

[76] Kevin J. Vanhoozer, "Augustinian Inerrancy: Literal Meaning, Literary Truth, and Literate Interpretation in the Economy of Biblical Discourse," in *Five Views on Biblical Inerrancy*, ed. J. Merrick and Stephen M. Garrett (Grand Rapids: Zondervan, 2013), 208–9.

[77] Kevin J. Vanhoozer, "Holy Scripture," in *Christian Dogmatics: Reformed Theology for the Church Catholic*, ed. Michael Allen and Scott R. Swain (Grand Rapids: Baker, 2016), 41.

[78] Malcolm B. Yarnell III, *God the Trinity: Biblical Portraits* (Nashville: B&H, 2016), 238.

[79] Yarnell, *God the Trinity*, 231–32; also, see Dockery, *Christian Scripture*, 20–24 (see introduction, n. 4).

Because of the need to speak clearly about "divine revelation," we believe that any doctrine of "revelation" must clearly affirm who the "divine" One is that is being revealed. The definition of "God" has too often been assumed rather than affirmed. We, therefore, must place first in our definition of revelation an affirmation that *the God who reveals himself is none other than God the Trinity.* This statement of priority holds true both for the Old Testament, which provides the building blocks for a doctrine of God as Trinity, and the New Testament, which clearly affirms that the God who saves us must be worshiped as Trinity. He is the one God in whose threefold "name" or identity new believers are baptized (Matt 28:19) and in, with, and by whom we are called into communion (2 Cor 13:13; Eph 2:19; Gal 4:4–6). The God who reveals himself in nature and conscience on the one hand and in special revelation and Scripture on the other hand is God the Trinity and no other. There is no God other than God the Trinity.

VI. Definition of Divine Revelation

With these twelve aspects of revelation identified, we are now prepared to provide a full definition of divine revelation. This definition will be offered in two sentences. Recognizing the priority of the identification of God as the Trinity, the One who is the Father and the Son and the Holy Spirit, will ground both sentences in theological orthodoxy. The first sentence focuses on the personal nature of divine revelation, while the second focuses on the propositional nature of divine revelation. Both sentences are true and require affirmation.

By speaking of "divine revelation" we mean that *God the Trinity from his absolute transcendence overcomes human blindness in an act of unexpected grace by personally disclosing unusual and life-giving knowledge about God, his world, and his work from creation to consummation, with a focus on the incarnation and redeeming work of Jesus Christ. The Eternal Logos, Jesus Christ, reveals himself and his saving work rationally and verbally in the written Word of God originally inspired by the Holy Spirit, illumined by the Spirit to his church today, and proclaimed to the world in the power of the Spirit through his church.*

While this detailed definition seeks to touch on the key points identified throughout this chapter, we can say the special revelation is God's manifestation of himself and his will to particular people in specific places. Though not in a complete way, we can still affirm the mystery of God himself is unveiled and God's truth is revealed. It can be said that special revelation is the declaration of truth about God, his character, and his actions in relationship with his creation. This self-manifestation is meaningful and intelligent, making known divine truth for the minds and hearts of the people of God.

This revelation is made known in the witness of biblical history over time, a progressive and developing manifestation of God, his will, and his truth in the Old Testament and then in the New. This development is complementary and not contradictory, progressing not from untruth to truth, but from a lesser to a fuller revelation (Heb 1:1–3). The Old Testament revelation is fulfilled in the New; the latter testament fulfills the former, even as the former testament grounds the latter. God's special revelation has been unfolded throughout redemptive history, ultimately being consummated in the person and work of the Lord Jesus Christ (John 1:1–18). This revelation, which has come to us in both words and acts has been divinely interpreted for us through the inspired writings of holy Scripture. God has initiated the revelation of himself to women and men, making it possible for those who place their faith in Christ to know God and to grow in relationship with him. Today, the Bible is the primary source of God's revelation; indeed, we can go so far as to say the Bible is a written revelation of the nature of God and his will for fallen humankind. These important truths will be developed in the remaining chapters of this volume.

2

The Two Ways of Revelation

Having examined the definition of revelation, we must now turn our attention to the two distinct ways through which the revelation of God comes to human beings. In the last chapter, we reviewed common biblical terms for revelation, then considered the personal aspects of revelation, the propositional aspects of revelation, and the necessity of affirming revelation as personal, propositional, and progressive. We emphasized the truth that revelation is a gracious act of disclosure to humanity by the trinitarian God. Our definition of divine revelation included these trinitarian, personal, and propositional dimensions. In the current chapter, we consider the two ways, or avenues or means, by which God reveals himself. In the next chapter, we rehearse and evaluate various natural theologies which principally depend upon one of those ways, general revelation.

I. Definitions

The two primary ways of divine revelation are typically classified under the technical terms of *general revelation* and *special revelation*. An adequate definition of either way of revelation should summarize the source, content, modes, and recipients of that way of revelation. We begin with a description of general revelation before defining special revelation. "General revelation," sometimes called "natural revelation,"[1] may be defined summarily as *God the Trinity's disclosure of certain truths to all human beings about himself and his relation to humanity through both external evidence and internal evidence.*

First, the *source* of general revelation is the one true God, who is the Trinity. We do not intend hereby to infer the doctrine of the Trinity is taught in general revelation. On the one hand, many theologians have followed Augustine of Hippo in discerning *vestigia Trinitatis*, "marks of the Trinity," in the human being particularly or in creation generally.[2] On the other hand, Karl Barth warned such efforts lead to "some alien God," for God reveals himself in Jesus Christ.[3] With due respect both for Augustine's positive approach and Barth's strong warning, we ourselves wish to remind Christians that the God who reveals himself in nature and conscience is the same God who reveals himself in the Bible. There is only one God who reveals himself. The fuller revelation of God as Trinity requires the special revelation of Jesus Christ. Prior to that special revelation in Jesus Christ, human beings receive only a limited portrait of God from general revelation.

Second, the *content* of general revelation does not include everything which human beings may find of interest. General revelation does not concern itself with everything which human beings have discovered about the natural world, history, religion, or human beings, but with certain truths. These certain truths focus on God himself and his relation to humanity. We shall have occasion below to consider these two major truths more fully. Third, the *modes* of general revelation include both external evidence and internal evidence. A general testimony to God is available outside humanity in creation or nature. A general testimony to God is also available within the human heart and conscience.

---

[1] Russell D. Moore, "Natural Revelation," in *A Theology for the Church*, rev. ed., ed. Daniel L. Akin (Nashville: B&H, 2014), 77–101.

[2] Augustine was focused upon discerning the Trinity through the human being made in his image rather than seeking to provide a proof for divine existence. Anna N. Williams, *The Divine Sense: Intellect in Christian Theology* (New York: Cambridge University Press, 2007), 155.

[3] Barth stood against *vestigia Trinitatis* precisely because it had been used to construct a correlation between humanity and the Trinity. Karl Barth, *Church Dogmatics*, ed. Geoffrey W. Bromiley and Thomas F. Torrance, (London: T&T Clark, 2004), I/1: 345–47.

Fourth, regarding *recipients*, the term "general" highlights the truth that the addressees of this way of revelation include all human beings. Because the human beings who receive divine revelation are sinners, we invariably distort revealed truth. As a result, important questions about how general revelation has been received and interpreted, or whether it has even been received at all, should chasten our conclusions from general revelation.

Our second technical theological term, "special revelation," must also be considered from the perspective of its source, content, modes, and recipients. In an earlier description of special revelation, we affirmed first that special revelation is "consistent with" yet also "distinct from" general revelation. After making this crucial statement, we identified four avenues of special revelation: "personal encounter with the Lord," "the mighty acts of God," "verbal/propositional revelation" from God, and "the incarnation" of the Second Person of the Trinity. All four of these avenues "coalesce beautifully in the person and work of Jesus Christ," who claims a "supremacy" in revelation "that cannot be exceeded." "The content of special revelation is primarily God himself," and God is in Christ.[4] Accordingly, then, the Christian understanding of the *source* and *content* of special revelation must be focused upon God in Christ. This identification of Christology as the center of special revelation is profoundly significant and absolutely indispensable.

Regarding the *modes* of special revelation, it can be said that "While we can identify Scripture as a mode of special revelation, along with God's words and acts, it must be acknowledged that Scripture and revelation are not identical." Not every instance of special revelation has been recorded in Scripture, as Scripture itself indicates (John 21:25). Nevertheless, "the Bible is a written revelation of God's nature and his will for fallen humankind."[5] The Bible is the Word of God.

Finally, regarding its *recipients*, the special revelation of God can be categorized as "primarily redemptive and personal."[6] Special revelation was treated synonymously by James Leo Garrett Jr. alongside the terms "historical or biblical." For Garrett, then, revelation entails a concrete or real event rather than an abstract or allusive one. Dwelling upon the historical and biblical context

---

[4] Dockery, "Special Revelation," 104–6 (see introduction, n. 24).
[5] Dockery, "Special Revelation," 107.
[6] Dockery, 105.

of special revelation, Garrett found two major "phases" of special revelation, "that which came to and through the people of Israel (Old Testament)" and "that which came in and through Jesus Christ (New Testament)."[7]

In addition to our primary terms, "general revelation" and "special revelation," we must consider two other major terms, "natural theology" and "revealed theology." Our first two terms consider the divine movement of revelation while the second two terms consider the human reception of that revelation. "Natural theology" has been defined as "the attempt to build a theological structure on the basis of general revelation apart from God's witness in the Scriptures and in Jesus Christ."[8] Although it derives from general revelation, natural theology should not be confused with general revelation. Revelation is a divine movement; theology is a human response. Natural theology is the human being's intellectual, moral, and spiritual response to God's revelation of himself in nature and conscience.

As a human response to divine revelation, natural theology will inevitably be characterized by human fallibility. This fallibility in natural theology does not impinge upon the perfection of God, who always reveals himself infallibly. Rather, the weakness of natural theology is due entirely to the intellectual limits, moral culpability, and spiritual bankruptcy of the fallen human beings engaged in this work. The frailty of natural theology is well attested in Scripture and in human history. Scripturally, the apostle Paul indicated that human beings used natural theology to manufacture idolatry and depravity by suppressing the truth of general revelation (Acts 14:8–18; 17:16–31; Rom 1:18–32). Historically, the multiplicity of false religions in the world is, from a Christian perspective, not due to a failure in general revelation but to the failure in what human beings do with that universal revelation. Recounting his own journey through many falsehoods to the truth of God in Christ, Augustine said, "The light is clouded over and the truth cannot be seen, although it is there before our eyes."[9] The problem is not with the light of God but with the human being who fails to receive his light properly.

---

[7] Garrett Jr., *Systematic Theology*, 1:105 (see chap. 1, n. 47).

[8] Moore, "Natural Revelation," 67.

[9] Augustine, *Confessions* 4.14; Saint Augustine, *Confessions*, trans. R. S. Pine-Coffin (New York: Penguin, 1961), 85.

When theologians and apologists refer to "revealed theology," they typically mean that theology which is derived from special revelation rather than from nature or conscience. Natural theology and revealed theology are deriving from the same source of revelation, God, but are responding to the two different ways of revelation. Revealed theology employs special revelation to arrive at its theological conclusions. Taking a large methodological and more trustworthy step beyond natural theology, revealed theology accepts the witness not only of nature and reason but also the witness of those who receive a direct revelation from God not otherwise available to human beings. In the Christian context, revealed theology privileges the witness of Scripture due to the inspiration and testimony of the Holy Spirit. Natural theology derives exclusively from general revelation, while revealed theology also derives from special revelation.

Since this entire volume is devoted to the topic of special revelation, this chapter and the following will deal primarily with general revelation. First, to demonstrate how general revelation is related to special revelation in terms of their being consistent with yet distinct from one another, we must garner relevant insights from Scripture. The Holy Bible, as the inspired and authoritative special revelation of God in written form, must be allowed to define the source, content, modes, and recipients of that revelation of God which comes more generally and allusively to humanity. To accomplish this end, we contemplate how the book of Romans correlates yet distinguishes general revelation and natural theology from special revelation. After surveying the witness of the remainder of the Christian canon, only then may we turn our attention to an historical description of the natural theologies derived from general revelation and offer our own. This chapter will focus upon the biblical witness, while the next will offer an historical and systematic response.

II. The Ways of Revelation in Romans

The book of Romans has been deemed "the most important piece in the New Testament" and "the purest gospel."[10] Its impact upon Christian

---

[10] "Diese Epistel ist das rechte Hauptstück des Neuen Testaments und das allerlauterste Evangelium." See Martin Luther, "Der Brief des Paulus an die Römer," in

history has been deep, profound, and repetitive. In 386, Augustine, the formative theologian for Western Christianity, converted to Christ while reading Romans 13.[11] In 1516, Martin Luther, the leading theologian of the Protestant Reformation, was transformed when he properly understood Rom 1:16–17.[12] In 1651, John Bunyan, author of *The Pilgrim's Progress*, was born again while considering the righteousness of Christ taught in Rom 3:28.[13] In 1738, John Wesley felt his heart "strangely warmed" after hearing Luther's *Preface to the Romans* read in a London church. His preaching was instrumental for the widespread awakenings of the eighteenth century.[14] In 1919, Karl Barth released the first edition of his *Römerbrief*, a theological commentary that began the turning of the tide against the intellectual ascendance of theological liberalism.[15]

The book of Romans is not merely historically significant. It is also canonically and theologically extremely important. Canonically, it is both the first and the longest of the epistles to appear in the New Testament. It is also the longest epistle of the apostle Paul. Theologically, Calvin Porter notes, "No other letter of Paul's has contributed more to the theological vocabulary of the church—gospel, sin, grace, faith, righteousness of God, hope, justification by faith, good works, and law. Important theological concepts and ideas have been derived either wholly or in part from Romans—original sin, free will, justification by faith alone, double-predestination, and sanctification."[16]

Luther Testament: Neues Testament und Psalmen mit Sonderseiten zu Luthers Leben und den Stätten seines Wirkens (Stuttgart: Deutsche Bibelgesellschaft, 1995), 50.

[11] Augustine, *Confessions* 8.12.

[12] Alister E. McGrath, *Luther's Theology of the Cross: Martin Luther's Theological Breakthrough* (New York: Basil Blackwell, 1985), 85–100.

[13] John Bunyan, *Grace Abounding to the Chief of Sinners* (London: Oliphant Anderson & Ferrier, ca. 1900), 100–101.

[14] Henry D. Rack, *Reasonable Enthusiast: John Wesley and the Rise of Methodism*, 3rd ed. (London: Epworth, 2002), 144.

[15] John Webster, *Barth* (New York: Continuum, 2000), 24–34.

[16] Calvin L. Porter, "Paul as Theologian: Romans," *Encounter* 65, no. 2 (Spring 2004): 109; also, see C. E. B. Cranfield, *Romans: A Shorter Commentary* (Grand Rapids: Eerdmans, 1985), 1–30; David G. Peterson, *Romans*, Biblical Theology for Christian Proclamation (Nashville: B&H, 2017), 1–30.

Like many others, Porter identified Rom 1:16–17 as the "theme" and "thesis" of the letter.[17] But he neglected to develop a central verb in that thematic passage for Paul's most theologically significant letter, a verb repeated in the very next verse in a formulaic way. The verb *apokalyptetai* means "is revealed" or "is uncovered." Paul says that both "the righteousness of God" and "the wrath of God" are revealed or uncovered. Central to the development of the thesis of Romans, therefore, is a twofold divine revelation. First, the divine attribute of the "righteousness" of God revealed in the gospel of God brings comfort to those who are reconciled believers in Jesus Christ. Second, the righteousness of God revealed in the law of God, available through both general revelation and special revelation, brings knowledge of the "wrath" of God against the unreconciled human being, the unbeliever. The thesis of Romans reads:

> For I am not ashamed of the gospel, because it is the power of God for salvation to everyone who believes, first to the Jew, and also to the Greek. For in it the righteousness of God is revealed [*apokalyptetai*] from faith to faith, just as it is written: The righteous will live by faith.
>
> For God's wrath is revealed [*apokalyptetai*] from heaven against all godlessness and unrighteousness of people who by their unrighteousness suppress the truth, since what can be known about God is evident among them, because God has shown it to them. (Rom 1:16–19)

After proposing his thesis about God's twofold revelation, the punitive righteousness of God against human sinfulness is first and extensively considered by Paul in his epistle to the Romans (1:18–3:20). Afterward, the redemptive righteousness of God available through justification by faith is developed in the second major section of his epistle (3:21–5:21). Later in the letter Paul deliberated upon the believer's transformation (6:1–8:39), the mystery of Israel (9:1–11:36), and various instructions for the Christian life (12:1–15:13). Confined by our assignment to the doctrine of divine revelation, we shall here limit our theological exegesis of Romans to the themes

---

[17] Porter, "Paul as Theologian," 116, 128.

of God's hiddenness, God's general revelation of the law, God's special revelation of the law and the gospel, the modes of the special revelation which saves, and the end or goal of special revelation.

1. The Hiddenness of God

In Rom 11:33, God's ways are described as, by nature "unfathomable" or "unsearchable," and "incomprehensible" or "inscrutable." To prove his point, Paul cited Job 41:11, Isa 40:13, and Jer 23:18 (Rom 11:34–35). Paul is teaching us that direct knowledge of God cannot be gained by any act of human will. Nor could it be understood by the natural human mind, even if a human being was somehow able to gain access to that knowledge. God's inscrutability is grounded in his utter independence. Theologians have learned to speak of God possessing divine aseity, by which we mean God has his origin from nowhere but himself—his existence depends upon his essence alone. The independence and self-referential existence of God means that, from our perspective, he remains radically transcendent. However, his transcendence does not keep God from becoming immanent to created persons by grace. He is Creator and, as such, the origin, sustenance, and end of all created things, including angelic and human persons.

Due to the difference between the divine nature and the human nature, God cannot naturally be known by his human creatures. However, God can bridge the divide and reveal himself to his creatures by grace. Thankfully, God's hiddenness is not the final act, for God reveals himself and his saving will through the special revelation of the gospel of Jesus Christ. Paul teaches that God acts on behalf of the revelation of his glory (Rom 11:36). Based on the apostle's description of God's hiddenness in Romans 11, Karl Barth argued, "in Christ Jesus the *Deus absconditus* is as such the *Deus revelatus*."[18] In the person of the divine-human person, Jesus Christ, "the hidden God" becomes to those who are granted the grace of hearing by the Holy Spirit of God, "the revealed God." The hiddenness

---

[18] Sean Winter, "God Revealed and Hidden: Barth's Exegesis of Romans 11:33–36," *Colloquium* 50, no. 1 (2018): 46–58; see Richard N. Longenecker, *The Epistle to the Romans: A Commentary on the Greek Text* (Grand Rapids: Eerdmans, 2016), 906–16.

of God is the set position for humanity, but God has chosen to disclose himself in the flesh of his only Son. Because the Son is eternally God, he has always known the nature of God. Because the Son became a human being, taking our nature upon himself in Jesus Christ, he can reveal God to humanity.

One of the most comprehensive terms which the apostle Paul used to describe God's movement from unknown eternity into known history is *mystērion*, which may be translated as "secret" or "mystery." Note how the revelation of God derives from the inscrutability of eternity but becomes evident to human beings in the progress of sacred history: First, the "mystery" of God's "predestined" decree was "kept silent for long ages" (Rom 16:25; 1 Cor 2:7; Eph 3:9; Col 1:26). There was no human access to this knowledge (Isa 52:15). Second, the substance of this now-revealed mystery is centered on the person of Jesus Christ and the gospel of his death and resurrection (Eph 1:9; Col 2:2; 1 Tim 3:16; cf. Rom 1:1–4). Third, Paul says, "the mystery was made known to me by revelation" (Eph 3:3). The apostles proclaimed that mystery to others. By faith the mystery comes to believers (Eph 5:32; Rev 1:20), who must hold the mystery "with a clear conscience" (1 Tim 3:9). It must also be proclaimed among the nations (Col 1:27; 4:3). Finally, the mystery will reach its denouement with the events surrounding the future Second Coming of Jesus Christ (Rom 11:25; 1 Cor 2:7; 15:51; 2 Thess 2:7; Rev 10:7; 17:5–7).

2. The General Revelation of the Law

The revelation of God in the book of Romans may be considered according to its two major ways and its two major contents. The two major *ways* by which God reveals himself are general revelation and special revelation, as described above. The two major *contents* of God's revelation are the judgment of his law and the promise of his gospel. The ways of God's self-disclosure stand in correlation with the contents of his revelation. Through the law, general revelation makes known God's judgment upon all men, while through the gospel, special revelation makes known God's promise of salvation. We may consider the contents of God's revelation according to the language of Paul's central theme as "the righteousness of God" (Rom 1:17) and "the wrath of God" (1:18). We begin with the wrath of God, the judgment of his law against the unrighteousness of humanity, which is disclosed in general revelation.

After setting out his thesis in Rom 1:16–17, Paul first describes the general revelation of God (1:18–21). That God will one day judge humanity is made available to humanity in general through nature, history, and conscience. God's law, available to his creatures since the beginning of time, tells certain things both about God's attributes, such as his invisibility and power, and about his activities, such as past creation and future judgment. The revelation accessible to all through nature and history renders human beings accountable to God for their sin (Rom 1:21). The problem with this general revelation resides not in the revelation itself, but in what fallen humanity does with this revelation. Fallen humanity perverts the truth about God and his activities. We thereby descend into idolatry and sinfulness.

The general revelation of the attributes of God and of his activities comes to the knowledge of the human mind experientially when the vestiges of the Creator in his creation impress themselves upon human observation. Among the "invisible attributes" (1:20) of God which Paul describes as generally available are the following: God can and does reveal himself. God has "eternal power." This indicates both that God is eternal and that his power has no limit. Also revealed is his *theiotēs*, "divine nature." Paul does not declare of exactly what God's nature subsists, but he maintains that we are aware that God has a divine nature. Paul is not speculating with the content of general revelation but demonstrating enough revelation remains available to all men such that they are "without excuse." General revelation is "understood through what he has made." General revelation provides sufficient knowledge of God to hold human beings accountable for their sin.

Shifting from theology to anthropology, Paul says general revelation concerns God's "wrath" against "two objects": human "ungodliness" and human "unrighteousness."[19] And what do human beings do with this significant yet limited knowledge of God and of ourselves? We exercise our personal agency, received upon being made in the image of God, but humans

---

[19] Douglas J. Moo, *The Epistle to the Romans*, The New International Commentary on the New Testament (Grand Rapids: Eerdmans, 1996), 102; also, see C. K. Barrett, *The Epistle to the Romans*, Harper's New Testament Commentaries (New York: Harper & Row, 1957), 31–38.

do not glorify or praise God with our agency as we should. Instead, "their thinking became worthless" and their hearts were "darkened" (1:21). Human beings became foolish and depraved, embracing theological perversity in heart, mind, and will. Three "parallel retribution sequences" comprise the remainder of Romans 1: Humanity "exchanged" divine truth for idolatry, so God "delivered them over" to their hearts (vv. 21–24). Humanity "exchanged" divine truth for deception, so God "delivered them over" to their passions (vv. 25–26a). Humanity "exchanged" the sexual relations God gave in nature for unnatural relations, so God "delivered them over" to their minds (vv. 26b–31).[20] The depraved human mind hereby reinforces its moral culpability and receives judgment.

Next, Paul indicated that knowledge of God comes not merely through observation of the outside world. Knowledge of God and his activity also comes innately through the human "consciences" (Rom 2:1–16). In the first two chapters of Romans, Paul outlined "two uses" or two avenues of natural revelation, one derived through observation, the other through internal witness.[21] Paul's description of the conscience is chaste, but it is enough to let human beings know there is a record being maintained in the divine court regarding one's actions. "Here conscience appears as an intuitive recognition, both in principle and in detail, of the distinction between right and wrong."[22]

God will "repay each one according to his works," differentiating those acts which are "good" from those which are "evil" (2:6–9). The Gentiles do not have Scripture, but "the work of the law" is nonetheless "written on their hearts." The "consciences" of human beings remind them that God remains fully aware of our moral guilt. The conscience works by allowing the "competing thoughts" of the human being to "accuse" or to "excuse" us before the future throne of divine judgment (vv. 15–16). Philosophers and theologians trace movements of conscience to a general knowledge among human beings regarding morality. The knowledge of God's "eternal law" developed

---

[20] Moo, *The Epistle to the Romans*, 96.

[21] These two uses "do not stand in conflict with one another, and in fact may be seen to interlock." Mark A. Seifrid, "Natural Law and the Purpose of the Law in Romans," *Tyndale Bulletin* 49, no. 1 (May 1998): 118.

[22] Kenneth E. Kirk, *The Epistle to the Romans in the Revised Version with Introduction and Commentary*, The Clarendon Bible (Oxford: Oxford University Press, 1937), 38.

historically through the subject of "natural law" manifested in "the laws of nations."[23] Divine law manifests itself in natural law, so that nations may form their laws.[24]

3. The Special Revelation of Both Law and Gospel

While the Jews are not in the murkier epistemological state of the Gentiles, they are nevertheless just as subject to God's wrath as the Gentiles. The Gentiles have some knowledge of God's will through nature, history, and conscience. The Jews are in considerably better shape, as far as revelation of the law goes. This is because the people of Israel "were entrusted with the very words of God," the special revelation of God through the Law of the Old Testament (Rom 3:2). However, because the Jews still disobeyed the revelation of God's law, they are likewise subject to God's wrath (2:25; 3:5). Whether it is through general revelation of God's law in nature or through special revelation of God's Law in writing, "both Jews and Gentiles are all under sin" (3:9, KJV). Paul proceeds with a liturgical tirade against universal human depravity drawn from the Psalms and Prophets (3:10–18). The whole world needs to shut its mouth, for all deserve God's wrath. The Law only reveals our sin. It cannot justify us (3:19–20).

Having outlined the revelation of God's wrath through both general revelation to all people and through special revelation to the people of Israel,

---

[23] Paul E. Sigmund, "Law and Politics," in *The Cambridge Companion to Aquinas*, ed. Norman Kretzmann and Eleonore Stump (New York: Cambridge University Press, 1993), 222–29. "An unjust law is a human law that is not rooted in eternal law and natural law. Any law that uplifts human personality is just. Any law that degrades human personality is unjust. All segregation statutes are unjust because segregation distorts the soul and damages the personality. It gives the segregator a false sense of superiority and the segregated a false sense of inferiority." Martin Luther King Jr., "Letter from Birmingham City Jail (1963)," in *A Testament of Hope: The Essential Writings and Speeches of Martin Luther King Jr.*, ed. James Melvin Washington (New York: HarperCollins, 1991), 289–302.

[24] The doctrine of natural law simultaneously grounds national laws and relativizes them. The emperor Darius recognized the relativization of the supposedly "irrevocable" law of the Medes and Persians through the divine preservation of Daniel in the Lions' Den. He later confessed both the eternality and ultimate power of "the living God" (Dan 6:8, 12, 15, 26–27); also, see David E. Garland, *Romans*, Tyndale New Testament Commentaries (Downers Grove: IVP, 2021), 84–97.

Paul returned to the revelation of God's righteousness in Rom 3:21–26. "But now, apart from the law, the righteousness of God has been revealed, attested by the Law and the Prophets" (3:21). On the one hand, the way of the revelation of the law, which makes us aware of God's impending judgment of wrath, cannot save a person. On the other hand, the way of the revelation of "the gospel," which makes us aware of God's gift of righteousness through faith in the death and resurrection of Jesus Christ, can save a person (1:16). The gospel has been clearly made available now, and it is focused upon the twofold nature of the person of Jesus Christ. He is both "Son of God," according to his deity, and "descendant of David, according to the flesh" (Rom 1:1–4). The gospel is also focused upon the twofold event of the work of Jesus Christ in his death and resurrection (1:4; 4:25; 10:9–10).

Paul twice referred in Rom 3:25–26 to *endeixin tēs dikaiosynēs autou*, "the demonstration of his righteousness." According to Walter Bauer, the noun *endeixis* refers to a "sign" or "demonstration," "something that points to or demonstrates something" and even "compels acceptance of something, mentally or emotionally."[25] The words of the gospel of Jesus Christ thereby prompt the hearer to believe and to be saved. The blood of Christ before the mercy seat of God allows God to pass over our sins. God is declared to be both "just" and the "justifier" of the one who believes in the special revelation of the gospel.

In his groundbreaking work on biblical hermeneutics and theological exegesis, Augustine argued we should similarly understand the "words" of Scripture to be meaningful and effective "signs." A word, like a sign, compels a person to think of something beyond the word or sign itself. A "sign" points to a "thing signified." Similarly, God inspired the biblical writers to use human language in such a way that it can point the reader or hearer to the otherwise inscrutable theological reality, the mystery of God the Trinity.[26]

---

[25] W. Arndt, F. W. Danker, W. Bauer, and F. W. Gingrich, *A Greek-English Lexicon of the New Testament and Other Early Christian Literature*, 3rd ed. (Chicago: University of Chicago Press, 2000).

[26] Augustine, *De Doctrina Christiana* 1.1–12, 2.1–4; Saint Augustine, *On Christian Teaching*, trans. R. P. H. Green (New York: Oxford University Press, 1999), 8–10, 30–31. We summarize the fuller teaching of Augustine about signs and things signified in the section on pre-critical exegesis in chapter 11 below. Regarding the modern discipline which evaluates the use of signs in human culture, please see the

When we receive the words about the gospel by faith, we receive the thing which is thereby effectively signified, eternal salvation, life with God in Christ by the Holy Spirit. Theologians may therefore speak of special revelation as conveying both the law and the gospel, while general revelation conveys only the law.

4. Three Modes of Saving Special Revelation

We have thus far discovered how Paul taught that the law of God provides the basis for his condemnation of all people. The revelation of the law of God comes to all humanity in two ways, through general revelation and through special revelation. But the revelation of the gospel of God, unlike the universally available law, is available only through special revelation. The only way a human person can possibly be saved is through receiving the special revelation of Jesus Christ and the good news of his death and resurrection for sinners.

Special revelation is centered upon the person of Jesus Christ. But he is also made instrumentally and epistemologically available to human beings through Scripture and proclamation. Three modes of the saving special revelation should be affirmed. First, Jesus Christ is the unique special revelation of God *in person*. The Word of God as a person comes to humanity for the purpose of our salvation (Rom 16:25; cf. John 14:6–11; Gal 1:12; 1 Pet 1:7, 13; Rev 1:1). Second, knowledge of the gospel of God in Christ originally came *in the proclamation* of Jesus Christ. The proclamation of who Jesus is and what he does was made by himself, by his prophets, and by his apostles. Third, knowledge of the gospel of God continues to be made available through the proclamation of the words of Christ put *in writing* by his apostles and prophets. The Bible is also, therefore, the Word of God.

The distinction between the three modes of the special revelation of human salvation requires some attention. The two modes of proclamation and Scripture are instrumental rather than finally causal, because they point to the primary special revelation of the person of Jesus Christ. These two

---

excellent introduction by Umberto Eco, *A Theory of Semiotics* (Bloomington: Indiana University Press, 1976), 3–29. Eco's description of the difference between denotation and connotation is particularly helpful. Eco, *A Theory of Semiotics*, 54–57.

modes are also intimately related to one another, for the original saving proclamation was recorded in writing, and those writings have now themselves become the content of effective proclamation by means of the Holy Spirit. Even as we maintain the distinction between the three modes of God's saving revelation in Jesus Christ, we must also emphasize their epistemological unity. Jesus is the special revelation of God who saves us personally and powerfully, while Scripture and proclamation are the revelation of God which introduce human beings to the person of Jesus Christ. Jesus Christ is the unique revelation of God ontologically and personally, while Scripture and proclamation participate in the revelation of God epistemologically and instrumentally.

Regarding the original proclamation, Paul says the gospel of God was "promised beforehand through his prophets in the Holy Scriptures" (Rom 1:2) and "attested by the Law and Prophets" (3:21). The gospel was in a preparatory sense available during the Old Testament period. While the mystery of the gospel was partially revealed and partially hidden to the patriarchs and prophets, the way of salvation was nevertheless made available to these ancient people through their exercise of faith in the promise of God concerning the coming Christ (Rom 4:3–9; cf. Heb 11). The revelation of salvation has since been fully revealed in the Lord Jesus Christ, as the apostles were led to attest (John 1:18; Acts 8:12; 10:36; 28:31; Rom 15:19; 2 Cor 1:19; Eph 3:8, etc.). Christ continues to be proclaimed even now, since the long-hidden mystery of salvation through Jesus Christ is hereby effectively "revealed and made known through the prophetic Scriptures" (Rom 16:26).

Following upon the central events of the death and resurrection of Jesus Christ, it is in the proclamation of the *rhēma*, "message," that one can be saved through calling back to God in faith. The phenomenological process of salvation described in Rom 10:4–21 is highly instructive. First, the message of Jesus Christ comes as a gift of divine freedom, apart from any human willfulness (vv. 5–7). Second, the message moves palpably through the preaching of those sent out by the church to the ears of sinners (vv. 14–15). Third, the hearer who responds in concurrent faith in and confession of the message is the one who will be saved (vv. 8–13). The process of salvation through proclamation is activated by the dynamic message from God rather than by the mind or will of the human recipient (vv. 16–17). The obstinance of Israel and the mercy of God to the nations is the reason for Israel's temporary rejection of the message of Christ (vv. 18–21).

5. The End of Special Revelation

Paul writes in Rom 10:4, "For Christ is the end [*telos*] of the law for righteousness to everyone who believes." Scholars hesitate when interpreting the word *telos* into English. Should the term be translated as "end" with the idea of "termination" or "cessation"? Or should it perhaps be translated as "goal" or "conclusion"? Translating *telos* as "end" in the sense of "termination" may diminish the law of God. But translating it as "goal" may downplay the finality of revelation in Jesus Christ. Whichever translation is chosen, salvation in Jesus Christ remains the terminus of divine revelation. The gospel of Jesus Christ is the end of the revelation of God. For Herman Ridderbos, the principal point and "fundamental structure" of Paul's preaching is that "the eschatological time of salvation" was "inaugurated with Christ's advent, death, and resurrection."[27] Paul encapsulates everything in Christ and his gospel (Eph 1:10; 1 Cor 2:2). Looking back, Ridderbos could say, "the Old Testament is the book of Christ." Looking forward, he concluded Paul's eschatology has a "fundamental Christological character." In summation, "Christ [is] the revelation of the mystery."[28]

Paul emphasized the "revealing" of God twice, regarding his righteousness and his wrath, in his thesis for the letter to the Romans (Rom 1:16–18). The third occurrence of the key verb *apokalyptō* for divine revelation appears in the eighth chapter. "For I consider that the sufferings of this present time are not worth comparing with the glory that is going to be revealed to us" (8:18). The threefold progress of *apokalyptō* in the book of Romans suggests revelation occurs in three stages. First, the *general revelation* of God available always to all human beings is focused upon the knowledge of God's impending wrath against sinners. Second, the *special revelation* of God available to those who have faith makes the knowledge of God's righteousness available through the gospel of Jesus Christ. This special revelation saves those who receive in faith the church's proclamation of the message of Scripture. Third, the *eschatological revelation* of God encompasses the glory of the God who awaits believers suffering during this age.

---

[27] Herman Ridderbos, *Paul: An Outline of His Theology*, 44 (see chap. 1, n. 39).
[28] Ridderbos, *Paul*, 51–52.

We also note that the eschatological revelation of God will bring together both believers and unbelievers. In the end, every human being will know that God reigns in righteousness, whether through the final display of his wrath upon unbelievers or the eternal display of his glory for the comfort of believers. Mirroring his threefold use of the verb *apokalyptō*, Paul also uses the noun for "revelation," *apokalypsis*, three times in the book of Romans. The first and second instances concern the coming judgment (2:5) and the future bodily resurrection (8:19). The third instance returns us to the comprehensive message of the mystery of Jesus Christ, who unites eternity and history in his unique person. The mystery was "kept silent for long ages," but it has now been revealed "through the prophetic Scriptures" and "according to my gospel and the proclamation about Jesus Christ." Glory belongs to God in Christ "forever" (16:25–27). The nominal use of "revelation" thus finally concerns the entire revelation of God's reign over all people in the openly revealed eschatological mystery of Jesus Christ.

III. General Revelation Elsewhere in the Canon

The two ways of revelation detailed in Paul's epistle to the Romans find reinforcement elsewhere in the biblical canon. Particularly significant passages appear in the Old Testament Psalter and the New Testament book of Acts. These texts correlate with Paul's fuller description of general revelation in the epistle to the Romans. Creation teaches about both God and humanity. The God described via nature in the books of the Psalms and of the Acts is One, unique, Creator, glorious, providential, good, and Judge. Human beings are described via nature as creatures, with a common ancestry, whose various nations are blessed and guided providentially, who receive illumination, who are driven to worship, and who are responsible before divine judgment. Even while the biblical canon avows the existence of general revelation, it also affirms the difficulty with theologies which arise thereof.

1. The Old Testament

Psalm 8 treats general revelation as a prompt for human beings both to praise God and to reflect upon their relationship vis-à-vis God and creation. Rolf Jacobson says the poetic structure highlights two objects of content:

"Psalm 8 is rich in both theology and anthropology."[29] Reflection upon
the glory of God in the "heavens" provides reasons for the human being to
inquire why God "made him little less than God." It also provides reasons
for humanity to ask why God "made him ruler over the works of your hands"
(Ps 8:5–6). If the poetry of Psalm 8 summarizes the twofold content of
general revelation (God and humanity in relation to God), the poetic structure of Psalm 19 reflects on avenues of revelation: Creation (Ps 19:1–6) and
Torah or Law (vv. 7–14).

In the first two verses of the Psalm 19, the avenues of general revelation
are said to include "the heavens" and "the expanse" as well as the progress of
"day" and "night." Their witness encompasses "the glory of God" and "the
work of his hands" through "speech" and "knowledge" (vv. 1–2). The next
verse, however, introduces a definitive ambiguity in general revelation. The
psalmist's expression of the opacity of general revelation is so great that Karl
Barth used this verse to help him argue that Scripture does not allow for
natural theology whatsoever. "In itself and as such the text of the cosmos is,
indeed, mute, as it says expressly in Ps. 19: 'Without speech, without words
and with inaudible voice' one day speaks to another and one night declares
to another."[30]

Barth was convinced both that Scripture does not support general revelation[31] and that natural theology leads to the conception of a different God
than the Christ revealed through Scripture.[32] While his protest serves as
an important reminder of the ambiguity in general revelation, Barth's utter
negation remains unusual. John Calvin, Rolf Jacobson, and John S. Feinberg

---

[29] Rolf A. Jacobson, "Psalm 8: A Natural Question," in *The Book of Psalms*, New
International Commentary on the Old Testament, ed. Nancy L. deClaissé-Walford,
Rolf A. Jacobson, and Beth LaNeel Tanner (Grand Rapids: Eerdmans, 2014), 127.

[30] Karl Barth, *Church Dogmatics*, ed. G. W. Bromiley and T. F. Torrance
(Edinburgh: T&T Clark, 1957), II/1:112.

[31] "What amputations (open or secret) have to be undertaken to make the biblical text really say what has to be said to find a biblical basis for natural theology."
Barth, *Church Dogmatics*, II/1:107.

[32] "Natural theology," which is so central to Roman Catholic theology, is "possible on the basis only of a mortal attack on the Christian doctrine of God, and it
certainly cannot be the case that this attack is the starting-point for the Christian
doctrine of God, and with it, dogmatics, and therefore the question of pure doctrine."
Barth, *Church Dogmatics*, II/1:85.

interpret the text differently. Calvin said creation uses a common language which speaks to men of every human language.[33] Jacobson concluded, "Verse 2 emphasizes that creation speaks a message about God and passes on knowledge of God; v. 3 denies that the message can be interpreted."[34] And following Franz Delitzsch, Feinberg said nature speaks of God "without uttering a single word."[35] We agree with Jacobson that Psalm 19 simultaneously affirms general revelation but denies that human beings receive this revelation properly, which mirrors our conclusions from Romans 1.

2. The New Testament

How should we interpret John 1:9, which speaks of Christ as "the true light" who came into the world and "gives light to everyone"? On the one hand, Leon Morris argued *panta anthrōpon*, "every man," is the object indicating divine action upon each person individually. The verse thereby supports "general illumination."[36] On the other hand, D. A. Carson argued this concerns the proclamation of Christ.[37] If the apostle John affirmed universal illumination, Jesus indicated human beings prefer darkness (John 3:19–20).

The New Testament records several instances in which Paul proclaimed the gospel to primarily pagan audiences. First, through Paul's preaching, the pagan Thessalonians turned from idolatry "to serve the living and true God" (1 Thess 1:9–10). Second, when preaching to the pagans of Lystra, Paul and Barnabas likewise demanded they repent of idolatry and worship "the living God" (Acts 14:15). They appealed to the providence of God over nature in providing both their bodies and their souls with goodness. The apostles employ nature to describe God with seven characteristics: He is One, living,

---

[33] John Calvin, *The Psalmes of David and Others, with M. John Calvin's Commentaries*, trans. Thomas East and James Middleton (London, 1571), 68.

[34] Jacobson, "Psalm 19: Tune My Heart to Sing Your Praise," in *The Book of Psalms*, 207.

[35] Feinberg, *Light in a Dark Place*, 66 (see introduction, n. 5).

[36] Leon Morris, *The Gospel According to John*, rev. ed., New International Commentary on the New Testament (Grand Rapids: Eerdmans, 1995), 84.

[37] D. A. Carson, *The Gospel According to John*, Pillar New Testament Commentary (Grand Rapids: Eerdmans, 1991), 123–24.

Creator, good, providential, patient, and Revealer.[38] However, the apostles kept one eye on the special revelation of the Old Testament. Martin Dibelius noted the evangelists' portrayal of God to the pagans, though appealing to nature, was "preached completely in Old Testament style."[39]

The third and fullest example of Paul's preaching to pagans, this time before the ancient academy in Athens, appears in Acts 17. As at Thessalonica and Lystra, Paul's sermon in the Areopagus involved a "convictional confrontation," though he stood now to challenge "the admitted ignorance of the purported intelligentsia of the ancient hedonistic world."[40] While Paul affirmed certain truths about God from pagan learning, he also contradicted important aspects of pagan natural theology. Drawing repeatedly from the Old Testament, Paul corrected the pagan understanding of God by affirming God's transcendence, providence, uniqueness, personhood, unity, and self-revelation (vv. 24–31).[41] "His argument is firmly based on biblical revelation."[42]

But Paul also cited the pagan poets Aratus and Epimenides during his effort to establish an immanent relation between God and humanity (v. 28), thereby undermining the Middle Stoic belief in the necessity of angelic intermediaries.[43] God's nature ought not be confused with the world, with human imagination, or with artistic representation (v. 29). Paul affirmed both the unity of humanity and the providential guidance of the history of human nations, as well as the human reception of divine benevolence and our desire to worship (vv. 26–27). Paul's academic sermon concluded with a reminder of the coming judgment of humanity and its need to respond to the gospel of the saving resurrection of Jesus Christ (vv. 30–31).

Paul warned the churches of the continuing challenge which human philosophies present to Christian theology. "Be careful that no one takes

---

[38] F. F. Bruce, *The Book of the Acts*, rev. ed., New International Commentary on the New Testament (Grand Rapids: Eerdmans, 1988), 277.

[39] Martin Dibelius, *Studies in the Acts of the Apostles*, trans. Mary Ling (New York: Scribner, 1956), 71n23.

[40] Malcolm B. Yarnell III, "Shall We 'Build Bridges' or 'Pull Down Strongholds?'" *Southwestern Journal of Theology* 49, no. 2 (Spring 2007): 209.

[41] Yarnell, "Shall We 'Build Bridges' or 'Pull Down Strongholds?'" 213–16.

[42] Bruce, *The Book of the Acts*, 335.

[43] Yarnell, "Shall We 'Build Bridges' or 'Pull Down Strongholds?'" 211–12.

you captive through philosophy and empty deceit based on human tradition, based on the elements of the world, rather than Christ" (Col 2:8). Rather than letting their minds and hearts be captured by vain philosophy, Paul encouraged the Colossians to rehearse the gospel they were taught and to rejoice in Christ (2:7). N. T. Wright says the particular "philosophy" in view here was advanced by Paul's synagogue rivals in Hellenistic Judaism.[44] Timothy was similarly warned to "guard what has been entrusted to you, avoiding irreverent and empty speech and contradictions from what is falsely called knowledge" (1 Tim 6:20). In Timothy's context, the challenge seemed to derive from heretics within the church advancing "fables, genealogy, and asceticism."[45]

Whether the challenge came from within the church or from without, and whether it derived ultimately from Judaism or from paganism, Paul was convinced the wisdom of God and the wisdom of the world ultimately contradicted one another. "For the Jews ask for signs and the Greeks seek wisdom, but we preach Christ crucified, a stumbling block to the Jews and foolishness to the Gentiles" (1 Cor 1:22–23). Jewish wisdom focused upon visible evidence while Greek wisdom encompassed both physics and metaphysics. Paul, however, deemed all human systems deficient in comparison to Christ. "Yet to those who are called, both Jews and Greeks, Christ is the power of God and the wisdom of God, because God's foolishness is wiser than human wisdom, and God's weakness is stronger than human strength" (1:24–25). Mark Taylor notes, "God's wisdom and power rest on a completely different basis from that of the world."[46] Both "wisdom" and "power" derive from the eternal person of Christ, and both are supremely manifested in his work upon the cross.

Our review of the first chapters in the book of Romans alongside other canonical texts has confirmed the existence of both general revelation and special revelation. It has shown the universal judgment enabled by general revelation and the promise of salvation through special revelation. It has also

---

[44] N. T. Wright, *Colossians and Philemon: An Introduction and Commentary*, Tyndale New Testament Commentaries (Downers Grove: IVP, 1986), 106–7.

[45] Thomas D. Lea and Hayne P. Griffin Jr., *1, 2 Timothy, Titus*, The New American Commentary (Nashville: B&H, 1992), 177.

[46] Mark Taylor, *1 Corinthians*, The New American Commentary (Nashville: B&H, 2014), 71.

provided the contours of a description of God and humanity through general revelation. Because of their biblical basis, the question of the natural manifestations of divine wisdom in relation to the special revelation of Jesus Christ would soon be taken up in the early church. The story of the struggle within the church and without over what humanity may say about God apart from any reference to special revelation needs to be rehearsed. In the next chapter, we therefore turn our attention to the natural theologies which have been put forward by those who identify themselves as Christian. Afterwards, we propose a chaste description of natural theology.

3

Natural Theology

From the days of the early church to today, Christians have been busily constructing and deconstructing natural theology from the sources of general revelation and special revelation. The subject of natural theology, which discusses humanity's supposed general knowledge of God, remains a hot topic today. What can human beings say about God and his human creatures without formal reference to God's revelation of himself to Israel and in Jesus Christ as recorded in Scripture? In this chapter, we rehearse some of the influential answers to this question.

We begin with the post-apostolic theologians of the early church, the Apologists, before proceeding to review the influential contributions of Jerome and Augustine in the West and the Cappadocians in the East. Next, we turn our attention to the efforts of the theologians of the Middle Ages and the Reformation to relate the knowledge of God through nature and by grace. During the modern period, both orthodox and heterodox theologians constructed theologies and anthropologies which reflect upon general revelation. Those conversations led to some intractable conflicts, including a bracing disagreement between two former colleagues which called into question the very reality of general revelation itself.

From a systematic theology perspective, we believe the lessons offered by the theologians of classical orthodoxy, by the Reformers, and by the theologians of the twentieth century best help the reader reflect on the possibility of a natural theology from human observations of nature and human attention to God's judgment through conscience. Drawing upon our review in the last chapter of the authoritative biblical revelation regarding general revelation, and in conversation with the natural theologies available in church history in this chapter, we shall conclude with certain reflections about humanity's natural knowledge of God and humanity in relation to God.

I. The Early Church Apologists

As the early church broadcast the gospel of Jesus Christ, they encountered an existing set of philosophies and theologies. In the ancient world, broadly speaking, a "philosopher" examined the optimal form of life, while a "theologian" was at best concerned with metaphysics, at worst with magic.[1] More than one attitude toward natural philosophy and natural theology may be broadly detected among early Christians, with individual theologians displaying complex responses. Patristic approaches to human learning, philosophical and theological, traversed a spectrum from comprehensive rejection on the one hand to uncritical identification on the other. The dominant attitude, that of critical appropriation, rested somewhere between the two extremes.

Justin Martyr, a second-century Apologist, considered Christianity the true philosophy and correlated those who accepted truth before the coming of Christ with Moses and the patriarchs. He believed classical philosophy coincided with biblical revelation in John's use of *logos* to describe Jesus Christ (John 1:1, 14; 1 John 1:1; Rev 19:13). "Christ is the Logos and those who at any time live in accordance with the Logos, to whatever degree, are in effect desiderate Christians."[2] Other notable Apologists like Clement of Alexandria and Hippolytus of Rome took similar approaches. Pagan philosophies like Stoicism were lauded for their moral rigor, while Platonism's affirmation of a transcendent world and its desire for beauty were deemed helpful.[3] Theology moved beyond these early efforts during the early church councils, as the topics of Trinity and Christology received careful definition, but the Apologists continued to receive appreciation.

---

[1] James M. Rist, "Christian Theology and Secular Philosophy," in *The First Christian Theologians: An Introduction to Theology in the Early Church*, ed. G. R. Evans (Malden, MA: Blackwell, 2004), 105.

[2] Rist, "Christian Theology and Secular Philosophy," 106.

[3] Rist, "Christian Theology and Secular Philosophy," 108.

Another group of Christians, however, garnered condemnations due to their uncritical appropriation of pagan philosophy. A loose religious movement known as Gnosticism blurred the boundaries between religions. Late-second and early-third-century theologians like Irenaeus and Tertullian treated Gnosticism "simply as a Christian heresy, an aberration brought about by the adulteration of sound apostolic doctrine with pagan philosophy, or even astrology and Greek religions, and charge the Simon Magus mentioned in Acts 8 as having originated it."[4] Adolf von Harnack deemed the Gnostics the first Christian theologians, who although condemned, nevertheless "led to the blending of Christianity with the ideas of antiquity, . . . Christianity conceived and formulated from the standpoint of the Greek philosophy of religion."[5] Harnack's Hellenization thesis, because it was applied to orthodox Christianity, has been vigorously and rightly disputed. However, that the Gnostics chose to revise Christian truth with pagan philosophy is undisputable. The common stock of Gnostic doctrines included dualism, hierarchy, inferior deity, syncretism, and redemption by elite knowledge.[6]

As Tertullian of Carthage disputed with Gnosticism and related heresies such as Marcionism and Sabellianism, his rhetoric sometimes appears to deny philosophy and natural theology. Due to his invective, some wrongly ascribe to Tertullian an utter dismissal of Greek philosophy and an irrational fideism.[7] Arguing against the Gnostics, Tertullian indeed asked, "What has Athens to do with Jerusalem? What harmony is there between the academy and the church? What between heretics and Christians? . . . Away with all attempts to produce a hybrid Christianity out of Stoic, Platonic, and dialectic components!"[8] However, Tertullian did not dismiss general revelation but affirmed its internal and external modes.[9] He also

---

[4] J. N. D. Kelly, *Early Christian Doctrines*, rev. ed. (New York: HarperCollins, 1960), 22.

[5] Adolf von Harnack, *The History of Dogma*, 7 vols. (Reprint; Eugene, OR: Wipf and Stock, 2020), II:14.

[6] Kelly, *Early Christian Doctrines*, 261-62.

[7] Eric Osborn, "Tertullian," in *The First Christian Theologians: An Introduction to Theology in the Early Church*, ed. G. R. Evans (Oxford: Blackwell, 2004), 144.

[8] Tertullian, *Prescription against Heretics* 7; Gerald Bray, "Tertullian," in *Shapers of Christian Orthodoxy: Engaging with Early and Medieval Theologians*, ed. Bradley G. Green (Downers Grove: IVP, 2010), 71.

[9] Tertullian, *Apology* 17.4; Osborn, "Tertullian," 147.

affirmed the Logos as a common link between philosophers like Zeno and Christian Scripture.[10] His purpose in denigrating philosophy was to encourage others not to privilege philosophy but to embrace Christ.[11] "We want no strange disputation once we possess Christ Jesus, no inquisition once we enjoy the Gospel. With our faith, we desire no further belief."[12] Tertullian's problem is not with philosophy *per se*, for he also found opportunity to praise philosophy.[13] His problem was with those who granted human philosophy the authority of a "special wisdom" which leads to "a whole river of speculation."[14]

II. Critical Appropriations

During the period of the ecumenical councils, Christians in the East struggled to find a way forward in their encounter with pagan learning. On one side of the spectrum, some like Emperor Julian, known as "the Apostate," due to his renunciation of Constantine's elevation of the church, "sought to break up the alliance between Christianity and Classical culture and to reclaim that culture for paganism."[15] Among Julian's classmates in Athens was Gregory of Nazianzus. Basil of Caesarea, Gregory of Nyssa, and Macrina, their sister, joined with Nazianzus in pursuing a different path, that of *critical appropriation*.[16] Nyssa responded to Julian, arguing Christians could use the language and culture of the Greeks without surrendering the uniqueness of the Christian faith.[17] The Cappadocians were willing, therefore, to use Greek philosophy both as a presupposition in theological construction and as an apologetic for witness.[18]

---

[10] Tertullian, *Apology* 21; Bray, "Tertullian," 72.

[11] Osborn, "Tertullian," 144.

[12] Tertullian, *Prescription against Heretics* 7; Bray, "Tertullian," 71.

[13] Tertullian, *Pallium* 4; Osborn, "Tertullian," 145.

[14] Tertullian, *To the Nations* 2.2; Bray, "Tertullian," 72–73.

[15] Jaroslav Pelikan, *Christianity and Classical Culture: The Metamorphosis of Natural Theology in the Christian Tradition with Hellenism* (New Haven, CT: Yale University Press, 1993), 11.

[16] Pelikan describes their approach toward Greek culture as "ambivalent identification." Pelikan, *Christianity and Classical Culture*, 17.

[17] Pelikan, 12.

[18] Pelikan, 36, 38.

Maintaining the distinction between Christian faith and pagan philosophy, even as they appropriated certain helpful aspects of learned Greek culture, was important to the Cappadocians. While they defended the use of Greek learning against the Apostate, they also warned against an *uncritical identification* between Christianity and Hellenism. Both rhetoric, the art of speaking, and dialectic, the art of logic, needed to be used with care. Eunomius was deemed a heretic precisely because he correlated Greek dialectics too tightly with Christian theology.[19] The theological method crafted by the Cappadocians was intended to preserve the truth of Scripture even as it enabled contemporary proclamation. Basil said Christians must first have recourse to Scripture and tradition before appropriating reason. Nyssa elevated Scripture's teachings above reason's "artificial conclusions." Nazianzus affirmed that human reason must come "under the guidance of Scripture." Macrina agreed that Scripture is "the rule and measure of every tenet."[20]

The Western fathers similarly settled on critical appropriation. Jerome, the great Bible translator, was driven from pagan learning in "a second conversion." Appreciation for classical writers led him to look down on Scripture's "uncouth style."[21] A dream accused him of being "a disciple of Cicero, not of Christ; for your heart is where your treasure is."[22] Adopting an attitude of *comprehensive rejection* toward pagan learning, Jerome thus refused to read the classics for more than a decade. Eventually, deeming a dream insufficient to bind his conscience, Jerome returned to the classics. He noted the Israelites took pagan women into their homes after ritual cleansing (Deut 21).[23]

Augustine provided a paradigm for the critical appropriation of natural theology which dominated Western theology and philosophy for nearly a millennium. In his writings, "revelation" and "illumination" function as coordinate terms for the way God encounters the human soul.[24] Augustine

---

[19] Pelikan, 25–26.

[20] Pelikan, 27–28, 36–37.

[21] J. N. D. Kelly, *Jerome: His Life, Writings, and Controversies* (Peabody, MA: Hendrickson, 1996), 41–42.

[22] Jerome, *Letter* 22; Kelly, *Jerome*, 42.

[23] Jerome, *Letter* 70; Kelly, *Jerome*, 43.

[24] "Only in the high Scholasticism of the thirteenth century does 'revelation' become restricted to strictly supernatural knowledge." Avery Dulles, *Revelation*

shortened the distance between how God speaks to man through nature and Scripture, even while maintaining the Bible speaks with "the highest, even the heavenly, pinnacle of authority."[25] The distance between general revelation and special revelation is bridged by the incarnation of Christ and through the conversion of the human will. The intellect must be guided by the will; faith must lead natural thought to true knowledge. "Do you wish to understand? Believe."[26]

Augustine worked through various natural theologies before coming to faith in Christ. He dismissed both pagan "mythical theology" and "civil theology" but deemed the "physical" or "natural theology"[27] propounded by certain Platonists helpful.[28] He detected correlations between his readings of Platonism and the prologue to the Gospel of John. "The Word, who is God, is the true Light, which enlightens every soul born into the world."[29] The eternal Christ enlightens every human mind, which is created in the divine image.[30] Natural theology comes externally from experience with nature and internally by reason. All science derives through the innate quality of natural reason implanted by the preincarnate Christ. However, the mind remains spiritually dark apart from the incarnation of Christ.[31]

Humanity needs not merely *scientia*, natural knowledge, but *sapientia*, gospel wisdom. The eternal Word speaks to all human beings, granting

---

Theology: A History (New York: Herder and Herder, 1969), 38.

[25] Augustine, *Epistle* 82, 5; Robert E. Cushman, "Faith and Reason in the Thought of St. Augustine," *Church History* 19, no. 4 (December 1950): 280.

[26] Augustine's dictum derives from Isaiah 7:9. "For understanding is the reward of faith. Therefore, do not seek to understand to believe, but believe that you may understand. For 'except you believe, you shall not understand.'" Augustine, *Tractatus* 29; Augustine, *Homilies on the Gospel of John*, in *Nicene and Post-Nicene Fathers*, ed. Philip Schaff, series I, vol. 7 (New York: Christian Literature, 1888), 301.

[27] Augustine, *Civitas Dei* 8.5–9; Saint Augustine, *The City of God*, trans. Marcus Dods (New York: Modern Library, 1993), 190–201.

[28] In his *Confessions*, Augustine traced his intellectual and religious journey through periods of appreciation for Cicero, astrology, Manichaenism, skepticism, and neo-Platonism before converting to Christianity. Saint Augustine, *Confessions*, trans. R. S. Pine-Coffin (New York: Penguin, 1961).

[29] Augustine, *Confessions* 7.9.

[30] Augustine, *De Trinitate* 14.4–6; Saint Augustine, *The Trinity*, trans. Edmund Hill (Brooklyn, NY: New City, 1991), 372–74.

[31] Augustine, *De Trinitate* 4.3.

natural theology, but the incarnate Word alone can grant redemptive theology.[32] Under the guidance of Platonist psychology, "I saw the Light that never changes casting its light over the same eye of my soul, over my mind." He says such natural theology "raised me up so that I could see that there was something to be seen, but also that I was not yet able to see it." The Word's universal illumination brings some knowledge of God to all human beings, prompting our desire for his glory, but universal illumination leaves the sinner in place. "I realized that I was far away from you."[33] The will of the fallen human being continually undermines reason, a reason continually maintained by the eternal Word, until the mind submits to the incarnate Word.[34] By divine grace Scripture prepares the mind for the beatific vision of the triune God of love, aided by the self-examination of the mind made in the image of God.[35] While we draw near now by faith, the perfect and peaceful vision of God will come only after the bodily resurrection.[36]

Augustine considered the relationship between natural human learning and biblical learning in his *On Christian Teaching*. When using "any branches of learning which are pursued outside the church of Christ," Christians must "discriminate sensibly and carefully between them." Some "should be entirely repudiated and treated with disgust." Those which assist human community should be retained.[37] Just as the wealth the Israelites gathered in Jerusalem was far superior to the wealth they took from the Egyptians, so is the "useful knowledge" gained from pagan books in comparison with Scripture. "For what a person learns independently of Scripture is condemned there if it is harmful but found there if it is useful. And when one has found there all the useful knowledge that can be learnt anywhere

---

[32] Cushman, "Faith and Reason in the Thought of St. Augustine," 273, 279.

[33] Augustine, *Confessions* 7.10.

[34] Cushman, "Faith and Reason in the Thought of St. Augustine," 281.

[35] Augustine, *De Trinitate* 15.10.

[36] Transformed by the image of God in Christ, humans will see God. "God will be so known by us, and shall be so much before us, that we shall see him by the spirit in ourselves, in one another, in Himself, in the new heavens and the new earth, in every created thing which shall then exist; and also by the body we shall see Him in every body which the keen vision of the eye of the spiritual body shall reach." Augustine, *Civitas Dei* 22.29.

[37] Augustine, *De Doctrina Christiana* 2.139; Saint Augustine, *On Christian Teaching*, trans. R. P. H. Green (New York: Oxford University Press, 1999), 63.

else, one will also find there, in much greater abundance, things which are learnt nowhere else at all, but solely in the remarkable sublimity and the remarkable humility of the Scriptures."[38]

III. On Nature and Grace

Augustine's works became set texts in the West. He wrote a work on "Nature and Grace" during the Pelagian controversy. The theologians of the Middle Ages and the theologians of the Reformation can trace many of their ideas to their readings of Augustine. The terms "nature" and "grace" are appropriate descriptors for the thoughts of leading medieval and Reformation theologians because they all appealed to nature and to grace in their own ways. On the one hand, Anselm of Canterbury and Thomas Aquinas gave prominence to nature in the construction of their theology. On the other hand, Martin Luther and John Calvin turned the conversation strongly toward grace. However, the medieval theologians did not forget grace, and the Reformation theologians did not forget nature.

Anselm defended his use of reason in a defensive letter to his mentor, Lanfranc of Bec, regarding the rational style of his *Monologion*. He asserted he was in accord with Scripture and Augustine, although the work was an independent thought exercise.[39] Lanfranc himself was the first to employ Aristotle in theological construction, but Anselm was first to cite the philosopher.[40] Anselm is well known among philosophers, apologists,

---

[38] Augustine, *De Doctrina Christiana* 2.151. "The gulf which separated a direct awareness of God from a human consciousness dislocated, as it were 'repressed', by the Fall, had been mercifully bridged through the Bible, by a marvelous proliferation of imagery." Peter Brown, *Augustine of Hippo: A Biography* (Los Angeles, CA: University of California Press, 1967), 262.

[39] Sandra Visser and Thomas Williams, *Anselm* (New York: Oxford University Press, 2009), 17.

[40] Lanfranc used Aristotle's categories of substance and accident in his debate with Berengar over the Eucharist. R. W. Southern, *Anselm: A Portrait in a Landscape* (New York: Cambridge University Press, 1990), 55. Anselm did not lean heavily upon Aristotle. Anselm, *Cur Deus Homo* 17; Anselm of Canterbury, *The Major Works*, ed. Brian Davies and G. R. Evans (New York: Oxford University Press, 1998), 346–47. Cf. Anselm, *De Grammatico* 10 and 17–19.

and theologians for his proofs for God's existence. However, he operated in an Augustinian and Platonic frame rather than an Aristotelian one. He also treated reason and revelation holistically. His treatises began in prayer, presumed Christian faith, and were written for Christians. The goal was to see God in eternity, attainable now in part through the spiritual purification of both *cogitatio*, empirical examination, and *meditatio*, pure reflection upon the essences of things.[41]

Technically, Anselm intended not to "prove" (*probare*) but "understand" (*intelligere*).[42] "For I do not seek to understand so that I may believe; I believe so that I may understand."[43] He used reason to demonstrate who God is and that God exists. In *Monologion*, he argued only "one nature" is "supremely good" and "supremely great."[44] Everything which exists necessarily exists through this "one," "the supreme." The supreme alone has "power-to-exist-through-oneself," while all other things participate in existence by creation from nothing through "the supreme being."[45]

In his next major treatise, *Proslogion*, Anselm set out what has become known as the "ontological argument" for the existence of God. He begins his argument in the form of a prayer to the Lord, "Now we believe that You are something than which nothing greater can be thought."[46] He argues from both logic and Scripture that "that-than-which-a-greater-cannot-be-thought" necessarily exists in both mind and reality.[47] According to Anselm, reason and revelation work together, for it is God who illumines the mind and leads it to proper understanding.[48]

Like Augustine and Anselm before him, Thomas Aquinas also proceeded from the perspective of a convinced Christian faith. He argued that

---

[41] Southern, *Anselm*, 78–79.

[42] "Certainly not one of Anselm's writings appeals to us as being addressed directly to those outside that is as an 'apologetic' in the modern sense." Karl Barth, *Anselm: Fides Quarens Intellectum: Anselm's Proof of the Existence of God in the Context of his Theological Scheme*, trans. Ian W. Robertson (London: SCM, 1960), 14, 62.

[43] Like Augustine, he appeals to Isaiah 7:9. Anselm, *Proslogion* 1.

[44] Anselm, *Monologion* 1–2.

[45] Anselm, *Monologion* 3–8.

[46] Anselm, *Proslogion* 2.

[47] Anselm, *Proslogion* 3.

[48] Anselm, *Proslogion* 4.

Christian doctrine requires both lower *scientia* and higher *sapientia*.[49] "Grace does not abolish nature but perfects it."[50] However, rejecting both Augustine's doctrine of illumination and Anselm's ontological argument for the existence of God, Aquinas developed a natural theology via sense perception "from effect to cause."[51] Aquinas distinguished between "the light of reason" or "the preambles of faith," which considers truths about God established in nature, and "the light of faith," which is infused by grace.[52]

Dedicated to discipleship, Aquinas deemed Aristotle's limited natural theology helpful to his own chaste theological method.[53] Each of his famous "five ways" prove the existence of God by starting from a different observation but each proceeds through a hierarchy of causes to the first cause, which is God.[54] Aquinas works both as a natural theologian and as a theologian of revelation, treating them as "two complementary forms of wisdom." This allows him to work either philosophically from nature to God or theologically from God to nature.[55]

Martin Luther emphasized divine grace and downplayed the spiritual dependability of reason and nature. Luther read Aristotle keenly in his early years and offered over a thousand comments on Aristotelianism in his own works.

---

[49] Frederick Christian Bauerschmidt, *Thomas Aquinas: Faith, Reason, and Following Christ* (New York: Oxford University Press, 2013), 51.

[50] Thomas Aquinas, *Summa Theologica*, trans. Fathers of the English Dominican Province (Westminster, MD: Christian Classics, 1981), Iae, q. 1, a. 8.

[51] Brian Davies, *The Thought of Thomas Aquinas* (New York: Oxford University Press, 1992), 22–25.

[52] Aquinas, *De Trinitate* q. 2, a. 3, in Thomas Aquinas, *Summa Contra Gentiles*, trans. Anton C. Pegis, 5 vols. (Notre Dame, IN: University of Notre Dame Press, 1975), 1:24–25.

[53] Bauerschmidt, *Thomas Aquinas*, 72–73.

[54] Etienne Gilson, *The Christian Philosophy of St. Thomas Aquinas*, trans. L. K. Shook (Notre Dame, IN: University of Notre Dame Press, 1956), 76–77. The five ways argue from the observation of "motion," "the nature of the efficient cause," "possibility and necessity," "the gradation to be found in things," and "the governance of the world." Aquinas, *Summa Theologica* Iae, q. 2, a. 3.

[55] Thomas Joseph White, *Wisdom in the Face of Modernity: A Study in Thomistic Natural Theology*, 2nd ed. (Ave Maria, FL: Sapientia, 2016), 71–74. White demonstrates natural theology from Aristotle to Aquinas is innocent of the Kantian accusation that it works from an *a priori* theological perspective as "ontotheology." White, *Wisdom in the Face of Modernity*, 1–30.

However, Luther rejected his nominalist predecessors, who favored Aristotle, because they allowed for a human role in justification. Rationalism and voluntarism were dismissed by the great Reformer with prejudice.[56] Instead, Luther emphasized the Pauline teaching that people use general revelation to craft idols.[57] Natural theology challenges the unique place which the cross of Christ must hold.[58] The old "theology of glory" must give way to the "theology of the cross." This does not mean Luther embraced irrationalism or entirely rejected general revelation, but he definitively negated its soteriological importance.[59]

John Calvin held a more robust view of general revelation. He recognized the book of nature alongside the book of Scripture, the latter providing clarity to the former.[60] In his opening discussion about human knowledge of God as Creator, Calvin posited a dialectic between human knowledge of God and of ourselves.[61] "The knowledge of God has been naturally implanted in the minds of men."[62] General revelation, therefore, inevitably shapes both theology and anthropology. In a highly respected academic biography of Calvin, William Bouwsma reviewed Calvin's rational and humanist background and progress yet ultimately biblical mindset. Bouwsma says Calvin believed both "the knowledge of faith" and "experimental knowledge" "work together."[63]

Calvin affirmed the utility of general revelation and reason. But he also affirmed its misuse. On the one hand, he detected "a sense of deity inscribed in the hearts of all." On the other hand, the human response to general revelation is corrupted by idolatry, for the human nature is "a perpetual factory of

---

[56] Huong Thi Tran, "Martin Luther's Views on and Use of Aristotle: A Theological-Philosophical Assessment," *Constantine's Letters* 13, no. 2 (2020): 125, 133–34.

[57] David Haines, *Natural Theology: A Biblical and Historical Introduction and Defense* (Landrum, SC: Davenant, 2021), 93–94.

[58] Luther, *Lectures on Romans* 1:18; Martin Luther, *Luther's Works*, ed. Jaroslav Pelikan, 55 vols. (St. Louis: Concordia; Philadelphia: Fortress, 1955–1986), 25:151–60.

[59] Haines, *Natural Theology*, 155–56.

[60] George H. Tavard, *The Starting Point of Calvin's Theology* (Grand Rapids: Eerdmans, 2000), 126.

[61] Calvin, *Institutes* 1.1.1; John Calvin, *Institutes of the Christian Religion*, ed. John T. McNeill, trans. Ford Lewis Battles (Philadelphia: Westminster, 1960), 35.

[62] Calvin, *Institutes* 1.3.

[63] William J. Bouwsma, *John Calvin: A Sixteenth Century Portrait* (New York: Oxford University Press, 1988), 158.

idols."[64] However, "even idolatry is ample proof."[65] There are signs of divinity in creation and in providence,[66] alongside "unfailing signs of divinity in man."[67] The moral judgment of the human conscience, for instance, is "an undoubted sign of the immortal spirit."[68] Alas, the Fall perverted the human will and the human reason. Reason is retained by fallen human beings, but it is "partly weakened and partly corrupted."[69]

Beyond the proofs for divine existence and human responsibility in nature and conscience, human beings require the Bible to function as "spectacles." The doctrines of the Bible refine the teachings of general revelation. "Scripture, gathering up the otherwise confused knowledge of God in our minds, having dispersed our dullness, clearly shows us the true God."[70] Calvin affirmed general revelation but recognized its insufficiency for salvation. Instead of general revelation, "Calvin grounded piety in the certainty of scriptural revelation."[71] While Scripture is manifestly reasonable,[72] only by "the testimony of the Holy Spirit" does a person receive "certainty" that the Bible is God's Word.[73] The Law, available both in nature and the Old Testament, pales before the gospel of the New Testament, which clearly reveals salvation in Jesus Christ alone.[74]

IV. Modern Theologies and Anthropologies

During the early modern period, philosophers widely engaged in natural philosophy and theology. René Descartes deployed ontological arguments for the existence and perfections of God, but he argued without conviction

---

[64] In Latin, *idolorum fabricam*. Calvin, *Institutes* 1.11.8.

[65] Calvin, *Institutes* 1.3.1.

[66] Calvin, *Institutes* 1.5.1–2.

[67] Calvin, *Institutes* 1.5.5.

[68] Calvin, *Institutes* 1.15.2. "An infallible indication that the spirit is immortal." Tavard, *Starting Point*, 174.

[69] Calvin, *Institutes* 2.1.8–9, 2.2.2, 2.2.12.

[70] Calvin, *Institutes* 1.6.1.

[71] Peter J. Leithart, "That Eminent Pagan: Calvin's Use of Cicero in Institutes 1.1–5," *The Westminster Theological Journal* 52 (1990): 5.

[72] Calvin, *Institutes* 1.8.1.

[73] Calvin, *Institutes* 1.7.5.

[74] Calvin, *Institutes* 2.9.1–2.

and without clarity.[75] According to John Locke, the "Law of Nature" reveals that God created human beings to receive freedom and equality.[76] Joseph Priestley crafted a similar anthropology from natural theology. Humanity must therefore obey God, pursue happiness, look out for the good of others, and respond to conscience.[77] Immanuel Kant crafted a popular threefold paradigm of the proofs for God's existence: "the cosmological," "the ontological," and "the physico-theological" or "design" arguments. Kant discounted each proof and doubted the "illusion" of metaphysics,[78] but his "categorical imperative" provided a fourth moral argument for the transcendental existence of God and for treating each human being as an end in himself.[79] As proponents of reason engaged with proponents of faith in hearty conversation, even conflict, two prominent series were established to promote natural theology, the Boyle Lectures during the early Enlightenment[80] and the Gifford Lectures during the nineteenth century.[81]

---

[75] Tom Sorell, *Descartes* (New York: Oxford University Press, 1996), 65–70.

[76] Locke contended for the same anthropology from Scripture. John Locke, *Two Treatises of Government*, 2nd ed. (New York: Cambridge University Press, 1967), 2.2.4–6.

[77] Malcolm B. Yarnell III, *John Locke's 'Letters of Gold'* (Oxford: Centre for Baptist History and Heritage, 2017), 36–38.

[78] Roger Scruton, *Kant*, rev. ed. (New York: Oxford University Press, 2000), 66–69.

[79] Scruton, *Kant*, 86, 95.

[80] Funded by the English scientist, Sir Robert Boyle, the Boyle Lectures were first delivered between 1692 and 1732, then revived in 2004. They are "widely regarded as the most significant public demonstration of the 'reasonableness' of Christianity in the early modern period, characterized by that era's growing emphasis upon rationalism and its increasing suspicion of ecclesiastical authority." Alister McGrath, "A Blast from the Past? The Boyle Lectures and Natural Theology," *Science and Christian Belief* 17, no. 1 (April 2005): 26.

[81] The Scottish lawyer Adam Lord Gifford established the Gifford Lectures for "promoting, advancing, teaching and diffusing the study of 'Natural Theology' in the widest sense of the term." This included "the Knowledge of God," "the knowledge of His nature and attributes," and "the knowledge of the relations which men and the whole universe bear to Him." Beginning in 1889, they have included philosophers, theologians, historians, and scientists like William James, John Dewey, Michael Polanyi, Jaroslav Pelikan, and Charles Taylor. John Haldane, "Scotland's Gift: Philosophy, Theology, and the Gifford Lectures," *Theology Today* 63, no. 4 (January 2007): 471. Cf. Larry Witham, *The Measure of God: Our Century-Long Struggle to Reconcile Science and Religion* (New York: HarperCollins, 2005).

During the seventeenth century, John Webster and William Dell argued against natural theologians' ecclesiastical elitism and lack of gospel focus. "What need is there then of our Philosophy, and of our Arts and Sciences to the Ministry of the New Testament?"[82] Two styles of natural theology responded to this thorough rejection of natural theology. First, thinkers from Oxford and London like John Wilkins and Robert Boyle pointed to the existence of law in an orderly universe. Second, the Cambridge Platonists carried the day with their appeal to the wonder of design in creation. The scientist, Henry More said, is "a Priest in this magnificent Temple of the Universe," who prompts the people to worship God through science.[83]

In the eighteenth century, "The Age of Reason," deists like Thomas Paine became so enamored with natural theology that they even denied special revelation. Repelled by the elite clergy's use of state coercion, they preferred "humanity," "morality," and "theology" without ecclesiastical dominance. Their natural theology was available to everyone through nature.[84] Most natural theologians, however, remained firmly committed to Scripture and church. For instance, natural theology was deemed "useful and indeed necessary for Reformed orthodoxy." Reformed theologians used natural theology to demonstrate God's existence, to identify certain attributes or perfections of God, and to encourage Christians.[85]

Philip Doddridge, the leading theologian of the dissenting academies, likewise "believed firmly" in natural theology. Doddridge evaluated eight proofs for God's existence, denying four of the proofs as inadequate but affirming four others. Doddridge discerned several natural attributes of God and believed God's inherent goodness requires all human beings to pursue

---

[82] William Dell, *The Stumbling Stone* (London: Giles Calvert, 1653), 27; Scott Mandelbrote, "The Uses of Natural Theology in Seventeenth-Century England," *Science in Context* 20, no. 3 (September 2007): 459.

[83] Henry More, *An Antidote against Atheism* (London: Roger Daniel, 1653), 103; Mandelbrote, "The Uses of Natural Theology," 471.

[84] He concluded, first, "That the idea or belief in a Word of God existing in print, or in writing, or in speech, is inconsistent in itself." Thomas Paine, "The Age of Reason (1794)," in *The Thomas Paine Reader*, ed. Michael Foot and Isaac Kramnick (New York: Penguin, 1987), 400, 450.

[85] Haines, *Natural Theology*, 168–69.

personal virtue.[86] Doddridge agreed that general revelation was available to all human beings, but he also affirmed that salvation requires the special revelation of Jesus Christ. The Holy Spirit must correct the failures of reason.[87] Thus, both establishment theologians and dissenting theologians practiced aspects of natural theology.

The famous American writer, Thomas Paine, detected "human rights" in natural theology.[88] His *Common Sense*, "a bestseller on a scale hitherto unknown," effectively "altered the course of history." Paine's idea that creation is "the first source of natural and human right" carried the American public and was enshrined in the Declaration of Independence of the United States.[89] His *The Rights of Man* was dedicated to George Washington and lauded by Andrew Jackson, and his ideas "still resonate" today.[90] Humanity, Paine wrote, received "unity and equality" originally from God.[91] Because freedom is "engraved in the heart of every citizen" by God, it cannot be withdrawn without tragedy.[92] Humanity's "natural rights," moreover, are the basis of "civil rights," and each person retains those rights.[93] Foundational among these rights is the "universal right of conscience," which relates every person directly to God.[94] Human beings create and recreate national "constitutions" to preserve their civil rights, whatever divine right monarchists might say.[95] Modern radical democratic theory was, through the writings of Paine and like-minded radicals in America, England, and France, thoroughly grounded in natural theology.

---

[86] Robert Strivens, *Philip Doddridge and the Shaping of Evangelical Dissent* (New York: Routledge, 2015), 86–88, 93–96.

[87] Strivens, *Philip Doddridge and the Shaping of Evangelical Dissent*, 97–98.

[88] "The great achievement of Paine was to have introduced the discussion of human rights, and of their concomitant in democracy, to a large and often newly literate popular audience." Christopher Hitchens, *Thomas Paine's Rights of Man: A Biography* (New York: Grove, 2006), 104.

[89] Hitchens, *Thomas Paine's Rights of Man*, 30, 36–38.

[90] Paine also drew upon Locke's theory of religious tolerance and Rousseau's social contract. Andrew Clapham, *Human Rights* (New York: Oxford University Press, 2007), 8.

[91] *The Thomas Paine Reader*, 215–16.

[92] *The Thomas Paine Reader*, 206–7.

[93] *The Thomas Paine Reader*, 217–18.

[94] *The Thomas Paine Reader*, 231–33.

[95] *The Thomas Paine Reader*, 220–22.

In the arena of apologetics, the English theologian William Paley offered an argument from design which dominated the major universities during the early nineteenth century.[96] Paley argued that just as a person who finds a watch in a field ascribes its complexity to a watchmaker, so creation indicates a Creator.[97] "There cannot be design without a designer; contrivance without a contriver; order without choice. . . . Arrangement, disposition of parts, subserviency of means to an end, relation of instruments to an use, imply the presence of intelligence of mind."[98] Working through numerous mechanical and organic examples from early modern science, Paley concluded that the cumulative weight of the evidence indicated a divine Designer.

After constructing his argument from design, Paley's highly influential book, *Natural Theology*, went on to describe the perfections of God. While special "revelations" necessarily correct natural theology, seven "natural attributes" of God are discernible: omnipotence, omniscience, omnipresence, eternity, self-existence, necessary existence, and spirituality.[99] Because this deity has "personality," he also has aseity, agency, power, and intelligence.[100] After divine unity, divine goodness places a moral duty upon humanity.[101] Even the presence of evil, framed by the right narrative, demonstrates God's goodness.[102] "The marks of design are too strong to be got over. Design must have had a designer. That designer must have been a person. That person is God."[103]

Late nineteenth century "natural philosophy," increasingly known simply as "science," left a mixed legacy for Christian theology. Two clerics named Charles defined the extreme positions taken by both Christians and non-believers in the new conflict, a conflict that continues to this day. The first Charles, Charles Darwin, rejected design theory. Darwin found Paley's

---

[96] Matthew D. Eddy and David Knight, "Introduction," in *Natural Theology: or Evidence of the Existence and Attributes of the Deity, Collected from the Appearances of Nature*, by William Paley, ed. Eddy and Knight (New York: Oxford University Press, 2006), xxiv–xxvi.

[97] Paley, *Natural Theology*, 7–8.

[98] Paley, 12.

[99] Paley, 230–33.

[100] Paley, 213–18.

[101] Paley, 271–73.

[102] Paley, 255.

[103] Paley, 229.

Natural Theology stimulating but was not convinced by the older man's summary rejection of proto-evolutionary theory. Instead, Darwin developed a "dynamic" or evolving view of nature and humanity from his own detailed scientific observations.[104]

The second Charles, Charles Hodge, began with the goal of bringing harmony between modern science and theology. He was personally enamored with science and encouraged others to join him in the effort to bring intellectual concord. Hodge even crafted a unique and still influential theological method from the same philosophical approach as "that which the natural philosopher adopts to ascertain what nature teaches."[105] However, the influential Princeton theologian increasingly reacted against modern science, particularly its anthropology.[106] Detecting a growing hostility from scientists against theologians, the second Charles responded sternly to the first Charles. Hodge conceded Darwin was not an atheist, but Hodge condemned Darwinism as essentially atheistic.[107] Its challenge to the design argument rendered Darwinism incompatible with Christianity.[108]

A fourfold spectrum of attitudes to general revelation thus developed during the modern period. First, theologians like Paine *depended exclusively* upon general revelation to define theology and anthropology. Second,

---

[104] Eddy and Knight, "Introduction," xxvii–xxviii. Cf. Paley, *Natural Theology*, 224–28.

[105] Ronald L. Numbers, "Charles Hodge and the Beauties and Deformities of Science," in *Charles Hodge Revisited: A Critical Appraisal of His Life and Work*, ed. John W. Stewart and James H. Moorhead (Grand Rapids: Eerdmans, 2002), 83. A much more favorable interpretation of the work of Hodge and other Princeton theologians can be found in Bradley Gundlach, *Process and Providence: The Evolution Question at Princeton, 1845–1929* (Grand Rapids: Eerdmans, 2013).

[106] "The portrait that emerges from my reading of the available sources reveals an unusually complex man, both rigid and flexible, dogmatic and open-minded, torn between his genuine love of natural knowledge and his loathing for what sometimes passed as science." Numbers, "Charles Hodge and the Beauties and Deformities of Science," 81, 93–96.

[107] Numbers, "Charles Hodge and the Beauties and Deformities of Science," 97.

[108] Hodge was also troubled by Darwin's reaction to the eye as indicating divine design, which was a key point in Paley's argument. Charles Hodge, *What Is Darwinism?: And Other Writings on Science and Religion* (New York: Scribner, 1874); Numbers, "Charles Hodge and the Beauties and Deformities of Science," 99; Paley, *Natural Theology*, 16–31. Also, see Gundlach, *Process and Providence*.

theologians like the Cambridge Platonists and Paley *defended* Christianity through the natural theology of design. Third, Reformed theologians and Dissenting theologians also deemed natural theology *helpful* in theology, anthropology, and ethics. However, they carefully maintained that the special revelation of the gospel was necessary for salvation, and that Scripture and the Holy Spirit correct reason. Fourth, theologians like Webster, Dell, and Hodge became *highly suspicious* of natural theology, although Hodge had already adapted his influential theological method to the modern scientific method.

V. "Yes!" and "No!"

During the twentieth century, Emil Brunner and Karl Barth engaged in a major conflict over general revelation and natural theology. Brunner grounded his doctrine of general revelation in Scripture, interacting extensively with the Reformers.[109] Brunner agreed with Calvin's identification of two "ways" of revelation, generally in nature and historically through redemption, but Brunner also recognized a third "way"—"the revelation of the last days."[110] He affirmed general revelation heartily but distinguished two separate approaches to natural theology, "the 'objective' natural theology of the Bible" and "the rationalistic, or Catholic, 'subjective' view."[111] Against medieval Thomism, Brunner denied natural theology could ground revealed theology. Moreover, natural theology must derive from Scripture.[112]

Brunner's formal system of general revelation and natural theology is worth rehearsing for its exegetical and Reformation conclusions. First, Scripture affirms general revelation but limits natural theology.[113] Second, general revelation is available universally through creation, reason, and natural law.[114] Third, human beings naturally pervert general revelation into idolatry.

---

[109] "This too is not a specifically Catholic, but a general Christian, doctrine; it is good Reformation doctrine, plainly biblical, and common to the Christian Church as a whole." Brunner, *Revelation and Reason*, 68 (see chap. 1, n. 7).

[110] Brunner, *Revelation and Reason*, 58–59, 62n.

[111] Brunner, 79.

[112] Brunner, ix, 59–62, 66.

[113] Brunner, 62.

[114] Brunner, 63, 70.

Fourth, general revelation nevertheless holds men responsible for their sin. Fifth, the burdened conscience creates a "contact point" for evangelism.[115] Sixth, while general revelation "makes man guilty it cannot free him from his sin."[116] Seventh, contrary to Karl Barth, who restricts revelation to personal redemption, Brunner argued both Scripture and nature reveal God objectively without regard to human subjectivity.[117] Brunner elsewhere argued the Scriptures don't merely "become" but "already are" the Word of God.[118]

Eighth, original sin severely reduced but did not eliminate the human capacity for general revelation: The *imago dei* remains in fallen human beings, although they are shorn of original righteousness. Human rationality likewise remains, although it is used with the wrong "attitude." God's law is written on the human conscience, yet it has been "darkened." God's civil law remains, but the moral law has been twisted.[119] Ninth, "it is true that all 'natural theology' is in principle idolatrous; but this does not mean that it is all equally remote from the truth."[120] Tenth, mirroring Augustine's use of John 1:9, Brunner says "the eternal Word" is "the principle of general revelation." The eternal Word's revelations of God through nature and conscience hold human beings "responsible" and "inexcusable." Only faith in a special revelation, "the saving revelation" of Jesus Christ, will remove the human "blindness" and "guilt" that general revelation discloses.[121]

Where Emil Brunner issued a qualified "Yes" to general revelation and natural theology, Karl Barth responded with an emphatic "No!" Barth attacked his former Swiss colleague in dialectical theology for endangering "the ultimate truth" by promoting a "theology of compromise" favorable to the German Christians who were syncretizing Christianity with National Socialism.[122] Barth argued for a tighter definition of revelation

---

[115] Brunner, 64–65.

[116] Brunner, 66.

[117] Brunner, 68.

[118] Emil Brunner and Karl Barth, *Natural Theology: Comprising "Nature and Grace" by Dr. Emil Brunner and the Reply "No!" by Dr. Karl Barth*, trans. Peter Fraenkel (1946; reprint, Eugene, OR: Wipf and Stock, 2002), 49.

[119] Brunner, *Revelation and Reason*, 70–72.

[120] Brunner, 72, 75.

[121] Brunner, 75–77.

[122] Brunner and Barth, *Natural Theology*, 69, 72.

which excluded numerous aspects of Brunner's natural theology. Barth said revelation is a "grace," not a human capacity; its only "subject" is Jesus Christ; and its only "method" is biblical exposition. There is effectively no such thing as "natural theology."[123] Barth accused Brunner of manufacturing a "point of contact" and "capacity for revelation," compromising grace and the Reformation.[124]

In his *Church Dogmatics*, Barth later returned to the problem of natural theology. He said Scripture must be misread to justify natural theology, as we noted in the previous chapter.[125] Roman Catholics who use natural theology introduce "a foreign god."[126] Their traditional "analogy of being" must be replaced by the biblical "analogy of faith."[127] Unbelievers, moreover, will rightly reject Christian natural theology.[128] In summary, Barth wrote, natural theology "makes out of the 'He' an 'it,' out of the becoming a being, out of the coming to us by God's revelation something existing and capable of proof even without revelation and otherwise than in faith."[129] Barth claimed to be a gentle person by nature, but he was incensed by Brunner's natural theology.

Brunner defended his doctrine of general revelation in several key areas. He said his idea of a "point of contact" concerned God's general grant of a capacity for "words" and "responsibility." He also said emphatically that the separate human ability to believe remains a special grace that comes through preaching the Word.[130] Brunner rejected three opposing errors: Roman Catholics based special revelation on general revelation; the radical Enlightenment philosophers exclusively affirmed general revelation; and Karl Barth entirely denied general revelation.[131] Brunner set himself over against all three positions. Brunner believed his views, not those of Barth, coincided with that of the Reformers.[132] Alister McGrath notes how the

---

[123] Brunner and Barth, 71, 75.

[124] Brunner and Barth, 78–109.

[125] Karl Barth, *Church Dogmatics*, ed. G. W. Bromiley and T. F. Torrance (Edinburgh: T&T Clark, 1957), II/1: 105.

[126] Barth, *Church Dogmatics*, II/1: 84.

[127] Barth, *Church Dogmatics*, II/1: 243.

[128] Barth, *Church Dogmatics*, II/1: 93.

[129] Barth, *Church Dogmatics*, II/1: 231.

[130] Brunner and Barth, *Natural Theology*, 31–32, 56–57.

[131] Brunner and Barth, 46–48.

[132] Brunner and Barth, 35–45.

Swiss theologian appeared somewhat ignorant of the contemporary German context developing in his country's northern neighbor.[133]

The German *Sitz im Leben* explains Barth's fighting spirit, but gross error elsewhere need not condemn a third party, especially when their theologies so radically diverge. Brunner clearly differentiated his idea of political order and denied general revelation was "tied at all" to certain nations.[134] This last caveat gets to the heart of the matter. Pursuing a Hegelian reading of national history, the liberal theologian Adolf von Harnack earlier argued the warlike Bismarck was "a special revelation of the intrinsic spirit of the [German] nation."[135] The German Christian movement similarly syncretized Christianity with Adolf Hitler's anti-Semitic racism through appeals to a supposed general revelation about the Führer in 1933.[136] Prominent theologians like Emmanuel Hirsch sadly reinforced these claims.[137] Isolated in Switzerland, Brunner wrote *Nature and Grace* at the very time Barth was leading the Confessing Church to contradict German syncretism through the Barmen Declaration.[138]

The debate between Barth and Brunner bequeathed an ongoing dilemma for Protestant theologians on the heels of developments from the early church through the Enlightenment. How should general revelation and

---

[133] Alister E. McGrath, *Emil Brunner: A Reappraisal* (Malden, MA: Wiley Blackwell, 2014), 114.

[134] Brunner and Barth, *Natural Theology*, 18, 51–52. For an appreciative critique, see Reinhold Neibuhr, "The Concept of 'Order of Creation' in Emil Brunner's Social Ethic," in *The Theology of Emil Brunner*, ed. Charles W. Kegley (New York: Macmillan, 1962), 265–71.

[135] Harnack assigned the individual to divine sovereignty and history to state sovereignty. J. C. O'Neill, "Adolf von Harnack and the Entry of the German State into Ware, July-August 1914," *Scottish Journal of Theology* 55 (2002): 16.

[136] Doris L. Bergen, *The Twisted Cross: The German Christian Movement in the Third Reich* (Chapel Hill: University of North Carolina Press, 1996), 11.

[137] Robert P. Erickson, "Emanuel Hirsch: Intellectual Freedom and the Turn toward Hitler," *Kirchliche Zeitgeschichte* 24, no. 1 (2011): 74–91.

[138] The Confessing Church denied general revelation: "We reject the false doctrine, as though the church could and would have to acknowledge as a source of its proclamation, apart from and besides this one Word of God, still other events and powers, figures and truths, as God's revelation." *The Barmen Declaration* 8.12; Eberhard Busch, *The Great Passion: An Introduction to Karl Barth's Theology*, trans. Geoffrey W. Bromiley (Grand Rapids: Eerdmans, 2004), 67.

natural theology be correlated with special revelation and revealed theology? Should theologians even construct a natural theology from general revelation, or should they depend upon Scripture alone? How might theologians avoid the idolatries which characterize sinful humanity's natural theologies? What exactly does general revelation teach about God, humanity, and their relationship? Perhaps if Brunner had been more attuned to Barth's context and Barth had been a little more patient with Brunner, their split may not have occurred or at least been so rancorous. Nevertheless, their opposing positions demonstrate both the inevitability of natural theology which Brunner saw, and the danger of natural theology which Barth detected.

VI. Systematic Theology Conclusions

From a systematic theology perspective, we conclude that while general revelation is sufficient to hold human beings accountable before God for their sinful actions, it is insufficient for the generation of the true faith which brings salvation in Jesus Christ. Regrettably, general revelation inexorably leads fallen human beings to suppress the truth about God and create their own idols.

There are three important uses for general revelation. In this chapter, we reviewed the proposals of many theologians and philosophers who constructed systems of thought and practice derived at least in part from general revelation. Their natural theologies included various proofs for the existence of God useful in apologetics, partial descriptions of the true God potentially helpful in the development of theology proper, and partial descriptions of human character and responsibility. We now offer our own conclusions from our reading of the biblical text and interaction with the history and philosophy of natural theology.

First, regarding the proofs for the existence of God, it should be noted these proofs neither do not nor need not convince everyone who hears them. Whether an intellect receives a particular proof for divine existence is not necessarily indicative of the presence of true faith or false faith. One person may accept a certain proof yet lack saving faith in Jesus Christ. Another person may reject a certain proof yet possess a saving faith in Jesus Christ. The proofs may and often will serve as intellectual aids in the deconstruction of atheistic, agnostic, or heretical views of God, but they do not guarantee the person who receives or rejects them will come to faith or not. The proofs for the existence of God, left on their own, are also used to construct pagan views of God which are both severely partial and thoroughly idolatrous.

Second, we must respond to the efforts of theologians who craft a view of God from general revelation. We agree that general revelation's partial descriptions of the true God can be helpful in the development of theology proper. After all, a natural reading of Scripture appears to affirm that there are certain truths about God which are revealed to the entirety of humanity through nature and conscience. According to Romans 1, among these are the truths that God reveals himself, that he is eternal, that he is powerful, that he is invisible, that he has a divine nature, that he demands from his creatures a moral accounting for their deeds, and that he is thereby also implicitly revealed as personal. Our review of other biblical texts which address general revelation indicate that God is One, that he is unique, that he is the Creator, that he is glorious, that he providentially guides the histories of his creatures, that he is good, and that he will judge his creatures righteously. If the Augustinian reading of John 1:9 is received, one can also say that God shows himself to every human being through the light which he makes available to their minds. We leave to the side accounts about the character and nature of God which are derived from general revelation alone, since Paul is clear that human beings inevitably pervert that revelation.

Third, we must respond to the efforts of theologians regarding general revelation's partial descriptions of both human character and human responsibility before God. As with God's existence and attributes, we prefer to limit our definite conclusions to a rehearsal of those truths about humanity which the biblical texts themselves explicate or, according to good human reasoning from Scripture, indicate are a definite fruit of general revelation. The early chapters of Romans indicate that we human beings are liable to the judgment of God for our ungodliness and unrighteousness, that we possess a moral agency, that we have utilized that agency irresponsibly, that we naturally suppress God's revelation of himself, that we pervert that revelation into idolatry, and that we are being prepared for judgment as a result. The human heart and its conscience bear witness to these moral claims. By implication from the revelation of human moral agency and of human responsibility before God, we also affirm the freedom of the human conscience. Article XVII of the Baptist Faith and Message states, "God alone is the Lord of the conscience, and He has left it free from the doctrines and commandments of men which are contrary to His Word or not contained in it." Historically and philosophically, the freedom of the human conscience in religion is the foundation and security of all natural human rights.[139]

Despite our positive conclusions about the utility of natural theology in apologetics and in the doctrinal development of orthodox theology and of orthodox anthropology, Karl Barth's remonstrances against the human propensity to make an idolatrous abstraction of God and for the indispensability of the supreme revelation in Jesus Christ remain relevant. Saving faith exclusively originates with divine election, requires knowledge of the gospel of Jesus Christ, and accompanies personal regeneration by the Holy Spirit. Only this one God, God the Trinity, can save a person, and any human being's lack of the saving knowledge of this God who is Trinity dooms himself or herself eternally. Special revelation remains necessary for the salvation of human beings, so we must turn our attention away now from the limited benefits of general revelation and toward the triune God's perfect revelation of himself in Holy Scripture.

---

[139] Andrew T. Walker, "Religious Liberty and the Public Square," in *First Freedom: The Beginning and End of Religious Liberty*, 2nd ed., ed. Jason G. Duesing, Thomas White, and Malcolm B. Yarnell III (Nashville: B&H, 2016), 146–48. Since the locus of the first human right is the individual human conscience responsible directly to God, the equality of human beings vis-à-vis other human beings is implied. A helpful and brief summary of these matters can be seen in Erickson, "Revelation," 5–10 (see chap. 1, n. 39).

4

The Nature of Truth and the Nature of Scripture

T he truth of God originates with the Father, is expressed through the Son, and is received in the Spirit, so that believers may be transformed for eternal fellowship with the trinitarian God. Subsequent to his revelation to Israel and supremely in the incarnate Christ, God works today in, with, and through the biblical canon as his chosen instrument. Our subject matter in this chapter is the nature of truth and the nature of Scripture. However, the history of theological discourse in the last few centuries has worked to inhibit access both to the nature of truth and to the truth of Scripture. We propose to recapture the scriptural description of truth through theological exegesis. Herein, we will first examine the taxonomy of truth, followed by the history of truth. We then proceed to a theological interpretation of the Gospel of John focused on the nature of truth and Scripture's relation to truth.

We believe Scripture is by nature "true" because Scripture is the gift of the triune God who is himself "Truth." God leads Christians to speak of Jesus as "the Voice of God" and "the Word of God." Scripture contains his very words, such that Scripture is also denominated "the Word of God." The nature of Scripture thereby depends upon and is maintained by the nature of the God who spoke his Word originally. And through the Spirit's inspiration and preservation of Scripture, his Word speaks truth to humanity today. Scripture leads us to affirm God the Trinity is truth by nature. It also leads us to speak of Scripture and the church as creatures of God which participate in his truth by grace. We must differentiate between the nature of God, who is supreme personal being, and the nature of Scripture, which is his divinely inspired literature. God is truth by nature; Scripture is truth by grace.

First, by nature, Moses ascribed the attribute of "truth" to Yahweh (Exod 34:6). The psalmist and the prophet Isaiah agreed (Ps 31:5; Isa 65:16). Buttressing this foundational claim, both John the Baptist and Jesus Christ ascribed God the Father in his divine nature the perfection of being "true" (John 3:33; 8:26). Furthermore, by virtue of being eternally, perfectly, and uniquely "begotten" of the Father (1:18; 3:16, KJV), Jesus Christ was accounted "full of grace and truth" by John the apostle (1:14). God the Son is, with God the Father, personally "the truth," a title the Son assigns himself (14:6). The Holy Spirit, by virtue of his personal, eternal, and ontological procession from God (15:26), is likewise accounted as "truth" by "the truth," the Son (14:17; cf. 1 John 5:6). Because God the Son and God the Spirit, in personal participation with God the Father, truly partake in the one divine nature, we must say that the three persons share simply, equally, and entirely the perfection of "truth." To speak of "truth" is to speak of the essence of God.

Second, by grace, God grants participation in his perfection of truth both to Scripture and to the people of God. As we shall see, the divine perfection of truth is granted instrumentally to Scripture through the inspiration of the Holy Spirit. This perfection is preserved in the canon by the Spirit. God grants a personal relationship through his Word and Spirit to people via the grace of Scripture. Jesus provides a title for the nature of Scripture in his prayer to the Father, "your Word" (17:17b). Through the grace of the Spirit and in the speech of the Son the Bible participates in the divine perfection of truth. In the same prayer, Jesus indicated the nature of the people of God progressively becomes truth through the grace of sanctification (17:17a). The human being receives these truths by grace through faith. The one who receives divine truth by grace also necessarily "lives by the truth" in his or her works (3:21).

I. Defining Truth Today

In his commendable theological essay, "The Nature of Truth," Thomas F. Torrance says a proposition "refers to a communication of one subject to another about something."[1] A "proposition" is used for constructing statements about beliefs.[2] While truth is more than propositional, this certainly does not imply that it is less than propositional. Biblical truth is not just some mystical encounter or vague experience that we have as a result of reading Scripture. The fact that truth is more than doctrine should never be used to imply that doctrine is not necessary or important. Truth would be unknowable and incommunicable without the doctrinal framework and propositional grounding that we are granted in Scripture.

Two extraordinary statements, "God is true," and "the Bible is true," are propositional. Such statements are indispensable to Christian theological discourse. Human beings necessarily use propositions, composed of words, to convey important truths, and theologians are no different.[3] For theology to exist, certain human words about God, by which God chose to reveal himself, must be received as true propositions. But these revealed statements about God and Scripture must be conceived representatively and as concretely as possible. When a Christian speaks of "God," he or she understands the one real personal being identified as Yahweh in the Old Testament and God the Father, the Son, and the Holy Spirit in the New Testament. Similarly, the "Bible" must be conceived concretely as the church's approved canon. "True" must be understood as concretely as possible. "God is true" and "the Bible is true" are propositions which must necessarily be affirmed by orthodox teachers.

However, it is quite common for theologians to switch from concrete truth statements to abstract truth statements. For instance, Thomas Aquinas

---

[1] Thomas F. Torrance, *Theological Science* (New York: Oxford University Press, 1969), 162. "Proposition" today indicates "content," while the medieval meaning of proposition indicated a "sign." Colwyn Williamson, "Proposition," in *The Oxford Companion to Philosophy*, ed. Ted Honderich (New York: Oxford University Press, 1995), 724.

[2] Alexander D. Oliver, "Abstract Entities," in *The Oxford Companion to Philosophy*, ed. Ted Honderich (Oxford: Oxford University Press, 1995), 3.

[3] Human beings have been identified as "verbivores," because we cannot exist without words. Stephen T. Davis, "What Do We Mean When We Say, 'The Bible Is True'?" in *But Is It All True? The Bible and the Question of Truth*, ed. Alan G. Padgett and Patrick R. Kiefert (Grand Rapids: Eerdmans, 2006), 86.

argued, "Truth is the conformity of the thing and the intellect."[4] All theologians, including the writers of this book, inevitably resort to such abstract propositions to convey important ideas. Our internal ideas about internal and external realities are conveyed through words. But the real things our ideas represent must retain correlation with the words we use to convey them. Theologians inevitably resort to abstractions to make the universal truths taught by Scripture evident to the minds of their audience. Propositions are necessary, and abstractions are useful, but abstract propositions can sometimes overshadow the concrete aspects of truth.

The Bible contains many other genres than the strictly propositional, genres such as narrative, poetry, command, and song. Truth comes through many linguistic forms. Scripture also applies truth in different ways. The human response to biblical truth may begin with propositional affirmation, but it must proceed to immediate personal faith and make progress toward faithfulness.

II. The Historic Diminishing of Truth

Among Western Christians, definitions of truth first began moving away from the eternally real and toward the humanly nominal during the late Middle Ages. Subsequently, the definition of truth was increasingly severed from its theological and personal root during the Enlightenment. In other words, truth was disentangled through the centuries from its personal foundation in God and reassigned to the anthropological and subjective phenomena of internal reason and external experience. Westerners came to believe human minds could and eventually should discern truth apart from reference to God's personal revelation. Reviewing these historical developments will shed light on the magnitude of the contemporary problem.

The classical theological exegesis of Scripture and interpretation of providence during the patristic and high medieval periods, represented in the

---

[4] Aquinas, *Questiones Disputatae de Veritate*, Q 1, Art 1, Responsio. Citing Augustine, Aquinas also argued that "all things are true by means of one truth, the truth of the divine intellect." Aquinas, *Questiones Disputatae de Veritate*, Q 1, Art 4, Responsio; Saint Thomas Aquinas, *The Disputed Questions on Truth*, trans. Robert W. Mulligan, James V. McGlynn, and Robert W. Schmidt, 3 vols. (Chicago: Henry Regnery, 1952–1954).

influential writings of first Augustine of Hippo and later Thomas Aquinas, connected linear history with the revelation of God. Augustine "aligned words (including the words of scripture) and created things by regarding them both as signs (*signa*) that point beyond themselves to the only true reality (*res*) worth knowing, namely, the Trinity."[5] Matthew Levering refers to this understanding as "participatory exegesis," because God was seen as revealing himself truly to human beings, first generally in creation then intensively through redemptive grace. The eternal Creator palpably interacted with his temporal creatures within and through history.[6]

The classical Christian consensus included five "premises": First, God guarantees the unity of the Old and New Testaments. Second, correct interpretation depends upon the human being's faith in "the triune Teacher." Third, the Bible is "the authoritative Word of God." Due to the work of the Holy Spirit, "the books of Scripture, firmly, faithfully and without error, teach that truth which God, for the sake of our salvation, wished to see confided to the sacred Scriptures." Fourth, the depth, power, and complexity of God's unitary voice is conveyed faithfully through the many human authors of Scripture. And fifth, "Scripture requires a hermeneutics of charity." In other words, interpreting God's providence in history and God's revelation in Scripture depends upon the Holy Spirit, who is love.[7]

Levering surveyed the theological exegesis of ten biblical commentators from the thirteenth through the twentieth centuries, comparing their various readings of John 3:27–36. This passage contains the claims of John the Baptist and the apostle John that "God is true" (v. 33); that God the Father sent his Son, who "speaks God's words" and "gives the Spirit without measure" (v 34); and that the "voice" of Christ must be received by human beings (v. 29). Augustine and Aquinas believed these texts ground human access to truth in trinitarian grace. However, in the fourteenth century, the nominalist

---

[5] Willemien Otten, "Nature and Scripture: Demise of a Medieval Analogy," *Harvard Theological Review* 88, no. 2 (April 1995): 261.

[6] Matthew Levering, *Participatory Biblical Exegesis: A Theology of Biblical Interpretation* (Notre Dame, IN: University of Notre Dame Press, 2008), 3–7, 18. Otten argued similarly that "standard medieval exegesis" said the truth regarding God "can be known through an understanding of the things that are made," including Scripture itself. Otten, "Nature and Scripture," 262.

[7] Levering, *Participatory Biblical Exegesis*, 83–84.

philosopher Duns Scotus helped foster a woeful shift away from biblical exegesis toward "autonomous humanism." The "Scotist rupture" introduced a wedge between human reason seeking truth and divine revelation.[8] Thus began a trend toward "the autonomy of history from theology," according to Matthew Levering.[9]

British theologian John Webster discerned a similar historical movement: "The sensible and intelligible realms, history and theology, were thrust away from each other, and creaturely forms (language, action, institutions) denied any capacity to indicate the presence and activity of the transcendent God."[10] The earlier understanding of revelation as coordinate with reason presumed God revealed himself rationally through Scripture and invited the reader to eternal life. The classical understanding was diminished. The trend away from the priority of divine truth intensified with the rise of the modern historical critical method. "Nowhere is modernity's effect on the interpretation of the NT more evident than in the fact that we can manage to read the NT and avoid acknowledging the question it puts about truth."[11] The modern method of Bible study focused exclusively upon history as a self-enclosed phenomenon. Any theological reading of the biblical text was now deemed an "add-on."[12]

Early Enlightenment philosophers in the seventeenth century, including René Descartes and John Locke, were typically confessing Christians, but their psychological emphases encouraged inward reliance upon human reason or outward reliance upon sensory experience. On the one hand, Descartes grounded the perception of truth within human self-reflection, providing an apparently universal and anthropological basis for epistemological certainty. On the other hand, Locke located the discernment of truth not within innate mental properties but with perceptions arising from the senses. Whichever method one followed, human beings increasingly trusted their own rational capabilities and elevated human

---

[8] Levering, 18–23.

[9] Levering, 45.

[10] Webster, *Holy Scripture*, 19–20 (see chap. 1, n. 73).

[11] C. Kavin Rowe, "What If It Were True? Why Study the New Testament," *New Testament Studies* 68, no. 2 (April 2022): 145.

[12] Levering, *Participatory Biblical Exegesis*, 53–61.

reason above divine revelation.[13] In a separate but influential development, Baruch Spinoza equated nature with God and argued Scripture must be read exclusively in a natural way.[14] The crisis over theological revelation deepened as academics followed Spinoza into treating Scripture primarily as history.

The anti-theological trend deepened in the eighteenth century. Germany's premiere philosopher defined "Enlightenment" as having "the courage to use your own understanding."[15] Immanuel Kant wished to free humanity from dependence upon existing authorities, especially the clergy and their theological dogma.[16] The French Enlightenment took an even more radical turn. The *philosophes* argued the *ancien regime*, supported by Roman Catholic clergy, had built their social and political hegemony through mass deception.[17] Many philosophers deemed it imperative to "destroy these false doctrines," including trust in biblical truth. Their goal was to guarantee human equality and freedom, but their means often involved not only anti-clericalism but anti-biblicism.[18] Casting about for a new understanding of truth, many modern people divorced truth from personal divine revelation and married it to rationalism or empiricism.

The definition of reason itself varied, with some setting reason against metaphysics and religious dogma, while others set rationalism against empiricism.[19] The earliest manifestations of pure "rationalism," "the doctrine that reason alone is a guide to truth," appeared in pre-Socratic Greek

---

[13] Felipe Fernandéz-Armesto, *Truth: A History and a Guide for the Perplexed* (New York: St. Martin's Press, 1997), 79–80.

[14] He deemed prophecy a product of the human imagination which contained moral rather than intellectual excellence. Steven Nadler, "Scripture and Truth: A Problem in Spinoza's *Tractatus Theologico-Politicus*," *History of Ideas* 74, no. 4 (October 2013): 623.

[15] Immanuel Kant, *An Answer to the Question: What Is Enlightenment?*, trans. H. B. Nisbet (New York: Penguin Books, 2009), 1.

[16] Kant, *An Answer to the Question*, 3–4.

[17] "'Public welfare' and 'religion' are the two pretexts used by oppressors to veil the truth." Lester Gilbert Crocker, "The Problem of Truth and Falsehood in the Age of the Enlightenment," *Journal of the History of Ideas* 14, no. 4 (October 1953): 593.

[18] Crocker, "The Problem of Truth and Falsehood in the Age of the Enlightenment," 577.

[19] Fernandéz-Armesto, *Truth*, 85–86.

philosophy.[20] Plato pictured reason as a means to "the divine and immortal and eternal."[21] Aristotle developed a canon of logic, including the syllogism and the laws of non-contradiction and the excluded middle, though tempered with common sense.[22] Enamored with Aristotle, the High Middle Ages have been characterized as an "age of reason," but in the modern period reason became an axiomatic reaction against religious faith. "The 'reason' exalted by the European enlightenment was mixed together out of other ingredients: hostility to authority, rejection of dogma, faith in the progressive thrust of history, interest in the mechanical models of the reality of the universe, and fascination with scientific method."[23] With his characteristic ability to expose self-delusion, Gilbert Chesterton responded that rationalism's denial of faith itself requires an act of faith in reason.[24] Modern rationalism's preeminent faith commitment is to abstract mathematics.[25]

"Empiricism," which depends upon human sensory perceptions of the natural world to obtain truth, can be found in ancient societies from Polynesia to Egypt to China to Greece. But these cultures counted their experience of nature one among many avenues to truth.[26] During the medieval period, Western thinkers revived interest in nature. Albert the Great defined "natural science" as "not simply receiving what one is told, but the investigation of causes in natural phenomena."[27] During the modern period, natural philosophers crafted scientific laws to describe nature's conduct. While the Roman church persecuted Galileo Galilei, most Western scientists in the early modern period still considered themselves Christian, as some scientists still do today.[28] Isaac Newton turned scientific thought in a mechanical direction and John Locke restrained innate truth, but natural

---

[20] Fernandéz-Armesto, 96.

[21] Fernandéz-Armesto, 100.

[22] Fernandéz-Armesto, 104–5.

[23] Fernandéz-Armesto, 110, 113.

[24] Fernandéz-Armesto, 82.

[25] Fernandéz-Armesto, 114–19.

[26] Fernandéz-Armesto, 123–45.

[27] Fernandéz-Armesto, 147.

[28] Johannes Kepler, Robert Boyle, and Isaac Newton, for instance, were Christian by confession. On the complex and dependent relationship of modern science upon Christianity, see Herbert Butterfield, *The Origins of Modern Science 1300–1800*, rev. ed. (New York: Simon & Schuster, 1957).

philosophy became highly skeptical with David Hume. The modern ideology of "empiricism" confined truth to manifestations of reality which are "observable and verifiable by sense perception."[29]

The Enlightenment emphasis upon truth as an abstract proposition universally accessible through either interior human reason or external human experience was hereby enthroned as the standard account of truth. Modern canons of reason remained dominant until radical forms of postmodernism turned the skepticism of the Enlightenment against itself. Modernity retained the idea of truth as universal, but postmodernity doubts every metanarrative.[30] John Caputo says the overarching problem that modernity presents to truth is its tendency toward "absolutism." Absolutism confuses the human being with God. The primary problem that postmodernity presents to truth is its tendency toward "relativism." "Relativism means there is no Truth, just a lot of competing truths, depending on your language, culture, gender, religion, needs, tastes, etc., and one is as good as another."[31]

Historically speaking, the premodern concept was that "God is truth," while modernity says, "Reason judges what is true," and postmodernity defines truth as "an event, where neither God nor reason enjoy pride of place."[32] Both modernity's absolutizing trust in human reason and human experience and postmodernity's relativizing of truth have rightly been rejected by Christians. Nevertheless, when the Western Christian sets out to describe "truth," his own language and culture immediately miscue his mental processes to lead away from truth as it is construed in the biblical canon. Truth for the Christian influenced by modernity is first and foremost "fact" or "data." Too often, the human being is assumed to grasp truth through the inductive exercise of his or her robust mental powers.[33]

---

[29] Fernandéz-Armesto, *Truth*, 153.

[30] John D. Caputo, *Truth: The Search for Wisdom in the Postmodern Age* (New York: Penguin, 2016), 4–5; also, see David S. Dockery, ed., *The Challenge of Postmodernism: An Evangelical Engagement*, rev. ed. (Grand Rapids: Baker, 2001).

[31] Caputo, *Truth*, 6–8.

[32] Caputo, 18.

[33] Kevin J. Vanhoozer, "Lost in Interpretation? Truth, Scripture, and Hermeneutics," *Journal of the Evangelical Theological Society* 48, no. 1 (March 2005): 94–96, 100.

We agree with the classical conception of truth as a grace of knowledge descending from a personal God above. Augustine and Aquinas were recalling the apostle John's affirmation that Jesus Christ possessed "the fullness of grace and truth" (John 1:14b). Alas, through a tortuous historical process, the divine grace of truth was replaced by a Pelagian approach to truth. Many human beings now believe they have immediate access to truth through the natural exercise of the human mind in concert with human observations invigorated by human willfulness. The Augustinian belief in the devastating impact of original sin absents itself from modern assumptions regarding human epistemology. Alongside this empowerment of the human, Modernity loosened the connection between truth and virtue. One may now conceivably hold intellectual truth without being morally faithful to other persons, whether they are divine or human.[34] The Gospel of John, however, providentially offers us the means by which we may reclaim the truth about truth.

III. Understanding Truth

The theological confrontation between Jesus and Pontius Pilate during the sentencing and crucifixion of Christ highlights the Bible's differentiation between concrete divine truth and human abstraction. In John 18, Jesus identified his own person with truth, prompting Pilate to decide what to do with Jesus's truth claims. Wondering about the teachings of Jesus, yet finally relinquishing them, Pilate rejected the divine origin of truth, the personal nature of truth, and the participative nature of truth. The importance of this key passage in the narrative of Christ's death and resurrection can hardly be overstated. Pilate's encounter with Christ was considered so central that the pagan magistrate's name was included by the early church in its universally accepted creeds. The Apostles' Creed and the Nicene Creed, which affirm that Jesus suffered under Pontius Pilate, have been widely used in Christian worship ever since.[35]

---

[34] To his credit, contrary to both defenders of the *ancien regime* and philosophers like Voltaire and Kant privileged morality. Crocker, "The Problem of Truth and Falsehood in the Age of the Enlightenment," 577–87.

[35] Only three human beings are named in the universal confessions of the early church: Jesus Christ, the Virgin Mary, and Pontius Pilate. Mary confirms the truth of his human birth; Pilate, his human death.

Jesus's discourse with Pilate presented truth in three primary senses: epistemically, ontologically, and participatively. Jesus is epistemically, the Teacher of Truth, for he conveys the message of heaven to earth so that we may know it. Jesus is ontologically Truth Incarnate, for he is the Son of God who is "the way, the truth, and the life" (John 14:6). He is as the eternally generate Son of God (John 1:18; 3:16) also, ontologically, one with the Father who is "true" (3:33; 7:28; 8:26; 10:30; 17:3) and one with "the Spirit of truth" (14:17; 15:26; 16:13). And Jesus provides through his humanity the Voice of God. With his voice, Jesus offers fallen human beings the opportunity to enter fellowship with God.

First, Jesus made an epistemic claim, identifying himself as the earthly witness to eternal truth. After affirming the divine origin yet currently recessive nature of his kingship, Jesus told Pilate, "For this purpose I was born and for this purpose I have come into the world—to bear witness to the truth" (John 18:37 ESV). Functioning as "the Teacher" (11:28; 13:13–14), Jesus in his personal speech-acts conveys truth from heaven. Through authoritative testimony, he bears witness on earth to a message from heaven. Jesus Christ speaks both universally and personally. Universally, he is the "true light" who enlightens everyone and has come into the world (John 1:9). Personally, he verified important truths for his disciples with either the adverb *alēthōs*, "truly" (cf. John 1:47), or the more common liturgical affirmation of truth borrowed from the Hebrew, *amēn* (cf. John 1:51; 3:3, 5, 11, etc.)[36] *Jesus is the Teacher of Truth.*

Second, profoundly, Jesus also identified truth with his own person. His statement that he has "come into the world" contains a vivid ontology. Jesus told Pilate that he has a personal and unique relationship with heaven. In the ancient world, a prophet, a sage, an oracle, or a teacher might serve as an epistemological mediator, a witness to truth. Jesus similarly claimed to mediate the knowledge of God, but he went much further, asserting his very person originates in eternity. Jesus believed, as we shall see more fully below, not only that he spoke truth instrumentally but that he was truth personally. His words mean "nothing less than the self-disclosure of God."[37] According

---

[36] See also Jesus's ascription of the adverb *kalōs* "correctly" or "fitly," to a proper human claim to truth (John 4:17).

[37] D. A. Carson, *The Gospel according to John*, Pillar New Testament Commentary (Grand Rapids: Eerdmans, 1991), 594; also, see F. F. Bruce, *The Gospel of John* (Grand

to Ignace de la Potterie's critical study of the use of *alētheia* in this gospel, John taught the relations between the divine persons, such that in Jesus is revealed "the unity between the divine persons" or "the Trinitarian life" and thereby "the mystery of the Incarnation of the Word."[38] Jesus claimed He is divine Truth in the world. *Jesus is Truth Incarnate.*

Third, Pilate was offered the opportunity to give his personal acquiescence to Jesus as both Teacher of Truth and Truth Incarnate. Jesus told Pilate, "Everyone who is of the truth listens to my voice." Through an "implicit invitation," Pilate was promised that, as a human being and through faith in Christ, he could share in truth itself.[39] The Gospel earlier said the "voice" of Jesus has power to raise the dead (5:25; 11:43) and that it guides his disciples into sure knowledge of the truth (10:3–5, 16, 27). The voice of Jesus was verified by the "voice" of the Father (12:28, 30). When Jesus speaks, he speaks in unison with God (5:36–38).[40] "As the incarnate Son, Jesus perfectly corresponds to the Father because the Father fully expresses himself in the person of his Son."[41] Presented the opportunity to be transformed morally via a decision to enter a personal relationship with the eternal Truth who had come in flesh, Pilate could have become a person "of the truth" (18:37d). He could have heard the voice of Christ with faith, participating in divine truth by the grace of the Spirit. The "voice" of God confronted Pilate in the face of Jesus Christ. *Jesus is the Voice of Truth.*

Alas, Pilate balked and chose to keep the truth of God presented in the person and voice of Jesus at an abstract distance. In verse 38, Pilate responded with a wave, "What is truth?" "Curt and cynical," Pilate dismissed the divine truth about Jesus with an aloof, dismissive query.[42] Even at a merely human level, Pilate refused to recognize the moral commitment required for a

---

Rapids: Eerdmans, 1983), 352–54.

[38] Ignace de la Potterie, *La Vérité dans Saint Jean*, vol. 1, *Le Christ et la vérité, L'Esprit et la vérité* (Rome: Biblical Institute, 1977), 277.

[39] Carson, *The Gospel according to John*, 595.

[40] Jesus is likewise the "Word" of God (John 1:1, 14). It is not without accident that the Word of God is directly identified with the incarnate one who is "full of grace and truth" (John 1:14).

[41] Bruce D. Marshall, *Trinity and Truth* (New York: Cambridge University Press, 2000), 279.

[42] Carson, *The Gospel according to John*, 595.

proper relation between persons. The magistrate understood the objective contours of truth, seen in his studied juridical conclusion, "I find no guilt in him" (18:38; 19:6 ESV). Pilate and the Jewish leaders united against Jesus treated written words as bearers of truth (19:19–22).[43] However, compelled by political tactic and surrendering to personal expediency, Pilate responded with the ascription of guilt to the guiltless one (18:39; 19:12, 15).[44]

"Truth" for Pilate became impersonal and amoral as he removed truth beyond his primary concern through a deliberation of will. Human abstractions of truth often try to move the objective basis of truth from its reference to God. The goal is to make truth malleable to the needs or ideas of the human being. Every human effort to remove truth from its reference to God in Christ is a move away from divine objectivity to human subjectivity. However, there simply is no objective truth apart from its reference to God in Christ. The Truth of God has "ultimate authority and ultimate objectivity."[45] Despite all his efforts to reduce truth through abstraction, to subject truth to his own definition, Pilate could not escape the messianic import of the Truth (19:19). He knew there was something divine about Jesus but lacked the faith necessary for saving knowledge (19:7–9, 11).

As with the canon in general, the Gospel of John makes the deity of Jesus clear, a deity that includes his ontology of Truth. We next consider the trinitarian nature of truth before proceeding to the trinitarian work of disseminating truth. We will then be prepared to turn our attention to the nature and function of Scripture.

IV. The Trinitarian Ontology of Truth

The Gospel of John may use the noun *alētheia*, "truth," generically or abstractly. But the abstract sense, which does not require personal response, is rare (John 4:18; 5:31; 7:26; 8:17). More often *alētheia* is explicitly grounded in the concrete personal nature of God as Trinity, and he commands a

---

[43] Pilate was warned of the eternal consequences of his actions (John 19:6–11).

[44] The Jews confronted Pilate with the prospect of defending himself before Caesar for dismissing the claims of a different "king," though Jesus already told Pilate he was not a king in the world's sense (John 18:36; 19:12).

[45] Torrance, *Theological Science*, 144–46.

response. "Truth" in the Fourth Gospel refers both to the nature of God and to the revelation of God. Divine ontology concerns who God is, in his nature, while divine economy concerns what God does, in his work, including his work of revelation. First, we must consider the triune ontology indicated by the Evangelist's use of *alētheia*. Afterwards, we may consider the triune economy, how God's truth is communicated to us via his Word. The trinitarian ontology of truth is discernible in three short texts from the Gospel of John. These texts identify Truth with the Father as its source, the Son as its fullness, and the Spirit as its perfection.

> The one who has accepted his testimony has affirmed that God is true. For the one whom God sent speaks God's words, since he gives the Spirit without measure. (John 3:33–34)

First, we note from the Fourth Gospel that *God the Father is the source of truth*. Jesus told the disciples through his prayer that to know God truly, one must know God as "true" (17:3). God is eternal truth, pure truth, simply truth. Thomas Aquinas perceived that "the personal God is the highest truth" and communicates "truth through word."[46] God the Father is the source of truth, ontologically within the eternal Trinity and historically without.[47] Focusing upon the economy of truth, Aquinas recalled its height and dignity in his inaugural academic sermon. God waters "from the heights of divine wisdom the minds of the learned," who in turn minister truth to others.[48] God, who is truth, provides truth by his Word to (and through) his creatures as an act of grace in his Spirit. In turn, the human being who accepts the testimony of Jesus affirms "God is true" (3:33).[49]

---

[46] Enrique Martinez, "God as Highest Truth According to Aquinas," *Religions* 12, no. 6 (2021): 1, 6.

[47] That we speak of the Father as "source" does not mean we believe there is a "hierarchy" within God, for the divine attributes are entirely possessed by all three persons as the one God. See Yarnell III, *God the Trinity* (see chap. 1, n. 78).

[48] *Rigans Montes*, in Thomas Aquinas, *Inaugural Lectures: Commendation and Division of Sacred Scripture*, trans. Ralph McInerny (New York: Penguin, 1998); Randall B. Smith, "Thomas Aquinas's Principium at Paris," in *Towards a Biblical Thomism: Thomas Aquinas and the Renewal of Biblical Theology*, ed. Piotr Roszak and Jörgen Vijgen (Pamplona, Espana: Ediciones Universidad de Navarra, 2018), 50–57.

[49] Paul places the truthfulness of God against the falsehood of sinners (Rom 3:4).

Jesus told him, "I am the way, the truth, and the life. No one comes to the Father except through me. If you know me, you will also know my Father. From now on you do know him and have seen him." (John 14:6–7)

Second, John teaches that *the Son of God is the fullness of truth.* "The Word of God" (1:1) is "the only begotten Son" (1:18, KJV) "from the Father" (1:14). Because the Father is perfect grace and perfect truth, John considers the Son equally "full of grace and truth" (1:14). The eternal generation of the Son indicates the ontological derivation of the Son from the person of the Father. The Son's eternal generation thus verifies his full participation by nature in the attributes and acts of God. Jesus Christ also can be identified as "the truth" (14:6). Though focused on defending both the personal and propositional nature of truth to evangelicals, Kevin Vanhoozer detected a correlation between Christ and truth, "There is a correspondence between what he says, what he does, and who he is. Jesus Christ is the truth because he is God-keeping-his-word; as God's 'kept' word, Christ not only bears but is the truth, a personal bearer of the way God is."[50]

In his first epistle, John provides clarification concerning the relation of Christ to God and the truth of God. We can hereby affirm the Son is not merely truth by generation but is truth because he is *autotheos,* "Godself." John writes, "And we know that the Son of God has come and has given us understanding so that we may know the true one. We are in the true one—that is, in his Son, Jesus Christ. He is the true God and eternal life" (1 John 5:20). Christ is here entitled, "the Son of God," "the true one," and "the true God."[51] Because Christ is the true God, he may give and "has given us understanding" to know "the truth." According to Webster, Jesus Christ is the Word of God who invites us into his sovereign "domain" so we can "share in his boundless knowledge of himself and all things."[52]

---

[50] Vanhoozer, "Lost in Interpretation?" 111.

[51] "For here the full identity of Jesus with God is recognized without reserve (note the article with *theos,* God)." Rudolf Schnackenburg, *The Johannine Epistles: Introduction and Commentary,* trans. Reginald H. Fuller (Tunbridge Wells, UK: Burns & Oates, 1992), 236.

[52] John Webster, *The Domain of the Word: Scripture and Theological Reason* (New York: T&T Clark, 2012), ix.

> And I will ask the Father, and he will give you another Counselor
> to be with you forever. He is the Spirit of truth. The world is unable
> to receive him because it doesn't see him or know him. But you
> do know him because he remains with you and will be in you.
> (John 14:16–17)

Third, the Gospel of John relates that *the Holy Spirit is the perfection of truth.* The One who comes from the Father and is sent by the Son is thrice identified as "the Spirit of truth" (14:17; 15:26; 16:13). In his first epistle, John described both the Spirit's identity and function. Economically, "the Spirit is the One who testifies." Ontologically, "the Spirit is the truth" (1 John 5:6). Just as Jesus bears a testimony from heaven, so the Spirit bears testimony from heaven. The epistemological work of the Spirit is twofold. First, he comes to "teach" and to "remind" the apostles (John 14:26) "into all the truth" (16:13). This led to the apostolic writings canonized in the New Testament. Second, he comes to "convict the world about sin, righteousness, and judgment" (16:8). The Holy Spirit, however, does not merely convey truth. The Spirit is, alongside the Father and the Son, truth in a personal ontological sense. According to Bruce Marshall, yes, the Spirit's "distinctive role" is to bring God's creatures to "their proper share in the divine life."[53] But the Spirit also has divine identity. "What the church identifies when it calls upon the Father, Jesus, and the Spirit is of course God," "the triune God."[54] The Spirit is God.

These statements of triune ontology, which place the Son and the Spirit in natural union with the Father, reinforce the classical tradition of Augustine and the Cappadocians. But these statements contradict the ideas of modern scholars like Bultmann and de la Potterie, who employ the historical critical method. Rudolf Bultmann demythologizes the teaching of John 1:14 regarding the fullness of truth in Jesus Christ so that John was reputed to "describe God's being," but "not 'in itself.'" Rather, John describes God's being "as it is open to man (in his receptivity) and in its activity toward man."[55] De la Potterie emphasized the work of the Spirit over

---

[53] Marshall, *Trinity and Truth*, 113.
[54] Marshall, 43.
[55] Rudolf Bultmann, *The Gospel of John: A Commentary*, trans. G. R. Beasley-Murray, R. W. N. Hoare, and J. K. Riches (Philadelphia: Westminster Press, 1971), 73.

against the person of the Spirit.[56] The depersonalization of truth we noted above, along with the diminishing of access to divine ontology, thereby dug insidious roots into modern biblical scholarship, Protestant and Roman Catholic alike.

For many scholars, even discussing ontology betrays a decidedly Hellenistic orientation that is presumed contrary to Hebrew and, therefore, biblical ways of thought. In a helpful response, Pierce Taylor Hibbs does not jettison ontology but argues for biblical ontology's unique character. The canonical doctrine of "reality" is radically dissimilar to the philosophical. Two major problems with the Aristotelian ontology of "substance" and "accident" immediately present themselves. First, there is no sense of relational person-hood involved in Aristotle's ontology. Second, there is no need for a personal God in Aristotelianism.[57] Like Hibbs, we do not argue for a Greek ontology. But unlike the modern critics, neither do we argue for an economy without a supportive ontology. Rather, we argue for a biblical ontology which enervates a biblical economy.

V. The Trinitarian Economy of Truth

Having outlined the trinitarian ontology of truth, we may now address its economy. Not only is God truth, but God can and does grant truth through divine communication. His truth is so powerful that when he speaks, things which were not come into existence. When God speaks, his truth creates the reality verbalized. Hibbs writes, "I *am* and you *are* because he *said*."[58] The divine being creates other beings by utterance. From the ground of his eternal being as "intra-Trinitarian communication," God creates beings through external acts of communication.[59] Scripture grounds creaturely ontology in divine ontology through his economy of revelation.

The covenantal name of the Lord (יהוה; *Yahweh*, derived from *hayah*) correlates God's revelation with his eternal being. "God replied to Moses,

---

[56] De la Potterie, *La Vérité dans Saint Jean*, 2:471.

[57] Aristotle's doctrine of a Prime Mover is impersonal. Pierce Taylor Hibbs, "World through Word: Towards a Linguistic Ontology," *Westminster Theological Journal* 79, no. 2 (Fall 2017): 358.

[58] Hibbs, "World through Word," 346.

[59] Hibbs, 348.

'I AM WHO I AM.' This is what you are to say to the Israelites: I AM has sent me to you'" (Exod 3:14–15).[60] The One who bears this covenantal name also bears the baptismal name (Matt 28:19). On the one hand, God's name expresses God's being. On the other hand, God's expressiveness creates all creaturely reality. Genesis 1:3 states, "Then God said, 'Let there be light,' and there was light." The creaturely verb of "being" (הָיָה; *hayah*) derives from the divine act of "speaking" (אָמַר; *'amar*). "The emphasis is on creation by speech as command."[61] "God spoke. That is the ontological grounds for all existence and the foundation of all the coherence in our experience."[62]

Scott Swain correctly concludes, "The Bible's metaphysical pattern of divine naming identifies the triune God as the self-subsistent source and goal of all things."[63] But we must also distinguish intra-trinitarian communication from the external act of communication. The trinitarian being and his internal processions are eternal. God is pure act. But God is, moreover, the transcendent One whose perfection grounds all other things. He is not dependent upon anything but is the origin of all things. Divine ontology necessarily precedes creaturely ontology. Creaturely being derives from the grace of communication by the divine being. We exist because God as Trinity wills, speaks, and perfects our creation.

In turn, we are created for responsive communion with God and with one another. The triune God above creation, who counts "truth" among his perfections, is necessarily the origin and end of truth within creation. Among the human creatures of God, there is an enthralling desire to participate in the truth of God. This is because humanity was made in the image of the One who is truth (Gen 1:26). Truth comes to God's creatures through God's revelation of his triune self. Truth returns with God's redeemed creatures

---

[60] Systematic and philosophical theologians are struck by the profundity of the verbs of being in God's self-naming: "I AM WHO I AM" and "I AM."

[61] Victor P. Hamilton, *The Book of Genesis: Chapters 1–17*, The New International Commentary on the Old Testament (Grand Rapids: Eerdmans, 1990), 119.

[62] Hibbs, "World through Word," 345.

[63] Swain also laments, "The metaphysical pattern of divine naming is the most understudied pattern of divine naming among recent works on the Bible and the Trinity." Scott Swain, "The Bible and the Trinity in Recent Thought: Review, Analysis, and Constructive Proposal," *Journal of the Evangelical Theological Society* 60, no. 1 (March 2017): 45–46.

through participation in him by faith. God the Trinity both reveals himself and enables the reception of his self-revelation.

First, John's doctrine of the triune economy of revelation teaches that *God the Trinity reveals himself.* There is a movement from God to the human being, which prompts a return movement from the human being to God. Truth has its source of revelation in God the Father. From the Father, truth comes to humanity "through Jesus Christ" (1:17). The Son testifies to the truth he hears from the Father (8:40; 16:7). In John, truth is twice paired with "grace" (1:14, 17) and once paired with "way" and "life" (14:6). Both pairings refer to the redemptive movement of God toward humanity in Jesus Christ. "If the Gospel of John identifies 'the truth, with Jesus Christ, the Word incarnate, the Epistle of 1 John identifies 'the truth' with the Holy Spirit, precisely in virtue of the Spirit's faithful witness to Jesus Christ."[64] Paul similarly identifies grace with the Spirit, who is the outflowing love of God (1 Cor 12:3; Rom 5:5).

Second, in addition to revealing himself, *God the Trinity enables the believer to receive his redemptive revelation.* The only way to worship God properly is "in Spirit and in truth" (4:24). Those who receive the Spirit know truth, but those who lack the Spirit fail to know him (14:17). The Spirit of God comes to the apostles "to guide them into all truth" (16:13). Alongside the Holy Spirit, the Word, who is "truth," brings sanctification in the truth of the Father (17:17, 19). The only way a human being may come to the Father is through the truth of the Son (14:6). Those who live "by the truth" given to them through the Word in the Spirit are able to come "to the light" of God the Father (3:21).

The things said in the Gospel of John immediately regard the direct auditors of Jesus Christ, especially his apostles. But how does God's creative and redemptive truth come to those who are not apostles? The Holy Spirit inspired the apostles to write down the truth they received, and the Holy Spirit led the church to preserve these apostolic writings in the biblical canon. The Gospel of John focuses upon the immediate reception of the truth by the apostles but also promises that divine truth will be made available to others through their witness.

---

[64] Marshall, *Trinity and Truth*, 180.

Third, the Gospel of John addresses *the transmission of the gospel*. The transmission of the gospel occurs in five ways: First, Jesus prayed for those who would come to faith and participate in the truth through "the word" of the apostles (17:20). Second, the prayer of Jesus included not just the apostles but all his disciples, who would be united in the triune glory (17:22) and love (17:23). Third, the apostles were specifically promised the Spirit would guide and lead them to recall all the truths taught by Jesus Christ, including things they had not yet learned (14:26; 16:12–14). Fourth, the Holy Spirit and the apostles would exercise coordinate ministries to glorify Jesus Christ (15:26–27). Fifth, the Spirit will convict the world of the truths about Jesus Christ, especially concerning "sin, righteousness, and judgment" (16:8). Unbelief in Jesus is the very definition of sin (16:9). Belief is the very definition of salvation (3:15).

Fourth, the Gospel of John *indirectly outlines the process of the canonization of the apostolic and prophetic writings*, which we now call the Holy Bible. Jesus foretold the process by which we have come to understand the apostles and prophets carry the revelation of God as Father, Son, and Holy Spirit. We will later rely upon biblical passages written by Paul and Peter to reconstruct the process of biblical inspiration and preservation. But John is concerned to disclose the process of revelation which precedes and authorizes the canon, and this process includes God the Father, his Word, and his Spirit, as well as the prophets and the apostles.

God the Father sent God the Son and God the Holy Spirit to bring truth into the world. The Voice of God, or Word of God, spoke to the apostles. He promised to continue speaking through the Holy Spirit to the apostles after his return to the Father. The apostles, empowered by the Holy Spirit, testified to the truth about Jesus Christ through preaching the gospel. The apostles were also led to continue their testimony to the eternal truth of God in Christ through their writings. Today God testifies of his truth to human beings via his chosen instruments of the scriptural canon and the church. "The fact of the canon tells us simply that the church has regarded these scriptures as the place where we can expect to hear the voice of God."[65] The Holy Bible is the written extension of the personal voice of God in Christ.

---

[65] Barth, unfortunately, next undermines inspiration, saying, "The proper attitude of preachers does not depend on whether they hold on to a doctrine of

The Gospel of John identifies "truth" both with the being of God and with the activity of God. From the perspective of systematic theology, to speak of divine truth being made known to humanity is to speak of revelation. Divine revelation discloses the important aspects of both divine ontology and divine economy. We learn through revelation of who God is and what he is doing. God creates by truly speaking life into existence. God renews the lives of his fallen creatures by speaking truth through the divine truth who came in the flesh. The "Spirit of Truth" then guided the apostles into the truth of Jesus Christ. Divine truth has been placed in the writings of the apostles (and prophets) through the Trinity's perfect work of revelation. God's Word is true because God himself is the Truth.

VI. The Ontology of Scripture

If the doctrine of revelation is concerned with divine ontology and divine economy, then in the doctrine of Scripture we must be concerned with ontology and economy. Scripture is important because it is the elect and ordinary means today for human beings to access God's redemptive revelation. But what is Scripture's ontology, and what is Scripture's economy? Before we examine the nature and function of Scripture, we must affirm Scripture is central to the divine economy. Jesus Christ is the personal "Word of God" (Rev 19:13), and Scripture is the written "Word of God." Scripture is the Word of God by grace but not the Word of God in person. Scripture is the created instrument through which God works effectively to bring human beings to give an account before him in person (Heb 4:12–13).

Evangelicals distinguish between the "nature of Scripture" and the "function of Scripture." Lutheran theologian Dale Huelsman affirms, "The *nature* of Scripture refers to its origin, efficacy, inspiration, infallibility, inerrancy, perspicuity or clarity, and sufficiency. The *function* of Scripture includes its authority, its effectiveness (not to be confused with efficacy), its role in unification and separation, its role as source and norm for Christian faith and

---

inspiration but on whether or not they expect God to speak to them there." Karl Barth, *Homiletics*, trans. Geoffrey W. Bromiley and Donald E. Daniels (Louisville: Westminster John Knox, 1991), 78.

life, and its ability to provide divine assurance and comfort."[66] The Bible is infallible, inerrant, clear, and sufficient, because God the Trinity provides Scripture with its truthful origin, effective agency, and inspiration. Scripture's various attributes and functions, discussed in later chapters, are true because Scripture participates by divine grace in and manifests triune truth.

First, by *origin*, we mean the Bible has its source in the words of the First Person of the Holy Trinity, God the Father. The Father is identified as "true" (3:33; 7:28; 8:26) and "the only true God" (17:3). When asked by Philip to reveal the Father, Jesus replied, "the one who has seen me has seen the Father" (John 14:9). In other words, the Person of Jesus Christ is united with the Person of the Father. The intra-trinitarian relations are so intimate that the Father and the Son are "in" one another (14:11). The transformative "words" and powerful "works" of the Son derive from the Father and are expressed in the Son (14:10). The Son's word originates with the Father and is effective (17:24). The Father is the eternal origin of the incarnate truth who the Son is (1:14) and of the transformative truth which the Son speaks (8:32; 18:37).

Second, by *effective agency*, we mean the Bible as the written Word of God continually and instrumentally presents the Second Person of the Holy Trinity, the living Word of God. The Prologue to John uses the language of "Word" to refer to Jesus Christ. John tapped into a rich terminology with significant roots in both the Hebrew theological and Greek metaphysical traditions: It was by (*'amar*), "uttering" or "saying," that God created during the six days of creation in Genesis 1. Among Hellenistic philosophers, the term *logos* indicated the universal source of thought and speech. John intended multiple correlations with Genesis 1 to "recall the first creation,"[67] a creation by revelation. *Logos* "points to the truth," "that it is of the very nature of God to reveal himself."[68] Jesus Christ, who both "is God" in identity and "with God" in distinction (John 1:1), is the revelation of God in human flesh

---

[66] Dale B. Huelsman, "The Nature and Function of Holy Scripture as Discussed in Nineteenth Century Lutheran Free Conferences: Part One," *Concordia Historical Institute Quarterly* 76, no. 3 (Fall 2003): 164.

[67] Leon Morris, *The Gospel according to John*, rev. ed., New International Commentary on the New Testament (Grand Rapids: Eerdmans, 1995), 64.

[68] Morris, *The Gospel according to John*, 66.

(1:14). This *logos* speaks the *rhēmata*, "sayings," of God; to reject his sayings is to reject God (12:48).

The words of Jesus are true because Christ himself is eternally true and truth. The Son participates in God by nature, so that whatever we say of the Father's nature must also be said of the Son. (Anything less than a full identification between the nature of the Father and the nature of the Son correlates to the grossest heresy, Arianism.) As we saw above, the Father's nature includes the perfection of "true" or "truth." Likewise, the Son is "true" or "trustworthy" (*alēthinos*) and "truth" (*alētheia*). Because he seeks the Father's glory, Jesus is "true" (7:18). He is the "true light" (John 1:9), "true bread" (6:32), and "true vine" (15:1). Sacramentally, his flesh is "true food" and his blood, "true drink" (6:55). God the Son is not only "true," but "truth" (1:14; 14:6; 17:19). Because the Son is truth, he always acts in truth. As noted in our discussion about his voice, Jesus speaks "truly" (*alēthōs* and *amēn*).

And the truthfulness or trustworthiness of Jesus carries into his message about himself and his work in the gospel. The divine testimony to Jesus is "truth" (8:40, 45; 16:7, 13; 17:17; 18:37), and that human testimony which is faithful to Jesus is also, by participation in the grace of the Spirit, also "truth" (5:33; 15:26). The divine "saying" or "testimony" from God in Christ or through the prophet and the apostle is "true" (4:37; 5:32; 8:14; 10:41; 19:35). On the irrefutable basis of the divine testimony to truth, guaranteed by Jesus Christ, the author of the Gospel concluded with epistemological confidence about his own writing, "He who saw this has testified so that you also may believe. His testimony is true, and he knows he is telling the truth" (19:35). By the grace of God, the apostles convey the truth of God about Jesus Christ through their testimony in speech and in literature.

Third, by *inspiration*, we mean the Third Person of the Holy Trinity, the Holy Spirit, carries along the writers of Holy Scripture such that we must refer to their writings as "God-breathed" (2 Tim 3:16). The Gospel of John does not explicate a doctrine of inspiration by the Holy Spirit but lays the theological basis for that doctrine: Jesus promised he and the Father would send "the Spirit of truth" to the apostles. The Spirit did not come to the world but to reside "in" and "remain with" the apostles (John 14:17). The Spirit worked with the minds of the apostles, reminding them of everything Christ taught and teaching them all things (14:26). Because the Spirit "who proceeds from the Father" testified about Jesus, the apostles are also empowered to "testify" about Jesus (15:26–27).[69] The Spirit can guide creatures into truth, because he participates in the divine nature with the Father and the Son. The Spirit "will speak whatever he hears," "will also declare to you what is to come," and will "take from what" belongs to Christ and "declare it to you" (16:13–15). This last passage demonstrates the full participation by nature of both the Son and the Spirit with the Father in the Godhead.[70]

While John focused on the apostles' role in conveying the truth in the power of the Holy Spirit, there are indications that truth is already being ascribed to their writings. We just mentioned the highest confidence of the apostle John that his written testimony is true. Elsewhere verified as true are the testimonies to the gospel by the prophet John the Baptist (5:33), the apostle John (19:35), Jesus Christ (8:40, 45; 16:7; 18:37), the Holy Spirit (15:26; 16:13), and the Father (17:17). Three divine persons and three human persons authenticate the truth of the gospel. The number of witnesses required to establish the truthfulness of a statement in a legal court are thereby sufficiently provided on earth and in heaven (Num 35:30; John 8:14–18). The truth of the gospel of Jesus Christ is verified on earth by the prophet, the apostle, and the Christ. The truth of Jesus Christ is verified in heaven by the Father, the Son, and the Holy Spirit.

The truth of Jesus Christ is verified in heaven and on earth because Jesus Christ participates as God fully in the source of truth in heaven and presents all truth through his very person upon earth. There is no truth outside the trinitarian God: Father, Son, and Spirit. All truth finds its coherence and consistency with Christ and the Trinity, "the highest truth," and nowhere else.[71] The divine Truth chose to reveal himself in Christ to the apostles. Through the apostolic witness gathered in Scripture under the guidance of the Holy Spirit the Truth still reveals himself today. This is the nature of Scripture: Scripture is God's expression of his truth in written form. Scripture is the voice of God and Christ heard by the apostles and prophets.

---

[69] "It is probable that the Counsellor's testimony is to be understood as effected through the witness of the disciples." Colin G. Kruse, *John: An Introduction and Commentary*, Tyndale New Testament Commentary (Downers Grove: IVP, 2003), 322.

[70] Yarnell, *God the Trinity*, 107–33 (see chap. 1, n. 78).

[71] Marshall, *Trinity and Truth*, 120–22.

Guided by the Holy Spirit they testify to him with the Spirit. Scripture is the Word of God which speaks today with the same veracity he spoke yesterday. Scripture's historic truthfulness derives from and expresses faithfully God's eternal truthfulness. On this basis, "we can gladly confess that the Bible is a dependable, truthful, trustworthy, faithful, and thus inerrant Word of God to humanity."[72]

VII. The Economy of Scripture

Finally, what is Scripture's economy? What is the Bible's function? As the continuation of the witness to God the Trinity by the prophets and the apostles, Scripture defines its own purpose. John's Gospel states the function of Scripture: "These are written so that you may believe that Jesus is the Messiah, the Son of God, and that by believing you may have life in his name" (20:31). Scripture was not written to satisfy the historian's curiosity, for Jesus "performed many other signs," but they are "not written in this book" (20:30). Scripture was not written to satisfy the scientist's curiosity about how the miraculous "signs" of Jesus might accord with natural law. Scripture contains beautiful poetry, but it was not written primarily for aesthetic pleasure. When Scripture addresses history or science or art, we believe it speaks truthfully, simply because Scripture is the Word of God, who is Truth. The Word's purpose is not to scratch the intellectual itch of fallen human minds. The Word's purpose is to transform human beings so they might "know the truth" and be "set free" by faith to eternal life with the Trinity (8:31–32).

The written Word is given to make wicked people holy. The Word is an elect instrument within the divine economy for the sanctification of humanity, so that the human being may approach the holy Judge who sits over creation (John 17:17).[73] God the Trinity confronts humanity with the fearful truth of its expected judgment through the proclamation of the Law and offers the gift of salvation through the proclamation of the gospel of Jesus Christ. The Gospel of John reveals God's ministry of confrontation through Word and Spirit. The Spirit's ministry of testimony to the truth of

---

[72] Dockery, *Christian Scripture*, 67 (see introduction, n. 4).
[73] Webster, *Holy Scripture*, 10.

the Word fosters a crisis requiring "decision."[74] The Holy Spirit convicts of sin, of judgment, and of righteousness. Judgment will come upon those who refuse to believe the truth of Jesus Christ (16:8–10). Chapters 3, 8, and 18 of John's Gospel narrate episodes of decision made during Truth's convictional confrontation with humanity.

In John 3, Nicodemus, a leading Pharisee, approached Jesus at night. He confessed Jesus was a teacher from God. In three "truly" statements, Jesus taught Nicodemus that, on the one hand, regeneration by the Holy Spirit (3:3, 5), and on the other, personal faith in Jesus (3:11–12), are prerequisite for entering God's kingdom. Personal regeneration by the Spirit and personal faith in the Son are coordinate within the moment of human salvation.[75] Jesus ended the night's discourse with a subsequent requirement: "But anyone who lives by the truth comes to the light, so that his works may be shown to be accomplished by God" (3:21). True salvation comes through regeneration by faith and necessarily exhibits faith in a transformed moral life. The One who is "the way, the truth, and the life" (14:6) never treated truth as separable from life and its conduct. "He is not the Truth apart from his whole course of His life and acts."[76] Jesus demands his disciple repent toward Truth with the whole life.[77] Morality and spirituality are inextricably bound together with the intellectual.

In chapter 8 of John's Gospel, the scribes and Pharisees accosted Jesus at the temple. Only two responses to the proclamation of divine truth in Jesus became possible. These responses are not merely mutually exclusive but radically opposed. Human beings who hear but do not believe in Jesus reject the truth (8:45–46). They reflect the deceptions of their "father," the devil, who "does not stand in the truth." The devil "speaks from his own nature;" literally, "out of his own things" (*ek tōn idiōn lalei*; 8:44). The nature of the devil as liar is entirely contrary to the nature of God as truth. Human beings must decide whether to participate in one nature or the

---

[74] Torrance, *Theological Science*, 153–54.

[75] Carson writes, "'to be born again' or 'to be born from above' must mean the same thing as 'to become children of God', to be 'born of God', by believing in the name of the incarnate Word." Carson, *The Gospel according to John*, 189.

[76] Torrance, *Theological Science*, 155.

[77] "True knowing is inseparable from true living and true living is living in the Truth of God as it is in Jesus." Torrance, *Theological Science*, 158.

other.[78] Unbelievers share in the things of the devil.[79] But human beings who hear and receive the truth of God by the Spirit are set free to participate in the truth (8:32; cf. 18:37). The person "from God" listens to his Word. Believers in Jesus Christ share in the divine truth accessible only through the Word.

The juxtaposition between these two possibilities for participation is striking. The auditor must decide between being a child of the devil or a child of God. Unbelievers are children of "your father the devil" (8:44a). Believers are those who receive the things that "the Father taught" Jesus (8:28). Believers become "children of God" by faith in his Word (1:12). Unbelievers participate in the things of the devil, while believers participate in the things of God. A person's spiritual, intellectual, and moral genealogy derives either from divine Truth or demonic deception.

Knowledge of the true God personally transforms human beings. To know the Son is to know the Father (14:7). To know the Spirit of truth requires knowing both the Son and the Father (14:17). And the only way a person may worship God is by worshipping via the Holy Spirit (4:24). The one who hears the Word of Christ and believes in God through Christ receives "eternal life" (5:24; cf. 8:51). But only people who truly continue in his Word are accounted "disciples" (8:31). In his detailed work on truth in John, de la Potterie followed the Spirit's subjective uniting of the disciple with truth through five major activities: doing the truth, knowing the truth, appropriating the truth, being liberated by the truth, and cooperating with the truth. The true believer embraces a life of truth and true worship of truth.[80]

In the third narrative, found in John 18, truth addresses both individual sinners and abusive social systems. Abusers of power are by degrees resistant to, fearful of, and hypocritical about truth.[81] Both Testaments present "a sustained contestation over truth in which conventional modes of power

---

[78] The language of "nature" applied to the devil is problematic, for evil may not have a nature *per se*, but is the contradiction of being and good. Donald A. Cross, "Augustine's Privation Account of Evil: A Defense," *Augustinian Studies* 20 (1989): 109–28. However, the language is rhetorically unavoidable here.

[79] Grant Osborne and Philip W. Comfort, *John and 1, 2, and 3 John*, Cornerstone Bible Commentary (Carol Stream, IL: Tyndale, 2007), 137.

[80] De la Potterie, *La Vérité dans Saint Jean*, 2:1014–19.

[81] George Orwell, *Orwell on Truth* (London: Harvill Secker, 2017).

do not always prevail."[82] Pharoah did not submit to truth, so his power was broken by God. Josiah properly submitted his exercise of power to truth. Both Elisha and Jesus spoke with life-giving truth to power. Christians today must continue to present truth to power. "The governor, on behalf of the empire, will continue to ask, 'What is truth?' And the apostles will continue to give answer, uncommonly unintimidated: 'We must obey God rather than any human authority' (Acts 5:29)."[83] The truth transforms individual sinners through Word and Spirit into disciples, who must speak of his truth to everyone, including rebellious rulers (Luke 12:11; Acts 4:26). Truth transforms both individual lives and whole societies.

Coming from God the Father as source, the Son as effective agent, and the Spirit as inspirer, the testimony of the Bible to truth graciously and effectively reveals who God is and what God commands and promises. God has empowered the written words of the prophets and the apostles with his agency. This instrumental agency of Scripture explains why terms like "word" and "truth" are applied not only to the person of Jesus Christ as revelation incarnate (e.g., Isa 55:9–12; John 1:1, 14), but also to the oral proclamation of divine revelation (e.g., Josh 3:9; Acts 6:2, 7) and to the prophetic and apostolic literature (e.g., Deut 27:3; Heb 4:12). The written Word of God, endowed by divine truth, continues to reveal truth which must be received with faith. Truth still works through the holy book and the holy voices who proclaim the law and the gospel so that fallen sinners will be transformed into righteous disciples.

---

[82] Walter Brueggemann, *Truth Speaks to Power: The Countercultural Nature of Scripture* (Louisville: Westminster John Knox, 2013), 6.

[83] Brueggemann, *Truth Speaks to Power*, 165.

5

Jesus Christ and the Bible

The Bible presents a message about God and his purposes. It describes the creation of the universe, including the direct creation of men and women in a paradise on earth. The Bible describes the call of Abraham, the giving of the law, the establishment of the kingdom, the division of the kingdom, and the captivity and restoration of Israel. Scripture sees humankind as fallen from a sinless condition and separated from God. The promise of a coming Messiah who will redeem men and women and reign as King appears throughout the Old Testament.[1]

The message of Holy Scripture proclaims that believers are restored to favor with God through the sacrifice of Jesus Christ. His sacrifice put an end to the Old Testament sacrificial system in which the blood of animals represented the handling of the sin problem. The New Testament reveals the Christ who brought salvation and describes how these prophecies about him were fulfilled. This unifying message ties the biblical library together. The Old Testament promises were fulfilled in the person of Jesus Christ, "the Son of Abraham" and "the Son of David" (Matt 1:1). At the beginning of his ministry, Jesus claimed that he had not come to abolish the law and the prophets, "but to fulfill them" (Matt 5:17). With the statement "law and the prophets," he endorsed the entire Old Testament, including its prophecies,

---

[1] D. A. Carson, *The God Who Is There: Finding Your Place in God's Story* (Grand Rapids: Baker, 2010); T. Desmond Alexander, *From Eden to the New Jerusalem* (Grand Rapids: Kregel, 2009).

promises, and priorities.[2] As several church fathers observed more than fifteen hundred years ago, the New is in the Old concealed; the Old is in the
New revealed. The overarching unity centers in Jesus Christ, who is the primary subject and key to interpretation of Holy Scripture.[3]

Jesus Christ is the central figure of divine revelation and the focus of
the Christian faith.[4] The Bible is our primary source of information about
Jesus. Yet, the Bible's testimony is amply supported by the impact of Jesus
Christ on the world of the first century. In this chapter we will provide an
overview of how Jesus is presented as the central figure of divine revelation,
which will include an examination of how Jesus interpreted Holy Scripture.
We will look both at Scripture's view of Jesus and at Jesus's understanding
of Scripture. We will also give attention to the significance of Jesus as both
divine and human as a model for the divine-human aspect of Scripture.

I. Jesus Christ, the Covenants, and
the Unity of Scripture

Jesus was born in Bethlehem of Judea, a few miles south of Jerusalem (Matt
1–2; Luke 2). In different ways and at various times God had spoken to his
people through his prophets (see Heb 1:1–2). The purposes of God were
made known through a series of covenants (see Gen 12; 2 Sam 7; Jer 31). In
these covenants, God's intent for establishing his kingdom and for redeeming humankind were progressively expressed. God's purposes were to be
accomplished through a descendant of David. The people of God in the

---

[2] See R. T. France, *Jesus and the Old Testament* (Vancouver: Regent College
Press, 1992); Chad Bird, *The Christ Key: Unlocking the Centrality of Christ in the
Old Testament* (Irvine, CA: 1517 Publications, 2021); Donald Macleod, "Jesus and
Scripture," in *The Trustworthiness of God: Perspectives on the Nature of Scripture*, ed.
Paul Helm and Carl R. Trueman (Grand Rapids: Eerdmans, 2002), 69–95.

[3] Wenham, *Christ and the Bible* (see introduction, n. 9); Wayne Grudem, John J.
Collins, and Thomas R. Schreiner, eds., *Understanding the Big Picture of the Bible: A
Guide to Reading the Bible Well* (Wheaton: Crossway, 2010).

[4] Christ is manifestly both "the Word of God" (John 1:1) and "the wisdom of
God" (1 Cor 1:24). See H. D. McDonald, *Jesus: Human and Divine: An Introduction
to Christology* (Grand Rapids: Zondervan, 1968); Carl F. H. Henry, *The Identity
of Jesus of Nazareth* (Nashville: Broadman, 1992); Donald G. Bloesch, *Jesus Christ:
Savior and Lord* (Downers Grove: IVP, 2005).

Old Testament looked forward expectantly to the coming of the promised King, their Messiah. In Jesus Christ these covenant promises found their ultimate fulfillment.[5]

The connection of three covenants noted above, the Abrahamic Covenant (Gen 12:1–3), the Davidic Covenant (2 Sam 7:12–16), and the new covenant (Jer 31:31–34) will help give us guidance for thinking about the unity of the Bible.[6] A covenant is a compact or agreement between two parties binding them to each other and to understandings of the other on each other's behalf. When one considers the theological meaning of covenant, the primary focus is on a gracious undertaking entered into by God for the benefit and blessing of men and women. A general characteristic of the Old Testament covenant is its unalterable and permanently binding character. In the ancient Near East when one party to the agreement was greatly superior in power to the other, the covenant had a one-sided emphasis. The ruler or one in authority, though, was expected to act in the best interest of his people. The covenants made by God with his chosen people were even more explicitly one-sided. God promises, "I will," and his word is binding. This is especially the case with the covenant between God and Abraham found in Genesis 12.[7]

1. The Abrahamic Covenant

This covenant was the initial announcement of the coming of the kingdom and its king. The declarations made by God in this covenant represent promises that he will surely bring to pass. These kingdom promises will accrue only to those individuals who manifest a true and living faith, expecting their fulfillment in the manifestation of God's kingdom. Thus, the first aspect is evident in this covenant to Abraham. God promised him a land, a seed, to make of him a great blessing, and to make his name great. Paul taught that

---

[5] Daniel Block, *Covenant: The Framework of God's Plan of Redemption* (Grand Rapids: Baker, 2021).

[6] Walter C. Kaiser Jr., *Recovering the Unity of the Bible: One Continuous Story, Plan, and Purpose* (Grand Rapids: Zondervan, 2015).

[7] Walter C. Kaiser Jr., *The Promise-Plan of God: A Biblical Theology of the Old and New Testaments* (Grand Rapids: Zondervan, 2008).

this covenant finds its fulfillment in Jesus Christ and those who have placed faith in him:

> Now the promises were spoken to Abraham and to his seed. He does not say, "and to seeds," as though referring to many, but referring to one, and to your seed, who is Christ (Gal 3:16).

> For if the inheritance is based on the law, it is no longer based on the promise; but God has graciously given it to Abraham through the promise (Gal 3:18).

> And if you belong to Christ, then you are Abraham's seed, heirs according to the promise (Gal 3:29).

Thus, God's kingdom plan, ultimately focused on Jesus Christ, was set forth from the beginning; nothing shall frustrate it. Yet, participation in the promise is restricted to those who manifest the faith and obedience of Abraham. God will see to it that his kingdom plan is carried out in history, but he will also see to it that none partake of the covenant who are in violation of the demands of faith. No person who finally presents to God a faithless and insincere heart will participate in kingdom blessings. Thus, faith in Christ and expectation of the kingdom is to be commended and desired.[8]

2. The Davidic Covenant

The promises to Abraham are expanded in God's covenant to David in 2 Samuel 7. The major themes of this covenant, namely the king and the kingdom, are vital to understanding God's plan for the ages as made in the canonical Scriptures. All the promises of the Davidic covenant have been fulfilled by and in Jesus Christ. God promised three things to David: he would have a son; David's throne would be established; and David's kingdom would be established forever. During Jesus's day, the people expected to see the Messiah come as a fulfillment of the promise to David. The genealogies

---

[8] Kenneth A. Mathews, *Genesis 11:27–50:26*, New American Commentary (Nashville: B&H, 2005), 104–19; Timothy George, *Galatians*, New American Commentary (Nashville: Broadman, 1994), 244–92.

of Jesus found in Matthew 1 and Luke 3 are vitally important because they establish Christ's descent from David and thus support the claim of Jesus of Nazareth as the Old Testament's promised Messiah. Just as the Abrahamic covenant is timeless, the Davidic covenant is timeless in that it looks ahead to the day when God will keep his promise and Jesus Christ will rule over all as King.[9]

3. The New Covenant

The purposes of God in the Abrahamic and Davidic covenants and the accompanying expectations regarding the establishment of the kingdom are expanded further through the prophets' words:

> "Look, the days are coming"—this is the LORD's declaration—"when I will make a new covenant with the house of Israel and with the house of Judah. This one will not be like the covenant I made with their ancestors when I took them by the hand to bring them out of the land of Egypt—my covenant that they broke even though I am their master"—the LORD's declaration. "Instead, this is the covenant I will make with the house of Israel after those days"—the LORD's declaration. "I will put my teaching within them and write it on their hearts. I will be their God, and they will be my people. No longer will one teach his neighbor or his brother, saying, 'Know the LORD,' for they will all know me, from the least to the greatest of them"—this is the LORD's declaration. "For I will forgive their iniquity and never again remember their sin." (Jer 31:31–34)

4. Covenant Fulfillment

The Old Testament includes two different lines of teaching about the Promised One, sometimes distinct and other times commingled. One of these lines claims that the Messiah would be a Redeemer who would restore

---

[9] Robert D. Bergen, *1, 2 Samuel*, New American Commentary (Nashville: Broadman, 1996), 338–41; also, see F. B. Huey Jr., *Jeremiah and Lamentations*, New American Commentary (Nashville: Broadman, 1993), 278–86.

humankind to a right relationship with God. This theme is most clearly developed around the idea of a Suffering Servant Messiah in Isa 52:13–53:12. Here the Messiah is pictured as one who would become an offering for the sins of men and women.

Another line of Old Testament teaching describes the Messiah as a coming King destined to restore Israel to its rightful place as God's people on earth. The promises portray the restoration as a time of peace and righteousness. Aspects of each purpose can be seen in the covenant promises and the prophetic pictures, though the details of the completion of these teachings remained somewhat unclear. The New Testament, however, interprets the Old Testament and announces that the promised Messiah had come in Jesus of Nazareth. Through his ministry, teachings, sacrificial death, and resurrection, Jesus fulfilled the messianic promises, accomplished the messianic mission, and provided for the salvation of the lost world. The New Testament also declares that Jesus will come again and reign as King, bringing peace and joy and righteousness.[10]

Jesus is introduced to us in the New Testament with a genealogy (Matt 1:1–17). The genealogy is followed by an account of his miraculous conception by the Holy Spirit (Luke 1:35); his later adoption by Joseph (1:18–25), his flight to Egypt, and his return to Galilee (2:1–23). Jesus is presented as the Messiah, the Son of David (1:1). He is made known to us as the obedient Son of God in the account of his baptism by John the Baptist (3:13–17) and his temptation by the devil (4:3–10). Jesus went about all Galilee teaching in the synagogues and preaching the gospel of the kingdom (Matt 4:23). Luke's introduction of Jesus also includes attention to the first synagogue sermon in Luke 4:18–19. After returning to his hometown of Nazareth, Jesus was asked to read in the synagogue. After reading Isa 61:1–3, he sat down and amazingly proclaimed, "Today, as you listen, this Scripture has been fulfilled" (Luke 4:21). Jesus is described as "the coming one" with reference both to his first coming (Matt 21:9; Luke 7:19) and to his second (2 Thess 1:10; Rev 1:7; 22:7). The New Testament throughout presents Jesus first coming as a fulfillment of Old Testament covenants, pictures, promises, and prophecies.

---

[10] Richard B. Hays, *Reading Backwards: Figural Christology and the Fourfold Gospel Witness* (Waco: Baylor University Press, 2014), 93–110.

The New Testament writers also looked forward to further fulfillment of God's promises and purposes in Christ.[11]

The establishment of the kingdom under a descendant of David was central to these expectations. Jesus spoke of a day when this kingdom would arrive in all its glory (Mark 9:1; Luke 19:11; 22:18). When Jesus began to announce that "the kingdom of God has come near" (Mark 1:15), he was not referring primarily to a physical kingdom. He called on his listeners to enter or receive God's kingdom (Matt 4:17), for this kingdom is both a present reality for God's people as well as a future promise. While this kingdom has a present aspect to it, it also has future expectations (Matt 19:28; 24:1–51; Mark 13:24–37; Luke 12:35–48; 21:25–28).[12] What was announced by Jesus was clearly taught by the apostles as well (1 Cor 15:51–58; 1 Thess 4:13–18; 2 Thess 1:7–10; 2 Pet 3:10–12; Rev 19:11–21).

5. Jesus Christ and the Unity of Scripture

Within the various and diverse settings and presentations in Scripture, there is an overarching unity that is focused on Jesus Christ, the ultimate revelation of God.[13] The variety is evident as one compares Leviticus to Acts, Isaiah to Hebrews, Proverbs to Matthew, Psalms to Romans, and Esther to Jude. While James D. G. Dunn and others have in recent years stressed the diversity in Scripture,[14] Kenneth Kantzer noted that the Christian church has solidly recognized an ultimate unity throughout the Bible. He added: "Only on this basis could it possibly be a revelation from a God of truth, and naturally also, only thus could it be a practical guide for our life and thought."[15]

---

[11] N. T. Wright, *Jesus and the Victory of God* (London: SPCK, 1996); Robert B. Sloan, *The Favorable Year of the Lord: A Study of Jubilary Theology in the Gospel of Luke* (Austin, TX: Schola, 1977).

[12] Russell Moore, *The Kingdom of Christ* (Wheaton: Crossway, 2004).

[13] John Piper, *Reading the Bible Supernaturally: Seeing and Savoring the Glory of God in Scripture* (Wheaton: Crossway, 2017).

[14] James D. G. Dunn, *Unity and Diversity in the New Testament: An Inquiry into the Character of Earliest Christianity* (London: SCM, 2006).

[15] Kenneth S. Kantzer, "Evangelicals and the Doctrine of Inerrancy," in *The Foundation of Biblical Authority* (Grand Rapids: Zondervan, 1978), 147–56; Kenneth S. Kantzer, "Systematic Theology as a Practical Discipline," in *Doing Theology for the*

A. M. Hunter, in his book *The Unity of the New Testament*, similarly maintained that there is a deep unity in the Bible which dominates and transcends its diversity.[16] C. F. D. Moule, while recognizing the distinctive individuality of the biblical authors and the diversity represented among them, observed: "The rainbow spectrum thus presented is undeniably thrown by one luminary alone. Common to every writing of the New Testament, without even the exception of the Epistle of James, is devotion to Jesus Christ."[17] Walter C. Kaiser Jr. has insightfully highlighted the Bible's storyline as one, continuous story, plan, and purpose, following the promise-fulfillment theme in his volume, *Recovering the Unity of the Bible*.[18] As John Stott claimed, "this combination of unity and diversity is exactly what we would expect, granted our belief in the double authorship of Scripture, the one mind and mouth of God speaking through the many minds and mouths of the human authors."[19]

The New Testament expands on the Old Testament story with a focus on Jesus Christ. He is the central figure of the New Testament and the focus of the Christian faith. God's purposes were to be accomplished through the seed of Abraham (Gal 3:16, 29), a descendant of David (Rom 1:3–4). As we have noted, this revelation was progressively revealed in two different lines about the Messiah. He would be both King and Redeemer. Aspects of each purpose can be observed in the covenant promises and the prophetic portraits. The New Testament interprets the Old Testament and announces that the promised Messiah had come in Jesus of Nazareth. In identifying Jesus as the Messiah, the New Testament authors affirm an essential unity between the Old and New Testaments. The New Testament, rooted in the Old Testament

---

People of God: Studies of J. I. Packer, ed. Donald Lewis and Alister McGrath (Downers Grove: IVP, 1996), 21–42.

[16] See A. M. Hunter, *The Unity of the New Testament* (London: SCM, 1957); also, see Ronald A. Ward, *The Pattern of Our Salvation: A Study of New Testament Unity* (Waco: Word, 1978).

[17] C. F. D. Moule, "Fulfillment Words in the New Testament: Use and Abuse," *New Testament Studies* 14, no. 3 (April 1968): 293–96; C. F. D. Moule, *The Birth of the New Testament* (London: SCM, 1981), 17; C. F. D. Moule, *The Origin of Christology* (Cambridge: Cambridge University Press, 1977).

[18] Kaiser, *Recovering the Unity of the Bible*, 69–182.

[19] John R. W. Stott, "Theology: A Multidimensional Discipline," in *Doing Theology for the People of God: Studies in Honor of J. I. Packer*, ed. Donald Lewis and Alister McGrath (Downers Grove: IVP, 1996), 4–6.

and acknowledged by Jesus to be the Word of God and the basis of his teaching and ministry (Matt 5:17; John 10:34–35), indicates Jesus understood his mission in a way that ran counter to the assumptions and expectations of his contemporaries—both his followers and his opponents. One thing is for sure: Jesus understood his mission as a fulfillment of the Scriptures, which is indicated both by his interpretation and teaching of Scripture, as well. We find similar patterns among his followers. This Jesus, who walked on the earth as teacher (Matt 5–7; 13) and healer (Matt 4:23–25; 8:16; 14:35–36; 15:30; 19:2), is the Son of Man (Matt 8:20; 9:6; 13:37; 20:28), the Son of David (Acts 13:34; Rom 1:3; 2 Tim 2:8), the Son of God (Matt 16:16; John 11:27), and Christ the Lord (Rom 10:9; Rev 19:16).[20]

"The Christ" is not a personal name, but a description meaning "the anointed one." Anointing is intimately associated with a divine commission to a royal, priestly, or prophetic ministry. At the zenith of Jesus's earthly ministry, we find Peter's great confession at Caesarea Philippi. It is revealed that Jesus is "the Christ, the Son of the living God" (Matt 16:16). To affirm Jesus as "the Christ" was to acknowledge that the one from Nazareth was the Messiah foreseen by Old Testament prophets, the one commissioned by God to redeem his people and complete God's redemptive plan. Sometimes, Jesus is addressed as Lord, which functions as the theological equivalent of the Old Testament name for God (*Yahweh*). With this expression, the early church proclaimed the deity of Jesus of Nazareth. As Lord, he is the one in whom the church places its faith and who will return as Lord of lords and King of kings (Rev 19:16).[21]

In identifying Jesus as Messiah and Lord, the New Testament authors affirm an essential unity between the Old Testament and the New. The New Testament, which is rooted in the Hebrew Scriptures, interprets and amplifies the Old Testament. The life and work of Jesus, therefore, were grounded

---

[20] Richard N. Longenecker, *Contours of Christology in the New Testament* (Grand Rapids: Eerdmans, 2005); Donald Guthrie, *New Testament Theology* (Downers Grove: IVP, 1981), 219–407.

[21] See George E. Ladd, *Theology of the New Testament* (Grand Rapids: Eerdmans, 1974), 142; Richard N. Longenecker, *The Christology of Early Jewish Christianity* (London: SCM, 1970), 70; D. A. Carson, "Matthew," in *The Expositor's Bible Commentary*, ed. Frank E. Gaebelein, 12 vols. (Grand Rapids: Zondervan, 1984), 8:363–75.

in the Old Testament, which Jesus acknowledged to be the Word of God, which cannot be broken (John 10:35), the Word on which he based his earthly life.[22]

II. Jesus Christ and the Old Testament

The teachings and practices of Jesus exemplified for his followers that his life and ministry fulfilled the Old Testament Scriptures.[23] He interpreted the Old Testament in a manner similar to contemporary Jewish interpreters, but his message and method were novel. His Christological reading of Scripture meant that Jesus interpreted the Old Testament in light of himself. For example, in John 5:39–40, Jesus said, "You pore over the Scriptures because you think you have eternal life in them, and yet they testify about me. But you are not willing to come to me so that you may have life." In John 5:46 Jesus said: "For if you believed Moses, you would believe me, because he wrote about me." Also, on the Emmaus Road with his disciples following the resurrection, Jesus said: "How foolish and slow you are to believe all that the prophets have spoken! Wasn't it necessary for the Messiah to suffer these things and enter into his glory?" Then beginning with Moses and all the Prophets, he interpreted for them the things concerning himself in all the Scriptures (Luke 24:25–27).

The method that Jesus used to interpret the Old Testament was entirely Christological, though he consistently treated the historical narratives as straightforward records of fact, such as references to: Abel (Luke 11:51); Noah (Matt 24:37–39; Luke 17:26–27); Abraham (John 8:56); Sodom and Gomorrah (Matt 10:15; 11:23–24; Luke 10:12); Lot (Luke 17:28–32); Isaac and Jacob (Matt 8:11; Luke 13:28); the manna (John 6:31, 49, 58); the wilderness serpent (John 3:14); David and the shewbread (Matt 12:3–4; Mark 2:25–26; Luke 6:3–4); David as a psalm writer (Matt 22:43; Mark 12:36; Luke 20:42); Solomon (Matt 6:29; 12:42; Luke 11:31; 12:27); Jonah (Matt 12:39–41; Luke 11:29–30, 32); and Zechariah (Luke 11:51). There

---

[22] Guthrie, *New Testament Theology*, 49–59.
[23] See John Rogerson, Christopher Rowland, and Barnabas Lindars, *The Study and Use of the Bible* (Grand Rapids: Eerdmans, 1988), 3–5; Guthrie, *New Testament Theology*, 955–57.

are repeated references to Moses as the giver of the law (Matt 8:4; 19:8; Mark 1:44; 7:10; 10:5; 12:26; Luke 5:14; 20:37; John 5:46; 7:19); the sufferings of the prophets (Matt 5:12; 13:57; 21:34–36; 23:29–37; Mark 6:4; Luke 6:23; 11:47–51; 13:34); and the creation narratives in Genesis 1 and 2 (Matt 19:4–5; Mark 10:6–8). As John Wenham notes, it is quite interesting that "the narratives that are the least acceptable to the so-called 'modern mind' are the very ones that he [Jesus] seemed most fond of choosing for his illustrations."[24]

The appeal to the lordship of Jesus Christ was understood to carry with it Christ's regard for the Old Testament as a revelation from God. In the New Testament, again and again we read of Jesus saying, "it is written" and "have you not read?"[25] As noted above, he quoted from all parts as being divinely authoritative, recognizing the Scriptures as a unity and not merely a compilation. H. D. McDonald observed that "to its pages he turned constantly for the vindication of his person and the validation of his mission; and he declared all the Scriptures to testify of him."[26] R. V. G. Tasker amplified:

> The testimony of our Lord to the Old Testament and his claim to divinity are, it would seem, more closely associated than many in our day are prepared to acknowledge. Those who had found Christ in those Old Testament Scriptures consequently found themselves bound to look at that unique literature primarily through the eyes of him who claimed to be the light of the world, our Lord and Savior Jesus Christ.[27]

We can see the Christological reading of the Old Testament in places like the temptation narratives (Matt 4:1–11; Luke 4:1–13), in which we find Jesus's own estimation of his status and calling. His answers in this context were taken from Deuteronomy 6–8, in which Moses, following the forty years of wandering in the wilderness, exhorted Israel to wholehearted

---

[24] Wenham, *Christ and the Bible*, 12–13.

[25] Wenham, 106–8.

[26] H. D. McDonald, "The Bible in Twentieth-Century British Theology," in *Challenges to Inerrancy: A Theological Response*, ed. Gordon Lewis and Bruce Demarest (Chicago: Moody, 1984), 100.

[27] R. V. G. Tasker, *The Old Testament in the New Testament* (London: Hodder & Stoughton, 1962), 23.

obedience and continued faith in God's provision for them. It was a time
of hunger and testing, preparatory to a special task, in which God disci-
plined the nation Israel to teach his people to worship only the true God
(Deut 8:5). Israel often failed to carry out the mission and call of God.
Jesus at the end of forty days, accepted afresh his messianic mission and his
status as the Son of God. His belief in his forthcoming resurrection seemed
to be motivated both by the promises of Israel's resurrection and by seeing the account of Jonah as a picture of his own resurrection (Jonah 1:17;
Matt 12:40). Jesus observed that his own experience was prefigured in the
Psalms of vindication and suffering. These Psalms were used both by individual Israelites and by corporate Israel (Pss 22; 41–43; 118; Matt 21:42;
23:39; 26:38; 27:46).[28]

R. T. France sums up the evidence of the Synoptic Gospels in these
words:

> He uses persons in the Old Testament as types of himself (David,
> Solomon, Elijah, Elisha, Isaiah, Jonah) or of John the Baptist
> (Elijah); he refers to Old Testament institutions as types of him-
> self and his work (the priesthood and the covenant); he sees in
> the experience of Israel foreshadowings of his own; he finds the
> hopes of Israel fulfilled in himself and his disciples, and sees his
> disciples as assuming the status of Israel; in deliverance by God,
> he sees a type of the gathering of men into the church, while the
> disasters of Israel are foreshadowings of the imminent punish-
> ment of those who reject him, whose unbelief is prefigured in that
> of the wicked in Israel and even, in two instances, in the arrogance
> of the Gentile nations.[29]

In these and other pictures in the Old Testament, Jesus saw foreshad-
owings of himself and his work. The result was that Jesus was rejected by
large sectors of the Jewish population, while the true people of God were
now to be found in the nascent Christian community. The history of Israel
had reached its decisive point in the coming of Jesus Christ. The whole of
the Old Testament was summed up in him. Jesus embodied in himself the

---

[28] France, *Jesus and the Old Testament*, 75.
[29] France, *Jesus and the Old Testament*, 76.

redemptive destiny of Israel. That status and destiny are to be fulfilled in the community of those who belong to him.[30]

Because Jesus is the fulfillment of God's purposes for Israel, words originally spoken of the nation could be rightly applied to him. Jesus is the key to understanding the Old Testament because everything points to himself. The New Testament writers, following the pattern of Jesus, interpreted the Old Testament as a whole and in its parts as a witness to Christ. It is not surprising that in providing different pictures of Jesus's life, the biblical writers saw that at almost every point he had fulfilled the Old Testament. This realization provides the key to the way Jesus understood and used the Old Testament.[31]

The Gospels indicate that Jesus viewed his mission as a fulfillment of the Scriptures and in a way that ran counter to the assumptions and expectations of his closest followers as well as his opponents. C. K. Barrett has noted: "The gospel story as a whole differs so markedly from current (i.e., first-century) interpretation of the Old Testament that it is impossible to believe that it originated simply in meditations of prophecy; it originated in the career of Jesus of Nazareth."[32]

It is not surprising that in providing different pictures of Jesus's life, the biblical writers saw that at almost every point his life had fulfilled the Old Testament. His birth had been foretold (Isa 7:14 = Matt 1:23; Mic 5:2 =

---

[30] See Baker, *Two Testaments, One Bible*, (see introduction, n. 18); D. A. Carson and H. G. M. Williamson, eds., *It Is Written: Scripture Citing Scripture. Essays in Honor of Barnabas Lindars* (Cambridge: Cambridge University Press, 1988); Klyne Snodgrass, "The Use of the Old Testament in the New Testament," in *New Testament Criticism and Interpretation*, ed. D. A. Black and David S. Dockery (Grand Rapids: Zondervan, 1991); Robert B. Sloan, "Use of the Old Testament in the New Testament," in *Reclaiming the Prophetic Mantle: Preaching the Old Testament Faithfully*, ed. George L. Klein (Nashville: Broadman, 1992); David S. Dockery, ed., "The Use of the Old Testament in the New Testament," *Southwestern Journal of Theology* (entire Fall 2021 issue); James M. Hamilton Jr., *Typology: Understanding the Bible's Promise-Shaped Patterns. How the Old Testament Expectations Are Fulfilled in Christ* (Grand Rapids: Zondervan, 2022); Averbeck, *The Old Testament Law for the Life of the Church*, 225–333 (see introduction, n. 8).

[31] C. K. Barrett, "The Old Testament in the New," in *Cambridge History of the Bible*, 4 vols. (Cambridge: Cambridge University Press, 1970), 1:377–411; Morna D. Hooker, *Studying the New Testament* (Minneapolis: Augsburg, 1982), 70–92.

[32] Barrett, "The Old Testament in the New," 1:405.

Matt 2:6); as had the flight to Egypt (Hos 11:1 = Matt 2:15); the slaughter of the innocent children by Herod (Jer 31:15 = Matt 2:18); and his upbringing in Nazareth (Matt 2:23). The overall impact of his ministry has been described (Isa 42:1–4 = Matt 12:17–21), as well as his use of parables in his teaching (Isa 6:9–10; Ps 78:2 = Matt 13:14–15, 35). The message of Jesus's passion is filled with allusions to the Old Testament, including accounts of the triumphal entry into Jerusalem (Zech 9:9 = Matt 21:5), the cleansing of the temple (Isa 56:7 = Matt 21:13), and the events surrounding the cross (John 19:24, 28, 36–37).[33]

Reading the Old Testament in a typological manner enabled the New Testament writers to point to a correspondence between people and events of the past and of the present or future.[34] Because of the abuses in the usage of typology by post-Reformation interpreters, many people today tend to ignore the typological method. But when carefully defined and distinguished from fanciful readings of Scripture, it can be considered a rightful category for understanding Christian interpreters of the first century. This approach can be distinguished from prophecy, where the text functions only, or primarily, as a prediction of the future, and from allegorical interpretation where the correspondence is found in the hidden meaning of the text and not in the history it presents.[35] Typological interpretation does not ignore the historical meaning of a text but begins with the historical meaning. Typological interpretation then is based on the conviction that certain events in the history of Israel prefigure a future time when God's purposes will be revealed in their fullness.[36]

---

[33] R. T. France, "The Formula-Quotations of Matthew 2 and the Problem of Communication," *New Testament Studies* 27, no. 2 (1981): 223–51; Donald Juel, *Messianic Exegesis: Christological Interpretation of the Old Testament in Early Christianity* (Philadelphia: Fortress, 1988); Hamilton, *Typology*.

[34] Dunn, *Unity and Diversity*, 86; Richard M. Davidson, *Typology in Scripture: A Study of Hermeneutical TYPOS Structures* (Berrien Springs, MI: Andrews University Press, 1981).

[35] See D. S. Russell, *The Method and Message of Jewish Apocalyptic: 200BC–AD100* (London: SCM, 1964).

[36] David S. Dockery, "Typological Exegesis: Beyond Abuse and Neglect," in *Reclaiming the Prophetic Mantle: Preaching the Old Testament Faithfully*, ed. George L. Klein (Nashville: Broadman Press, 1992); Leonhard Goppelt, *TYPOS: The Typological Interpretation of the Old Testament in the New*, trans. Donald H. Madvig (Grand Rapids: Eerdmans, 1982), 61–208.

Jesus is recorded as pointing out typological correspondence between earlier events in redemptive history and circumstances connected with his person and ministry. Richard Longenecker has suggested three examples where Jesus invoked the correspondence theme: (1) Matt 12:40, where Jesus paralleled the experience of Jonah and his own approaching death and entombment; (2) Matt 24:37, where the relationship was drawn between the days of Noah and the days of "the coming Son of Man"; and (3) John 3:14, where Jesus connected the elevation of the serpent in the wilderness to his own approaching crucifixion. In each case, "Jesus viewed these Old Testament events as typological, pointing forward to their fulfillment in his person and ministry—not just analogies that could be drawn for the purpose of illustration."[37] The following Old Testament themes regularly find correspondence in the New Testament: paradise (Isa 11:6–8); the exodus and wilderness wanderings (Isa 43:16–21); David (Isa 11:1); and Moses (Deut 18:15–18).[38]

Apart from the literal usage of the Old Testament for moral injunctions, the other approaches Jesus used for reading the Old Testament have an obvious Christological reference. No one single image or pattern, no one motif or theme can adequately express this concept, yet what is emphasized throughout the New Testament is that numerous themes, images, and motifs of revelation and response are fulfilled in Jesus Christ. The note of Philip's jubilant words, "we have found the one Moses wrote about in the law (and so did the prophets)" (John 1:45), was echoed by the Gospel writers as the way to interpret the Old Testament events, pictures, and ideas. It was not so much one fulfillment idea, but a harmony of notes presented in a variety of ways. The teaching of Jesus and his hermeneutical practices became the direct source for much of the early church's understanding of the Old Testament.[39]

G. K. Beale has offered four helpful summary points for understanding the Gospel writers' approach to reading the Old Testament in light of Jesus Christ:

---

[37] Richard N. Longenecker, *Biblical Exegesis in the Apostolic Period* (Grand Rapids: Eerdmans, 1975), 34.

[38] Russell, *Method and Message of Jewish Apocalyptic*, 283–85.

[39] See F. F. Bruce, *New Testament Development of Old Testament Themes* (Grand Rapids: Eerdmans, 1968), 20–21; Baker, *Two Testaments, One Bible*; S. Lewis Johnson Jr., *The Old Testament in the New: An Argument for Biblical Inspiration* (Grand Rapids: Zondervan, 1980), 53–80.

(1) Christ corporately represents the true Israel of the Old and New Testaments; (2) history is unified by a wise and sovereign plan, so that the earlier parts of canonical history are designed to correspond typologically and to point to latter parts of inscripturated history; (3) the age of end-time fulfillment was inaugurated with Christ's first coming; and (4) in light of these latter two, the later parts of biblical history interpret earlier parts—a trend already begun by later Old Testament tradition with respect to earlier Old Testament books—so that Christ, as the goal of history, is the key to interpreting the ultimate interpretive aims of various Old Testament passages and narratives.[40]

The church appears to have taken Jesus's own interpretation of Scripture and its themes as paradigmatic for their continued exegetical endeavors. As C. F. D. Moule maintains when summarizing the approach of the New Testament writers, "At the heart of their biblical interpretation is a Christological and Christocentric perspective. Jesus became the direct and primary source for the church's understanding of the Old Testament."[41] What was needed was a hermeneutical perspective that could transform the Torah into the messianic Torah. Thus, through the pattern that Jesus had set and his exalted lordship through the Holy Spirit, Jesus served as the ongoing source and guide for reading the Old Testament Scriptures as seen in Acts, Paul, the book of Hebrews, Peter, John, and the rest of the New Testament. The Gospel writers also provide the framework and groundwork for Jesus's authentication of the New Testament.

III. Jesus Christ and the New Testament

In the Gospels we learn that Jesus interpreted his own life and ministry in light of the Scriptures. We learn, too, that he accepted the full authority and divine authorship of the Old Testament. In addition, he claimed truth for his

---

[40] Beale, *The Erosion of Inerrancy in Evangelicalism*, 227 (see introduction, n. 1); also, see Henri Blocher, "The 'Analogy of Faith' in the Study of Scripture," in *The Challenge of Evangelical Theology* (Edinburgh: Rutherford House, 1987), 29–31.

[41] Moule, *The Birth of the New Testament*, 58.

own teaching. We know that the New Testament was written after Jesus's life on earth. What then was his relationship to the New Testament?

During his ministry on earth Jesus invested in the training and formation of his followers in manifold ways. Among these, twelve were given special attention and a special commission (Mark 3:14). It is impossible to speak with certainty about the methods Christ used to teach his disciples. Probably, however, Jesus instructed his disciples in ways similar to those used by the rabbis of his day. He is referred to as teacher ("rabbi" and "teacher" are vitally related ideas). The rabbis thought of themselves as bearers of truth or of the true tradition. It was their task to pass on truth to approved disciples, who memorized their teachings. The disciples of Jesus must have committed themselves to intensive instruction. After they received special commissioning, they gave themselves to the Word of God and to teaching and preaching. The church followed the example of the disciples by continuing steadfastly in their teaching (Acts 2:42; 6:2).

Before and after his resurrection Jesus indicated that his disciples would have authority to teach and build his church in his name (Matt 16:16–20; 28:18–20). As the Father had sent Jesus, Jesus sent the apostles (John 20:21). In the name of Jesus, repentance and forgiveness were to be proclaimed (Luke 24:47). All these things were fulfilled in the early church through Christ's gift of the Holy Spirit to the apostles. The Spirit brought events to their remembrance and led them into all truth (John 14–17). In this way the Spirit of God led the apostles in ministry and mission. The apostles' words were confirmed by Jesus through the inspiration of the Spirit. Paul's commissioning to preach and teach was different from that of the other apostles, but Jesus's affirmation of Paul's work was quite similar (Acts 9). Therefore, there is good reason to maintain that Jesus authenticated the work of the apostles in the work of writing Scripture.[42] John Wenham observes that "To Christ, his own teaching and the teaching of his Spirit-taught apostles were true, authoritative, inspired. To him, what he and they said under the direction of the Spirit, God said. To him, the God of the New Testament was the living God; and in principle the teaching of the New Testament was the teaching

---

[42] Some aspects of this section have been adapted from David S. Dockery, *Biblical Interpretation Then and Now: Contemporary Hermeneutics in the Light of the Early Church* (Grand Rapids: Baker, 1992), 23–44.

of the living God."[43] Thus, we see the Old and New Testaments stamped with Christ's own authority.

Over the past two hundred years much debate in scholarly circles has wrestled over the question of Jesus Christ. These discussions have led to the "quest for the historical Jesus," "the new quest for the historical Jesus," "Christologies from below," "Christologies from above," and the so-called Jesus Seminar, which we will briefly seek to summarize in the following paragraphs.

The purpose of the "quest" was to reconstruct the Gospels and the sources behind them to interpret and understand Jesus in purely historical and human categories. The phrase achieved widespread usage from the title of Albert Schweitzer's (1875–1965) volume, *The Quest for the Historical Jesus* (1906). Originally published as *From Reimarus to Wrede*, Schweitzer summarized more than 250 authors who, from the end of the eighteenth century to the beginning of the twentieth, investigated the life of Jesus. The primary scholars examined were H. S. Reimarus (1694–1768), H. E. G. Paulus (1761–1851), F. D. E Schleiermacher (1768–1834), D. F. Strauss (1801–1874), and W. Wrede (1859–1906). Reimarus separated the teachings of Jesus from what the apostles taught about him, suggesting that the apostles' teaching was a fabrication of their own theology. Paulus continued this line of thinking and rejected the miraculous events in the life of Jesus, claiming that the observers of those events misunderstood natural events as "miracles." Paulus generally distrusted anything outside of rational thought.[44]

Schleiermacher's *Leben Jesu* was published posthumously in 1864 based on lecture notes transcribed by a student. Schleiermacher differentiated between the Jesus of history in the Synoptic Gospels and the Christ of faith presented in the Fourth Gospel. Strauss, perhaps as radical as any "questor," rejected the idea that God could intervene in this world. He thus rejected the idea of incarnation and reconstructed the gospel story in mythological fashion. What was created by Schleiermacher and Strauss was a false either/or

---

[43] Wenham, *Christ and the Bible*, 123.

[44] See Colin Brown and Craig Evans, *History of the Quests for the Historical Jesus*, 2 vols. (Grand Rapids: Zondervan, 2022); D. E. Nineham, "Schweitzer Revisited," in *Explorations in Theology 1* (London: SCM, 1977), 112–33.

choice: either Jesus was historical or supernatural; either he was the Jesus of the Synoptic presentation or of the Johannine picture.[45]

Wrede argued that the Gospels were not intended to be historical works but were written as biased theology; thus, the historical Jesus could not be discovered in the Gospels. Schweizer reviewed all of these and with J. Weiss (1863–1914) concluded that the kingdom proclamation of Jesus should be understood from a thoroughgoing eschatological perspective. Rudolf Bultmann (1884–1976) declared that the historical Jesus was inaccessible to the historian.[46] Most nineteenth- and early twentieth-century New Testament scholars felt the importance of acknowledging this movement. T. W. Manson's infamous words point to this seeming necessity: "Indeed, it may be said of all theological schools of thought: By their lives of Jesus ye shall know them."[47] Problems were created by wrongly emphasizing either/or choices when the Gospel picture is clearly both/and. Jesus is historical (man) and supernatural (God), and the portraits in the Synoptics and the Gospel of John are complementary and not contradictory. Jesus inaugurated the kingdom, but the kingdom awaits a consummation.

The psychological quest closed with Bultmann but was reopened by his students John Robinson and Ernst Käsemann. Their existential quest was no more profitable than the previous one. It should be noted that several British and American scholars, such as J. Jeremias, C. H. Dodd, T. W. Manson, Vincent Taylor, F. F. Bruce, I. Howard Marshall, Darrell Bock, Craig Blomberg, D. A. Carson, Greg Beale, and numerous others, rejected this entire approach, raising opposition to both the old quest and the new one.[48]

---

[45] For a brief overview of the "quests," see Malcolm B. Yarnell III, "Eschatology," in *Historical Theology for the Church*, ed. Jason G. Duesing and Nathan Finn (Nashville: B&H, 2021), 368–71.

[46] D. Luhrmann, *An Itinerary for New Testament Study*, trans. I. Bowdon (Philadelphia: Trinity, 1989), 67–69; also, see Rudolf Bultmann, *The History of the Synoptic Tradition*, trans. John Marsh (New York: Harper, 1968).

[47] T. W. Manson, "The Failure of Liberalism to Interpret the Bible as the Word of God," in *The Interpretation of the Bible*, ed. C. W. Dugmore (London: SPCK, 1944), 92.

[48] I. Howard Marshall, *I Believe in the Historical Jesus* (Grand Rapids: Eerdmans, 1977).

Much attention has been given to the relationship between the "Jesus of history" and the picture presented of him in the New Testament. It, however, seems both clear and sufficient to say that Jesus created the church; the church did not create Jesus. So, the words of Jesus were not created by the church; the words of Jesus became the foundation and cornerstone for the church and its writings. We need to see what the New Testament writers believed about Jesus. Our purpose in doing so is to help to establish a model for the written Word of God by looking at the living Word of God.[49]

The apostle John proclaimed, "In the beginning was the Word, and the Word was with God, and the Word was God" (John 1:1). John identified the eternal Word with Jesus (John 1:14, 18). He is very God of very God. Before his death he prayed, "Now, Father, glorify me in your presence with that glory I had with you before the world existed" (John 17:5). His own prayer affirms his preexistence. These themes are echoed in the epistles as well (Phil 2:5–11; Col 1:15–16). Claims to Jesus's preexistence are simultaneously claims to his deity. Thus, when we point to Jesus, we say that he is God (Heb 1:8; Rom 9:5). Not only does God live through Jesus and with Jesus, but also Jesus himself is God (John 1:1).

Yet, Jesus is also portrayed as a man. His humanity is taken for granted in the Synoptic Gospels. Other points in the Bible witness to his humanity in particular as if it might have been called into question or its significance neglected.[50] Mark's Gospel focuses on Jesus's humanity. Luke and Matthew present the birth stories and some aspects of his human life. Luke even emphasizes Jesus's human development (Luke 2:40, 52). John more than any other writer pictures Jesus's humanity. His humanity was like ours, except without sin. His humanity was visible for all to see (John 1:14; 1 John 1:1–2). As we have already noted, he was regarded as a teacher or a rabbi (John 1:38; 3:2; 9:2; 11:8). Jesus grew tired (John 4:6), grew thirsty (John 4:7), and displayed genuine emotions (John 11:33–35). These are all traits of genuine humanity.

The New Testament identified him as "Jesus of Nazareth" (Acts 2:22; 4:10; 22:8). He was seen, heard, and touched by his disciples. To deny

[49] David F. Wells, *The Person of Christ: A Biblical and Historical Analysis of the Incarnation* (Westchester, IL: Crossway, 1984).
[50] Barrett, "Old Testament in the New," 405.

the genuine humanity of Jesus in the early church was viewed as heresy (1 John 4:2–3). Because of his humanity Jesus has the ability to "sympathize with our weaknesses." He "has been tempted in every way as we are, yet without sin" (Heb 4:15). The early church confessed Jesus was a real man. However, he was a unique man, as evidenced by his virgin birth and resurrection. His significance as a man is not found in comparison with others but rather in contrast with others.[51]

In his complete humanity Jesus remained sinless. He always did the will of his Father (John 10:37; 14:10; 15:10; 17:4). Jesus was called "the righteous one" (1 John 2:1), the "holy one" (Acts 2:27), "the light of the world" (John 8:12), "faithful and true" (Rev 19:11), for he knew no sin (2 Cor 5:21; 1 Pet 2:22). The New Testament simultaneously affirms his humanity, his real temptations (Matt 4:1–11), and his complete sinlessness. Unquestionably, the New Testament affirms his uniqueness as fully God and fully man.[52]

The tension created by the confession of his full deity and his full humanity has created intense debate throughout church history. Some have emphasized one or the other—either his deity or his humanity, resulting in less than orthodox teachings. The deity of Christ has been denied by some (like the Ebionites, the Arians, and modern-day equivalents). Others have denied the reality of his humanity, who, like the Docetists, thought he only appeared to be God. Still others think he was a human who was adopted as divine at his baptism.[53]

Combinations of these faulty views have claimed that Jesus is God, but his humanity is incomplete. Similarly, others have maintained his humanity but have been less than clear about his deity. The classic Christian tradition has always been clear that Jesus Christ is both fully God and fully man.[54]

---

[51] See the carefully stated and historically supported defense of this approach in Gerald L. Bray, *Creeds, Councils, and Christ: Did the Early Christians Misrepresent Jesus?* (Downers Grove: IVP, 1984).

[52] Bloesch, *Jesus Christ*; James Leo Garrett Jr., "Reappraisal of Chalcedon," *Review and Expositor* 71, no. 1 (1974): 31–47.

[53] Donald G. Bloesch, *Essentials of Evangelical Theology: Volume 1: God, Authority, and Salvation*, 2 vols. (San Francisco: Harper and Row, 1978), 127–46.

[54] The highly regarded formula of the Council of Chalcedon of 451 says, "We all with one voice teach the confession of one and the same Son, our Lord Jesus Christ: the same perfect in divinity and perfect in humanity, the same truly God and truly man, of a rational soul and a body; consubstantial with the Father as regards his

He is one person with two natures. The two natures are united in one person without forming a third nature or two separate persons.[55]

Moreover, for our purposes in this volume, we recognize the implications of the lordship of Jesus Christ, the second person of the Trinity, for a doctrine of scriptural authority. In his teaching, he maintained that he came to fulfill the Law and the Prophets, saying, "For truly I will tell you, until heaven and earth pass away, not the smallest letter or one stroke of a letter will pass from the law until all things are accomplished" (Matt 5:18). Jeff Bingham notes that the apostles followed the teaching of Christ on these matters: "The Lord's words in Matt 5:17–29 teach that Scripture, in all its parts, corresponds to reality."[56] R. T. France offers a helpful interpretive paraphrase: "The law, down to its smallest details, is as permanent as heaven and earth, and will never lose its significance; on the contrary, all that it points forward to will in fact become reality."[57] The words of Jesus in John's Gospel underscore this teaching with the affirmation that Scripture "cannot be broken," meaning it cannot be annulled or set aside.

Finally, we see in his high priestly prayer the clear acknowledgement that God's "word is truth" (John 17:17). Thus, as John Frame concludes,

---

divinity, and the same consubstantial with us as regards his humanity; like us in all respects except for sin; begotten before the ages from the Father as regards his divinity, and in the last days the same for us and for our salvation from Mary, the virgin God-bearer, as regards his humanity; one and the same Christ, Son, Lord, only-begotten, acknowledged in two natures which undergo no confusion, no change, no division, no separation; at no point was the difference between the natures taken away through the union, but rather the property of both natures is preserved and comes together into a single person and a single subsistent being; he is not parted or divided into two persons, but is one and the same only-begotten Son, God, Word, Lord Jesus Christ, just as the prophets taught from the beginning about him, and as the Lord Jesus Christ himself instructed us, and as the creed of the fathers handed down to us." Norman F. Tanner, ed., *Decrees of the Ecumenical Councils*, vol. 1 (Washington, DC: Georgetown University Press, 1990), 86–87.

[55] Carl F. H. Henry, ed., *Jesus of Nazareth: Savior and Lord* (Grand Rapids: Eerdmans, 1966).

[56] Bingham, "Biblical Inspiration, Authority, and Canonicity," 106 (see introduction, n. 23).

[57] R. T. France, *The Gospel of Matthew*, The New International Commentary of the New Testament (Grand Rapids: Eerdmans, 2007), 186; also, see David S. Dockery and David E. Garland, *Seeking the Kingdom: The Sermon on the Mount Made Practical for Today* (Wheaton: Harold Shaw, 1992), 41–70.

Scripture can never "fail or lose its authority."[58] Jesus Christ is not only central to the Scriptures, but he is also the one who holds all things together (Col 1:17) and the one around which all Christian beliefs cohere.

IV. Jesus Christ and the Bible: Implications

The central figure in God's revelation is Jesus Christ, who is also the ultimate revelation of God (Heb 1:1–2). The Old Testament looked forward to Jesus's coming. Jesus understood his life and ministry in light of the Old Testament. Jesus Christ, the Son of God incarnate, who claimed divine authority for all that he did and taught, not only affirmed the absolute authority of the Old Testament, but also unreservedly submitted to it. His reading of the Old Testament was shaped by his own messianic mission. At the heart of his own interpretation of Scripture was a Christocentric perspective. Jesus thus became the direct and primary source for the church's understanding of the Old Testament.

Jesus stamped his authority on Scripture by his submission to it and by his commissioning of the apostolic witness. Jesus discipled and commissioned his followers to pass on his teaching to others, who would do the same with following generations (Matt 28:18–20; 2 Tim 2:2). His "authority" comes from the Father (Matt 11:27; 28:18) and marks his power to heal (Matt 9:35), to teach (Matt 7:29), to command (Matt 8:9), to cast out demons (Matt 8:29–32), and to forgive sins (Matt 9:6–8). His authority is both heavenly and earthly, a comprehensive statement that points to the divine character of this authority. His authority, seen previously during Jesus's earthly ministry, attains a new status from the human perspective as he receives from the Father his preexistent glory and authority. His authority is also placed upon the writings of the apostles in the New Testament. The Spirit of God, who was given to the apostles to enable them to carry out their task, directed their writings to focus on the life, ministry, death, resurrection, and exaltation of Christ. The New Testament equally affirms the deity and the humanity of Jesus.[59]

---

[58] Frame, *The Doctrine of the Word of God*, 120 (see introduction, n. 27).
[59] Erickson, *Christian Theology*, 1124–39 (see introduction, n. 3). See Grant R. Osborne, *Matthew*, Exegetical Commentary on the New Testament (Grand Rapids:

The overall picture in Scripture and in the history of the church is that Jesus possessed inwardly and demonstrated outwardly the very nature of God himself (Col 1:15–16; 2:9).[60] The opening verse of John's Gospel is a categorical affirmation of Jesus's full deity (also, John 14:9; 17:5). The same is true for the distinctive "I Am" statements of John's Gospel (John 6:35; 8:12; 10:7–9, 11–14; 11:25; 14:6; 15:1–5).[61] These passages, along with Rom 9:5, Titus 2:13, and Heb 1:1–8, show that any attempts to make Jesus to be merely a great teacher or prophet are inadequate. It is necessary that Christ be both God and man, for only as a sinless man could he fittingly die for others as the redeemer of humanity. And only as God could his life, ministry, and redeeming death have infinite value, satisfying the demands of God to deliver others from death and the wrath to come.[62]

We must not think of Jesus Christ as only a human person or only a divine person. We must confess him as the unique divine-human person possessing all the essential qualities of both the human and divine natures. We affirm the uniqueness of Jesus, acknowledging his lordship and the exalted view of him confessed by the early church as fully God and fully man. Countering Arius, a presbyter in the church of Alexandria, the Council of Nicaea in 325 contended that "only God himself, taking on human flesh and dying in our flesh can effect a redemption that consists in being saved from sin, death, and corruption, and in being raised to share the nature of God himself." The council declared their belief in "one Lord Jesus Christ, the only begotten son of God, begotten of his Father before all worlds, God of God, Light of Light, very God of very God, begotten, not made, being of one substance with the Father."[63]

Zondervan, 2010), 1078–79; and Jonathan Pennington, *Heaven and Earth in the Gospel of Matthew* (Grand Rapids: Baker, 2007), 203–6.

[60] David W. Pao, *Colossians and Philemon*, Exegetical Commentary on the New Testament (Grand Rapids: Zondervan, 2012), 84–117.

[61] Carson, *The Gospel according to John*, 288–89, 358 (see chap. 4, n. 37).

[62] Christopher W. Morgan, *Christian Theology* (Nashville: B&H, 2021); also, Travis Dickinson, *Logic and the Way of Jesus* (Nashville: B&H, 2022), 31–52; Samuel J. Mikolaski, "Jesus Christ: Prophet, Priest, and King," in *Basics of the Faith: An Evangelical Introduction to Christian Doctrine*, ed. Carl F. H. Henry (Bellingham, WA: Lexham, 2019), 188–96.

[63] Carl F. H. Henry, "New Dimensions in Christology," in *New Dimensions in Evangelical Thought*, ed. David S. Dockery (Downers Grove: IVP, 1998), 299–316;

If Jesus was not one substance with the Father, the first great council said, then he was neither worthy to be worshipped nor capable of redeeming the world. Recognizing who Jesus Christ is, his affirmation of Scripture, and his approach toward it and interpretation of it have important and significant implications for our understanding of Scripture as the written Word of God. Harold O. J. Brown, in his work on "The Arian Connection: Presuppositions of Errancy," contends that failing to confess Scripture as the divine-human book, which is inspired of God's Spirit, fully truthful, inerrant, and ultimately authoritative has serious implications for the church today in the same way that the issues of Arianism did for the fourth century, impacting our bibliology, our Christology, our anthropology, and our pneumatology.[64]

V. The Divine-Human Authorship of Scripture

Drawing upon the analogy of orthodox Christology while recognizing that the parallel is not exact, we can begin to formulate a doctrine of Scripture as a divine-human book. John Feinberg cautions in his massive defense of a traditional understanding of the full truthfulness and authority of Scripture, *Light in a Dark Place: The Doctrine of Scripture*, that this analogy is not identity.[65] Taking a different approach from Feinberg, Peter Enns, in *Inspiration and Incarnation: Evangelicals and the Problem of the Old Testament*, has, from our perspective, wrongheadedly appealed to the incarnational analogy to challenge traditional understandings of inspiration and inerrancy.[66] Enns

---

J. I. Packer and Thomas C. Oden, *One Faith* (Downers Grove: IVP, 2004); Thomas C. Oden, *The Rebirth of Orthodoxy* (San Francisco: HarperCollins, 2003); Stephen R. Holmes, *Listening to the Past: The Place of Tradition in Theology* (Grand Rapids: Baker, 2002).

[64] Harold O. J. Brown, "The Arian Connection: Presuppositions of Errancy," in *Challenges to Inerrancy: A Theological Response*, ed. Gordon Lewis and Bruce Demarest (Chicago: Moody, 1984), 383–402; also, see Harold O. J. Brown, *Heresies: The Image of Christ in the Mirror of Heresy and Orthodoxy from the Apostles to the Present* (New York: Doubleday, 1984).

[65] See Feinberg, *Light in a Dark Place*, 205–18; also, J. I. Packer, "Calvin's View of Scripture," in *God's Inerrant Word: An International Symposium on the Trustworthiness of Scripture*, ed. John W. Montgomery (Minneapolis: Bethany, 1974), 102–4; Bloesch, *Holy Scripture*, 117–30 (see introduction, n. 2).

[66] Peter Enns, *Inspiration and Incarnation* (Grand Rapids: Baker, 2005).

contends that just as Jesus was fully human (and his humanity was not eclipsed by his deity), the dual authorship of Scripture means that there will be genuine marks of its human authors. Such markers of human limitation, according to Enns, help us to see that the Bible is a genuinely human book, not just a divine book.[67]

In a more balanced manner, Luis Alonso Schökel, the distinguished Roman Catholic scholar, claims that:

> Just as the substantial Word of God was made in the likeness of men in every respect "except sin," so also the words of God, as expressed in human language, are in every respect assimilated to human discourse, except error. Such is the *sunkatabasis* of condescension of God in his providence which already St. John Chrysostom magnificently extolled and again and again affirmed to be present in the Sacred Books.[68]

Likewise, the Dutch theologian Herman Bavinck notes the parallel:

> The *Logos* became *sarx*, and the Word became Scripture. . . . Christ became flesh, a servant, without seemliness or majesty, the one despised of men; He descended to the lower regions of the earth, and became obedient even to the death of the cross. And so also has the Word, the divine revelation which has entered the creaturely realm, the life and history of human beings and peoples, in all the human forms of dreams and visions, of research and reflection, even down to human weakness, contempt and disrepute; the

---

[67] See the insightful review of the proposal by Enns by John Frame, "Review of Peter Enns, *Inspiration and Incarnation*," in *The Doctrine of the Word of God* (Phillipsburg, PA: P&R, 2010), 499–516; also, see responses that offered different proposals from that of Enns: Vern Poythress, "Adequacy of Human Language and Accommodation," in *Hermeneutics, Inerrancy, and the Bible*, ed. Earl D. Radmacher and Robert D. Preus (Grand Rapids: Zondervan, 1984); J. I. Packer, "The Adequacy of Human Language," in *Inerrancy*, ed. Norman Geisler (Grand Rapids: Zondervan, 1980), 197–226.

[68] Luis Alonso Schökel, *The Inspired Word: Scripture in the Light of Language and Literature*, trans. Francis Martin (New York: Herder and Herder, 1965), 52.

Word became writing, and as a writing was subject to the lot of all writings.[69]

A common objection to the divine-human authorship of Scripture is that in the end it amounts to Docetism, but, as Henri Blocher has noted, that "presupposes the parallel."[70] While emphasizing the human aspect of Scripture and the diversity of genres or speech-acts, Kevin Vanhoozer still stresses that "as commissioned divine-human discourse, the Bible is not only authorized but, in providential fashion, *authored* by God."[71] In conclusion, let us reflect on this summary from Blocher concerning the divine-human authorship of Scripture, which he prefers to call the Bible's "double author-ship." The advantages of this model, Blocher says,

> draw attention to the centrality of the Incarnation for the divine speaking in history. Since the Fall, God communicates with fallen humankind on the basis of the Son's incarnation—through instru-ments who "extend" his human role. This incarnation itself, as ortho-dox theologians perceived, is grounded in God's eternal being on the distinction between God and his Word and Son: God *monogenēs* is the *alter ego* of the Father, the perfect expression of God in himself, and thus the principle of all revelation (John 1:18). His incarna-tion manifests his *unique* (exclusively divine) ability to become what he was not without ceasing to be what he was, or rather who he is eternally. His union with created being in *one* person, the wonder of wonders, making closer the bond of creation, is *the closer than which none can be conceived* (to paraphrase St. Anselm). In the economy of redemptive grace, since the apostles and the prophets are to be seen as joined to his humanity, the hypostatic union is the precise

---

[69] Herman Bavinck, *Reformed Dogmatics: Prolegomena*, ed. John Bolt and trans. John Vriend, 4 vols. (Grand Rapids: Baker, 2003), 1:380–82.

[70] Henri Blocher, "God and Scripture Writers: The Question of Double Authorship," in *The Enduring Authority of the Christian Scriptures*, ed. D. A. Carson (Grand Rapids: Eerdmans, 2016), 531.

[71] Kevin J. Vanhoozer, "Word of God," in *Dictionary for Theological Interpretation of the Bible*, ed. K. J. Vanhoozer (Grand Rapids: Eerdmans, 2005), 853.

foundation of the union of God and human speakers or writers in the same speech-act.[72]

With the divine-human authorship of Scripture demonstrated, let us turn our attention to the closely related topics of biblical inspiration and canonicity. As we do so, we note that the divine-human aspects can never be ignored. The unity of Scripture and its meaning are found in Jesus Christ, the founder and foundation of the Christian faith, who is one person with two natures. He is the Suffering Servant as well as the eternal God. In acknowledging his lordship, we submit also to his lordship over Holy Scripture and surrender to its authority for our lives. Thus, our doctrinal confession regarding Scripture must match our love for him, our belief in him, our service for him, and our submission to him as King of kings and Lord of lords, the one who declared that "the Scripture cannot be broken" (John 10:35).

---

[72] Henri Blocher continues, "Since the Unique Son (*unigenitus*, "only begotten," was the traditional rendering; it keeps the flavor of traditional faith) became a man, the consistency of human reality under divine inspiration is established beyond all question. In him human speech reaches its ordained end: mediating truth and life." Blocher, "God and Scripture Writers," 540.

6

The Inspiration of the Bible

T he Bible is a book written by numerous human authors over several centuries. At the same time, the Bible is also the Word of God. In this chapter we will further discuss aspects of the divine-human authorship of the Bible and its implications for articulating an understanding of the Bible's inspiration. The Bible cannot be rightly understood without grasping that the Bible is completely the Word of God and completely the words of human authors. As we noted at the conclusion of our previous chapter, it may not be entirely appropriate to draw a direct correspondence between the Bible and Jesus Christ. Yet, just as the conception of Jesus came by the miraculous overshadowing of the Holy Spirit (Luke 1:35), so Scripture is the product of the Spirit's inspiration (2 Tim 3:16). Jesus took on humanity through a human mother, so the Bible has come to us in human language through human authors. Jesus, the God-Man, is the living Word of God, and the Bible, the divine-human Scripture, is the written Word of God. It is quite inadequate to affirm that the Bible is only partly the Word of God or partly the words of human authors.

The Bible is the Word of the infinite, all-knowing, eternal God; it speaks eternal truth that is applicable to readers of all time, beyond those who initially received it. The Scriptures are also the words of godly men to specific contexts addressing problems, questions, and challenges within certain communities and situations. It is possible to overemphasize the divine aspect of Scripture to the neglect of the Bible's real humanity, and it is also possible to overemphasize the human aspect of the Bible and miss its divine nature.

In articulating the doctrine of biblical inspiration, we must confess both the divine and the human aspects of inspired Scripture.

The Protestant Reformation of the sixteenth century recovered critical evangelical doctrines, especially the doctrines of justification by faith, the authority of Scripture, and the priesthood of all believers. Regarding the first of these necessary doctrines, Martin Luther argued justification is "that article by which the church stands or falls."[1] Luther was correct, but the history of the church since the rise of modern methods of Bible study proves something similar should be said of the inspiration and preservation of divine revelation in its written form: The Holy Spirit's inspiration and preservation of Scripture are those articles by which the church's doctrine of Scripture stands or falls.[2]

We teach not only biblical inspiration but also biblical preservation, because the Spirit of God did not cease working after he inspired the prophets and the apostles to write their original autographs. The preservation into the canon of these inspired documents in the history of the church is also due to the sovereign guidance of the Holy Spirit. The inspiration of the biblical text rendered it inerrant; the preservation of the canon rendered it infallible. There are, therefore, two indispensable aspects of the sovereign Spirit's work upon Holy Scripture: the inspiration of the prophetic and apostolic writings, and the preservation of those inspired writings in the biblical canon. The doctrines of inspiration and preservation thus provide the structure for these central chapters of this book on special revelation and Scripture.

We believe the two major doctrines considered in this and the next chapter are indispensable for any responsible doctrine of revelation. The Holy Spirit's works of inspiration and preservation provide the church with the standard to which all claims of theological authority must have constant

---

[1] The proverb itself derives from later Lutheranism, but it certainly captures Luther's sentiments. Justin Taylor, "Luther's Saying: 'Justification Is the Article by Which the Church Stands or Falls,'" The Gospel Coalition, August 31, 2011, https://www.thegospelcoalition.org/blogs/justin-taylor/luthers-saying/.

[2] Warfield argues similarly regarding *sola scriptura*. "This is the corner-stone of universal Protestantism; and on it Protestantism stands, or else it falls." Again, "'The word of God written' stands through all the ages as a changeless witness against human additions to, and corruptions of, God's truth." Fred G. Zaspel, *The Theology of B. B. Warfield: A Systematic Summary* (Wheaton: Crossway, 2010), 118–19.

reference. We cannot know God apart from his revelation of himself, and he has chosen to inspire and preserve a text for the purpose of revealing himself authoritatively to the church today. We begin our discussion of the Spirit's leading work in the triune gift of revelation with a description in this chapter of the inspiration of the prophets and apostles and their writings. We proceed in the next chapter to an investigation of the Spirit's work of preservation through the church's canonization of the inspired documents.

I. Preliminary Definition

In the modern period the one theologian "best known as the theologian of the doctrine of inspiration" was, "without doubt," Benjamin Breckenridge Warfield.[3] Warfield wrote some 1,500 pages to construct from Scripture and history a strong defense of the doctrine of biblical inspiration for his contemporaries.[4] It is somewhat difficult to find a singular statement regarding a final definition from his multitude of investigations into the doctrine. However, he begins his most popular essay on the subject with this simple definition: "Inspiration is, therefore, usually defined as a supernatural influence exerted on the sacred writers by the Spirit of God, by virtue of which their writings are given Divine trustworthiness."[5]

Warfield's influential definition includes the following four aspects: First, inspiration is supernatural or divine in origin. Second, the activity of inspiration brings two subjects, the Holy Spirit and the human writers, into a close relationship which has been variously described as "concursive" or "organic."[6] Third, inspiration begins with consideration of a process that includes the writers but extends also to the produced literature,

---

[3] Zaspel, *The Theology of B. B. Warfield*, 63.

[4] Zaspel, 114.

[5] "Inspiration," originally published in the first edition of *The International Standard Bible Encyclopedia*, alongside related essays expounding and defending the doctrine of biblical inspiration, may be found in the first volume of his collected works. Benjamin Breckinridge Warfield, *Revelation and Inspiration*, The Works of Benjamin B. Warfield, 10 vols. (New York: Oxford University Press, 1932; Reprint, Grand Rapids: Baker, 2003), 1:77–78.

[6] Warfield typically uses the language of "concursus" to describe the relation between divine initiative and human instrumentality. Bavinck prefers the language of "organic." Bavinck, *Reformed Dogmatics*, 1:431 (see chap. 5, n. 69).

the writings. Finally, inspiration results in the certainty and thus authority of the writings of the prophets of the Old Testament and the apostles of the New Testament. We will begin fleshing out our definition of inspiration with the initiative of the divine author and the instrumentality of the human authors.

II. The Work of God and the Work of Humanity upon the Bible

Because our gospel did not come to you in word only, but also in power, in the Holy Spirit, and with full assurance. (1 Thess 1:5a)

Since the advent of Historical Critical Exegesis with the works of Baruch Spinoza in the late seventeenth century, modern scholars engaged in biblical studies have typically divided into two large camps. In the one camp stand those who affirm the church's Scriptures are distinctly human books like any other. The Bible, they argue, should be treated with the same critical tools as any other human construction. Interpreters must depend primarily upon historical, literary, social, and other sciences to derive the meaning of the original human author(s) in the context of its intended reception by the original human audience.[7] While one might characterize the advocates of this approach as "liberal," there are some in this first camp who would not carry that label yet treat the biblical text primarily as an anthropological document in their hermeneutical approach.

In a second camp stand those, including the present authors, who affirm the Holy Bible is indeed a human book, but it is also a divine book. We believe accepting the doctrines of divine revelation and inspiration by the divine Holy Spirit are necessarily foundational for proper hermeneutics. The second camp invites the readers of Scripture to recognize the biblical text's nature as truth, receive its authority as supreme, and engage in its interpretation with respect for God the Trinity's activities of revelation, inspiration, preservation, and illumination. Most scholars in this

---

[7] See the section entitled, "Critical Exegesis," in chapter 12 for further discussion of Spinoza and his followers.

camp are also careful to affirm the human nature of the biblical text. The Bible was manifestly written by human beings but under the guidance of the Holy Spirit. However, some in this camp have been tempted to treat the Bible primarily as a divine text without due regard for its simultaneous human character.

This division into merely two camps, as already indicated, should not be taken simplistically. The two major camps are themselves divided, and individual theologians sometimes evince movement both between the camps and within the camps. To bring clarity to the scholarly divisions, Kevin Vanhoozer helpfully identifies four primary claims regarding the relationship of God with the world in the construction of the biblical text. We have rearranged his categories to reflect a spectrum moving from those which are more human in orientation to those which are more divine. The third group's position seems to align best with the Bible's own description, explicit and implicit, of itself, as we shall presently see.

There are four primary views of the correlation between the divine inspiration of the biblical authors and the human authorship of those biblical texts. When affirmed, this relationship is sometimes described as "concursus" or "concursive authorship." The four primary models of concursive authorship are as follows:

1. *Naturalism*: Proponents of naturalistic approaches "ascribe no causal agency to God in relation to Scripture or anything else." God may be the object of the text, but God is not the subject of the text.

2. *Weak Divine Authorship*: While God exercised influence upon the biblical writer, according to the weak view, "there is no guarantee that the human authors will go along with it." God accepts the human author's failures such that "there are not only factual but ideological (and theological) errors in the biblical texts." God is involved in the production of the text, but he exercises an anemic influence.

3. *Strong Divine Authorship*: Those holding the strong view bind the act of divine revelation with the biblical text through what has become known as the doctrine of plenary verbal inspiration. In the strong view, "God makes communicative initiatives in order to share what is his with others." Scripture is, therefore, manifestly "God's

Word." God's purpose in sending his Word is "to invite and orient us to be in a right relationship to God."

4. *Extreme Divine Authorship*: God's sovereignty is "dictatorial" toward humanity, for God "dictates" his words to the prophet who functions as an amanuensis. "Extreme authorship entails a dictation theory, according to which Scripture's human authors are passive mouth-pieces, mere puppets in the hands of God." Unfortunately, with this model, God may be charged both with violating human freedom and initiating evil.[8]

We believe the strong divine authorship view of concursive authorship reflects best the phenomena of Scripture. The fully divine work of the Holy Spirit, operating in close relation with the fully involved human authors, is clearly taught in the classic New Testament texts from which a doctrine of biblical inspiration may be crafted. Moreover, strong divine authorship becomes immediately evident when the reader opens almost any page of the canon. For instance, just now we find the prophet Ezekiel clearly affirmed a robust form of divine concursive authorship when he as a human prophet wrote, "This is what the Lord God says" (Ezek 46:16). Before reviewing the classic biblical texts which address the doctrine of biblical inspiration, it may be helpful to rehearse the common models of biblical inspiration advocated by contemporary scholars.

III. Models of Biblical Inspiration

While we may classify scholars according to their views of the relationship between the divine and the human authors of Scripture, their efforts to give the full meaning of biblical inspiration also require delineation. Modern scholars have offered numerous models of biblical inspiration. Warfield outlined three primary models of inspiration: common inspiration, partial inspiration, and plenary verbal inspiration.[9] In his survey of several modern systematic theologians who tried to define views of inspiration, James Leo

---

[8] Vanhoozer, "Holy Scripture," 31–34 (see chap. 1 n. 77).
[9] Zaspel, *The Theology of B. B. Warfield*, 114–16.

Garrett Jr. found they typically identified anywhere from four to six different theories of inspiration. Seeking a measure of comprehension, Garrett himself outlined seven theories of biblical inspiration.[10] Elsewhere, we evaluated yet two more views not discussed by Garrett.[11]

Seeking to provide simplicity and clarity, we now organize the various theories evaluated by previous scholars into four major groups. These groups of theories of biblical inspiration are here arranged along a spectrum according to their general acceptability among contemporary evangelicals. We begin with the least acceptable view and conclude with the most acceptable. We exclude those views, such as natural inspiration and common inspiration, which effectively deny the doctrine. The four groups of theories of biblical inspiration below have multiple Christian adherents who sometimes take divergent approaches.

1. Dictation Theories

Dictation theories correlate with the "extreme divine authorship" approach to the concursive activity of Scripture's authors noted above. One advocate, the twentieth-century Fundamentalist John R. Rice, referred to this as "word-for-word inspiration." Rice properly desired to protect the perfection of Scripture against modernist denigrations. His reaction, however, was so strident that he denied even obvious stylistic differences between the various human authors.[12] Some aspects of the "appropriated discourse" theory have the appearance of a dictation theory with its illustration of a corporate executive's secretary, though this is not its intention.[13] Herman Bavinck dismissed

---

[10] "Mechanical dictation with inerrancy," "verbal inspiration with inerrancy," "dynamic or limited verbal inspiration," "different levels or degrees of inspiration," "partial inspiration," "universal Christian inspiration," and "natural inspiration." Garrett Jr., *Systematic Theology*, 1:131–33 (see chap. 1, n. 47).

[11] The two additional views were the "encounter" view of Karl Barth and the "appropriated discourse" view of Nicholas Wolterstorff. Dockery, "Special Revelation," 128–31 (see introduction, n. 24).

[12] Garrett, *Systematic Theology*, 1:131 and 131n.

[13] Wolterstorff, alas, ends with a text only partially inspired. Dockery, "Special Revelation," 131.

dictation theory due to its mechanical and coercive qualities,[14] which we
have elsewhere associated with the docetic heresy.[15]

2. Partial Theories

The partial theories arose in prominence alongside the Enlightenment.
Modernist theologians diminished both God's role in the process of inspiration
and the resulting written product. "The Enlightenment philosophies emphasized the primacy of nature, a high view of reason, and a low view of sin, an
anti-supernatural bias, and encouraged revolt against the traditional understanding of authority."[16] Many of the critics against whom Warfield strove,
such as Charles Briggs, argued Scripture was inspired by degrees or only in
certain parts.[17] Some argued the biblical writers were given enhanced yet merely
human spiritual insight.[18] Others said the biblical writers operated with various
levels of inspiration, from superintendence to suggestion.[19] Karl Barth argued
the words of Scripture become the Word of God in existential encounter.
Diverging between his theory and his practice, Barth denied Scripture's entire
truthfulness but treated Scripture with reverence.[20] Many of the partial views,
such as the so-called "illumination theory," reflect the tendencies of Ebionism.[21]

3. Dynamic Theories

Dynamic theories of inspiration became popular among moderately conservative evangelicals like Abraham Kuyper, Edgar Young Mullins, and Donald

---

[14] Bavinck, *Reformed Dogmatics: Prolegomena*, 431–32.

[15] Dockery, "Special Revelation," 129. Docetism, an early heresy, discounted the
humanity of Christ.

[16] Dockery, "Special Revelation," 128.

[17] Zaspel, *The Theology of B. B. Warfield*, 122–23.

[18] This is often referred to as the "illumination view," but it should not be confused with the distinct doctrine of illumination, which states that the reader or hearer
of Scripture is led by the Spirit to recognize the truth in Scripture. Cf. Garrett,
Systematic Theology, 1:132; Dockery, "Special Revelation," 129.

[19] Garrett, *Systematic Theology*, 1:132.

[20] Dockery, "Special Revelation," 129–30.

[21] Dockery, "Special Revelation," 129. Ebionism was an early heresy which
undermined the deity of Christ.

Bloesch. These highly respected theologians recognized an ameliorating fitness in modernity's concern for the human. Their basic idea seems to be that God inspired the ideas or the content of the biblical revelation while the human authors were free to choose style and words used in its written revelation. The Bible is deemed true in the arena of doctrine and ethics, but it may not necessarily reflect history and science with accuracy. This view has been criticized for failing to deal adequately with the relationship between concepts and words. Moreover, although they affirm divine leadership in the process of inspiration, dynamic theories underplay the product of inspiration.[22]

4. Verbal Plenary Theory

The verbal plenary view of biblical inspiration remains the overwhelmingly preferred view among American evangelicals. The verbal plenary theory makes five critical claims about what biblical inspiration entails: the Bible's divine author inspired the human authors to write all the words in the original written autographs.

First, the Holy Spirit is the divine and sovereign subject of inspiration. The origination of both Old and New Testament texts belongs with the *divine author*. Not merely the Spirit, but each person of the Holy Trinity must be identified with the origin of revelation, including its written form. "Every good and perfect gift," including the good and gracious Holy Scripture, comes "down from the Father of lights" (Jas 1:17). And Jesus Christ, who sent the Holy Spirit into the church, remains "the pioneer and perfecter of our faith" (Heb 12:2). Nevertheless, the Spirit takes the lead in bringing the biblical text into existence by inspiration and in preserving it by canonization.

Second, the *human author* is, along with the Trinity, also fully involved in the process of writing, though under divine direction.[23] The collaborative process between the one divine and many human authors has been described

---

[22] Garrett, *Systematic Theology*, 1:131; Dockery, "Special Revelation," 130–31.

[23] "The Scriptures, in other words, are conceived by the writers of the New Testament as through and through God's book, in every part expressive of His mind, given through men after a fashion which does not violence to their nature as men, and constitutes the book also men's book as well as God's, in every part expressive of the mind of its human authors." Warfield, *Revelation and Inspiration*, 99; David S. Dockery, "The Divine-Human Authorship of Inspired Scripture," in *Authority*

as "double-authorship," "dual-sided authorship," "co-authorship," "concursive operation," "concursus," and "organic inspiration."[24] Warfield argued the
human authors' intelligence and moral agency remain fully involved. As in
personal salvation, inspiration requires full engagement by both God and
the human being.[25] Bavinck agreed: "God never coerces anyone. He treats
human beings, not as blocks of wood, but as intelligent and moral beings.
The Logos, in becoming flesh, does not take some unsuspecting person by
surprise, but he enters into human nature, prepares and shapes it by the Spirit
into his own appropriate medium."[26]

Third, verbal plenary inspiration considers not merely the human writers but also their writings, which were recognized and later collected in the
biblical canon. Both the process of writing and the product of the biblical texts, *the original autographs*, are the objects of inspiration.[27] "Because
Scripture finds its origin in God and because the Holy Spirit superintended
the writers," we must also conclude the resulting text is "the product of
God's breath."[28]

Fourth, this verbal theory of inspiration includes every portion of the
original autographs. Inspiration is not partial in any way but "plenary," or
entire. "Everything in Scripture is God's word."[29] While our claim to plenary
inspiration is also a matter of faith, it has a firm basis in biblical exegesis, as
we shall see in our review of the classical texts on inspiration below.

Fifth, this plenary inspiration theory is also thoroughly *verbal*. Inspiration
by the Holy Spirit extends "beyond the direction of thoughts to the selection
of words (thus, the adjective, 'verbal')."[30] God's direction of the very words
neither diminishes the humanity of the text nor removes the mystery of the

---

and Interpretation: A Baptist Perspective, ed. Duane Garrett and Richard R. Melick
(Grand Rapids: Baker, 1987).

[24] Warfield, *Revelation and Inspiration*, 23–24, 26–27; Zaspel, *The Theology of B.
B. Warfield*, 137–38; Bavinck, *Reformed Dogmatics: Prolegomena*, 435–48.

[25] Warfield, *Revelation and Inspiration*, 24–25; Zaspel, *The Theology of B. B.
Warfield*, 137.

[26] Bavinck, *Reformed Dogmatics: Prolegomena*, 432.

[27] Dockery, "Special Revelation," 131.

[28] Feinberg, *Light in a Dark Place*, 185.

[29] Feinberg, 188.

[30] Dockery, "Special Revelation," 131.

process. Neither does the "verbal" aspect of inspiration diminish truth claims that "meaning is located at the sentence level and beyond."[31]

The Old Princeton theologians and their evangelical successors explicated this verbal plenary view because they believed it was the view Scripture presumed for and taught of itself. Warfield argued certain Christological and apostolic pronouncements clearly teach this view, particularly statements found in 2 Timothy 3, 2 Peter 1, and John 10. He also evaluated the way the titles which Scripture assigns to itself advanced this view, including "scripture" and "the scriptures,"[32] as well as "the oracles of God."[33] Besides these exalted titles, certain formulae in Scripture correlate biblical statements with God's speech, including "it says," "scripture says," and "God says." The biblical phenomena led Warfield to describe the Scriptures as "living words still speaking to us" and "the crystallized voice of God." It was "all one to the New Testament writers whether they said, 'God says' or 'Scripture says.'"[34]

Warfield likewise argued the verbal plenary view has been historically presumed by the church from its earliest days. It is "the church-doctrine," a claim he strived at length to support.[35] Speaking to modern Christians, Warfield concluded the plenary verbal view of inspiration "is the foundation of our Christian thought and life, without which we could not or could only with difficulty, maintain the confidence of our faith and the surety of our hope."[36] Agreeing that the verbal plenary view was fundamental, Charles Hodge bound it inextricably with the Christian faith itself. "Faith therefore in Christ involves faith in the Scriptures as the word of God, and faith in the Scriptures as the word of God is faith in their plenary inspiration."[37]

The present authors affirm verbal plenary inspiration. We believe this model for understanding biblical inspiration best accounts for the content,

---

[31] Dockery, 132.

[32] Warfield, *Revelation and Inspiration*, 115–65.

[33] Warfield, 335–91.

[34] Warfield, 300–1, 332.

[35] Warfield, 52, 234–78.

[36] Warfield, 73.

[37] Mark A. Noll, ed., *The Princeton Theology 1812–1921: Scripture, Science, and Theological Method from Archibald Alexander to Benjamin Breckinridge Warfield* (Grand Rapids: Baker, 1983), 137.

design, and character of Scripture and the human circumstances of the Bible's composition.[38] A review of three biblical texts, which may be described collectively as *loci classici* for the doctrine of biblical inspiration, further demonstrates the verbal and plenary nature of that inspiration.

IV. The First *Locus Classicus* of Biblical Inspiration

And you know that from infancy you have known the sacred Scriptures, which are able to give you wisdom for salvation through faith in Christ Jesus. All Scripture is inspired by God and is profitable for teaching, for rebuking, for correcting, for training in righteousness, so that the man of God may be complete, equipped for every good work. (2 Tim 3:15–17)

The apostle Paul held a high view of Scripture. For him, the sacred text conveys indispensable teaching regarding both the law and the gospel to its contemporary hearers. "Paul regarded the Scriptures as the very words of God which were written for the ethical instruction of Christians and as a testimony to the gospel."[39] Paul believed the Scriptures were meant to be learned today, for they were "written," personally, "for us" (Rom 4:23–24; 1 Cor 9:10), even "to us" (1 Cor 10:11).

The primary text for those seeking to discover Paul's doctrine of biblical inspiration is 2 Tim 3:15–17. As noted in our chapter on the sufficiency of Scripture, this text's primary purpose is to establish the truth that God's Word accomplishes, that for which God sent it. But an indispensable building block in Paul's construction of the sufficiency of Scripture is the inspiration of Scripture. Scripture is sufficient to fulfill God's eternal purposes precisely because Scripture is inspired by God's eternal Spirit.

The critical term Paul uses in 2 Timothy 3 has often been translated in Western theology as "inspired," due to the Vulgate's rendering of the

---

[38] Dockery, "Special Revelation," 132.

[39] Brian S. Rosner, "'Written for Us': Paul's View of Scripture," in *A Pathway into the Holy Scripture*, ed. Philip E. Satterthwaite and David F. Wright (Grand Rapids: Eerdmans, 1994), 81. Paul's doctrinal view was "in large measure the standard Jewish view." Rosner, "Written for Us," 103.

Greek with the Latin *inspirata*.[40] Unfortunately, this translation, which was carried into the evangelical tradition of English translations by William Tyndale,[41] connotes an internal activity of the human writer. With this translation, the human being could perhaps be considered inspired by virtue of his own nature. Warfield disagreed vehemently. "The Greek term has, however, nothing to say of *in*spiring or *in*spiration; it speaks only of a 'spiring' or 'spiration.'"[42] In the Greek text the emphasis falls not upon the human author but upon the divine author. The writing was "breathed out by God," such that the text may be described as "the product of the creative breath of God."[43] Evangelical scholars now prefer to render *theopneustos* as "God-breathed."[44]

The text states *pasa graphē theopneustos*, which may be translated in several ways. The primary options are:

Option 1: "All Scripture is God-breathed."
Option 2: "Every Scripture is God-breathed."
Option 3: "Every (or all) inspired Scripture that is God-breathed."

The historical-grammatical interpretation depends on the literary intent of Paul. In his writings, the singular *graphē* may refer to a particular text of Holy Scripture (1 Tim 5:18) or to Holy Scripture in general (Gal 3:8–13, 22). Paul uses *graphē* in Galatians to indicate multiple texts from the Old Testament. Likewise, in 2 Timothy, Paul already cited multiple texts (2 Tim 2:7, 19; 3:8–9, 11) and will cite more (4:14, 17–18) to establish

---

[40] "Omnis scriptura divinitus inspirata," *Biblia Sacra Vulgatae Editionis, Sixti V et Clementis VIII* (London: Bagster, [n.d.]), 155.

[41] "For all scripture geven by inspiracion of God." *The New Testament: The Text of the Worms Edition of 1526 in Original Spelling*, ed. W. R. Cooper, trans. William Tyndale (London: The British Library, 2000), 452. Cf. "For all Scripture, inspired of God," in *The Wycliffe New Testament (1388): An Edition in Modern Spelling with an Introduction, the Original Prologues and the Epistle to the Laodiceans*, ed. W. R. Cooper (London: The British Library, 2002), 365.

[42] Warfield, *Revelation and Inspiration*, 79.

[43] Warfield, 79.

[44] Cf. W. D. Mounce, *The Pastoral Epistles*, Word Biblical Commentary (Nashville: Word, 2000), 565–67; Philip H. Towner, *The Letters to Timothy and Titus*, The New International Commentary on the New Testament (Grand Rapids: Eerdmans, 2006), 589.

his teaching. Paul's typical usage of the term pushes us away from the third translation option.

Moreover, Paul cited the plural regarding the biblical text in 2 Tim 3:15 with the related term *grammata* rather than *graphē*. With this term, *grammata*, Paul was indicating all the particular "letters" of the Hebrew Bible. Therefore, we should expect his use of the second term, *graphē*, will likewise encompass every Hebrew letter. In other words, Paul has in view not merely a portion but the entirety of the biblical "text." These literary phenomena indicate multiple problems will arise with those who choose the third translation.

A further problem with the third option is theological in nature. Through elevating the human exegete, diminishing the divine author, and atomizing the Scripture text, biblical critics may presume for themselves the capability to identify those texts which are God-breathed and those texts which are not. At that point, some may find opportunities to embrace or dismiss those passages he or she finds personally advantageous or personally disadvantageous, which invites irresponsible scholarship. For these reasons, literary and theological, we reject the third option with prejudice. Paul did not say "every Scripture that is God-breathed" in the sense that "not all Scripture is God-breathed." Rather, he taught that "all" Scripture, corporately (option 1), or "every" Scripture, distributively (option 2), is breathed by God.

The way Paul has already treated the Old Testament as sufficient "text by text" in this letter,[45] just as he typically does in his other letters, indicates the apostle likely has in mind that every single text is inspired even while referring to the whole biblical text. In other words, both the first and second interpretive options may stand. "Whether Paul, looking back at the Sacred Scriptures he had just mentioned, makes the assertion he is about to add, of them distributively, of all their part, or collectively, of their entire mass, is of no moment: to say that every part of these Sacred Scriptures is God-breathed and to say that the whole of these Sacred Scriptures is God-breathed, is, for

---

[45] Towner, *The Letters to Timothy and Titus*, 587. Towner has been helpful here, but he fails to discern that Paul refers to more than one sacred text in Galatians 3. Also, see George Knight III, *The Pastoral Epistles*, The New International Greek Testament Commentary (Grand Rapids: Eerdmans, 1992), 25; Robert Yarbrough, *The Letters to Timothy and Titus*, The Pillar New Testament Commentary (Grand Rapids: Eerdmans, 2018), 428–30.

the main matter, all one."[46] Whether one chooses to translate *pasa* with the corporate term "all" or the distributive term "every," we must recognize the apostle already presupposed both approaches to the biblical text were true.

Finally, the apostle Paul confirms all the "letters" are *hiera*, "sacred" or "holy" (2 Tim 3:15), on the basis that the entire "text" was "God-breathed" (2 Tim 3:16). The holiness of the entire contents of the biblical text ultimately depends upon the grace of the One who is holiness by nature. The Holy Spirit conveys the grace of the Holy One through sanctified human writers to the Holy Bible. Divine sanctification comes upon the human authors, and through the human authors the Holy Spirit sanctifies the text. Every human author is set apart and purified by God for God's purpose of the self-revelation of himself through their writings. Each human letter in the entire text is thereby rendered sacred. While Paul specifically considered the Hebrew Bible in this passage, the truth of inspiration necessarily extends to the writings of the apostles of the New Testament as well as the prophets of the Old Testament. Peter will, therefore, summarily classify the writings of Paul "with the rest of the Scriptures" (2 Pet 3:16). God originally breathed the entire Bible, such that one should say every book, indeed every letter, of the Old Testament and the New Testament is sacred.

V. The Second *Locus Classicus* of Biblical Inspiration

> For we did not follow cleverly contrived myths when we made known to you the power and coming of our Lord Jesus Christ; instead, we were eyewitnesses of his majesty. For he received honor and glory from God the Father when the voice came to him from the Majestic Glory, saying "This is my beloved Son, with whom I am well-pleased!" We ourselves heard this voice when it came from heaven while we were with him on the holy mountain. We also have the prophetic word strongly confirmed, and you will do well to pay attention to it, as to a lamp shining in a dark place, until the day dawns and the morning star rises in your hearts. Above all, you know this: No prophecy of Scripture comes from the prophet's own interpretation, because no prophecy ever came by the will of man;

---

[46] Warfield, *Revelation and Inspiration*, 80.

instead, men spoke from God as they were carried along by the
Holy Spirit. (2 Pet 1:16–21)

The second major text which describes the biblical doctrine of inspiration comes from the leading apostle of the Christian church, Peter.
Where Paul provided a didactic understanding of biblical inspiration,
Peter provided a pneumatic understanding. Peter offers not only a solid
doctrine of the Spirit's origination of the biblical text but also the process
of revelation which settled in the text via inspiration. The entire process
begins with the initial revelation, continues in the inspiration and then
the canonization of the written revelation, and ends with its illumination
and proclamation via the executive activity of the sovereign God the Holy
Spirit. Five truths about the Spirit's act of inspiration may be garnered
from this text.

First, the process of revelation begins with Peter's affirmation that the
apostolic witness is *true*. Their witness is not characterized by "cleverly con-
trived" narratives. Cunning humanity has an ability to contrive "myths" from
the fecundity of our own fallen imaginations. Peter is emphatic no such thing
occurred in true prophecy. Rather, just as Scripture itself demands juridical
facts be established by more than one eyewitness, so we must consider the
apostle's testimony is not idiosyncratic but part and parcel of the common
testimony of the whole apostolic body. "We ourselves heard this voice," Peter
says. The revelation of God is utterly true and cannot be characterized as
falsehood whatsoever.

Second, Peter describes exactly who they heard and what they heard.
They heard God the Father speak to them in a *verbal* way. The early revelation to the disciples at the Mount of Transfiguration (Matt 17:5–6) simultaneously grounded revelation in the doctrine of the Trinity and explicitly
defined revelation as verbal. Regarding the doctrine of the Trinity, we ought
to remember that the God who reveals himself is "the Father," the First
Person of the Holy Trinity. The Father revealed the truth to the disciples
that "Jesus Christ" is his "beloved Son," whom orthodox tradition considers
the Second Person of the Holy Trinity. The way we know these foundational claims are true is due to the inspiration and interpretation of "the Holy
Spirit," who is the Third Person of the Holy Trinity. With regard to the doctrine of verbal inspiration, Peter says they received a particular message from

the Father regarding his Son. These words are cited by Peter as constitutive of the revelation.

Third, after the act of revelation, which comes via sight as well as hearing, there is an affirmation of the *utility* of the "prophetic word." The words of God, which the apostles received indirectly through the prophets, foreshadowed the words which the apostles later received directly from the Lord himself. Indeed, the apostles treated the Father's direct revelation as a confirmation of the prophets' mediated revelation. The written words of the prophets, which the people of God already possessed, thus participate in the divine act of revelation. The previous revelation of the prophets was subsequently confirmed in the direct experience of revelation granted to the apostles from God.

Fourth, Peter explains the prophets' words were of *divine origination*, not initiated by human willing. Having established the truth of the written prophecy through contemporary divine revelation, Peter said, "No prophecy ever came by the will of man." Rather than using their own imaginations, the prophets simply conveyed the words of God. They were able to do so because they were "carried along by the Holy Spirit" (2 Pet 1:21). The term *pheromenoi* means "borne," "led," or "carried" from one place or one idea to another. Employed here in the passive, the verb indicates the Holy Spirit's initiating role in inspiration.[47] "Speaking thus under the determinative influence of the Holy Spirit, the things they spoke were not from themselves but from God."[48] The prophet comes to know revealed truth only through the Spirit of God guiding the prophet to that truth.

Fifth, just as the inspiration of the prophetic words was not due to human speculation but to divine condescension, so the reader's interpretation is not due to human speculation but divine *illumination*. The proper interpretation of the words of God inspired by the Holy Spirit

---

[47] "The pass. is also used of the prophets who spoke as they were *pheromenoi* 'impelled' by the Holy Ghost, 2 Pt. 1:21." Konrad Weiss, "*pherō*, etc.," in *Theological Dictionary of the New Testament*, ed. Gerhard Kittel, Geoffrey W. Bromiley, and Gerhard Friedrich, 10 vols. (Grand Rapids, Eerdmans, 1964–1976), 9:58. Also, see Thomas R. Schreiner, *1, 2 Peter and Jude*, Christian Standard Commentary (Nashville: B&H, 2020), 379–87.

[48] Warfield, *Revelation and Inspiration*, 82.

must be provided by the Holy Spirit who inspired them in the first place. He is the One who shines the light upon, or we might say, "illumines" the written Word so that we might pray for the inspired Word to be interpreted properly. It would do persons well to "pay attention" as they interpret the prophetic word. Feinberg argues that in verse 20 *epiluseōs*, "interpretation," is concerned not with the readers' or hearers' contemporary interpretation but with the prophet's own inspired understanding. We agree with Feinberg's interpretation here.[49] However, Peter in a previous verse (v. 19) was concerned that his readers understand the Word is also confirmed through acceptance of the divine "light" in their "hearts." Divine illumination for the sake of human interpretation, emphasized early in this Petrine passage, remains a theological conclusion which must be drawn from this passage.

The leading apostle's discussion of prophecy indicates that the revelation of God is true, that it comes with words, that it is profoundly useful, that it derives from God, and that it is ultimately interpreted properly through and only through the divine illumination of the hearer or reader by the Holy Spirit. In response to these profound truths about God's process of inspiring the prophets and the apostles, we believe the contemporary Christian exegete must learn to pray for the Holy Spirit to guide his or her interpretation of the inspired biblical text.

VI. The Third *Locus Classicus* of Biblical Inspiration

Jesus answered them, "Isn't it written in your law, 'I said, you are gods'? If he called those to whom the word of God came 'gods'—and the Scripture cannot be broken—do you say, 'You are blaspheming' to the one the Father set apart and sent into the world, because I said: I am the Son of God?" (John 10:34–36)

After expositing our first two *loci classici* of biblical inspiration, Warfield spent even more time with the words of Jesus in John 10:35.[50] However, Feinberg does not include this text among his "key governing passages" for

[49] Feinberg, *Light in a Dark Place*, 132.
[50] Warfield, *Revelation and Inspiration*, 84–87.

the doctrine of biblical inspiration, although he was aware of it.[51] Preferring succinctness, Garrett focused upon our first two texts.[52] Bavinck included John 10 at important points in his discussion of biblical inspiration, alongside 2 Timothy 3 and 2 Peter 1.[53] While some express difficulty with its interpretation, we believe this text must be received as a significant witness to the personal Word's involvement in the inspiration of the written Word. The Lord's teaching in the flesh grounds what we have already discovered from his apostles in the undivided work of the Trinity.

Jesus first affirmed the Jewish view of the "law," treating it synonymously with the term "Scripture." Warfield adds, canonically speaking, "prophecy" must also be deemed a synonym.[54] The three terms of Scripture, law, and prophecy were treated by our Lord in a close correlation. Jesus's reference to the psalmist's declaration (Ps 82:6) as "Scripture [which] cannot be broken" indicates written prophecy is inviolable. *Luthēnai*, the term which the CSB translates as "broken," is derived from *luō*. In Rabbinic and New Testament literature, *luō* is often paired with *deō* to convey the formal religious binding or loosing of a person (cf. Matt 16:19; 18:18).[55] Many scholars believe the context of the term *luthēnai* in John 10 indicates Psalm 82 "must be fulfilled."[56] Because God promised to act, he will necessarily bring this Christological event to pass.[57]

---

[51] Feinberg, *Light in a Dark Place*, 113–15, 116–49.

[52] Garrett, *Systematic Theology*, 1:125–26. Cf. Dockery, "Special Revelation," 113–15.

[53] Bavinck, *Reformed Dogmatics*, 1:394–97, 422–28.

[54] Warfield, *Revelation and Inspiration*, 85.

[55] "The customary meaning of the Rabbinic expressions is equally incontestable, namely, to declare forbidden or permitted, and thus to impose or remove an obligation, by a doctrinal decision." Friedrich Büchsel, "deō," in *Theological Dictionary of the New Testament*, 2:60.

[56] Cf. Richard Jungkutz, as discussed in Carson, *The Gospel according to John*, 397–98 (see chap. 4, n. 37).

[57] Similarly, in Matt 5:18, Jesus stated that no part of God's Law will *parelthē* ("pass," "perish," or stated as prophecy, "remain unfulfilled"). While we often distinguish the genre of law from that of prophecy, both terms function for the whole product of divine inspiration. When God's Word speaks, his act is sure. This prophetic truth, that "God speaks and acts according to his speech," gives us a glimpse of eternity and providence. It also grounds every biblical genre in divine willing,

In a pair of fascinating articles, Anthony Hanson affirms this prophetic interpretation. Building on previous commentary by Westcott, Lagrange, and Barrett, Hanson traces the origin of Psalm 82 to the preincarnate activity of the eternal "Word," "the Son of God." Noting similar trends in Rabbinic and Qumran literature, Hanson agreed Psalm 82 is a messianic prophecy in origin and fulfillment. This prophecy came from the eternal divine Word and was completed when the Word became incarnate in Jesus Christ.[58] While the psalm includes human beings among those empowered to render judgment, such that as instruments of divine activity they may be classified "among the gods" (Ps 82:1) and "sons of the Most High" (v. 6), Jesus's reference ought not be read merely as a handy prooftext for assigning the term "god" to a human being.[59] Rather, Jesus in particular is the One who is "God," and who will "die" (v. 7) and "rise up" (v. 8).

Jesus is himself the God who inspires Scripture. He is God the eternal Word, the Son of God who gave the prophecy in the genre of a psalm to ancient Israel. He is the Son of God, the premiere human judge, who became flesh, died, and was raised to life. He directly and personally fulfilled the prophecy he previously provided. John 10 demonstrates Psalm 82 was inspired by the Word preincarnate and fulfilled by the Word incarnate. Jesus affirmed "the Scripture cannot be broken," because he is "the word of God" who originally "came" to the ancient prophets in word only. After coming to the prophets in word, the Word came to the New Testament apostles in both word and flesh (cf. Heb 1:1–2). Jesus is the Messiah of Israel, the divine Word who spoke previously through the human prophets and who speaks now in the flesh. His Jewish contemporaries understood the original meaning all too well, for they again sought to seize and kill Jesus for his claim to divine identity (John 10:33, 39).

---

speech, and act. Through law, God commands and will judge. Through prophecy, God promises and will fulfill. Through poetry, God comes near, and so on.

[58] A. T. Hanson, "John's Citation of Psalm LXXXII," *New Testament Studies* 11, no. 2 (January 1965): 158–62; Hanson, "John's Citation of Psalm LXXXII Reconsidered," *New Testament Studies* 13, no. 4 (July 1967): 363–67.

[59] Warfield, Morris, and Carson adopt this more limited interpretation, which has Jesus treating the prophecy as "a rather run-of-the-mill passage." Cf. Morris, *The Gospel according to John*, 468 (see chap. 4, n. 67).

Along with the Spirit of God, therefore, the Son of God was involved in the inspiration of the biblical text. Moreover, not only the Spirit and the Son, but the Father too originates revelation and inspiration. Jesus declared of Peter's confession, a confession central to the Gospels as literature, "flesh and blood did not reveal this to you, but my Father in heaven" (Matt 16:17). Such phenomena undergird the orthodox patristic claim that all three Persons of the Holy Trinity are indivisibly involved in all the divine works. Revelation, inspiration, and illumination are the common work of the Word and of the Father as of the Holy Spirit. According to Augustine, the work of the divine persons is "inseparable."[60] Both the Word and the Spirit were "sent into the world" from "the Father" to make the revelation of God available to the apostles (John 14:24, 26).

Inspired by the divine Trinity, the prophets and the apostles wrote what they heard. The divine Word spoke previously through the prophets, but he became flesh and spoke directly to the apostles. Today, the divine Word and the divine Spirit still speak from the Father to all who hear the witness of the prophets and the apostles in the unbroken biblical text. God the Trinity, the Father, the Word, and the Spirit, not only originate by inspiration but remain active in the church's reception of that inspiration.

VII. The History of the Doctrine of Biblical Inspiration

Historically, the church's teaching about the inspiration of Scripture developed from a focus upon the divine author toward a recognition of the necessary inclusion of the human authors. The early church understood God the Trinity inspired Scripture. Because it is inspired, Scripture must be received as the Word of God. Convinced of divine inspiration, the church fathers sometimes downplayed human participation. The Medieval and Reformation periods continued the same ideas while questioning the relation of oral tradition to the written text. Operating from a positive attitude toward human reason, the modern period focused upon human participation in the origins of the biblical text. Modern evangelical theologians recognized an organic relation between the divine and human authors of the text, while

---

[60] Augustine, *De Trinitate* 1.15; Saint Augustine, *The Trinity*, trans. Edmund Hill (New York: New City Press, 1991), 76.

liberal theologians diminished the divine role, and radical theologians outright denied it.

Both the early church and early Judaism deemed the Hebrew Scriptures
the Word of God. Jewish writers like Philo and Josephus believed the
prophets received their words from God in an ecstatic state lacking personal
consciousness.[61] With this emphasis upon divine authorship, an approach
having many things in common with the dictation theory became the prevailing view in the early church. Early Christian apologists envisioned the
human authors as musical instruments upon which God played.[62] The
fathers affirmed all three persons of the Holy Trinity are involved. According
to John Chrysostom, it is "one and the same God whom both the Old and
the New Testament proclaim, who is praised and glorified, the Trinity."
"Through the Holy Spirit, therefore, both the law and the prophets, the
evangelists and apostles and pastors and teachers spoke. All scripture, then,
is given by inspiration of God and is also assuredly profitable."[63]

During the Middle Ages, the divine authorship of the biblical text continued to be emphasized, and the divine author was the trinitarian God. For
Bonaventure, Scripture "originates, not in human research, but in divine revelation from the Father, through the Son, in the Holy Spirit."[64] The human
writer was commonly compared to a secretary. But theologians like Thomas
Aquinas began to provide a more subtle account of the human authors' role.
On the one hand, "the Holy Spirit is the principal author of Scripture." On
the other, "John is the author of the Principal Gospel."[65] In Aristotelian fashion, Aquinas ascribed to God "principal efficient cause," while the human
was "instrumental."[66] Sometimes, the Spirit's inspiration was ascribed to
persons and texts other than that of the Bible. For instance, councils were

---

[61] Bavinck, *Reformed Dogmatics*, 1:402–3.

[62] Bavinck, 1:404.

[63] John of Damascus, *Exposition of the Orthodox Faith* 4.17. cited in Brad East,
The Doctrine of Scripture (Eugene, OR: Cascade, 2021), 25.

[64] Bavinck, *Reformed Dogmatics*, 1:406.

[65] Peter M. Candler Jr., "St. Thomas Aquinas," in *Christian Theologies of Scripture:
A Comparative Introduction*, ed. Justin S. Holcomb (New York: New York University
Press, 2006), 75.

[66] Gerald O'Collins, *Inspiration: Towards a Christian Interpretation of Biblical
Inspiration* (Oxford: Oxford University Press, 2018), 15.

accounted authority through the supposed special presence and guidance of the Holy Spirit.

Inspiration received attention during the Protestant Reformation. Martin Luther and John Calvin applied the doctrine to the writers through whom God spoke and the purpose for which he spoke.[67] Calvin continued to refer to inspiration as dictation, but like Aquinas showed sensitivity regarding the dual authorship of the text. The previous revelation shared orally was placed in writing through inspiration. He recognized that different biblical writers require different interpretations due to differences in time and context. Calvin taught that the Holy Spirit testifies to the truth of Scripture as the Word of God.[68] His doctrine of the testimony of the Holy Spirit to the veracity of Scripture remains consequential for contemporary bibliology.

Reformed theologians have more recently been criticized for retaining a mechanical theory of inspiration where the human authors functioned as "secretaries" and "amanuenses."[69] However, there were genuine attempts at adopting a more holistic view.[70] In their zeal to defend a high view of Scripture, some Reformed churches in the late seventeenth century made the dubious claim that even the vowel-points in the Hebrew were inspired.[71] Overreacting to such claims, scholars like William Sanday concluded inspiration did not necessarily result in infallibility in matters of text, grammar, science, or history.[72] Sanday thought Protestant scholars could link historical criticism with basic confessional orthodoxy.[73] On the positive side, both Lutheran and Reformed Scholastic theologians refuted the Roman Catholic council of Trent, which had ascribed inspiration to tradition.[74]

---

[67] Anthony C. Thiselton, *The Thiselton Companion to Christian Theology* (Grand Rapids: Eerdmans, 2015), 484–85.

[68] Randall C. Zachman, "John Calvin," in *Christian Theologies of Scripture*, 115–19.

[69] Michael S. Horton, "Theologies of Scripture in the Reformation and Counter-Reformation: An Introduction," in *Christian Theologies of Scripture*, 86.

[70] Bavinck, *Reformed Dogmatics*, 1:415.

[71] William Sanday, *The Oracles of God: Nine Lectures on the Doctrine of Biblical Inspiration* (New York: Longmans, 1894), 20–21.

[72] Sanday, *The Oracles of God*, 35–36.

[73] Sanday, 84.

[74] Bavinck, *Reformed Dogmatics*, 1:408.

After the Enlightenment, the agency of the human writers began to be emphasized. The prophets and apostles were recognized as being fully involved in their writing. It became evident there were human sources behind various Old Testament and New Testament writings, including oral traditions and written chronicles. This set off a great search for the original sources. The modern definitions of inspiration which developed in response to the Enlightenment range from the radical and the liberal to the neo-orthodox and the postliberal to the evangelical. As described above, evangelicals moved toward concursive views of inspiration.

At the other end of the spectrum, radical philosophers like Voltaire rejected biblical inspiration outright. The radicals were "completely finished with Scripture, shed all feelings of reverence toward it, and frequently have nothing but mockery and contempt for it."[75] The leading German theologian at the turn of the nineteenth century, Friedrich Schleiermacher, helped define the liberal response to the Enlightenment. Schleiermacher denied biblical inspiration was clearly grounded in Scripture. He affirmed the authors were inspired but according to their "whole freedom of personal productivity." To him, inspiration did not mean the writers were given the words to use.[76]

Karl Barth, objecting to the lack of orthodoxy in theological liberalism, recovered some aspects of the traditional relationship between Scripture and the Word of God. But Barth also said Scripture as a human construction contained certain errors. He bypassed inspiration to focus on the gracious decision of God to engage the reader of Scripture. The Bible, he argued, becomes the Word of God only in the divine-human encounter.[77] In the neo-orthodoxy of Barth, the doctrine of biblical inspiration was denied or, we might say,

---

[75] Bavinck, 1:420.

[76] Jeffrey Hensley, "Friedrich Schleiermacher," in *Christian Theologies of Scripture: A Comparative Introduction*, ed. Justin S. Holcomb (New York: New York University Press, 2006), 172–74.

[77] "In this event the Bible is God's Word. . . . The Bible is God's Word to the extent that God causes it to be His Word, to the extent that He speaks through it. . . . The Bible, then, becomes God's Word in this event . . ." Karl Barth, *Church Dogmatics: The Doctrine of the Word of God*, 2nd ed., ed. G. W. Bromiley and T. F. Torrance, trans. G. W. Bromiley (Edinburgh: T&T Clark, 1975), I/1:109–10. He objected, therefore, to Protestant orthodoxy's "fatal slide into the doctrine of inspiredness." Barth, *Church Dogmatics*, I/1:114.

effectively replaced by the distinct if related doctrine of biblical illumination.[78] If Barth located inspiration in the relation between God and the reader while objecting both to post-Reformation scholasticism and post-Enlightenment liberalism, postliberal theologians in the Yale School located inspiration in the received narrative of the community of faith while objecting both to experiential-expressive liberalism and cognitive-propositional evangelical-ism.[79] We believe that none of the radical, liberal, neo-orthodox, or postliberal options account properly for Scripture's high doctrine of inspiration.

VIII. Conclusion

While we appreciate the movement toward orthodoxy represented in the work of Karl Barth, we disagree with his circumventing of the inspiration of Scripture so that Scripture only becomes the Word of God. Rather, we believe with the church fathers, the medieval theologians, and the Reformers that the Bible was inspired by the Holy Spirit as the executor of the will and the word of the triune God. As a divine grace, Scripture must always be accorded the status of being the perfect Word of the living God in written form. We believe the Bible was supernaturally inspired, that the human authors were fully involved in the process of writing, and that the resultant text is also inspired and sufficient for fulfilling God's purposes, retaining normative external authority in Christian doctrine and practice. We affirm the Bible's divine authorship, such that the best existing theological model for explaining biblical inspiration remains the verbal plenary theory. Warfield properly denominated the Holy Bible "the crystallized voice of God" and "living words still speaking to us," for the Bible's inspiration by the Holy Spirit renders it always valuable, beautiful, dynamic, and incontestable. God's written Word speaks to us today with the same divine power as it spoke to its original hearers. Let us trust it, read it, apply it, and teach and proclaim it as God's inspired written Word.

---

[78] Mary Kathleen Cunningham, "Karl Barth," in *Christian Theologies of Scripture*, 189–90.

[79] Mike Higton, "Hans Frei," in *Christian Theologies of Scripture*, 220–37. The terms "experiential-expressive" and "cognitive-propositional" were famously proposed by Frei's colleague, George Lindbeck. Lindbeck, *The Nature of Doctrine: Religion and Theology in a Postliberal Age* (Philadelphia: Westminster John Knox, 1985).

7

The Preservation and Canonization of the Bible

We have explored the Holy Spirit's inspiration of the biblical writers to record the revelation of God's law to Israel and of God and his gospel in Jesus Christ. We have affirmed Scripture must be denominated the written Word of God. However, since the Spirit's inspiration terminated in the original autographs, we must attend to the Holy Spirit's preservation of the inspired writings for the sake of transmitting the Word to other times and places. In his preserving work, the Spirit leads the church to recognize the biblical canon, thereby extending to subsequent generations the written Word. The preservation of the Scriptures in the biblical canon assures the church an infallible text with normative authority for dogmatic confession and moral obedience. The canon preserves the inspired writings so saving truth may continue to be disseminated through translation, interpretation, and proclamation to new people groups.

The following traditional canonical account may not satisfy higher critics. For instance, James Barr objected that the New Testament "contains absolutely no discussion of questions about whether this or that book was canonical."[1] Barr's naïve literalism fueling his theological skepticism need not, however, stymie believers. Unlike modern critics, we believe the principles prompting the church's canonization of Scripture derive from the

---

[1] James Barr, *Holy Scripture: Canon, Authority, Criticism* (New York: Oxford University Press, 1983), 62.

biblical text. Evangelicals and other scholars have been accounting for how Scripture itself requires the doctrine of canonicity.[2] Our own account of the canon, while organized theologically, likewise develops the witness of Scripture to itself as authoritative text. We believe the church was not merely informed by Scripture but compelled by God through his Word and Spirit to recognize the inspired writings then collect them into a canon. The canon received the theological authority needed to regulate the worship, doctrine, and life of the church through the ages. The biblical arguments in this chapter justify the theology which drove the church to recognize the canon.

We start our discussion of the Holy Spirit's work of preserving the Bible with the transcendent eternality of God and his Word. God the Creator remains transcendent even as his eternal Word condescends by grace to take on creaturely form. The written Word similarly came by the grace of the Holy Spirit, as he inspired the prophets and apostles both to speak and to write. The Spirit extended divine revelation after Christ's ascension, first inspiring the apostolic writings, and Christ promised to guide and protect the church as it proclaimed the Word in the power of his Spirit. God's Spirit preserves the Word in the church and guides the church to disseminate that Word, thereby continually edifying the church. The Spirit led the church to recognize the inspiration and authority of the prophetic and apostolic writings; the church responded by collecting the prophetic and apostolic writings in their canon. The canon thus provides the basis for translation, interpretation, and theological construction.

I. The Transcendent Word Condescends by Grace

LORD, your word is forever; it is firmly fixed in heaven. Your faithfulness is for all generations; you established the earth, and it stands

---

[2] Michael J. Kruger, *The Question of Canon: Challenging the Status Quo in the New Testament Debate* (Downers Grove: IVP, 2013); John C. Peckham, *Canonical Theology: The Biblical Canon, Sola Scriptura, and Theological Method* (Grand Rapids: Eerdmans, 2016), 16–47; Feinberg, *Light in a Dark Place*, 469–86 (see introduction, n. 5). Though not an evangelical, Brevard Childs makes a similar claim, stating, "the concept of canon was not a late, ecclesiastical ordering which was basically foreign to the material itself, but that canon-consciousness lay deep within the formation of the literature." Brevard S. Childs, *Biblical Theology: A Proposal* (Minneapolis: Fortress, 2002), 39.

firm. Your judgments stand firm today, for all things are your servants. If your instruction had not been my delight, I would have died in my affliction. I will never forget your precepts, for you have given me life through them. I am yours; save me, for I have studied your precepts. The wicked hope to destroy me, but I contemplate your decrees. I have seen a limit to all perfection, but your command is without limit. (Ps 119:89–96)

In the Lamed (ל) section of the 119th Psalm, the Word of God is clearly and repeatedly ascribed the perfection of eternality. The divine Word is "forever," because it is "firmly fixed in heaven," the place of God's habitation. From this transcendent reality, God graciously condescends with blessings for believing humanity through his revelation. Seven blessings are conveyed in his eternal Word: First, God is always faithful to his Word. Second, his judgments remain firm. Third, avoiding death depends on human loyalty to his Word. Fourth, his Word brings life. Fifth, hope for eternal salvation comes through his Word. Sixth, his Word preserves persons from wickedness. Seventh, the psalmist concludes that while his creatures reflect God's perfection only in a limited way, God's Word remains utterly perfect. Imperfect creatures can reflect upon their Creator,[3] but a profound gap separates his eternal perfection from our sinful creatureliness.

The eternally divine Word remains transcendent above, yet in an act of divine grace becomes immanent to his human creatures by the means of his proclaimed Word and his written Word but supremely in the personal Word's incarnation. Martin Luther differentiated between the eternal divine Word and the creaturely agents of his Word with the terms "spiritual things" and "temporal things." Temporal things, Luther said, are "trifling, they can be poured out into another." Spiritual things are "beyond grasp, and therefore they can hardly be put forth to the outside and given meaning by the tongue."[4] Luther argued that while eternal spiritual reality necessarily eludes our grasp by nature, God uses temporal creatures

---

[3] "The nature of the Lord is also reflected in everything he has created." Willem A. VanGemeren, "Psalms," in *The Expositor's Bible Commentary*, ed. Frank E. Gaebelein, 12 vols. (Grand Rapids: Zondervan, 1991), 5:752.

[4] Luther, *First Lectures on the Psalms*, in *Luther's Works*, ed. Hilton C. Oswald, 55 vols. (St. Louis: Concordia Publishing House, 1974), 10:211.

to convey life by grace. "God uses our words, whether Gospels or prophetic books, as tools with which He Himself writes living words in our
hearts."[5] The prophet or apostle, as a human creature, lacks the divine
agency required to initiate grace, but God uses them as instruments to
convey eternal truth.[6]

The eternal Word is the Son of God, divine by nature. He entered creation through his incarnation as Jesus Christ. Due to his sacred person-
hood and his transcendent divinity, the eternal Word must be distinguished
from both the proclaimed Word and the written Word about him, though
they are intimately related. The incarnate Word is personally divine, but
the proclaimed Word and the written Word are servant creatures of God.
"Scripture is," as Bavinck wrote, "the servant form of revelation."[7] The mediating servants of Scripture and proclamation temporally participate in the
divine economy via the grace of the Holy Spirit.[8] The proclaimed words of
the prophets and the apostles, perfected by divine grace, must not be confused with the transcendent reality of the personal Word, the eternal Son of
God—nor must they be divorced from them. "Long ago God spoke to our
ancestors by the prophets at different times and in different ways. In these
last days, he has spoken to us by his Son" (Heb 1:1–2a). The servant words
of revelation known as Scripture and proclamation culminate in the personal
revelation of the eternal Word.

While a fundamental differentiation must be made between the
Lord God and his created instruments of proclamation and Scripture,
the unity between the divine Word and his instrumental words remains
unbroken by divine fiat.[9] The promises of Psalm 119 presume a continual
correlation between God's perfection in origin and Scripture's perfection

---

[5] Luther, *First Lectures on the Psalms*, 212.

[6] "Therefore, O prophet, it is for you to utter and be the pen. You can openly
proclaim out of the fullness of your heart and spirit, but you cannot openly pour out
the Spirit Himself, nor can you infuse Him and so make others feel the feeling you
have." Luther, *First Lectures on the Psalms*, 212.

[7] Bavinck, *Reformed Dogmatics*, 1:380 (see chap. 5, n. 69).

[8] "The direct Word of God meets us only in this twofold mediacy." Karl Barth,
Church Dogmatics, trans. G. W. Bromiley, 2nd ed. (Edinburgh: T&T Clark, 1975),
I/1:121.

[9] "We have been speaking of three different forms of the Word of God and not
of three different Words of God." Barth, *Church Dogmatics*, I/1:120.

in condescension. The eternal Lord chose to be our faithful, life-giving, and protecting Savior by means of his incarnate Word. The eternal Word spoke human words to the apostles and the prophets, and the apostles and the prophets spoke those words to their contemporaries. The words of the apostles and prophets were the media by which the Word spoke to humanity. These words of divine revelation were then committed to Scripture for continuing access among new people groups and their subsequent generations.

The traditional distinction between "nature" and "grace" may be helpful in distinguishing this truth about the Word of God as God and the Word of God using chosen creaturely media:[10] The nature of the Word of God as God, ontological truth, is distinguishable from the grace of the Word of God as Scripture and proclamation, epistemological truth. On the one hand, the person of Jesus Christ is the Word of God *by nature*. On the other hand, the prophetic and apostolic preaching of the Word and their deposition of it in written form are the Word of God *by grace*. The written Word calls us to participate by faith in the eternal perfection of the personal Word by the perfecting grace of the Holy Spirit. While the media of Scripture and proclamation are creaturely, they are nonetheless the Word of God, even if by grace rather than by nature.

II. Revelation Continues through the Written Word

The doctrine of biblical inspiration, detailed in the last chapter, asserts the Holy Spirit guided the prophets both to speak and to write. The inspired writings of the Old Testament participate in the perfection of God by grace because the Holy Spirit "carried along" the prophets (2 Pet 1:21). The Lord Jesus Christ promised his apostles they would also receive the Holy Spirit's guidance to remember from, to receive more regarding, and to testify to him. The Spirit's superintending work in biblical revelation required the church to render an account for the truth that the inspired writings of the inspired prophets of the Old Testament and the inspired apostles of the New Testament would be continually preserved.

---

[10] Eugene TeSelle, *Augustine the Theologian* (1970; Reprint, Eugene, OR: Wipf and Stock, 2002), 164, 200–204.

Declaring the Spirit's guidance of his apostles' minds and of the Spirit's continuing presence with the apostles' testimony to the world was the burden of our Lord's Paraclete promises before his crucifixion, resurrection, and ascension. First, Jesus promised the Spirit would come and remain with the disciples (John 14:16–18). He would bring to their minds both the things which Jesus already taught them plus additional revelation beyond that which he conveyed during his earthly ministry (14:25–26; 16:12–14). Second, Jesus also promised the Holy Spirit would accompany the apostles' testimony (15:26–27) to bring conviction to the world (16:7–11). In other words, the Spirit guarantees the apostolic memory and empowers the apostolic testimony.

The Spirit's work did not cease with his inspiration of the writings of the apostles and the prophets. The Spirit continued to accompany their witness through the preservation of their testimony in writing and the subsequent illumination of their written testimony to those who hear it. The Spirit who inspired the original autographs associated with the apostles also guided the early churches to recognize the authority of their testimony to Christ. The early churches responded by collecting their writings as a guide or "rule" (*kanōn*) for their own public testimony to Christ. The church's testimony to Christ continues to be guided by the Holy Spirit, from the act of inspiration through the act of personal faith. "The Bible was revelation, but the revelatory process was complete only when its word was believed by the sinner."[11]

Because of two further promises of Christ to his church, we trust he will continually preserve his church through various actions, including the gift of the canon. Christ's first promise was always to protect his church, even against the assault of the demonic (Matt 16:18). His second promise was to guide the church, for the Holy Spirit is Christ's eternally present gift of himself to the church. Above, we outlined the promise of guidance through an examination of his Paraclete promises. Due to these two other promises, those of protection and of continuing guidance, we affirm the Holy Spirit always guides and protects the testimony of the prophets and the apostles to the church: In the days of the apostles, the Spirit of God

---

[11] Peter Jensen, *The Revelation of God*, Contours of Christian Theology (Downers Grove: IVP, 2002), 233.

guided and protected their testimony to the church. Through the history of the church, the Holy Spirit guided and protected the apostolic testimony of the church. Today, the Holy Spirit continues to protect and guide the church's apostolic testimony.

Jesus Christ, by the gift of his Spirit from the Father, continually guides and protects his church in the face of two major challenges—persecutions by the world and the failures of the church itself.[12] The church of Jesus Christ may never claim present perfection for herself, for she is being sanctified, just as individual Christians are being sanctified. The church may fail at times, but she shares in Christ's victory at the Cross even now by faith and will share in his final victory by hope. Jesus Christ will always guide and protect his church until he comes to take her to himself at his Second Coming (Rev 19). Christ guides and protects, and builds, his church through the gift of the Holy Spirit, who maintains fellowship with the church and accompanies her continuation of the apostolic testimony to Christ.

III. Preservation, Dissemination, and Edification

The Holy Spirit's guidance and protection of the apostles and the church is focused upon his continuing work with the written Word of God. His work may be described as the preservation of the Word, the dissemination of the Word, and the edification of the church of Jesus Christ. Jesus promised his church it would have an intimate relationship with the Holy Spirit, who will accompany their testimony. Jesus said the Holy Spirit "will testify about me." Establishing the intimate relation between the church's external witness and the Spirit's internal witness, Jesus went on to command, "You also will testify" (John 15:26–27). The Spirit's testimony empowers the church's testimony. As the people of God respond in faith to the dissemination of the

---

[12] Lee Martin McDonald believes "the first discernible moves" toward fixing the canon arose during the Diocletian persecution, when church leaders had to identify which books they might safely turn over to their Roman persecutors. McDonald, *The Origin of the Bible: A Guide for the Perplexed* (New York: T&T Clark, 2011), 26. The Donatist controversy arose during the same persecution when compromised bishops became identified as *traditores*, traitors, for having handed over the holy texts to be burned. Brown, *Augustine of Hippo*, 215 (see chap. 3, n. 38).

Word, the church is edified. The apostles' testimony, guided by the Spirit, is both preserved and disseminated by means of the canon of books we know as the Holy Bible.

First, the *preservation* of the Word of God in the canon began after the Holy Spirit guided the prophets and apostles to record the spoken Word in written texts. These texts were then conveyed from one person to another and one congregation to another through the handing on of the gospel by the church. These texts were recognized by the early churches and further preserved through a process of collecting them into the "canon." We shall have more to say about the historical process of canonization and the apparent criteria for canonization in the following sections.

Second, the *dissemination* of the Word of God occurs whenever the Scriptures of the canon are proclaimed within the congregations and especially beyond the congregations to the world. The ongoing mission of the church of Jesus Christ requires the dissemination of the Word of God, which Word enables personal confessions of faith (Rom 10:14–17). The second book of Luke, which may equally be entitled "the Acts of the Apostles" or "the Acts of the Holy Spirit,"[13] records the first efforts of the church to disseminate the Word of God to more and more people. Acts is marked by "the pervasive emphasis on the dominant role of the Holy Spirit in the expansion of the gospel."[14] The early church grew in strength and in numbers as the Word of God was proclaimed to new people groups.

Third, the *edification* of the church took four major leaps as new people were incorporated through proclamation. The structure of the book of Acts indicates four seminal growth points: First, in Acts 2 with the Jews gathered in Jerusalem, then in Acts 8 with the Samaritans, followed in Acts 10 with God-fearing Gentiles, and finally in Acts 19 with disciples of John the Baptist.[15] These four major movements of apostolic testimony in the power

---

[13] F. F. Bruce, *The Acts of the Apostles: The Greek Text with Introduction and Commentary*, 2nd ed. (Grand Rapids: Eerdmans, 1952), 1, 30.

[14] Bruce, *The Book of the Acts*, 12–13 (see chap. 2, n. 38).

[15] Wayne E. Ward, *The Holy Spirit*, Layman's Library of Christian Doctrine (Nashville: Broadman, 1987), 92. Jack MacGorman identified a threefold outline, including Ward's third and fourth movements together. J. W. MacGorman, *Acts: The Gospel for All People*, Adult January Bible Study (Nashville: Convention Press, 1990), 5.

of the Holy Spirit show the early church's initial fulfillment of the command given by Christ in Acts 1:8: "But you will receive power when the Holy Spirit has come on you, and you will be my witnesses in Jerusalem, in all Judea and Samaria, and to the ends of the earth." The promise is the power of his Spirit; the command is for the church to be his witness. The book of Acts ends with Paul testifying to the gospel in the heart of the Roman Empire (Acts 28:14–31).

The continuing commission for the church of Jesus Christ, the community which preserves and disseminates the testimony to the gospel of Jesus Christ "to the ends of the earth" for the purpose of the edification of the church, is why Christians translate the Bible. Therefore, translation is related to the works of preservation, dissemination, and edification. The need for translation to reach a growing number of people groups is evidenced as early as the gift of tongues in Acts 2:6: "When this sound occurred, a crowd came together and was confused because each one heard them speaking in his own language." By means of this supernatural gift of translation, the earliest Christian preachers and teachers were able to proclaim the Word of God to people from various places in their own languages. "What was significant was that the various *vernacular* languages of these peoples were being spoken."[16]

The church's subsequent acts of natural translation resulted in the spread of the gospel during the early centuries into the continents of Asia, Africa, and Europe.[17] This was followed by various mission movements throughout church history, including the Modern Missions Movement, which began after the British Baptist preacher, William Carey, was sent to India in 1793. Carey translated the Bible for the first time into Bengali, Oriya, Marathi, Hindi, Assamese, and Sanskrit. The example provided by Carey and the Baptist Missionary Society which supported him encouraged many other evangelical Christians to start similar efforts. The church's acts of translation

---

[16] I. Howard Marshall, *The Acts of the Apostles: An Introduction and Commentary*, Tyndale New Testament Commentaries (Grand Rapids: Eerdmans, 1980), 70.

[17] For a substantial history of the church written from the perspective of its mission, see Kenneth Scott Latourette, *A History of Christianity*, rev. ed. (Peabody, MA: Prince Press, 2007). For a more global view, see Philip Jenkins, *The Lost History of Christianity: The Thousand-Year Golden Age of the Church in the Middle East, Africa, and Asia—And How It Died* (San Francisco: HarperOne, 2009).

continue today through such movements as the Wycliffe Bible Translators.[18] Reflecting his work in the early church, the Modern Missions Movement and its efforts at universal translation have been preceded by prayer for the Holy Spirit to move.[19]

The typical means by which the living Word of God is now made known to people occurs after the written Word of God is translated into their own languages. Training in literacy, sometimes even the creation of written language to accompany the existing oral language, also helps fulfill the church's goal. We shall have more to say about the practice of Bible translation as the link between canonization and interpretation via establishing the critical text toward the end of this chapter.

Spirit-empowered preachers and teachers, using the languages of their recipient people groups, proclaim orally what has been preserved in writing for the purpose of proclamation. In the central volumes of his magisterial *God, Revelation and Authority*, Carl Henry affirmed the importance of recognizing the superintending work of the Holy Spirit in the whole historical process of conveying God's revelation. The Spirit superintended the original inspiration of the writers and the compilation of their writings in the canon, and he continues to superintend the church as it sends "spirit-anointed couriers" to "forward the ongoing task of proclamation" today.[20]

Despite Henry's helpful Spirit-led approach to the doctrine of revelation, Peter Jensen identified three tendencies which challenge contemporary

---

[18] Edward L. Smither, *Christian Mission: A Concise Global History* (Bellingham, WA: Lexham, 2019).

[19] Several Northamptonshire Baptists were led by John Sutcliff to read and pray for what Jonathan Edwards advocated in his Humble Attempt, that God "would appear for the help of his church, and in mercy to mankind, and pour out his Spirit, revive his work, and advance his spiritual kingdom in the world, as he has promised." Michael A. G. Haykin, "'Until the Spirit be poured upon us from on High': Prayer and Revival among the English Particular Baptists in the Eighteenth Century," *Presbyterian and Reformed Journal* 12, no. 1 (January 2020): 83, 87–91. Cf. Haykin, "John Sutcliff and the Concert of Prayer," *Reformation and Revival* 1, no. 3 (1992): 65–88.

[20] Henry, *God, Revelation and Authority*, 1:476 (see chap. 1, n. 32). Also, see R. Laird Harris, *Inspiration and Canonicity of the Bible: An Exegetical and Historical Study* (Grand Rapids: Zondervan, 1971); Yarnell, "Whose Jesus? Which Revelation?" 33–53 (see chap. 1, n. 31).

Protestant reception of the Holy Spirit's continuing ministry vis-à-vis the written Word of God. First, after the Reformation, "there was a stress on the biblical source of revelation, which tended to formalize the process of revelation so that it simply became the knowledge of the Scriptures. Where the idea of illumination was carefully made subservient to the word, the work of the Spirit became 'invisible' and might just as well not have existed." The doctrine of inspiration swallowed and suppressed the doctrine of illumination.[21] A second tendency, found among those deeply influenced by Immanuel Kant and Karl Barth, denied or at least severely diminished the inspiration of Scripture. In opposition to the first tendency, these theologians allowed illumination to subsume inspiration.[22] A third tendency was to stress the "inner light," so that the Spirit began to be treated as a second source of revelation separate from the Word.[23]

Jensen encouraged Protestants to avoid the errors in each of these three modern tendencies by affirming the Spirit's original work of inspiration and by affirming his continuing work, including his illumination of the Word to unite people by faith with God in Christ.[24] We believe the coinherence of the Word with the Spirit, advocated by the Reformers, offers contemporary evangelicals a helpful model for avoiding these modern errors.[25] Let us now turn our attention to the history of the preservation of the canon under the continuing guidance of the Holy Spirit so that the church's "spirit-anointed couriers" possess an authoritative and transformative word to proclaim.

IV. The Early Development of the Canon

Although we no longer possess the inspired autographs, sufficient copies render the manuscript tradition reliable. The original autographs of the prophets and apostles were treasured and used so often in both Jewish worship

---

[21] Jensen, *The Revelation of God*, 234.

[22] Jensen, 235, 252.

[23] Jensen, 235.

[24] Jensen, 245–50.

[25] The evangelical Anabaptist, Pilgram Marpeck, offered a helpful and balanced approach to correlating the Word with the Spirit. Malcolm B. Yarnell III, *The Formation of Christian Doctrine* (Nashville: B&H Academic, 2007), 82–90.

and Christian worship it became necessary to make copies to replace the originals. And as synagogues and churches gathered in new places, they too required access to the sacred texts, prompting more copies. This process repeated itself through the generations. The Christian churches today have been bequeathed a substantial number of copies, both early and medieval, so that even a skeptic must admit, "the textual critic of the New Testament is embarrassed by the wealth of material."[26] Martin Hengel agrees that, especially in comparison with other manuscripts from the ancient period, "the attestation of the original [scriptural] text is so strong that practically all the secondary alterations to the text and interpolations can be picked up in the unbelievably multiple textual tradition."[27]

Contrary to prejudiced discounting by radical critics in the modern period,[28] the ancient manuscript tradition yields a text for our use today which may be described as "authoritative" and "sufficient," as well as "infallible," that is to say, free from doctrinal error.[29] Henry, the leading intellectual of twentieth-century American evangelicalism, affirmed the original manuscripts are definitively "inerrant" or "without error," while the manuscript tradition of copies are "infallible" or "not prone to error."[30] The copies we have today "reliably convey the Word of God."[31] The analysis of this textual

---

[26] Bruce M. Metzger and Bart D. Ehrman, *The Text of the New Testament: Its Transmission, Corruption, and Restoration*, 4th ed. (New York: Oxford University Press, 2005), 51. Metzger and Ehrman were comparing the New Testament material with copies of other ancient texts.

[27] Martin Hengel, *The Four Gospels and the One Gospel of Jesus Christ*, trans. John Bowden (Harrisburg, PA: Trinity Press International, 2000), 29.

[28] Hengel, a prominent critic himself, decries the radical critics' unwarranted methods. Hengel, *The Four Gospels and the One Gospel of Jesus Christ*, 143–44. A sustained insider's critique of radical criticism may be found in Eta Linnemann, *Historical Criticism of the Bible: Methodology or Ideology: Reflections of a Bultmannian Turned Evangelical*, trans. Robert W. Yarbrough (Grand Rapids: Baker, 1990); Eta Linnemann, *Is There a Synoptic Problem? Rethinking the Literary Dependence of the First Three Gospels*, trans. Robert W. Yarbrough (Grand Rapids: Baker, 1992).

[29] See the chapters in this book on sufficiency and inerrancy. Also, see Malcolm B. Yarnell III and David S. Dockery, "The Authority and Sufficiency of Scripture: An Introduction," in *The Authority and Sufficiency of Scripture*, ed. Adam W. Greenway and David S. Dockery (Fort Worth: Seminary Hill Press, 2022), 1–19.

[30] Henry, *God, Revelation and Authority*, 4:220n.

[31] Henry, 4:220.

tradition is the ongoing work of biblical scholars dedicated to preserving an infallible copy of the original text.

But how did we progress from the inerrant autographs of the apostles to our infallible text of today? How were the texts effectively preserved for the church's continuing use through the ages? From a theological perspective, we take it as a matter of faith that the Bible continually reveals God's will and way in our midst by virtue of the inspiring grace, the preserving grace, and the illuminating grace of the Holy Spirit.[32] Jesus promised the Spirit would guide the church "into all the truth" (John 16:13). He also promised the Holy Spirit would accompany the words of truth proclaimed by the church, thereby ensuring their words bring life (John 6:63).

From an historical perspective, the beginnings of canon formation are detected within the Bible. The *biblia* and *membranae* which Paul directed Timothy to deliver refer, respectively, to the roll form of the Hebrew Scriptures and the codex form of Paul's own writings (2 Tim 4:13). In other words, the apostolic church received as inspired that which we now call the Old Testament, even while it was learning to recognize inspiration in the writings of the apostles. Their writings were collected in the canon of the New Testament.[33] Because the apostles commanded or presumed their writings would be read in congregational gatherings (Col 4:16; 1 Cor 5:9; 2 Cor 7:8), the written apostolic deposit was accorded authority within the Christian community.

The implication of granting authority equally to the Scriptures of Israel and the writings of the apostles and their immediate associates stems from the earliest generation. For instance, the second epistle of Peter places the writings of Paul among "the rest of the Scriptures" (2 Pet 3:15–16). The apostles likewise recognized the authority of their own writings was equivalent to those of the prophets. "The same Holy Spirit who inspired the prophets was

---

[32] "The very divine reality which the interpreter strives to grasp, is the very One who grasps the interpreter. The Christian doctrine of the role of the Holy Spirit is not a hermeneutical principle, but that divine reality itself who makes understanding of God possible." Childs, *Biblical Theology*, 69.

[33] Moule, *The Birth of the New Testament*, 182–83 (see chap. 5, n, 17). Henry argues that while there are other writings used in the Old Testament and that the apostles seemed to have written other letters, only those which were inspired made it into the canon. Henry, *God, Revelation and Authority*, 408.

active in themselves. That is quite enough to explain how Peter could have put Paul alongside the Old Testament writers in this verse."[34] Similarly, the fifth book of the apostle John echoes the fifth book of the prophet Moses in warning against the alteration of the inspired written text (Deut 4:2; 12:32; Rev 22:18–19).

Barr was correct in stating the Bible offers no canonical list, but the theological basis for its formation is nonetheless revealed therein. The authority accorded to the writings of the prophets was both implicitly and explicitly recognized by Jesus and the apostles. Due to the authorization granted by Jesus Christ along with the inspiration of the Holy Spirit, prophetic authority extended to the apostles or to their approved associates. Malicious alteration of the writings of either the Hebrew prophets or the Christian apostles was strictly forbidden. The church was compelled to recognize and preserve the inspired, authoritative writings.

The church recognized and preserved the inspired, authoritative writings through the "canon." The Hebrew term *qaneh*, indicated a "stick," a branch of a tree or bush. However, when its length was standardized, a *qaneh* could also be used as a "measuring rod."[35] The Greek term *kanōn*, carried the same original natural and utilitarian meanings. The latter meaning could be extended to indicate a standard "rule" or "list."[36] Three utilitarian canons became important in the early church. The canon as a "rule," "norm," or "standard" of faith appeared first.[37] But by the fourth

---

[34] Michael Green, *The Second Epistle General of Peter and the General Epistle of Jude: An Introduction and Commentary*, rev. ed., Tyndale New Testament Commentaries (Grand Rapids: Eerdmans, 1987), 161.

[35] The densest concentration of references to *qaneh* occurs in Ezekiel 40–42.

[36] McDonald, *The Origin of the Bible*, 14.

[37] In the second century after Christ, the idea of canon was also applied to the basic content of the Christian faith. This use of canon was known variously as the "rule of truth," "ecclesiastical rule," and, most commonly, "rule of faith." The content of the rule of faith could vary in specific form but it typically included the central truths of God as Trinity and the gospel work of Jesus Christ. While the terminology of canon as rule of faith was used by Tertullian, Origen, and Augustine, its most relevant early proponent was Irenaeus, who used the term often in his writings from the latter part of the second century. The rule of faith simultaneously derived from Scripture and provided the key to interpreting Scripture. Irenaeus and Tertullian both emphasized its biblical origin. The canon of faith was utilized afterwards by orthodox teachers, often in direct response

century, two other meanings were in use: church councils, mimicking the Jerusalem gathering in Acts 15, referred to their rules as canons. Around the same time, the third major concept of the canon, the canon as a "list" of approved texts for use in Christian worship and discourse developed. "A list in itself may represent a norm."[38]

Following R. P. C. Hanson, F. F. Bruce defines this third meaning of canon as "the list of writings acknowledged by the Church as documents of divine revelation."[39] The particular details regarding the development of the biblical canon as a list of approved books "are shrouded in mystery," at least from the modern historian's perspective.[40] Part of the mystery derives from the fact that even of the Christian titles we know from the second century, only 15 percent of these known texts survived systemic persecution, neglect, and the vagaries of time.[41] However, the early church set out to be faithful to the person and teachings of Jesus, and by divine grace, succeeded. Part and parcel of their fidelity necessarily entailed honoring the sacred Scriptures approved by Christ and written about him. The collection of these Scriptures comprises our biblical canon.

Writing in the last decade of the first century, Clement of Rome lauded the Corinthian church for once "carefully attending to His words" and being "inwardly filled with His doctrine." "The commandments and ordinances of the Lord were written upon the tables of your hearts."[42] Clement quotes liberally from the text of the Hebrew prophets. He affirms "the Scriptures"

---

to the heresies which cropped up and misused Scripture. Tomas Bokedal, "The Rule of Faith: Tracing Its Origins," *Journal of Theological Interpretation* 7, no. 2 (Fall 2013): 233–55; Everett Ferguson, *The Rule of Faith: A Guide*, Cascade Companions (Eugene, OR: Wipf and Stock, 2015). See this book's concluding chapter on biblical interpretation for more detail about the continuing relevance of this use of canon.

[38] Einer Thomassen, "Some Notes on the Development of Christian Ideas about a Canon," in *Canon and Canonicity: The Formation and Use of Scripture*, ed. Einer Thomassen (Copenhagen: Museum Tusculanum Press, 2010), 10.

[39] F. F. Bruce, *The Canon of Scripture* (Downers Grove: IVP, 1988), 17.

[40] Metzger and Ehrman, *The Text of the New Testament*, 272.

[41] Hengel, *The Four Gospels and the One Gospel of Jesus Christ*, 55.

[42] 1 Clement 2; "The First Epistle of Clement to the Corinthians," in *The Apostolic Fathers with Justin Martyr and Irenaeus*, ed. Alexander Roberts, James Donaldson, and A. Cleveland Cox, Ante-Nicene Fathers, 10 vols. (1885; Reprint, Peabody, MA: Hendrickson Publishers, 1994), 1:5.

are "the true utterances of the Holy Spirit," but his references to "that which is written" largely concern the Hebrew Scriptures.[43] After rehearsing "ancient examples" of faithfulness to Christ from the Old Testament, Clement also considered Peter and Paul. The apostles are "the most recent spiritual heroes" and "in our own generation."[44] Clement's references to the literal "words of the Lord Jesus" are fragmentary. While he deemed Christ supremely authoritative, Christ's own *logia* were likely available to Clement only through oral means.[45] He does, however, make scattered references to the writings of Paul, Peter, James, and the letter to the Hebrews.[46]

A generation after Clement, Justin Martyr became a pagan convert to Christ and employed philosophy to aid his Christian witness. Justin's writings indicate an implicit development of the canon.[47] He believed the divine Word speaks in the persons of the Father and the Son and the Spirit.[48] The preincarnate Word spoke to all men of reason but was born of a virgin "one hundred and fifty years ago."[49] "The prophetic Spirit" used the Hebrew prophets to foretell important future events, and Jesus taught his followers to interpret the prophets in reference to himself.[50] Like Clement, Justin

---

[43] 1 Clement 3, 4, 45; *The Apostolic Fathers*, 5–6, 17.

[44] 1 Clement 5; *The Apostolic Fathers*, 6.

[45] 1 Clement 13, 42, 46; *The Apostolic Fathers*, 8, 16–17. Chapter 13 of Clement's letter includes seven *logia* or sayings of Jesus which resemble sayings from the gospel accounts. Michael Strickland concludes, the "early Christian writers, including the gospel authors, were careful to accurately and faithfully combine reliable oral tradition with their accepted written sources." Michael Strickland, "The Integration of Oral Jesus Tradition in the Early Church," *Early Church Studies* 5, no. 1 (2015): 133–37.

[46] 1 Clement 33, 36, 47, 49; *The Apostolic Fathers*, 14–15, 18.

[47] Hans von Campenhausen, *The Fathers of the Church: Combined Edition of The Fathers of the Greek Church and The Fathers of the Latin Church*, trans. W. Kohlhammer, L. A. Garrard, and Manfred Hoffmann (Peabody, MA: Hendrickson, 2000), 5–15.

[48] Justin, *Apology* 36–39; "The First Apology of Justin," in *The Apostolic Fathers*, 175.

[49] Justin, *Apology* 46; *The Apostolic Fathers*, 178. Justin has a vigorous understanding of general revelation. Justin *2 Apology* 10; "The Second Apology of Justin," in *The Apostolic Fathers*, 191.

[50] Justin, *Apology* 31; *The Apostolic Fathers*, 173. Justin believed the translation of the Hebrew prophets into Greek at the request of Ptolemy was perfected "by divine power." Justin *Oration* 13; in "Hortatory Address to the Greeks," in *The Apostolic Fathers*, 278–79.

interpreted the Old Testament at length, especially in his *Dialogue.* Justin also said the early church regularly gathered on Sundays to read publicly from "the writings of the prophets" and from "the memoirs of the apostles."[51] Justin also called these memoirs, "Gospels."[52] The public reading of the prophetic and apostolic writings during worship was a way of recognizing their inherent authority.

The authority of the prophetic and apostolic writings was recognized in the second-century church, but modern scholars disagree about the catalyst for fixing a canonical list of inspired writings. That they defined the canon is certain;[53] what prompted that development is debated. The role of Marcion is at issue. A near contemporary of Justin, Marcion disliked the God he perceived at work in the Old Testament and the Hebraic portions of the New Testament. He thus admitted only an edited version of Luke and ten letters of Paul. Some scholars say the orthodox fathers may have been compelled to begin defining the biblical canon in response to Marcion.[54] Martin Hengel disagrees vehemently, "The four-Gospel collection did not result from the attempt to defend the 'apostolic' Jesus tradition against his radical attack. It was the other way around."[55] Settling the argument over Marcion's agency is unnecessary. Scripture affirms heresies will be used by God providentially to highlight approved teachers (1 Cor 11:19).

---

[51] Justin, *Apology* 67; *The Apostolic Fathers*, 186.

[52] Justin, *Apology* 66; *The Apostolic Fathers*, 185.

[53] "The story of the formation of what is known as the New Testament 'canon' is a story of the demand for authority." Moule, *The Birth of the New Testament*, 178.

[54] Thiselton, *Companion*, 484. Campenhausen opined, "the first Christian canon remains his peculiar and unique creation, one in which neither churchman nor gnostic anticipated him." Campenhausen, *The Formation of the Christian Bible*, trans. J. A. Baker (Philadelphia: Fortress, 1972), 148; Also, see Dockery, "Special Revelation," 139–40 (see introduction, n. 24); Adam Harwood, *Christian Theology: Biblical, Historical, and Systematic* (Bellingham, WA: Lexham, 2022), 91–113.

[55] Hengel argues that efforts to reduce the Gospels by excision (as with Marcion) or to harmonize them (as with Tatian) were unsuccessful, "because the (three or) four Gospels had already largely found recognition before him [Marcion], and because from the beginning names from the apostolic age were connected with these Gospels." Hengel, *The Four Gospels and the One Gospel of Jesus Christ*, 55–56. Hengel believes his opponents in this matter were driven by "latent anti-Jewish modern liberal Protestantism." Hengel, *The Four Gospels and the One Gospel of Jesus Christ*, 33.

By the late second century, identifying the accepted Christian authors and their writings became a matter of importance. The growing cadre of Gnostic gospels, acts, and epistles often used the names of apostles surreptitiously to gain legitimacy.[56] In response, pastors like Irenaeus of Lyons felt duty bound to protect the flock from wolves "whose language resembles ours, while their sentiments are very different."[57] The case of the *Gospel of Peter* provides an instructive example. Around 200, the bishop of Antioch withdrew his previous approval of the text in the church. Serapion's reason for excluding the *Gospel of Peter* included its pseudonymity: "We receive both Peter and the other apostles of Christ," but "the writings which falsely bear their names we reject, as men of experience, knowing that such were not handed down to us."[58] The bishop also detected that text's unorthodox content, after reading it carefully in comparison with apostolic writings already in widespread church use. Serapion concluded the spurious gospel "breathes an entirely different atmosphere from that of the canonical Gospels."[59] Serapion objected both to its pseudonymity and its departure from the canon of faith, which had come to him with the apostolic witness.[60]

V. Criteria for Recognizing the Canon

Traditional Christian theology affirms a book's inclusion in the canon depends ultimately upon the identification of its inspiration by the Holy Spirit.[61] Uncomfortable with relying only on the internal criterion of the testimony of the Holy Spirit, some theologians have sought to identify the external factors which helped the church recognize a particular prophetic or apostolic text was inspired. Once its inspiration was identified, a text

---

[56] Willis Barnstone and Marvin Meyer, *The Gnostic Bible* (Boston: Shambhala, 2003).

[57] Irenaeus, *Against Heresies*, Preface; *The Apostolic Fathers*, 315.

[58] Eusebius, *Ecclesiastical History* 6.12; Moule, *The Birth of the New Testament*, 193.

[59] Moule, *The Birth of the New Testament*, 193.

[60] At issue was its insufficient view of Christ's humanity. Craig D. Allert, "The State of the New Testament Canon in the Second Century: Putting Tatian's Diatessaron in Perspective," *Bulletin of Biblical Research* 9 (1999): 15.

[61] Barr calls this the "really strict old-fashioned view," as if something established is necessarily errant. Barr, *Holy Scripture*, 49.

could and should be included in the canon, thus sealing its authority for the church. Because of the paucity of early sources, the process of canonization is somewhat mysterious from the modern-day historian's perspective. But we believe the church was consciously guided by the Spirit to recognize the inspired texts which should be included in the canon.[62]

Correlating the intrinsic value given to a text by the inspiration of the Holy Spirit with the church's recognition of that inspiration is key to describing canonization.[63] Two aspects must be held together in the discussion about the verification of a particular text for inclusion in the canon: On the one hand, Bavinck correctly states, "The canonicity of the Bible books is rooted in their existence. They have authority of themselves, by their own right, because they exist. It is the Spirit of the Lord who guided the authors in writing them and the church in acknowledging them."[64] On the other hand, we can detect external criteria useful for verifying texts for the canon, as with Serapion's evaluation of the *Gospel of Peter.*

Scholars examining the early church's external logic for recognizing the biblical canon speak of "tests," "principles," "factors," or "criteria" for canonization. They do not mean, however, that early church leaders were quality inspectors standing in a Bible factory with a checklist evaluating texts. Nor should it be assumed anyone today may employ such tests to determine whether a new text, or a newly discovered ancient text, might be added to the canon.[65] Rather, identifying a criterion helps disclose the rationale behind the early church's decisions. They inform us as to how the church became convinced a document qualified as Holy Scripture.[66] Dimitris Kyrtatis

---

[62] Kyrtatis agrees, "the New Testament canon was the product of a conscious decision not a cumulative, haphazard and happenstance process." Dimitris J. Kyrtatis, "Historical Aspects of the Formation of the New Testament Canon," in *Canon and Canonicity: The Formation and Use of Scripture,* ed. Einar Thomassen (Copenhagen: Museum Tusculanum Press, 2010), 32.

[63] Peckham says a text's divine appointment renders it a member of the "intrinsic canon." Peckham, *Canonical Theology,* 5–6.

[64] Bavinck, *Reformed Dogmatics: Prolegomena,* 401.

[65] Cf. Dietrich Ritschl, *The Logic of Theology: A Brief Account of the Relationship between Basic Concepts in Theology,* trans. John Bowden (Philadelphia: Fortress, 1987).

[66] "The Canon has not been produced, as some say, by a single act of human beings, but little by little by God, the director of minds and times." Valentin Loescher, *De Causa Linguae Ebraea* (1706), cited in Bavinck, *Reformed Dogmatics: Prolegomena,* 400.

argues that even before the final decisions were recorded in episcopal and conciliar writings, there was a "canon principle" at work compelling church-men to define the canon.[67] Once acknowledged, the church's canonical list became the normative authority for identifying texts as usable in worship and in doctrine.

We may describe the first criterion as *the test of worship* or liturgy.[68] Canonization allowed churches to identify texts which were suitable for reading during public Christian worship. Recognition for suitability in wor-ship was implied in the time of Justin Martyr, as noted above. Providing more depth, the Muratorian Fragment (ca. 180) identified such texts as the *Shepherd of Hermas* neither as Scripture nor as spurious. The fragment opined that the writing of Hermas, whose brother was the bishop of Rome (ca. 140), "ought indeed to be read; but it cannot be read publicly to the people in church."[69] Despite its clear correlation of a canon based on acceptable use in worship, the test of liturgy was primarily a lagging indicator or concluding factor rather than a leading indicator. A text's use in worship rested upon the authority it had already garnered in the churches. An authoritative text must convey faithfully the apostolic teaching about Jesus and our reconciliation with God. In other words, the leading external test of a canonical text was its conveyance of the gospel of Jesus Christ in accord with the rule of faith.

The second but more significant criterion, therefore, was *the gospel test*, which compared a text to the rule of faith received from the apostles. Timothy was instructed, "Hold on to the pattern of sound teaching that you have heard from me" (2 Tim 1:13a). This pattern was centered on "the faith and love that are in Christ Jesus" (2 Tim 1:13b). The gospel test asks whether a certain text preserves "the faith delivered to the saints once for all" (Jude 3). The New Testament is filled with admonitions to know and pro-claim the received standard of teaching about faith in Christ. It was not only providential but necessary for the church to recognize its pattern of teaching. In turn, this pattern became the conceptual standard in Christian worship

---

[67] Kyrtatis, "Historical Aspects," 32–34.

[68] Thomassen, "Some Ideas," 19–20.

[69] Edmon L. Gallagher and John D. Meade, *The Biblical Canon Lists from Early Christianity: Texts and Analysis* (New York: Oxford University Press, 2017), 181; Michael F. Bird, *What Christians Ought to Believe: An Introduction to Christian Doctrine through the Apostles' Creed* (Grand Rapids: Zondervan, 2016), 35.

and theology. As previously noted, this first "canon," the church's use of the apostolic teaching pattern as a "norm," preceded the church's recognition of the "canon" as a standard "list" of inspired books. The canon of faith as a norm achieved confessional status in early forms like the Old Roman Creed, which lay behind today's widely used Apostles' Creed. Michael Bird argues the credal canon and the literary canon thus developed together in a "symbiotic relationship." "The two entities were mutually creating and mutually reinforcing."[70] The gospel test or rule of faith both derived from the apostolic testimony and provided the key for accepting or rejecting texts.

The third criterion, *the apostolic test*, lent key support to the gospel test. The criterion of apostolicity privileged the witness of Christ's immediate followers during his earthly ministry. The apostolic test treated a text as worthy of inclusion in the canon because its teaching was conveyed by the apostles of Jesus Christ, and they were directly authorized by Christ to teach his words. The apostolic criterion asks whether an apostle called by the risen Lord wrote a text or approved its contents. Jesus's earthly disciples, including Peter, John, and Matthew, were called through post-resurrection appearances, so their writings were naturally deemed authoritative. Saul was converted after the death of Christ, but he was called to join the apostolate directly through an appearance of Christ and was renamed Paul. The apostolate included Jesus's brothers in the flesh, James and Jude, who were called after the resurrection. The disciples of these apostles included Mark, Luke, and the author of Hebrews. Their writings were thus deemed apostolic by approval.

The Gospels of Matthew and John were written by apostles, while the Gospels of Mark and Luke were written by disciples of Peter and Paul. Peter resided in Rome toward the end of his earthly ministry, and Mark's Gospel seems to have been approved by him. The early church came to include four Gospels in the biblical canon. Each was considered apostolic, but many churches likely used only one at first. For instance, Mark was used first in Rome and little elsewhere. One positive byproduct of Constantine's influence was in the provision of the collection of all four Gospels to major churches in the empire. It subsequently became common to include Matthew, Mark, Luke, and John together.[71] Through recognizing the four Gospels as a unit,

---

[70] Bird, *What Christians Ought to Believe*, 30.
[71] Kyrtatis, "Historical Aspects."

the churches were united, orthodoxy was established, and freedom in worship encouraged.

VI. Did the Church Create or Recognize the Canon?

Augustine wrote, "For my part, I should not believe the gospel except as moved by the authority of the Catholic Church."[72] Wrenched from its context, Augustine's statement might perhaps be interpreted as granting the church authority over the Christian faith. If so, the church's authority would be sufficient to create the canon of the Scriptures which convey the faith. But such a grand claim would be contested by evangelicals on one side and skeptics on the other. The critical question before us now is, "Did the church create the biblical canon or did it merely canonize what it recognized as inspired?" There are three primary answers regarding the church's authority in either creating or recognizing the biblical canon. We may refer to them as the Tridentine view, the Reformation view, and the Liberal view.

1. The Tridentine View

Roman Catholic apologists during the sixteenth century appealed to Augustine's statement to assert the church's authority, defend papal tradition, and refute the Protestant doctrine of *sola scriptura*. Protestant apologists disputed the Roman interpretation of Augustine, but Romanists during the Tridentine period believed apostolic authority resided supremely in the episcopal succession centered in the bishop of Rome.[73] The Roman council of Trent (1545–1563) treated unwritten tradition as inspired revelation, seemingly creating two streams of revelation.[74] The First Vatican Council

---

[72] Augustine was arguing hotly against naming Mani an apostle of Jesus Christ rather than carefully crafting an axiom relating the church to the faith. Augustine, *Against the Epistle of Manichaeus*, 5; Philip Schaff, ed., *Augustine: The Writings against the Manichaens, and against the Donatists*, Nicene and Post-Nicene Fathers, First Series, 14 vols. (1887; Reprint, Peabody, MA: Hendrickson, 1994), 4:131.

[73] Jaroslav Pelikan, *The Christian Tradition: A History of the Development of Doctrine*, 5 vols. (Chicago: University of Chicago Press, 1984), 4:342–43.

[74] "The council clearly perceives that this truth and rule are contained in written books and in unwritten traditions which were received by the apostles from the

(1869–1870) retained Trent's respect for tradition and advanced the doctrine of papal infallibility. However, Vatican I clarified the Roman theology on the canon, declaring the canon was authoritative, not due to the church, nor due to an inerrant text, but because Scripture was "written under the inspiration of the holy Spirit."[75]

2. The Reformation View

From the beginning of the Reformation, Protestants deemed the canon authoritative, not by reason of the church's authority, but because the early church recognized the Spirit's inspiration. The writings collected in the canon had "imposed themselves on the church by their intrinsic apostolic authority."[76] The Reformation view located apostolic authority within the canon by reason of the Spirit's inspiration. The church's agency was entirely instrumental. "Authentically canonical Scripture was self-verifying."[77] If Protestants needed to speak of apostolic succession, they located it in the apostolic writings rather than the episcopal office, much less the episcopal office of Rome.

3. The Liberal View

Liberal theologians like Adolf von Harnack portrayed the early church as comprised of powerful warring factions. Harnack deemed Gnostics and fellow

---

mouth of Christ himself, or else have come down to us, handed on as it were from the apostles themselves at the inspiration of the holy Spirit." Council of Trent, Session 4; Norman P. Tanner, ed., *Decrees of the Ecumenical Councils*, 2 vols. (Washington, DC: Georgetown University Press, 1990), 2:663.

[75] First Vatican Council, Session 3; Tanner, *Decrees of the Ecumenical Councils*, 2:806. The Tridentine view has had a revival of sorts in the modern period, with critics like William J. Abraham, who considered the canon as "epistemic criteria" an ecclesiastical innovation. William J. Abraham, *Canon and Criterion in Christian Theology* (Oxford: Oxford University Press, 1998), 1–2. For a thorough evangelical critique of Abraham's concept of canon, see Feinberg, *Light in a Dark Place*, 456–67.

[76] Oscar Cullmann, *La Tradition: Problème Exégétique, Historique et Théologique* (Paris: Delachaux et Niestlé, 1953). See relevant translations and discussion in Yarnell, *The Formation of Christian Doctrine*, 128–33.

[77] Pelikan, *The Christian Tradition*, 4:340.

enthusiasts like Marcion the first theologians. Marcion's elevation of the writings of Paul at the expense of the Old Testament prompted powerful churchmen to restrict authority to a sacred canon comprised of Pauline texts alongside the Old Testament and various Hebrew Christian texts. This process of canonization led the church to treat the Spirit and the apostles as "correlative conceptions." The Holy Spirit did not, in the liberal view, inspire the writings which led the church to recognize the canon. Rather, the doctrine of inspiration by the Holy Spirit was invented to buttress the authority of the canon.[78]

Contemporary evangelicals affirm the inspiration of the texts collected in the canon and thus embrace the Reformation view. The written Word possesses intrinsic authority. While scholars speak of tests of canonicity, the inclusion of a particular text within the authoritative canon is ultimately based upon the church's Spirit-led reception and recognition of that text's original inspiration. The church's role is to discern, not to determine. The churches' declarations about the biblical canon do not grant theological authority but recognize its prior existence. Divine inspiration grants authority to a text; ecclesial canonization simply acknowledges the authority of that text. For evangelicals, the two key doctrines of the Spirit's original inspiration of the inerrant prophetic and apostolic texts and of the Spirit's continuing preservation of infallible copies of their texts through the churches' recognition of an authoritative canon constitute a theological *sine qua non*.

It will be helpful to remember the church is both a human and a divine institution. The church was established by Jesus Christ (Matt 16:18) and has been granted his continual presence (Matt 18:15–20). As noted above, Christ promised to guide and protect the apostolic witness by his Holy Spirit. The people of Christ are "the people of God" (Heb 11:25). The church is thus manifestly a triune institution. But the church is also comprised of human creatures. As an historical institution, the church's complex process

---

[78] Adolf von Harnack, *The History of Dogma*, trans. Neil Buchanan, 7 vols. (1961; Eugene, OR: Wipf and Stock, 1997), 2:53–54. Cf. Bart D. Ehrman, *Lost Christianities: The Battles for Scripture and the Faiths We Never Knew* (New York: Oxford University Press, 2003).

of recognizing the biblical canon need not pose a stumbling block to its reception. The historic church was granted divine truth through the inspired apostles' written texts.[79] We believe God's Spirit led the early church to recognize these writings and collect them into a canon considered authoritative by virtue of inspiration.

VII. The Two Testaments

The canon developed in two large phases. First was the church's reception of the Hebrew Bible, which Christians came to call the Old Testament. Second came the church's recognition of the apostolic writings, which they called the New Testament.

1. The Reception of the Old Testament

The Hebrew Bible was affirmed by the Lord Jesus Christ. He clearly stated neither a "jot" nor a "tittle" of the Law would pass away or remain unfulfilled (Matt 5:18 KJV). "Jesus' use of the Old Testament texts rests on his conviction that these writings were the revelation of God through faithful prophets, a conviction that is decisive for his interpretation of Scripture and that surfaces explicitly in a number of places in the Gospels."[80] Following Christ, his disciples adopted their Lord's view of Scripture. "What was indispensable to the Redeemer must always be indispensable to the redeemed."[81]

Moreover, Jesus read the Hebrew Scriptures through a Christological hermeneutic encompassing the entire threefold division of the Old Testament (Luke 24:27, 32, 44–48). Having conveyed his high view of Scripture and his hermeneutic to his disciples, it should come as no surprise that their writings are filled with citations, quotations, and allusions to the Messiah taken from

---

[79] On the Reformed distinction between the communicable as opposed to the incommunicable attributes of God, see Garrett Jr., *Systematic Theology*, 1:234–35 (see chap. 1, n. 47).

[80] E. Earle Ellis, *The Old Testament in Early Christianity: Canon and Interpretation in the Light of Modern Research* (Grand Rapids: Baker, 1991), 126.

[81] This early twentieth-century dictum by G. A. Smith was reaffirmed in Bruce, *The Canon of Scripture*, 276.

Hebrew law, prophecy, and poetry.[82] For instance, the first Christian sermon exposited the gospel of Jesus Christ through Old Testament prophecy (Acts 2:14–40). Similarly, the book of Hebrews is an extended sermon upon Old Testament Messianic texts.

The five books of Moses, the *Torah*, were the first Hebrew writings accorded authoritative status, as seen in the rediscovery and reception of Deuteronomy in the days of the last great king of Israel (2 Kgs 22:8–11; 23:2–3). The Jews subsequently recognized the writings by and about the Prophets, the *Nevi'im*, as well the authority of various Writings, the *Ketuvim*. The official adoption of a Jewish canon of Scripture, which Christians began to call the "Old Testament" in the second century,[83] has been disputed. Stephen Chapman argues the debate has been complicated by confusion over the meanings of "Scripture," "canon," and "canonization." He suggests the Jews gradually recognized the full canon of Hebrew Scripture after receiving its "core canon."[84] The people of God recognized the written "Scriptures" were inspired, so the people of God accorded the Scriptures the status of an authoritative "canon" through a process known as "canonization."

Jewish tradition held that Ezra compiled the canon while leading the returned exiles to hear, interpret, and covenant to obey the law of Moses (Neh 7:73b–8:18; Ezra 10:1–4). Offering the earliest date by a Christian scholar for a relatively complete canon, Roger T. Beckwith argued its collection occurred at least by the time of Judas Maccabeus in 165 BC. The first-century Jewish historian, Josephus, indicated the Hebrew canon was set by 100 BC, mentioning twenty-two books. Certain texts, such as the Minor Prophets, which Christians today divide into two or more books were combined in his count.

Two canon traditions existed in early Judaism, the "Palestinian canon" and the "Hellenistic canon." It was said the Hellenistic canon was translated

---

[82] The detailed 1,239-page project of Gregory Beale and Donald Carson is but one demonstration of the dependence of the New Testament upon the Old Testament. G. K. Beale and D. A. Carson, *Commentary on the New Testament Use of the Old Testament* (Grand Rapids: Baker, 2007).

[83] McDonald, *The Origin of the Bible*, 16–18.

[84] Stephen B. Chapman, "The Canon Debate: What It Is and Why It Matters," *Journal of Theological Interpretation* 4, no. 2 (Fall 2010): 273–94.

and agreed upon by seventy scribes, thus providing the common name for
the Greek Old Testament, the Septuagint (LXX), literally, "the seventy."
Both Jewish canon traditions recognized the same twenty-two books, but
the Hellenistic canon included several other books written after 200 BC.
These additional books were deemed "Deuterocanonical," which means they
came second in or to the canon, by early eastern Christians. They were called
"Apocrypha" by Western Christians.[85] Liberal scholars once argued the rabbinic Council of Jamnia closed the canon in AD 90. However, the Jamnian
hypothesis is now panned by both Jewish and Christian scholars. Instead, a
"general consensus" regarding the canon of Hebrew Scripture likely occurred
well before the Fall of Jerusalem in AD 70.[86]

For their part, Christians assumed the Old Testament was settled by
the time of Jesus. Our Lord affirmed its three sections, and he and his
apostles made prolific references to its books. The status accorded the
Deuterocanonical or Apocryphal books has not been entirely settled, but
the New Testament does not explicitly treat any of them as canonical. The
Roman Catholic and Eastern Orthodox churches honor these extra books,
but Western Protestants downplay their importance. On the one hand,
Roman Catholics do not place these texts in the same category of inspiration as the Old and New Testaments. On the other hand, Martin Luther
considered the Apocrypha "useful" even if not inspired.[87]

2. The Recognition of the New Testament

Our New Testament books were written by the apostles and their approved
disciples during the first century, with the latest contribution possibly being

---

[85] Garrett, *Systematic Theology*, 1:138–39. Among the fourteen books in the
Apocrypha are important historical texts like 1 and 2 Esdras, Judith, the Wisdom of
Solomon, Ecclesiasticus, and 1 and 2 Maccabees.

[86] Robert C. Newman, "The Council of Jamnia and the Old Testament Canon,"
The Westminster Theological Journal 38, no. 3 (Spring 1976): 349. Cf. Jack P. Lewis,
"Jamnia after Forty Years," *Hebrew Union College Annual* 70–71 (1999–2000): 259.

[87] Jerome did not include the Apocrypha in the canon, considering them *libri
ecclesiastici* rather than *libri canonici*. *The Oxford Dictionary of the Christian Church*,
2nd ed., ed. F. L. Cross and E. A. Livingstone (New York: Oxford University Press,
1974), 70–71. Augustine at first included them but later referred to them as books
outside the church. Thiselton, *Companion*, 29–30.

the Revelation of John around AD 90. The four Gospels of Matthew, Mark, Luke, and John were all written "well within the natural life span of the apostolic generation."[88] According to Justin, the Gospels were "drawn up" either by "his apostles" or by "those who followed them."[89] Matthew and John presumably belong in the first category, while Mark and Luke belong in the latter.[90] Irenaeus referred to the Gospels collectively as the "quadri-form Gospel," which alone should be received. His view ultimately prevailed among the churches.[91]

Irenaeus leaned heavily on the apostolic test while refuting Gnostic teachings. He pointed out the orthodox, unlike the Gnostics, could trace their teachings through their churches to the apostles. Irenaeus himself guaranteed apostolic teaching through Polycarp, the bishop of Smyrna he knew as a child. And Polycarp was taught directly by the apostles.[92] Eusebius of Caesarea similarly says the three Synoptic Gospels were approved by the apostle John. "He accepted them and bore witness to their truthfulness." In his own Gospel John filled the gaps left by the other Gospels.[93] The Pauline letters seem to have been collected early and passed around the churches.[94] The longest decisions over the inclusion of certain texts occurred with certain catholic epistles as well as Revelation, the latter due to its earthy millenarianism.[95]

---

[88] Moule, *The Birth of the New Testament*, 185.

[89] Justin, *Dialogue* 103; "Dialogue with Trypho," in *The Apostolic Fathers*, 251.

[90] Papias, a contemporary of Justin, provides details regarding the authorship of the Gospel of Mark. Papias repeatedly affirmed the efforts of Peter's protégé: Mark "wrote down accurately whatever he remembered" from Peter, "made no mistake in thus writing some things as he remembered them," and "took especial care, not to omit anything he had heard, and not to put anything fictitious into the statements." Papias *Fragment* 6; "Fragments of Papias," in *The Apostolic Fathers*, 155.

[91] Dimitris J. Kyrtatis, "Historical Aspects of the Formation of the New Testament Canon," in *Canon and Canonicity*, ed. Thomassen, 39–43.

[92] Irenaeus, *Against Heresies* 3.3.2–4; *The Apostolic Fathers*, 415–16.

[93] Eusebius, *Ecclesiastical History* 3.24; Philip Schaff and Henry Wace, eds., *Eusebius: Church History, Life of Constantine the Great, and Oration in Praise of Constantine*, Nicene and Post-Nicene Fathers, Second Series, 14 vols. (1890; Reprint, Peabody, MA: Hendrickson, 1994), 1:153.

[94] Thomassen, "Some Ideas," 16–17.

[95] Thomassen, "Some Ideas," 22–23. Andreas Caesariensis, writing around 500, wrote, "With regard to the inspiration of the book (Revelation), we deem it

Eusebius divided the various candidates for the New Testament canon into three categories: First came the "undisputed" writings, "which according to ecclesiastical tradition are true and genuine and commonly accepted." The undisputed "catalogue," by the early fourth century, included "the holy quaternion of the Gospels," the Acts of the Apostles, the Pauline epistles, 1 Peter, and 1 John. Second came the "disputed writings," which were accepted by some churches. These disputed writings included the epistles of James, Jude, and 2 Peter, as well as 2 John, 3 John, and the Apocalypse. Eusebius believed the disputed works would be settled "at the proper time" through reference to "the testimony of the ancients." In a third category, Eusebius placed the "rejected" writings, including the Shepherd of Hermas, the Acts of Paul, and the Apocalypse of Peter. Some rejected works were unobjectionable, while others were definitively heretical. The latter included many "cited by the heretics under the name of the apostles."[96]

Christian writings indicate implicit acceptance of the bulk of the New Testament books by the end of the second century. The earliest Christian writers treated the apostolic books both referentially and reverentially.[97] Irenaeus utilized nearly all our current twenty-seven books and defended them at length against pretenders.[98] The first extant and complete canonical list including all the current New Testament books is found in an annual festal letter of Athanasius. Writing in 367, he delimited the New Testament canon to twenty-seven books, commending their deferential use as "the springs of salvation."[99] The first local Western councils to affirm the complete canon met in the late fourth century. Augustine

---

superfluous to add another word; for the blessed Gregory Theologus and Cyril, and even men of still older date, Papias, Irenaeus, Methodius, and Hippolytus, bore entirely satisfactory testimony to it." Papias *Fragment* 8; *The Apostolic Fathers*, 155.

[96] Eusebius, *Ecclesiastical History* 3.24–25; *Eusebius*, 153–57.

[97] We must be careful not to assume every reference ascribes authority. Instead, each reference in the early fathers must be read in its context. Such a task is beyond the confines of this study. Cf. McDonald, *The Origin of the Bible*, 41.

[98] Kyrtatis, "Historical Aspects," 39. Campenhausen sees Irenaeus as instrumental in developing the Christian idea of an authoritative canon. Campenhausen, *The Formation of the Christian Bible*, 182.

[99] Athanasius, *Epistula Festalis* 39.18–19; *The Biblical Canon Lists from Early Christianity*, 123–24.

agreed with their conclusions, referring to "the authority of the great majority of catholic churches, including of course those that were found worthy to have apostolic seats and receive apostolic letters."[100] The first major council to affirm the biblical canon was Trent, but its decrees were never received as authoritative either among Protestants or the Eastern Orthodox. Whatever a council says, the conclusive evidence remains not a conciliar declaration but the Christian consensus in recognizing a text's inspiration.[101]

VIII. From Canonization to Interpretation via Translation

Before interpreting Scripture and developing theology, we must correlate three disciplines within biblical studies: canon studies, translation, and hermeneutics. Hermeneutics as the discipline of interpretation must be carefully distinguished from the logically prior yet closely related disciplines of canonization and translation. First, there is *canonization*. The recognition and demarcation of the canon of Scripture identifies the authoritative text which should be made available to people in each receiving culture. Second, there is the process of *translation*. The translation of the canon makes the text available to people and churches in new cultures with different languages. Third comes *hermeneutics*, the science of interpretation. The churches are empowered by and responsible to the Spirit of God for receiving and interpreting as well as obeying and proclaiming the Word of God, which requires further translation.

The identification of an authoritative text through the process of canonization precedes both its translation and its interpretation. Identifying the best available texts in the canon is a sub-discipline within canon studies known today as "textual criticism." Textual criticism in some sense was evident as early as Origen but experienced a renaissance during the early sixteenth century. Desiderius Erasmus of Rotterdam helped renew

---

[100] Augustine, *On Christian Teaching* 2.8.12.24; *The Biblical Canon Lists from Early Christianity*, 226.

[101] Bruce, *The Canon of Scripture*, 279.

textual criticism by compiling an authoritative edition of the Greek New Testament. This Renaissance-inspired textual tradition is now known as the Textus Receptus.[102] Erasmus attended to the significant linguistic differences between the Greek textual tradition and the Roman Catholic Church's official Latin translation, the Vulgate. The Textus Receptus helped Catholic Humanists and Protestant Reformers identify not only textual problems within the Vulgate but also Western theological divergences.

Despite the significance of the Textus Receptus in prompting the Western Church to reform itself theologically, it relied heavily upon medieval Byzantine texts. These relatively late texts themselves required correction by reference to newly discovered older extant texts. One important example concerns the so-called Johannine Comma of 1 John 5:7–8, which seemed to provide a strong proof for the doctrine of the Trinity.[103] Comparison between the numerous available texts, from the early church through the medieval period, demonstrate the Johannine Comma is doubtless a late scribal addition.[104] The field of textual criticism continues to build upon yet correct the Textus Receptus.

During the nineteenth and twentieth centuries, the labors of Brooke Foss Westcott and Fenton John Anthony Hort in Cambridge, England,[105]

---

[102] Erasmus of Rotterdam, *Novum Instrumentum Omne* (Basel, 1516). "Textus Receptus" refers to the tradition of printed Greek New Testaments before 1633, including editions by Robert Stephanus and Theodore Beza. These editions provided Reformation Protestants with the authoritative text used in translation and interpretation.

[103] The addition, which was likely a scholarly comment later included in the text, reads, "testify in heaven: the Father, the Word, and the Holy Spirit, and these three are one. And there are three who bear witness on earth." On the hermeneutical difficulties generated by the Johannine Comma, see Yarnell, *God the Trinity*, 8–9 (see chap. 1, n. 78).

[104] Metzger provides the standard technical account. Metzger and Ehrman, *The Text of the New Testament*, 146–48, 162. Bart Ehrman has been roundly criticized for making mercurial revisions, causing significant omissions, and introducing numerous scribal errors into his edition of Metzger's classic description of textual criticism. D. C. Parker, "Review Article: The Text of the New Testament," *Journal of Theological Studies* NS, 57 (2006): 551–67.

[105] Brooke Foss Westcott and Fenton John Anthony Hort, *The New Testament in the Original Greek: The Text Revised* (New York: Harper and Brothers, 1881).

alongside those of Eberhard Nestle and Kurt Aland in Münster, Germany,[106] were instrumental in providing a critical text.[107] Technical scholars agree the critical Greek text we now possess is highly reliable.[108] From a theological perspective, James Leo Garrett's conclusion is widely accepted: "Actually only a small portion of the Bible is under any uncertainty as to its textual authenticity, and no major doctrine is imperiled by any alternate textual readings."[109] While scholars continue to clarify minor divergences, the dogmas of the Christian faith are clearly affirmed in the critical text.

Utilizing the best critical text, translators of the canon have typically provided first portions of Scripture, then eventually the entire Bible, to new churches in their own languages. Translation thus depends upon two other disciplines: It is bound by the canon and its textual critical apparatus on the one side and marked by choices regarding interpretation on the other side. Translation is, therefore, a mediating discipline within biblical studies. Its own responsibilities should not be underplayed. Translators must be skillful with the original languages, skillful with the receptor language, and careful not to impose their own denominational or personally peculiar interpretations upon the new translation. This is where dependence upon the rule of faith, available in the credal legacy of the universal church, becomes necessary.

---

[106] The Nestle-Aland text of the New Testament is currently in its 28th edition. *Novum Testamentum Graece* (Stuttgart: Deutsche Bibelgesellschaft, 2017). For the Hebrew text, see *Biblia Hebraica Stuttgartensia*, ed. A. Alt, O. Eißfeldt, P. Kahle, R. Kittel et al. (Stuttgart: Deutsche Bibelgesellschaft, 1984). Cf. *Biblia Sacra Utriusque Testamenti Editio Hebraica et Graeca* (Stuttgart: Deutsche Bibelgesellschaft, 1994).

[107] Kurt Aland's Institute for New Testament Textual Research at the University of Münster and the worldwide United Bible Societies serve in distinct ways as central agencies for preserving and disseminating the best critical text from the manuscript tradition today.

[108] "Thus in nearly two-thirds of the New Testament text, the seven [critical] editions of the Greek New Testament which we have reviewed are in complete accord, with no differences other than in orthographical details (e.g., the spelling of names, etc.). Verses in which any one of the seven editions differs by a single word are not counted. This result is quite amazing, demonstrating a far greater agreement among the Greek texts of the New Testament during the past century than textual scholars would have suspected." Kurt Aland and Barbara Aland, *The Text of the New Testament: An Introduction to the Critical Editions and to the Theory and Practice of Modern Textual Criticism*, 2nd ed. (Grand Rapids: Eerdmans, 1995), 29–30.

[109] Garrett, *Systematic Theology*, 1:154.

It is, moreover, wise that the creation of a translation be performed in community. The adoption or revision of a translation awaits critical reception by churches in the host culture. Once the canonical text has been translated and critically received, the text must then be interpreted by new churches in healthy dialectical conversation with the churches of Jesus Christ through the ages. It is to the subject of the Bible's truthfulness, as well as to the historic and modern practices of moving from Scripture to theology, that we now turn.

8

The Truthfulness and Inerrancy of Scripture

In what sense might we be able to confess that Scripture, which contains evidence of genuine human authorship and of being written in a time-related context, remains also theologically normative for all times and places? Must we conclude that Scripture is wholly descriptive, and that the student of Scripture is little more than an antique keeper or, at best, an historian who displays his or her exhibits in a museum dedicated merely to the past? We believe such a descriptive approach is entirely unacceptable, because it fails to account for the dynamic experience of the biblical authors and their communities of faith with the eternal God, an experience that continues to this day.[1] Perhaps we might rephrase the question: Does any Bible student completely accept a descriptive approach? Is not the real issue to what extent is the Bible normative for the contemporary church? Even Rudolf Bultmann, who maintained that first-century cultural patterns cannot be considered normative, nevertheless sought to reinterpret those patterns for the contemporary church.[2]

In chapter 4, we considered how truth is grounded in the very nature of God himself. We also argued that God graces Scripture with his ultimate truth. In subsequent chapters, we established the profound relationship of sacred Scripture to God through the divine-human person of Jesus Christ

---

[1] Guthrie, *New Testament Theology*, 953–82 (see chap. 5, n. 20).

[2] Rudolf Bultmann, *New Testament Theology*, trans. K. Grobel (New York: Scribners, 1955).

and by the inspiration of the Holy Spirit. In this chapter, we are now ready to advocate more fully the truthfulness of Scripture as that attribute which makes the Holy Bible theologically and ethically normative for every human being in every culture. We begin with an affirmation of the normativity of Scripture, followed by a review of the history of the truthfulness, authority, and trustworthiness of Scripture in the eyes of the church. We then proceed to a definition of biblical inerrancy, followed by a series of affirmations.

I. Holy Scripture as Normative

Although the cultural background and environment have radically changed since the biblical writings were penned, the human condition has not changed. It is to the human condition, men and women created in the image of God, yet fallen, that the unity of the biblical message speaks in a normative manner. We maintain this confession for the following four reasons: the Scriptures are the result of divine inspiration; they proclaim the saving acts of God; they are historically proximate to the saving acts of God; and they are based on the prophetic-apostolic authority.[3] Even with cultural advancements and scientific progress, the need of men and women for a right standing before God and right relationship with God remains unchanged. The reason is that even the advancing wisdom and knowledge of the world cannot help humanity in the ultimate aspects of life (see 1 Corinthians 1–4). The basic problem is the same across the ages: How are sinful humans to approach a holy God, and how are these persons to live in relationship to the life-giving Spirit of God?

We believe divinely inspired teaching concerning God and matters relating to God and his creation (*sub specie Dei*) are normative and sufficient for the life and practice of the followers of Christ in all contexts and cultures. When such matters are proclaimed and confessed in the twenty-first century, however, it may also be necessary for teachers to contextualize applications that awaken modern readers to an awareness that the Bible

---

[3] R. P. C. Hanson, *The Bible as a Norm of Faith* (Durham, UK: University of Durham Press, 1963), 7; Hanson, *Tradition in the Early Church* (London: SCM, 1962), 213–24; H. E. W. Turner, *The Pattern of Christian Truth: A Study in the Relations between Orthodoxy and Heresy in the Early Church* (London: Mowbray, 1954); and E. J. Carnell, *The Case for Orthodox Theology* (Philadelphia: Fortress, 1959).

speaks in relevant ways to contemporary issues in church and society.[4] When Scripture is approached from this perspective, it will be necessary to determine underlying principles for all portions of Scripture that address the contemporary situation, even if the direct teaching of Scripture is somehow limited by cultural-temporal factors (e.g., 1 Cor 16:20; Eph 6:5; 1 Tim 5:23). Believers will recognize that this is the case because of the two-sided character of Scripture. Because it is authored by humans in specific contexts, certain teachings may be contextually limited; but because Scripture is divinely inspired, the underlying principles remain normative and applicable for the church in every age. When approaching the Bible, recognizing its authoritative and normative character, we can discover truth[5] and its ramifications for the answers to life's ultimate questions as well as guidelines and principles for godly living in the twenty-first-century world.[6] Before exploring the question of the Bible's truthfulness, it will be informative to see what key leaders and thinkers throughout the history of the church have believed about the Bible's truthfulness, including those who have raised questions about the reliability and dependability of the Bible.

II. The Truthfulness of the Bible: A Historical Overview

1. The Patristic Period

Much early and widespread evidence indicates that the early church in near unanimity confessed the truthfulness and authority of the Scriptures. Justin Martyr held that the human authors of Scripture were moved by the

---

[4] John Jefferson Davis, "Contextualization and the Nature of Theology," in *The Necessity of Systematic Theology*, ed. John Jefferson Davis (Grand Rapids: Baker, 1980), 169–85; Clark Pinnock, *Scripture Principle* (San Francisco: Harper and Row, 1984), 210–21; David Hesselgrave, "Contextualization and Revelational Epistemology," in *Hermeneutics Inerrancy, and the Bible*, ed. Earl D. Radmacher and Robert D. Preuss (Grand Rapids: Zondervan, 1986), 693–764; John D. Morrison, *Has God Said? Scripture, the Word of God, and the Crisis of Theological Authority* (Eugene, OR: Pickwick, 2006).

[5] Anthony C. Thiselton, "Truth," in *Dictionary of New Testament Theology*, ed. Colin Brown, 3 vols. (Grand Rapids: Zondervan, 1979), 3:874–902.

[6] Anthony C. Thiselton, *The Two Horizons* (Grand Rapids: Eerdmans, 1980), 432–38.

"Divine Word,"[7] who also described inspiration in terms of the Holy Spirit playing a musician upon the soul of the inspired human author.[8] While some such statements might be constructed to diminish the role of human authors, Irenaeus recognized both divine and human authorship[9] in the process of divine inspiration, concluding that the Scriptures are perfect: "Being most properly assured that the Scriptures are indeed perfect, since they were spoken by the Word of God and His Spirit."[10] Like Justin and Irenaeus, we could also point to Barnabas, Clement of Rome, Athenagoras, Tertullian, Clement of Alexandria, Origen, Cyprian, John Chrysostom, and others.

Augustine insisted upon accepting the inspiration and authority of the Bible and linked Scripture's truthfulness to its trustworthiness.[11] For Augustine, if a book was accepted in the canon, then one should accept it as true and trustworthy: "But in consequence of the distinctive peculiarity of the sacred writings, we are bound to receive as true whatever the canon shows to have been said by even one prophet, or apostle, or evangelist. Otherwise, not a single page will be left for the guidance of human fallibility."[12]

Augustine considered it unacceptable to admit error or imperfection with respect to the Bible:

> For if you admit into such a high sanctuary of authority one false statement as made in the way of duty, there will not be left a single sentence of those books which, if appearing to any one difficult in practice or hard to believe, may not by the same fatal rule be explained away, as a statement in which intentionally, and under a sense of duty, the author declared what was not true.[13]

---

[7] Justin Martyr, *First Apology* 36.

[8] Justin Martyr, *Address to the Greeks* 8. A similar musical analogy is made by Athenagoras in *A Plea for the Christians*, 9, where he speaks of the "prophets, who lifted in ecstasy above the natural operations of their minds by the impulses of the Divine-Spirit, uttered the things with which they were inspired, the Spirit making use of them as a flute-player breathes into a flute."

[9] Irenaeus, *Against Heresies* 4.9.

[10] Irenaeus, *Against Heresies* 2.28.2.

[11] A. D. R. Polman, *The Word of God According to St. Augustine*, trans. A. J. Pomerans (Grand Rapids: Eerdmans, 1961).

[12] Augustine, *Reply to Faustus the Manichean* 11.5.

[13] Augustine, *Letters* 28.3; see also *Letters* 40.5.

Again, he claimed:

> I have learned to yield such respect and honor only to the canonical books of Scripture; of these do I most firmly believe that the authors were completely free from error. And if in these writings I am perplexed by anything which appears to me opposed to truth, I do not hesitate to suppose that either the *manuscript is faulty*, or the translator has not caught the meaning of what was said, or I myself have failed to understand it.[14]

Augustine affirmed that the Bible reported events truthfully, including miraculous events,[15] and he also affirmed the continuity of the Old and New Testaments within the single Christian canon.[16]

Augustine's affirmations about Scripture's perfection were not based on any naïve understandings regarding challenging questions about the biblical text. Augustine was aware of such issues, but he reasoned that the Scriptures were divinely inspired and, therefore, without error.[17] Eugene TeSelle, noting Augustine's towering influence not only in the early church, but continuing for centuries thereafter, stated that Augustine had confidence that whatever has been discovered about the world on the basis of reliable evidence cannot be inconsistent with the Bible.[18] After a review of the early church's understanding of the nature of the Bible, Stephen Presley

---

[14] Augustine, *Letters* 82.1.3.

[15] See the statements about Jonah in Augustine, *Letters* 102.33: "Let him, therefore, who proposes to inquire why the Prophet Jonah was three days in the capacious belly of the sea monster, begin by dismissing doubts as to the fact itself; for this did actually occur; and did not occur in vain."

[16] Augustine, *Sermon on the New Testament Lessons* 32:8: "We must fear, lest the divine precepts should be contrary to one another. But no: let us understand that there is the most perfect agreement in them, let us not follow the conceits of certain vain ones, who in their error think that the two Testaments in the Old and New Books are contrary to each other."

[17] Among such references see *Commentary on Romans* 111.7 and *Letters* 82.3. Typical of Augustine's view of these issues is his statement in *Reply to Faustus* 11:5: If we are perplexed by an apparent contradiction in Scripture, it is not allowable to say, the author of this book is mistaken; but either the manuscript is faulty, or the translation is wrong, or you have not understood."

[18] Eugene TeSelle, *Augustine*, Abingdon Pillars of Theology (Nashville: Abingdon, 2006).

offers this summary: "There is no doubt that the early fathers of the church believed that God had spoken through Christ and that Christ delivered his teaching to the apostles. . . . This assumption reminds us that the inspiration of Scripture has been the normative testimony of the church from the earliest days."[19]

2. The Medieval Period

Such was the respect for Scripture in the Middle Ages that Jaroslav Pelikan concludes of the times, "The authority of Scripture was supreme over that of reason; it was supreme over other authorities as well."[20] This position is reflected in Pope Leo the Great, Bonaventure, Anselm, Bernard of Clairvaux, William of Ockham, and others. Thomas Aquinas, in his *Summa Theologica*, which was penned in the thirteenth century, affirmed the infallibility and authority of Scripture when he took up the question of whether sacred doctrine was a matter of argument. He concluded that sacred doctrine "does not argue in proof of its principles," but "from its principles it may prove something else."[21] Aquinas demonstrated his belief that sacred Scripture, which is divine revelation, is such a "principle" and an "infallible truth" making a clear distinction between the authority of the Scripture and the authority of the "doctors of the Church."[22] The authority of the canonical Scriptures serves as "incontrovertible proof" for sacred doctrine while the authority of the church

---

[19] Stephen Presley, "Scripture and Tradition," in *Historical Theology for the Church*, ed. Jason G. Duesing and Nathan A. Finn (Nashville: B&H, 2021), 86.

[20] Jaroslav Pelikan, *The Christian Tradition: A History of the Development of Doctrine: The Growth of Medieval Theology (600–1300)*, 5 vols. (Chicago: University of Chicago Press, 1978), 3:121–22. He illustrates the point: "It was said of Anselm, for example, that he reposed such trust in Scripture that everything in it was unquestionably true for him and he made it his supreme goal to conform his faith and thought to the authority of Scripture."

[21] Aquinas, *Summa Theologica* 1.1.8. Thomas made his point from Titus 1:9, in which the overseer must hold to the "trustworthy message" and rebuke those who contradict sound doctrine.

[22] The gist of his position is that the first principles, in any "science," cannot be argued but must be accepted. Sacred Scripture is such a first principle. He then said that our faith rests on infallible truth (*infallibli veritati*). Sacred Scripture is, therefore, infallible truth.

fathers is merely "probable" because Scripture is divine revelation, and the works of the fathers are not.[23]

A central question raised during this period was, what is the relationship between the authority of Scripture and the tradition of the church? In the fourteenth century, John Wyclif penned a defense of the Bible called *On the Truth of Holy Scripture*, which called for people to understand the Scriptures by comparing the Bible with the Bible rather than thinking that the Bible was to be understood in light of the fathers. Moreover, Wyclif called the Bible the written Word of God both explicitly and implicitly.[24] The historian Heiko Oberman, in his magisterial work *The Dawn of the Reformation*, noted that some medieval thinkers agreed with Wyclif's approach that Scripture is not opposed to tradition nor in competition with it so long as tradition is seen as a servant to Scripture. Others, however, thought of the tradition, which included the fathers, the councils, and the pope, as an equal authority with Scripture. While the place of tradition in relation to Scripture became one of the primary issues during the Reformation, it is nevertheless the case that the truthfulness and divine authority of the Bible as well as ongoing faithful devotion to it was not in doubt during the 1,000–year stretch of Christian history from Augustine to Martin Luther.[25]

3. The Reformation Period

Martin Luther affirmed that the Bible is "God's Word written—presented in letters, as Christ is the eternal Word presented in human nature."[26] Because it truly is the Word of God, the Bible must be heard and loved by God's people.[27] Convicted of the truthfulness of the Scriptures, Luther

---

[23] *Summa Theologica* 1.1.8, quoting Augustine to this effect.

[24] William M. Marsh, "Scripture and Tradition," *Historical Theology for the Church*, 170–71.

[25] Heiko Oberman, *The Dawn of the Reformation: Essays in Late Medieval and Early Reformation Thought* (Edinburgh: T&T Clark, 1992).

[26] Martin Luther, *Weimarer Ausgabe*, 48:31, cited by A. Skevington Wood, *Captive to the Word: Martin Luther, Doctor of Sacred Scripture* (Grand Rapids: Eerdmans, 1969), 135.

[27] Martin Luther, *Lectures on Genesis*, in *Luther's Works*, vol. 2., ed. Jaroslav Pelikan (St. Louis: Concordia, 1960), 97.

reasoned, "we must remain content with them and cling to them as the perfectly clear, certain, sure words of God which can never deceive us or allow us to err."[28] While Luther respected the church fathers, they were not granted the same authority as the Bible, because the Bible is perfect and the fathers were not: "But everyone, indeed, knows that at times they [the fathers] have erred, as men will; therefore, I am ready to trust them only when they give me evidence for their opinions from Scripture, which has never erred."[29]

Luther adopted the commitments representative of Augustine as well as the late medieval church's understanding that the inspired Scriptures of the Old and New Testaments serve as the foundation of all belief and practice. Luther's teachers had taught the young monk that the inspired Scriptures were the authority on which his teaching was to be based. As Hermann Sasse has observed, "It has to be stated that he (Luther) took over the traditional doctrine of Scripture as having been given by inspiration of the Holy Spirit."[30] Luther never questioned this doctrine, nor did he try to create a different understanding of biblical inspiration and authority even while he developed a new approach to interpretation. He had no hesitation in declaring the entirety of the Bible to be God's Word. As Kenneth Hagan noted, Luther was a medieval Augustinian monk who inherited the tradition of Scripture as the *sacra pagina*.[31] Luther maintained this deep commitment

---

[28] Martin Luther, *Confession concerning Christ's Supper*, in *Luther's Works*, vol. 37, ed. Robert H. Fischer (Philadelphia: Fortress, 1961), 308.

[29] Martin Luther, *Defense and Explanation of All the Articles*, in *Luther's Works*, vol. 32. *Career of the Reformer II*, ed. George W. Forell (Philadelphia: Fortress, 1958), 11.

[30] Hermann Sasse, *Luther and the Word of God*, in *Accents in Luther's Theology: Essays in Commemoration of the 450th Anniversary of the Reformation*, ed. Heino O. Kadal (St. Louis: Concordia, 1967), 84.

[31] Kenneth Hagan, "The History of Scripture in the Church," in *The Bible in the Churches: How Various Christians Interpret the Scriptures*, ed. Kenneth Hagan (Milwaukee: Marquette University Press, 1994), 1; Timothy George, *Theology of the Reformers* (Nashville: B&H, 2013), 79–86; Mark D. Thompson, *A Sure Word on Which to Stand: The Relation of Authority and Interpretive Method in Luther's Approach to Scripture* (Eugene, OR: Wipf & Stock, 2007), 47–53; Hans J. Hillerbrand, ed., *The Reformation: A Narrative History Related by Contemporary Observers and Participants* (Reprint; Grand Rapids: Baker, 1978), 32–103; and Rhyne Putman, "Baptists, *Sola*

throughout his life. Shortly before his death, Luther stated, "Thus we attribute to the Holy Spirit all of Holy Scripture."[32]

It is important to clarify that Luther did not reject Christian tradition, the church fathers, nor the confessional statements from the important church councils of the fourth and fifth centuries. He did, however, contend that the authority of Scripture took priority over these matters; in fact, post-biblical Christian confessions were normed by Scripture so that Scripture was the norming norm rather than the other way around. Luther's well-known words at the Diet of Worms in 1521, which epitomize the Reformation's prioritizing of Scripture over church tradition in all matters, are worth repeating:

> Unless I am convinced by the testimony of the Scriptures or by clear reason for I do not trust in the pope or councils alone, since it is well known that they have often erred and contradicted themselves, I am bound by the Scriptures I have quoted, and my conscience is captive to the Word of God. I cannot and will not retract anything since it is neither safe nor right to go against conscience.[33]

Let us turn our attention to the second generation of Reformers and the work of John Calvin in Geneva. Calvin likewise affirmed the inspiration, authority, and perfection of the Scriptures. The Scriptures are God's Word, because they are spoken by God himself,[34] and because they are from God, they are "the certain and unerring rule."[35] Calvin affirmed that believers could observe the veracity of Scripture and that in the Bible the Christian can see the majesty of God which moves the Christian toward obedience, but this is not true of the unbeliever:

Scriptura, and the Place of Christian Tradition," in *Baptists and the Christian Tradition: Toward an Evangelical Baptist Catholicity,* ed. Matt Y. Emerson, Christopher W. Morgan, and Lucas Stamps (Nashville: B&H, 2020), 39–44.

[32] *On the Last Words of David* (1543) in *Luther's Works,* 15:275.

[33] Luther, *Luther's Works,* 32:112; see Erik M. Heen, "Scripture," in *Dictionary of Luther and the Lutheran Tradition,* ed. Timothy J. Wengert (Grand Rapids: Baker, 2017), 673–76.

[34] John Calvin, *Institutes of the Christian Religion,* 1.7.1–4.

[35] John Calvin, *Commentary on the Book of Psalms,* 5.11.

But even if one clears God's Sacred Word from man's evil speaking, he will not at once imprint upon their hearts that certainty which piety requires. Since for unbelieving men religion seems to stand by opinion alone, they, in order not to believe anything foolishly or lightly, both wish and demand rational proof that Moses and the prophets spoke divinely. But I reply the testimony of the Spirit is more excellent than all reason. For as God alone is a witness of himself in his Word, so also the Word will not find acceptance in men's hearts before it is sealed by the inward testimony of the Spirit.[36]

The magisterial Reformers remained consistently Augustinian in their approach to the full truthfulness of Holy Scripture, as might be expected from their roots in the Augustinian tradition.

4. The Challenge of Modern Liberalism

In the modern period there arose divergent opinions about the truthfulness and authority of Scripture. John Wesley, the founder of Methodism, affirmed that "the Scripture therefore of the *Old and New Testament* is a most solid and precious system of divine truth. Every part thereof is worthy of God; and all together are one entire body, wherein is no defect, no excess."[37] His affirmation of the inerrancy of the Bible is clear: "If there be any mistakes in the Bible, there may as well be a thousand. If there be one falsehood in that book, it did not come from the God of truth."[38] The evangelical orthodoxy was soon, however, challenged by modern liberalism.

The influence of Enlightenment thought, including Cartesian methodological doubt, Humean skepticism, and naturalistic deism, created a milieu in which doubts were raised about the nature of Scripture as well as its

---

[36] Calvin, *Institutes of the Christian Religion* 1.7.4; see also 1.7.5.

[37] Robert W. Burtner and Robert E. Childs, eds., *John Wesley's Theology: A Collection from His Works* (Nashville: Abingdon, 1982), 18. Also see the helpful summary of Roman Catholic teaching on the nature of Scripture in Thomas G. Guarino, "Scripture," in *Evangelicals and Catholics Together at Twenty* (Grand Rapids: Brazos, 2015), 38–52.

[38] John Wesley, *Works of John Wesley: Journal from September 13, 1773 to October 24, 1790*, 4 vols. (Grand Rapids: Zondervan, 1958), 4:82.

truthfulness and authority. In the case of the deists, their questions included whether God could even reveal himself as the Bible claimed. In this larger context, some theologians and biblical scholars began to interrogate the traditional orthodox doctrine of Scripture.

The initial steps in this direction took place in England during the seventeenth century. As Otto Heick observed, the English deists "will always be known as the group which took the first steps to inaugurate radicalism into Christian theology."[39] He noted that the German rationalists and the French naturalists followed the lead of the deists, who affirmed a natural religion without miracles, without God's providential intervention in history, and without the divine inspiration of sacred Scripture. Bruce Demarest identified three stages in the development of deistic thought. Initially, they mediated between supernaturalism and naturalism by claiming that some religious truths lie above reason and are communicated by revelation. Later deists asserted that religion contains nothing above reason, meaning that revelation must be understood completely within the framework of human reason. The final stage denied revelation altogether while prioritizing autonomous reason. Matthew Tindal (1657–1733) went so far as to reject the very idea of special revelation, pointing to natural revelation as sufficient for men and women. David Hume (1711–1776), a Scottish philosopher, went further and endorsed religious skepticism.[40]

The eighteenth-century German rationalists maintained that human reason was the primary source of religious knowledge. They eventually denied the need for God to make himself known in Scripture. Gotthold Lessing (1729–1778) maintained that all revealed religion is basically nothing more than a reconfirmation of the religion of reason.[41] Enlightenment historians summarized the position of the rationalists by saying, "Grant inspiration and you bind us down to the belief that all contents of Scripture are true. You force us to believe what our reason does not comprehend."[42] Confidence in

---

[39] Otto W. Heick, *A History of Christian Thought*, 2 vols. (Philadelphia: Muhlenberg, 1946), 2:53.

[40] Bruce Demarest, "The Bible in the Enlightenment Era," in *Challenges to Inerrancy*, ed. Gordon Lewis and Bruce Demarest (Chicago: Moody, 1984), 16–23.

[41] Demarest, "The Bible in the Enlightenment Era," 26–28.

[42] John F. Hurst, *History of Rationalism* (New York: Eaton and Mains, 1865), 200–201.

the Bible was undermined throughout Germany and other parts of Europe. This philosophical and theological rationalism provided much of the foundation for the rise of historical criticism, whose effect will be considered in the next few chapters. H. S. Reimarus (1694–1768) and Lessing subsumed biblical revelation under the role of reason.[43] While English deism and German rationalism ran their course, the presuppositions which shaped both movements, including the autonomy of reason, the loss of divine inspiration, the rejection of biblical miracles, and the culturally bound character of the Bible resulting in a denial of the Bible's truthfulness, have continued to exercise ongoing influence on how the Bible has been understood for the past three centuries.

Lessing insisted that modern men and women no longer needed guidance from God or from Scripture. His work on the *Education of the Human Race* (1780), combined with *Religion within the Limits of Reason Alone* (1793) by Immanuel Kant (1724–1804), shaped the intellectual landscape of the day. Kant sought to rescue the Christian faith from a prevailing skepticism by distinguishing between "pure" rational reason and "practical" moral reason.[44] By categorizing Christianity as practical reason, he limited the value of the Bible to matters of morality and ethics. In this context, Romanticism, which is easier to describe than to define, began to permeate religious thought.[45] Harold O. J. Brown observed that "Romanticism was less a movement in favor of religion that an artistic-literary movement that became religious."[46] Many who had become dissatisfied with rationalist approaches, extolled Christianity as the highest religious experience within which other religious

---

[43] Adapted from David S. Dockery, "New Testament Interpretation: A Historical Survey," in *Interpreting the New Testament*, ed. D. A. Black and David S. Dockery (Nashville: B&H, 2001), 28–31.

[44] Nathan A. Finn, "Scripture and Authority," in *Historical Theology for the Church*, 252–54.

[45] Johannes Zachhuber, "Religion vs. Revelation? A Deceptive Alternative in Twentieth-Century German Theology," in *Religious Experience and Contemporary Theological Epistemology*, ed. L. Boeve, Y. De Maeseneer, and S. Van Den Bossche (Leuven: Leuven University Press, 2005), 305–9; Avery Dulles, *Models of Revelation* (Maryknoll, NY: Orbis, 1992), 6–7.

[46] Harold O. J. Brown, "Romanticism and the Bible," in *Challenges to Inerrancy: A Theological Response*, ed. Gordon R. Lewis and Bruce Demarest (Chicago: Moody, 1984), 52.

expressions could be accommodated. As Nathan Finn notes, "they valued human feelings and emotions over rational autonomy and emphasized the subjective elements of religion over objective truth claims."[47]

For Friedrich Schleiermacher, the Christian faith, as set forth in his *On Christian Faith*, is understood to begin with and to be sustained by a feeling of dependence on God. Christianity was deemed to be rooted in the religious experience of men and women rather than in Christian Scripture.[48] The Bible was recognized as inspirational but not inspired in the same way it had been affirmed for centuries by orthodox Christians. The father of theological liberalism thus argued the authority of Holy Scripture cannot be the foundation of faith in Christ. By the early nineteenth century, the locus of authority had now moved from God and the message he has made known in Scripture to humans and their subjective religious experience.

In theological liberalism, the Bible possessed no unique character; it was essentially a human book.[49] Such notions of the Bible became more common with the rise of post-Enlightenment anti-supernaturalism, typified by the nineteenth-century German biblical scholar David Strauss. To Strauss the miracles of the Bible were myths, inventions of the imaginative disciples of Jesus.[50] Through the influence of Schleiermacher, Strauss, Adolf von Harnack (1851–1930), and many others, liberalism became prominent across Europe and North America in the late nineteenth and early twentieth centuries.

5. Further Shifts from Classic Orthodoxy

In the early twentieth century, Karl Barth led what appeared at first to be a complete revolt against classical theological liberalism. Central to Barth's theology was a radical emphasis on the transcendence of God and a return to a conception of dogmatics that takes seriously the Bible as a source for

---

[47] Finn, "Scripture and Authority," 253.

[48] See Friedrich Schleiermacher, *The Christian Faith*, ed. H. R. Mackintosh and J. S. Stewart (Reprint; Edinburgh: T&T Clark, 1960).

[49] Gregg Allison, *Historical Theology* (Grand Rapids: Zondervan, 2011), 70; also see the perceptive and insightful thoughts of Roger Olson, *Against Liberal Theology* (Grand Rapids: Zondervan, 2022), 1–74.

[50] David F. E. Strauss, *Life of Jesus*, 3:383.

theology. While Barth attempted to recover the authority of the Bible in the church and theology, he did not recover a fully orthodox understanding of the nature and inspiration of Scripture. With respect to its nature, Barth distinguished the Bible from revelation itself, saying: "Therefore when we have to do with the Bible, we have to do primarily with this means, with these words, with the witness, which as such is not itself revelation, but only—and this is the limitation—the witness to it."[51] For Barth, the Word of God is perfectly revealed in Jesus Christ; the Scriptures are a witness, though imperfectly, to the perfect revelation of the God-Man. It is the church's responsibility to preach the Scriptures. Barth contends that as they are preached, the Holy Spirit works to make the Bible become the Word of God to the people. Barth believed that "we call the Bible the Word of God only when we recognize its human imperfection in face of its divine perfection, and its divine perfection in spite of its human imperfection."[52]

For Barth, then, the locus of inspiration shifted. Instead of an inspired biblical text penned by authors under the inspiration of the Holy Spirit, Barth located divine inspiration in the event of preaching, particularly in the context of the church. God's people experience a divine-human encounter when the preached word becomes the Word of God.[53] Barth's influence on twentieth- and early twenty-first-century theology has been enormous.[54] His views of revelation and Scripture have become popular even among some evangelicals. To the contrary, Roger Nicole contended that Barth's view of Scripture, that the Bible becomes the Word of God, reflects a form of Christological adoptionism rather than an orthodox model.[55] Similarly, Donald Bloesch suggested that though Barth, Brunner, Niebuhr and others emphasized the theological unity of the

---

[51] Karl Barth, *Church Dogmatics*, ed. G. W. Bromiley and T. F. Torrance, trans. G. T. Thompson and Harold Knight (Edinburgh: T&T Clark, 1956), I/2:463.

[52] Barth, *Church Dogmatics*, I/2:508.

[53] Barth, *Church Dogmatics*, I/2:203–79, 473–537, 743–58.

[54] One person greatly influenced by Barth was Donald Bloesch, who contends that when one compares Barth with some evangelicals, the more thoroughly scriptural engagement is often found in Barth. See Bloesch, *Holy Scripture* (see introduction, n. 2).

[55] See Roger Nicole, "The Neo-Orthodox Reduction," in *Challenges to Inerrancy*, 121–36.

Scriptures, they were "unable to hold together the divine and human sides of Scripture."[56] Thus, they fostered "a Nestorian approach to the Bible in which the divine word and human word are only loosely associated and never function in an indissoluble unity."[57]

Rudolf Bultmann and Paul Tillich, among other neo-orthodox and existential thinkers, in a much more sweeping manner than Karl Barth discounted the truthfulness of the Bible at many points, particularly matters such as history, geography, natural science, and others. Again, Nicole's summary is apt: "In spite of some favorable developments in the vanguard of the movement, such as the renewal of interest in biblical theology and in biblical preaching, we are compelled to the conclusion that the failure to recognize the Holy Scripture as intrinsically the Word of God has weakened the whole attitude toward Holy Writ."[58] Even beyond these neo-orthodox and existentialist theologians, process theology and liberation theology "eviscerated" the truthfulness and authority of the Bible.[59]

The Dutch theologian, G. C. Berkouwer, shifted in his thought over the years from an affirmation of the classic understanding of the truthfulness of the Bible to a more functional understanding of the Bible, which has influenced many post-conservative theologians such as Jack Rogers and Donald McKim, and a host of contemporary thinkers. Rogers and McKim, building on the theology of Berkouwer and the historiography of Ernest Sandeen, asserted that the doctrine of inerrancy is a relatively new development and the current debate surrounding the issues is based, in part, on a misunderstanding about the use of the term "infallibility."[60] While they acknowledge that the term "infallible" has been commonly used to refer to the Bible, they denied it was basically synonymous with the term "inerrancy." Shifts from

---

[56] Bloesch, *Holy Scripture*, 31.

[57] Bloesch, 31.

[58] Nicole, "Neo-Orthodox Reduction," 144.

[59] Vernon Grounds, "Scripture in Liberation Theology: An Eviscerated Authority," in *Challenges to Inerrancy*, 317–46.

[60] G. C. Berkouwer, *Studies in Dogmatics: Holy Scripture* (Grand Rapids: Eerdmans, 1975); Jack Rogers and Donald McKim, *Authority and Interpretation of the Bible* (San Francisco: HarperCollins, 1980); Ernest Sandeen, *The Roots of Fundamentalism: British and American Millenarianism, 1800–1930* (Chicago: University of Chicago Press, 1970).

previous commitments to biblical inerrancy were simultaneously seen in the writings of some evangelical thinkers.[61]

John Woodbridge, in his response titled *Biblical Authority*, and John Feinberg, in his volume on the doctrine of Scripture, have made the case that inerrancy and infallibility, while having distinctions of meaning, are basically synonymous. These two terms have been used interchangeably in theological discourse throughout church history.[62] If there is a distinction, infallibility, as noted by J. I. Packer and Roger Nicole, is actually the stronger term, meaning both that the Bible is incapable of error and that it cannot deceive or mislead.[63] Kevin Vanhoozer has made a similar observation, "Scripture is therefore indefatigable in its illocutionary intent. It encourages, warns, asserts, instructs, commands—all infallibly. Note that this makes inerrancy a *subset of* infallibility."[64]

Some contemporary scholars like Berkouwer, Rogers, McKim, and others want to apply the term "infallible" only to the salvific message of the Bible rather than affirming that the Bible is also truthful when it speaks of history, geography, and related matters. We will see in a later chapter that several twentieth-century Baptists attempted to do something similar in their affirmations of Scripture. The meaning given to "infallible" in this volume is consistent with the classical meaning of the term, not with the revised meaning of some recent scholars. Even James D. G. Dunn, who does not affirm biblical inerrancy, has stated that while there have been others who define

---

[61] Bernard Ramm, *After Fundamentalism: The Future of Evangelical Theology* (San Francisco: Harper & Row, 1983); Clark Pinnock, *The Scripture Principle* (San Francisco: Harper & Row, 1984), and the account of Daniel Fuller in George Marsden, *Fuller Seminary and the New Evangelicalism* (Grand Rapids: Eerdmans, 1987).

[62] See John D. Woodbridge, *Biblical Authority: Infallibility and Inerrancy in the Christian Tradition* (Grand Rapids: Zondervan, 2015); Woodbridge, "The International Council on Biblical Inerrancy," *Presbyterian* 48, no. 1 (Spring 2022): 37–59; Feinberg, *Light in a Dark Place*.

[63] Roger Nicole, "James I. Packer's Contribution to the Doctrine of Inerrancy," in *Doing Theology for the People of God: Studies in Honor of J. I. Packer*, ed. Donald Lewis and Alister McGrath (Downers Grove: IVP, 1996), 175–90.

[64] Kevin J. Vanhoozer, "The Semantics of Biblical Language," in *Hermeneutics, Authority, and Canon*, ed. D. A. Carson and John D. Woodbridge (Grand Rapids: Zondervan, 1986), 94–95.

infallibility in a different sense, biblical scholars and theologians like E. J. Young have defined it as equivalent to inerrancy.[65] Young claims:

> In all parts, in its very entirety, the Bible, if we are to accept its witness to itself, is utterly infallible. It is not only that each book given the name of Scripture is infallible but, more than that, the content of each such book is itself Scripture, the Word of God written and, hence, infallible, free entirely from the errors which adhere to mere human compositions. Not alone moral and ethical truths, but to all statements of fact does this inspiration extend.[66]

More will be said about these important matters later in this chapter, but for now we continue the survey recognizing that the functional approach of Berkouwer, Rogers, and McKim has had significant influence.

Influenced by these shifts toward a more functional understanding of the Bible's infallibility, the post-conservative reconstruction of Scripture, as reflected in Stanley Grenz and John Franke in their work on *Beyond Foundationalism: Shaping Theology in a Postmodern Context*, rejected a realistic-objectivistic understanding of knowledge and the world. They noted that Scripture is inspired and authoritative only in the sense that the Spirit speaks to the community through the Bible, not because the Bible is inherently God-breathed. It is not the Bible as a book that is authoritative, but the Bible as the instrumentality of the Spirit; the biblical message spoken by the Spirit through the text is theology's norming norm. Affirming that both tradition and the believing community serve as sources of authority similar to Scripture, Grenz and Franke suggested the biblical text is not the determining norm, but only its message, since Scripture is not to be equated with the Word of God.[67]

In response, Osvaldo Padilla claims that post-conservatives "often emerge as dangerously close to elevating community over Scripture (or giving both

---

[65] James D. G. Dunn, "The Authority of Scripture according to Scripture," *Churchman* 96, no. 3 (1982): 105–6.

[66] E. J. Young, *Thy Word is Truth* (Grand Rapids: Eerdmans, 1963), 48.

[67] Stanley J. Grenz and John Franke, *Beyond Foundationalism: Shaping Theology in a Postmodern Culture* (Louisville: Westminster John Knox, 2001); Curtis Freeman, *Contesting Catholicity: Theology for Other Baptists* (Waco: Baylor University Press, 2014); and East, *The Doctrine of Scripture*, (see chap. 6, n. 63).

equal authority) and to an extreme form of perspectivalism."[68] He continues, "what is 'original' in post conservatism is simply a synthesis of postmodern thought and postliberal theological method with certain types of evangelical influence."[69] Blurring distinctions between inspiration and illumination, Grenz, influenced both by Wolfhart Pannenberg and George Lindbeck, said that the reason why the church confessed the inspiration of Scripture was because the early Christians experienced the power of the Spirit of God via these writings.

The inspiration and truthfulness of the Bible for post-conservatives, then, is more a matter of the church's confession rather than of the intrinsic nature of the scriptural texts. Thus, in an instrumentalist or functional manner, Scripture is the vehicle through which the Spirit speaks. They are thus reluctant to affirm the words of Scripture as the Word of God.[70] While the post-conservatives are to be commended for taking seriously the need to understand our postmodern context, their view of Scripture does not do justice to what the Bible claims for itself. Rather than affirming that the Bible has an inherent authority due to its divine authorship and Spirit-inspired character, as Padilla and others have noted, they view the truthfulness and authority of Scripture in a dynamic manner as the Holy Spirit appropriates the biblical text and speaks through it to the believing community.[71] The post-conservatives disjoined the Bible from the Word of God.

The modern and postmodern movements, from the English deists to the contemporary post-conservatives, thus fostered significant shifts away from the orthodox conception of the Scriptures as the divinely inspired, authoritative Word of God. Theological liberalism largely reduced the

---

[68] Osvaldo Padilla, "Postconservative Theologians and Scriptural Authority," in *The Enduring Authority of the Christian Scriptures*, ed. D. A. Carson (Grand Rapids: Eerdmans, 2016), 656.

[69] Padilla, "Postconservative Theologians," 666–68.

[70] Stanley J. Grenz, *Theology for the Community of God* (Nashville: B&H, 1994).

[71] See responses in Gary L. W. Johnson and Ronald N. Gleason, *Reforming or Confirming? Post-Conservative Evangelical Theology and the Emerging Church* (Wheaton: Crossway, 2008); Millard J. Erickson, Paul Helseth, and Justin Taylor, eds., *Reclaiming the Evangelical Center* (Wheaton: Crossway, 2004); R. Scott Smith, "Non-Foundational Epistemologies and the Truth of Scripture," and Michael C. Rae, "Authority and Truth," in *The Enduring Authority of the Christian Scriptures*, 831–98.

Bible to a disparate set of human religious testimonies that bear no particular authority for faith and practice. Even the neo-orthodox revolt against liberalism, led by Karl Barth, did not adequately return to a biblical view of Scripture. Some have not only questioned the truthfulness of the Bible but have questioned whether such an affirmation adequately represents the consensus of Christians through the years. But Donald Bloesch rightly points to the continuity of an orthodox affirmation of Scripture through the centuries:

> Contrary to what is commonly believed in liberal and neoorthodox circles, there is a long tradition in the church that represents the teaching of Scripture as being without error. References to the Scriptures as *inerrabilis* are to be found in Augustine, Aquinas, and Duns Scotus. The adjective *infallibilis* was applied to Scripture by John Wycliffe and Jean de Gerson. Luther and Calvin described the Bible as being infallible and without error.[72]

It is to expressions of the orthodox tradition in contemporary evangelicalism that we now briefly turn our attention.

6. Orthodoxy Reaffirmed

The orthodox tradition regarding Scripture can be traced through the early church, the medieval period, and the Reformation, as well as through the Puritans, the Protestant Scholastics, and the Pietists into contemporary evangelicalism. Clarity and greater definition have come in response to the challenges fostered by the modern period. Nevertheless, these affirmations were consistent extensions of what Christian leaders through the centuries long maintained. Some of the most important responses came from the Princeton theologians Charles Hodge, A. A. Hodge, B. B. Warfield, and J. Gresham Machen as they defended the historic orthodox view of Scripture biblically, theologically, philosophically, and pastorally.

---

[72] Bloesch, *Holy Scripture*, 33–34. Also, Avery Dulles, in *Models of Revelation*, notes that this traditional view of Scripture has been the dominant view throughout Christian history, 36. In addition, see David S. Dockery and Timothy George, *The Great Tradition of Christian Thinking* (Wheaton: Crossway, 2012).

A. A. Hodge and Warfield, in their classic article on "Inspiration" in 1881 not only demonstrated the truth of biblical inspiration by the Holy Spirit but also convincingly set forth the case for the full truthfulness and authority of the Bible.[73] Of interest is the fact that they used the terms "inspiration" and "infallibility" to describe Scripture without using the term "inerrancy" even once. It was as though they were anticipating the later awkward approaches of Berkouwer, Rogers, and McKim. Similar observations could be made about the important contribution of Basil Manly Jr. with his *The Biblical Doctrine of Inspiration, Explained and Verified* (1888).

Richard Lovelace, the eminent American church historian, maintained that the views of the Princeton theologians in the nineteenth and early twentieth centuries were not merely an echo of Protestant orthodoxy, for its germinal core had already been clearly stated by Augustine, the foundational theologian of the Christian church.[74] Thus, the influential work of Hodge and Warfield was not, as some have suggested, a new departure which diverges from a previous tradition of limited or partial truthfulness. Rather, the Princeton scholars offered a comprehensive restatement of the classical orthodox position.

As the twentieth century began, the "modernist/fundamentalist" controversy moved publicly into full force. In 1910, the "five fundamentals" were clarified by the Northern Presbyterians reflecting on earlier versions spelled out by the Niagara Prophecy Conference in the 1890s. These doctrinal tenets, which focused on the full and complete inspiration and authority of Scripture, the virgin birth of Jesus Christ, the deity of Christ, the atoning death and resurrection of Christ, and the historical reality of biblical miracles, were aimed at the primary challenges offered by proponents of liberalism.[75] A series of 90 articles were included in a multi-volume publication titled *The Fundamentals* (1910–1915), edited by R. A. Torrey and funded by Lyman Stewart and Milton Stewart. This collection was well reasoned, serious, calm, thoughtful,

---

[73] A. A. Hodge and B. B. Warfield, "Inspiration," *The Presbyterian Review* 2, no. 6 (1881): 225–60.

[74] Richard Lovelace, "Inerrancy: Some Historical Perspectives," in *Inerrancy and Common* Sense, ed. Roger Nicole and J. Ramsey Michaels (Grand Rapids: Baker, 1980), 15–48.

[75] See David S. Dockery, "Southern Baptists, Evangelicalism, and the Christian Tradition," *Baptists and the Christian Tradition*, 267–92.

not shrill, and generally quite persuasive. More than thirty of these articles articulated and defended the nature, truthfulness, and authority of Scripture.[76]

In 1949, evangelical scholars formed the Evangelical Theological Society (ETS), which expected all members annually to confess their commitment to the inerrancy of Scripture. During the twentieth century, key evangelical scholars representing various denominational traditions authored major works affirming the full truthfulness of Scripture.[77] Among these many important works were contributions by E. J. Young, Carl F. H. Henry, J. I. Packer, Kenneth Kantzer, Robert Preus, D. A. Carson, John Woodbridge, Millard Erickson, Mark Thompson, John Feinberg, and Paul Feinberg, among others. The best summary of the doctrine of these and dozens of other evangelical thinkers came together in 1978 in the work known as the *Chicago Statement on Biblical Inerrancy*. Concerned about widespread defection away from a belief in the Bible's complete truthfulness, this articulated statement clearly affirmed and carefully defended both the infallibility and inerrancy of Scripture. It also denied that the truthfulness of the Bible can be limited to matters of faith and practice alone.

III. The Inerrancy of Holy Scripture

Having examined the normativity of Scripture and having looked at representative viewpoints of significant Christian thinkers through the centuries, we must ask how we can confess the complete truthfulness, dependability, trustworthiness, and reliability of Scripture. This issue must be addressed because of ongoing misunderstandings in contemporary discussions about the Bible, and because the doctrine of the Bible's truthfulness or inerrancy is the corollary of our affirmations regarding the verbal plenary view of the Bible's inspiration. While the term "inerrancy" continues to be subject to misunderstanding, even after so many carefully stated works on the subject, it remains, when thoughtfully defined, a helpful and informative theological term to describe the results of biblical inspiration.

---

[76] See R. A. Torrey, ed., *The Fundamentals*, 12 vols. (Reprint; Los Angeles: Bible Institute of Los Angeles, 2017).

[77] David F. Wells and John D. Woodbridge, eds., *The Evangelicals: Who They Are, What They Believe, and Where They Are Changing* (Nashville: Abingdon, 1975).

These misunderstandings have resulted from false associations of the term with a literalistic hermeneutic and/or dictation theories of inspiration. Additional problems have developed from careless statements on the part of advocates who have been overzealous in their defense of the doctrine (some of whom have even denied the constructive use of textual criticism) or who have concentrated unduly on issues of preciseness, exactness, and "errors," when the focus should instead be primarily placed on the issues of truthfulness, reliability, and dependability. While passages such as Psalm 119, Matt 5:17–19, and John 10:35 point to the Bible's own self-witness of what is understood by those who affirm the inerrancy of Scripture, we need to acknowledge that inerrancy is primarily the proper implication of inspiration. In these discussions about the nature of Holy Scripture, some have attempted to make a case for the slippery slope that takes place when individuals, groups, or denominations move away from a commitment to the Bible's full truthfulness. While there are certainly clear examples to provide serious words of caution, drawing such slippery-slope implications must be done thoughtfully, respectfully, and carefully.

The doctrine of the Bible's truthfulness or inerrancy is important primarily for theological and epistemological reasons. Individual salvation is not dependent on one's confession of biblical inerrancy, but consistent theological method and instruction need the foundation of inerrancy in order to continue to maintain an orthodox confession in salvific matters for the present generation and the generations to come.[78] Thus, we see that inerrancy, as a corollary of inspiration, is a foundation upon which other theological building blocks are laid. With these words of warning behind us and an awareness of the complexity of the issue, let us suggest a definition that builds on and draws from the *Chicago Statement,* as well as

---

[78] On theological method, see Malcolm B. Yarnell III, *The Formation of Doctrine* (Nashville: B&H, 2007); Rhyne Putman, *The Method of Christian Theology: An Introduction* (Nashville: B&H, 2021); Glenn R. Kreider and Michael J. Svigel, *A Practical Primer on Theological Method: Table Manners for Discussing God, His Works, and His Ways* (Grand Rapids: Zondervan, 2019); Kevin J. Vanhoozer, "From Bible to Theology," in *Theology, Church, and Ministry,* ed. David S. Dockery (Nashville: B&H, 2017); and Graham A. Cole, *Faithful Theology: An Introduction* (Wheaton: Crossway, 2020). On Psalm 119 as an example of the Bible self-attestation of its own truthfulness, see Zemek, *The Word of God in the Child of God* (see introduction, n. 18).

the works of J. I. Packer, Millard Erickson, John Feinberg, and especially Paul Feinberg.[79]

We define "inerrancy" in this way: *When all the facts are known, the Bible (in its original writings), properly interpreted in light of the culture and communication means that had developed by the time of its composition, will be shown to be completely true (and therefore not false) in all that it affirms, to the degree of precision intended by the biblical authors, in all matters relating to God and his creation.* We trust that the careful construction of our definition will help those who have misunderstood the doctrine to discern what biblical inerrancy is and what it is not, perhaps leading them to reevaluate their initial opposition. This definition seeks to be faithful to the phenomena of Scripture and to the theological affirmations in Scripture about the truth of God. We also appeal to the best examples in Christian history of those who have sought to affirm and defend the full truthfulness of the Bible. It will be helpful at this point to provide a brief five-part commentary regarding our definition.

1. *"When all the facts are known."* Our definition of inerrancy begins from the Augustinian vantage point of faith that seeks understanding. We certainly recognize that we may not have all the information necessary on this side of the eschaton to settle some of the complex issues found in Scripture. It is also likely that our sinful, finite minds may misinterpret some facts and information we do have. Thus, we should exercise caution with things we might not understand until all the facts are known. An eschatological framing is, therefore, implicit in this statement, although we also believe it is necessary to discover as many facts as possible now.[80]

---

[79] See similar statements in Millard J. Erickson, *Christian Theology*, 221–40; Paul D. Feinberg, "The Meaning of Inerrancy," in *Inerrancy*, ed. Norman L. Geisler (Grand Rapids: Zondervan, 1979), 267–304; John Feinberg, *Light in a Dark Place*, 236–46 (see introduction, n. 5); Louis Igou Hodges, "Scripture," in *New Dimensions in Evangelical Thought*, ed. David S. Dockery (Downers Grove: IVP, 1998), 209–34; James Emery White, "Inspiration and Authority of Scripture," in *Foundations for Biblical Interpretation*, ed. David S. Dockery, Kenneth A. Mathews, and Robert B. Sloan (Nashville: B&H, 1994), 19–35; Robert Saucy, *Scripture* (Nashville: W Publishing Group, 2011); among others.

[80] Thompson, *The Doctrine of Scripture*, 141–43 (see introduction, n. 29); William Kynes and Greg Strand, *Evangelical Convictions* (Minneapolis: Free Church Publications, 2011), 56–65.

2. *"The Bible (in its original writings)."* Inerrancy applies to all aspects of the Bible as originally written. A claim to biblical inerrancy must be limited to the original words of the biblical text. Reference to these original writings is not restricted to some lost codex but is an affirmation relating to the original words written by the prophetic-apostolic messengers. Thus, our confessions of both inspiration and inerrancy apply to translations to the degree that those translations represent accurately the original words. We certainly can express great confidence in our present translations. Therefore, our qualifying statement regarding the original writings is not intended as an apologetic sidestep but is a theological appeal to the providential oversight and veracity of God in the conduct of his superintending work of both inspiration and textual preservation.[81] Affirming the inerrancy of the original autographs is never intended to remove trust from our present-day translations, whether one has access to the KJV, NKJV, NIV, NASB, NRSV, ESV, CSB, NET, or another translation accepted among the true churches of the Lord Jesus Christ. Instead, affirming even the inerrancy of the typical translation ensures and confirms the true faith available in that translation. The translations also rest on a sure foundation.

3. *"Properly interpreted in light of the culture and the communication means that had developed by the time of its composition."* Our definition of biblical inerrancy recognizes that statements concerning the nature of the biblical text cannot be separated completely from hermeneutics. While hermeneutical issues must be distinguished, they cannot be divorced. Before any truth or falsehood can be recognized, it is necessary to know whether a text has been interpreted properly. The textual intention must be recognized and matters of precision and accuracy must be judged with attention to the culture and means of communication that had developed by the time of the text's composition. The text, as a guideline, should be interpreted with literary, grammatical, historical, contextual, canonical, and theological matters in mind,

---

[81] Greg L. Bahnsen, "The Inerrancy of the Autographa," in *Inerrancy*, ed. Norman L. Geisler (Grand Rapids: Zondervan, 1980), 172–89; Paul Helm, "The Idea of Inerrancy," in *Enduring Authority of the Christian Scripture*, 899–919; Feinberg, *Light in a Dark Place*, 307–20, including his response to A. T. B. McGowan, *The Divine Spiration of Scripture: Challenging Evangelical Perspectives* (Downers Grove: IVP, 2009).

as our chapters on biblical interpretation and application make clear. The context, background, genre, and purpose of the writing must be considered in matters of biblical interpretation.[82]

The highly regarded sociologist Christian Smith has argued that the reality of multiple and incompatible interpretations to any single biblical text has rendered all claims to inerrancy vacuous. In *The Bible Made Impossible*, he contends:

> The very same Bible—which Biblicists insist is perspicuous and harmonious—gives rise to divergent understandings among intelligent, sincere, committed readers about what it says about most topics of interest. Knowledge of "biblical" teachings, in short, is characterized by *pervasive interpretive pluralism*. What that means in consequence is this: in a crucial sense it simply does not matter whether the Bible is everything that Biblicists claim theoretically concerning its authority, infallibility, inner consistency, perspicuity, and so on, since in actual functioning the Bible produces a pluralism of interpretations.[83]

Smith suggests that the church should abandon inerrancy and inspiration as the starting point for a doctrine of Scripture and should instead embrace a Christocentric hermeneutic which is flexible enough to glean truth from the Bible without senseless devotion to believing everything the Bible teaches is true in a literal sense. But Smith errs when he suggests

---

[82] This is one of the real strengths of Clark Pinnock's *Scripture Principle*, 197–202. Pinnock's earlier work, *Biblical Revelation* (Chicago: Moody, 1971) is, in our opinion, a more consistent explanation of the doctrine of Scripture, but his discussion of the relationship of inspiration to interpretation in the latter work is a most important contribution. E. D. Radmacher and R. D. Preus, eds., *Hermeneutics, Inerrancy, and the Bible* (Grand Rapids: Zondervan, 1984); J. I. Packer, "Infallible Scripture and the Role of Hermeneutics," in *Scripture and Truth*, ed. D. A. Carson and John D. Woodbridge (Grand Rapids: Baker, 1983), 321–56; and Bloesch, *Holy Scripture: Revelation, Inspiration, and Interpretation*; also, Millard J. Erickson, "Donald Bloesch's Doctrine of Scripture," in *Evangelical Theology in Transition: Theologians in Dialogue with Donald Bloesch*, ed. Elmer M. Colyer (Downers Grove: IVP, 1999), 77–97.

[83] Christian Smith, *The Bible Made Impossible: Why Biblicism Is Not a Truly Evangelical Reading of Scripture* (Grand Rapids: Brazos, 2011), 17. Emphasis original.

biblical inerrancy requires uniformity of interpretation across the spectrum of fallen humanity. Just because there is disagreement over correct interpretation does not mean that a correct interpretation does not exist, nor does it mean the problem of multiple interpretations is caused by the Bible itself. Smith wrongly suggests that pervasive interpretive pluralism defeats inerrancy, when in reality all the phenomenon demonstrates is that the Bible is not equally clear to every interpreter. The Bible itself accounts for this phenomenon, and the doctrine of the clarity of Scripture, as we will see later in this volume, is robust enough to handle multiple and divergent interpretations from its flawed interpreters without denying its truthfulness or perspicuity.

4. *"Will be shown to be completely true (and therefore not false), in all that it affirms, to the degree of precision intended by the biblical authors."* An important aspect of this definition is the evaluation of whether the Bible is inerrant in terms of truthfulness and falseness rather than in terms of error or lack of precision. This moves the discussion away from grammatical mistakes or the lack of precision in reports. Inerrancy, on the one hand, must not be associated with strict tests of precision in which careless harmonization efforts attempt to bring about a precision uncommon and alien to the text itself.[84] On the other hand, we cannot shift the emphasis to such overly general and less meaningful definitions of inerrancy and infallibility as merely willful deceit.[85] Erickson, Thompson, and Feinberg have correctly maintained that the issue is and has always been about truthfulness and reliability, not just

---

[84] It seems to us that the kind of undue concern for excessive harmonization, as exhibited in Harold Lindsell's *Battle for the Bible* (Grand Rapids: Zondervan, 1976), 174–76, is more confusing than helpful in demonstrating the full truthfulness of the Bible. Even though Lindsell does not include precision or preciseness as an aspect of his definition of inerrancy, he nevertheless confuses the issue with his focus on excessive harmonization. A more constructive approach to this matter of harmonization can be found in Craig L. Blomberg, "The Limits of Harmonization," in *Hermeneutics, Authority, and Canon*, ed. D. A. Carson and John D. Woodbridge (Grand Rapids: Zondervan, 1986).

[85] Rogers and McKim, *Authority and Interpretation*, 3, define the nature of Scripture in terms of the lack of willful deception. See the response by Richard Muller, *The Study of Theology: From Biblical Interpretation to Contemporary Formation* (Grand Rapids: Zondervan, 1991).

functional matters of purpose.[86] We must not confuse Enlightenment understandings of precision or exactness with faithful communication means at the time when Scripture was written.

One more observation seems appropriate at this point in considering the definition of biblical inerrancy. Some have inferred from the ongoing theological conversation that inerrancy may not be the best term to describe Scripture. Even if this is the case, inerrancy, like inspiration, has become firmly imbedded in the theological literature. It is best to emphasize careful definitions rather than to attempt to adopt new terminology or to pass over the conversation entirely. We need to be reminded that the concept of inerrancy is more important than the word itself.[87]

5. *"In all matters relating to God and his creation."* Our definition states that inerrancy is not limited merely to "religious" or "spiritual" matters. Such a delimitation would create, or at least provide the framework for, an improper dualism between the physical and the spiritual. We affirm that inerrancy applies to all areas of knowledge since all truth finds its source in God. However, issues of history and science must be evaluated considering the communication means at the time of inscripturation. Modern canons of science and historiography and their concerns for exactness were not the standards for first century and yet earlier authors. These matters of nature and history must be analyzed with consideration for the author's intended level of precision, which most likely should be seen in terms of phenomenological observation.[88]

---

[86] Erickson, *Christian Theology*; Thompson, *The Doctrine of Scripture*; Feinberg, *Light in a Dark Place*.

[87] This is an important point made several times by J. I. Packer. See the select bibliography of J. I. Packer's writings on Scripture in *Doing Theology for the People of God*, 184–89. James Leo Garrett Jr. prefers the terms "dependability" or "reliability" when discussing the "truthfulness" or "inerrancy" of Scripture. Garrett Jr., *Systematic Theology*, 1:179–92 (see chap. 1, n. 47). In response to our common mentor, we agree that the underlying point is to approach Scripture as the written Word of God with teachable humbleness without finding fault. However, we also believe it remains important to make the effort, as we tried to do here and as others attempted elsewhere, to define carefully what is meant by "inerrancy." Cf. Calvin, *Institutes of the Christian Religion* 1:18.4.

[88] Adapted from Dockery, *Christian Scripture*, and Dockery, "The Inerrancy and Authority of Scripture: Affirmation and Clarifications," 13–36, (see introduction, n.

IV. Affirmations Regarding Biblical Inerrancy

After reflecting through this brief commentary on our definition, we can maintain that inerrancy primarily points to theological and epistemological matters. In providing a statement about an inerrant Bible, we must be cautious with "slippery slope" theories. However, it is vitally important to recognize that missions, evangelism, faithful Christian living, and zeal for ethical application of Scripture have almost always declined after defection from a high view of Scripture. We know that God can, and certainly does, overrule departures from orthodoxy; church history bears testimony to this truth. We must also avoid unnecessary associations with a literalistic, stilted approach to interpretation, but we dare not dissociate the issue of the Bible's truthfulness from hermeneutics. We affirm the Bible's self-witness concerning its truthfulness and reliability.[89] We also recognize biblical inerrancy is an important corollary of God's truthful nature and of Scripture's direct teaching about its divine inspiration, an inspiration which is verbal, plenary, and concursive. All Scripture finds its source in God, who through his Word and by his Spirit superintended the process of inspiration in such a way that it can be affirmed that "all Scripture is inspired by God" (2 Tim 3:16; 2 Pet 1:21).

We must seek a view of inerrancy that is consistent with the divine-human nature of Scripture. This means the phenomena must be accounted for, and Scripture's witness to itself and its divine character must be satisfied. Such an approach is not entirely dependent on a correspondence view of truth, although many of the affirmations of Scripture can be verified. Most of the theological and ethical statements in Scripture lie outside the realm of current verification and point to an eschatological expectation; thus a coherence view of truth is more applicable and encompassing for all of Scripture. We can work from a correspondence view of truth when we account for eschatological realities. Realizing these issues, we can gladly confess that the

---

15); also, Carl Trueman, "The God of Unconditional Promise," in *The Trustworthiness of God: Perspectives on the Nature of Scripture*, ed. Paul Helm and Carl Trueman (Grand Rapids: Eerdmans, 2002), 175–91.

[89] See Gleason L. Archer Jr., "The Witness of the Bible to Its Own Inerrancy," in *The Foundation of Biblical* Authority, ed. James Montgomery Boice (Grand Rapids: Zondervan, 1978), 85–99, who points to both explicit and implicit references to the Bible's self-witness.

Bible is a dependable, reliable, truthful, trustworthy, faithful, and thus infallible and inerrant Word of God to humanity.[90]

The Bible, like other forms of human communication, is certainly more than true assertions. Communication involves emotions, aesthetic and affective abilities, and the will, in addition to propositional statements. Certainly, praise is more than a propositional statement. While a psalm may include a declaration of God's faithfulness, it is true even if it is not principally a proposition. The same can be said for ethical commands. So, although we affirm the inerrancy of the Bible, the idea of total trustworthiness better describes the whole of the Bible and its uniqueness. It is important to say more than just that the Bible's propositions are true, though we certainly wish to say no less than this. We can joyfully affirm that all aspects of Christian Scripture are totally reliable.[91]

While truth is more than propositional, as previously noted this certainly does not imply that it is less than propositional. Biblical truth is not just some mystical encounter or vague experience that people have as a result of reading Scripture. The fact that truth is more than doctrine should never be used to imply that doctrine is unimportant. Truth would be unknowable and incommunicable without the doctrinal framework and propositional grounding we find in the Bible. Thus, we can affirm the Bible's total truthfulness, its coherence, and its perspicuity and clarity made possible by the witness of the Holy Spirit. The Bible focuses on Jesus Christ, is applicable for the church, and is affirmed to us by the testimony of the Holy Spirit in our hearts. Without these presuppositions we cannot move forward in understanding how Scripture should be rightly interpreted or applied to our lives.[92]

---

[90] John Jefferson Davis, *Theology Primer: Resources for the Theology Student* (Grand Rapids: Baker, 1981), 20–21; also, the important discussion in Feinberg, *Light in a Dark Place*, 248–54. We have discussed these matters in greater detail in an earlier chapter.

[91] Kevin J. Vanhoozer, *Biblical Authority after Babel: Retrieving the Solas in the Spirit of Mere Christianity* (Grand Rapids: Brazos, 2016); Kevin J. Vanhoozer and Daniel J. Treier, *Theology and the Mirror of Scripture: A Mere Evangelical Account* (Downers Grove: IVP, 2015).

[92] Feinberg, *Light in a Dark Place*, 235–53; Smith, "Non-Foundational Epistemologies," 833–43; Joel R. Beeke and Paul M. Smalley, *Reformed Systematic Theology: Revelation and God* (Wheaton: Crossway, 2019), 276–79; 376–81.

Before turning to matters regarding interpretation and application as well as the Bible's authority and sufficiency, we summarize our discussion to this point in the volume by affirming the Bible's two-sided divine-human character. Equally, we have observed that the Bible testifies to its own divine nature and inspiration. Divine inspiration should be understood primarily as referring to the final product, the written text, although we desire to avoid any unnecessary tension between the Spirit's enablement of the human authors of the text and the inspiration of the written text itself. It is our conclusion, however, that a view of the inspiration limited to the human authors alone is insufficient. While focusing on the product of inspiration—the inscripturated text—we do not want to ignore the purpose and process of inspiration. Inspiration is ultimately for salvific purposes, including teaching, reproof, correction, and training in righteousness, so that believers can be equipped for godliness, faithful service, and good works (2 Tim 3:16–17).[93] The process of inspiration includes the training and preparation of the authors, their research, and their use of witnesses. As a result, we can posit that the Bible is simultaneously the Word of God and the words of the prophetic-apostolic messengers.

We believe it is important to note at this point that inspiration does not mean God dictated all of Scripture, for this fails to account for the human activity. Neither can it be affirmed that the Bible is merely a human book, whose authors due to a spiritual sensitivity produced inspiring and inspirational works of literature. Not only must inspiration recognize the human authorship and the divine character of Scripture; it must not divorce God's deeds from his words. Neither must we create dichotomies between thoughts and words, processes and product, writers and written word, or God's initiating impulse and his complete superintending work. A comprehensive verbal, plenary, and concursive view of inspiration is essential.[94]

This understanding of biblical inspiration applies to all of canonical Scripture, including the process, the purpose, and ultimately the product. It asserts that by the concursive action of God the Scriptures are, in their entirety, both the work of the Holy Spirit and the work of human authors.

---

[93] See D. A. Carson, *Collected Writings on Scripture* (Wheaton: Crossway, 2010), 55–110.

[94] Morrison, *Has God Said?*, 186–220.

Such a view of inspiration is not only plausible but necessarily important for affirmations of truth. We believe a plenary, verbal, inclusive view of inspiration alone does justice to the theological teachings and the phenomena within the biblical text.

We examined these conclusions in light of the human authorship of the Bible. We recognized that a concursive view of inspiration accounted for the style, personality, background, and context of the human authors. We noted the possibility of confessing a concursive view because the human authors were not autonomous but were men of faith, functioning in the communities of faith with an awareness of God's direction in their lives. Consistent with our view of the genuine humanness of the biblical text is the need to notice the cultural-temporal factors involved. Recognition that the writers were bearers of the image of God, however, opens up the possibility of qualifying historical and cultural distance. This is due to the belief that the writers, along with their readers and hearers, had memories of the past, consideration of the present, and expectations of the future. This allows for the possibility of cross-cultural and cross-temporal communication.

The reality of human authorship is evidenced by the variety of emphases in Scripture, the different writing styles, and the development within the Old and New Testaments as well as among the writers themselves. This variety is complementary and not contradictory. The variety of Scripture has a genuine unity that is not forced on the text but is present and evident as a result of divine inspiration.[95] With Scripture, we have unity, not uniformity, and variety, not discrepancy.[96] God communicates with his people through various writers using various genres and styles, including law, poetry, prophecy, narrative, wisdom literature, historical accounts, gospels, and letters (Heb 1:1–2). The variety, while quite real, may create apparent discrepancies that are challenging to reconcile, but they do not constitute contradictions.[97] The diversity can be understood within the one true story of God's

---

[95] Webster, *Holy Scripture* (see chap. 1, n. 73).

[96] Daniel Fuller, *The Unity of the Bible: Unfolding God's Plan for Humanity* (Grand Rapids: Zondervan, 2000).

[97] See Gleason L. Archer Jr., *The Encyclopedia of Bible Difficulties* (Grand Rapids: Zondervan, 1982); Vern S. Poythress, "Understanding an Alleged 'Contradiction,'" in *Inerrancy and Worldview: Answering Modern Challenges to the Bible* (Wheaton: Crossway, 2012), 153–57.

redemptive plan for his people in and through the Lord Jesus Christ, the living Word of God.[98]

While the concept of biblical inerrancy continues to raise red flags in some contexts and remains a subject of misunderstanding among others, we believe it remains an adequate term to describe the results of the Holy Spirit's work of inspiration. J. I. Packer has identified four problems linked with some models of inerrancy. He suggests inerrancy is often misunderstood because of:

1. *Bad Apologetics.* It is sometimes built on faulty rationalistic apologetics.
2. *Bad Harmonization.* It often forces the Bible to say what it does not say with bad harmonizations.
3. *Bad Interpretation.* It often is preoccupied with what are actually minor aspects of the Bible and a failure to focus on its central message.
4. *Bad Theology.* The Bible is often treated as merely a source of information; thus, its Christocentric dimension is missed.[99]

Certainly, there are real challenges. Still Packer maintains the need to affirm inerrancy because when rightly understood, (1) it affirms biblical inspiration, (2) it provides interpretative guidance, and (3) it safeguards biblical authority.[100]

V. Both the Word and the Spirit

Christians have historically affirmed the objective reality of God's revelation to his people and the subjective witness and affirmation of God's Spirit.[101] The combination of both these important affirmations remains both needful and helpful. Doing so helps us to guard against over-spiritualizing and

---

[98] See Vaughn Roberts, *God's Big Picture: Tracing the Storyline of the Bible* (Downers Grove: IVP, 2003); Preben Vang, *The Bible Story: From Genesis to Revelation* (Nashville: B&H, 2019).

[99] J. I. Packer, "Notes on Biblical Inerrancy," Lecture 12 (Regent College, Fall 1978).

[100] See J. I. Packer, "Infallibility and Inerrancy," in *New Dictionary of Theology*, ed. D. Wright, S. Ferguson, and J. I. Packer (Downers Grove: IVP, 1988), 337–39.

[101] Donald G. Bloesch, *A Theology of Word and Spirit* (Downers Grove: IVP, 2005).

over-personalizing revelation. John Calvin addressed this issue during the time of the Reformation:

> The Holy Spirit so inheres in his truth, when he expresses in Scripture, that only when its proper reverence and dignity are given to the Word does the Holy Spirit show forth his power. . . . The children of God . . . see themselves without the Spirit of God bereft of the whole light of truth, so are not unaware that the Word is the instrument by which the Lord dispenses the illumination of his Spirit to believers. For they know no other Spirit than him who dwelt and spoke in the apostles, and by those oracles they are continually recalled to the hearing of the Word.[102]

We must be wary of the errors involved when over-spiritualizing or over-personalizing the text. But James Boice also observes that the combination of the objective work of the Word and the subjective work of the Spirit also keeps us from the error of rationalizing God's truth:

> That error was evident in the diligent Bible study habits of the scribes and Pharisees in Jesus' time. The scribes and Pharisees were not slothful students. They were meticulous in their pursuit of Bible knowledge, even to the point of counting the individual letters of the Bible books. Yet, Jesus rebuked them saying, "You search the scriptures, because you think that in them you have eternal life; and it is they that bear witness to me" (John 5:39).[103]

The witness of the Spirit guides God's people to affirm the full truthfulness of God's written Word. Without the ministry of God's Spirit, the truthfulness of God's Word will never impress itself adequately on one's life. While the work of the Spirit is primary,[104] we need to mention other

---

[102] Calvin, *Institutes of the Christian Religion*, I.9.3.

[103] James Montgomery Boice, *The Sovereign God* (Downers Grove: IVP, 1978), 65.

[104] Graham A. Cole, *He Who Gives Life: The Doctrine of the Holy Spirit* (Wheaton: Crossway, 2007), 259–80; J. Theodore Mueller, "The Holy Spirit and the Scriptures," in *Revelation and the Bible*, ed. Carl F. H. Henry (Grand Rapids: Baker, 1958), 265–82; also see Malcolm B. Yarnell III, *Who Is the Holy Spirit?: Biblical Insights into His Divine Person* (Nashville: B&H, 2019).

witnesses to the Bible's truthfulness.[105] We noted earlier in this book the importance of the Bible's testimony to itself and of the witness of the Lord Jesus to the Bible. In addition, we can point to the superiority and coherence of the Bible's doctrinal and ethical teaching. This truth leads to another, which is that the biblical writers would not have affirmed the Bible as divine if they knew in their hearts that the teaching was merely their own.

In chapter 6, we observed the overall unity of the Bible, while acknowledging its genuine diversity. This profound unity is evident because behind the work of more than forty human authors is the remarkable superintending work of the One, divine Author. We must not forget the overarching accuracy of Scripture, the fulfillment of prophecy, and the preservation of Scripture over thousands of years. Not to be left out is the reality that lives are transformed by the reading, hearing, and application of the Bible, including the transformation in our own lives and the ongoing process of sanctification (John 17:17). Throughout the history of Christianity, it has proven true, over and over again, that the gospel of Jesus Christ operating through the enabling work of the Holy Spirit by means of the written Word of God renews and transforms human lives. Together, this combination of witnesses leads us to affirm the Bible is the fully truthful, inspired, inerrant, and authoritative written Word of God.

VI. Conclusion

We have noted the plausibility of maintaining the normative character of Scripture while simultaneously affirming the historical situation of the human authors and the time-relatedness of the biblical text. Because of the basic needs shared by men and women of all ages and ethnicities in all times, places, and cultures, the central message of Scripture speaks in a normative and authoritative manner. Beyond this we have acknowledged that Scripture speaks not only to pietistic and religious needs but to the truth of and about God, and to the ramifications affecting all matters related to life

---

[105] John Piper, *A Peculiar Glory: How the Christian Scriptures Reveal Their Complete Truthfulness* (Wheaton: Crossway, 2016), 195–280; William D. Mounce, *Why I Trust the Bible: Answers to Real Questions and Doubts People Have about the Bible* (Grand Rapids: Zondervan, 2021).

and godliness. We believe that all canonical Scripture is inspired and ought therefore to be described as completely truthful, infallible, reliable, dependable, trustworthy, and inerrant. We have argued that biblical inerrancy should be carefully defined to avoid overstatement or improper associations with a dictation theory of inspiration.

We believe, therefore, that it is important, even epistemologically necessary, that the people of God carefully articulate, affirm, and confess a statement concerning Scripture that maintains with equal force both the divine and human aspects of the Bible. We can have confidence in the Bible, the written Word of God, as a true and trustworthy guide for all aspects of life. Even with the challenges related to interpreting Holy Scripture, we accept the difficulties and humbly affirm the truthfulness of God's written Word without finding fault. Now, let us turn our attention to the important characteristics of biblical authority and sufficiency.

9

The Sufficiency and the Authority of Scripture

Orthodox Christians wisely affirm and refuse to relinquish certain attributes of Scripture, including its authority, sufficiency, inerrancy, and infallibility. These biblical attributes are grounded in the perfections of God and conveyed by Christ Jesus through the Holy Spirit's inspiration of the prophets and the apostles to their writings. Due to the Bible's origin in God's perfect revelation of himself, we affirm the inerrancy of the original autographs and the infallibility of the canonical text which the Holy Spirit has preserved for the church. These doctrines remind us that the Holy Bible remains thoroughly dependable, trustworthy, and true.

This chapter focuses on two attributes which result from the Bible's inspiration by the Holy Spirit: the authority of Scripture and the sufficiency of Scripture. Preliminary definitions of biblical sufficiency and biblical authority may prove useful as we begin. Biblical sufficiency is concerned with the purpose of Scripture; biblical authority is concerned with its normative value. First, the doctrine of "the sufficiency of Scripture" states that God enabled his written Word to bring life to believers.[1] Second, "the supreme or final authority of the Bible" means that Scripture's authority resides "always

---

[1] The sixth article in the premiere English Reformation confession, The Thirty-Nine Articles, is entitled, "Of the Sufficiency of the Holy Scriptures for Salvation." *The Book of Common Prayer* (New York: Oxford University Press, 1969), 694.

above any creeds or confessions of faith or church councils or private religious experiences or opinions."[2]

Because these biblical attributes originate from their relationship to God, the first three sections below consider "the Word of God," "the Sufficiency of God," and "the Authority of God." After establishing their theological basis, we can turn to a detailed definition of the derivative doctrines of "the Sufficiency of Scripture" and "the Authority of Scripture." We will then consider their practical implications in a section entitled, "Clarifying Biblical Sufficiency and Biblical Authority." We conclude with what we believe will be a helpful set of "Affirmations and Denials." Our hope is to encourage readers to maintain both biblical sufficiency and biblical authority as gifts to the church from the God who has perfect sufficiency and entire authority.

I. The Word of God

In two powerful passages, the prophet Isaiah discloses that God invests his Word with eternal power and sends it into the world to accomplish his own will. The first states, "The grass withers, the flowers fade, but the word of our God remains forever" (Isa 40:8). The second says, "So my word that comes from my mouth will not return to me empty, but it will accomplish what I please, and will prosper in what I send it to do" (55:11). The term, "the Word of God," and near terms, like "the Word of the Lord," are found throughout the Old and New Testaments.

"Word of God" is used in three significant ways in the Bible. First, the apostle John reveals the profound mystery that the eternal Christ is personally the Word of God who became a human being in Jesus (John 1:1, 14). Second, alongside the Word of God who is the Second Person of the Trinity, Paul affirmed his own preaching should be received as the Word of God (1 Thess 2:13). Third, both John and the author of Hebrews inform us the Bible may also be identified as the Word of God, having come in written form through the Old Testament prophets and the New Testament apostles (John 10:35; Heb 4:12). James Leo Garrett Jr. thus concluded, "the Bible is at the same time the Word of God and the words of human beings."[3]

---

[2] Garrett, *Systematic Theology*, 1:205 (see chap. 1, n. 47).
[3] Garrett, *Systematic Theology*, 1:182.

We must carefully maintain these biblical distinctions between the incarnate Word of God, the preaching of the Word of God, and the Word of God written by the apostles. The *incarnate Word* is the person of Jesus Christ, who was sent from the Father and appeared to the apostles. The *written Word* is the coordinate testimony of the prophets and the apostles alongside the Holy Spirit, who was given by Jesus Christ to his human servants. The *proclaimed Word* is comprised of the Law and of the gospel delivered through both the Old Testament prophets and the New Testament apostles. Jesus promised the testimony of the Spirit would inform the testimony of his apostles (John 15:26–27), and he continues to do so today through the church's continual preaching of their written testimony.

At this point, it might be helpful to distinguish between *nature* and *grace*, the ontological nature of God within himself and the economic grace of God toward his creatures. The incarnate Word possesses the fullness of God by nature. The Holy Spirit possesses the fullness of God by nature too (John 16:15). However, it was by the grace of the Holy Spirit, rather than by nature, that the apostles and prophets recorded the written Word regarding the incarnate Word. The holiness or perfection of the Spirit is granted as an act of revelatory grace to the testimony of the apostles and the prophets (2 Pet 1:19–21). Our regular and sufficient access to saving knowledge of the incarnate Word today comes by means of the words of the prophets and the apostles, who were inspired by the Spirit (2 Tim 3:16). By grace, the written words of the biblical authors are adequate to convey to us the truth of the incarnate Word of God by nature.

We may confidently say that the written Word, the Holy Bible, shares in the perfections of God by grace. This is clearly the case, for instance, with the trinitarian attribute of "truth" (John 1:14; 14:6, 17, etc.), which was conveyed to the apostles as the words of the Father and the Son (John 17:17), as we noted at length in chapter 4. These simultaneously divine and apostolic words, in turn, came to the early church in spoken form and in written form. Once the word of truth is written down, it can thereafter be spoken to others as the word of truth. God thereby continues to reveal himself today through the revelation given to the prophets and the apostles and recorded by them yesterday. The Christian church has, since its early days, been at its best when it proclaims their writings, collected in the Bible, as the true Word of God.

To illustrate the unity and distinctions regarding the Word of God, we may refer to tradition, philosophy, and liturgy. First, borrowing from patristic language, we may affirm the incarnate Word of God, Jesus Christ the Lord, is divine *by nature*. The written and oral forms of the Word of God share in certain communicable attributes of God, but *by divine grace*. Second, a philosophical way to make this distinction states that, in the first place, Jesus is the Word of God *ontologically*, in his being. In the second place, the writings of the prophets and apostles along with their proclamation today are the Word of God *epistemologically*, by way of knowledge. Third, in a liturgical vein, we properly *worship* the person of the Word of God, the eternal Son, because he is God. During our worship, public or private, we *respect* the gifts of the written Word and the proclaimed Word because they testify to God. We learn to worship the person of the Word of God through the written and spoken testimony of the Word of God.

II. The Sufficiency of God

The divine movement of grace by participation can also be seen in the way God shares his "sufficiency" with the biblical writers' testimony through granting them the accompanying testimony of his Holy Spirit. Because God is sufficient in himself, we know his self-revelation is sufficient to speak through his ministers and make their words sufficient for that which God designs. The Greek noun *ikanotēs* means "competency," "adequacy," or "sufficiency." Sufficiency is treated in the New Testament as a first principle belonging to the nature of the triune God. By extension, the grace of sufficiency proceeds from God's Spirit to the church through the biblical writers' ministry.

The grounding of competency in God himself and the sharing of his competency by the grace of his Spirit working through his apostles is outlined in 2 Cor 3:5–6. The Greek term for sufficiency is there used three times, once each in the adjectival, nominal, and verbal forms. Paul writes,[4]

---

[4] "Letter" in this passage refers not to the written quality of Scripture but to the crushing demand of the old covenant external law. Paul Barnett, *The Second Epistle to the Corinthians*, The New International Commentary on the New Testament (Grand Rapids: Eerdmans, 1997), 176–77.

It is not that we are competent [*ikanoi*] in ourselves to claim any-thing as coming from ourselves, but our adequacy [*ikanotēs*] is from God. He has made us competent [*ikanōsen*] to be ministers of a new covenant, not of the letter, but of the Spirit. For the letter kills, but the Spirit gives life.

In other words, the apostle Paul's ministry does not derive from his human competence. As with all Christian ministers, his competence must come from above by divine grace rather than from within by human nature. The sufficiency of the apostolic ministry is a gift of grace from God himself. This grace accompanied the apostle's proclamation of the gospel of Jesus Christ through the powerful working of the Holy Spirit. Today, when the Christian teacher or preacher opens the written Word of God to proclaim it, the Holy Spirit continues to accompany the proclamation of the apostolic teaching about Christ, but this time through the Word-guided testimony of the minister.

Later in the same epistle, Paul described God's "grace" (*charis*) as "sufficient" (*arkei*) for whatever God sends it to do (2 Cor 12:9). Our confidence in God and his work has nothing whatsoever to do with human creatures. Rather, our confidence results from knowing the grace of God's Spirit accompanies the apostolic words to make them sufficient to accomplish God's will and reveal God's incarnate Word, Jesus Christ. God is sufficient in himself to accomplish that which he wants done. Therefore, through the sufficient grace of his Holy Spirit, God is entirely capable of accomplishing his will via the instrumentality of his Word—foremost by his Word incarnate, then by his Word in Scripture, and finally by his Word in voice.

III. The Authority of God

Timothy George argues the Old Testament description of God as *Shaddai*, typically translated into English as "Almighty," is "better rendered as 'God the All Sufficient.'"[5] A related Hebrew Old Testament term is *Yahweh Sabaoth* (lit. "Lord of Hosts"). Both Hebrew names for God were translated into the Septuagint as *pantokrator*, which derives from the Greek words for

---

[5] Timothy George, "The Nature of God: Being, Attributes, and Acts," in *A Theology for the Church*, rev. ed., ed. Daniel L. Akin (Nashville: B&H, 2014), 167.

"all" and "power."[6] The biblical terms for "power" or "sovereignty" applied to God were summarily evaluated by Garrett, who concluded, "An adequate concept of the power of God should include the fullness or plenitude of his power to execute and fulfill his purpose."[7]

The meanings of "power" and "authority" are sometimes sharply divided in modern literature, but the New Testament uses the terms both in parallel and synonymously. For instance, Paul in Eph 1:21 uses the terms *exousia* ("authority") and *dynamis* ("power") alongside *archē* ("ruler") and *kyriotēs* ("dominion") to indicate that Christ possesses the plenitude of all power and authority.[8] Moreover, although often rendered "authority," *exousia* can also carry the English meanings of "freedom," "right," and "power."[9]

In his exegetical treatment of the New Testament term *exousia*, Silva divided biblical "authority" into three theological categories: "God's authority," "the authority of Jesus," and "the authority of believers." First, the Greeks noticeably used the term "only of people." The pagan mind was consumed with defining human authorities, but the Bible grounds all authority in God. From his perfection of "absolute freedom," God determines individual destinies (Luke 12:5) and guides history to accomplish his purposes (Acts 1:7). The trinitarian God delegates authority to both human beings and angels (Matt 10:5–8; John 19:10–11; Rev 6:8; 20:4), but he also promises final judgment over all who were given authority (Rev 20:11–12). For instance, Satan has authority over this world (John 14:30; Eph 2:2; Col 1:13), but his abuse of his limited authority prompts the judgment of God (John 16:11; Rev 20:1–3).[10]

Second, Jesus possesses "plenipotentiary authority," an entire divine authority without any limit whatsoever.[11] In his earthly ministry, Jesus

---

[6] Moisés Silva, "κράτος," in *New International Dictionary of New Testament Theology and Exegesis*, 2nd ed., 5 vols. (Grand Rapids: Zondervan, 2014), 2:741.

[7] Garrett, *Systematic Theology*, 1:219–20, 257–59.

[8] "Various designations of authority are piled up to emphasize the supremacy of Christ." F. F. Bruce, *The Epistles to the Colossians, to Philemon, and to the Ephesians*, The New International Commentary on the New Testament (Grand Rapids: Eerdmans, 1984), 273.

[9] Silva, "ἐξουσία," in *New International Dictionary of New Testament Theology and Exegesis*, 2:216.

[10] Silva, "ἐξουσία," 2:216–19.

[11] Silva, "ἐξουσία," 2:220.

demonstrated profound authority—authority over demons (Luke 4:36), over the temple (Mark 11:11–17), and over human sicknesses (Matt 10:1). He had unique authority in his teaching (Matt 7:29), in his revelation of God (11:27), and in sending his apostles (28:19–20). Eternally, he has divine authority to give his own life and take it up again (John 10:18), to forgive sins (Matt 9:2–8), and to raise the dead. Proving himself the Son of God through his resurrection, Jesus said, "All authority has been given to me in heaven and on earth" (28:18). The ascription of entire authority covers not only matters upon earth but the ascription of entire authority to each of the three persons together within the eternal Godhead.[12] Divine authority is also manifest in the divine titles given to Jesus. With God the Father, the Son shares the titles of "Lord" (Rom 10:9; 1 Cor 12:3) as well as "KING OF KINGS AND LORD OF LORDS" (Deut 10:17; Dan 2:47; Rev 19:16).[13]

Third, regarding the church, Christ's possession of divine authority allows him to command his disciples to do his will by going on mission (Acts 1:8). Christ has the authority to send the Holy Spirit (John 14:12–17; 15:26). He gave the Holy Spirit to the apostles to recall all he had taught them (14:26) and to guide them into all truth (16:12–15). It is from Christ's authority via the inspiration of Scripture by the Holy Spirit that the authority of the apostles and the prophets, and the consequent authority of their writings, derive (2 Tim 3:15–17; 2 Pet 1:19–21). It is due to the presence of the testimony of the Holy Spirit with the testimony of the disciples to the world (John 15:26–27) that the apostolic and prophetic testimony preserved in Scripture has the convicting authority to save people (16:7–11).

In ancient times, the attempt to lessen the authority of Jesus Christ as the eternal Son of God was part and parcel of the greatest heresy in the history of the universal church, Arianism. In modern times, the challenge of Arianism remains, but there also arose an attack upon the authority of the Bible. The challenge of rationalist criticism which developed during the

---

[12] This is not the place to discuss the novel teaching of eternal functional subordination, or eternal relations of authority and submission, which is held by some modern evangelicals, except to say that it is widely doubted.

[13] "The name emphasizes the universal sovereignty of the warrior Christ in his eschatological triumph over all the enemies of God." Robert H. Mounce, *The Book of Revelation*, rev. ed., The New International Commentary on the New Testament (Grand Rapids: Eerdmans, 1977), 356.

Enlightenment has joined the challenge of Arianism to become one of the most debilitating problems facing the church today.[14] Arianism challenges the authority of the personal Word of God, while radical criticism challenges the authority of the written Word of God. Both challenges must be identified, rebuked, and corrected.

IV. The Sufficiency of Scripture

God's written Word is sufficient to accomplish the task for which God sends it. But what does God want his Word to accomplish? We have elsewhere defined the intention of God in his Word in terms of salvation, holiness, and good works. "The Word was written for instruction and encouragement (Rom 15:4), to lead to saving faith (2 Tim 3:15), to guide people toward godliness (2 Tim 3:16b), and to equip believers for good works (2 Tim 3:17)."[15] We drew upon the second major passage which speaks of "sufficiency" in the New Testament, which is also the *locus classicus* for the doctrine of biblical inspiration.

Before reviewing that passage again, it is important to consider a reminder that all biblical revelation remains always focused upon Jesus Christ. "Jesus Christ is the center to which everything in Scripture is united and bound together—the beginning and the end, creation and redemption, humanity, the world, the fall, history, and the future." Dockery warns against the many problems which will result "if this overriding unity is ignored."[16] The written Word of God must never be interpreted apart from continual reference to the incarnate Word of God.

While the terms concerning sufficiency in 2 Corinthians are closely related and deal with God, the terms concerning sufficiency in 2 Tim 3:15–17 are various and concerned with the divine power within and the divine purpose for the biblical text:

> And you know that from infancy you have known the sacred
> Scriptures, which are able [*dunamena*] to give you wisdom for

---

[14] Ben Witherington III, *The Living Word of God: Rethinking the Theology of the Bible* (Waco: Baylor University Press, 2009), 241.

[15] Dockery, "Special Revelation," 113 (see introduction, n. 24).

[16] Dockery, "Special Revelation," 113.

salvation through faith in Christ Jesus. All Scripture is inspired by God and is profitable [*ōphelimos*] for teaching, for rebuking, for correcting, for training in righteousness, so that the man of God may be complete [*artios*], equipped [*exērtismenos*] for every good work.

Many theologians correctly emphasize the truths that the Scriptures are both "sacred" and "inspired" by God. These two statements concern the awesome nature of Scripture, which must be stated clearly to our critical age. However, these significant descriptions were originally intended to prepare the reader for the primary point of the passage. "But this statement on the divine authority of every text of Scripture is really preliminary to the main topic of the verse, which comes in the second predicate adjective."[17] The nature of Scripture is established so that the functional sufficiency of Scripture may be developed. In verse 15, Paul had written that Scripture was *dunamena*, "able," to perform God's will. In verse 16, Paul now states that Scripture is also *ōphelimos*, "profitable." Both of these terms affirm the sufficiency of Scripture to carry out God's intentions for it.

There are two other terms which concern the movement of "sufficiency," and these are related to the person and work of the believer. A person who is *artios*, "complete," has been fitted properly for a task. The complete "man of God," or "person of God,"[18] is the believer who has been equipped by Scripture for fulfilling the work of the ministry God bestowed upon his people. The wordplay between the nominal adjective *artios* (lit. "completion" or "full outfitting") and its related participial verb *exērtismenos*, "equipped," is striking.[19] The sufficiency which begins with God and is granted to the Word of God finds its penultimate end in the person of God prepared to minister God's Word to others.

But what is it that Scripture is sufficient to perform through the minister? According to this second major biblical passage regarding the sacred text's "sufficiency," Scripture has a twofold function: God inspired Scripture, intending that it should, first, bring "wisdom for salvation" and, second, bring

---

[17] Towner, *The Letters to Timothy and Titus*, 590 (see chap. 6, n. 44).
[18] Towner, *The Letters to Timothy and Titus*, 592.
[19] Towner, 593.

"righteousness" for entire sanctification displayed in good works. We may locate these two purposes of the sufficiency of Scripture systematically in the doctrine of salvation. Scripture is powerful and profitable for the proclamation which prompts our salvation and for our salvation's completion in holiness. The Holy Spirit inspired Paul to convey to believers the saving purpose which God intends Scripture to fulfill.

God's soteriological purposes are both quite specific and completely glorious. The first purpose of biblical sufficiency is to equip the people of God with the form of proclamation which leads to human salvation. The way of salvation is disclosed in the dialectic between Law and Gospel. The law instructs the hearer regarding his or her personal responsibility and failure before God. The gospel then instructs the hearer regarding the free offer of salvation intended for every sinner who believes in the atoning death and justifying resurrection of Jesus Christ. Scripture, through both the law and the gospel together, sufficiently provides human beings who will hear it with the opportunity to be justified.

The second purpose of biblical sufficiency may be categorized according to the related ideas of personal holiness ("so that the man of God may be complete") and of God-honoring communal edification and human flourishing ("equipped for every good work").[20] We conclude, therefore, that Scripture is sufficient for the purposes of God. And God's purposes for Scripture, which has been made sufficient by grace for the tasks he gave to Scripture, are our justification and our sanctification. The person of God is enabled to receive the grace which fulfills these tasks by the divinely chosen means of the biblical texts.

V. The Authority of Scripture

The authority of Scripture and the authority of the proclamation of Scripture are grounded in the nature of the Bible as the Word of God. The New Hampshire Confession of Faith (1833) and the Baptist Faith and Message (1925, 1963, 2000) borrow language from a letter written by the philosopher John Locke. This language has stood the test of time because

---

[20] Cf. Bingham, "Biblical Inspiration, Authority, and Canonicity," 96–97 (see introduction, n. 23).

it encapsulates so very well orthodox Christian beliefs about the author of Scripture, the sufficiency of Scripture, the truthfulness of Scripture, and the inerrancy of Scripture. These four doctrines of Scripture are intimately bound with one another. Locke and the Baptists said the Holy Bible "has God for its author, salvation for its end, and truth, without any mixture of error, for its matter."[21]

First, God is the ultimate "author" of Scripture by means of the Holy Spirit's verbal plenary *inspiration* of the biblical writers and their writings. Second, the "end" or goal or purpose of Scripture is human "salvation." The second part of Locke's famous sentence succinctly defines the *sufficiency* of Scripture. Third, the "matter" of Scripture is "truth." Locke was a Christian philosopher standing near the headwaters of the Enlightenment and was aware of the challenges to truth which were mounting. Baptists incorporated his statement, because they recognized "truth" is something which comes from God and stands in judgment of human reason. The matter of truth, ultimate truth, is not an idea to be constructed by human effort but a gift to be received by divine revelation. This is the doctrine of biblical *truthfulness*. Fourth, the truth is "without any mixture of error." The assaults of radical biblical criticism were directed at the truthfulness of the Bible, which the radical critics believed was filled with errors. Their speculative criticisms are defeated by means of the Christian's faith statement that the Word of God is perfect or without error, or in another word, *inerrant*.

The three biblical attributes of biblical sufficiency, biblical truthfulness, and biblical inerrancy derive from the fact that Holy Scripture participates by grace in the authority of the "author" of Scripture. Later in its article on the Bible, after affirming the author of the Bible is God, the Baptist Faith and Message addresses a fourth biblical attribute, the authority of Scripture. The confession states Scripture is "the supreme standard by which all human conduct, creeds, and religious opinions should be tried." The "authority" of Scripture is divine because the "author" of Scripture is divine; Scripture's authority derives from God's authority. Since the Word of God himself is the origin and the end of all authority, his written Word remains today the

---

[21] On Locke's reception by the Baptists, see Malcolm B. Yarnell III, "The Baptists and John Locke," in *Baptist Political Theology*, ed. Thomas S. Kidd, Paul D. Miller, and Andrew T. Walker (Nashville: B&H, 2023), 97–122.

final authority among human beings. Where Scripture speaks, it speaks with divine authority.

Our belief in the authority of Scripture originates not, however, with our dogmatic tradition. The Bible first affirmed the authority of Scripture in numerous ways. In his first epistle to the church of Thessalonica, the apostle Paul heartily affirmed the church's initial reception of his preaching. "This is why we constantly thank God, because when you received the word of God that you heard from us, you welcomed it not as a human message, but as it truly is, the word of God, which also works effectively in you who believe" (1 Thess 2:13). Paul admitted his humanity and fallibility in numerous places, so he understood any good from him was simply instrumental, a movement entirely dependent upon divine grace (1 Tim 1:15; 1 Cor 15:9–10). Likewise, Paul recognized his human words could claim no authority over other lives whatsoever. Rather, the apostolic words have authority over human lives because they come from God through the apostles.

Scripture's authority continues through the transmission of the biblical texts written by the Old Testament prophets and New Testament apostles. The Word of God continues to possess divine authority through the whole process of transmission. The process of transmission can be described in this way: First, the work of the Holy Spirit of God is to guide the church continually into the truth about Christ and God. Second, the Spirit of God inspired the biblical text in the beginning (2 Tim 3:16). Third, the Spirit of God preserves the teachings of Christ for the church in the biblical canon (John 14:16–17, 25–26; 15:26–27; 16:7–15). Fourth, the Spirit of God illumines the biblical text to its readers, interpreters, and hearers (2 Pet 1:19–21). The Spirit guides the tradition of the church focused upon Christ, the prophets, and the apostles. However, the church must also be careful not to allow "human tradition," for they "nullify" God's Word (Mark 7:6–13; cf. Isa 29:13).

The infallible authority of the Holy Bible must be differentiated from fallible human authority. There are numerous biblical references which buttress the authority of Scripture by referring the authority of its words to the eternal God. The written Word is the Word of the Lord, and it must be respected as such. To King Jehoiakim, who was unhappy with God's warnings, Jeremiah was told to write, "You have burned the scroll." Therefore, in judgment, God says, "I will punish him." "I will bring on them . . . all the disaster, which I warned them about, but they did not listen" (Jer 36:29–31). The written Word is the Word of the Holy Spirit. The author of Hebrews cited the prophets, describing their writings as what "the Holy Spirit says" (Heb 3:7). The writings of the prophets are what God once "said," "has spoken," and now "says" (Heb 4:3, 4, 5). The specific words of the prophets long ago are ascribed authority today because they derive from the eternal God. "He specified this speaking through David after such a long time" (Heb 4:7). The authority of Scripture is eternal, moving across time, space, and culture to speak now whatever the eternal God wants spoken, in the past, in the present, and in the future.

VI. Clarifying Biblical Sufficiency and Biblical Authority

In a prior discussion of special revelation, we provided some clarifying details regarding the sufficiency of Scripture: First, the sufficiency of Scripture is extremely important. It is a "foundational" and "necessary" doctrine.[22] Second, we must be careful not to misuse the doctrine of the sufficiency of Scripture. The English Reformers agreed. In their article on the sufficiency of Scripture, they state, "Holy Scripture containeth all things necessary to salvation." Therefore, "whatsoever is not read therein, nor may be proved thereby is not to be required of any man, that it should be believed as an article of faith, or thought requisite or necessary for salvation."[23]

The early British Baptists agreed with the English Reformers and positively united the sufficiency of Scripture with the authority of Scripture. "The Holy Scripture is the only sufficient, certain, and infallible rule of all saving knowledge, faith, and obedience."[24] The Second London Confession likewise focuses the sufficiency of Scripture upon "saving knowledge, faith, and obedience." It also clarified the sufficiency of Scripture by noting general revelation was insufficient for bringing salvation. We therefore offered three similar qualifications regarding our use of biblical sufficiency: First,

---

[22] Dockery, "Special Revelation," 146.

[23] Book of Common Prayer, 694.

[24] *The Second London Baptist Confession of Faith* (London, 1689; Reprint, Pensacola, FL: Chapel Library), ch. 1.

the teaching of Scripture is sufficient for God's purposes but *not exhaustive* for our purposes. As we argued previously, "the Scriptures do not provide exhaustive teaching." For instance, Scripture does not speak to everything about creation from a scientific perspective. After all, the Bible devotes only one chapter to describing the divine act of creation.[25] We must submit to Scripture's declared sufficiency and not seek to add to its sufficiency with our own ideas.

Second, we previously noted that the doctrine of scriptural sufficiency "does not suggest that *creeds and confessions* have no place in the life of the church." Scripture provides the basis for the church to discern its necessary dogmas and to put them in language useful for instruction and for liturgy. Of course, the doctrine of sufficiency does remind us that credal statements must themselves derive from Scripture.[26] The necessary teachings of the universal church regarding the central dogmas of the Trinity and of Jesus Christ have been summarized in the ecumenical creeds. And the biblical basis of these universal creeds has been well established.[27] Scripture also teaches important matters beyond the basics of the "rule of faith" or "analogy of faith," and those doctrines must also be taught. But the center of Scripture in Jesus Christ may not be diminished.

Third, Scripture does not address some of the *mundane matters* of life, such as Scripture is not intended to teach you how to tie your shoes, even though you need to learn such to function in certain societies. This reminds us that God works not only through special revelation but through his common gift of wisdom to all human beings. Scripture provides its readers and hearers with sufficient spiritual and moral principles by which we should conduct ourselves in this world. Scripture ought not be treated as a manual for baking bread or splitting atoms. Instead, Scripture prompts us to provide bread for the poor and wisdom to navigate challenging decisions.

We also have said, as we come expectantly to Scripture to lead us sufficiently, we should remember Scripture must be read with reference to its various genres rather than as mere "cookbook-like instructions." The Word's

---

[25] Dockery, "Special Revelation," 146.

[26] Dockery, 146.

[27] On the biblical basis of the Nicene doctrine of the Trinity, see Yarnell, *God the Trinity* (see chap.1, n. 78).

primary concern is "to tell us who God is and who we are," and from there, to bring us to a right relationship with God. Rather than treating Scripture with an infantile, glib, and facile attitude expecting easy answers, biblical sufficiency invites us into a living relationship with God in Jesus Christ by the power of the Holy Spirit. The long and arduous path of biblical discipleship is a process that only a minority of today's postmodern generations, trained in the immediate gratification school of pragmatism, seem equipped to endure.[28]

Because it is sufficient for God's purposes, we come to Scripture to proclaim Christ and to receive salvation. God uses his written Word to address us at the point of our deepest need, our own human hearts. The human heart is prone to self-delusion and wickedness, but God's Word dynamically acts as God's agent to judge the thoughts and intentions of the human heart (Heb 4:12). We must "give an account" to the One who approaches us in his Word (Heb 4:13). We are typically unaware of our own intentions, so God's external Word opens our eyes to the depths of our personal depravity, bringing conviction through the internal work of the Holy Spirit (John 16:8–11). He thus prepares us to receive the good news of Jesus Christ, which brings forgiveness. The dynamic working of God, his Word, and his Spirit upon the receptive human being involves an ongoing process. God's ultimate purpose is to bring us the holiness required for communion with a Holy God. The written Word of God works sufficiently and authoritatively as God by his Holy Spirit speaks directly to the human heart in need of salvation and growth in godliness.

Where the Particular Baptists began their approach to the Bible with a careful definition of the sufficiency of Scripture, the General Baptists began their approach with a careful definition of the authority of Scripture. Echoing what we have argued above, they wrote, "The Authority of the holy Scripture, dependeth not upon the Authority of any Man, but only upon the Authority of God, who hath delivered and revealed his mind therein unto us." Scripture's authority derives from God's authority alone. The General Baptists also defined the purpose of Scripture's authority. Believers ought to "endeavour to frame their Lives, according to the direction of God's Word, both in faith and practice, the holy Scriptures being

---

[28] Dockery, "Special Revelation," 147.

of no private Interpretation, but ought to be interpreted according to the
Analogie of Faith, and is the best Interpreter of it self; and is sole Judge in
Controversie." To conclude their high view of Scripture's authority, they
rebuked other traditions for appealing to other norms: "And no Decrees
of Popes, or Councils, or Writings of any Person whatsoever, are of equal
Authority with the sacred Scriptures."[29]

It is important to note that the early Baptists affirmed the normative
authority of Scripture as supreme. Their extremely high view of biblical
authority did not, however, keep them from seeing the potential utility of
other sources. Christian theological sources, like those found in ecumenical
councils or in personal writings, may possess limited authority, but not "equal
Authority." Both of the early major Baptist groups, the General Baptists
and the Particular Baptists, drew upon language from the major ecumenical creeds in their confessions. The General Baptists even republished the
Apostles' Creed, the Nicene Creed, and the Athanasian Creed.[30] They recognized that Christians never interpret the Bible on their own. Because the
Spirit is the interpreter of Scripture, and all Christians receive the Spirit, we
must have exegetical conversation within our local churches and with the
universal church in general.

Recognizing the authority of the Bible as providing the source and norm
of all theological discussion, Garrett employed the Latin term, *suprema scriptura*, to describe the normative authority of the Bible.[31] After reviewing the
biblical basis and the historic responses, Garrett crafted five statements to
describe "the nature of biblical authority:" First, "The Bible is authoritative
primarily as a book of religion or of divine revelation." Second, "The authority of the message of the Bible transcends the societal, geographical, and
chronological matrix of the biblical books," contrary to the claims of cultural
relativists. Third, "The authority of the Bible is that of the sovereign God,
who commands and persuades but does not coerce human beings." Fourth,
"The Bible is authoritative as it is accurately and faithfully interpreted in its
historical context and by the criterion of Jesus Christ, who as the promise

---

[29] *An Orthodox Creed: Or, A Protestant Confession of Faith* (London, 1679;
Reprint, Fort Worth: Center for Theological Research, 2006), art. 37.
[30] *The Second London Baptist Confession of Faith*, ch. 2; *An Orthodox Creed*, art. 38.
[31] Garrett, *Systematic Theology*, 1:206.

and the fulfillment is the central personage and theme of the Bible." Fifth, "The Bible is authoritative as the Holy Spirit bestows illumination."[32]

VII. Affirmations and Denials regarding Authority and Sufficiency

As a summary for the proper way to honor the doctrines of the sufficiency and authority of Scripture, we offer some significant affirmations and denials. These affirmations and denials may occur explicitly or implicitly. Three necessary affirmations provide a positive baseline for recognizing the doctrines in practice. Afterward, we consider three common denials of biblical sufficiency and biblical authority. Sadly, some will affirm these doctrines in word even while they deny them in deed.

Affirmations

First, behind the written Word of God stands the grace of the God who is sufficient and authoritative by nature. Scripture is sufficient because God is sufficient and has chosen to grace the biblical authors and the biblical canon. Scripture is authoritative because God is the source of all authority and has granted his personal authority to the biblical authors and their texts. The Christian theologian would do well never to sunder the attributes of the written and proclaimed Word of God from the gift of God.

Second, those who look to the Bible to discover the revelation of God concerning the renewal of their personal relationship with God effectively affirm the doctrine of scriptural sufficiency. The Bible is God's Holy Word and is intended to bring human beings into a holy relation with himself. God sent his Word to show us his Law, indicating his will for us and our disobedience of that will, and to show us his gospel, indicating the death and resurrection of Jesus Christ brings forgiveness to believers. Look to the Bible to improve your walk with God, receiving as a personal word of repentance its "teaching," "rebuking," "correcting," and "training." Orthodox Christians affirm the doctrine of scriptural sufficiency in both attitude and action. You may thus draw toward complete holiness, displaying good works.

---

[32] Garrett, *Systematic Theology*, 1:208–9.

Third, orthodox Christians in the modern era affirm the authority of Scripture. Two historical movements have caused them to hone their appreciation for biblical authority. First, coming out of the Reformation, they have learned to distinguish between the fallible tradition of the church and the infallible authority of the Bible. Second, confronted by the challenges of radical historical biblical criticism, orthodox Christians have learned to appreciate the authority of Scripture vis-à-vis reason. The Reformation taught them to keep Scripture's authority above human tradition; the Enlightenment taught them to keep Scripture's authority above human reason. The doctrine of biblical inerrancy has been important in buttressing this aspect of Scripture's authority.

Denials

First, those who look to the Bible to find support for their human agendas effectively deny the doctrine of the sufficiency of Scripture. The Bible is God's Word intended to carry out God's saving purpose. People who appeal to the Word of God but use it for their own human purposes violate the first table of God's Law, which commands men not to use the "name" or authority of God "in vain," that is, for human purposes (Exod 20:7; Deut 5:11). Ungodly agendas are typically imposed upon the "sheep" of God through the forceful and deceptive actions of a spiritual "wolf." Garrett noted that, contrary to such human authoritarianism, "The authority of the Bible is that of the sovereign God, who commands and persuades but does not coerce human beings and who redeems or liberates but does not enslave human beings."[33]

Second, those who elevate their tradition or reason above God's written Word likewise deny the doctrine of biblical authority. The promotion of tradition may occur explicitly as in the case of Tridentine Catholicism. But it may occur implicitly among Protestants who say they "correctly teach the word of truth" (2 Tim 2:15) but are actually "invalidating God's command" with their own ideas (Mark 7:9). The promotion of reason occurs explicitly when higher critics study the Bible carefully but reject its claims in favor of popular canons of rationality. Through his terminology of *suprema scriptura*, Garrett rightly recalled that, although we consult other sources of theology, such as tradition, experience, or reason, Scripture alone remains the

---

[33] Garrett, *Systematic Theology*, 1:208.

supreme source of theology. Theology includes intellectual and moral teachings. Moreover, one may elevate human traditions and human rationality in two ways, by addition or by negation. If you require someone to affirm a certain teaching which cannot be supported in Scripture, you deny Scripture is sufficient by adding to it. Conversely (and equally perversely), if you require someone to deny a certain teaching which cannot be found in Scripture one way or the other, you deny Scripture is sufficient by subtracting from it.

Third, those who elevate a widely disputed interpretation which is not central to the Christian faith may deny the sufficiency of Scripture. If Christians who honor and interpret the biblical text do not come to a disputed interpretation but are nevertheless rejected for their reluctance to adopt that disputed interpretation, the argumentative person or group implies Scripture is incapable (i.e., insufficient) of bringing a certain truth to the universal church. The same warning applies to those who neglect a central teaching of the Christian faith, whether that be a key doctrine about God, Christ, the Holy Spirit, the image of God, salvation, or even an essential eschatological doctrine like the bodily resurrection. A good measure of what is a non-negotiable teaching may be found in the widely accepted Nicene Creed, Apostles' Creed, and Athanasian Creed.

This summarization through various affirmations and denials brings into sharp focus the practical implications of maintaining proper doctrines of the authority of Scripture and of the sufficiency of Scripture. Having examined the doctrines of revelation, the two ways of general revelation and special revelation, natural theologies and the nature of Holy Scripture, as well as Jesus Christ and the Bible and the divine-human authorship of Scripture, followed by the Holy Spirit's inspiration and preservation of Scripture along with the various attributes of Scripture, including inerrancy, infallibility, authority, and sufficiency, we are now prepared to turn next to detailed considerations for moving from Scripture to theology.

10

From Biblical Interpretation to Theology, Part I

Having established the doctrine of the Bible's inspiration by the Holy Spirit, and then having considered the implications of inspiration upon the product of sacred Scripture, we are now prepared to turn in the remainder of this book toward a description of how the church has both responded and ought to respond to the Spirit's illumination of the biblical text. Carl F. H. Henry stated in the twelfth of his fifteen theses on divine revelation that the Holy Spirit "superintends" the entire process of communicating divine revelation to humanity. Henry argues, correctly we believe, that the Holy Spirit engages in two major works of superintendence vis-à-vis the Holy Bible. First, the Spirit communicates divine revelation "by inspiring the prophetic-apostolic writings."[1] Recognizing the seminal importance of biblical inspiration, we thus wrote chapters 6 through 9 to highlight the Spirit's perfect work of breathing upon the text which also resulted in certain perfections or attributes being granted to the biblical canon.

In the Holy Spirit's second major work, according to Henry, the Third Person of the Trinity superintends the communication of divine revelation "by illuminating and interpreting the scripturally given Word of God."[2] In light of the significance of the Spirit's second great work with the Bible, that of illumining the text to provide human beings with the proper understanding

---

[1] Henry, *God, Revelation and Authority*, 2:13 (see chap. 1, n. 32).
[2] Henry, *God, Revelation and Authority*, 2:13.

of God and his creation and of human salvation in Christ Jesus, we therefore necessarily turn in the remaining chapters of this book to a description of the church's interpretation of the Bible under the guidance of the Holy Spirit. In this chapter, we begin with a review of the important spiritual and biblical principles revealed in Scripture for its own interpretation. We then review the earliest Christian hermeneutical method as governed by the apostolic "rule of faith." The literal and spiritual methods of pre-critical exegesis in the post-apostolic and medieval periods are then described. In chapter 11, we rehearse the Reformers' emphasis upon the historical and grammatical senses of the biblical text before perceiving and criticizing the Enlightenment hermeneutic known as the historical-critical method. We propose the way forward for evangelicals is through a careful reappropriation of the theological exegesis of Scripture which honors the rule of faith centered upon the Trinity and Jesus Christ. In our penultimate chapter, we will then review the Baptist tradition before concluding with an important discussion about the proper understanding and application of the sacred writings today.

I. Holiness and Humility

In him we have redemption through his blood, the forgiveness of our trespasses, according to the riches of his grace that he richly poured out on us with all wisdom and understanding. He made known to us the mystery of his will, according to his good pleasure that he purposed in Christ as a plan for the right time—to bring everything together in Christ, both things in heaven and things on earth in him. (Eph 1:7–10)

Before the believer may speak of hermeneutics, exegesis, or proclamation, one must consider one's personal attitude in the project of moving from Scripture to theology. The Christian interpreter is a disciple of Jesus Christ who must continually depend in faith upon her or his Lord for the ability to interpret the Bible. At the end of the classical period, Augustine perceived rightly that Scripture hides truth before it reveals truth. Like Paul, the bishop of Hippo argued the Bible is "veiled" to the unbeliever, but the divine Spirit has "removed the veil" of the repentant person (2 Cor 3:14–18). So, he resorted to prayer. "Grant me, then, space for my meditations on the hidden things of Your Law, nor close them fast against those who knock. Not for nothing have you willed so many pages to be written in veiled secrets. . . . Complete your work in me, O Lord, and open these pages to me."[3]

Augustine asserted the only way to interpret Scripture is through appropriating the theological virtues of faith, hope, and love. When the interpreter has these three, he "may approach the task of handling these books with confidence."[4] The whole of life is a process by which God unveils himself by the Spirit through the words of Scripture and the signs of the sacraments[5] to the human being, culminating in the blessed vision. For Augustine, the process of interpretation began with "fear of God" and moved through holiness to knowledge of God. The exegete moves through fortitude, compassion, and purification to enjoy the wisdom of God.[6] Gregory of Nazianzus likewise prioritized holiness in the pursuit of theology. Theology "is not for all people, but only for those who have been tested and have found a solid footing in study, and, more importantly, have undergone, or at the very least are undergoing, purification of body and soul."[7] Theology entails a continual ascent by the human being to the vision of God.[8]

During the Middle Ages, Christians who lived under various voluntary rules followed a careful discipline so they might more easily hear God in Scripture. "The mode of reading taught in the monastic schools was *lectio divina*, a slow, patient, reflective 'chewing' and ruminating which made the texts so studied ineradicably part of the furnishings of the minds which thus

---

[3] Helpful models for this chapter and the one to follow can be found in Kevin J. Vanhoozer, "From Bible to Theology," in *Theology, Church, and Ministry*, 233–56 (see chap. 8, n. 78); and Kevin J. Vanhoozer, "May We Go Beyond What Is Written After All? The Pattern of Theological Authority and the Problem of Doctrinal Development," in *The Enduring Authority of the Christian Scriptures*, ed. D. A. Carson (Grand Rapids: Eerdmans, 2016), 747–94. Also, see Augustine, *Confessions* 11.2.2; Brown, *Augustine of Hippo*, 262 (see chap. 3, n. 38).

[4] Augustine, *De Doctrina Christiana* 1.95–96; Saint Augustine, *On Christian Teaching*, trans. R. P. H. Green (New York: Oxford University Press, 1997), 29.

[5] The Latin *sacramentum* means "sign."

[6] Augustine, *De Doctrina Christiana* 2.16–23.

[7] Gregory of Nazianzus, *Oration* 27.3; Saint Gregory of Nazianzus, *On God and Christ: The Five Theological Orations and Two Letters to Cledonius*, trans. Frederick Williams and Lionel Wickham (Crestwood, NY: St. Vladimir Seminary's Press, 2002), 27.

[8] Gregory of Nazianzus, *Oration* 28.2–3.

absorbed them." The biblical literacy of a monk like Anselm allowed him
to seek understanding for his deep faith. He also read and cited previous
theologians like Augustine, Jerome, and Gregory the Great, but "as points of
departure for his own often wholly original thought."[9] A devotional mindset
attendant to Scripture was not, however, everywhere ascendant.

Martin Luther thus challenged the religious leaders of the late Medieval
church, who came to the Word of God with the arrogance of their own
minds and wills. Some Roman Catholic scholastic theologians presumed
they brought dogmatic light to the "obscurity" or "darkness" of the Bible.
Luther disagreed vehemently, believing the Word of God exercised its own
divine agency, shedding light upon the reader.[10] The light of the Word shin-
ing in the darkness humbles and destroys the pride of humanity. Luther said,
"But the fact is that if the Word of God comes, it comes contrary to our
thinking and our will. It does not allow our thinking to stand, even in those
matters which are most sacred, but it destroys and eradicates and scatters
everything."[11] Jeremiah similarly wrote that the Word comes "to uproot and
tear down, to destroy and demolish, to build and plant" (Jer 1:10).

Ulrich Zwingli, the Reformer of Zürich, also argued for the submission of the human mind to God as one approaches the Bible. This requires
suspending human teaching and praying for help from God. The trinitarian
frame of Zwingli's description is striking in its subtlety. "If you want to speak
on any matter, or to learn of it [Scripture], you must first think like this:
Before I say anything or listen to the teaching of man, I will first consult the
mind of the Spirit of God: 'I will hear what the Word of God will speak.'
Then you should reverently ask God for his grace, that he may give you his
mind and Spirit, so that you will not lay hold of your own opinion but of
his."[12] From Jeremiah to Anselm to Zwingli, the Word of God acts as the

---

[9] Brian Davies and G. R. Evans, eds., "Introduction," in *Anselm of Canterbury: The Major Works* (New York: Oxford University Press, 1998), xxi.

[10] Roland F. Ziegler, "Luther and Lutheran Orthodoxy: *Claritas* and *Perspicuitas Scripturae*," *Concordia Theological Quarterly* 81 (2017): 119–36.

[11] Martin Luther, *Lectures on Romans: Scholia*, Luther's Works, 55 vols. (St Louis, MO: Concordia Publishing House, 1972), 25:415.

[12] Ulrich Zwingli, "Of the Clarity and Certainty of the Word of God (1522)," in *Zwingli and Bullinger*, trans. Geoffrey W. Bromiley, Library of Christian Classics (Philadelphia: Fortress, 1953), 88–89.

divine agent by which God confronts sinners and saves believers, who come to the text with humility.

Speaking to those living after the advent and dominance of modern scholarship, Donald Bloesch describes a fourfold "process" for the one who wants to come to know the Word of God: First, we must come to the Bible with reverence and humility. Second, we must read the Bible with careful examination, which he describes as "criticism," although not in its modern acidic sense. Third, we must allow God's Word to judge the personal presuppositions which we bring to the text. Fourth, we must pray and be willing to learn from God's Holy Spirit.[13] Humility is both a prerequisite and a product of coming to know the Word of God.

Both Martin Luther and Donald Bloesch, one theologian living before the Enlightenment and one after the Enlightenment, arrived at similar theological conclusions regarding the need for reverence before God and thus humility in the human person dealing with the Holy Bible. They both perceived the Word of God was present and working in, with, and through the biblical text. The author of Hebrews pictures Scripture as the Word of God examining and judging the listener. The Word acts with penetrating agency to transform the reader (Heb 4:12–13).

Those Christians who wish to take the next step of constructing an orthodox theology from their encounter with the Holy Bible must come to the text with deep reverence toward God. We must also exercise humility regarding our own severe limits and thus necessary dependence upon God in the task of perceiving, explaining, and applying the text. The benefits of modern scholarship, with its incredible advances in the human reading of a manifestly human text, must be balanced by a recognition of the limits in humanity's own capabilities to deal with a manifestly divine text.

Believers must never forget that God's Spirit is the ultimate agent in the entire process which includes the inspiration, preservation, interpretation, proclamation, and reception of God's Word. First, Scripture was composed by human authors in certain times, places, and cultures, but it was inspired by the Holy Spirit as its ultimate author. Second, Scripture has been canonized, translated, and disseminated by the church with the Holy Spirit being its ultimate preserver. Third, Scripture's proper interpretation within the church

---

[13] Bloesch, *Holy Scripture*, 178–79 (see introduction, n. 2).

depends upon the Holy Spirit as its ultimate interpreter. Fourth, modern preachers and teachers, like the prophets in Scripture itself, must be careful to teach only what the Word of God says. Fifth, Scripture's reception among human beings likewise depends upon the church as its mediate witness but the Spirit as its ultimate witness. With Christian dependence upon the grace of the Spirit demonstrated, let us turn to the task of interpretation, which is described in the academic discipline of hermeneutics.

II. The Bible's Hermeneutic for the Bible

A few definitions regarding interpretation may be required here. "Hermeneutics" concerns the art and science of interpreting a literary text.[14] "Biblical hermeneutics" concerns the art and science of interpreting Holy Scripture in particular. Many systems of interpretation have been applied to the reading of the Bible, and many useful things may be learned from these various approaches. However, we argue there exists a core hermeneutic for reading Scripture correctly, the biblical hermeneutic which undergirds all true interpretation. Scripture's internal hermeneutic, simple yet multivalent, is preferable to any other hermeneutic on its own. We believe the Lord Jesus provided that hermeneutic, that the Spirit inspired the prophets and apostles to recall that hermeneutic, and that in his continuing work of illumination the Spirit continues to lead all faithful expositors—in whatever day, of whatever place, in conversation with whatever covenantal community—in the sacred endeavor to recall that hermeneutic.

Geerhardus Vos contended in his inaugural address as a professor of biblical theology that "The Bible contains besides the simple record of divine revelations, the further interpretation of these immediate disclosures of God by inspired prophets and apostles."[15] We agree that Scripture provides the

---

[14] "It is a science because it is guided by rules within a system; and it is an art because the application of the rules is by skill, and not by mechanical imitation." Bernard Ramm, *Protestant Biblical Interpretation: A Textbook of Hermeneutics*, 3rd ed. (Grand Rapids: Baker, 1970), 1.

[15] Geerhardus Vos, "The Idea of Biblical Theology as a Science and as a Theological Discipline: Inaugural Address," in *Inauguration of the Rev. Geerhardus Vos, Ph.D., D.D., as Professor of Biblical Theology* (New York: Anson D. F. Randolph and Company, 1894), 33.

reader with its own interpretive key. As a self-consciously Reformed theologian, Vos was, of course, merely extending the Protestant commonplace that "Scripture interprets Scripture." Orthodox Protestants and evangelicals perceive that the Lord providentially made available the Bible's interpretation of itself in the way that it highlights its key message regarding the gospel. This rule of faith, centered on the Trinity and the person and work of Jesus Christ, provides a superior hermeneutic than if we were to interpret the Bible according to a method alien to the Spirit-inspired canon.

Tracing the interaction between the Old Testament and the New Testament, and within each testament, may help us discern this biblical hermeneutic derived from the Bible in its simplicity and complexity. The recent growth in intra-canonical biblical studies, led by scholars such as Gregory K. Beale, Richard B. Hays, and Gary E. Schnittjer, have been instrumental in a post-critical reclamation of a biblical approach to biblical interpretation.[16] As alluded to above, Paul reminds us that the Spirit must interpret the Spirit. By theological extension, we may say, the Spirit-inspired text must be interpreted according to the leading of the same Spirit, and he leads us into the mind of Christ.[17] Scripture provides numerous examples of how the

---

[16] G. K. Beale and D. A. Carson, eds., *Commentary on the New Testament Use of the Old Testament* (Grand Rapids: Baker, 2007); Gregory K. Beale, *A New Testament Biblical Theology: The Unfolding of the Old Testament in the New* (Grand Rapids: Baker, 2011); Beale, *Handbook on the New Testament Use of the Old Testament: Exegesis and Interpretation* (Grand Rapids: Baker, 2012); Richard B. Hays, *Echoes of Scripture in the Letters of Paul* (New Haven, CT: Yale University Press, 1989); Hays, *Reading Backwards*, (see chap. 5, n. 10); Hays, *Echoes of Scripture in the Gospels* (Waco: Baylor University Press, 2016); Hays, *Reading with the Grain of Scripture* (Grand Rapids: Eerdmans, 2020); Gary Edward Schnittjer, *Old Testament Use of Old Testament: A Book-by-Book Guide* (Grand Rapids: Zondervan, 2021).

[17] "Now God has revealed these things to us by the Spirit, since the Spirit searches everything, even the depths of God. For who knows a person's thoughts except his spirit within him? In the same way, no one knows the thoughts of God except the Spirit of God. Now we have not received the spirit of the world, but the Spirit who comes from God, so that we may understand what has been freely given to us by God. We also speak these things, not in words taught by human wisdom, but in those taught by the Spirit, explaining spiritual things to spiritual people. But the person without the Spirit does not receive what comes from God's Spirit, because it is foolishness to him; he is not able to understand it since it is evaluated spiritually. The spiritual person, however, can evaluate everything, and yet he himself cannot be

community of God within Scripture was led through the illuminating work of the Spirit to interpret Scripture.

For instance, after the horrors of the Exile brought about by Israel's disobedience to God's Word, carefully recalling the writings of Moses and the prophets became a primary concern. During the return to the land, the priest Ezra led the Israelites to proclaim, hear, and interpret the Law. According to Neh 8:3, Ezra "read" the Law publicly while the people gathered in Jerusalem as one and "listened attentively." Several Levites were tasked with interpreting the Law to the people, "translating" it so they could understand its meaning (Neh 8:7–8). The Hebrew word *meprash*, often rendered "translating," derives from a term meaning to "make distinct," "separate," even "explain."[18] This is one example of how the people were led to perceive and renew their worship of the Lord through the interpretation of Scripture. The community's interpretation at the time depended upon a special priesthood faithful in pedagogy. Alas, however, ancient Israel's teachers did not always remain faithful, as the Old Testament prophets amply testify (cf. Jer 23:9–40; Ezek 34:1–24; Dan 9:4–14, etc.). We must turn, therefore, to the New Testament to see how the eternal priest and greatest teacher, Jesus Christ, perfectly revealed that hermeneutic then conveyed it to his disciples.

The New Testament use of a Greek compound term derived from *hermeneutēs* may be particularly instructive in helping contemporary scholars learn and emulate the Christological development of hermeneutics. *Diermēneuō*, which means "translate," "explain," or "interpret," is used in Luke 24:27 to describe how Jesus taught the fulfillment of the Old Testament prophecies had occurred in his own death and resurrection. The post-resurrection appearances of Jesus Christ as teacher proved normative for the entire development of Christian hermeneutics. He first taught the women, then two disciples on the road to Emmaus, and finally the disciples gathered in Jerusalem. Jesus instructed his awestruck auditors that he, the Messiah himself, was the interpretive key to "all the Scriptures." His hermeneutic

---

evaluated by anyone. 'For who has known the Lord's mind, that he may instruct him?' But we have the mind of Christ" (1 Cor 2:10–16).

[18] The returning Israelites may have needed the Hebrew text not only explained but also translated into Aramaic. Traditionally, Ezra is also seen as prompting the identification of the Old Testament canon.

covered every portion of Scripture, conveying the proper interpretation of "the Law of Moses," the Torah; "the Prophets," both the historical prophets and the writing prophets; "and the Psalms," inclusive of all the poetic writings (Luke 24:44). Through his own canonically comprehensive, personally authoritative, and explicitly Christ-centered exegesis, Jesus powerfully "opened their minds to understand the Scriptures" (Luke 24:45; cf. v. 32).

The apostles received, reflected upon, and passed on the exegesis of Jesus, as seen, for example, in their rehearsal of the Lord's interpretations of key messianic texts in the Old Testament. If we examined the apostolic use of the Messianic prophecies in 2 Sam 7:11b–16, Psalm 110, and Isa 52:13–53:12, among many other such passages, it becomes clear that the person and work of Jesus the Christ, as provided by the Lord Jesus, is the hermeneutical key to the Christian Scriptures. To demonstrate this claim, a review of the use of Dan 7:13 first by Jesus then by the apostles in their New Testament writings should suffice. The identification of the person described in Daniel as "one like a son of man" (Aramaic *kebar enash*; cf. Hebrew *ben-adam*) has prompted much discussion, ancient and modern. The term "son of" typically indicates that a particular person belongs to a class or group. It is one of the most common terms in the Hebrew Bible. The description, "the son of man," began as a general classification but transitioned to a messianic title over time.

In the first instance, the Lord God applied the description to his prophet Ezekiel (Ezek 2:1, etc.), who was active near the beginning of the Exile. There, it seemed to be a way of identifying the human prophet as one of the people. The description may also allude to the prophet's vision of God, because "on the throne, high above, was someone who looked like a human" (1:26b). An allusive correlation between humanity and deity, perhaps building on the earlier Mosaic language of the image of God, was thus broached. This divine-human allusion received further clarity through the oracles of a later exilic prophet. With Daniel, the phrase "son of man" also transitioned from the realm of class or group to become more narrowly applied to a particular person.

While describing the judgments of God upon human empires, the prophet Daniel wrote, "I continued watching in the night visions, and suddenly one like a son of man was coming with the clouds of heaven. He approached the Ancient of Days and was escorted before him. He was given dominion and glory and a kingdom, so that those of every people, nation, and language should serve him. His dominion is an everlasting dominion that will not pass away, and his kingdom is one that will not be destroyed" (Dan 7:13–14). Walter Wink collected six possible interpretations, the fifth of which was adopted early in church history.[19] The typical Christian interpretation looks to Jesus as the "one like a son of man," who comes "with the clouds" to "the Ancient of Days," God the Father.

The reference of Jesus to himself as "the Son of the Man" occurs over eighty times and in all four Gospels. It appears both early and often (cf. Matt 8:20; Mark 2:10; Luke 5:24; John 1:51). Uniquely and repeatedly adopted by Jesus as a self-referent, even higher critical scholars admit the provenance of this Christological symbol or title is doubtlessly rooted in the self-same words of Jesus.[20] The title was subsequently applied to Jesus Christ by the writing apostles and their assistants. The early church thus concluded Jesus as "the Son of the Man" is the One who approaches God the Father on his eternal throne to receive everlasting dominion. Christian attention transitioned to other titles, but this undoubtedly ancient title remains a witness to the very early and very high Christology of both Jesus and the apostles.

Most significantly in his own history of self-awareness, Jesus referred to Daniel's vision at the critical moment during his trial. The High Priest confronted Jesus in the courtroom setting, asking him to declare plainly whether he was "the Messiah, the Son of God." The response of Jesus was electric in its impact upon the unbelieving Jews and deeply instructive for Christians afterwards. Jesus replied to the accusatory High Priest, "You have said it." Leaving no room for doubt regarding his self-understanding, Jesus continued, "I tell you, in the future you will see *the Son of Man seated at the right hand* of Power and *coming on the clouds of heaven*" (Matt 26:64; cf. Mark 14:60–65; Luke 22:66–71). Jesus thereby made public, in a dramatic and consequential way, his previously private claim to be the Messiah who has come from God and returns to God, proclaiming himself equal with God (cf. John 10:30–33; 16:28). Jesus's own self-reference in the context of citing Daniel 7 sealed his judgment by the Sanhedrin.

---

[19] These include the nation of Israel, Michael as the guardian of Israel, a messiah, God himself, Jesus Christ, and an ambiguous symbol. Walter Wink, *The Human Being: Jesus and the Enigma of the Son of the Man* (Minneapolis: Fortress, 2002), 53.
[20] Wink, *The Human Being*, 19–22.

After his resurrection, the apostles used Jesus's particularization regarding the description to identify the connection between the historical and eternal aspects of the person and work of Christ. "The Son of the Man" became shorthand for the Christian contention that Old Testament prophecy was fulfilled when Jesus as the Messiah suffered, died, and arose from the dead to rule at the right hand of the Father. The women at the empty tomb were reminded, "'He is not here, but he has risen! Remember how he spoke to you when he was still in Galilee, saying, "It is necessary that the Son of Man be betrayed into the hands of sinful men, be crucified, and rise on the third day."' And they remembered his words" (Luke 24:6–8). The core of the gospel message as fulfillment of Daniel's vision was given to the women first. Jesus soon after delivered the same interpretation to two male disciples on the road to Emmaus (Luke 24:25–26), then to all the disciples gathered in Jerusalem (Luke 24:45–46). Christ thus presented himself to all his followers in his very first appearances as "the Son of Man." Jesus is the One Person who inhabits the boundary encompassing both divine identity and human identity.

The Gospels were not alone in identifying Christ Jesus as the fulfillment of Daniel's prophecy. The Apocalypse of John described Jesus as the One "coming with the clouds" (Rev 1:7; cf. 1 Thess 4:17). Building on the teaching of Jesus and furthering their import, Paul taught that Christ is the perfect human being. Where Adam brought sin to humanity, Christ is "the one man" through whom the gift of righteousness is made present (Rom 5:12–21). Christ is the "second man" after Adam, "the man of heaven" who perfects the broken image of humanity (1 Cor 15:46–49). Christ is the Mediator who, as "the man" Jesus, is both the One with God and the One with humanity, ransoming human beings through his blood (1 Tim 2:5–6). Beale and D. A. Carson have collected extensive scholarly discussions concerning a dozen such references to Dan 7:13–14 in the New Testament.[21]

Jesus taught his disciples during his earthly ministry to discern the Christological nature of ancient Israel's sacred texts. Jesus then reaffirmed

---

[21] Beale and Carson, eds., *Commentary on the New Testament Use of the Old Testament*, 87–90, 93–95, 133–39, 184–85, 227–29, 292–93, 328, 378–80, 391–92, 475–76, 1090–91, 1102. Schnittjer identifies nine references in the New Testament to Dan 7:13–14. Schnittjer, *Old Testament Use of Old Testament*, 617.

this hermeneutic during his post-resurrection sojourn prior to his ascension to the Father's throne. The disciples later repeatedly returned to the same passages in their sermons and letters, along with making many similar references to the Hebrew Bible in their proclamation of the gospel. Christ Jesus himself is the key to the Christian interpretation of Scripture, and he himself provided this key, this biblically derived biblical hermeneutic, to the early church.

III. The Canon of Faith and the Canon of Scripture

But is there a way to formalize the interpretation of Scripture offered by Christ and collected in the New Testament? Is there a "standard" or "rule" which will help one read Scripture faithfully? The spiritual person who approaches the biblical text senses both its clarity and its dynamism. There is an utter simplicity to the message of Scripture, centered in the person and work of Jesus Christ, but there is also a profound complexity which emanates from that Christological center. By the sovereign power of the Holy Spirit God the Father calls the hearer of the Bible to a relationship with the triune self in Christ Jesus. Due to the divine work of Scripture, its fundamental saving message can be understood by the young novice. Accessible and unconfused in its core message, the Bible also continually opens new and unexpected treasures for the most experienced scholar.

The Bible's message is a mystery both hidden and revealed. A review of the idea of "mystery" as developed in Paul's epistle to the Ephesians may help us perceive how the early church perceived and proclaimed its basic rule of faith. Gregory Beale and Benjamin Gladd have shown how the hermeneutical model held by the Old Testament prophet Daniel was adopted and used by Jesus and the apostles in the New Testament. While we must always be careful not to presume a term is used theologically in the same way across Scripture, for context always remains key, the Old Testament use of *raz* (Aramaic) and the New Testament use of *mysterion* demonstrate a common "technical" range of meaning.[22]

---

[22] G. K. Beale and Benjamin L. Gladd, *Hidden but Now Revealed: A Biblical Theology of Mystery* (Downers Grove: IVP, 2014), 20–21.

Beale and Gladd analyze and synthesize the meaning of "mystery" as a hermeneutic in both the Old and New Testaments. According to this model, the God of entire wisdom and power reveals himself or his will in a "deep" and "hidden" manner (Dan 2:22). This initial revelation was real but required a further revelation from God to be understood more fully, an "interpretation" (Aramaic *pesher*; Dan 2:4–5, etc.). The New Testament appropriated Daniel's hermeneutical model to show the Old Testament is fulfilled in Christ and his good news of the kingdom (cf. Matt 13:11; Col 1:26–27; 2:2–3).[23] Even in the New Testament, however, which offers the fuller revelation of the mystery in Christ, the revelation of God is hidden from unbelievers in the paradox of the cross and the resurrection. This profound mystery unites Jews and Gentiles in Christ and defeats the evil kingdom of this world.[24]

The Mystery of Scripture

Paul's use of "mystery" in the epistle to the Ephesians has been particularly helpful to Christians in determining the substantial outline of the Christian faith. Four major aspects of the mystery of Scripture may be garnered with primary reference to the book of Ephesians. First, we learn that the mystery was partially hidden but has now been revealed. Second, the mystery is focused on Christ and his good news. Third, the mystery is continually revealed through Scripture and its proclamation. Fourth, God must himself bring the believer to receive the wisdom of Christ through the illuminating work of his Holy Spirit.

1. *The Mystery Revealed.* The mystery was hidden within the depths of the Trinity's eternal and inscrutable counsel from before creation. This mystery concerns God's will, which was "hidden for ages in God who created all things" (Eph 3:9). Humanity could not go up into heaven to gain access to this mystery (Eph 4:10; Rom 10:6–8). The mystery was revealed in part to Israel but has now been fully revealed in Christ Jesus. This mystery is, moreover, made known only by the divine grace of "revelation" (Eph 3:3).

---

[23] Beale and Gladd, *Hidden but Now Revealed*, 29–46, 328–38.
[24] Beale and Gladd, 321–28.

2. *Two Indispensable Aspects.* There are two major aspects to this mystery which was hidden in eternity but has now been revealed in history. The mystery is correlated in the first place with the person of "Christ" (Eph 3:4), and it is correlated in the second place with his saving work in "the gospel" (Eph 6:19). As Paul wrote in another great theological epistle, identification of the person of Jesus as Lord and confession that God has raised him from the dead are both necessary for salvation (cf. Rom 10:9–10). The identification of the person of Christ as both God and man, and the confession of his work in the gospel of his death and resurrection: These are the two indispensable aspects of saving faith. The Lord Jesus Christ and his good news for humanity are what God planned to, and did, make "known" (Eph 1:9).

3. *Two Ordinary Means.* Salvation, Paul discovered personally through an appearance by the risen Lord, requires encounter with God in Christ and prompts external confession in baptism (Acts 9:1–20). While the apostles themselves were visibly encountered by Christ, other Christians ordinarily now encounter Christ through the witness of the apostles. Their writings continue to make Christ and his gospel known in subsequent history. As Paul wrote, "by reading this you are able to understand my insight into the mystery of Christ" (Eph 3:4). Paul also asks for prayer, "that the message may be given to me when I open my mouth to make known with boldness the mystery of the gospel" (Eph 6:19). In other words, the apostolic message recorded in Scripture and the proclamation of that message are the ordinary means for how people may come to know Christ Jesus and his gospel.

4. *The Necessity of the Holy Spirit's Work of Illumination.* Receiving the truth of the mystery, however, is not recognized by every person who hears of the gospel, as the disciples of Jesus recognized (John 14:22). Paul, therefore, prayed that the Ephesians would be given the Holy Spirit by the Father, so that they might receive the revelation of God with requisite "wisdom" (Eph 1:17). As Paul discussed with the Romans, some have been shown the revelation of God but are blind to its meaning (Rom 10:16–21). The person who wishes to interpret the mystery with the appropriate "wisdom" must be guided by the Holy Spirit into the "mind of Christ" (1 Cor 2:6–16).

We would contend that the church has been and must continue to be guided into interpretive wisdom by the Holy Spirit. One evidence of the work of the Spirit upon the early church to bring the church to the mind of Christ may be found in the standard of faith to which the earliest Christian theologians appealed. The "rule of faith" (Lat. *regula fidei*) is the common term for the earliest church's compilation of its theological wisdom. The central doctrines of the Christian faith were themselves derived from the writings which were later officially recognized as the biblical canon.

By reading such apostolic texts as these "mystery" passages from the book of Ephesians, the early church came to recognize the canon of the faith even before they clearly described the boundaries of the canon of Scripture. The language of "canon" has been applied to various Christian items and practices in Christian history. The first use of "canon" or "rule" concerned the "rule of faith" as a central set of Christian teachings. The second use of "canon" concerned the collection of recognized biblical texts, which we reviewed in chapter 7. Later historical references to "canon" in the sense of various church rules included the words used in the Lord's Supper, the canon laws which regulated the lives of clergy and laity, and an office in an episcopal cathedral.[25] We shall consider here the earliest use of "canon," because it helps one perceive how the early church interpreted the inspired writings.

IV. The Rule of Faith in the Early Church

Irenaeus of Lyons was a second-century theologian who held off the advances of various Gnostic heresies by appealing to the teaching of the apostles contained in their writings. Gnostics presumed they had an elite knowledge of God and called people to become their disciples. Irenaeus responded that true knowledge of God came to the people in the church through the writings of the apostles granted to the churches. The "Great Church," of which Irenaeus was a bishop, was being pulled apart as Gnostics like Marcion and Valentinus reduced the symphony of the diverse church's common witness to Christ. According to John Behr, Irenaeus drew from the four Gospels to describe the "canon of truth" (*regula veritatis*) or "canon of faith" (*regula fidei*) which functioned, in modern terms, as a "single hypothesis" or "first

---

[25] Anthony C. Thiselton, "Canon," in *The Thiselton Companion to Christian Theology* (Grand Rapids: Eerdmans, 2015), 186–87.

principle" for interpreting Scripture. With the Great Church, Irenaeus discerned "the coherence of Scripture as a mosaic of Christ."[26]

D. Jeffrey Bingham rehearses Irenaeus's vivid metaphor contrasting the proper approach of the orthodox with the pernicious approach of the Gnostics to the interpretation of Scripture, "Put together properly, Irenaeus said, the parts of Scripture were like a mosaic in which the gems or tiles form the portrait of a king. But the Gnostics rearranged the tiles into the form of a dog or fox."[27] In summary, says Irenaeus, the heretics were compelled to separate themselves from the church because they elevated themselves above the Scripture to which the church submitted: "By transferring passages, and dressing them up anew, and making one thing out of another, they succeed in deluding many through their wicked art in adapting the oracles of the Lord to their opinions."[28]

The Gnostics' interpretation of Scripture involved not the outright denial of the text but its pernicious rearrangement and misappropriation to justify their false interpretation. In response, the early orthodox Christians, like Origen and Irenaeus as well as Tertullian and Clement, argued that the proper interpretation of Scripture depends upon access to the apostolic tradition available in the common preaching of the apostolic texts preserved in the churches. The apostolic tradition of interpretation is summarized in the canon of faith held by those churches who had access to the apostles and their writings, often through having been established by the apostles.

Irenaeus's own presentation of the rule of faith interacted deeply with Paul's language of economy and recapitulation expressed in Eph 1:9–10. His structural thought concentrated upon two major doctrines: the three persons of the Trinity and the gospel of Jesus Christ. Here is one instance from his seminal work, *Against Heresies*, wherein we italicize to highlight the trinitarian structure of the early church's orthodox faith:

---

[26] John Behr, *Irenaeus of Lyons: Identifying Christianity* (New York: Oxford University Press, 2013), 10–11.

[27] D. Jeffrey Bingham, "One God, One Christ, One Salvation: Irenaeus 'The Peacemaker' was the Early Church's Best Warrior against the Gnostic Heresy," *Christian History and Biography* 96 (Fall 2007): 19.

[28] Irenaeus, *Haeresis* 1.8.1, in Alexander Roberts and James Donaldson, eds., *The Apostolic Fathers, Justin Martyr, Irenaeus*, Ante-Nicene Fathers, 10 vols. (1885; Reprint, Peabody, MA: Hendrickson, 1994), 1:326.

The Church, though dispersed throughout the whole world, even to the ends of the earth, has received from the apostles and their disciples this faith: *in one God the Father* Almighty, Maker of heaven, and earth, and the sea and all things that are in them; *and in one Christ Jesus, the Son of God,* who became incarnate for our salvation; *and in the Holy Spirit,* who proclaimed through the prophets the dispensations [or economies], and the advents, and the birth from a virgin, and the passion, and the resurrection from the dead, and the ascension into heaven in the flesh of the beloved Christ Jesus, our Lord, and His [future] manifestation from heaven in the glory of the Father "to gather all things into one," and to raise up anew all flesh of the whole human race.[29]

Irenaeus concluded with a description of the final judgment with eternal condemnation for the impenitent and eternal glory for the redeemed. Tomas Bokedal discovered six common aspects of the rule of faith in the works of Irenaeus, Clement, and Tertullian, among others. The ancient "rule of faith" (1) derives through the church's tradition, (2) focuses upon the gospel of Jesus Christ, (3) affirms the three persons of the Trinity, (4) demonstrates variety while holding tight the basic frame of the gospel and the Trinity, (5) depends upon the apostolic writings, and (6) reflects the *nomina sacra* as recorded in the earliest available manuscripts of the New Testament. (The *nomina sacra* are significant, because the respect shown to the divine names in these authoritative manuscripts demonstrate that the early Christians revered the three persons of the Trinity.)[30]

A younger contemporary of Irenaeus, Origen, witnesses to the origin and end of the rule of faith. The son of a martyr and teacher of grammar, Origen also became a *grammatikos* in Alexandria, the "city of books."[31] To aid in catechizing for the Christian faith, he learned literary and philosophical

---

[29] Irenaeus, *Haeresis* 1.10.1; in *The Apostolic Fathers, Justin Martyr, Irenaeus,* 1:330–31.

[30] The technical term, *nomina sacra*, refers to the scribal practice of abbreviating a divine name. Abbreviations were applied to the names of the Father and the Son, then also the Holy Spirit. Tomas Bokedal, "The Rule of Faith," 238–39.

[31] Ronald E. Heine, *Origen: Scholarship in Service of the Church* (New York: Oxford University Press, 2010), 13–22.

principles from the Greeks. Aristarchus of Samothrace developed a system of interpreting Homer by Homer, and Origen advocated a similar rule for interpreting Scripture by Scripture, "interpreting spiritual things by spiritual."[32] Origen used these advanced literary skills to provide a critical edition of the Old Testament, write numerous theological commentaries, and launch the discipline of systematic theology with his *On First Principles*. One might say Origen contributed to all three of the primary academic disciplines now required for moving from Scripture to theology: biblical studies, biblical theology, and systematic theology. Origen argued the biblical text, whose every word comes from the Holy Spirit, remains "veiled" to all but those whom the same Spirit enlightens (2 Cor 3:14–16). The "key of David" that opens the biblical text is the coming of Christ Jesus. Scripture retains its deepest mystery, even as the Spirit reveals the rule of faith that points the redeemed to God in Christ with the Holy Spirit.[33]

Bokedal's first point, that the rule of faith is derived through the church's tradition, confronts those of us who count ourselves heirs of the Reformation with the need to remember historical context. Clifton Black's point that "scriptural theology" is technically "proto-Trinitarian," rather than trinitarian in the sense of Nicaea and Chalcedon, likewise reminds us that theology develops from Scripture within tradition.[34] During the sixteenth century, Reformers of all types necessarily challenged the concept that tradition should be accepted as normative alongside Scripture. The theological weight with which Roman Catholic apologists loaded tradition required that tradition itself come under critique. Moreover, it became apparent to the Reformers that there were doctrines attached to tradition which could not be adequately demonstrated from Scripture. Medieval teachings regarding papal primacy, purgatory, and penance are but three well-known examples of the controverted nature of these late traditions.

Contrary to the situation which developed over a thousand years later, Irenaeus and his colleagues in the first three centuries were not appealing to a hidden, extrabiblical teaching. Indeed, appeals to a secret, extrabiblical

---

[32] Heine, *Origen*, 23.

[33] Heine, *Origen*, 132–41.

[34] C. Clifton Black, "Biblical Theology Revisited: An Internal Debate," *Interpretation* 70, no. 4 (October 2016): 409–411.

tradition were made by their Gnostic opponents. To the contrary, Irenaeus appealed to the teaching of the apostles in their publicly available writings. The tradition of the orthodox churches was directly verified in the written texts of the apostles. The difference between the early church and the late medieval church a millennium later was made clear by a leading Reformation scholar, Heiko Oberman: "Irenaeus insists that the rule of faith or the rule of truth is faithfully preserved by the apostolic Church and has found multiform expression in the canonical books. There is an unbroken continuation of the preached kerygma into Holy Scripture. One may speak here of an 'inscripturisation' of the apostolic proclamation which in this written form constitutes the foundation and cornerstone of faith."[35] The canon of faith is the canon of apostolic Scripture.

Each of these factors allows us to see that the two major teachings of the Christian faith—the Trinity and the gospel of Jesus Christ—were received from the earliest disciples first through personal interaction with the apostles then maintained by faithful resort to the apostolic gospels and letters. The structure and the content of "the rule of faith" is very similar to the Old Roman Creed and its descendant, the Apostles' Creed. The Apostles' Creed, upon which Rufinus of Aquileia wrote a famous commentary in the early fourth century, remains the most widely accepted creed in Christian history.[36] The Nicene Creed incorporates the structure and content of the rule of faith but develops it in more conceptual depth to answer and move past the great Arian heresies. The Apostles' Creed was universally reaffirmed for Baptists during both the inaugural meeting of the Baptist World Alliance in 1905 and its centennial in 2005.[37] From a propositional perspective, we believe the rule of faith, as repeated in the Apostles' Creed, should be accepted as the adjudicative hermeneutical key to the Bible. The *regula fidei* is not imposed upon the biblical text but develops from that text.

Any theological interpretation of Scripture today would do well to start from the perspective conveyed by the rule of faith. There are numerous

---

[35] Oberman, *The Dawn of the Reformation*, 272 (see chap. 8., n. 25).

[36] Tyrannius Rufinus, *A Commentary on the Apostles' Creed*, trans. J. N. D. Kelly, Ancient Christian Writers (New York: Newman Press, [n.d.]).

[37] *The Word of God in the Life of the Church: A Report of International Conversations between the Catholic Church and the Baptist World Alliance, 2006–2010* (Falls Church, VA: Baptist World Alliance, 2013), 103.

reasons for doing so, including that it is (1) centered upon the Lord Jesus Christ, (2) developed from the apostolic preaching conveyed in the canonical writings, (3) grounded in the theological literature of the earliest church fathers, (4) respectful of the dogmatic history of the universal church, and (5) broadly affirmed by the free churches, especially the Baptists.[38] Beginning our interpretation of the Bible with the rule of faith demonstrates respect for God as Trinity, for Christ Jesus as Lord, for the priority of the apostolic witness, for the unity of the church of Jesus Christ across time and space, and for our own Baptist tradition.

The ancient rule of faith, preserved within the major creeds, has provided Christians through the centuries with the propositional rudiments for the Christian faith. The basic minimum of these first principles includes the identity of the three persons of God the Trinity, the fully human and fully divine identity of the one Lord Jesus Christ, and the saving work of Jesus Christ from his divine preexistence and human incarnation through his death and resurrection to his ascension and second coming. The rule of faith, moreover, does not constrict Christian liberty but provides the necessary control for guiding faithful yet free theological interpretation. From a rational perspective, biblical interpretation is impossible without the rule of faith. Eric Osborn writes, "The rule of faith did not limit reason to make room for faith, but used faith to make room for reason. Without a credible first principle, reason was lost in infinite regress."[39] The Holy Spirit led the early church to recognize simultaneously the literary canon of apostolic proclamation and the basic interpretive canon provided by apostolic proclamation.

Luther took over the early church's high respect for Scripture and its rule of faith, even as he elevated Scripture above later tradition.[40] For Luther,

---

[38] Matthew Y. Emerson, Christopher W. Morgan, and R. Lucas Stamps, eds., *Baptists and the Christian Tradition: Towards an Evangelical Baptist Catholicity* (Nashville: B&H, 2020); Yarnell, *The Formation of Christian Doctrine*, 187–92 (see chap. 7, n. 25).

[39] Eric Osborn, "Reason and the Rule of Faith in the Second Century," in *The Making of Orthodoxy: Essays in Honour of Henry Chadwick*, ed. Rowan Williams (New York: Cambridge University Press, 1989), 57. See Dockery, *Biblical Interpretation Then and Now*, 68–73, 94–97 (see chap. 5, n. 42).

[40] "It must be observed that Luther did not reject Christian tradition, the church fathers, nor the confessional statements from the important church councils of the fourth and fifth centuries." David S. Dockery, "Martin Luther's Christological

the trinitarian Christ with his gospel, as proclaimed by the apostles, remains the principle by which Scripture must be interpreted. This is as relevant for interpretation of the Old Testament as it is for the New Testament. The theological heirs of Luther's Protestant Reformation thereby came to speak of the close-fitting relationship between the "material principle" and the "formal principle" of their faith. Like the patristic rule of faith, the Reformation material principle concerns the basic content of the Bible, which for the Protestants is that faith in Jesus Christ as risen Lord justifies the sinner. The formal principle of the Reformation is that Scripture always rules as the normative authority in theology. These material and formal principles are conceptually distinct but inseparable. The two principles "strictly taken constitute but two sides of one and the same principle, which resolves itself into the maxim, *Christ all in all.*"[41] There can be no division between basic Christian orthodoxy and the proper view of Scripture as the perfect Word of God.

V. Pre-Critical Exegesis: Literal and Spiritual

During the Patristic and Medieval periods, the church developed a hermeneutic which was historically and grammatically literal yet also deeply theological. For instance, through his skilled literary studies of the biblical text, Athanasius concluded that the "scope" or "intent" or "drift" of Scripture fosters a distinction between Christ's humanity and deity even as it maintained his centrality and unity. According to James Ernest, for Athanasius, "the scope of Scripture is the incarnation of the Word for the sake of human salvation."[42] Athanasius argued the Arians failed to interpret Scripture correctly regarding its central figure, Jesus Christ. The heretics did

---

Principle: Implications for Biblical Authority and Biblical Interpretation," in *The Reformation and the Irrepressible Word of God: Interpretation, Theology, and Practice*, ed. Scott M. Manetsch (Downers Grove: IVP, 2019), 45.

[41] Philip Schaff, *The Principle of Protestantism as related to the Present State of the Church*, trans. John W. Nevin (Chambersburg, PA: Publication Office of the German Reformed Church, 1845), 93.

[42] James D. Ernest, "Athanasius of Alexandria: The Scope of Scripture in Polemical and Pastoral Context," *Vigiliae Christianae* 47, no. 4 (December 1993): 342.

not understand that Christ is the fully divine Son of God through eternal generation who became a human being to work our salvation with God. "Now the scope and character of Holy Scripture, as we have often said, is this,—it contains a double account of the Saviour; that He was ever God, and is the Son, being the Father's Word and Radiance and Wisdom; and that afterwards for us He took flesh of a Virgin, Mary Bearer of God, and was made man."[43]

Modern scholars have often separated the "Alexandrian" school of interpretation, which began with Origen and was characterized by allegorical exegesis, from the "Antiochene" school, which began with Lucian and was characterized by literal exegesis.[44] However, this paradigm has been challenged more recently for ignoring the reality that both schools prioritized the literal and used the figurative.[45] It is true that with some texts, Alexandria was more concerned with a figurative reading where Antioch focused upon the literal. But both schools were deeply committed to expositing the theological and moral meanings of the text. These findings correct the longstanding modern assumption that Alexandria was carried away with theological fancy while Antioch was more reliably historical. Antioch should not be seen as a precursor of the modern historical-critical method, which isolated and elevated the historical.[46] Antioch, moreover, was tied to the development and propagation of the Arian heresy.[47]

---

[43] Athanasius, *Contra Arianos* 3.29; Ernest, "Athanasius of Alexandria: The Scope of Scripture," 351.

[44] On the origin of the Alexandrian school, see Heine, *Origen: Scholarship in Service of the Church.*

[45] This approach is a slight adjustment from our previous work, though we still think the distinction between the allegorical approach in Alexandria and the typological approach in Antioch is worth noting. Please see Dockery, *Biblical Interpretation Then and Now,* 75–128; also, David S. Dockery, "The Value of Typological Exegesis," in *Restoring the Prophetic Mantle,* ed. George L. Klein (Nashville: Broadman, 1992), 161–78. Also, see Gerald Bray, *How the Church Fathers Read the Bible: A Short Introduction* (Bellingham, WA: Lexham, 2022).

[46] Darren M. Slade, "Patristic Exegesis: The Myth of the Alexandrian-Antiochene Schools of Interpretation," *Socio-Historical Examination of Religion and Ministry* 1, no. 2 (2019): 155–176.

[47] On Lucian, the Antiochene school, and the Arians, see Glanville Downey, *A History of Antioch of Syria from Seleucus to the Arab Conquest* (Princeton, NJ: Princeton University Press, 1961), 337–42.

The impact of Origen, the father of the Alexandrian school, upon subsequent theological exegesis should not be underestimated. "More than any
other figure in the fields of hermeneutics, exegesis, and spirituality, he would
be the grand master." Alongside Augustine of Hippo, he has been named,
"the doctor of the spiritual sense of history." While his legacy was marred
by the assaults of Jerome and Justinian, his modern theological biographer
catalogued his great influence as "the prince of commentators."[48] Origen was
willing to utilize the language of Greece and the literary devices of Greek
grammar. However, he was motivated to work from his Christian spirituality
and for the purpose of Christian catechizing. Origen's adoption of allegory
helped him correlate the Old Testament with the New Testament. His threefold method of interpretation developed from his extension of 1 Thess 5:23
to the whole human response to Scripture. He remained firmly grounded in
"the sense of Christ."[49] The allegorical hermeneutic built upon Paul's decla-
mation of the Jewish rejection of God's revelation in 2 Corinthians 3. God
was previously veiled in the law of Moses but is now seen in Jesus Christ.

The Origenian hermeneutic thus held two primary senses: The first
sense is that of the "letter," identified with the law, Israel, and history. The
second sense is that of the "spirit," identified with the mystery or allegory of
Jesus Christ.[50] Origen justified his method, not by appealing to Greek pagans
but with Paul's reference to allegory in his early epistle to the Galatians 4.[51]
Origen systematically correlated the apostle's covenantal use of *allēgoreō*
of Galatians with his Christological use of *mysterion* in Ephesians. Origen
and his many disciples identified the key of their "spiritual" interpretation

---

[48] Henri de Lubac, *Medieval Exegesis: The Four Senses of Scripture*, trans. Mark
Sebanc, vol. 1 (Grand Rapids: Ecrdmans, 1998), 159, 173.

[49] De Lubac, *Medieval Exegesis*, 1:143–50.

[50] Henri de Lubac, *Medieval Exegesis: The Four Senses of Scripture*, trans. E. M.
Macierowski, vol. 2 (Grand Rapids: Eerdmans, 2000), 25–36.

[51] "These things are being taken figuratively, for the women represent two
covenants" (Gal 4:24a). Bauer defines ἀλληγορέω as "to use analogy or likeness to
express something." Walter Bauer, *A Greek-English Lexicon of the New Testament and
Other Early Christian Literature*, trans. Frederick William Danker, 3rd ed. (Chicago:
University of Chicago Press, 2000). Following Origen, Jerome noted Paul's moral
application of the old covenant to Christians in 1 Corinthians 10. De Lubac,
Medieval Exegesis, 2:9.

of Scripture with Christ and his cross.[52] The terms, "mystical," "allegorical," and "typological" were synonymous for him with "spiritual." Modern historical critics dislike Origen and his dominant place within patristic and medieval Christian theological exegesis, but it is noteworthy that Origen grounded his exegesis first in history then continually in the historical and theological Jesus Christ. Modern critics, on the other hand, have been quick to assign myth to the biblical text itself and to diminish Christ. The difference between Pagan allegory and Christian allegory were "radical" in foundation, method, and frame of mind.[53]

For Augustine of Hippo, the words of Scripture are integral to the divine economy. Before the fall, humanity had direct access to God, but this knowledge was lost when man sinned, averting his eyes from God. God now bridges the gap in humanity's knowledge of God through Scripture. However, the saving knowledge of Christ through Scripture is hidden until the Spirit removes the veil from the human mind with repentance. On the one hand, the Holy Spirit's work of illumination is foundational to the hermeneutics of the leading Western church father.

On the other hand, while the mystery of Christ is unveiled by the Spirit, the believer must yet learn to read the Bible properly. According to his Oxford translator, Augustine wrote his classic treatise, *On Christian Teaching*, as "a guide to biblical theology," and the object of biblical theology is the blessed vision of God.[54] The Bible is the instrument of salvation whose words act as signs directing our minds to God.

Augustine's theory of signs, introduced in book I of *On Christian Teaching*, became integral to Western hermeneutics and theology up to and well through the Protestant Reformation. "All teaching is teaching of either things or signs, but things are learnt through signs." Some "things," like words, may function as "signs" pointing toward other things. "Things" themselves may be classified either as for "use" or for "enjoyment." "To enjoy something is to hold fast to it in love for its own sake. To use something is to apply whatever it may be to the purpose of obtaining what you love." The

---

[52] De Lubac, *Medieval Exegesis*, 2:6–7, 83–98.

[53] De Lubac, *Medieval Exegesis*, 2:10–19.

[54] R. P. H. Green, "Introduction," in *On Christian Teaching*, by Augustine, viii, xii.

word-signs of Scripture point toward the ultimate thing, God, who alone is to be enjoyed.[55]

In book II, Augustine offered three simple rules for inductive interpretation of the canon: "know these books," "examine them carefully and diligently," and allow "the more obvious parts to illuminate obscure expressions."[56] Ambiguities multiply when interpreters fail to perceive the difference between "literal" language and "metaphorical" or "figurative" language. Literal word-signs point more directly to a thing; figurative word-signs work indirectly via something else. The literary key for Augustine rotates around the difference between the literal and the figurative. The literal always retains priority, while the figurative requires theological wisdom. Reference should also be made to the original languages of Greek and Hebrew, and various translations must be conferred.[57] Augustine also encouraged Christians to learn generally from the disciplines of the academy, including history, the natural sciences, the arts, and logic.[58]

In book III, Augustine offered interpretive rules when ambiguity over the literal meaning remains. He presumed the need to obtain "reliable texts derived from the manuscripts," a discipline known in modernity as textual criticism. He also presumed the priority of the "literal usages." However, if the literal meaning remains ambiguous, then "we must consult the rule of faith."[59] After alternative interpretations have been filtered through the rule of faith, one must "consult the context" within the canon.[60]

Several of Augustine's hermeneutical rules are literary: Figurative texts must only be interpreted figuratively; literal texts, literally.[61] Other rules are moral: "Scripture enjoins nothing but love, and censures nothing but lust." Thus, any harsh word from God is intended to destroy lust.[62] In Old

---

[55] Augustine, *De Doctrina Christiana* 1.3, 1.8, 1.12.

[56] Augustine, *De Doctrina Christiana* 2.26–31.

[57] Augustine, *De Doctrina Christiana* 2.32–40.

[58] Augustine, *De Doctrina Christiana* 2.104–138.

[59] The rule of faith is established by the church through the clear passages of the Bible. Augustine, *De Doctrina Christiana* 3.1–3.

[60] Augustine, *De Doctrina Christiana* 3.4.

[61] Augustine, *De Doctrina Christiana* 3.20, 3.33. He provides some detail regarding grammar, too. Augustine, *De Doctrina Christiana* 3.87–91.

[62] Augustine, *De Doctrina Christiana* 3.36, 3.39.

Testament interpretation, these rules become more important.[63] An interpreter may ascribe multiple meanings to an ambiguous passage but must
limit meaning to what "can be shown from other passages" and "does not run
counter to the faith."[64] Augustine also evaluates the seven metaphorical or
theological rules of Tyconius the Donatist.[65] In learning to move wisely from
Scripture to theology, the interpreter must be careful to hear his teacher,
to memorize Scripture, "and especially—this is paramount, and absolutely
vital—to pray for understanding."[66] Augustine thus began and ended interpretation with an appeal to the Spirit.

VI. Medieval Appropriation of the
Literal and the Spiritual

During the Middle Ages, theological exegesis settled into a fourfold (or
threefold) method. In his version of the way theology should be gathered
from Scripture, Thomas Aquinas centers on the statement of Gregory
that "in one sentence, while Scripture describes a fact, it reveals a mystery."
Aquinas's famous description of the fourfold method summarizes the tradition launched by Origen and buttressed by Augustine. There are two primary
senses: The "first sense, the historical or literal," contains such genres as direct
"history" and "etiology" and the more allusive "analogy" and "parabolical."
Second is "the spiritual sense, which is based on the literal, and presupposes
it." The spiritual sense never undermines history. The spiritual sense encloses
three subsidiary senses: The "allegorical sense," wherein the "the things of the
Old Law signify the things of the New Law," in other words, the Lord Jesus
and his work. The "moral sense," which looks to the Lord for "what we ought
to do." And the "anagogical sense," which looks forward "to eternal glory."[67]

---

[63] Augustine, *De Doctrina Christiana* 3.60.

[64] Augustine, *De Doctrina Christiana* 3.84.

[65] Augustine, *De Doctrina Christiana* 3.92–133.

[66] Augustine, *De Doctrina Christiana* 3.134.

[67] History is concerned with factual narrative; etiology, statements of causation;
analogy, comparisons; and the parabolical, figures and anthropomorphisms. These
literal senses derive, as one might expect, from Augustine. Thomas Aquinas, *Summa
Theologica*, trans. Fathers of the English Dominican Province, vol. 1 (Westminster,
MD: Christian Classics, 1948), 7.

Gregory the Great's commentary on Job describes the way Scripture acts with unique sovereign agency to bring human beings from earth to heaven and convey delight without ceasing to the simple and to the learned.[68] The medieval method of moving from Scripture to theology through the later fourfold method possessed its inappropriate examples. But the medieval theologians nevertheless retained history even as they pursued the spirit. Alas, modern critics doubt history and leave the spiritual end unknown. Medieval theologians recognized the control of allegory and the unity of the two testaments resided in the rule of faith. Christ remained the goal, the intent, and the sense of Scripture.[69] Medieval exegetes were reminded in the fourfold method that the point is not history but the God whom history reveals. The earthly Jerusalem leads to the new Jerusalem. Scripture calls for conversion to Christ. "Allegory signifies a conversion of intellect, tropology of morals, anagogy of desires. Allegory builds up or edifies faith, tropology charity, anagogy hope."[70]

---

[68] "Holy Scripture far excels all knowledge and all lore without comparison, to say nothing of it telling forth what is true. It bids to the heavenly country; it changes the heart of him that reads it from earthly desires to the embracing of things above. By its obscurer statements it exercises the strong, and by its humble strain speaks gently to the little ones. It's neither so shut up, that it should come to be dreaded, nor so open to view as to become contemptible. By use it removes weariness and is the more delighted in the more it is meditated on. The mind of him who reads it, by words of a low pitch it assists, and by meanings of a lofty flight it uplifts; in some sort it grows with the persons reading, that by uninstructed readers it is in a manner reviewed, and yet by the well instructed is always found new. So then to say nothing of the weightiness of the subjects, it goes beyond all forms of knowledge and teaching even by the mere manner of its style of speaking, because in one and the same thread of discourse, while it relates the text, it declares a mystery, and has the art so to tell the past, that merely by that alone it knows how to announce the future, and the order of telling remaining unaltered, is instructed by the very self-same forms of speech at once to describe things done before, and to tell things destined to be done." Gregory the Great, *Moralia* 20.1. Translation adapted from John Henry Parker, J. G. F., and J. Rivington, *Morals on the Book of Job*, vol. 2 (London: 1844), part 4.

[69] "All of Scripture contains faithful testimonies to Christ." *Universitas scripturarum, in qua sunt fidelia testimonia Christ.* Rupert of Deutz, "Prologue to the Minor Prophets," *Patrologia Latina* 168, 9B. Cf. De Lubac, *Medieval Exegesis*, 2:93.

[70] Robert E. McNally, "Medieval Exegesis," *Theological Studies* 22, no. 3 (September 1961): 453.

Following negative comments from the Reformers,[71] modern scholars such as Bernard Ramm, Walter C. Kaiser Jr., and many others have dismissed the possibility of multiple meanings. Today, most scholars from various traditions, including evangelicals such as D. A. Carson, Grant Osborne, Kevin Vanhoozer, G. K. Beale, Royce Gruenler, and others, call for biblical interpreters to prioritize the one primary meaning in the text, the literal or historical.[72] However, both Roman Catholic scholars and evangelical scholars, including some of those just mentioned, seem open to the idea of seeing a fuller meaning in the biblical texts.

The Reformation scholar David Steinmetz famously argued that "The medieval theory of levels of meaning in the biblical text, with all its undoubted defects, flourished because it is true." Steinmetz's concluding words are still widely cited: "Until the historical-critical method becomes critical of its own theoretical foundations and develops a hermeneutical theory adequate to the nature of the text which it is interpreting, it will remain restricted—as it deserves to be—to the guild and the academy, where the question of truth can

---

[71] Luther rejected a famous poem about the fourfold method as "impious verses." "This approach of dividing up Scripture into four compartments strikes him as introducing otiose and questionable divisions, which serve neither faith nor morals. With just a few exceptions, all of Protestantism followed his lead." De Lubac, *Medieval Exegesis*, 1:9.

[72] "The curse of the allegorical meaning is that it obscures the Word of God and had it not kept the Gospel truth central it would have become cultic and heretical. In fact, this is exactly what happened when the gnostics allegorized the New Testament. The Bible treated allegorically becomes putty in the hands of the exegete." Ramm, *Protestant Biblical Interpretation*, 30. "In the course of the eighteenth century [biblical interpretation] came to signify not so much a literary depiction which was literal rather than metaphorical, allegorical, or symbolic but rather the single meaning of a grammatically and logically sound propositional statement." Hans W. Frei, *The Eclipse of the Biblical Narrative: A Study in Eighteenth and Nineteenth Century Hermeneutics* (New Haven, CT: Yale University Press, 1974), 9. Also see David S. Dockery, "Study and Interpretation of the Bible," in *Foundations for Biblical Interpretation*, ed. David S. Dockery, K. A. Mathews, and Robert B. Sloan (Nashville: B&H, 1994), 36–54. Even Walter C. Kaiser Jr. has shown an openness to a fuller spiritual meaning. See Kaiser, "Hermeneutics and Evangelical Theology," in *The Foundations of Evangelical Theology: Essays in Honor of John S. Feinberg*, ed. Gregg R. Allison and Stephen J. Wellum (Wheaton: Crossway, 2015), 51–65. We will amplify on these thoughts later in this volume.

be endlessly deferred."[73] However, as mentioned above, the medieval church conveyed not merely the biblical canon and the rule of faith, along with the literal and grammatical senses of interpretation, to subsequent generations. It also cultivated a high regard for subsequent tradition that the Reformation opponents of Rome were compelled to refute so that they might recover the primacy of Holy Scripture in theological construction.

VII. Reforming Exegesis

The Christian renaissance of the fifteenth and sixteenth centuries prepared the ground for the Protestant revolution in theological exegesis. "Of the many tributaries which contributed to the flow of the Reformation, by far the most important was Renaissance humanism."[74] These Christian humanists were interested in reviving the faith even while they undermined church tradition. They were dedicated to recovering the classics, thinking critically, and expressing themselves with eloquence. The Renaissance slogan of *ad fontes*, "to the sources," encapsulated their desire to go behind the medieval collections of Scripture and the church fathers. The humanists wanted to recover the classic texts and their meaning from the confusing glosses and systems of the late medieval scholastic theologians.[75] Driven by Valla's discovery through philology that the Donation of Constantine was a later forgery manufactured to justify the bishop of Rome's territorial acquisitions, they became interested in what else might be corrected.

Erasmus of Rotterdam was the leading late Renaissance humanist, and his early writings influenced the subsequent fractured traditions in Western Christianity.[76] Erasmus's publication of Valla's notes on the Greek

---

[73] David C. Steinmetz, "The Superiority of Pre-Critical Exegesis," *Theology Today* 37, no. 1 (April 1980): 38; also, see David S. Dockery, "The History of Pre-Critical Interpretation," *Faith and Mission* 10, no. 1 (Fall 1992): 3–33.

[74] Alister E. McGrath, *Reformation Thought: An Introduction*, 3rd ed. (Malden, MA: Blackwell, 1999), 3.

[75] Erasmus's anti-Scholasticism pervades his writing but is particularly poignant in his witty *Encomium Morae*. Desiderius Erasmus, *Praise of Folly*, trans. Betty Radice (New York: Penguin, 1994).

[76] Erasmus's faith, exemplified in his *Enchiridion militis Christiani*, "Handbook of the Christian Knight," may be characterized as Christ-centered, scriptural, critical, lay-oriented, and warmly moral. *The Enchiridion of Erasmus*, trans. Raymond

New Testament in 1505, followed by the publication of his own *Novum Testamentum* in 1516, generated great excitement. "It seemed to many, such as Luther, that God in his providence had given the church the key (in the new humanist textual and philological tools) by which the New Testament experience of Christ could be unlocked and made available."[77] *Novum Testamentum* provided a basic Greek text, encouraged vernacular translation, and called into question late medieval doctrines regarding penitence, the number of the sacraments, and Mary as the repository of grace.[78] Erasmus later broke with Luther as schism became apparent, but he was credited with laying the egg Luther hatched.

The Reformers were stung by accusations they were teaching novelties with their doctrines of justification, the sacraments, and the church. But encouraged by the humanist critique of scholastic obscurities and recovery of the original biblical languages, they subjected the tradition to theological criticism. They also rebelled against papal and conciliar claims to interpretive authority, advocating instead the supreme authority, sufficiency, and clarity of the biblical text. Papal, episcopal, and conciliar excommunications were handed down, and the European states sporadically threatened dissenters with fiscal penalties, imprisonment, even execution. This turbulent environment prompted a wholesale reevaluation of medieval hermeneutics by the Reformers. Their reevaluation established a benchmark for future theological exegesis.

Martin Luther was a Bible professor at the new University of Wittenberg. He provided his students with the text of the original language, encouraging translation and personal commentary. Trained in medieval exegesis but increasingly beholden to humanist principles, Luther's use of the fourfold

---

Himelick (Bloomington, IN: Indiana University Press, 1964). See David S. Dockery, "A Fresh Look at Erasmus: Foundations for Reformation Hermeneutics," in *Evangelical Hermeneutics*, ed. Michael Bauman and David Hall (Camp Hill, PA: Christian Publications, 1996), 53–76.

[77] McGrath, *Reformation Thought*, 45.

[78] McGrath, *Reformation Thought*, 54–55. William Tyndale was influenced by Erasmus's preface of the *Novum Testamentum* to pursue his own translation of the entire Bible, thereby launching the modern tradition of English translations. For a contemporary translation of *Paraclesis*, see Desiderius Erasmus, *Christian Humanism and the Reformation: Selected Writings*, ed. John C. Olin (New York: Harper & Row, 1965), 92–106.

method was replaced by a focus upon the literal sense of the text. His primary tools became history and grammar. Emphasizing the literal, he accused patristic and medieval Bible commentators of jettisoning history in favor of allegory let loose from the original meaning of the text. Luther retained a spiritual sense, but it was explicitly and intentionally derived from the literal sense. "Luther did not intend his spiritual interpretation as an innovation. He was conscious of the fact that he was doing nothing else than the Lord and the apostles had done in their use of Scripture."[79]

Luther's exact relationship with later historical criticism is disputed. On the one hand, he clearly believed the Bible is the Word of God. The Word for Luther was first and foremost oral, as it was for the apostles, but their living proclamation of the Word was written down to preserve it. The Bible is the Word of God yet remains a creature not the Creator.[80] On the other hand, Luther occasionally practiced historical criticism, as when he detected contradictions. "This is hardly reason, however, to consider him one of the fathers of historical criticism; for he makes such critical remarks only occasionally and he places no weight on them."[81] He also engaged in theological criticism. "Whatever does not teach Christ is certainly not apostolic, even though St. Peter or St. Paul teaches it."[82] This helps explain his attitude to the epistle of James. "He was not critical, for example, in the name of reason or in the name of a scientific worldview or the modern understanding of existence." The Bible remained "the book written by the Holy Spirit" with "infallible authority."[83]

While Martin Luther believed, like other classical thinkers, that the Bible is the Word of God, he also protested against traditional practices which allowed the imposition of alien ideas alongside and even in the name of the biblical text. Luther's highly popular treatises broadcast far and wide the formal Reformation doctrine of *sola scriptura*, which asserts that the

---

[79] Paul Althaus, *The Theology of Martin Luther*, trans. Robert C. Schultz (Philadelphia, PA: Fortress, 1966), 96–97.

[80] Bernard Lohse, *Martin Luther's Theology: Its Historical and Systematic Development*, trans. Roy A. Harrisville (Minneapolis: Augsburg, 1999), 188.

[81] Althaus, *The Theology of Martin Luther*, 82.

[82] Luther, *Luther's Works*, 35:396; cited in Althaus, *The Theology of Martin Luther*, 83.

[83] Althaus, *The Theology of Martin Luther*, 86.

Holy Bible provides the authoritative norm by which the church itself must be judged. Luther's elevation of the Word of God, and of the human conscience held captive to the Word of God, loosened the traditional connection between the church and Scripture by bringing the latter under the former. Yet Luther loosened that connection, not to diminish the Christian faith but to preserve it. Luther advocated the "formal principle" of *sola scriptura* to preserve the "material principle" of justification by faith alone, which he discovered therein.[84]

Another way to think of it is that Martin Luther discovered a hinge between the church and Scripture. Earlier Christian thinkers like Irenaeus of Lyons, Basil of Caesarea, and Augustine of Hippo presumed the church was the champion of Scripture. They integrated the church tightly with Scripture. But Luther discovered the church's clerical hierarchy could not be trusted to uphold that integration without presuming upon it for its own purposes. The authority of the church had been inappropriately used to inhibit the proper reception of Scripture. Papal and conciliar interpretations were granted an inspiration and an authority which should have been ascribed only to Sacred Scripture.[85] Luther discovered the hinge between the Bible and the leadership of the community which interprets the Bible. Therefore, Luther himself functions as an appropriate historical hinge between the movements known as pre-critical exegesis and critical exegesis. In the next chapter, we explore Reformation hermeneutics before turning to radical critical developments in the fields of biblical studies and biblical theology.

---

[84] The language of "formal" and "material" applied to these Reformation doctrines derives from the nineteenth century. Timothy George, "What the Reformers Thought They Were Doing," *Modern Age* 59, no. 4 (Fall 2017): 22.

[85] Gerald L. Bray, *Doing Theology with the Reformers* (Downers Grove: IVP, 2019), 42–87.

11

From Biblical Interpretation to Theology, Part II

In the previous chapter, we discussed the church's development of theology from Scripture, first by noting the widespread call to ground the theological exegesis of Scripture in prayer to the Spirit of God for illumination. We then examined how God through Scripture provided the means for interpreting Scripture. The incarnate Word delivered his own theological hermeneutic for his followers to interpret the written Word. In summary, Jesus Christ is "the exegete of Scripture." Afterwards, we recalled the canon of faith, which centers on the gospel of Jesus Christ, who brings human reconciliation with God the Trinity. The canon of faith, or rule of faith, developed both from and alongside the canon of the sacred Scriptures. In summary, Jesus Christ as the God-Man who died and arose again is also "the exegesis of Scripture." We then examined the development of pre-critical exegesis of the Bible from the early church through the Middle Ages, noting various theologians' appeals to the literal and spiritual senses of Scripture. Compelled to criticize the failures of the church from the normative Scripture of the church, Martin Luther became a hinge between classical faith and critical evaluation.

Because the Reformers held to the classical faith yet criticized the church's exegesis from its own Scripture, the Protestant Reformation stands between the eras of "pre-critical exegesis" and "critical exegesis." In the present chapter, we continue our consideration of the way Christians have moved from biblical interpretation to theology by first examining the hermeneutics of Luther and similar critical theologians during the Reformation. Afterwards, we introduce the post-Reformation disciplines of biblical studies, biblical theology, and the theological interpretation of Scripture. The first two disciplines, biblical studies and biblical theology, progress from one to the other and may broadly be described as "critical exegesis." The third discipline recalls certain practices from pre-critical exegesis even as it retains certain practices from critical exegesis. The theological interpretation of Scripture may thus be described as "post-critical exegesis."

VIII. Reformation Exegesis

Bernard Ramm identified six principles by which Martin Luther interpreted Scripture.[1] These six principles, along with two others, are generally indicative of the Reformation approach to theological exegesis. First, Luther affirmed the text calls for faith in the reader. With due respect to Ramm, we believe this "psychological principle" might better be entitled, *the justification principle*. The language of "justification" recalls Luther's central doctrine and avoids modern overtones in the term "psychology." Ramm's primary point, that Scripture must be approached with faith, remains intact.

Second, *the authority principle* looked not to church or tradition but to the biblical text as supreme. While the relationship between Luther and historical criticism is ambiguous, Luther certainly engaged in ecclesiastical criticism. Lohse notes, "in the course of his dispute with Rome, he was forced more and more to give Scripture critical value against specific traditions and doctrinal opinions in tension with or actually opposed to Scripture." The Bible requires "faith" from us, while the fathers express only their "opinion."[2]

Third, *the literal principle* includes a rejection of fanciful allegory, acceptance of the primacy of the original languages over Latin, and prioritization of the grammatical meaning and historical context of a passage. Luther's elevation of history and grammar with the literal principle should not be taken as a rejection of the spiritual sense of Scripture. The Word of God was not divided from the Spirit of God. The letter of the Old Testament requires the

---

[1] Ramm, *Protestant Biblical Interpretation*, 52–57 (see chap. 10, n. 14).
[2] Lohse, *Martin Luther's Theology*, 187 (see chap. 10, n. 80).

spirit of the New Testament to receive its full meaning. "The New Testament is nothing but a revelation of the Old; it is as if somebody had a sealed letter and later on broke it open."[3]

Luther's fourth teaching on interpretation, *the sufficiency principle*, employs both the priesthood of all believers and the clarity of Scripture to affirm, "The competent Christian was sufficient to interpret the Bible, and the Bible is sufficiently clear in content to yield its meaning to the believer."[4] The priesthood of all believers for Luther was not to be taken in an individualistic sense. He retained the community as important, though he reduced the authority of the papacy and elevated the primacy of conscience.

We would classify *the clarity of Scripture* as a fifth distinct principle in Luther's interpretive framework. Scripture has an "outer clarity" found in the literal sense, but its "internal clarity" depends upon the Holy Spirit, who removes "internal obscurity" from the sinner's heart.[5] The correlation of the outer letter with the inner spirit became a prominent feature of exegesis in numerous branches of the Reformation.

Sixth came *the Christological principle*. Luther looked to Christ Jesus as the key to every biblical text. Ramm criticized Luther for treating the Christological principle in an allegorical way, but Luther was well within the Christian tradition and uses a method reflected in the Bible itself. Luther taunted Erasmus, "Take Christ from the Scriptures, and what else will you find in them?"[6] Luther appealed continually both to the immediate historical context of the individual text and to the Christological rule over the entire canon. His affirmation of that general rule was, moreover, firmly rooted in the immediate context of countless individual texts. Althaus affirms that, for Luther, Christ is simultaneously "the sole content of Scripture" and "the Lord and King of Scripture."[7]

Seventh, Ramm affirms that Reformation exegesis was characterized by *the Law-Gospel principle*. Luther distinguished between two aspects of the

---

[3] Luther, *Luther's Works*, 52:41; cited in Lohse, *Martin Luther's Theology*, 192.

[4] Ramm, *Protestant Biblical Interpretation*, 55. This principle helped create a complex battlefield within Protestant hermeneutics between the interpreter and the church and the academy and the church.

[5] Lohse, *Martin Luther's Theology*, 195.

[6] Luther, *Luther's Works*, 33:26; cited in Lohse, *Martin Luther's Theology*, 189.

[7] Althaus, *The Theology of Martin Luther*, 74, 79 (see chap. 10, n. 79).

one Word of God. There is "the Law," which brings the sure condemnation upon sinful humanity, and "the Gospel," by which God freely offers to sinners the grace of salvation by faith in Jesus Christ. It is important to note Luther found the gospel in both testaments, even if it was often in shadow in the Old Testament. Similarly, the law is also found in both testaments, though muted by grace in the New Testament.

In addition to the clarity principle above, Ramm's list should be supplemented with an eighth principle from Luther's thought. Along with many other Reformers, Luther believed *sacra scriptura sui ipsius interpres*, "Holy Scripture is its own interpreter." When the interpreter encounters obscurity in a particular text, it is best to resort to one of the many clearer passages in the Bible. The eighth and final Reformation hermeneutical principle is *the Scripture interprets Scripture principle*. This principle interacts with the literal principle in immediate contexts and the Christological principle in the canon.

Luther's hermeneutical approach provided a general standard from which the other Reformers could draw, because they found themselves in substantial agreement with him over against the Roman Catholic Church. However, reviewing a few other prominent figures and movements will demonstrate a definite variety in the hermeneutics of the major Reformation traditions. The interpretive principles of Reformed theologians like Ulrich Zwingli, Martin Bucer, and John Calvin differed at significant points from Martin Luther. Moreover, the evangelical Anabaptists and the English Reformers came under the influence of both Luther and the Reformed but pursued their distinct agendas.

Ulrich Zwingli stands at the headwaters of both the Reformed movement and the Anabaptist movement. He presented one of the earliest and most effective teachings on Scripture's clarity. Against scholastic claims to illumine Scripture, Zwingli asserted Scripture possessed an inherent ability to foster right thought about God. "God's Word brought with it its own clarity and enlightenment."[8] In contrast to Luther, Zwingli emphasized the

---

[8] Ulrich Zwingli, *Of the Clarity and Certainty of the Word of God* (1522), in *Zwingli and Bullinger*, trans. Geoffrey W. Bromiley, Library of Christian Classics (Philadelphia: Fortress, 1953), 77. "Note, you cavillers, who have no trust in the Scriptures, that it is the Word of God, which is God himself, that lighteth every

role of the Spirit and was willing to adopt aspects of the fourfold method. For instance, he appealed to the moral and mystical senses of Scripture, even while prioritizing the natural sense.[9] A humanist who preached Scripture text-by-text, in a method described as *lectio continua*,[10] Zwingli said he garnered his thoughts from Scripture directly and not from Luther.[11] His spiritual and metaphorical approach to the Eucharist prompted Luther and the Lutherans to accuse Zwingli and the Reformed of being "sacramentarians" and "enthusiasts."[12]

The Dominican Martin Bucer met Luther at the Heidelberg Disputation of 1518. Pursuing Reformation, he became the leading pastor in Strasbourg, where he shepherded a young John Calvin and disputed with the Anabaptist Pilgram Marpeck. During the Augsburg Interim, he went into exile and ended his days at the University of Cambridge. Bucer's theological approach has been described as "Christocentric ethical spirit mysticism."[13] He rejected Luther's law-gospel dialectic in favor of a legalistic reading. He also rejected Marpeck's identification of a progression between the old and new covenants.

---

man. Away then with that light of your own which you would have to give the Word of God with your interpreters." Zwingli, *Of the Clarity and Certainty of the Word of God*, 79.

[9] W. P. Stephens, *The Theology of Huldrych Zwingli* (New York: Oxford University Press, 1986), 73–77. Stephens treats Zwingli's theological exegesis under six headings: "The Spirit and the Word," "The Spirit and the Letter," "Context and Comparison," "Faith," "The Old Testament," and "The Natural, Moral, and Mystical Sense." Stephens, *The Theology of Huldrych Zwingli*, 59–73.

[10] Timothy George, *Reading Scripture with the Reformers* (Downers Grove: IVP, 2011), 236–38.

[11] Stephens, *The Theology of Zwingli*, 50.

[12] In the context of the Reformation, "Enthusiasts" are those "who contrive the idea that God draws people to himself, enlightens them, makes them righteous, and saves them without means, without the hearing of God's Word, even without the use of the holy sacraments." Robert Kolb and Timothy J. Wengert, eds., *The Book of Concord: The Confessions of the Evangelical Lutheran Church*, trans. Charles Arand, Eric Gritsch, Robert Kolb, William Russell, James Schaaf, Jane Strohl, and Timothy J. Wengert (Minneapolis: Fortress, 2000), 493, 504, 608–9. Paul L. Maier, "Fanaticism as a Theological Category in the Lutheran Confessions," *Concordia Theological Quarterly* 44, no. 2–3 (July 1980): 173–81.

[13] H. E. Weber, *Reformation, Orthodoxie und Rationalismus* (1937), I, 1, 203, cited in Henning Graf Reventlow, *The Authority of the Bible and the Rise of the Modern World*, trans. John Bowden (London: SCM, 1984), 74.

Bucer emphasized the role of the Holy Spirit. The Spirit's inspiration provided Scripture with its objectivity. The Spirit worked through the human
intellect. Citing John 1:9, he also believed the Logos illumines the intellect of the elect. Bucer's spiritual-intellectual and "completely unhistorical"
approach to Scripture, described as a form of "biblicism," came to dominate
English Protestantism until the Enlightenment.[14]

John Calvin drew upon Zwingli and Bucer to fashion a "synthesis of
the work of the exegete, the systematic theologian, and the preacher."[15]
Calvin's synthetic method of theological exegesis still exercises a profound
influence upon Protestant evangelicals, including the present authors. John
Leith writes, "Calvin's theology can properly be described primarily as
commentary upon Scripture as a whole and secondarily as commentary
upon the way the church had read Scripture in its theology and creeds.
Theology clarifies and focuses the message of Scripture."[16] In contrast to
both Luther and Zwingli, Calvin emphasized the natural sense to the near
exclusion of allegory.[17] History and grammar dominated his exegesis of the
Bible. Any figurative sense was assumed to have "a natural coherence" with
its literal sense.[18]

The French humanists with whom Calvin trained struggled in the
Sorbonne against scholastic theologians who used the mystical sense to
control biblical translation and dogmatic instruction.[19] This helps explain
Calvin's strongly negative reaction to allegory. Nevertheless, he too retained
the priority of Christ and canon over biblical theology. Any difficulties in
theological interpretation[20] of the natural sense were handled by appeal to
the canon of Scripture and the analogy of faith. Calvin's definition of the

---

[14] Reventlow, *The Authority of the Bible and the Rise of the Modern World*, 75–82.

[15] John H. Leith, "John Calvin: Theologian of the Bible," *Interpretation* 25, no.
3 (July 1971): 331.

[16] Leith, "John Calvin," 334.

[17] Leith, "John Calvin," 337.

[18] Hans W. Frei, *The Eclipse of Biblical Narrative: A Study in Eighteenth and
Nineteenth Century Hermeneutics* (New Haven, CT: Yale University Press, 1974), 27.

[19] Bernard Cottret, *Calvin: A Biography*, trans. M. Wallace McDonald (Grand
Rapids: Eerdmans, 1995), 54–56.

[20] "Theological interpretation of Scripture" receives a fuller definition in the
section on post-critical exegesis below.

analogy of faith is assumed rather than defined, although by most accounts it appears related to the ancient rule of faith expressed in the creeds.[21]

Calvin consulted the church fathers but freely departed from them when he deemed best.[22] In contrast to Luther's law-gospel dialectic and the Anabaptists' emphasis on progressive revelation, Calvin emphasized the unity of the canon to the point there remained no substantial difference between the old and new covenants. While he eschewed allegory, Calvin was willing to pursue abstractions of predestination and ecclesiology in his theological interpretation. Christ appears in shadow in the Old Testament and is clearly revealed in the New Testament.[23] Locating the origin of "the ancient church" in Old Testament Israel, Calvin justified infant baptism and clerical appeals to the state to assist the work of the church.[24]

The evangelical Anabaptists first came into prominence in Zürich. They incorporated important elements from Zwingli, including his overwhelming desire to hear the Word of God and respond obediently to the Spirit. They assumed his memorial view of the Lord's Supper but diverged over the intended recipients of baptism and the authority of the state. The differences between the theological method of the Anabaptists and the Reformed are most striking in the way they relate the Old Testament to the New Testament. The Anabaptists differentiated the covenants and their sacraments, while the

---

[21] Leith, "John Calvin," 344. Calvin made early use of the Apostles' Creed and organized his Institutes accordingly. George H. Tavard, *The Starting Point in Calvin's Theology* (Grand Rapids: Eerdmans, 2000), 125–28. Leith's criticism of Calvin's ambiguity is bracing. "Calvin's failure to develop either an analogy of faith or an analogy of love led to serious difficulties in his theology. On the one hand Calvin could write that we are to find Christ in the Scripture. On the other, he could use Scripture to justify infant damnation and brutality that cancelled all human sentiments." Leith, "John Calvin," 342.

[22] "Calvin does not use the Fathers in the way a medieval commentator used his ancient authorities." Calvin uses the Fathers but not because "he needs their authority to strengthen his argument." David C. Steinmetz, *Calvin in Context* (New York: Oxford University Press, 1995), 136.

[23] Frei, *The Eclipse of Biblical Narrative*, 21, 31–35; Leith, "John Calvin," 339–40.

[24] Malcolm B. Yarnell III, "The Potential Impact of Calvinist Tendencies upon Local Baptist Churches," in *Whosoever Will: A Biblical-Theological Critique of Five-Point Calvinism*, ed. David L. Allen and Steve W. Lemke (Nashville: B&H, 2010), 215–31.

Reformed conflated them.[25] Reifying 1 Corinthians 14, Zwingli developed a school, "the Prophecy," to train clergy in exegesis and proclamation.[26] But the Anabaptists extended the responsibility for biblical literacy, theological judgment, and proclamation to the entire congregation, even as they retained pastoral leadership. Stuart Murray concludes the Anabaptists thereby developed a unique "congregational hermeneutic."[27]

The English Reformers received their theological method from the continent, at first from the German Lutherans, but they later forged deep ties with the Swiss Reformed. The Bible translator and commentator William Tyndale interacted with the Lollards, Erasmus, Luther, and the Reformed theologians.[28] But Bucer's co-laborer, Thomas Cranmer, the Archbishop of Canterbury and Oxford martyr, permanently shaped the hermeneutics of the English reformation with his liturgical formulae.[29] The deepest theological conversations within the English context still today swivel upon what God demands of his people in worship. This tendency is as true for breakaway groups like the Baptists and the Methodists as for adherents to the Church of England. The hermeneutical and theological conflicts of the long English Reformation have focused upon the questions of what Scripture requires in worship, "the regulative principle," as opposed to what Scripture allows, "the indifference principle."[30] Arguments during the Reformation ran deep over what the Bible required of man rather than what the Bible is. This liturgical

---

[25] Yarnell, *The Formation of Christian Doctrine*, 90–104 (see chap. 7, n. 25).

[26] George, *Reading Scripture with the Reformers*, 238–40.

[27] Stuart Murray, *Biblical Interpretation in the Anabaptist Tradition* (Scottdale, PA: Herald Press, 2000), 157–85.

[28] Carl R. Trueman, *Luther's Legacy: Salvation and English Reformers 1525–1556* (New York: Oxford University Press, 1994), 44–81.

[29] Malcolm B. Yarnell III, *Royal Priesthood in the English Reformation* (New York: Oxford University Press, 2013), 179–244.

[30] Matthew Ward, *Pure Worship: The Early English Baptist Distinctive* (Eugene, OR: Pickwick, 2014); Diarmaid MacCulloch, *The Later Reformation in England 1547–1603* (London: Macmillan, 1990), 44–63, 152–62; Nigel Atkinson, *Richard Hooker and the Authority of Scripture, Tradition and Reason: Reformed Theologian of the Church of England?* (Carlisle, Cumbria, UK: Paternoster, 1997); Reventlow, *The Authority of the Bible and the Rise of the Modern World*, 118–34; Walter Howard Frere and C. E. Douglas, eds., *Puritan Manifestoes: A Study of the Origin of the Puritan Revolt* (London: SPCK, 1954).

and sometimes legalistic biblicism shifted toward historicism, rationalism, and moralism in the Enlightenment.

IX. Critical Exegesis: Biblical Studies

During the European Enlightenments of the seventeenth and eighteenth centuries, the Bible was subjected to the intellectual reader. With roots in the Dutch, English, and German Enlightenments, the modern higher critical method of Bible study took rationalist individualism into unorthodox territory. Biblical inspiration, if affirmed at all, was diminished. The Bible was increasingly treated like any other book. The historical and grammatical concerns of the Reformation were retained, but the Reformers' criticism of the church was turned against the church's canon. Early modern philosophers sought freedom from authoritarian clerics who used the coercive measures available within the various European states to persecute heretics and free thinkers. The modern historical critical method of Bible study emerged from this revolutionary political, religious, and intellectual milieu.

The earliest major critic was a Dutch philosopher, Baruch Spinoza. As a young man, Spinoza was excommunicated from his Amsterdam synagogue for arguing that the human soul is impermanent, that the Jews are not exceptional, and that the Hebrew Scriptures are merely human.[31] Later, his friend Adriaan Koerbagh attacked the ascendant Reformed clergy and treated their authoritative Bible as a human book.[32] At the instigation of incensed Calvinist clergy, Koerbagh was thrown in prison, where he died in late 1669. Spinoza issued a Latin response, *Tractatus Theologico-Politicus*, to the matter in early 1670. The book outraged the hardline Voetian Reformed clergy, who blamed the nation's decline on such infidelity and demanded state intervention. Clerical affectations for civil authority prompted Spinoza to denounce their intellect, piety, and intolerance. He also trumped their interpretation of

---

[31] While the harsh *cherem* against him does not list the charges, these are the most probable reasons gathered from his later reflections. Steven Nadler, *Spinoza: A Life*, 2nd ed. (New York: Cambridge University Press, 2018), 153–58.

[32] For Koerbagh's own view of Scripture and its interpretation, see Nadler, *Spinoza*, 310–11.

Scripture. In turn, they considered his work "a book forged in hell," which "ought to be buried forever in an eternal oblivion."[33]

Instead, the publicity brought Spinoza great fame and prompted Northern European universities to train their clergy through disputation with the book. "The uproar over the Treatise is, without question, one of the most significant events in European intellectual history, occurring as it did at the dawn of the Enlightenment."[34] Spinoza became "the supreme philosophical bogeyman."[35] His views on Scripture were vilified, but his invitation to freedom of thought beguiled. Spinoza's philosophy, including his views on the nature and study of Scripture, worked their way into the European mind. Alas, the Bible was reduced from holy Scripture to mere human text.[36] "More than any other work, it laid the foundation for modern critical and historical approaches to the Bible."[37] As such, Spinoza's *Theological-Political Treatise* requires our attention.

Spinoza's goal was to provide for the good of the Dutch republic, but such good must come through freedom for philosophy, which entailed removing clerical pretensions to "divine authority."[38] The clergy "dream that the most profound mysteries lie hidden in the Sacred Texts, wear themselves out searching for these absurdities, neglecting the rest, which are useful." To undermine clerical inventions, which "in their madness they attribute to the Holy Spirit, and strive to defend with utmost force and violent

---

[33] Steven Nadler, *A Book Forged in Hell: Spinoza's Scandalous Treatise and the Birth of the Secular Age* (Princeton, NJ: Princeton University Press, 2011), xi, 38–51.

[34] Nadler, *A Book Forged in Hell*, xi.

[35] Jonathan I. Israel, *Radical Enlightenment: Philosophy and the Making of Modernity 1650–1750* (New York: Oxford University Press, 2001), 159.

[36] Michael C. Legaspi, *The Death of Scripture and the Rise of Biblical Studies* (New York: Oxford University Press, 2011), 3–26.

[37] Nadler, *A Book Forged in Hell*, 240.

[38] "We see that almost everyone peddles his own invention as the word of God, concerned only to compel others to think as he does, under the pretext of religion. We see that the Theologians have mainly been anxious to twist their own inventions and fancies out of the Sacred texts, to fortify them with divine authority." Baruch Spinoza, "*Theological-Political Treatise* (1670)," in *The Collected Works of Spinoza*, ed. Edwin Curley, vol. 2 (Princeton, NJ: Princeton University Press, 2016), 170.

affects," Spinoza called believers to adopt "the true method of interpreting Scripture." Readers would thereby be able to "free our minds from theological prejudices."[39] Spinoza offered a rational approach: "To interpret Scripture, it is necessary to prepare a straightforward history of Scripture and to infer from the mind of Scripture's authors, by legitimate inferences, as from certain data and principles."[40]

There are three logical parts to Spinoza's method of moving from Scripture to theology, each of which contributes to the nascent disciplines of biblical criticism and biblical theology. First, readers must use the original languages, especially Hebrew, in which Spinoza himself was adept and offered numerous corrections in interpretation. Second, the reader must carefully "collect" and "organize" the sentences of Scripture from a logical perspective. The "true meaning" of the text is distinct from but correlated with the witness of nature. Metaphors should be distinguished from literal statements, and readers should depart from the literal "as little as possible."[41] Third, the historical aspect of the text must be taken seriously. The interpreter must identify the best available text. The reader must discern the author, the temporal context, the recipient, and the occasion of the writing.

After considering the text, its language, and its history, the critical reader must separate those teachings which are eternal and universal from those teachings unique to a particular author. Spinoza detected five eternal truths: "that a unique and omnipotent God exists, who alone is to be worshipped, who cares for all, and who loves above all those who worship him and who love their neighbor as themselves."[42] While much of what Spinoza argues would be non-controversial to the contemporary evangelical, he also offers advice which undermines the biblical text itself. "We must use great caution here not to confuse the intention of the Prophets and Historians with that of the Holy Spirit or with the truth of the matter."[43]

---

[39] Spinoza, *Theological-Political Treatise*, 170–71.
[40] Spinoza, 171.
[41] Spinoza, 173–74.
[42] Spinoza, 176.
[43] Spinoza, 178.

While Spinoza's public faith was allusive,[44] he doubted the Spirit's verbal plenary inspiration of the biblical text. The prophets were given to strong imaginations.[45] And whatever the narrative conveys, "the Decalogue does not teach God's very words, but only their meaning."[46] Finally, the clergy not only place Aristotelian and Platonic views on the text and force their faith on others, but they are strong advocates that Scripture is "everywhere true and divine."[47] It is the persecutors who are strongest for the illumination of the Holy Spirit. Absolutely clear to the average reader are its indispensable teachings about morality and love.[48] Spinoza says the natural light of the human intellect apart from the Spirit is sufficient for the interpretation of the biblical text.[49] In conclusion, he argued the authoritative interpretation of Sacred Scripture is "in each person's hands, because it is a matter of each person's right."[50]

Meanwhile, Protestant scholastics in England at first maintained a strict orthodoxy, even as they developed individualistic intellectualist readings of the Bible. "The Protestant Principle" advocated by William Chillingworth became an axiom accepted across denominational boundaries. Chillingworth wrote, "That all things necessary to salvation are evidently contain'd in Scripture."[51] Expressing England's *Zeitgeist*, Chillingworth objected to Rome's claims to authority and any tyranny over the conscience. The necessary doctrines for salvation are limited to a recognition of Jesus Christ, whose followers are marked by rationality and morality. He asserted that every Bible reader is capable of naturally perceiving Scripture's meaning,

---

[44] Spinoza conceded an exalted place for Christ as the only one with direct access to "the mind of God" but doubted the churches' Christological dogma. Spinoza, *Theological-Political Treatise*, 84–85. The "true Universal faith," which he detected among honorable people in all the churches, shows itself in the fruit of the Holy Spirit, especially in "justice" and "loving-kindness." Nadler, *Spinoza*, 392. A French Catholic acquaintance classified Spinoza a "Jewish Protestant." Nadler, *Spinoza*, 362.

[45] Spinoza, *Theological-Political Treatise*, 79.

[46] Spinoza, 80. The quote regarding the Decalogue could be taken as placing inspiration at the level of meaning rather than words.

[47] Spinoza, 71.

[48] Spinoza, 185.

[49] Spinoza, 186.

[50] Spinoza, 191.

[51] William Chillingworth, *The Religion of Protestants a Safe Way to Salvation* (Oxford: Leonard Lichfield, 1638), "Preface," 5v.

with negligible reference to the Holy Spirit.[52] Instead, the interpreter's tools are the Apostles' Creed, human reason, and basic morality.[53]

In his insightful essay on the rise of biblical criticism, Henning Graf Reventlow traced the morality and rationality of the humanist tradition and the left wing of the Reformation through the Puritans and the Latitudinarians to the eighteenth-century English Deists.[54] Deistic efforts to promote "the right to free thinking independently of any given authority" pitted them against the "priestcraft" and "superstition" of persecuting clergy. The Deists and other free thinkers challenged the priests and their appeals to the biblical text, helping foster the modern historical critical method.[55] Arguing the Bible is a human book generated in other times and places using other languages and various customs of transmission, these radical critics turned from clerical dogma to the historical origin of the biblical texts.

Anthony Collins is an exemplar of Deism. An acquaintance of John Locke, Collins pressed rationalism further than the great Christian philosopher, restricting truth to its propositional form. His goal was "to prove the necessity of the use of Reason to distinguish Falsehood from Truth in matters of Revelation." The "real meaning" of Christian Scripture must be distinguished from its "literal meaning," which Collins rejected.[56] He employed textual criticism and canonical criticism, narrowing acceptable hermeneutics to the simple historical style of the Old Testament. Scandalized by New Testament typology and allegory, he canonized the Old Testament portions he could accept as original. Collins remained a practicing Anglican who affirmed "the excellency of original primitive Christianity" in its morality but was perceived as "an open opponent of Christianity."[57]

---

[52] Chillingworth's goal is to undermine Roman elitism. There are a few references to the interpreter's need for the Holy Spirit, but his emphasis is that there exists a plain meaning in the text via the Spirit's work upon the apostles. Cf. Chillingworth, *The Religion of Protestants*, 36–37, 94–95, 131, 141, 145–47, 171–76, 337.

[53] Reventlow, *The Authority of the Bible and the Rise of the Modern World*, 147–52.

[54] Reventlow, 69–72.

[55] Reventlow suggests that developments in biblical criticism during the English Enlightenment prompted both the American and German Enlightenments. Reventlow, 411–14.

[56] Anthony Collins, *Essay concerning the Use of Reason in Propositions* (1707), 17–18, 20; cited in Reventlow, *The Authority of the Bible and the Rise of the Modern World*, 355.

[57] Reventlow, 365–69.

Radical criticism came to dominate the universities on the European continent during the nineteenth century. Friedrich Schleiermacher's lectures to the University of Berlin on "Hermeneutics and Criticism" were published posthumously in 1838. He advocated the art of "criticism" to determine the proper text and the art of "hermeneutics" to understand the text.[58] The interpreter must search for only one meaning, which is determined through analyzing the objective historical context and the subjective psychology of the literary author.[59] Against "the presupposition of another era," the Holy Spirit's role should be bypassed in favor of anthropological study.[60] The critical pursuits of the academy diverged from the life of the church as hermeneutics became "a systematic, self-contained discipline."[61]

In 1860 Benjamin Jowett introduced the ascendant German anthropological orientation in biblical studies to the University of Oxford in England with his thesis, "Interpret the Scripture like any other book."[62] Jowett argued one must dismiss all theological traditions and recognize discrepancies in the text. The critic must sense only one meaning, reject allegories, and limit typology. Jowett disallowed canonical unity since it depended upon "the idea of a Spirit."[63] Critics must find meaning behind the text in a revelation still in "progress."[64] His novel goal of getting behind the text back to one origin still dominates the academic discipline.

X. Five Higher Critical Methods

The radical critics' historical, social, and linguistic studies resulted in the development of "higher criticism" or "critical studies." These studies were often carried out with speculative excess. Due to their dissipations,

---

[58] Friedrich Schleiermacher, *Hermeneutics and Criticism and Other Writings*, trans. Andrew Bowie (New York: Cambridge University Press, 1998), 3.

[59] Schleiermacher, *Hermeneutics and Criticism*, 24.

[60] Schleiermacher, 16, 81.

[61] Christopher Bryan, *Listening to the Bible: The Art of Faithful Biblical Interpretation* (New York: Oxford University Press, 2014), 5.

[62] Benjamin Jowett, "The Interpretation of Scripture," in *Religious Thought in the Nineteenth Century: Illustrated from Writers of the Period*, Bernard M. G. Reardon (New York: Cambridge University Press, 1966), 315.

[63] Jowett, "The Interpretation of Scripture," 318.

[64] Jowett, 320–23.

"criticism" is generally taken as a negative statement about the Bible. However, contemporary biblical scholars prefer to use more neutral definitions. Amy Balogh and Douglas Mangum argue the negative presuppositions behind its historic development "are not a necessary part of biblical criticism."[65] They prefer to define criticism neutrally as "the academic evaluation and analysis of the biblical text."[66] Mindful of the need to exercise discernment, a summary review of five higher critical methods may be helpful. These five do not exhaust the increasing number of critical methods but are historically significant. The higher critical methods include historical criticism, source criticism, form criticism, redaction criticism, and canonical criticism.

Historical criticism at a basic level refers to the search for information regarding the immediate author, the intended recipient, the date, and the historical background to a particular text in Scripture. Most commentaries on Scripture today, both conservative and liberal, utilize this type of criticism. Historical criticism aims to disclose the context of the biblical writing. However, academic historical criticism becomes a problem for the church's reading of Scripture when writings from the extracanonical context are employed to diminish the claims of the canon. For instance, scholars like James D. G. Dunn and Tom Wright used the texts of Second Temple Judaism to recast Paul's doctrine of justification. While our understanding of divine righteousness may be deepened by reference to contemporary Jewish texts, they must not be allowed to marginalize Paul's emphasis upon God's radical grace in justification.[67]

Source criticism refers to the search for the various literary sources which were or may have been used by the biblical authors to construct their texts.[68] Source criticism has been used effectively to outline similarities and differences between the four Gospels. It prompted most (though not all) source

---

[65] Amy Balogh and Douglas Mangum, "Introducing Biblical Criticism," in *Social and Historical Approaches to the Bible*, ed. Mangum and Balogh, Lexham Methods Series (Bellingham, WA: Lexham, 2019), 7.

[66] Balogh and Mangum, "Introducing Biblical Criticism," 2.

[67] Malcolm B. Yarnell III, "Christian Justification: A Reformation Baptist View," *Criswell Theological Review*, New Series 2, no. 2 (Spring 2005): 86–89.

[68] Cf. Amy Balogh, Dan Cole, and Wendy Widder, "Source Criticism," in *Social and Historical Approaches to the Bible*, 55–98.

critical scholars to identify Mark as the first of the Gospels.[69] Many also perceived a yet unidentified source behind the non-Marcan similarities between Matthew and Luke (the so-called Q document).[70] The extended German-dominated projects to separate the life of Jesus, on the one hand, from the teachings of the early church, on the other hand, have been characterized by speculations regarding the original sources and their inclusion in the Bible. Albert Schweitzer outlined and dismissed much of the source-critical work done on the life of Jesus, which reached a nadir with the publication of David Friedrich Strauss's *The Life of Jesus, Critically Examined* in 1835. Strauss separated the strict history of Jesus from the "mythical" supernatural elements ascribed to him. Schweitzer's own proposal involved interpreting Jesus as a disappointed apocalyptic visionary who simply died.[71] Ferdinand Christian Baur of Tübingen famously argued the New Testament is characterized by two original forms of the gospel. The gospel of the original disciples was Jewish in character, while the gospel of Paul was Hellenistic. The "Tübingen School" of New Testament studies long argued this conflict lay behind the apostolic writings and the triumph of Hellenism.[72] Adolf von Harnack famously put forward the thesis there is a radical difference between the simple moral teaching of the Jewish Jesus and the church's dogmatic Hellenization of Christianity.[73]

A series of scholarly studies in the eighteenth and nineteenth centuries similarly developed a source-critical approach to the Old Testament.

[69] Carl Lachmann first made this observation in 1835. J. K. S. Reid, *The Authority of Scripture: A Study of the Reformation and Post-Reformation Understanding of the Bible* (London: Methuen, 1957), 17.

[70] Q is short for *Quelle*, the German word for "source." Burnett Hillman Streeter, *The Four Gospels, A Study of Origins: Treating of the Manuscript Tradition, Sources, Authorship, and Dates* (London: Macmillan, 1924).

[71] Albert Schweitzer, *The Quest of the Historical Jesus: A Critical Study of Its Progress from Reimarus to Wrede*, trans. W. Montgomery (London: Black, 1911). Schweitzer was motivated by the ethics of Jesus. On his life and eschatology, see Malcolm B. Yarnell III, "Eschatology," in Duesing and Finn, *Historical Theology for the Church*, 369–71 (see introduction, n. 10).

[72] Martin Werner, *The Formation of Christian Dogma: An Historical Study of its Problem*, trans. S. G. F. Brandon (German ed.: 1941; ET: New York: Harper & Brothers, 1957), 3–9.

[73] Adolf von Harnack, *What Is Christianity?*, 2nd ed., trans. Thomas Bailey Saunders (New York: Putnam, 1904).

These scholars finally perceived four major editorial traditions with diverse chronologies which went into the construction of the Hebrew Torah which we possess today. The radical critics ultimately divided the Pentateuch as a document into four intricately interwoven strands based on the supposed literary and theological characteristics of its various editors: J (Yahwist), E (Elohim), D (Deuteronomist), and P (Priestly). This Documentary "Theory" or "Hypothesis," which received its definitive form in the work of Julius Wellhausen,[74] has not gone without significant correction by liberal scholars and challenges from conservative scholars.[75] Alas, however, "although the Wellhausenian view has been so modified subsequently as to be well-nigh abandoned, this has not everywhere resulted in a more sympathetic evaluation of the Pentateuch."[76]

Form criticism assesses the supposed oral traditions which existed prior to their collection in written form. Form criticism was lauded for allowing modern scholars to discern the church was involved in collecting the sayings of and fashioning pericopes about Jesus, but it has been criticized for lacking respect for the oriental memory and early records of the original eyewitnesses.[77] Jesus's authoritative promise that the Spirit would lead

---

[74] Gleason L. Archer, *A Survey of Old Testament Introduction*, rev. ed. (Chicago: Moody, 1994), 89–98.

[75] Archer identified nine deficiencies which undermine the JEDP hypothesis. Liberal criticism: "1. Employs circular reasoning, 2. Textual evidence is devalued in favor of Hegelian dialectic, 3. Assumes lower literary standard for Hebrew authors than contemporaries, 4. Gives pagan documents prior credibility over Scripture, 5. Assumes a purely human origin for Israel's religion, 6. Artificially concocted 'discrepancies' are manipulated as proof text for biblical error, 7. Espouses literary duplication or repetition as demonstrating diverse authorship, 8. Claims 'scientific reliability' for dating of documents according to a theory of evolution, 9. Assumes a superior knowledge of ancient history over original authors who lived 2,000 plus years closer to the events which they record." Archer, *A Survey of Old Testament Introduction*, 89–112.

[76] William Sanford LaSor, David Allan Hubbard, and Frederic William Bush, *Old Testament Survey: The Message, Form, and Background of the Old Testament* (Grand Rapids: Eerdmans, 1982), 58.

[77] Three errors with this key plank of form criticism have been identified. First, Vincent Taylor, himself a translator of form criticism, said the form critics' presentations of the early accounts were abstracted. Second, Martin Hengel pointed to the "undeniable" link between the eyewitnesses and the events they conveyed. Third, Richard Bauckham established that the time between the events and their

the apostles to remember correctly is also conveniently set aside. Rudolf
Bultmann used form criticism to "demythologize" the supernatural elements
of the New Testament. He treated the New Testament writings as products
of the early church which are different from the person and teaching of Jesus
himself. "Here, too, great caution is demanded by the nature of our sources.
What the sources offer us is first of all the message of the early Christian
community, which for the most part the church freely attributed to Jesus.
This naturally gives no proof at all that the words which are put into his
mouth were actually spoken by him." Through the process of form criticism,
the "oldest layer" of the teaching of Jesus must be separated from "whatever betrays the specific interests of the church or reveals characteristics of
later development." These later layers placed on top of the teaching of Jesus
"must be rejected."[78] Even liberal critics have, however, deemed Bultmann's
mode as characterized by "irrational skepticism."[79] We shall have more to say
about Bultmann's influence upon biblical theology in the next section. More
recently, scholars have used form criticism to trace a biblical statement's later
use rather than to speculate about its origin.[80]

Among more recent forms of biblical criticism are the movements known
as redaction criticism and canonical criticism. *Redaction criticism*, building on
the productions of form criticism, examines the editorial decisions of the
various biblical writers. For instance, a redaction critic will examine how the
author(s) of the biblical books of the Chronicles developed the moral aspects
of the kings who are discussed in the biblical books of the Kings. Rehoboam
is more clearly culpable in his morals in 2 Chronicles 12 than in 1 Kings 14.
Again, Manasseh becomes an example of repentance in 2 Chronicles 33,

---

literary records were short and well within the lifetimes of the eyewitnesses. Richard
Bauckham, *Jesus and the Eyewitnesses: The Gospels as Eyewitness Testimony*, 2nd ed.
(Grand Rapids: Eerdmans, 2017), 7.

[78] Rudolf Bultmann, *Jesus and the Word*, trans. Louis Pettibone Smith and
Erminie Huntress Lantero (London: Collins Fontana, 1958), 17. The form critical
approach of Bultmann, which divides the Bible into layers to be received or rejected,
contradicts the attitude of Jesus to Scripture. Bultmann passes over the dichotomy
between his own low view of Scripture and Jesus's high view of Scripture without any
sense of the irony. Bultmann, *Jesus and the Word*, 51–53.

[79] Werner, *The Formation of Christian Dogma*, 12.

[80] Gretchen Ellis, "Form Criticism," in *Social and Historical Approaches to the
Bible*, 99–135.

a matter passed over in 2 Kings 21.[81] Again, redaction criticism has been helpful in extricating the particular theological concerns of the four Gospel writers, although it can be less concerned with the historical aspects of their writings. E. Earle Ellis and R. T. France are two evangelicals among many who have pursued this approach to good benefit.[82]

Canonical criticism has also proven beneficial, particularly in correcting the long-term trends toward the atomization of Scripture within both biblical studies and biblical theology. Canonical criticism retains the distinctions between the biblical texts but recognizes they also contextualize one another. Due to its relationship with biblical theology, this recently developed form of higher criticism remains marginal in biblical studies.[83] Although he rejects the phrase itself, Brevard S. Childs became prominent within the movement of canonical criticism by calling for the text to be evaluated critically as a document of the believing community. "The term 'canon' points to the received, collected, and interpreted material of the church and thus establishes the theological context in which the tradition continues to function authoritatively for today."[84] Because the early church received both the Old Testament and the New Testament, a theology for the whole Bible has hereby again become possible. The testaments maintain a "discrete witness" while the canon shapes their reception "much like a *regula fidei*."[85] John Sailhamer also rejects the phrase, because he sees "canon" as authoritative for the church and "criticism" as an attempt to get behind the text.[86]

Evangelical theologian Leo Garrett turned a critical eye upon criticism itself. He first distinguished "textual criticism" as a "science" from the higher

---

[81] Jeffery Leonard, "Redaction Criticism," in *Social and Historical Approaches to the Bible*, 163–94.

[82] France, *The Gospel of Matthew*, (see chap. 5, n. 57); R. T. France, *The Gospel of Mark*, The New International Greek Text Commentary (Grand Rapids: Eerdmans, 2002); E. Earle Ellis, *The Gospel of Luke*, rev. ed., New Century Bible (London: Marshall, Morgan, and Scott, 1974).

[83] Ron Haydon and David Schreiner, "Canonical Criticism," in *Literary Approaches to the Bible*, ed. Douglas Mangum and Douglas Estes, Lexham Methods Series (Bellingham, WA: Lexham, 2017), 37.

[84] Childs, *Biblical Theology: A Proposal*, 40 (see chap. 7, n. 2).

[85] Brevard S. Childs, *Biblical Theology of the Old and New Testaments: Theological Reflection of the Christian Bible* (Minneapolis: Fortress, 1992), 71, 95, 209.

[86] Haydon and Schreiner, "Canonical Criticism," 41–42.

criticisms, which are "studies." Drawing upon the modernist penchant to prioritize the objective over the subjective, Garrett concluded to the contrary, "The subjective factor seems to play a greater role under these methods than under textual criticism."[87] He noted that the common opinion in biblical studies was that "the assured results of biblical criticism" should be accepted. However, Garrett warns that such enthusiasm should be tempered by "the criticism of criticism." A genuine "assessment process" will "sometimes confirm the conclusions of biblical criticism and at other times invalidate such conclusions." Garrett was especially critical of three prominent critical movements: The attempt of Ferdinand Christian Baur to describe the early church as "a clash" between Pauline and Petrine parties; the source-document hypothesis of Graf, Kuenan, and Wellhausen; and the theory of Rudolf Bultmann that the Gospel of John was a Hellenistic or Gnostic development rather than a Hebrew one.[88] We reaffirm Garrett's critical approach to both the biblical critics and their critical methods.

XI. Critical Exegesis: Biblical Theology

In its simple sense, "biblical theology"[89] occurs whenever Christians receive truth about God from their canon. Christian history is replete with examples of pastoral theologians who sensibly garnered theology from Scripture as they proclaimed it to the people—from Athanasius to Augustine to Bernard to Luther. Despite widespread diversity in some areas, pre-critical biblical theology broadly interpreted the doctrines of Scripture as trinitarian in origin, Christological in focus, and fully canonical in extent. The previous sections on patristic, medieval, and reformation biblical studies make this clear. For more than fifteen centuries, Scripture was taken prima facie as the Word of God inspired by the Holy Spirit and thus authoritative for the Christian church. However, each central biblical and theological claim was criticized in modern biblical studies. The theology of the Bible has, likewise, been

---

[87] Garrett, *Systematic Theology*, 1:160.

[88] Garrett, *Systematic Theology*, 1:161–63.

[89] The term, "biblical theology," was first used in the late 1750s in several Pietistic works. Rudolf Bultmann, *Theology of the New Testament*, vol. 2, trans. Kentrick Grobel (New York: Scribner's Sons, 1955), 242, 242n.

subjected to reexamination, prompting some to engage in the "remaking" of theology to reach modern society.[90]

"Biblical theology" as a modern critical discipline is typically traced to the 1787 lecture of Johann Philipp Gabler, "On the Proper Distinction Between Biblical and Dogmatic Theology and the Specific Objectives of Each." Gabler began by affirming "the sacred books, especially of the New Testament, are the one clear source from which all true knowledge of the Christian religion is drawn." The major problem of opposing interpretations arose for five reasons: "the occasional obscurity of the sacred Scriptures," "reading one's own opinions and judgments into the Bible," "a servile manner of interpreting it," and "the neglected distinction between religion and theology." The final reason concerns "an inappropriate combination of the simplicity and ease of biblical theology with the subtlety and difficulty of dogmatic theology."[91]

Gabler excavated the distinction between biblical theology and dogmatic theology into a gulf. On the one side is "religion," which secures happiness "in this life and the life to come." Religion "is passed on by the doctrine in the Scriptures" and "is every-day, transparently clear knowledge." On the other side lies "theology," which is "subtle, learned knowledge, surrounded by a retinue of many disciplines." Theology is a "field elaborated by human discipline and ingenuity" and "experiences various changes." Gabler raised the "clear," "sacred," and "historical" nature of biblical theology above the "subtle," "human," and "shifting" nature of dogmatic theology, parroting the humanist and modernist prejudice against "the thick gloom of barbarity" in scholastic and dogmatic theology.[92]

Gabler justified his method in Paul's reference to "worthless elements" (Gal 4:9). He argued the biblical theologian must distinguish the various

---

[90] Maurice Wiles, *The Remaking of Christian Doctrine: The Hulsean Lectures 1973* (London: SCM, 1974). On Wiles's liberal theological method, see Yarnell, *The Formation of Christian Doctrine*, 42–48.

[91] Johann Philipp Gabler, *De Justo Discrimine Theologiae Biblicae et Dogmaticae Regundisque Recte Utriusque Finibus*, in John Sandys-Wunsch and Laurence Eldredge, "J. P. Gabler and the Distinction between Biblical and Dogmatic Theology: Translation, Commentary, and Discussion of His Originality," *Scottish Journal of Theology* 33, no. 2 (April 1980): 134–35.

[92] Gabler, *De Justo Discrimine*, 136–38.

historical concerns of the writers from "the true sacred ideas typical of each author."[93] The biblical theologian, "diligently isolating the opinions of each," will arrive through contrast and comparison at "the happy appearance of biblical theology, pure and unmixed with foreign things." "When these opinions of the holy men have been carefully digested, carefully referred to the universal notions, and cautiously compared among themselves, the question of their dogmatic use may then profitably be established."

Gabler does not address how his "universal notions," which control the process, are derived. Gabler, perhaps unreflectively or naively, believes these indefinite "basic elements," "true sacred ideas," or "universal notions," which the biblical theologian presumes to know, also enjoy inherent authority in theology. The biblical theologian possesses an innate capability to show, somehow without dogma but "with unambiguous words the form of faith that is truly divine, the *dicta classica* properly so called, which can then be laid out as the fundamental basis for a more subtle dogmatic scrutiny."[94] The father of modern biblical theology thereby granted his own discipline a dogmatic authority he denied to the church.

Buttressed with self-referential authority, the new discipline went in directions Gabler might regret. Gabler recognized diversity among the biblical authors but maintained the reality of "universal notions." Others emphasized the human diversity and forsook the sacred unity. After Georg Lorenz Bauer's one-volume *Theologie des Alten Testaments* and four-volume *Theologie des Neuen Testaments* were published between 1796 and 1802, the field divided into Old Testament theology and New Testament theology. Scholars increasingly treated the theologies of the various biblical authors and their texts in isolation from each other, even in opposition to one another. Ferdinand Christian Baur, it will be remembered, proposed a division between Peter's Jewish theology and Paul's Hellenism, prompting the Tübingen school to trace theology according to his idealist history of a bifurcated biblical text. Conservative theologians proposed a historical method which treated the Bible more respectfully. J. C. K. Hofmann's method of

---

[93] Gabler hereby violated his own historical-grammatical principles. Gabler, *De Justo Discrimine*, 139–41.

[94] Gabler, *De Justo Discrimine*, 142–43.

Heilsgeschichte, "salvation-history," organized the canonical books according to the eschatological progress of God's redemptive plan.[95]

Julius Wellhausen's critical division of the Old Testament into editorial traditions had a devastating effect upon Old Testament theology. Israel's religion was now largely traced according to its underlying editorial traditions rather than according to a canonical unity. "Wellhausen's work marks the beginning of the period that saw the apparent death of OT theology and the victory of the discipline called the 'history of the religion of Israel.'"[96] Even conservative scholars largely ceased writing Old Testament theology for nearly half a century after Wellhausen. While Wellhausen's documentary hypothesis has been challenged and other critical methods introduced, the historical critical method continues to influence many Old Testament scholars. Those who still follow the history of the religion of Israel approach generally refuse to treat the Old Testament literature with privilege, dislike prescriptive interpretations, follow the supposed history "behind the text" rather than the history in the text, and do not link the Old Testament with the New Testament.[97]

A Swiss scholar, Walther Eichrodt, shocked the field in 1933 with the first volume of his magisterial *Theology of the Old Testament*. While remaining thoroughly conversant with historical critical tools, Eichrodt issued a sharp challenge, saying, "It is high time that the tyranny of historicism in OT studies was broken and the proper approach to our task re-discovered."[98] Eichrodt rejected Wellhausen's approach, but neither would he let dogmatics impose its abstract scheme. The text should provide its own center, which he identified with the doctrine of "Covenant" arranged in three principal categories: "God and the People," "God and the World," and "God and Man."[99] The renewal was soon joined by the English Baptist Henry Wheeler

---

[95] George Eldon Ladd, "Biblical Theology, History of," in *The International Standard Bible Encyclopedia*, ed. Geoffrey W. Bromiley, 4 vols. (Grand Rapids: Eerdmans, 1979), 1:499.

[96] Ladd, "Biblical Theology," 500.

[97] Brittany Kim and Charlie Trimm, *Understanding Old Testament Theology: Mapping the Terrain of Recent Approaches* (Grand Rapids: Zondervan, 2020), 34–50.

[98] Walther Eichrodt, *Theology of the Old Testament*, trans. J. A. Baker, 2 vols. (Philadelphia: Westminster Press, 1961), 1:31.

[99] Eichrodt, *Theology of the Old Testament*, 1:32–35.

Robinson, the Dutch Reformed Theodoor Christiaan Vriezen, and the German Lutheran Gerhard von Rad.[100] The field of Old Testament theology continues to see new contributions from more traditional perspectives.[101]

Meanwhile, the field of New Testament theology became the center of the academic struggle over Christianity. In 1897, William Wrede went beyond Gabler by rejecting both "New Testament" and "theology" as inappropriate. Perceiving the deceptive dogmatic imposition enclosed within Gabler's method, Wrede proposed "a purely historical discipline."[102] Concern for the canon as inspired revelation must be surrendered; other early sources must be elevated. The "religion" of the early church should be engaged "scientifically" in a "disinterested" manner, and every "dogmatic" declaration surrendered.[103] The modern academic must objectively portray what Israel, Judaism, and the early church had "believed, thought, hoped, required, and striven for."[104] Through his own important essay, Wrede created the "history of religion" approach, which still dominates the university context of biblical theology.[105] God and his church were denied any meaningful role, for "history has its own laws."[106] In effect, the individual scholar's perception of history achieved an apotheosis by displacing divine revelation.

Adolf Schlatter's intricate 1909 response to Wrede established him as the most substantial critic of this history of religion approach. Schlatter agreed the scholar must suspend his dogmatic goal to discern "what was once true

---

[100] Ladd, "Biblical Theology," 502. Von Rad uses the documentary hypothesis but thinks the unhistorical claims of the Old Testament have a theological truth behind them. Kim and Trimm, *Understanding Old Testament Theology*, 44–46.

[101] Kim and Trimm, 14–30.

[102] William Wrede, "The Task and Methods of 'New Testament Theology,'" in *The Nature of New Testament Theology: The Contribution of William Wrede and Adolf Schlatter*, ed. Robert Morgan, Studies in Biblical Theology, 2nd series, vol. 25 (London: SCM, 1973), 69.

[103] Wrede, "The Task and Methods of 'New Testament Theology,'" 70–71.

[104] Wrede, 84.

[105] Reflecting on Wrede's influence upon the field of "biblical theology," Clifton Black wryly noted, "In academic scholarship precious little of it is either 'biblical' or 'theological.'" C. Clifton Black, "Biblical Theology Revisited: An Internal Debate," *Interpretation* 70, no. 4 (October 2016): 399.

[106] Wrede, "The Task and Methods of 'New Testament Theology,'" 73.

for others," but only for a time.[107] The "dogmatic question may not be set aside," because "the New Testament word" "confronts us with the claim that we should be affected by it in all our character and without reserve."[108] The church's canon calls the listener to "choose" in the presence of Christ and his Spirit; this makes Wrede's "abstractions" impossible. The New Testament requires a dogmatic response to a "real event."[109]

For Schlatter, New Testament theology is where "the struggle for and against Christianity" is now waged, and Wrede's appeal to "the historian's objectivity is self-deception."[110] Since reason and faith are inextricably intertwined, the historian must identify his own "presuppositions."[111] "We have to be clear that historical criticism is never based on historical fact alone, but always has roots in the critic's dogmas, too."[112] Step by step, Schlatter unmasked the alien dogmas of the historicists posing as biblical theologians, restored the unity of the canon, and recalled the discipline to the Christian faith.[113] "Schlatter turned Wrede's fundamental critique against himself: if the New Testament's authors had been illegitimately 'modernized' into dogmaticians, then neither should they be modernized as Troeltschian historians."[114]

Rudolf Bultmann's *Theology of the New Testament* "is generally acknowledged as the twentieth century's most important experiment in New Testament theology."[115] Bultmann followed Wrede's lead in treating first of Jesus, then the early church, followed by Paul and John. According to

---

[107] Adolf Schlatter, "The Theology of the New Testament and Dogmatics," in *The Nature of New Testament Theology*, 118. Schlatter believed the Reformation appeal to the authority of the biblical canon required the maintenance of the distinction between dogma and history, but the Enlightenment unfortunately divorced dogma and history. Schlatter, "The Theology of the New Testament and Dogmatics," 123, 127–28, 130–31.

[108] Schlatter, 122.

[109] Schlatter, 129–34.

[110] Schlatter, 124.

[111] Schlatter, 127.

[112] Schlatter, 155.

[113] A slim version of Schlatter's method is available in Robert Yarbrough, "Adolf Schlatter's 'The Significance of Method for Theological Work: Translation and Commentary,'" *Southern Baptist Journal of Theology* 1, no. 2 (Summer 1997): 64–76.

[114] Black, "Biblical Theology Revisited," 401.

[115] Black, 404.

Bultmann, the "message" of Jesus is "a presupposition" for the New Testament but Jesus himself did not preach the *kerygma*. The *kerygma* about Jesus came from "the earliest church and not before," so its theology begins there.[116] He said the assertion that Jesus possessed a "messianic consciousness" is "legend."[117] The church ascribed the resurrection to Jesus, who did not see himself as the suffering Servant of Isaiah 53.[118] Within the early church, "The proclaimer became the proclaimed." Jesus became the "Son of Man," but not yet the eternal "Son of God." The early Jewish church proclaimed Jesus simply as the Messiah.[119]

By contrast, he argued the early Hellenistic church's *kerygma* transformed the Hebrew Christ into a deified Greek "Lord" requiring worship.[120] Moving inexorably forward by degrees, Bultmann speculated that Paul toyed with Gnosticism to make Jesus fulfill its redeemer-myth.[121] Paul, he argued, "became the founder of Christian theology" by syncretizing Christianity "within the Hellenistic frame." Paul also shifted Jesus's saving message of the kingdom to salvation by righteousness.[122] In his second volume, Bultmann said John's Christology, which was later and independent of Paul, was also Hellenized. The two apostles "formed" Christ "after the pattern of the Gnostic Redeemer-myth."[123]

Bultmann undercut Scripture's veracity, but this was unimportant to him. The "vitality" of the New Testament "faith" is demonstrated in the way it "understandingly masters its constantly new historical situation."[124]

---

[116] Rudolf Bultmann, *Theology of the New Testament*, vol. 1, trans. Kendrick Grobel (New York: Scribner's Sons, 1951), 3; see Dockery, *Biblical Interpretation Then and Now*, 164–69 (see chap. 5, n. 42); also, David A. Black and David S. Dockery, ed., *New Testament Criticism and Interpretation* (Grand Rapids: Zondervan, 1991).

[117] Bultmann, *Theology of the New Testament*, 1:27.

[118] Bultmann, *Theology of the New Testament*, 1:31.

[119] Bultmann, *Theology of the New Testament*, 1:33–35, 42–43. Bultmann says "Son of God" was ascribed to Jesus, but only as a royal title. Bultmann, *Theology of the New Testament*, 1:50.

[120] Bultmann, *Theology of the New Testament*, 1:124.

[121] Bultmann, *Theology of the New Testament*, 1:164–83.

[122] Bultmann, *Theology of the New Testament*, 1:187–89

[123] Rudolf Bultmann, *Theology of the New Testament*, vol. 2, trans. Kendrick Grobel (New York: Scribner's Sons, 1955), 6.

[124] Bultmann, *Theology of the New Testament*, 2:237.

Perhaps tipping his hat to Schlatter, who argued for the necessity of a dog-matic meaning, Bultmann exercised *Sachkritik*, "content criticism." He denied the theological claims of the text for an incarnate God-Man and proposed existentialism in its place.[125] Ironically enough, Bultmann's move has been identified as a modern successor to allegorical interpretation. Content criti-cism "'gets around' obstinate pieces of tradition by re-interpretation, instead of removing them."[126]

Martin Werner provides an endpoint to the twentieth century biblical theology movement born in liberalism and matured in Bultmann. For his part, Werner pitted the "eschatological" theology of "Primitive Christianity" against the later "Hellenistic mystery-religion of Early Catholicism." He agreed with Baur that Paul's teaching was a "departure point." He also agreed with Schweitzer that the "delay of the Parousia" was instrumental in fostering a different theology within the early church and the biblical documents.[127] Appropriating Harnack's Hellenization of Christianity thesis, Werner con-cluded there was a "transition to the dogma of the divinity of Christ" away from the primitive Jewish theology of messianic humanity.[128] From Baur and Schweitzer to Bultmann and Werner, the discipline of biblical theology moved significantly away from Christian orthodoxy.

However, Bultmann's deconstruction project was not alone in emphasiz-ing *kerygma* during the twentieth century. In a more traditional vein, C. H. Dodd examined the preaching of the apostles and discovered their emphasis on the gospel of Jesus Christ provided the Christian center of the Bible. The apostles proclaimed that God sent his Son to become the Messiah, to die on the cross, and to arise from the dead, so that believers may come into the Kingdom of God.[129] While Dodd's eschatology was criticized, his historical-theological project has been taken up by many. Oscar Cullmann verified the

[125] Morgan, *The Nature of New Testament Theology*, 36–51.
[126] Morgan, 43.
[127] Werner, *The Formation of Christian Dogma*, 40–55.
[128] Werner, 213–18.
[129] C. H. Dodd, *The Apostolic Preaching and Its Developments: Three Lectures with an Appendix on Eschatology and History*, rev. ed. (London: Hodder and Stoughton, 1963).

historical center of the Christian faith, recalling the conservative *Heilsgeschichte*. However, Cullmann downplayed claims regarding the nature of Christ.[130]

Despite the desacralizing work of scholars like Wellhausen, Wrede, and Bultmann, contemporary scholars continue to argue for the utility of biblical theology. Andreas Köstenberger deems Gabler's argument "hermeneutically sound, theologically astute, well argued, and altogether timely."[131] With less optimism, Peter Stuhlmacher says, "the primary duty of Biblical Theology is (in my opinion) to discover and develop the original historical meaning and the theological claims of the biblical texts." Both history and dogma are necessary because the church recognizes it is a creature of the Word.[132] New Testament theologies continue to be written by scholars in both evangelical and mainline traditions. The whole canon has risen in importance again, even as its distinct theologies are respected. The biblical theologies of Childs,[133] Stuhlmacher,[134] and Beale[135] represent three highly regarded efforts.

Robert Morgan concludes the discipline has now effectively divided into three groups. First, *the history of religion approach* to the theology of the New Testament is concerned only with historical exegesis, discerning what the ancient writers and their audiences perceived about God and the world. Following Wrede, these scholars reject dogmatic readings. Second, *the*

---

[130] "All points of this redemptive line are related to the one historical fact at the mid-point." That mid-point is "the death and resurrection of Jesus Christ." Oscar Cullmann, *Christ and Time: The Primitive Christian Conception of Time and History*, trans. Floyd V. Filson (Philadelphia: Westminster, 1950), 32–33. Ladd, "Biblical Theology," 503.

[131] Andreas Köstenberger, "Editorial," *Journal of the Evangelical Theological Society* 55, no. 1 (March 2012): 1.

[132] "Creatura verbi." Peter Stuhlmacher, *How to Do Biblical Theology*, Princeton Theological Monographs (Eugene, OR: Pickwick, 1995), ix–x. As with Lutheran biblical scholars generally, Stuhlmacher identifies the center of New Testament theology with the righteousness of Christ. The "Christological clamp" unites the Old and New Testaments; Christ's resurrection "caused the formulation of the New Testament confessions and traditions;" the Holy Spirit provided the apostles with "inspired words;" and whoever believes in Christ may participate in his Kingdom. Stuhlmacher, *How to Do Biblical Theology*, xxv, 11, 25–26, 63.

[133] Childs, *Biblical Theology of the Old and New Testaments*.

[134] Peter Stuhlmacher, *Biblical Theology of the New Testament*, trans. Daniel P. Bailey (Grand Rapids: Eerdmans, 2018).

[135] Beale, *A New Testament Biblical Theology*, (see chap. 10, n. 16).

biblical theology approach prioritizes historical exegesis of the text but is open to contemporary theological discussion. For example, Bultmann affirmed Wrede's historical judgment, but incorporated Schlatter's call for contemporary meaning through his peculiar appropriation of Martin Heidegger's existentialism. Third, *the theological interpretation of Christian Scripture approach* utilizes historical exegesis but emphasizes its theological concern. "Like dogmatics, explicit theological interpretation is primarily addressed to an ecclesial readership."[136] To this third approach, we now turn our attention.

XII. Post-Critical Exegesis: The Theological Interpretation of Scripture

Striving against the substantial Christian witness of eighteen prior centuries, academic study of the biblical text had largely severed itself from the life of the church during the nineteenth and twentieth centuries. The radical critics took the Bible apart page-by-page, "determined not merely to be free from church decrees, as Jowett wished, but also from the texts themselves."[137] These academics maintained their work was "objective," but they exercised a destructive "hermeneutic of suspicion." Two distinctly modern notes have come to characterize the academy: "facile reductionism" and a modernist privileging of "the latest narrator" over the supposed "guile or stupidity" of the biblical writers.[138]

Suspicion toward Scripture sank deep roots in Western culture not only through biblical studies departments in the major universities but also through the social, philosophical, and psychological influences of Karl Marx, Friedrich Nietzsche, and Sigmund Freud.[139] Other movements also hindered modern Christians who sought to move from Scripture to theology. Immanuel Kant, the highly influential modern philosopher, created an

---

[136] Robert Morgan, "New Testament Theology as Implicit Theological Interpretation of Christian Scripture," *Interpretation* 70, no. 4 (2016): 389.

[137] Bryan, *Listening to the Bible*, 8.

[138] Bryan, 29–30.

[139] Marx deemed biblical religion an opiate to repress the masses. Nietzsche claimed Christianity promoted mental weakness. Freud said the requirement for a heavenly Father was rooted in disappointment over earthly fathers. Bryan, 36–37; Walter Wink, *The Bible in Human Transformation*, 2nd ed. (Minneapolis: Fortress, 2010).

approach to epistemology, "transcendental idealism," which limited access to all metaphysical reality. Kant categorized metaphysics, including theology, under the "logic of illusion."[140] In response, Friedrich Schleiermacher, "the most significant theologian between John Calvin and Karl Barth," reconnected epistemology with theology through the feeling of absolute dependence. However, Schleiermacher's Romanticist liberalism pointed humanity inward to reflect upon its own piety, decoupling Christian theology from its traditional relation to objective truth.[141] In recent decades, both liberal and conservative scholars have protested against both the destructiveness of biblical criticism and the reduction of biblical theology.

From the liberal side, a prominent member of the Jesus Seminar flatly declared, "Historical biblical criticism is bankrupt."[142] Walter Wink provided five reasons for declaiming his own discipline: its method is "inconsistent" with the texts; its "objectivism" creates a "false consciousness;" its technique limits answers from the text; its proponents isolate themselves from the church; and the end of modernity makes this modern method "obsolete."[143] Wink alleged radical critics silenced the voice of God's word by sealing a Faustian pact with the devil to suspend judgment.[144] Wink proposed the critics exorcise themselves. "Criticism rounds upon the critic. There is a further work of destruction, but this time a destruction of what destroys, a deconstruction of the assurances of modern man. There is another kind of suspicion, but this time a suspicion lodged against ourselves."[145] Wink invited his fellow critics to renounce Satan, participate in the text, and be freed for communion.[146] Alas, Wink's anthropocentrism prevented him from

---

[140] The "phenomenal" is experimentally measurable, while the "noumenal" is variously intuited. Kant's anti-metaphysical bias makes theological interpretation "difficult at the least and impossible at the worst." Yarnell, *God the Trinity*, 102–3 (see chap. 1, n. 78). Scruton, *Kant*, 1, 54–72 (see chap. 3, n. 78); Shao Kai Tseng, *Immanuel Kant*, Great Thinkers (Phillipsburg, NJ: P&R, 2020), 110–15.

[141] Hensley, "Friedrich Schleiermacher," 165–68, 179 (see chap. 6, n. 76); see Dockery, *Biblical Interpretation Then and Now*, 161–64.

[142] Wink, *The Bible in Human Transformation*, 1.

[143] Wink, 2–12.

[144] Wink, 18–26.

[145] Wink, 26.

[146] Wink, 58–60.

calling on the only One who could possibly assist the self-referential liberal project, the transcendent God.[147]

From the traditional side, numerous scholars are identifying a better way to move from text to theology. John Webster credited Karl Barth with proposing the newest form of exegesis, now known as "theological interpretation of Scripture." Before Barth, hermeneutical efforts were strongly anthropocentric. "But his achievement is to have offered a theological account of the nature of Scripture and its interpretation that makes appeal to divine revelation rather than the interpreting subjects, and to have undertaken a dogmatic work that both recommends and illustrates the deference of doctrine to the Bible."[148] Most modern historians point to Barth's commentary on Romans as the public watershed in this turn toward the radical priority of divine grace. However, from a private perspective, Barth's immersion in "the strange new world within the Bible" once he began preaching regularly seems more significant.[149]

To create a common taxonomy for the developing movement, Kevin J. Vanhoozer brought together many well-regarded historical theologians, systematic theologians, philosophical theologians, and biblical scholars, including Craig G. Bartholomew, Henri Blocher, Alister McGrath, and I. Howard Marshall, as well as Alan Torrance, Nicholas Wolterstorff, and N. T. Wright, among others.[150] Bartholomew and Heath A. Thomas went further and crafted *A Manifesto for Theological Interpretation* to give form to the broad-based movement. It includes twelve planks: 1. move beyond modernity to recover the church's history of exegesis; 2. become "informed by a robust, creative theology of Scripture;" 3. reconnect interpretation "with the church;" 4. retain history but according to a "theological claim" and "Christological articulation of that claim;" 5. retain philosophy but in accord with the "Trinitarian God;" 6. recognize the "canon is the ground and basis of all theological interpretation;" 7. attend to the canon as "*tota Scriptura*;" 8. recall the church's mission "is a central thread;" 9. aim "to hear the voice of God" and experience transformation

---

[147] "Divinity is not a qualitatively different reality; quite the reverse, *divinity is fully realized humanity.*" Italics his. Wink, *The Human Being*, 29 (see chap. 10, n. 19).

[148] John Webster, "Barth, Karl," in *Dictionary for Theological Interpretation of the Bible*, ed. Kevin J. Vanhoozer (Grand Rapids: Baker, 2005), 84.

[149] Karl Barth, *The Word of God and the Word of Man*, trans. Douglas Horton (Gloucester, MA: Peter Smith, 1978), 28–50.

[150] Vanhoozer, ed., *Dictionary for Theological Interpretation of the Bible*, 7–12.

in Christ; 10. reintegrate the "foundational articles" of the Christian faith; 11. affirm theological commentary is not only possible but necessary; 12. and practice theological interpretation "for all of life," incorporating our narrative into the biblical narrative.[151]

We affirm the importance of the theological interpretation of Scripture for four major reasons among others. First and foremost, theological interpretation emphasizes the power and transcendence of God by recalling revelation is an act of divine grace. Second and closely related to the first reason, theological interpretation retains the Reformation priority of the canon of Scripture as the authoritative norm correcting every dogmatic tradition. Third and without contradicting *sola scriptura*, theological interpretation reintroduces to contemporary Christians the profound exegetical treasures in the tradition of the universal church.[152] Finally, theological interpretation invokes the necessity of reading Scripture with Jesus Christ at the center.

We believe that this approach, the theological interpretation of Scripture, is valid for twenty-first-century interpreters. This interpretative model recovers the canonical and the theological, for it builds upon yet takes evangelicals a step beyond the grammatical and historical interpretation of the biblical text. Christological and ecclesial interpretations, when consistent with the literary and historical context of the biblical books, should be encouraged. This allows us to read the experiences, promises, and prophecies of the Old Testament authors in their context, while pointing us to the eternal gospel of Christ that they themselves promised beforehand (Rom 1:1–4).

---

[151] Craig G. Bartholomew and Heath A. Thomas, eds., *A Manifesto for Theological Interpretation* (Grand Rapids: Baker, 2016), 1–26. Standing somewhere between theological interpretation and the older disciplines, Christopher Bryan identified three tasks to pursue: listen to "the individual voices" in the Bible; consider them "in relation to the whole of Scripture;" and "ask how all that relates to the continuing life and witness of the Church up to and including today." Bryan, *Listening to the Bible*, 45.

[152] Criticizing the "modern chauvinism" he once taught, Thomas C. Oden lauds the "young fogeys" who are renewing contemporary knowledge of traditional orthodoxy. Oden, *The Rebirth of Orthodoxy: Signs of New Life in Christianity* (New York: HarperSanFrancisco, 2003), 8–10. Both Oden and Timothy George have helped prompt a renaissance in historical biblical exegesis with their separate multi-volume series, *Ancient Christian Commentary on Scripture* and *Reformation Commentary on Scripture*.

With Nicholas Piotrowski and James Innell Packer,[153] we believe there is much insight and spiritual wisdom to be gained from this approach to interpretation and application. In doing so, however, one must never divorce a passage from its historical background. The canonical-theological interpretation will not stop at the grammatical-historical but will seek the eternal and Christological sense of the passage for the enrichment of teaching and preaching Scripture for the edification of the church. Ultimately, the Bible is to be interpreted through the centrality of Jesus Christ, who himself affirmed the complete veracity of, and lived his life in fulfilment of the sacred Scripture. The central message of the Bible remains the foundation on which the people of God can work together while moving forward in faithful witness, ministry, and mission, offering the transforming gospel of Jesus Christ to a fallen, hurting, and watching world.

---

[153] Nicholas Piotrowski, *In All the Scriptures: The Three Contexts of Biblical Hermeneutics* (Downers Grove: IVP, 2021); J. I. Packer, "Reading the Bible Theologically," in *ESV Systematic Theology Study Bible*, ed. Christopher W. Morgan and Stephen J. Wellum (Wheaton: Crossway, 2017), 1660–63. Cf. David S. Dockery, "Author? Reader? Text? Toward a Hermeneutical Synthesis," *Theological Educator* 38 (Fall 1988): 7–17. For a tribute to the recently deceased Packer, see Malcolm B. Yarnell III, "Theology for Worship: A Gift from James Innell Packer (1926–2020)," *Credo Magazine*, July 24, 2020, https://credomag.com/2020/07/theology-for-worship-a-gift-from-james-innell-packer-1926-2020/.

12

The Bible in Baptist Life

This chapter will seek to provide an overview of the way the Bible has been understood in Baptist life, with particular reference to the Southern Baptist Convention.[1] Traditionally, Baptists have been a confessional people, but have been cautious not to grant to any confessional statement or creed greater authority than Holy Scripture. Still, Baptists have published numerous confessions of faith since the early years of the seventeenth century.[2] In the initial section of this chapter, it will be our purpose to note a few of these important statements regarding the inspiration and authority of Scripture, statements which have appeared in representative Baptist confessions from the seventeenth century to the present.

I. Baptist Confessions and the Authority of Scripture

1. Article 23 of Thomas Helwys's *Confession* (1611) offers the following high view of Scripture:

   That the scripture off the Old and New Testament are written for our instruction, 2 Tim 3:16 and that we ought to search them for they testifie off CHRIST, Io. 5:29, and therefore to

---

[1] For a fine overview of Baptist movements and thinkers, see Anthony L. Chute, Nathan A. Finn, and Michael A. G. Haykin, *The Baptist Story* (Nashville: B&H, 2015).

[2] William L. Lumpkin and Bill J. Leonard, eds., *Baptist Confessions of Faith*, 2nd ed. (Valley Forge, PA: Judson, 2011).

bee used with all reverence, as concerning the Holie Word off God, which onlie is our direction in all things whatsoever.

2. A characteristic General Baptist understanding of Scripture was set forth in Article 23 of the *Standard Confession* (1663):

    That the Holy Scripture is the rule whereby Saints both in matters of Faith, and conversation are to be regulated, they being able to make men wise unto salvation, through Faith in Christ Jesus, profitable for Doctrine, for reproof, for instruction in righteousness, that the man of God may be perfect, thoroughly furnished unto all good works, 2 Tim 3:15,16,17. John 20:31. Isa 8:20.

3. The Particular Baptists adopted the *First London Confession* in 1644, predating the Westminster Confession. Articles 7 and 8 state:

    The Rule of this Knowledge, Faith, and Obedience, concerning the worship and service of God, and all other Christian duties, is not man's inventions, opinions, devices, lawes, constitutions, or traditions unwritten whatsoever, but only the Word of God contained in the Canonical Scriptures.

    In this written Word of God hath plainly revealed whatsoever He hath thought needfull for us to know, believe, and acknowledge, touching the Nature and Office of Christ, in whom all the promises are yea and Amen to the praise of God.

4. *The Second London Confession* (1677, 1689) tends to follow the wording and emphases of the Westminster Confession and Savoy Declaration statements on Scripture. This is certainly the case in terms of placement within the confession, where the articles on Scripture have been moved to the first sections of the document. In addition to articles on the biblical canon (21), a denial of the authority of the apocrypha (93), statements on illumination (6), the original languages (8), and the perspicuity of Scripture regarding the salvation of sinners, the *Second London Confession* affirms:

    The Holy Scripture is the only sufficient, certain, and infallible rule of all saving Knowledge, faith, and Obedience.

(4) The Authority of the Holy Scriptures for which it ought to be believed dependeth not upon the testimony of any man, or Church; but wholly upon God (who is truth itself) the author thereof, therefore it is to be received, because it is the Word of God.

(5) We may be moved and induced by the testimony of the Church of God, to an high and reverent esteem of the Holy Scriptures . . . and it doth abundantly evidence itself to be the word of God; yet, not withstanding, our full persuasion, and assurance of the infallible truth, and divine authority thereof, is from the inward work of the Holy Spirit, bearing witness by and with the Word in our Hearts.

(9) The infallible rule of interpretation is the Scripture itself: And therefore when there is a question about the true and full sense of any Scripture (which is not manifold but one) it must be searched by other places that speak more clearly.

(10) The supream judge by which all controversies of Religion are to be determined, and all Decrees of Counsels, opinions of ancient Writers, Doctrines of men, and private Spirits, are to be examined, and in whose sentence we are to rest, can be no other but the Holy Scripture delivered by the Spirit, into which Scripture so delivered, our faith is finally resolved.

5. *The Orthodox Creed* (1678). Article 37, which is positioned at the conclusion of the confession maintains that the "Scriptures are given by the inspiration of God, to be the Rule of faith and life."

6. *The Philadelphia Confession* (1742) repeats the Second London Confession's articles on divine revelation.

7. *The New Hampshire Confession of Faith* (1833)

   Article One: We believe that the Holy Bible was written by men divinely inspired, and is a perfect treasure of heavenly instruction; that it has God for its author, salvation for its end, and truth, without any mixture of error, for its matter; that it reveals the principles by which God will judge us; and therefore is, and shall remain to the end of the world, the true centre of Christian union, and the supreme standard by which all human conduct, creeds, and opinions should be tried.

8.   *The Abstract of Principles* (1858)

The Scriptures are given by inspiration of God, and are the only sufficient, certain, and authoritative rule of all saving knowledge, faith, and obedience.

9.   Article One of the *Baptist Faith and Message* (1925)

We believe that the Holy Bible was written by men divinely inspired, and is a perfect treasure of heavenly instruction; that it has God for its author, salvation for its end, and truth, without any mixture of error, for its matter; that it reveals the principles by which God will judge us; and therefore is, and will remain to the end of the world, the true center of Christian union, and the supreme standard by which all human conduct, creeds, and religious opinions should be tried.

10. Article One of the *Baptist Faith and Message* (1963)

The Holy Bible was written by men divinely inspired and is the record of God's revelation of Himself to man. It is a perfect treasure of divine instruction. It has God for its author, salvation for its end, and truth, without any mixture of error, for its matter. It reveals the principles by which God judges us; and therefore is, and will remain to the end of the world, the true center of Christian union, and the supreme standard by which all human conduct, creeds, and religious opinions should be tried. The criterion by which the Bible is to be interpreted is Jesus Christ.

11. Article One of the *Baptist Faith and Message* (2000)

The Holy Bible was written by men divinely inspired and is God's revelation of Himself to man. It is a perfect treasure of divine instruction. It has God for its author, salvation for its end, and truth, without any mixture of error, for its matter. Therefore, all Scripture is totally true and trustworthy. It reveals the principles by which God judges us, and therefore is, and will remain to the end of the world, the true center of Christian union, and the supreme standard by which all human conduct, creeds, and religious opinions should be tried. All Scripture is a testimony to Christ, who is Himself the focus of divine revelation.[3]

Some may question the importance of such confessional statements in a volume in which we have contended for the final authority of Scripture over the ministerial authority of tradition, creeds, and confessions. Their confessional statements, however, show that for four centuries Baptists have been willing to articulate their views about Scripture and acknowledge those convictions in their official documents.[4] Historian Heiko Oberman helpfully distinguished between Scripture as magisterial authority and confessions and traditions as secondary authority. In this regard, Baptists have followed the paths of many patristic and early medieval theologians, as well the Reformers.[5]

Both General and Particular Baptists in the seventeenth century agreed on the importance and role of confessional statements.[6] The Orthodox Creed of 1678 affirmed that the Nicene, Athanasian, and Apostles' Creeds "ought thoroughly to be received and believed." Article 38 acknowledges

---

[3] One can observe changes and revisions from the 1833 New Hampshire statement to the 1925, 1963, and 2000 versions of the Baptist Faith and Message. See Herschel H. Hobbs, "Southern Baptists and Confessionalism: A Comparison of the Origins and Contents of the 1925 and 1963 Confessions," *Review and Expositor* 76, no. 1 (Winter 1979); and Thomas J. Nettles, "Creedalism, Confessionalism, and the Baptist Faith and Message," in *The Unfettered Word: Southern Baptists Confront the Authority-Inerrancy Question*, ed. Robison B. James (Waco: Word, 1987), 138–54.

[4] See the helpful account in Joseph D. Wooddell, "The Scripture," in *Baptist Faith and Message 2000: Critical Issues in America's Largest Protestant Denomination*, ed. Douglas K. Blount and Joseph D. Wooddell (Lanham, MD: Rowman & Littlefield, 2007), 1–12.

[5] See Heiko A. Oberman, *Forerunners of the Reformation: The Shape of Late Medieval Thought*, trans. Paul L. Nybus (New York: Holt, Rinehart, and Winston, 1966).

[6] Putman, "Baptists, *Sola Scriptura*, and the Place of Christian Tradition," in *Baptists and the Christian Tradition*, 27–54 (see chap. 8, n. 31).

Baptists believe these important statements of faith from the early church "may be proved, by the most undoubted authority of holy Scripture, and are necessary to be understood by all Christians; and to be instructed in knowledge of them, by the ministers of Christ, according to the analogy of faith, recorded in the sacred scriptures, upon which these creeds are grounded." The confession goes on to recognize that such statements serve as "a means to prevent heresy in doctrine, and practice."[7]

In the third decade of the twentieth century, Southern Baptists were preparing to articulate their shared confession in the Baptist Faith and Message (1925). Edgar Young Mullins, the primary architect of this important document, insisted that confessional statements were vital for the survival of denominations and faith traditions, saying "a denomination controlled by a group who have no declared platform is heading for the rocks."[8] Furthermore, Mullins added:

> The Baptist denomination has never allowed creeds to be imposed upon it by others. But Baptists have always insisted upon their own right to declare their beliefs in a definite, formal way, and to protect themselves by refusing to support men in important places as teachers and preachers who do not agree with them.[9]

Moreover, he noted:

> If a group of men known as Baptists consider themselves trustees of certain great truths, they have an inalienable right to conserve and propagate those truths unmolested by others inside the denomination who oppose such truths. The latter have an equal right to unite with another group agreeing with them.[10]

Baptist confessional statements serve as important aspects of the larger interpretive tradition. The statements are not infallible like Scripture. Nevertheless, they serve as helpful indicators of the illumination of the

---

[7] Orthodox Creed (1678), article 38. Also, see Matthew Pinson, *Arminian and Baptist: Explorations in a Theological Tradition* (Nashville: Randall, 2015), 153–69.

[8] E. Y. Mullins, "Baptists and Creeds," in *The Axioms of Religion*, comp. R. Albert Mohler Jr., ed. Timothy George and Denise George (Nashville: B&H, 1997), 189.

[9] Mullins, "Baptists and Creeds," 189.

[10] Mullins, 190.

Holy Spirit, who enables and guides us as we seek to articulate our beliefs about holy Scripture.[11] We will now turn our attention from Baptist confessions to Baptist theologians and leaders as we seek to discern the consensus represented among Baptist thinkers through the years on the key doctrine of doctrine revelation. Our survey will not attempt to engage with every significant thinker in Baptist life, for that would entail a much longer survey than can be afforded by the purposes of the present book. However, the magnificent and unmatched work on *Baptist Theology* by James Leo Garrett Jr. offers guidance for those looking for greater detail regarding these and like matters.[12] Particular attention will be given below to Southern Baptist thought since the middle of the nineteenth century.

II. A Brief Survey of the Bible among Baptist Theologians

Baptist theology, in common with Baptist churches, can be traced to two common English sources. From English separatism arose the General Baptists who sought asylum in the Netherlands around 1608–9. This group, initially under the leadership of John Smyth (d. 1612), rejected infant baptism and began *de novo* believer's baptism by affusion. Based on his commitments to the authority of Scripture, Smyth offered new insights regarding church government and worship, in addition to baptism. General Baptist theology reflected key aspects of Arminianism, stressing universal atonement, thus the name "general." Thomas Helwys (1570–1615), who was baptized by Smyth, led a small contingent of the first English Baptists back to England and planted the first Baptist congregation on English soil at Spitalfields near London in 1612.

In addition to General Baptists, there were also the Particular Baptists, influenced by streams of Calvinism, who appear to have formed their first congregation in 1638. Confessional statements reflecting the commitments of each group to Scripture were cited earlier in this chapter. Similar patterns

---

[11] James Leo Garrett Jr., "Biblical Authority According to Baptist Confessions of Faith," *Review and Expositor* 76:1 (Winter 1979): 43–54.

[12] James Leo Garrett Jr., *Baptist Theology: A Four-Century Study* (Macon, GA: Mercer University Press, 2009).

were charted in America, where in 1639, a year after the first Particular Baptist church was formed in London, a Baptist congregation was started in Providence, Rhode Island by Roger Williams (1603–1684). While only a Baptist for a short while, Williams nevertheless affirmed the importance of scriptural authority as the basis for his views on the church, baptism, and religious liberty.[13]

Clear affirmations regarding the inspiration and authority of Scripture are evident in the writings of the earliest Baptist theologians. Thomas Grantham (1634–1692), apparently the first Baptist systematic theologian, in his *Christianismus Primitivus* (1678) balanced the normative priority of Scripture with the importance of tradition and confessional statements.[14] Dan Taylor (1738–1816), a leading General Baptist of the next generation, affirmed the significance of the Bible's truthfulness and an orthodox understanding of Christology, alongside the general atonement and the need for gospel proclamation. Of great consequence was his volume on *The Truth and Inspiration of the Scriptures* (1790).[15] At a time in Baptist history when both General and Particular Baptists faced spiritual and theological decline, Taylor's leadership brought renewal, and paved the way for the establishment of the Baptist Union in 1813. Great British Baptist pastors from Dan Taylor and John Gill (1697–1771) to Alexander Maclaren (1826–1910) and Charles Spurgeon (1834–1892) reflect an overarching commitment to the inspiration and infallibility of sacred Scripture. Their orthodoxy was representative of the majority of Baptists on both sides of the Atlantic.

In America, Baptists grew rapidly in the years surrounding the American Revolution. The earliest theological commitments in America echoed those of the Particular Baptists in England, as reflected in the Philadelphia Confession (1742). Moderating influences upon Calvinistic soteriology developed by the turn of the nineteenth century, as can be observed in the New Hampshire Confession (1833). An important work defending the

---

[13] See helpful resources regarding the shaping of Baptist life such as H. Leon McBeth, *The Baptist Heritage: Four Centuries of Baptist Witness* (Nashville: Broadman, 1987); James E. Tull, *Shapers of Baptist Thought* (Valley Forge, PA: Judson, 1972).

[14] Thomas Grantham, *Christianismus Primitivus* (London: Francis Smith, 1678).

[15] William H. Brackney, "Dan Taylor," in *The Baptists* (New York: Greenwood, 1988), 271–72.

truthfulness of Scripture and the distinctiveness of the Christian faith by New England Baptist Thomas Baldwin was entitled *Catechism or Compendium of Christian Doctrine and Practice* (1816).[16] The Baptist missionary movement, greatly influenced by the theological commitments of Andrew Fuller (1754–1815), made significant gains and likewise shaped aspects of Baptist thinking during this time. Francis Wayland (1796–1865) ranked as one of the premier intellects of his day and taught theology at Andover Seminary and Brown University. Wayland's *Notes on the Principles and Practices of Baptist Churches* (1856) circulated widely and served as a source of encouragement for those seeking to build their churches in a faithful manner on the gospel of Jesus Christ and the authority of the Bible.[17]

As the nineteenth century drew to a close, however, British Baptists found themselves in the midst of a struggle known as the Downgrade Controversy, which involved both Spurgeon and John Clifford (1836–1923). Clifford advocated forms of biblical criticism and theological-scientific synergism that were rejected by stricter Baptists who appreciated Spurgeon's commitment to the inerrancy of Scripture. Spurgeon withdrew from the Baptist Union in 1887, while Clifford continued as England's foremost Baptist stateman. Clifford exerted strategic leadership not only in the British Baptist Union but also in the Baptist World Alliance at the turn of the century. Two Southern Baptist presidents, E. Y. Mullins and George Washington Truett (1867–1944), however, fostered a more conservative theological tradition in the latter institution. The issues debated during the Downgrade Controversy set the agenda for ongoing controversies on both sides of the Atlantic in the twentieth century.[18]

Baptists were not exempt from the inroads of liberalism. Leading exponents of liberal trends included William Newton Clarke (1841–1911), Shailer Mathews (1836–1941), and Harry Emerson Fosdick (1878–1969). A social gospel theology was pioneered by Walter Rauschenbusch

---

[16] William H. Brackney, *A Genetic History of Baptist Thought* (Macon, GA: Mercer University Press, 2004), 225–28.

[17] See David S. Dockery, "Looking Back, Looking Ahead," in *Theologians of the Baptist Tradition*, ed. Timothy George and David S. Dockery (Nashville: B&H, 2001), 338–60.

[18] Lewis Drummond, *Spurgeon: Prince of Preachers* (Grand Rapids: Kregel, 1992), 669–714.

(1861–1918) and a mediating theology, influenced by personal idealism, was brilliantly expounded by Augustus Hopkins Strong (1836–1921). Clarke taught New Testament and theology at Toronto Baptist Seminary and Colgate Theological Seminary for almost three decades. His many impressive works included *The Use of the Scriptures in Theology* (1905), *Sixty Years with the Bible* (1909), and his classic contribution, *An Outline of Christian Theology* (1909). Clarke developed a semi-existential methodology that centered on Jesus's life and teachings as the revelation of God and the interpreter of human experience.[19]

Like Clarke, Mathews claimed a most impressive Baptist heritage. After studying at Newton Theological Institute, Mathews taught briefly at Colby College before beginning his distinguished career at the University of Chicago Divinity School. More than any other early twentieth-century Baptist, Mathews embodied liberal ideology. Shaped by German critical approaches to biblical and theological studies, by evolutionary understandings of religious history, and by a basic commitment to a social gospel, Mathews boldly defended modernism. His works on *The Social Teaching of Jesus* (1897) and *The Faith of a Modernist* (1924) expressed Christianity primarily in terms of human need and human freedom. His salient insights challenged traditional theological constructions and established the theological agenda for northern Baptists for decades.

The popular preacher who brought the thoughts of Clarke and Mathews to a wider audience was the pulpit giant Harry Emerson Fosdick. Fosdick was a scholar who, at various intervals, taught at Union Theological Seminary for almost four decades while pastoring three churches in the New York City area. The peak of his popularity came while he served as the eloquent pastor of the Park Avenue Baptist Church (subsequently renamed the Riverside Church). His challenge to traditional Christianity came in a famous sermon delivered in 1922 with the title, "Shall the Fundamentalists Win?" He popularized liberal Baptist theology in his considerable writings and sermons. His thought can be observed in his two most well-known works, *Christianity and*

---

[19] R. V. Pierard, "Theological Liberalism," in *Evangelical Dictionary of Theology*, ed. Daniel J. Treier and Walter A. Elwell, 3rd ed. (Grand Rapids: Baker, 2017), 488–90.

Progress (1922) and *The Modern Use of the Bible* (1924).[20] Reaction to modernist thought came from Baptist fundamentalists, especially William Bell Riley (1861–1947), J. Frank Norris (1877–1952), and T. T. Shields (1873–1955), as well as John R. Rice (1895–1980). By 1926, those who were militant for the fundamentals had failed to expel the modernists from Baptist conventions, creating the beginning of various independent Baptist movements.[21]

Two important women who pioneered women's causes and shaped Baptist life and thought were Susan E. C. Griffin (1851–1926) and Helen Barrett Montgomery (1861–1934). Griffin was the first woman to receive ordination among American Baptists (1893) when she and her husband were called as pastors of a Baptist church in Elmira Heights, New York. For a decade prior to this call, the couple had served as missionaries in India. A gifted linguist, speaker, and administrator, she effected the union of women's societies of the Free Baptist General Conference and the Northern Baptist Convention. Montgomery was another key figure in the developing role of women in Baptist life. She prepared numerous Bible study aids, but her most esteemed accomplishment was her *Centenary Translation of the New Testament* (1924). She organized the initial World Day of Prayer, and in 1920, amid the Modernist-Fundamentalist controversy, she presided over the national meeting of the Northern Baptist Convention.

Harold Henry Rowley (1890–1969) treated the theological significance of the Old Testament from the vantage point of redemption, election, and worship. He contended that the Bible, the Word of God, was both divine and human and yielded only to the ultimate authority of Jesus Christ, the living Word of God. These views were adequately articulated in *The Relevance of the Bible* (1942), *The Authority of the Bible* (1949), and *The Unity of the Bible* (1953). He helped to advance the serious study of the Old Testament among Baptists. Rowley argued persuasively that the Old Testament should

---

[20] Garrett, *Baptist Theology*, 304–18; Kenneth Cauthen, *The Impact of American Religious Liberalism* (New York: Harper & Row, 1962).

[21] Garrett, *Baptist Theology*, 318–27; George W. Dollar, *A History of Fundamentalism in America* (Greenville, SC: Bob Jones University Press, 1973); Bobby D. Compton, "J. Frank Norris and Southern Baptists," *Review and Expositor* 79:1 (Winter 1982): 63–84; O. S. Hawkins, *In the Name of God: The Colliding Lives, Legends, and Legacies of J. Frank Norris and George W. Truett* (Nashville: B&H, 2021).

be rediscovered and communicated in terms of its abiding significance for the church and Christian theology.

Martin Luther King Jr. was the leading voice in the civil rights crusade of the 1960s and the foremost advocate of nonviolent strategies for addressing social problems. He pastored churches in Montgomery, Alabama, and Atlanta, Georgia, before being assassinated in Memphis, Tennessee, in 1968. His doctoral dissertation focused on the theology of Paul Tillich. He was also influenced by the social teachings of Walter Rauschenbusch. King founded the Southern Christian Leadership Conference and worked with Gardner Taylor to form the Progressive National Baptist Convention. His important work on racial reconciliation and economic justice appealed to the authority of the Bible, particularly the teachings of Jesus. The influence of King's view of biblical Christianity upon the American civil rights tradition is unparalleled.

The contributions of Southern Baptists to theology, church, and ministry were informed by these developments in the nineteenth and twentieth centuries. Prior to the beginning of the Southern Baptist Convention in 1845 and the establishment of The Southern Baptist Theological Seminary in 1859, John L. Dagg (1794–1884), president and professor of theology at Mercer (1844–54), was considered the most prominent theologian among Baptists in the South.

Subsequently, the first hundred years of institutional Southern Baptist theology were largely shaped by a small group of scholars and theologians. James P. Boyce (1827–88), Basil Manly Jr. (1825–92), and John A. Broadus (1827–95), all members of the first generation of faculty and leaders at Southern Seminary, along with A. T. Robertson (1863–1934), E. Y. Mullins (1860–1928), and W. O. Carver (1868–1954), shaped the next generation of leaders. Of similar importance were Benajah Harvey Carroll (1843–1914) and Walter Thomas Conner (1877–1952), who influenced the thought and ministry of thousands of students at Southwestern Baptist Theological Seminary during its first four decades. These theologians helped shape, guide, and influence Southern Baptists as they entered and maintained the period of their greatest growth, but it would be hard to overestimate the influence of Mullins at Southern and Conner at Southwestern.[22]

---

[22] See David S. Dockery, *Christian Scripture* (Nashville: B&H, 1995), 177–215; also, the contribution of W. Wiley Richards, *Winds of Doctrine: The Origin*

III. Nineteenth-Century Southern Baptists and Biblical Authority

The first one hundred years of theology in Southern Baptist life was largely shaped by Dagg, Boyce, Manly, Broadus, and Carroll. John L. Dagg was the initial shaper of Southern Baptist theology. Among the many works from the pen of the former Mercer president was an article on the "Origin and Authority of the Bible" (1853), later included in his popular systematic, *A Manual of Theology* (1858).[23] Dagg simultaneously led the way for Southern Baptists and mirrored them in almost all areas of theology, including the doctrine of Scripture. Dagg characterized Scripture as fully inspired, infallible, and authoritative. He understood the Spirit's inspiration to be the means by which revelation was conveyed to human minds and the means by which this revelation was put in permanent form as a written document. Dagg maintained that inspiration guaranteed that God's people had received a revelation from God which must be characterized as infallible and authoritative. He believed "infallibility" meant the Bible was completely truthful in all its statements. Furthermore, Dagg argued this understanding was entirely consistent with human authorship; the Bible was divine truth without error.[24]

The most important Baptist work on special revelation in the nineteenth century was certainly Basil Manly Jr.'s *The Bible Doctrine of Inspiration* (1888), which was published as a response to the resignation of Old Testament professor C. H. Toy at Southern Seminary.[25] Both Manly and Boyce disagreed with Toy's doctrine of Scripture and its practical implications. Manly argued that an uninspired Bible would furnish no infallible standard of thought, no authoritative rule for obedience, and no ground for confidence and everlasting hope. Infallibility for Manly and Boyce meant "without error;" indeed, there is nothing in their writings to imply they distinguished between

---

and Development of Southern Baptist Theology (Lanham, MD: University Press of America, 1991); David Lyle Jeffrey, *We Were a Peculiar People Once: Confessions of an Old-Time Baptist* (Waco: Baylor University Press, 2023).

[23] J. L. Dagg, *A Manual of Theology* (Charleston, SC: Southern Baptist Publication Society, 1858).

[24] Mark E. Dever, "John L. Dagg," in *Theologians of the Baptist Tradition*, 52–72.

[25] Basil Manly Jr., *The Bible Doctrine of Inspiration: Explained and Vindicated* (New York: A. C. Armstrong and Sons, 1888).

infallibility and inerrancy. An inseparable relationship between inspiration, infallibility, and authority was held in Manly's work. This diminishes the idea that the change of wording between the term "infallible" in the Second London Confession and the word "authoritative" in the seminary's confessional statement, the Abstract of Principles, involved a change of meaning. Manly carefully defined inspiration as "that direct divine influence that secures the accurate transference of truth into human language by a speaker or writer, so as to be communicated to another."[26] While affirming plenary inspiration, Manly refuted any theory of mechanical dictation, because it ignored genuine human authorship. He believed every aspect of Scripture is infallibly true and divinely authoritative.

John A. Broadus, who authored a splendid volume on *Matthew* in The American Commentary series, wrote "Three Questions as to the Bible" (1883). Broadus gave the positive answer of "completely" to the question, "To what extent ought we to regard the sacred writings of the Old and New Testaments as inspired?" In 1887, he basically agreed with the conclusions of Dagg and Manly in his work, "The Paramount and Permanent Authority of the Bible," though Broadus was more independent and creative in his articulation.[27] We must, however, recognize that the failure of several of these key nineteenth-century leaders to address the important question of slavery detracts from their contributions in the area of bibliology.

Perhaps with less scholarly erudition, but with greater persuasive power, B. H. Carroll, the founder and first president of Southwestern Seminary, sounded similar commitments in the Southwest. His widespread reputation as the champion of Baptist orthodoxy in Texas and beyond was closely associated with his doctrine of Scripture. He confessed the Bible to be the written revelation of God. While noting a close relationship between revelation and inspiration, he nevertheless went to great lengths to differentiate between revelation, inspiration, and illumination. Carroll enthusiastically emphasized that the inspiration of Scripture ensures a perfect standard of instruction and conviction and a profitable work for correction and training in righteousness.

---

[26] Manly Jr., *Bible Doctrine of Inspiration*, 37.
[27] David S. Dockery, "The Broadus-Robertson Tradition," in *Theologians of the Baptist Tradition*, 90–114; David S. Dockery and Roger D. Duke, eds., *John A. Broadus: A Living Legacy* (Nashville: B&H, 2008).

While recognizing the biblical writers were moved along by the Holy Spirit, Carroll rightly stated that inspiration applies primarily to the writings of Scripture.[28] Carroll rejected all forms of limited or partial inspiration, saying that "when you hear the silly talk that the Bible contains the Word of God and is not the Word of God, you hear a fool's talk."[29] Having observed Charles Spurgeon's efforts to push back against the tides of modernism in Great Britain, Southwestern Seminary's founder was always ready as an apologist and polemicist to affirm biblical orthodoxy and counter liberalism, heresy, or schism.[30] Directly or indirectly, these Southern Baptist thinkers were influenced by the old Princeton Seminary theologians, as well as by British Baptists like Fuller and Northern Baptists like Wayland and Alvah Hovey (1820–1903).

As noted earlier, Baptists have drawn up authoritative confessions of faith as guides for belief, practice, and fellowship. These statements leave a clear impression regarding what Baptists believed about the doctrine of the Bible. While there were different emphases in these Baptist confessions and among the leaders who wrote them, they exhibited strong agreement on the divine origin and inspiration of Scripture. Baptists generally affirmed that revelation is personal, propositional, and progressive, that the Bible has its source in God, that its inspiration is plenary, and that it is the Word of God written, fully truthful and authoritative.[31]

Still, due to the influence of Enlightenment thought coming from one direction and deep pietistic tendencies coming from another, a shift could be observed toward deemphasizing the Bible's authority. Tensions rose as some made claims that authority belonged only to Jesus over his people. While sounding pious, it is strange that some Baptist thinkers could ignore the words of Jesus himself. Our Lord trusted the Scriptures and attested to their authority without reservation (Matt 5:17–19; John 10:35). In response, thinkers such as Gill, Taylor, and Fuller noted that to affirm the lordship of Jesus Christ calls for his followers to yield to Christ's own teaching and practice regarding the sacred Scriptures.

---

[28] B. H. Carroll, *Inspiration of the Bible* (New York: Revell, 1930).

[29] Carroll, *Inspiration of the Bible*, 20.

[30] James Spivey, "Benajah Harvey Carroll," in *Theologians of the Baptist Tradition*, 163–80.

[31] Garrett, *Systematic Theology*, 1:155–67.

The consensus regarding the inspiration and authority of Scripture that we have briefly surveyed began to be challenged in the initial decades of Southern Baptist life. In 1867, Thomas F. Curtis, who taught theology at several Baptist colleges along the East Coast and served as director of the SBC Home (Domestic) Mission Board from 1851 to 1853, questioned the early consensus regarding the inspiration and infallibility of Scripture. Curtis's *The Human Element in the Inspiration of the Sacred Scriptures* emphasized the freedom of the human authors, denying the infallibility of the Bible. He emphasized the aspects of Scripture he found to be experientially true. He believed his favored teachings were communicated in fallible ways by the biblical writers.[32]

C. H. Toy affirmed the Boyce-Manly-Broadus tradition when he initially joined the Southern Seminary faculty in 1869 with a presentation titled, "The Claims of Biblical Interpretation on Baptists." A decade later, this brilliant Old Testament scholar published a series of articles in the *Religious Herald* (1879–1880) articulating a position similar to Curtis. Toy raised questions regarding the trustworthiness of Scripture in response to evolutionary theory and historical criticism.[33] The proposals from Curtis and Toy were met with resounding pushback, not only from Manly, but in coming years from A. T. Robertson, John R. Sampey, C. Tyree, J. M. Frost, T. T. Eaton, F. H. Kerfoot, as well as Landmarkist leaders James M. Pendleton and J. R. Graves, among others. Jeter, editor of the *Religious Herald*, immediately answered Toy with three articles on the "Inspiration of the Bible" and an edited volume entitled *Baptist Doctrines* in 1880.

Both Robertson and Sampey, two brilliant biblical scholars at Southern Seminary, advocated for the inerrancy of Scripture during the early years of their careers, as indicated in the annual sessions of the Baptist Congress for the Discussion of Current Questions. Robertson authored "The Relative Authority of Scripture and Reason" (1892)[34] and Sampey defended the

[32] Thomas F. Curtis, *The Human Element in the Inspiration of Sacred Scripture* (New York: Appleton, 1867).

[33] Mikael C. Parsons, *Crawford Howell Toy: The Man, the Scholar, the Teacher* (Macon, GA: Mercer University Press, 2019); also, see Mark A. Noll, *America's Book: The Rise and Decline of a Bible Civilization, 1794–1911* (Oxford: Oxford University Press, 2022), 534.

[34] See Dockery, "The Broadus-Robertson Tradition," 107–11.

complete truthfulness of the Bible in his faculty address on "The Interpretation of the Old Testament." In 1921, at the Conference on Baptist Fundamentals, Sampey articulated his belief in the sufficiency and veracity of the Old Testament. He gladly affirmed that God's revelation is progressive and culminates in Christ, concluding Scripture is entirely inspired and infallible.[35] The discussion regarding the infallibility of Scripture dominated theological discussions in the Southern Baptist Convention during the last two decades of the nineteenth century. The conversation reached its zenith with a compendium edited by J. M. Frost called *Baptist Why and Why Not* (1900).[36] The opening essays by Frost, Eaton, and Kerfoot expressed the consensus Baptist position on the Bible. Frost, the first president of the Baptist Sunday School Board, explained in the introduction that the foundation of all the articles in the book was built on the presupposition the Bible is inerrant. He stated: "We accept the Scriptures as an all-sufficient and infallible rule of faith and practice, and insist upon the absolute inerrancy and sole authority of the Word of God."[37]

This brief overview should help put to rest the idea that the doctrine of biblical inerrancy is a recent innovation in Southern Baptist life. The last two decades of the nineteenth century and the initial decades of the twentieth century are filled with writings representing an affirmation of the complete infallibility and authority of Scripture. In addition to the above authors, we note the contribution of Edgar Estes Folk, editor of the *Baptist and Reflector*. Folk urged the next generation to maintain "loyalty to God's Word in God's Book" in the Sunday School Board publication, *Letters to My Son* (1909).[38] His thought followed that of Edwin Charles Dargan (1892–1907), a leading theologian at Southern Seminary, who argued in *Doctrines of the Faith* (1905) from tradition, the Bible's internal witness, and Scripture's overall character that the Bible is God's authoritative revelation.[39]

---

[35] Gregory A. Wills, *Southern Baptist Theological Seminary, 1859–2009* (Oxford: Oxford University Press, 2009), 311–12.

[36] J. M. Frost, ed., *Baptist Why and Why Not* (Nashville: Baptist Sunday School Board, 1900).

[37] Frost, *Baptist Why and Why Not*, 12.

[38] E. E. Folk, *Baptist Principles: Letters to My Son* (Nashville: Baptist Sunday School Board, 1909).

[39] E. C. Dargan, *Doctrines of the Faith: A Convenient Handbook for Use in Normal Classes, Sacred Literature Courses, and Individual Study* (Nashville: Baptist Sunday

The door, however, had been opened in Southern Baptist life for what was being boldly articulated by Ezekiel Gilmon Robinson (1815–1894), president of Rochester Seminary, and Clarke at Colgate Seminary. Both Robinson and Clarke had declared an affirmation of biblical inerrancy to be untenable. In his influential *Outline of Christian Theology* (1894), Clarke wrote, "the Bible itself releases us from all obligation to maintain its complete inerrancy, in the sense of freedom from all inaccuracy and incorrectness of statement, and shows us a higher quality in which is manifest a higher purpose than that of inerrancy."[40] Henry Wheeler Robinson (1872–1945), an influential British Baptist theologian, offered a perspective quite similar to Robinson and Clarke. One could add the names of Shirley Jackson Case (1872–1947) and Ernest DeWitt Burton (1856–1925), who were associated with the Baptist work at the University of Chicago, along with Rauschenbusch at Rochester. The influence of these thinkers led A. H. Strong, the highly regarded theologian and President of Rochester Seminary at the turn of the twentieth century, to slightly adjust his views on inspiration and infallibility in his widely circulated *Systematic Theology*. While continuing to affirm his evangelical and Baptist commitments, Strong focused on the efficacy of the Bible and its main purpose rather than its ontology.[41] All these moves influenced the events which arose during the first half of the twentieth century in Southern Baptist life.

IV. Early Twentieth-Century Southern Baptist Thinkers

E. Y. Mullins served as the fourth president and as professor of theology at the Southern Baptist Theological Seminary from 1899 to 1928. He has been called America's most neglected theologian. Literary critic Harold Bloom referred to Mullins as the Luther, Calvin, or Wesley of Southern Baptist life. Mullins brought creativity in theological method with his emphasis on pietism and personalism as he wrestled with how to maintain his

---

School Board, 1905).

[40] William Newton Clarke, *An Outline of Theology*, 2nd ed. (London: T&T Clark, 1900), 35.

[41] Carl F. H. Henry, *Personal Idealism and Strong's Theology* (Wheaton: VanKampen, 1951); Grant Wacker, *Augustus H. Strong and the Dilemma of Historical Consciousness* (Macon, GA: Mercer University Press, 1985).

commitments to biblical authority and historical orthodoxy while engaging the Enlightenment's emphasis on experience and individualism. Nowhere are these various matters better illustrated than in his systematic theology with the revealing title *The Christian Religion in Its Doctrinal Expression* (1917).[42] Not only was his book used as a textbook at both Southern and Southwestern seminaries for decades, but Mullins also powerfully influenced W. T. Conner, who served at Southwestern for thirty-nine years. Mullins's emphases on the role of experience and his work on the relationship between science and Scripture paved the way for twentieth-century Baptists to raise new questions and explore new approaches regarding the nature and interpretation of Scripture.

Mullins criticized the conclusions of German theologian Friederich Schleiermacher (1768–1834), the "Father of Theological Liberalism," while borrowing aspects of his methodology, including the emphasis on religious experience.[43] Mullins intentionally attempted to restate and recontextualize the theology of Dagg, Boyce, and Manly. His shift included some change in content, but it was primarily one of methodology for the changing context of the twentieth century. The methodological changes, however, had significant influence for the generations which followed him. Mullins was particularly cautious in how he acknowledged Scripture as revelation, providing nuance to what had been stated by Dagg and Manly in the previous generation. Similarly, while affirming the Bible's inspiration, he was not comfortable affirming the Bible's inerrancy, though he never publicly affirmed error or contradiction in Scripture.

A major shift for Mullins was his insistence that the authority of the Bible was limited to the religious life of the Christian believer, a change reflected in the 1925 Baptist Faith and Message. The most important shift in the thinking of this leading Southern Baptist statesman was his emphasis on experience, which drew upon William James, Boston personalism, and

---

[42] E. Y. Mullins, *The Christian Religion in Its Doctrinal Expression* (Philadelphia: Judson, 1917); see David S. Dockery, *Southern Baptist Consensus and Renewal: A Biblical, Historical, and Theological Proposal* (Nashville: B&H, 2008), 175–84.

[43] On the theological method of Mullins, see Malcolm B. Yarnell III, "Changing Baptist Concepts of Royal Priesthood: John Smyth and Edgar Young Mullins," in *The Rise of the Laity in Evangelical Protestantism*, ed. by Deryck Lovegrove (New York: Routledge, 2002), 236–52.

Schleiermacher's pietism. Near the end of his life and ministry, it needs to be noted that Mullins stressed that the Bible is a fully reliable and authoritative guide in his 1923 address to the Southern Baptist Convention on "The Dangers and Duties of this Present Hour." Mullins there concluded that the Bible is "God's revelation of himself and is the sufficient and authoritative guide" for all of life. Similar emphases can be found in his major publication, *Christianity at the Crossroads* (1924).[44]

Walter Thomas Conner influenced theological commitments and directions at Southwestern Seminary in a similar manner to Mullins at Southern. Conner's most important contribution to the subject of biblical authority is contained in *Revelation and God* (1936)[45] and *Christian Doctrine* (1937).[46] Conner not only studied with Mullins, but also with Calvin Goodspeed and Carroll at Southwestern, with Strong and Rauschenbusch at Rochester, and with Mathews at the University of Chicago. During his tenure, the influence of Goodspeed and Carroll waned while that of Mullins and Strong increased. Conner wrote with regular and numerous appeals to the biblical text, but his work was also shaped by the emphasis on experience found in Schleiermacher's methodology and the pragmatism and empiricism of William James.

Conner emphasized the personal nature of revelation and did not discuss either inerrancy or infallibility. He sought to balance carefully the divine and human aspects of Scripture but seemed even less comfortable with the idea of inerrancy than Mullins, although inerrancy had been clearly espoused by both Carroll and L. R. Scarborough, his two presidents at Southwestern. Like Mullins, he stressed the Bible's trustworthiness and authoritative character for the spiritual dimensions of life. His ultimate concern was with the function of Scripture in leading men and women toward freedom in Christ. The bottom line for Conner was the authoritative character of Scripture. He maintained the only way to realize true freedom is by submission to the Bible in and through which God's authority is

---

[44] E. Y. Mullins, *Christianity at the Crossroads* (Nashville: Baptist Sunday School Board, 1924); see William E. Ellis, *A Man of Books and a Man of the People* (Macon, GA: Mercer University Press, 1985). Also, see Noll, *America's Book*, 534–35.

[45] W. T. Conner, *Revelation and God: An Introduction to Christian Doctrine* (Nashville: Broadman 1936).

[46] W. T. Conner, *Christian Doctrine* (Nashville: Broadman, 1937).

made known.[47] Both Mullins and Conner contended for historic orthodoxy. However, their methodologies, combined with hesitancy to articulate biblical infallibility or inerrancy, set a trajectory away from Dagg, Boyce, Manly, Broadus, Carroll, and Scarborough.

Before concluding our survey of key Baptist thinkers in the first half of the twentieth century, we must look at William Owen Carver (1868–1954), who taught New Testament, missions, and world religions at Southern Seminary for more than four decades. For many years, he also served as editor of that seminary's journal, *Review and Expositor.* Carver pushed against Southern Baptist tendencies toward sectarianism, parochialism, Landmarkism, and fundamentalism. He also championed the Baptist distinctives of freedom and individualism, emphasizing spiritual experience more than doctrine. Carver pioneered work in missiology and world religions for Baptists, while also penning a warm-hearted work on Paul's letter to the Ephesians (1949).

Carver's prolific book reviews in *Review and Expositor* were as engaging and insightful as they were numerous. He once reviewed thirty books in one issue alone in 1914. We often learn more from Carver and about Carver in these reviews than in his other publications. Regarding the relationship of science and Scripture, Carver suggested Christians should not expect the Bible to contain an outline of science or other related fields. The creation story, he maintained, was a work of art, which is theologically trustworthy but not scientifically accurate. Scripture, also like a work of art, beckons personal interpretation. He thought the Word of God does not become revelation until it becomes the experience of a person.

While Carver pushed back against fundamentalism and Landmarkism, he did not think of himself as a theological liberal, describing himself as one who presented moderating and mediating views on most things. On the first page of *The Making of American Liberal Theology: Idealism, Realism, and Modernity, 1900–1950,* Gary Dorrien claims that "the essential idea of

---

[47] See the interpretive and biographical information in James Leo Garrett Jr., "The Theology of Walter Thomas Conner" (Th.D. dissertation, Southwestern Baptist Theological Seminary, 1954); Stewart Albert Newman, *W. T. Conner: Theologian of the Southwest* (Nashville: Broadman, 1964). Also, see Dwight Moody, "The Bible," in *Has Our Theology Changed: Southern Baptist Thought Since 1845,* ed. Paul A. Basden (Nashville: B&H, 1994), 7–40. We have been helped by Moody's thoughtful interpretation of Dagg, Manly, Carroll, Mullins, and Conner.

liberal theology is that all claims to truth, in theology as well as in other disciplines, must be made on the basis of reason and experience, not by an appeal to external authority."[48] While Carver may not have been a self-identified theological liberal, he certainly demonstrated a great appreciation for liberal thinkers and an openness to their methodological appeal to reason and experience.

The emphasis on religious experience found in Mullins, Conner, and especially Carver indicates that the tendencies of modernism were beginning to find a home among Southern Baptist intellectuals, even during the first half of the twentieth century. While not stated explicitly, these constituted early markers toward progressive thought in Southern Baptist life prior to the 1960s. For Carver, the Word of God in the Scriptures never meant primarily and specifically the Bible, or any section of the Bible. He thought of Scripture as the "chief medium" of God's revelation, one that becomes the Word of God when encountered by pious individuals, meaning the interpretive act served as the key. Carver's influence on teachers, missionaries, and pastors, not to mention the powerful Woman's Missionary Union, was measurably significant.[49]

Carver's voice was quite influential, but a strong chorus developed to counter his approach even during his lifetime. In a major work published by the Baptist Sunday School Board in 1922 with the title *Fundamentals of the Faith*, William B. Nowlin critiqued historical approaches to the Bible and supported the Scripture's own self testimony to its complete inspiration.[50] New Testament scholar Harvey Eugene Dana (1888–1945) defended the historical reliability of the Bible in *The Authenticity of the Holy Scriptures* (1923).[51] James Josiah Reeve (1866–1946), a professor at Southwestern

---

[48] Gary Dorrien, *The Making of American Liberal Theology: Idealism, Realism, and Modernity, 1900–1950* (Louisville: Westminster John Knox, 2003), 1.

[49] See the important work on Carver's life and thought in Mark R. Wilson, *William Owen Carver's Controversies in the Baptist South* (Macon, GA: Mercer University Press, 2010); also, see John J. Carey, *Carlyle Marney: A Pilgrim's Progress* (Macon, GA: Mercer University Press, 1980).

[50] William Dudley Nowlin, *Fundamentals of the Faith* (Nashville: Baptist Sunday School Board, 1922).

[51] James Leo Garrett Jr., "The Bible at Southwestern Seminary during Its Formative Years: A Study of H. E. Dana and W. T. Conner," *Baptist History and Heritage* 21, no. 4 (October 1986): 29–41.

Seminary who had previously embraced historical-critical methods and conclusions, contributed an article for *The Fundamentals* (1915). In the contributed essay, "My Personal Experience with Higher Criticism,"[52] Reeve
reflected on his change in views and affirmed the absolute truthfulness of
Scripture while critiquing the dangers of historical criticism.

The inerrancy of Scripture was popularized by the pulpit oratory of
Robert Greene Lee (1886–1978). Lee also penned *The Word of God: Not
Broken and Not Bound* in 1930.[53] Oates Charles Symonds Wallace (b. 1856)
in *What Baptists Believe* (1934) discussed the need for the Scriptures, the process of their writing, and the purpose of the Scriptures.[54] In his conclusion, he
reaffirmed the 1833 New Hampshire Confession and the 1925 Baptist Faith
and Message terminology that the Bible is "a perfect treasure of heavenly
instruction." That same year, the Sunday School Board also published *The
Book We Teach* by Jesse Burton Weatherspoon (1886–1964). Weatherspoon
maintained that the Bible is a book of revelation and sure guidance, and
that it is not only a book about Christian faith but for Christian mission
and education.[55] In 1936, Josiah Blake Tidwell (1870–1946), professor at
Baylor University, authored *Thinking Straight about the Bible or Is the Bible
the Word of God*. In many ways, Tidwell's book reflected the Southern Baptist
consensus about the nature of Scripture during its first one hundred years.
He reflected a closer kinship with Manly and Carroll than with Mullins,
Conner, or Carver. Tidwell identified direct and indirect claims regarding
the Bible's inspiration and absolute truthfulness, followed by fourteen proofs
for the complete veracity and divine origin of the Bible.[56]

Yet it must be observed that the syncretistic position of Carver, which
Carver reported was the latter position of Sampey and other Southern

---

[52] J. J. Reeve, "My Personal Experience with Higher Criticism," in *The Fundamentals: A Testimony to the Truth*, ed. A. C. Dixon and R. A. Torrey (1917; Grand Rapids: Baker, 1980).

[53] R. G. Lee, *The Word of God: Not Broken and Not Bound* (Orlando: Christ for the World, 1930).

[54] O. C. S. Wallace, *What Baptists Believe* (Nashville: Baptist Sunday School Board, 1934).

[55] J. B. Witherspoon, *The Book We Teach* (Nashville: Baptist Sunday School Board, 1934).

[56] J. B. Tidwell, *Thinking Straight about the Bible or Is the Bible the Word of God* (Nashville: Broadman, 1936).

Seminary scholars, coupled with openness not only to the methodology of historical criticism but in some cases to its conclusions, paved the way for shifts in the doctrine of biblical inspiration and authority in the post-World War II era of that seminary in particular. Nevertheless, a strong consensus among scholars, pastors, and denominational leaders remained regarding a high doctrine of Scripture. This diverse group from various regions of the country affirmed with deep convictions the common heritage regarding the divine origin, the complete truthfulness, and the full authority of the Bible. The commonly held conviction across Southern Baptist life during the first century of its existence was that the Bible is the inspired, written, reliable, and authoritative Word of God.

V. Southern Baptist Life and Thought after World War II

The growth of the Southern Baptist Convention was fueled in unprecedented ways by the "Million More in '54" campaign, an initiative seeking to enroll one million new Sunday school members for the calendar year. While the results fell short of the lofty goal, it was nevertheless an amazing year with some 750,000 people added to the Sunday school rolls, the largest membership increase in one year ever recorded in the convention's history. The year also marked the passing of Carver in 1954, two years after the death of Conner. The SBC entered the second half of the twentieth century an efficiently run and largely unified organization. The convention's new consensus, which historian Bill Leonard labeled "the grand compromise,"[57] tended toward adherence to a unified programmatic model alongside an assumed orthodoxy. Southern Baptist orthodoxy, therefore, had as much to do with one's selection of the right program as it did with an understanding of right beliefs. Pragmatism was the order of the day, a situation not unlike religious trends in the rest of American Protestantism.[58]

---

[57] Bill J. Leonard, *God's Last and Only Hope* (Grand Rapids: Eerdmans, 1990).
[58] This is not to find fault with the programmatic emphasis in Baptist life, which sadly has largely been lost. This programmatic emphasis helped to provide identity for Southern Baptists as a people as well as a framework for faithful ministry and effective outreach.

In the 1940s and 1950s there appeared examples of basic continuity with the doctrinal affirmations of previous generations. One may consult the popular works of William Richardson White (1892–1977) of Baylor University, "The Authoritative Criterion" in *Baptist Distinctives* (1946)[59]; John Benjamin Lawrence (1871–1968) of the Home Mission Board, "The Word and Words of God" and "The Bible, Our Creed" in *Southern Baptist Home Missions* (1952, 1957)[60]; and John Clyde Turner (1879–1974) of North Carolina, "That Wonderful Book" in *These Things We Believe* (1956). Their writings indicate a widespread and ongoing commitment to the trustworthiness and authority of Scripture during this period. However, changes were taking place.[61]

New models of what it meant to be a Baptist emerged, influenced by aspects of Enlightenment thinking, the rise of individualism, and the frontier mindset, as well as in reaction to any kind of fundamentalism. It is hard to know for sure how much the shifts and theological restatements initiated by Mullins, Conner, and Carver can be traced to reactions to Fundamentalist leaders like J. Frank Norris and W. B. Riley, but the tensions present therein should not be ignored. Certainly, these new directions were influenced by renewed understandings of a commitment to the priesthood of the believer (rather than the priesthood of all believers) and to the soul competency of the individual. Southern Baptists treasured their denomination's and their nation's cultural legacies of freedom.

In such an environment, a person could read the Bible for himself or herself, perhaps influenced by higher critical approaches to biblical interpretation, while still celebrating the experience and freedom of being a Baptist. The Southern Baptist seminaries and colleges, and publishing house and mission boards, who were held together through close relationships with ministers and leading laity in the tens of thousands of tall-steepled First Baptist churches, town churches, and county-seat churches which dotted the

---

[59] W. R. White, "The Authoritative Criterion," in *Baptist Distinctives* (Nashville: Convention, 1946).

[60] J. B. Lawrence, "The Word and Words of God," in *Southern Baptist Home Missions* (Nashville: Convention, 1952); Lawrence, "The Bible, Our Creed," in *Southern Baptist Home Missions* (Nashville: Convention, 1957).

[61] J. Clyde Turner, "That Wonderful Book," in *Things We Believe* (Nashville: Convention, 1956).

landscape from Virginia to Texas and beyond, were influenced by and fostered the individualist mindset.

The 1960s and 1970s were marked by increasing conflict amid the introduction of new theological voices, particularly those of Eric Charles Rust (1910–1991) of Southern Seminary,[62] Frank Stagg (1911–2001) of Southern Seminary and New Orleans Seminary,[63] Dale Moody (1915–1992) of Southern Seminary,[64] and Morris Ashcraft (1922–2011) of Southern Seminary, New Orleans Seminary, and Southeastern Seminary.[65] These influential teachers and writers furthered the changes initiated by Mullins and Carver, and Conner to a lesser degree. Together this group of thinkers, beholden to Mullins in particular, made carefully nuanced statements which did not equate the Bible with revelation in the same way as previously stated by Dagg, Manly, and Carroll. For these more radical theologians, the primary characteristic of the Bible was found in its spiritual authority, not its inspiration or inerrancy.

Following Mullins, this new generation insisted the authority of the Bible should be limited to the religious life of the Christian believer, seemingly overemphasizing the characteristic affirmation regarding the Bible's authority in "faith and practice." Following A. H. Strong, they were more comfortable with a dynamic model of inspiration rather than the verbal plenary view. Mullins in his volume on *Baptist Beliefs* (1912) had carefully commended the plenary view's intent to preserve and maintain the authority of the Bible as the very Word of God, but he also saw little difference between the dynamic or inductive approach to biblical inspiration and the plenary or deductive view of biblical inspiration. The difference between the two models, Mullins claimed, was primarily one of method.

These post-World War II theologians also demonstrated an openness to evolutionary theory and biblical criticism. Mullins had raised important concerns about the use of critical methodology which tended to reject historical fact and major on speculative reconstruction. As has been observed,

---

[62] Eric Rust, *Nature and Man* (London: Lutterworth, 1953); Eric Rust, *Salvation History: A Biblical Understanding* (Richmond: John Knox, 1962).

[63] Frank Stagg, *New Testament Theology* (Nashville: Broadman, 1962).

[64] Dale Moody, *The Word of Truth* (Grand Rapids: Eerdmans, 1981).

[65] Morris Ashcraft, *Christian Faith and Beliefs* (Nashville: Broadman, 1984).

particularly for Mullins, Conner, and Carver, the most significant shift came with their emphasis on spiritual experience. Again, Mullins, in his contribution to *The Fundamentals,* defended the Bible and the truthfulness of Christianity on the undeniable basis of religious experience as recorded in the Bible and confirmed by Christians through the centuries.

Southern Baptists in the 1960s and 1970s struggled to deal with the challenges of increasing urbanization, growing denominational bureaucracies, territorial expansion, and new emphases in theology. The crises which dominated the final quarter of the twentieth century, the years of great denominational controversy, were also coming into fuller view. Biblical scholars and theologians in the middle of the twentieth century wrestled particularly with the rise of biblical criticism. Both academics and pastors sought to combine a belief in biblical authority with the use of critical methodologies. These struggles came into public view during debates over the publication in 1961 of *The Message of Genesis* by Ralph H. Elliott (1925–2022), professor of Old Testament at Midwestern Baptist Theological Seminary,[66] followed by conflict over publication in 1969 of the commentary on "Genesis" written for the *Broadman Bible Commentary* by British Baptist Gwynne Henton Davies (1906–1998). Both Elliott and Davies questioned the veracity and historicity of Genesis 1–22.[67]

Many of the public issues with which the Convention wrestled during this period dealt with the history of the Old Testament. But the influence of form criticism was beginning to be seen on the New Testament side as well due to growing appreciation for the work of Rudolf Bultmann. Bultmann's influence was reflected in the work of Professor Robert Cook Briggs (1915–2009), among several others. Briggs taught New Testament at Union

---

[66] Ralph Elliott, *Message of Genesis* (Nashville: Broadman, 1961); also, see Ralph Elliott, *The "Genesis Controversy" and Continuity in Southern Baptist Chaos* (Macon, GA: Mercer University Press, 1992).

[67] G. Henton Davies, "Genesis," in *The Broadman Bible Commentary*, ed. Clifton J. Allen (Nashville: Broadman, 1969). The controversy surrounding the *Broadman Bible Commentary* should not detract from the recognition that Southern Baptists had now produced a major work of biblical scholarship that provided exegetical help for many students and pastors. The contributions of Roy L. Honeycutt, William Hull, Dale Moody, Jack MacGorman, and Ray Summers were especially commendable, though their critical conclusions often detracted from their overall contributions.

University in Tennessee and at Southeastern Baptist Theological Seminary in Wake Forest, North Carolina, during the 1950s and 1960s. Struggles over the teaching of those influenced by Bultmann between 1957 and 1965 dealt not only with the use of historical criticism, but with the place of Darwinism in the theological arena. Southeastern Seminary witnessed a clash between the older commitment to the authority of Scripture on the one hand and the critical approach to Scripture of three seminary professors on the other.[68]

In his systematic theology, *The Word of Truth: A Summary of Christian Doctrine Based on Biblical Revelation*, Dale Moody affirmed a comprehensive view of biblical inspiration which allowed for the use of historical criticism and the embrace of evolutionary theory. A brilliant thinker, with significant insights in the areas of Christology, ecclesiology, and eschatology, Moody taught theology at Southern Seminary for four decades, where his chief mentor had been Carver. In addition to his two degrees from Southern, Moody also studied with Paul Tillich, Karl Barth, Emil Brunner, and Oscar Cullman. Moody's Southern Seminary colleague in Old Testament theology at this time was Eric Rust, who penned significant works in the area of history, biblical theology, and apologetics, including *Nature and Man in Biblical Thought* (1953) and *Salvation History: A Biblical Interpretation* (1962). Rust embraced the use of historical criticism, while seeking to explore the worlds of theology and science, having also been trained in mathematics, physics, and chemistry. Southern Seminary historian E. Glenn Hinson referred to Rust as "the apostle to an age of science and technology."[69]

Few books have had the influence in Southern Baptist life as that of Frank Stagg's *New Testament Theology*. Stagg had lengthy faculty tenures at both New Orleans Baptist Theological Seminary and at Southern Seminary. Houston Baptist University president Robert Sloan later criticized Stagg's "moral influence theory" of the atonement of Christ, his modalism, his

---

[68] H. Mitchell Simpson, "The Conflicting Hermeneutics of Rudolf Bultmann and A. T. Robertson: Dimensions of Biblical Authority in the Southern Baptist Convention" (PhD Dissertation, Florida State University, 1986). Simpson identifies Briggs, William C. Strickland, and Harold H. Oliver as the proponents of Bultmann's hermeneutics.

[69] E. Glenn Hinson, "Eric Charles Rust: Apostle to an Age of Science and Technology," in *Science, Faith, and Revelation: An Approach to Christian Philosophy*, ed. Robert Patterson (Nashville: Broadman, 1979).

de-apocalypticizing of New Testament eschatology, and his rupturing of the New Testament canon based on the wedge he drove between Jesus and Paul. Stagg taught that the cross of Jesus Christ represented the revelation of the divine self-denial which was always at the heart of God. He believed his view would help believers find their authentic existence as God's creatures. Stagg rejected biblical inerrancy and suggested that Paul, having been influenced by the culture of his day, was in error on key matters, including the role of women.[70]

Morris Ashcraft taught theology for decades at both Midwestern and Southeastern seminaries and also served as dean at both institutions. Ashcraft authored *Christian Faith and Beliefs*, which emphasized experience and existential belief over a more objective and historical understanding of the Christian faith. He stressed the personal nature of revelation and failed to affirm a particular model of biblical inspiration. He rejected biblical inerrancy yet sought to affirm biblical authority. While all four of these thinkers were highly influential across the Southern Baptist Convention, each one pointed the theological trajectory of Southern Baptists in different directions than those proposed by Dagg, Boyce, Manly, Broadus, and Carroll. And while these four theologians furthered the thought of Mullins and Carver, their teachers might have been taken aback by their increasingly radical conclusions. Their contemporaries in the churches, who were also students of Mullins and Conner, certainly became alarmed.

Wally Amos Criswell (1909–2002), the second legendary pastor of the First Baptist Church of Dallas, personified the popular grass roots theology of the Southern Baptist Convention. As became apparent during the 1980s and 1990s, Criswell's outlook on Scripture represented a numerical predominance across the convention. The denomination thus entered the second half of the twentieth century divided between the progressivism which characterized the moderate leadership in denominational agencies and seminaries and the popular traditionalism in the pulpits. Southern Baptist conservatives reacted negatively to a changing American culture, regarding the 1960s as heading toward insanity. Living in a time of presidential assassinations, racial

---

[70] See the penetrating analysis of Stagg's theology in Robert Sloan, "Frank Stagg," in *Baptist Theologians*, ed. Timothy George and David S. Dockery (Nashville: Broadman, 1990), 496–517.

unrest, and civil rights protests, along with rock-and-roll celebrations, "love-ins," "sit-ins," and Vietnam war protests, these traditionalists lambasted these trends and recommitted themselves to a completely truthful Bible. Nowhere was this better illustrated than in the classic volume by Criswell published while he was convention president in 1969, *Why I Preach That the Bible Is Literally True*.[71]

Two other popular preachers were greatly admired across the SBC spectrum. One of these was Herschel Harold Hobbs (1907–1995); the other was William Franklin "Billy" Graham (1918–2018). Hobbs has often been called "Mr. Southern Baptist." He preached for eighteen years on the "Baptist Hour," was president of the Southern Baptist Convention from 1961 to 1963, and chaired the 1963 Committee for updating The Baptist Faith and Message. Hobbs held to a high view of biblical inspiration while embracing a quasi-Arminian perspective of salvation and an amillennial eschatology.[72] On the other hand, Graham, the most well-known interna-tional evangelist in the history of Christianity, was a member of the First Baptist Church of Dallas. Graham proclaimed a simple gospel to hundreds of thousands of people, introduced by his characteristic phrase, "the Bible says." Graham's appealing message was undergirded by commitment to a completely truthful Bible, augmented by a "deeper life" approach to the Christian life and by an apocalyptic dispensational eschatology, which was similar to Criswell's views.[73]

The consensus represented by Criswell, Hobbs, and Graham provided a framework for the traditionalists to appeal boldly to a fully truthful and authoritative Bible, contending this was the message needed for the times. The conservatives or traditionalists charged that the moderate leader-ship of the SBC had moved too far from the historic consensus of previ-ous generations. They appealed to Criswell's *Why I Preach That the Bible Is*

---

[71] W. A. Criswell, *Why I Preach That the Bible Is Literally True* (Nashville: Broadman, 1969).

[72] Hershel H. Hobbs, *My Faith and Message* (Nashville: Broadman, 1993).

[73] Billy Graham, *Just as I Am: The Autobiography of Billy Graham* (San Francisco: HarperCollins, 1997); See the account of Graham's commitment to biblical author-ity in Matthew McKellar and David S. Dockery, "The Authority and Sufficiency of Scripture for Pastoral Ministry and Preaching," in *The Authority and Sufficiency of Scripture*, 103–16 (see chap. 7, n. 29).

Literally True, while the progressives rallied around the widely circulated article, "Shall We Call the Bible Infallible?" by William Hull (1930–2013), who served as provost at Southern Seminary and dean of their School of Theology.[74] Certainly, as noted earlier, Manly, Frost, and Carroll, along with numerous others, espoused the full truthfulness of the Bible, even readily employing the terms "infallible" and "inerrant" to describe the nature of Scripture. Both Mullins and Conner employed the language of the 1925 Baptist Faith and Message, that Scripture is "truth, without any mixture of error." However, they did so without confessing a verbal or plenary view of biblical inspiration.

With the rise of historical criticism, new approaches to biblical interpretation and new ways of describing the Bible's nature were articulated. Many progressives were no longer comfortable describing the Bible in the tradition of Carroll or Manly. As a matter of fact, the doctrine of biblical inerrancy was explicitly affirmed by only a small minority of faculty members and denominational leaders in the 1970s. Many in the academy considered biblical inerrancy obscurantist, wrongly associating it with the view of inspiration known as mechanical dictation.[75] The SBC entered the decade of the 1980s as a diverse movement, but it was now facing its own version of the "modernist-fundamentalist" controversy which roiled the northern denominations in the 1920s.

VI. The Closing Decades of the Twentieth Century

When Southern Baptists attempted to reaffirm a commitment to the full truthfulness and authority of Scripture in the closing decades of the twentieth century, they generally needed to look beyond the teaching theologians at the SBC seminaries for guidance. Just as Boyce and Manly learned from the nineteenth-century Princeton theologians, and just as Mullins and

---

[74] William E. Hull, "Shall We Call the Bible Infallible?" *The Baptist Program* (1970), and in *Perspectives in Religious Studies* 37, no. 2 (Summer 2010): 211–12. See the critique in John Feinberg, *Light in a Dark Place*, 268 (see introduction, n. 5).

[75] It is true that the fundamentalist leader John R. Rice in *Our God-Breathed Book* at times affirms mechanical dictation, but such a charge is misleading when applied to the large number of Baptists and evangelicals who affirm the full truthfulness, infallibility, and inerrancy of Scripture.

Conner had learned from A. H. Strong, many Southern Baptist academics turned to Carl F. H. Henry, Francis Schaeffer, J. I. Packer, Millard Erickson, Kenneth Kantzer, D. A. Carson, John Woodbridge, and other voices from the broader evangelical landscape.[76] Southern Baptists were calling for a return to Manly's position, though now in an updated version enabled by several decades of discussion regarding Scripture, which culminated in the Chicago Statements on Biblical Inerrancy (1978), Biblical Hermeneutics (1982), and Biblical Application (1986).

The Baptist Sunday School Board (now known as Lifeway) attempted to address the issues by choosing the doctrine of Scripture as the convention's doctrine study for 1983. Russell Dilday, the president of Southwestern Baptist Theological Seminary, was invited to write *The Doctrine of Biblical Authority*, which was published in 1982.[77] Dilday had written his dissertation on Mullins. Dilday affirmed a dynamic theory of inspiration as well as the authority of the Bible even more clearly than either Mullins or Conner. Dilday also pointed out what he believed were the weaknesses of the inerrancy position in a manner similar to Jack Rogers and Donald McKim in their *The Authority and Interpretation of the Bible*.[78]

During the 1970s and 1980s, several works were penned either challenging or upholding the inerrancy of Scripture. A volume supporting the inerrancy position was written by two authors who served at Southwestern Seminary at the time. In *Baptists and the Bible*, L. Russ Bush III and Thomas J. Nettles attempted to show that a high view of biblical authority had been the primary view of Scripture throughout Baptist history.[79] The book met with mixed reviews and was countered by a series of essays, edited by Robison James of Richmond University, titled *The Unfettered Word*. James pointed to the fact that the inerrancy position was not represented among key Baptist

---

[76] References to the contributions of these scholars has been referenced at various places in the previous chapters of this volume.

[77] Russell Dilday, *The Doctrine of Biblical Authority* (Nashville: Convention, 1982).

[78] Jack Rogers and Donald McKim, *The Authority and Interpretation of the Bible: An Historical Approach* (San Francisco: Harper and Row, 1979).

[79] L. Russ Bush and Tom J. Nettles, *Baptists and the Bible: The Baptist Doctrines of Biblical Inspiration and Religious Authority in Historical Perspective* (Chicago: Moody, 1980).

theologians of the twentieth century.[80] Others tried to differentiate between infallibility and inerrancy, accepting the former and rejecting the latter.

In a carefully nuanced article in a 1986 issue of *Review and Expositor* entitled "Biblical Authority: A Treasured Baptist Heritage," Roy L. Honeycutt, the president of Southern Seminary, contended that an affirmation of biblical inerrancy was inconsistent with Baptist tradition. Yet, he also claimed the Bible was authoritative and binding in all matters of faith and practice,[81] adopting a position similarly articulated by New Testament scholar R. Alan Culpepper.[82] The two seminary presidents, Dilday and Honeycutt, mirrored key aspects of the Rogers-McKim proposal. For the next decade, more heat than light was generated by both sides, though steadily the inerrancy position gained a hearing. Many people thought inerrancy was only a position associated with denominational politics, which sadly was probably the case for some. Baptist pastors and theologians, however, found informed and helpful guidance from key evangelical thinkers and younger Southern Baptist theologians.[83]

The dean of Southern Baptist theologians, James Leo Garrett Jr., taught at Southwestern Seminary (1949–59), Southern Seminary (1959–73), and Baylor University (1973–79) before returning to teach at Southwestern in the 1979–80 academic year for another two decades. He concluded his career as Distinguished Professor of Theology Emeritus in the early years of the twenty-first century. A student of Conner, Garrett wrote a Th.D. dissertation on Conner's theology in 1954. He completed a splendid two-volume systematic theology in the 1990s as well a massive work on *Baptist Theology: A Four-Century Study* in 2009, which constitutes the finest source on the history of Baptist thought ever published.[84] As with other topics, Garrett modeled both conviction and charity when

[80] Robison B. James, ed., *The Unfettered Word* (Waco: Word, 1987).
[81] Roy L. Honeycutt, "Biblical Authority: A Treasured Heritage," *Review and Expositor* 83, no. 4 (Fall 1986): 605–22.
[82] R. Alan Culpepper, "Scripture," in *A Baptist's Theology*, ed. R. Wayne Stacy (1999; Macon, GA: Smyth and Helwys, 2021), 79–100.
[83] See David S. Dockery, "The Crisis of Scripture in Southern Baptist Life: Reflections on the Past, Looking to the Future," *Southern Baptist Journal of Theology* 9, no. 1 (Spring 2005): 36–53.
[84] Garrett, *Systematic Theology*; Garrett, *Baptist Theology*.

dealing with the topic of scriptural authority. He treasured the authority of Scripture, advocating for its supremacy in comparison to tradition, reason, experience, or any other proposed source of authority. Garrett joined Conner in offering an important articulation of the divine-human authorship of Scripture, affirming the Bible to be reliable, dependable, truthful, trustworthy, and infallible.[85]

The publication of a multi-volume commentary series, called The New American Commentary, which launched in 1991, provided a much-needed resource regarding both the Old Testament and the New Testament for Baptist scholars, pastors, and students from within the SBC and for the larger evangelical community. Every author in the series was asked to affirm the Chicago Statement on Biblical Inerrancy. The title of the series built on the nineteenth-century commentary project, *The American Commentary*, which was edited by Alvah Hovey and included an outstanding volume on the Gospel of Matthew by John Broadus, the second president of Southern Seminary.[86]

In 1992, Southern Baptists once again focused on *The Doctrine of the Bible* in their annual doctrinal study. This widely circulated doctrinal study book affirmed that God's revelation of himself was both personal and propositional. Moreover, it clearly acknowledged the Bible is inspired, fully truthful, inerrant, sufficient, and authoritative. It affirmed Scripture's literary diversity was more than a historic accident or decorative device and served as a vehicle for imaginative thought and creative expression about things difficult to grasp. This recognition of literary diversity provided a realization of the human aspect in Scripture, reminding readers to balance divine and human authorship of the Bible. Building on the works of Carl Henry, J. I. Packer, Millard Erickson, and D. A. Carson, as well as Paul and John Feinberg, among others, the 1992 doctrine study maintained the Bible attested its own inspiration, which can be characterized as plenary and concursive. The verbal plenary view of inspiration stresses that what the Bible affirms is completely true.[87] This view of Scripture has now become characteristic of leaders and

---

[85] Garrett, *Systematic Theology*, 1:108–82.
[86] *The New American Commentary*, ed. David S. Dockery and E. Ray Clendenen (1991–present).
[87] See David S. Dockery, *The Doctrine of the Bible* (Nashville: Convention, 1991).

faculty members across the denomination, placing most Southern Baptist academics solidly within evangelicalism, attested annually by the large number of Southern Baptists who actively participate in the meetings of the Evangelical Theological Society.

During this same period, eight theologians, representing a continuum of thought across Southern Baptist life, including progressives, feminists, moderates, evangelicals, and conservatives, participated in a series of open forums in Richmond, Virginia, and Louisville, Kentucky, and Birmingham, Alabama. After the conversations, the various positions were published, with opportunities for response by each participant, in a Broadman Press volume. The attempt to move "beyond the impasse" made clear the real differences between the various positions. This important book was published in 1992 with the title *Beyond the Impasse? Scripture, Interpretation, and Theology in Baptist Life.*[88] The question mark in the title highlighted the lack of consensus.

Beginning in the 1990s, Southern Baptists not only turned to the writings of evangelicals to shape their thought, but looked to evangelical institutions to help fill key faculty positions in the seminaries and colleges,[89] and to write for the denominational publishing house.[90] Carl Henry, whose church membership was at Capitol Hill Baptist Church in Washington, D.C., a cooperating Southern Baptist congregation, authored a six-volume work on the doctrine of Scripture called *God, Revelation, and Authority.*[91] Henry was the quintessential evangelical, and this massive work was the *magnum opus* of his highly influential multi-decade career. While Henry served as a model of faithfulness regarding the truthfulness of Scripture throughout his life and

---

[88] Robison B. James and David S. Dockery, eds., *Beyond the Impasse? Scripture, Interpretation, and Theology in Baptist Life* (Nashville: B&H, 1992).

[89] These evangelical institutions included Trinity Evangelical Divinity School, Gordon-Conwell Seminary, Dallas Theological Seminary, Denver Seminary, Bethel Seminary, Western Seminary (Oregon), and others.

[90] For example, there have been about sixty graduates from Trinity Evangelical Divinity School to teach at Southern Baptist related colleges, universities, and seminaries in recent decades.

[91] Originally published by Word Books from 1976 to 1983, it was reprinted and reissued by Crossway a decade later. Carl F. H. Henry, *God, Revelation, and Authority* (see introduction, n. 6).

ministry, sadly, a long list of other Baptists shifted over time in their position regarding the Bible.

Among Baptist evangelicals, the ambivalences of Bernard L. Ramm (1916–1992) in *After Fundamentalism*,[92] Clark Pinnock (1937–2010) in *The Scripture Principle*,[93] and Stanley Grenz (1950–2005) in *Beyond Foundationalism*,[94] remind us of the need for ongoing steadfastness and faithfulness, even in the light of the expanding cultural challenges of our day. In 2013, Albert Mohler, president of Southern Seminary, pushed back against the proposals offered by such postconservative evangelicals in a chapter titled, "When the Bible Speaks, God Speaks: The Classic Doctrine of Inerrancy."[95] And in 2020 and 2022, Chris Morgan of California Baptist University and Adam Harwood of New Orleans Seminary winsomely articulated their influential commitments to the truthfulness and authority of Scripture in their new systematic theologies.[96]

The leading evangelical Baptist theologian of the late nineteenth and early twentieth centuries, A. H. Strong, once sadly vacillated regarding an affirmation of inerrancy. However, reevaluating events in his own seminary and denomination, Strong warned in 1918, three years prior to his death, that "We Baptists must reform or die."

> What is the effect of [radical historical criticism] upon our theological seminaries? It is to deprive the gospel message of all definiteness, and to make professors and students disseminators of doubts. . . . The result of such teaching in our seminaries is that the student, unless he has had a Pauline experience before he came has all his

---

[92] Ramm, *After Fundamentalism*, (see chap. 8., n. 61).

[93] Pinnock, *Scripture Principle*, (see chap. 8, n. 4).

[94] Grenz and Franke, *Beyond Foundationalism*, (see chap. 8, n. 67). Similar approaches in Baptist life have been offered by Freeman, *Contesting Catholicity* (see chap. 8, n. 67); Steven R. Harmon, *Baptist Identity and the Ecumenical Future: Story, Tradition, and the Recovery of Tradition* (Waco: Baylor University Press, 2016).

[95] Mohler, "When the Bible Speaks, God Speaks: The Classic Doctrine of Biblical Inerrancy," 29–58 (see introduction, n. 17).

[96] Christopher W. Morgan, *Christian Theology: The Biblical Story and Our Faith* (Nashville: B&H, 2020); Harwood, *Christian Theology*, (see chap. 7, n. 54). Also, see Malcolm B. Yarnell III and David S. Dockery, "The Authority and Sufficiency of Scripture: An Introduction," in *The Authority and Sufficiency of Scripture*, 1–20.

early conceptions of Scripture and Christian doctrine weakened, has no longer any positive message to deliver, loses the ardor of his love for Christ; and at graduation leaves the seminary, not to become a preacher or pastor as he had once hoped, but to sow his doubts broadcast, as a teacher in some college, as editor of some religious journal, as secretary of some Young Men's Christian Association, or as agent of some mutual life insurance company. This method of interpretation switches off upon some sidetrack of social service many a young man who otherwise would be a heroic preacher of the everlasting gospel. The theological seminaries of almost all our denominations are becoming so infected with this grievous error, that they are not so much organs of Christ as they are organs of Antichrist. This accounts for the rise, all over the land, of Bible schools, to take the place of seminaries. . . . We are losing our faith in the Bible, and our determination to stand for its teachings. We are introducing into our ministry graduates who have lost their faith in him and their love for him. The unbelief in our seminary is like a blinding mist slowly settling down upon our churches, and is gradually abolishing, not only all definite views of Christian doctrine, but also all conviction of duty to "contend earnestly for the faith" of our fathers. . . . We are ceasing to be evangelistic as well as evangelical, and if this downward progress continues, we shall in due time cease to exist. This is the fate of Unitarianism today. We Baptists must reform or die.[97]

Intriguingly, Mullins sounded similar concerns as he neared the conclusion of his service in "Duties and Dangers of this Present Hour," an address to the annual meeting of the SBC in 1923.[98]

---

[97] Augustus Hopkins Strong, *A Tour of the Missions: Observations and Conclusions* (Philadelphia: Griffith and Rowland, 1918). See the section on Scripture and missions on pages 169–77. For helpful historical perspectives on the importance of biblical authority, see Putman, "Baptists, *Sola Scriptura,* and the Place of the Christian Tradition," 27–54; also see the overviews offered in the chapters by Stephen O. Presley, William M. Marsh, Matthew Barrett, and Nathan Finn in *Historical Theology for the Church,* ed. Jason G. Duesing and Nathan A. Finn (Nashville: B&H, 2021).

[98] E. Y. Mullins, "Duties and Dangers of this Present Hour," addressed at the Southern Baptist Convention in 1923; and Mullins, *Christianity at the Crossroads*

In the twenty-first century, the commitment of Baptists globally to the inspiration, truthfulness, and authority of Scripture is readily apparent on every continent. Two examples, among many which could be offered, come from Asia and Africa. In *Baptist Systematic Theology* (2016), Dongsun Cho, Yong-Su Cho, and Jeremiah Kim heartily affirm the infallibility and inerrancy of Scripture.[99] The importance of biblical authority is likewise echoed in *Theology Under the Mango Tree: A Handbook of African Christian Theology* (2013) by Emiola Nihinlola.[100] In light of the struggles among Baptists during the last century, we continue to teach our many outstanding students from North America and from other places around the globe that it is wise to state clearly that sacred Scripture is the written Word of God by virtue of its plenary and concursive inspiration by the Holy Spirit and that this results in the Bible's dependability, infallibility, inerrancy, authority, and sufficiency.

VII. Conclusion

This chapter has focused on developments in the doctrine of Scripture in Baptist life from the mid-nineteenth century through the beginning of the twenty-first century. Baptists in general, and Southern Baptists in particular, continue to struggle in numerous areas, but at least one major denomination has clearly decided the doctrine of the full truthfulness of the Bible cannot be ignored, de-emphasized, or eliminated from the discussion. Together, Baptists and other convictional evangelicals can help churches enable and educate leaders and enhance worship in order to bring about renewal across our country and around the globe so that the churches of Jesus Christ can grow and mature in obedience to the command of our Lord, who commissioned us to evangelize, disciple, baptize, and teach.[101]

(Nashville: Baptist Sunday School Board, 1924).

[99] Dongsun Cho, Yong-Su Cho, and Jeremiah Kim, *Baptist Systematic Theology* (Seoul, Korea: Jordan, 2016).

[100] Emiola Nihinlola, *Theology Under the Mango Tree: A Handbook of African Christian Theology* (Logos, Nigeria: Fine Print and Manufacturing, 2013).

[101] Such is the intention of the volume edited by James Leo Garrett Jr., *We Baptists* (Franklin, TN: Providence House, 1999).

As Baptists re-establish the foundation of the inspiration, authority, and sufficiency of Scripture, with recognition of who we are and consistent with our heritage, let us move beyond an articulation of the nature of Scripture and with heads, hearts, and hands seek to follow faithfully the divinely inspired, completely truthful, and fully authoritative and sufficient written Word of God.

CONCLUSION: UNDERSTANDING AND APPLYING THE BIBLE TODAY

On the basis of the above investigations into divine revelation, we conclude that God truly revealed himself to the prophets and in Jesus Christ, and that his revelation of himself was preserved in Holy Scripture through the Holy Spirit's work of inspiration. We affirm the authority of the inerrant and infallible Scripture, assured that we may place complete epistemological confidence in the truthful, reliable, authoritative, and sufficient Word of God. We believe these truths about divine revelation provide a safeguard against the erosion of the faith. We trust these convictions, grounded in Scripture, will enable us to relate to one another in love and humility, will bring about true Christian fellowship, and will result not only in the furtherance of orthodoxy and rejection of liberalism,[1] but that they can serve as the proper foundation for a renewal of orthopraxy, worship, and service. For these practical goods to occur, the steps to understanding and applying Scripture in our day must also be considered.

We believe that biblical inerrancy primarily points to epistemological and theological matters. While such affirmation should not be equated with salvation, it is certainly important to recognize that zeal for missions,

---

[1] See the important insights in Roger E. Olson, *Against Liberal Theology: Putting the Brakes on Progressive Christianity* (Grand Rapids: Zondervan, 2022), 1–74, who in a more nuanced way also agrees with J. Gresham Machen that liberalism and historic Christianity are not two versions of the same thing, but two different religions. See J. Gresham Machen, *Christianity and Liberalism* (New York: Macmillan, 1923).

evangelism, and the ethical application of Scripture have declined when a high view of Scripture has gone into decline. We, therefore, recognize that interpretation and application are connected not only to a right understanding of the Bible's message but to a right understanding of the Bible's nature. Because of the multifaceted character of the Bible, its practical uses have been displayed in a variety of forms. This conclusion explores some of these uses, reviewing their derivation from the historic church's interpretation of the Bible and outlining basic principles of interpretation for application which have been deemed helpful in the modern period. We then offer some concluding observations regarding the application of the Bible to our twenty-first-century context.

I. The Biblical Pattern of Interpretation for Application

As previously observed, the writers of the New Testament adopted a Christological understanding of the Old Testament, following a pattern based on the way Jesus Christ himself read the Hebrew Scriptures. Using the rabbinic practices of the day, the apostles also employed various hermeneutical strategies. For instance, moral injunctions were generally interpreted in a literal way. Other Old Testament passages received Christological interpretation, primarily through the use of typology.[2] It remains difficult to point to one single image, pattern, motif, or theme which can adequately express the apostles' interpretative approach to the Old Testament other than to stress that they grounded their exegesis in the Christology, the gospel of Jesus Christ, which the church soon came to call the rule of faith.

The New Testament emphasizes that numerous themes, images, and motifs of revelation and response are fulfilled in the person and work of Jesus Christ. Philip's exclamation, "We have found the one" (John 1:45), was echoed by the New Testament writers as the way to interpret Old Testament events, pictures, and ideas. There was not so much one fulfillment idea, but a harmony of notes presented in a variety of ways which all pointed to

---

[2] Hamilton, *Typology*, (see chap. 5, n. 30); Dockery, *Biblical Interpretation Then and Now*, 23–44 (see chap. 5, n. 42); Rogerson, Rowland, and Lindars, *The Study and Use of the Bible*, 2:3–5 (see chap. 5, n. 23).

him. Moreover, Jesus became the direct and primary source for the church's Christological understanding of the Old Testament. Through his example and through his exalted lordship and the work of the Holy Spirit, the Lord himself provided the early church with its approach to Scripture. This Christological and trinitarian perspective can be found at the heart of the apostles' message.[3]

From the earliest days of Christian history, Christians individually and the church corporately have used the Bible in a variety of ways. This rich heritage influences today's Christians in the ways they use the Bible for individual and corporate purposes as well.[4] The Christian heritage of using Scripture includes its uses as a text for preaching or teaching; a source for understanding life; a guide for worship; a wellspring to formulate Christian liturgy; a primary source for the formulation of theology; a guide for pastoral care; and a font for sustenance and spiritual formation in the Christian life as well as for literary aesthetic enjoyment.

The first and primary use of the Bible was in the church's worship. It is imperative to remember that biblical interpretation was performed through the church's use and understanding of the living sacred text, not through the theoretical and abstract analysis of scholarship. Following the pattern established in the Jewish synagogue, the exposition of the sacred Word was of utmost importance in the church's worship. This pattern started with Jesus's own exposition of Isaiah 61 at the beginning of his ministry, when he interpreted in light of his own messianic mission (Luke 4:16–22). The same practice was continually followed in the early church's worship (Acts 13:14–44; 14:1; 17:1; 19:8) and continued into the post-apostolic period, as we saw in chapter 7 with the testimony of Justin Martyr.

In 1 Tim 4:13, Paul exhorted young Timothy to devote attention to the public reading of Scripture. Paul encouraged personal study in 2 Tim 2:15, but such practices were not available to all. Public Scripture reading was

---

[3] See the discussion in G. K. Beale, ed., *The Right Doctrine from the Wrong Text? Essays on the Use of the Old Testament in the New* (Grand Rapids: Baker, 1994); Piotrowski, *In All the Scriptures*, 52–73, 121–62 (see chap. 11, n. 153).

[4] William W. Klein, Craig L. Blomberg, and Robert L. Hubbard Jr., *Introduction to Biblical Interpretation* (Dallas: Word, 1993), 377–99; also, Piotrowski, *In All the Scriptures*, 1–18.

therefore given the highest priority. That Scripture was given by the inspiration of God and was able to make the hearer wise unto salvation, which is in Jesus Christ alone (2 Tim 3:15–17), was the deepest conviction of the apostles. Thus, the reading and exposition of Scripture in public worship to point to Jesus was central. The model Christian service, like the service in the synagogue, was a service dedicated to hearing and responding to the Word of God. Early Christian worship was a Word-of-God service.

As a result, throughout the history of the church, theological construction has been vitally related to, if not inseparable from, biblical interpretation. The basis of all faithful theology in the history of the church depends upon the reading and sound theological interpretation of Scripture.[5] Moreover, most if not all theological deviations have been associated with the neglect of biblical truth or with a faulty interpretation of biblical texts. The ongoing thorough and faithful theological interpretation and application of the teachings of the Holy Bible remain essential for the health of the Christian church.

II. A Short History of Interpreting Scripture for Application

As we observed in chapters 10 and 11, on moving from biblical interpretation to theology, a dual heritage developed over the course of church history. One part of that heritage maintains that Scripture's meaning is found only in its primary literal or historical sense; and the other considers Scripture's ultimate meaning to rest in (or even allegorically beyond) its plenary or full spiritual sense. From this distinction between the literal and the spiritual, several models and combinations of models developed for interpreting Scripture in the early church.[6] Both the Old and New Testaments were interpreted according to their textual, canonical, and theological meaning. The biblical canon provided guidelines for validating both typological and allegorical

---

[5] See the final section of chapter 12 above. Cf. Kevin J. Vanhoozer, ed., *Dictionary for Theological Interpretation of the Bible* (Grand Rapids: Baker, 2005).

[6] Gerald Bray, *Biblical Interpretation: Past and Present* (Downers Grove: IVP, 1996), 14–76; Karlfried Froehlich, "Church History and the Bible," in *Biblical Hermeneutics in Historical Perspective* (Grand Rapids: Eerdmans, 1991), 1–18.

interpretations of itself, such that the historical meaning always remained primary, while the deeper spiritual meaning was allowed to rise.[7] A text was not to be interpreted apart from its larger context, the biblical canon and its inherent canon of faith.

The canon of faith, or rule of faith, which emphasized theological, Christological, and soteriological concerns, thus played a dominant role, as we saw in chapter 10. A balanced and multifaceted hermeneutic thus emerged to influence interpretive practices in the medieval period as well as in post-Reformation times. These practices were influenced by (1) pastoral and theological concerns, as well as (2) presuppositions that viewed the text from the standpoint of faith. These methods produced interpretations that emphasized the edification of the church and the love of neighbor, but primarily the knowledge of and love for God.[8]

After Augustine, the Western church, following John Cassian (d. 433), subscribed to a theory of the fourfold sense of Scripture: (1) The literal sense of Scripture could, and usually did, nurture the virtues of faith, hope, and love. When it did not, the interpreter could appeal to the three additional senses, with each sense corresponding to one of the theological virtues of faith, hope, and love (1 Cor 13:13). (2) The allegorical sense referred the text to the church and its faith, what it must believe. (3) The tropological or moral sense referred to individuals and how their actions should correspond to love. (4) The anagogical sense pointed to the church's eschatological expectation, considering those aspects of the text which corresponded to its hope. For example, the city of Jerusalem, in all its appearances in Scripture, could be understood literally as a Jewish city, allegorically as the church of Jesus Christ, tropologically as the souls of people, and anagogically as the heavenly city. This fourfold sense characterized medieval interpretation.[9]

Thomas Aquinas wanted to establish the spiritual sense even more securely in the literal sense than it had sometimes been grounded in earlier

---

[7] Beryl Smalley, *The Study of the Bible in the Middle Ages* (Oxford: Blackwell, 1952), 1–36.

[8] Bray, *Biblical Interpretation*, 125–27; Carol Harrison, "Augustine," in *Dictionary for Theological Interpretation of the Bible*, 76–78.

[9] Gillian R. Evans, *The Language and Logic of the Bible: The Earlier Middle Ages* (Cambridge: Cambridge University Press, 1984).

medieval thought. He returned to Augustine's distinction between things and signs, but due to his Aristotelianism he preferred to speak of "things" and "words." In Scripture, things designated by words can themselves have the character of a sign. Aquinas maintained the literal sense of Scripture has to do with the sign-character of things. Thus, he was able to demonstrate the spiritual sense of Scripture was always based on the literal sense and derived from it. Also, he equated the literal sense with the meaning of the text intended by the author.[10]

Erasmus, the brilliant Renaissance scholar, paved the way for Martin Luther and John Calvin by rediscovering the priority of the historical sense of Scripture.[11] Erasmus exemplified the finest in Renaissance scholarship that returned to the original sources.[12] The ultimate source to which he returned was the Greek New Testament, whose text he helped bring into print. Returning to the sources requires a truly historical understanding of ancient texts, but Erasmus also desired that the texts bring edification to the readers through the spiritual sense too. His hermeneutic developed a more critical-historical and philological approach as he matured, though he always, following his hero Origen, emphasized the spiritual sense.[13]

As significant and innovative as Erasmus's works were for the recovery of biblical interpretation, thus also for the renewal of its application, the pivotal figures from the Reformation period remain Luther and Calvin. In the early years of the sixteenth century, Luther initiated and fostered a hermeneutical revolution, which some have called a Copernican revolution in biblical inter-pretation that changed the course of history.[14] The Protestant Reformation

---

[10] David C. Steinmetz, "The Superiority of Precritical Exegesis," *Theology Today* 27 (1980): 31–32; Thomas Aquinas, *On Interpretation*, trans. J. T. Oesterle (Milwaukee: Marquette University Press, 1962).

[11] David S. Dockery, "The Foundation of Reformation Hermeneutics: A Fresh Look at Erasmus," in *Evangelical Hermeneutics*, ed. Michael Bauman and David Hall (Camp Hill, PA: Christian Publications, 1995), 53–76.

[12] Jerry H. Bentley, *Humanist and Holy Writ* (Princeton: Princeton University Press, 1983); J. W. Aldridge, *The Hermeneutics of Erasmus* (Richmond: John Knox, 1966), 16, who observed that Erasmus maintained multiple sources including classi-cal philosophy and the Church fathers, but the Scriptures remained the chief source.

[13] R. P. C. Hanson, *Allegory and Event: A Study of the Sources and Significance of Origen's Interpretation of Scripture* (London: SCM, 1959), 360.

[14] Bray, *Biblical Interpretation*, 171–73.

would have been impossible apart from Luther's approach to both the Old Testament and the New. In a very real sense, Luther was the father of evangelical biblical interpretation; his influence has been incalculable.

Luther brought together an understanding of a literal approach to Scripture and his distinctive Christological interpretation of Scripture. The first priority for Luther was the commitment to Scripture as the supreme and final authority for theology and life, for faith and practice, free from all ecclesiastical authority or interference. Luther proposed guidance for interpreting the Bible at several times in his life, but taken together, he offered six consistent points worthy of our observation. Luther insisted on:

1. the necessity of grammatical knowledge;
2. the importance of considering the times, circumstances, and conditions of the text;
3. the importance of identifying the literary context;
4. the need for faith and the Spirit's illumination;
5. the importance of keeping what he called the "proportion of faith" for maintaining the clarity of Scripture, often called the analogy of faith principle, which at times he also labeled the "body of doctrine" or the "rule of faith"; and
6. the necessity of referring all Scripture to Christ.[15]

Luther's stress on a fuller sense found in the Christological meaning of Scripture linked the practice of the Reformers with the patterns of the early church. And Calvin, the most consistent interpreter of the Reformation, emphasized the grammatical and the historical as the foundation for developing the spiritual message from the Bible. Always insisting Scripture interprets Scripture, Calvin rejected allegorical interpretation, emphasized the necessity of examining the historical and literary context, and compared Scriptures which treated common subjects.[16] The works of both Luther and Calvin evidence a rigorous use of applied theological exegesis.

---

[15] Kolb, *Martin Luther and the Enduring Word of God*, 98–100.

[16] P. A. Verhoef, "Luther and Calvin's Exegetical Library," in *Calvin Theological Journal* 3, no. 1 (April 1968): 5–20; also, B. A. Gerrish, *The Old Protestantism and the New: Essays on the Reformation Heritage* (Chicago: University of Chicago Press, 1982), 51–68.

After the Reformation, the historical-critical approach to the Scriptures, which stressed the importance of the historical but over against rather than in preparation for the theological interpretation of the Bible, began to develop. As discussed above, the rationalism of René Descartes, Thomas Hobbes, Baruch Spinoza, and John Locke greatly influenced the development of historical-critical studies. Philosophical and theological rationalism provided historical criticism with its foundation, an approach developed more fully by Johann Salamo Semler and Johann David Michaelis. Hermann S. Reimarus and Gotthold E. Lessing subsumed biblical revelation under the role of reason, while Friedrich Schleiermacher combined aspects of pietistic experience with rationalism and romanticism to develop new initiatives in biblical hermeneutics. Schleiermacher said the historical-critical approach helped disclose the intention of the biblical authors in the context of their day, but he raised serious questions regarding what that message might mean to readers and hearers in a different age and cultural context. In so doing, he became not only the "Father of Theological Liberalism," but also the "Father of Modern Hermeneutics."[17]

Though interesting, these approaches have limited value in helping us understand the meaning and significance of inspired Scripture for the church today due to their dismissive approach to theology. Gerhard Maier, in 1977, published *The End of the Historical-Critical Method,* describing the many shortfalls of the historical-critical approach to the Scriptures. Maier argued that only a thoroughgoing theological approach to the Bible could restore life to the work of biblical hermeneutics.[18] His work has been supported to some degree by Peter Stuhlmacher in his 2018 *Biblical Theology of the New Testament.*[19] Even more remarkable was the volte-face of Eta Linnemann, who rejected the historical-critical agenda as carefully presented in her 2001 *Historical Criticism of the Bible: Methodology or Ideology?*

---

[17] F. D. E. Schleiermacher, *Hermeneutics: The Handwritten Manuscripts,* ed. Heinz Kimmerle, trans. James Duke and Jack Forstman (Missoula, MT: Scholars, 1977). Note the influence of the historical-critical interpretation of Scripture on the quest for the historical Jesus. Colin Brown and Craig A. Evans, *History of the Quests for the Historical Jesus,* 2 vols. (Grand Rapids: Zondervan, 2022).

[18] Gerhard Maier, *The End of the Historical-Critical Method,* trans. Edwin W. Leverenz and Rudolph F. Norden (St. Louis: Concordia, 1977).

[19] Stuhlmacher, *Biblical Theology of the New Testament,* (see chap. 11, n. 134).

Reflections of a Bultmannian Turned Evangelical.[20] David Steinmetz, in 2011, published *Taking the Long View: Christian Theology in Historical Perspective*, in which he stated again his belief in the superiority of pre-critical exegesis.[21]

We now take a brief look at key insights from American and British scholars before turning our attention to the work of interpretation for application. While innovative questions were being pursued in Europe, we must not neglect the able exegesis carried out in North America during these centuries. America's greatest theologian, Jonathan Edwards (1703–1758), undertook two major exegetical projects seeking to advance a Reformed theological exegesis, though he was open to multiple levels of meaning in the biblical text as ably noted by Douglas Sweeney. Edwards was not bound to the literal sense but assumed every passage held the possibility for deeper meanings. In the same passage he often found a literal meaning, a statement about Christ, the church, and last things (heaven/hell). Edwards's spiritual approach has greatly influenced American pulpits for more than two centuries.[22]

An insistent echo of the Calvinist tradition's grammatical-historical exegesis was advanced at Princeton Seminary in the nineteenth century. Charles Hodge published masterful volumes on Romans and Ephesians, as well as 1 and 2 Corinthians, from 1835 to 1859. Other Princetonians also advanced the theological exposition of Scripture, a method that influenced the work of John Gresham Machen and Ned B. Stonehouse. The Old Princeton approach, combined with the British evangelical understanding of biblical

---

[20] Eta Linnemann, *Historical Criticism of the Bible: Methodology or Ideology? Reflections of a Bultmannian Turned Evangelical*, trans. Robert Yarbrough (Grand Rapids: Kregel, 2001).

[21] David C. Steinmetz, *Taking the Long View: Christian Theology in Historical Perspective* (Oxford: Oxford University Press, 2011).

[22] Douglas A. Sweeney, *Edwards the Exegete: Biblical Interpretation and Anglo-Protestant Culture on the Edge of the Enlightenment* (Oxford: Oxford University Press, 2016); David P. Barshinger and Douglas A. Sweeney, eds., *Jonathan Edwards and Scripture: Biblical Exegesis in British North America* (Oxford: Oxford University Press, 2018); also, Stephen J. Stein, "The Quest for the Spiritual Sense: The Biblical Hermeneutics of Jonathan Edwards," in *Harvard Theological Review* 70, no. 1–2 (January-April 1977): 99–113.

interpretation, has greatly shaped the contemporary American evangelical understanding of New Testament interpretation.[23]

British scholarship in the nineteenth century was led by the erudite Cambridge trio of B. F. Westcott and F. J. A. Hort, whose importance in developing the critical text were reviewed in chapter 7, and of J. B. Lightfoot, the bishop of Durham, who wrote excellent commentaries on especially the Pauline epistles. Lightfoot, Westcott, and Hort reached conclusions regarding the integrity of the text which generally differed from their more radical German counterparts. The exacting scholarship of the Cambridge trio has continued through the capable work of British scholars like F. F. Bruce, I. Howard Marshall, and N. T. Wright, among others.[24]

Baptists in America also made significant contributions to biblical studies. Moses Stuart, the great nineteenth-century Andover scholar, primarily concentrated his work in Old Testament but also wrote important New Testament commentaries that interacted with critical European scholarship. In the early twentieth century, Archibald Thomas Robertson, a prolific Greek New Testament scholar, wrote commentaries, grammatical works, and textual studies. This Southern Baptist's multi-volume *Word Pictures* remains a standard for pastors and teachers. George Eldon Ladd exemplified some of the best in twentieth-century scholarship with his first-rate New Testament theology, his studies on the kingdom in the New Testament, and his pioneering efforts in New Testament criticism.

The past seventy years have seen substantial contributions to evangelical biblical scholarship both in Great Britain and the United States through such commentary series as *New International Commentary, Baker Exegetical Commentary, Pillar Commentary, NIV Application Commentary, Word Biblical Commentary, Zondervan Exegetical Commentary, Tyndale Commentary,* IVP *Biblical Commentary, New American Commentary, Christian Standard Commentary,* and *Kregel KERUX Commentary,* among others. Individual

---

[23] John H. Gerstner, "The Contributions of Charles Hodge, B. B. Warfield, and J. Gresham Machen to the Doctrine of Inspiration," in *Challenges to Inerrancy,* ed. Gordon Lewis and Bruce Demarest (Chicago: Moody, 1984), 347–81; M. Silva, "Old Princeton, Westminster, and Inerrancy," in *Inerrancy and Hermeneutic,* 67–80.

[24] F. F. Bruce, "The History of New Testament Study," in *New Testament Interpretation,* ed. I. Howard Marshall (Grand Rapids: Eerdmans, 1977), 21–59.

biblical commentaries, from the critical to the practical, have also poured forth from evangelical pens.

III. Modern Hermeneutics

At this point, we turn to a review of the various ways modern Christians have learned to interpret the biblical text. Such a review will be helpful in suggesting how useful or not certain hermeneutical methods are for determining both the original meaning and the contemporary significance and application of a text. We begin with the genesis of modern hermeneutics, followed by an evaluation of the shift toward existential and reader-response theories. We then describe recent approaches which seek to take the author, the text, the reader, and the Holy Spirit seriously.

1. The Author-Oriented Genesis of Modern Hermeneutics

Friedrich Schleiermacher, who was greatly influenced by the romanticism of his day, argued that interpretation consisted of two categories, the grammatical and the psychological. For Schleiermacher, psychological interpretation was related to the author's intention, and he articulated some of the most incisive statements found in hermeneutical literature on the principles for grasping what an author willed to communicate. His grammatical hermeneutics were largely dependent on the work of J. A. Ernesti's 1761 *Institutio Interpretis Novi Testament*. The interpreter's goal focused on sharing a life relationship with the author. Understanding, then, involved more than rethinking what an author thought. Schleiermacher contended that if this reliving could take place, then the interpreter could understand the author's work as well as, or even better than, the author.

2. From the Author-Oriented Approach to Existential and Reader-Oriented Approaches

The most prominent approach to biblical studies in both Protestant and Roman Catholic schools of interpretation until the middle of the last century was an author-oriented approach with connections to the Schleiermacher tradition, sometimes called the "literal-grammatical" or "historical-contextual" methods of interpretation. In an early edition of *A Short History of the Interpretation of the Bible*, Robert M. Grant affirmed a similar position. Grant did this while recognizing some Christians had shifted toward existential and reader-oriented hermeneutics under the influence of Martin Heidegger, Rudolf Bultmann, and Hans-Georg Gadamer, who questioned the possibility of determinate meaning and objectivity. This shift in understanding was generated from the interpreter's existential awareness of human possibilities. The interpreter became the source of meaning as emphasis moved from the author to the reader, even to the "care" of the reader's being.[25]

That Bultmann was primarily responsible for Heidegger's hermeneutical insights entering the field of biblical studies in the twentieth century is well known. Bultmann and Heidegger were once colleagues at the University of Marburg.[26] For Bultmann the objective language of the New Testament was insignificant; instead, he was interested in the existential possibilities for the human being projected through the text. In his *Theology of the New Testament*, he wrote, "In the beginning, faith is the term which distinguishes the Christian congregation from the Jews and the heathen, not orthodoxy (right doctrine)." The latter, along with its corporate heresy, arises out of the differences which develop within the Christian congregations.[27] New Testament doctrine, couched in the objectifying mode of language Bultmann called "myth," was to be interpreted in terms of the primordial possibilities of the human being for faith. What Bultmann intended by his radical program of demythologizing was not the removal of myth but rather its existential interpretation. Bultmann's chief interest in reading biblical texts was to have a personal encounter. By de-emphasizing the cognitive aspects of the biblical text and shifting the notion of interpretation to encounter, Bultmann redirected the focus of New Testament interpretation. However, as Gerald Bray has chronicled,

---

[25] Robert M. Grant, *A Short History of the Interpretation of the Bible* (New York: Macmillan, 1963), 186–88.

[26] Rudolf Bultmann, *Theology of the New Testament*, trans. K. Grobel, 2 vols. (New York: Scribner's, 1955), 2:130–35; Rudolf Bultmann, *Kerygma and Myth*, ed. Hans W. Bartsch (London: SPCK, 1953).

[27] Bultmann, *Theology of the New Testament*, 135.

his approach failed to find universal academic acceptance and was thoroughly rejected by evangelical scholars.[28]

Karl Barth, for example, argued that Bultmann's method failed to take serious consideration of the intended reference of the discourse which often transcends both the language and the user of language. Bultmann implied that no matter what the biblical texts stated, their ultimate subject matter was human existence. All would agree that the biblical texts arose from human existence, but when interpretation is exclusively oriented toward human existence, the theological and cognitive aspects are reduced. When Bultmann demythologized Jesus and the writings of the apostles by conforming them to existential categories, he was not allowing the New Testament texts to speak for themselves.[29]

3. Returning to the Text

Robert Grant's words remain quite applicable for us today: "It would appear the primary task of the modern interpreter is historical, in the sense that what he is endeavoring to discover is what the texts and contexts he is interpreting meant to their authors in their relationship with their readers." In 1967, a University of Virginia literary scholar, E. D. Hirsch Jr., published *Validity in Interpretation*, which advocated an author-oriented, normative hermeneutic. He followed this work in 1976 with *The Aims of Interpretation*. Working within the tradition of general hermeneutics, Hirsch called for a grammatical and historical interpretation which attempts to grasp the meaning an author intended to convey in what was written. Hirsch's influence in biblical interpretation has been praised by many scholars in various traditions and fields.

Hirsch distanced himself from the Schleiermacher tradition, however, by maintaining it was not the task of the interpreter to have access to the mental process by which an author produced a work.[30] He affirmed

---

[28] Bray, *Biblical Interpretation*, 429–443.

[29] Karl Barth, *Rudolf Bultmann: Ein Versuch ihn zu Verstehen*, Theologischen Studien und Kritiken 34 (Zürich: Evangelischer Verlag, 1952).

[30] E. D. Hirsch Jr., *The Aims of Interpretation* (Chicago: University of Chicago Press, 1976), 17–18; see E. D. Hirsch Jr., *Validity in Interpretation* (New Haven, CT: Yale University Press, 1967).

the author's verbal meanings can be grasped because the interpretation of texts is concerned with shareable meanings. Hirsch contended that authors choose language conventions that will bring to readers' minds the things they are attempting to communicate. Thus, readers can also know what the authors wanted to share with their audience by words. Language is efficient in transmitting meaning because it consists of conventions, elements the society using that language has agreed should stand for all its various aspects of common experience. Thus, "an author's verbal meaning is limited by linguistic possibilities but is determined by his actualizing and specifying some of these possibilities."[31] The meaning of words is thus limited to the context determined by the author. Interpreters cannot, therefore, understand what writers meant except through reference to that which they actually wrote.

Within biblical studies, G. B. Caird has summarized the capacity of interpretation this way:

> We have no access to the mind of Jeremiah or Paul except through their recorded words. *A fortiori*, we have no access to the word of God in the Bible except through the words and the minds of those who claimed to speak in his name. We may disbelieve them, that is our right; but if we try, without evidence, to penetrate to a meaning more ultimate than the one the writers intended, that is our meaning, not theirs or God's.[32]

Hirsch's position on the author-oriented approach claims the task of the interpreter is to understand what an author meant at the time of the writing. This approach is possible, because a text's meaning is controlled by language

---

[31] Hirsch, *Aims of Interpretation,* 47–48; See Walter C. Kaiser Jr., "Hermeneutics and Evangelical Theology," in *Building on the Foundations of Evangelical Theology,* ed. Gregg R. Allison and Stephen J. Wellum (Wheaton: Crossway, 2015), 51–65; David S. Dockery, "An (Author-Oriented) Historical Model," in *Hermeneutics for Preaching,* ed. Raymond Bailey (Nashville: Broadman, 1992), 27–52.

[32] G. B. Caird, *The Language and Imagery of the Bible* (Philadelphia: Westminster, 1980), 61. Caird has discussed the concept of "meaning" and discovering meaning in Scripture as carefully as anyone (see pp. 32–61). He distinguishes between meaning (referent), meaning (sense), meaning (value), meaning (entailment), and meaning (intention). We are primarily concerned in this discussion with matters of intention and sense.

conventions which exist between the speaker and hearer, or the author and reader.[33] Agreeing with Hirsch, Paul Ricoeur, likewise observed:

> As concerns of procedures of validation by which we test our guesses, I agree with Hirsch that they are closer to a logic of probability than a logic of empirical verification. To show that an interpretation is more probable in light of what is known is something other than showing that a conclusion is true. In this sense, validation is not verification. Validation is an argumentative discipline comparable to the judicial procedures of legal interpretation. It is a logic of uncertainty and of qualitative probability. . . . A text is a quasi-individual, the validation of an interpretation to it may be said, with complete legitimacy, to give a scientific knowledge of the text.[34]

The most important contribution of Hirsch's theory to biblical studies is the distinction between meaning and significance. *Meaning* is what the writer intended to convey when addressing his original readers. Hirsch, however, suggested the more important or meaningful a text is, the greater the possibility of a deeper, fuller meaning. The *significance* of the text, therefore, includes all the various ways a text can be read and applied beyond the author's intention. G. K. Beale, following the insights of Kevin Vanhoozer in *Is There a Meaning in This Text*, observed:

> Interpretation seeks an understanding of an earlier author's original meaning. No interpretation ever reproduces an author's original meaning exhaustively, but it can achieve a truly approximate, partial, and adequate understanding, so that there are essential points

---

[33] Hirsch, *Aims of Interpretation*, 48; Caird, *Language and Imagery of the Bible*, 61. Also, see William E. Cain, *The Crisis in Criticism* (Baltimore: Johns Hopkins University Press, 1984); Suresh Ravel, *Metacriticsm* (Athens, GA: University of Georgia Press, 1981); Susan R. Horton, *Interpreting Interpreting* (Baltimore: Johns Hopkins University Press, 1979); Lenore Langsdorf, "Current Paths Toward an Objective Hermeneutic," *Criswell Theological Review* 2 (1987): 145–54; Janet Martin Soskice, *Metaphor and Religious Language* (Oxford: Clarendon, 1985).

[34] Paul Ricoeur, *Hermeneutics and the Human Sciences: Essays on Language, Action, and Interpretation*, ed. and trans. John B. Thompson (Cambridge: Cambridge University Press, 1980), 212; also, see William J. Abraham, "Intention and the Logic of Interpretation," *Asbury Theological Journal* 43, no. 1 (1988): 11–25.

of overlap between the original meaning and the apprehension of that meaning.[35]

Thus, as Vanhoozer, Beale, and others suggest, the distinction between meaning and significance needs to be maintained if one does not hold to the presuppositions of existentialism, reader-response criticism, or deconstructionism. Otherwise, the original meaning and its contemporary relevance collapse, and the meaning of the text becomes merely a reflection of the interpreter's own purely socially constructed thoughts.[36]

"Exegesis" focuses on the primary, normative meaning of the biblical text, whereas "exposition" entails revealing the fuller meaning or significance of the biblical text in line with the way the early church read Scripture through the vehicles of typological and allegorical interpretation with regard for the text's *sensus plenior* (fuller meaning) as ruled by the analogy of faith. The goal of interpretation, then, is not to psychologize an author but rather to determine the author's purpose as revealed in the linguistical structure of the text. In other words, the goal of interpretation concerns itself with what the author achieved. Ricoeur stressed that generally when one reads a text, the author is not present to be questioned about any ambiguous meaning. This is certainly true concerning the human authors of the biblical text.[37]

Ricoeur, like Hirsch, maintains a text's meaning is intelligible across the historical and cultural distance that separates contemporary readers from the biblical text. Because of the nature of writing, the text opens a possible world to the interpreter (the text world); the interpreter may enter that world and

---

[35] Beale, *The Erosion of Inerrancy in Evangelicalism*, 236 (see introduction, n. 1); Kevin J. Vanhoozer, *Is There Meaning in This Text? The Bible, the Reader, and the Morality of Literary Knowledge* (Grand Rapids: Zondervan, 2009).

[36] Beale, *The Erosion of Inerrancy in Evangelicalism*; D. A. Carson, *The Gagging of God* (Grand Rapids: Zondervan, 1996), 57–137; Royce G. Greunler, *Meaning and Understanding* (Grand Rapids: Zondervan, 1991); 74–86.

[37] Paul Ricoeur, *Essays on Biblical Interpretation*, ed. L. S. Mudge (Philadelphia: Fortress, 1980); Paul Ricoeur, *Interpretation Theory: Discourse and the Surplus of Meaning* (Fort Worth: Texas Christian University Press, 1976); also, see Kevin J. Vanhoozer, *Biblical Narrative in the Philosophy of Paul Ricoeur* (Cambridge: Cambridge University Press, 1990); Graeme Nicholson, *Seeing and Reading* (Atlantic Highlands, NJ: Humanities, 1984).

appropriate the possibilities it offers. When this event occurs, the meaning of the text is actualized in the interpreter's understanding. What is understood or appropriated, then, is the text itself, the result of the author's writing. Thus, the goal of biblical interpretation is to understand meaning from the vantage point of what the author actually wrote or to focus on the text as the result of the author's writing.[38] When studying Holy Scripture, we seek to grasp the author's meaning by, with, and through the enablement of the Holy Spirit.[39]

Recent studies in Speech-Act Theory have been quite helpful for describing the role of the Holy Spirit in interpretation. According to this theory, all speech is "performatory"; that is, speakers do things when they speak, whether it be to command, bless, complain, request, or so on. Each speech act is made up of the "locution" (the speaking and writing of words and sentences for the purpose of communicating), the "illocution" (what speakers do with their locutions, such as explain, bless, curse, command, and so forth), and the "perlocution" (what actually eventuates due to a speaker's speech acts as the reader responds, such as changes in behavior, mood, thinking, or other responses). The Holy Spirit inspired the original locutions of the biblical text.

Vanhoozer notes that when the Bible is read today, the Holy Spirit illumines the Word of God by bringing to bear the weight of authority (what Speech-Act Theory terms illocutionary force) on the reader, enabling him or her to recognize that the biblical words are the Word of God and ought to be obeyed. The Spirit then enables and effects the proper response to the illocution through bringing about understanding and application which are

---

[38] Paul Ricoeur, *The Conflict of Interpretations: Essays in Hermeneutics*, ed. Don Ihde (Evanston: Northwestern University Press, 1974); also, see William L. Hendricks, "Learning from Beauty," *Southwestern Journal of Theology* 29, no. 3 (1987): 19–27.

[39] Daniel Fuller, "The Holy Spirit's Role in Biblical Interpretation," in *Scripture, Tradition, and Interpretation*, ed. W. Ward Gasque and William Sanford LaSor (Grand Rapids: Eerdmans, 1978), 189–98; Fred H. Klooster, "The Role of the Holy Spirit in the Hermeneutic Process: The Relationship of the Spirit's Illumination to Biblical Interpretation," in *Hermeneutics, Inerrancy, and the Bible*, ed. Earl D. Radmacher and Robert D. Preus (Grand Rapids: Academie Books, 1984), 451–72; also, Craig S. Keener, *Spirit Hermeneutics: Reading Scripture in Light of Pentecost* (Grand Rapids: Eerdmans, 2016).

consistent with the meaning originally inspired.[40] Modern hermeneutical theory has shifted over recent centuries from stressing the human author's intention to stressing the reader's existential response to recovering the text's own meaning in light of its historical and literary context.

IV. Approaching Biblical Interpretation

Before identifying steps involved in the process of biblical interpretation for the sake of understanding and application, certain issues need to be addressed. Each biblical document and each part of a biblical document must be studied in its context, which includes not only its historical context but its immediate literary context as well. We believe it is necessary to recognize multiple contexts, to commit to reading the text with Christian presuppositions, and to remember the place of interpretation is in and with the church, both local and universal.

1. Recognizing Multiple Contexts

With the help of the Spirit of God who inspired Holy Scripture, the responsible interpreter must develop a basic understanding of the following, insofar as he or she is able: the biblical languages, the types of literature employed in the Bible, the historical and cultural backgrounds, the geographical conditions, and the life situations of the biblical authors, the readers, and the hearers. The meaning of some written material is seldom clearly self-evident. Especially is this the case for an ancient document like the Bible, which was written for people who lived in different cultural and historical settings. Exposing the issues identified requires asking several questions of the biblical text under consideration:

a.   Who was the biblical writer and who were the recipients?
b.   What was the cultural-historical setting of the writer and the recipients?
c.   What did the words which were used mean at the time of writing?

---

[40] Vanhoozer, *Is There a Meaning in This Text?* 209–14; Kevin J. Vanhoozer, *First Theology: God, Scripture, and Hermeneutics* (Downers Grove: IVP, 2002), 154–58.

d. What was the author's purpose for writing? More specifically, why did he write what was written, and why did he write in the way it was written?

e. What key textual terms and ideas point toward a better understanding?

f. What are the theological, Christological, and canonical implications of the biblical text being studied?

g. What is the significance of the text for believers in the contemporary church?

Nicholas Piotrowski, in his recent volume, *In All the Scriptures,* beautifully expounds the concept that there are three contexts of biblical interpretation: (1) the literary context, (2) the historical context, and (3) what could be summarized as the canonical, redemptive, Christological, or theological context. He warns us not to skip the literary and historical contexts of interpretation in our zeal to attain the theological or Christological significance of a passage.[41]

2. The Necessity of Christian Presuppositions

Personal presuppositions also must be acknowledged before interpretation is attempted. All understanding requires an interpretative framework or knowledge context. The more knowledge the reader has about a text, the more likely it can be understood properly. If the Bible is God's revelation to his people, which is the presupposition represented by both authors of this volume, then the first qualification, the essential qualification, for a full understanding of the Bible is to know the revealing God. In order to know God, one must enter a relationship with him through faith in the Lord Jesus Christ, enabled by the Holy Spirit. Only those who believe and trust in God can rightly understand what God has spoken in his Word.[42] It is impossible

---

[41] Piotrowski, *In All the Scripture,* 74–197.

[42] In other words, the historic orthodox tradition of humble faith commitment exemplified by Gregory of Nazianzus in the East and Augustine of Hippo in the West, described at the beginning of chapter 10 above, remains necessary for Bible expositors today.

to truly understand and apply the biblical text if one denies there is a God or denies the Bible comes from God.[43]

A second necessary commitment, which unfolds from the first presuppositional commitment, is the willingness to submit to the text and believe what it says. For those of us who accept the Bible as a sacred text, as the church's book, as God's self-revelation, as we have repeatedly affirmed in this volume, the Christian interpretation of the Bible must rise above the base level of grammatical-historical exegesis. The theological significance of a passage simply must not be ignored. Grammatical-historical interpretation helps discover the original meaning in a particular text, but theological exegesis presupposes the underlying theological unity in the Bible. Only when it is remembered that the Bible is a gift of the triune God, as well as a truly human text, may a proper perspective of its diversity be appreciated.[44]

3. The Place of the Church

In other words, to understand the Bible theologically so that we may obey its teachings rightly, the illuminating work of the Holy Spirit is required. The ministry of the Holy Spirit of God provides the resource for such faithful understanding of God's Word. The illuminating work of the Holy Spirit utilizes hard work and proper principles of hermeneutics. However, the Spirit ultimately enlivens the text so it can be properly understood and applied to the lives of believers, not only individually but also corporately. The latter aspect, the importance of the church as a community of biblical interpretation, may not be ignored.

Contemporary interpreters of the biblical text must be constantly aware of the modern temptations toward presentism and individualism. Christian interpreters rightly recognize their participation in the body of Christ. We interpret biblical texts for the good of others in the community of faith. The church is likewise the instrument the Spirit uses to provide accountability for interpretation and for protection against wrong-headed, solipsistic, and

---

[43] Grant R. Osborne, *The Hermeneutical Spiral: A Comprehensive Introduction to Biblical Interpretation* (Downers Grove: IVP, 2006), 407, 516–17.
[44] Beale, *Erosion of Inerrancy in Evangelicalism*, 246–59.

heretical approaches to the canon. The believing community provides a check against the self-referential conclusions which inevitably arise from limited circumstances.[45] Craig Bartholomew reminds us that "ecclesial reception of the Word is primary."[46] The church is indispensable in hermeneutics.

Alongside honoring the church's expression in local covenanted communities (Matt 18:15–20), we must recognize Jesus Christ established a worldwide fellowship which crosses temporal, social, and cultural boundaries (Matt 16:18; 28:18–20; Eph 1:22–23; 2:18–22, etc.). This means that a particular meaning and significance should make sense to others in Christ's universal church, not just to those Christians gathered in a particular local congregation.[47] The universal and worldwide nature of the church requires responsible biblical interpreters become adept in historical theology. Eccentric, errant, and heretical interpretations of Scripture become easier to identify, to rebuke, and to correct when the interpreter adopts a humble attitude and remains in conversation with other times and places in the Great Tradition of the one church of the one Lord Jesus Christ, which is indwelt by the one Holy Spirit and exists for the glory of the one living God. Responsible theologians honor the foundational work of interpretation performed by those who served previous generations.[48] We must learn from those who followed Christ before us.

---

[45] Craig G. Bartholomew, *Introducing Biblical Hermeneutics: A Comprehensive Framework for Hearing God in Scripture* (Grand Rapids: Baker, 2015), 544–45; Donald G. Bloesch, *Holy Scripture* (Downers Grove: IVP, 1994), 193; Plummer, *40 Questions about Interpreting the Bible*, (see introduction, n. 26).

[46] Bartholomew, *Introducing Biblical Hermeneutics*, 9.

[47] Beale, *Erosion of Inerrancy in Evangelicalism*, 261–65; Piotrowski, *In All the Scriptures*, 259–64; Bartholomew, *Introducing Biblical Hermeneutics*, 543–44; Even if one does not agree with all aspects of works by McCaulley and Richards, there is much to be learned from engaging their thoughtful presentations. See Esau McCaulley, *Reading Scripture While Black* (Downers Grove: IVP, 2020); E. Randolph Richards and Brandon J. O'Brien, *Misreading Scripture with Western Eyes* (Downers Grove: IVP, 2012). Helpful guidance is provided by Whan Kim, "The Reliability and Authority of the Bible," in *ESV Global Study Bible*, ed. J. I. Packer, Wayne Grudem, and Ajith Fernando (Wheaton: Crossway, 2012), 1872–73.

[48] George, *Reading Scripture with the Reformers*, (see chap. 11, n. 10); Christopher A. Hall, *Reading Scripture with the Church Fathers* (Downers Grove: IVP, 1998);

V. A Proposed Model for Biblical Interpretation

Scriptural interpreters must acknowledge their ecclesial setting; our own churches' confessions regard the Bible as the inspired, inerrant, and authoritative Word of God. Interpreters should also recognize the possibility that the biblical text in its canonical context contains a theological meaning which may be fuller than what might have been understood by the human author at the time it was written. The more significant the text, the more this is likely to be true. Because of the divine nature and canonical shape of the Bible, a passage may have a deeper significance which by its divine nature is beyond entire human comprehension. Indeed, the theological meaning may exceed the conscious intention of the original human author or the understanding and application of the original readers.[49]

Gregory Beale observed that if one presupposes a divine author over both the individual texts and the whole canon, then the expansion of earlier texts in later ones is part of one holistic if complex authorial act of communication. Though it remains necessarily mysterious, a viable hermeneutic recognizes Holy Scripture's *sensus plenior*.[50] If the presence of a "fuller sense" is possible, how can the meaning and significance of the biblical text be determined? What guidelines exist to limit fanciful excesses?

Yarnell, *The Formation of Christian Doctrine*, 178–80 (see chap. 7, n. 25).

[49] William Sanford LaSor, "The *Sensus Plenior* and Biblical Interpretation," in *Scripture, Tradition, and Interpretation: African American Biblical Interpretation as an Exercise in Hope*, 260–77. For warnings in this regard, see Douglas J. Moo, "The Problems of Sensus Plenior," in *Hermeneutics, Authority, and Canon*, ed. D. A. Carson and John D. Woodbridge (Grand Rapids: Zondervan, 1986), 175–211; Vern Poythress, "Divine Meaning of Scripture," *The Westminster Theological Journal* 48, no. 2 (Fall 1986): 241–79.

[50] G. K. Beale, *Erosion of Inerrancy in Evangelicalism*, 235–46; G. Reventlow, *Problems of Biblical Theology in the Twentieth Century* (London: SCM, 1986), 37–47; D. A. Carson, "Mystery and Fulfillment: Toward a More Comprehensive Paradigm of Paul's Understanding of the Old and New," in *Justification and Variegated Nomism*, ed. D. A. Carson, Peter T. O'Brien, and Mark A. Seifried (Tübingen: Mohr Siebeck, 2004), 410–34; Beale and Gladd, *Hidden but Now Revealed*, (see chap. 10, n. 22). The classic work on *sensus plenior* was authored by Raymond Brown, *The "Sensus Plenior" of Sacred Scripture* (Baltimore: St. Mary's University, 1955).

1. Guidelines for Interpretation

The guidelines for developing the *sensus plenior* in a responsible theological and ethical manner are already located within the biblical text as located in the biblical canon. The meaning and the significance of a specific biblical text must be consistent with the canonical message of the Bible. We offer the following guidelines for perceiving the fuller sense of sacred Scripture:

  a. Approach the text with the faith presupposition that the triune God is the source and end of Scripture. This requires acknowledging that God provides the Bible with its overall unity as well as its truthfulness, authority, and sufficiency.
  b. Affirm both the human authorship of the biblical text and its divine origin.
  c. Regard the biblical text in its literary and historical context as the place where meaning is concentrated.
  d. Recognize that the historical and literary meaning of the Bible is the primary meaning, but that the literal may not limit spiritual meaning.
  e. Understand that a single text resides in a larger canonical context; thus, Scripture serves as the best commentary on Scripture.
  f. Acknowledge the possibility of a deeper meaning and significance in the prophetic-apostolic witness, pointing to a typological or Christological understanding.
  g. Pray for the Holy Spirit's illumination to enable the work of interpretation.
  h. Expect the Bible's significance to speak to the interpreter's contemporary concerns.
  i. Always interpret the Bible in light of the centrality of Jesus Christ.[51]

It is true that the reader participates in understanding the biblical text. Yet the reader does not determine meaning. There are contextual markers in the text itself, intentionally planted to indicate an objective meaning mediated

---

[51] Several important books on biblical interpretation offer similar guidelines. A helpful example is Gordon D. Fee, *New Testament Exegesis* (Philadelphia: Westminster, 1983), 60–77; also, Piper, *Reading the Bible Supernaturally*, (see chap. 5, n. 13).

by the biblical text. While stressing the historical and literary meaning of the text, concern for the text's significance for the contemporary reader must not be neglected. The concept of the text's significance is certainly important, though not equal to the importance of a text's meaning.

Focusing upon meaning in the biblical text acknowledges a text's verbal meaning, which can be construed only on the basis of its own linguistic possibilities. These possibilities are not given from some other realm but must be learned or approximated within a particular linguistic system. According to Ricoeur, appropriated textual understanding is nothing other than the disclosing power of the text itself as it bridges the gulf between reader and author. A text is certainly historical in its origin, but the Spirit is also present in power to communicate its sense and significance, thereby opening a world to its contemporary reader. In this sense the Scripture possesses ongoing significance for contemporary readers.[52] We maintain this is true because of the work of the Holy Spirit who both inspired the biblical text when it was written and who illumines the Scripture for contemporary readers.[53]

2. Bridging the Distance between the Author(s) and the Interpreter

We propose readers take the following steps for helping to span the distance between author and interpreter. The interpreter should begin in prayer, observe the text, translate it, and perform basic exegesis. Afterwards, the interpreter must move through interpretation to theological understanding so that the reader may proclaim the significance of the text in the church and to the world for the sake of applying its truths in a salutary way.

a. *Introduction.* The interpretive process begins with prayer. God's direction and enablement must be sought at each step; only then should textual inquiry begin.[54] The following questions help introduce the issues: (1) What presuppositions do interpreters bring to the biblical text? Some already

---

[52] Ricoeur, *Interpretation Theory*, 1–24.

[53] Christopher W. Morgan, *Christian Theology: The Biblical Story and Our Faith* (Nashville: B&H, 2020), 82–83; Grudem, *Systematic Theology*, 105–11 (see introduction, n. 27); Frame, *The Doctrine of the Word of God*, (see introduction, n. 27).

[54] Thompson, *The Doctrine of Scripture*, 181–85 (see introduction, n. 29).

identified are faith, a spirit of obedience, the expectation of the illuminating work of the Holy Spirit, a commitment to the reliability of the biblical text, and recognition of the contextual setting within the community of faith by affirming that the Scriptures are fully inspired and constitute a truthful, divine-human book.[55] (2) What is the author's historical situation? (3) What is the cultural context out of which the author wrote?[56]

b. *Observation.* When observing a text, an interpreter should look for key terms and structural signals, such as conjunctions, particles, and so forth. These signals or text markers, help indicate the interpretive limits of the text. While the basic unit for consideration is the paragraph, individual sentences and words also must be considered. Credible interpretation is more than basic etymology, however, and an examination of the text's structure in paragraph units will help reveal the major idea being communicated by the author.

c. *Translation.* Through textual criticism and comparison of various translations, an interpreter can establish the text for investigation. Most interpreters will work from one basic (and favorite) translation, doing minimal comparison with other translations. We believe that a thoughtful comparison and consideration of several good translations should precede the interpretive process. The use of original languages is extremely helpful, if not mandatory, for the serious interpreter.

d. *Basic Exegesis.* The genre (or kind) of the text must be considered next. It may be poetry, narrative, prophetic, parabolic, gospel, epistolary, or apocalyptic. Once the genre is determined, basic work with Bible dictionaries, concordances, and grammars should commence. Many suggest that diagramming a sentence flow at this point will be beneficial for identifying the major emphases of the text. Gordon Fee's step-by-step instructions for analyzing the text with the use of sentence flow charts may be helpful in this process.[57] For certain genres, discovering the plot or macrostructure of the text will be necessary at this stage of the interpretive process.

---

[55] See the insightful observations on the relationship between hermeneutics and the spiritual life in Bruce K. Waltke, *The Dance between God and Humanity: Reading the Bible Today as the People of God* (Grand Rapids: Eerdmans, 2013), 301–12.

[56] Piotrowski, *In All the Scriptures*, 97–120.

[57] We also recommend the guidance provided by Scott Duvall and Daniel Hays in *Grasping God's Word: A Hands-On Approach to Reading, Interpreting, and Applying*

e. *Interpretation.* This step is the most important in seeking the textual meaning from an author-oriented and text-oriented perspective. The question that interpreters need to ask is, "What did the text mean in its historical setting to its initial readers or hearers?" Afterwards, the investigation moves from asking *what* to *why,* "Why was it written this way?" An examination of commentaries and background resources will help interpreters to trace the historical context as well as historic interpretations of the passage. Such consultation with others in the history of the church helps to guide interpreters toward grasping the meaning of the text in its literary and canonical context.[58]

f. *Theological Discernment.* Determining the theological significance of the passage involves exploring additional questions:[59] (1) What does the text mean to contemporary readers? (2) What cultural factors may need to be contextualized or retranslated in order to be understood?[60] (3) How does the passage reflect the Bible's fuller canonical meaning?[61] Beale reminds us of the importance for twenty-first-century interpreters not to fail to recognize the importance of our larger global context, saying that "theological globalism is nothing more than the different members of the body of Christ needing one another."[62]

---

the *Bible* (Grand Rapids: Zondervan, 2020); Fee, *New Testament Exegesis;* Gordon Fee and Douglas Stuart, *How to Read the Bible for All Its Worth* (Grand Rapids: Zondervan, 1982).

[58] Dockery, "Study and Interpretation of the Bible," in *Foundations for Biblical Interpretation,* 36–54 (see chap. 10, n. 72).

[59] See important discussions of canonical and theological interpretation in Robert B. Sloan, "Canonical Theology of the New Testament," in *Foundations for Biblical Interpretation,* 565–94; Daniel J. Treier, "Contemporary Theological Hermeneutics," in *Dictionary for Theological Interpretation of the Bible,* 787–93; Kevin J. Vanhoozer, "What Is Theological Interpretation of the Bible?," in *Dictionary for Theological Interpretation of the Bible,* 19–25; Charles M. Wood, *The Formation of Christian Understanding* (Philadelphia: Westminster, 1981), and Rhyne Putman, *In Defense of Doctrine: Evangelicalism, Theology, and Scripture* (Minneapolis: Fortress, 2015), 173–208, 375–400.

[60] David Hesselgrave, *Communicating Christ Cross-Culturally* (Grand Rapids: Zondervan, 1978); D. A. Carson, ed., *Biblical Interpretation and the Church: The Problem of Contextualization* (Nashville: Nelson, 1984).

[61] Beale and Gladd, *Hidden but Now Revealed.*

[62] Beale, *Erosion of Inerrancy in Evangelicalism,* 264–65.

g. *Christological Focus.* The Christological principle or rule of faith, as found in the doctrine of Jesus, the apostles, the early church, and the Reformers, especially Martin Luther, should best be understood and implemented today. As noted by Piotrowski, this theological principle informs the literary and historical construction of the text. The literary, historical, and theological approaches are thus complementary and coherent. The Christological principle is valid for twenty-first-century interpreters as a canonical and theological principle, taking us a step beyond the grammatical-historical method.

Christological interpretations developed with the rule of faith in mind, when consistent with the literary and historical context as well as with the teaching of the New Testament, should be encouraged. The experiences, promises, and prophecies of Israel point to the gospel of Jesus Christ promised beforehand through the prophets in the Holy Scriptures (see Rom 1:1–4).[63] There is great insight and spiritual wisdom to be gained from this approach to theological interpretation and application. In doing so, one must remember, however, never to divorce a passage from its literary or historical background.[64] A canonical and theological interpretation will not stop at the grammatical-historical level but will seek the Christological sense of the passage for the enrichment of the spiritual teaching and proclamation of Scripture and for building up and strengthening the church.[65]

h. *Proclamation of the Text's Significance for the Church.* Two more questions need to be explored: (1) How can the historical meaning and the contemporary significance be communicated to our contemporary context? How will the text be heard and understood today?[66] This final step

---

[63] Piotrowski, *In All the Scriptures*, 121–97.

[64] See Daniel I. Block, "Old Testament Theology," in *Theology, Church, and Ministry*, ed. David S. Dockery (Nashville: B&H, 2017), 192–216, who proposes that we should think of Christ as the goal of Old Testament study rather than thinking of Christ as the center of Old Testament interpretation and theology. Similarly, Piotrowski encourages readers not to rush past the historical context of the Old Testament in seeking Christ in the Old Testament. See Piotrowski, *In All the Scriptures*, 74–96.

[65] Robert W. Jenson, *A Theology in Outline: Can These Bones Live?* (Oxford: Oxford University Press, 2016), 85–87.

[66] John R. W. Stott, *Between Two Worlds* (Grand Rapids: Eerdmans, 1982); Robert Smith Jr., *Doctrine that Dances: Bringing Doctrinal Preaching and Teaching to*

points us toward the importance of ecclesial interpretation and scriptural application, as well as to the teaching and preaching of Scripture for the body of Christ.

VI. The Application of Scripture

As we have tried to make clear in this concluding chapter thus far, the immediate goal of interpretation is to seek to ascertain the authorial/textual meaning of a passage in its historical context as well as its broader canonical context. However, we also assert the ultimate goal of the process of interpretation within a biblical worldview is to hear the Word of God and seek to be obedient to its call. We must love God with all our minds and hearts, and grasping the truths of Scriptures through study is one way we do so. However, if we simply stop with mentally understanding the text while failing to apply it to life, we fall short of loving God in a well-rounded manner. Just as James warned about the failure to let true faith be seen in works (Jas 2:14–17), so interpretation without application is problematic.[67]

What guidelines might be helpful for us as we seek to encourage faithful application for the followers of Christ? The order of topics addressed in this chapter has been quite intentional. We must do the work of serious study and interpretation prior to the work of application. This may seem obvious, but the temptation to rush ahead to a practical application is often a real one for both young believers and seasoned students of Scripture. To reverse the right order opens the door to reading an application into the biblical text rather than allowing the Spirit to shape the application in accordance with the text's meaning.

The evangelical interpreter will want to develop the points of application directly from the text itself. He or she can proceed well by asking several questions: What does this text teach us about God? About ourselves? About

---

Life (Nashville: B&H, 2008); David S. Dockery, "Preaching and Hermeneutics," in *A Handbook for Contemporary Preaching*, ed. Michael Duduit, rev. ed. (Nashville: B&H, 2018), 142–50.

[67] Michael Horton, *Pilgrim Theology: Core Doctrines for Christian Disciples* (Grand Rapids: Zondervan, 2011), 70–71.

our church? About our service to others and our involvement in and engagement with the world?[68]

An important point to remember, especially for those called as teachers (Jas 3:1), involves applying the passage to our own lives before seeking to apply it to the lives of others.[69] We want to make applications as specific as possible, doing so in a way that is consistent with the meaning of the text in its historical and canonical meanings. If we try to make specific applications that are not consistent with the clear teaching of Scripture, it may lead to legalism or license or other faulty practices that are inconsistent with the overall teaching of the Bible. Application involves the integration of the biblical teaching into our lives, including the encouragement of connecting our lives with others.[70] We need to ask the Spirit of God to help us understand that the Bible is God's authoritative Word for us. Such contemporary issues as decision-making and ethical practices demand biblical answers and applications.[71]

Some biblical teachings are specific, universal commands which speak directly to people in all cultures. Some general teachings have universal application, while some biblical principles have implicit authority. Some matters can be addressed only by finding guidelines that can be applied to a specific issue or question.[72]

Some contemporary issues are not addressed specifically in Scripture. These include questions such as: Where should we work? What school should we attend? Whom should we marry? Which church should take our membership? These matters require thoughtful reflection on biblical

---

[68] David S. Dockery and George H. Guthrie, *The Holman Guide to Interpreting the Bible* (Nashville: B&H, 2004), 71–85.

[69] Eugene Peterson, "Eat This Book: The Holy Community at Table with the Holy Scriptures," *Theology Today* 56, no. 1 (1999): 5–7.

[70] Graeme Goldsworthy, *Gospel-Centered Hermeneutics: Foundations and Principles of Evangelical Biblical Interpretation* (Downers Grove: IVP, 2006), 251–57.

[71] Roy B. Zuck, "The Role of the Holy Spirit in Hermeneutics," *Bibliotheca Sacra* 141:562 (April-June, 1984): 120–30; also, see Payne, *Carl F. H. Henry on the Holy Spirit* (see chap. n. 50).

[72] Harvie M. Conn, "Normativity, Relevance, and Relativism," *Inerrancy and Hermeneutic*, ed. Harvie M. Conn (Grand Rapids: Baker, 1988), 186–89.

principles which likely give general rather than specific guidance.[73] Thus, the answers to practical questions like these, of which the list is long, must be dealt with a careful reading of Scripture under the guidance of the Holy Spirit within the context of the believing community, trusting the Lord for wisdom and understanding.[74]

There are various principles in the Bible, principles which must be discovered, but the difficult work in discerning them does not in any way indicate that the Bible is irrelevant for our lives. The general teachings of Scripture reveal God's will in a variety of ways. The direct, implied, and applied principles of Scripture cross temporal, social, linguistic, and cultural barriers. The Bible's clarity, adequacy, sufficiency, and authority for modern women and men should be affirmed, even as we remember how the Bible can and does speak at various levels and in various ways. The direct commands and indirect principles of the sacred writings remain relevant for addressing both the moral issues and other difficult challenges of our day.[75]

The Bible is to be regarded as the ultimate standard of authority for God's people. The Bible derives its authority and sufficiency from the self-revealing and self-authenticating God.[76] The Bible's authority can and does communicate across cultural, geographical, linguistic, and cultural differences. But we must go back to the historical setting of the text to ensure we have interpreted the eternal truths rightly before returning to our contemporary context with practical and pastoral words of application.[77] Inspired Scripture is authoritative and must be faithfully interpreted, taught, applied, and practiced. The Holy Spirit's illuminating work helps bring clarity to the Word of God. Likewise, the Spirit leads people to

---

[73] Elliot E. Johnson, *Expository Hermeneutics: An Introduction* (Grand Rapids: Zondervan, 1990), 225–31.

[74] Michael Lawrence, *Biblical Theology in the Life of the Church* (Wheaton: Crossway, 2010).

[75] Yarnell and Dockery, "The Authority and Sufficiency of Scripture," (see. chap. 7, n. 29).

[76] Feinberg, *Light in a Dark Place*, 387–425 (introduction, n. 5).

[77] J. I. Packer, *Truth and Power: The Place of Scripture in the Christian Life* (Wheaton: Harold Shaw, 1996).

recognize the authority of Scripture and encourages Christians to respond to and obey its message.[78]

While Scripture does not speak directly to every contemporary issue, the Bible's principles guide believers to make application for their entire lives so that believers may live in a God-honoring manner.[79] For example, technology can become either an instrument through which we fulfill our role as God's stewards or an object of worship that will eventually rule us. We gain wisdom from meditation on Scripture to help us understand how best to use this critical tool of twenty-first-century life. For another example, sexuality has become a major topic for those living in the third millennium. The Bible teaches that sexuality is good within a heterosexual and monogamous covenant of mutual self-giving marriage. More examples could be given of how the Bible offers principles to guide us in thinking wisely about education, the environment, the arts, science, history, poverty, wealth, work, and relationships.[80]

Regarding these and like important issues, M. Daniel Carroll R. and Darrell L. Bock maintain that "the Bible handles ethical topics with a depth

---

[78] Graham A. Cole, "*Sola Scriptura:* Some Historical and Contemporary Perspectives," *Churchman* 104, no. 1 (1990): 20–22; Osborne, *The Hermeneutical Spiral*, 441–51.

[79] Thompson, "The Sufficient Word," 27–44 (see introduction, n. 33).

[80] Justin A. Bailey, *Interpreting Your World: Five Lenses for Engaging Culture* (Grand Rapids: Baker, 2022); Christopher Watkin, *Biblical Critical Theory: How the Bible's Unfolding Story Makes Sense of Modern Life and Culture* (Grand Rapids: Zondervan, 2022); Charles Colson and Nancy Pearcey, *How Now Shall We Live?* (Wheaton: Tyndale, 1999); David S. Dockery and John Stonestreet, eds., *Life, Marriage, and Religious Liberty* (Nashville: Fidelis, 2019); David S. Dockery, ed., *Created in the Image of God: Applications and Implications for Our Cultural Confusion* (Nashville: Forefront, 2023); John D. Woodbridge, "The Authority of Holy Scripture: Commitments for Christian Higher Education in the Evangelical Tradition," in *Christian Higher Education: Faith, Teaching, and Learning in the Evangelical Tradition* (Wheaton: Crossway, 2018), 59–80. See the various chapters in *The Oxford Handbook of Evangelical Theology*, ed. Gerald R. McDermott (Oxford: Oxford University Press, 2010): "Politics," by Eric Gregory, 389–401; "Economics," by John Lunn, 402–17; "The Arts," by Roger Lundin, 418–33; "Science," by Alister McGrath, 434–48; "Sexuality," by Robert A. J. Gagnon, 449–64; "Race," by Timothy Tseng, 465–80; and "The Vulnerable-Abortion and Disability," by C. Ben Mitchell, 481–96. Also, see Autumn Alcott Ridenour, *Sabbath Rest as Vocation: Aging Toward Death* (London: T&T Clark, 2018).

that reflects their complexity. What some see as a cacophony, hopelessly confused, and confusing for modern appropriation is in fact inspired appreciation for the intricacy of some issues."[81] Moreover, they offer these wise words:

> Ultimately, treatment of these issues must be located within the
> entire canon, the divinely authoritative Scripture. Biblical ethics
> must take into account all that God says on a topic, not playing
> books and texts against one another or arbitrarily choosing one
> over another.[82]

We should approach Scripture with the expectation that it will lead us
sufficiently as we seek to be salt and light each day. Yet we should remember
Scripture must be read with reference to its various genres rather than as if it
contained cookbook-like instructions or was composed merely of legal code.
The primary concern of the written Word of God is to tell us who God is
and who we are, to bring us to a right relationship with God and to guide us
into true worship of God and personal Christlikeness. Let us remember that
Scripture invites us to a living relationship with God in Jesus Christ by the
power of the Holy Spirit.[83]

Living with a Holy Spirit-prompted desire, God's people respond to
the Bible's message and authority, which brings reproof and correction
(2 Tim 3:16), resulting in contrition, discipleship, and enablement for a life
of worship and service (2 Tim 3:17). Abiding in biblical authority brings
about training in righteousness that bears on Christians and their integrity
in the marketplace. Scripture guides Christians who must speak to matters
of injustice in society and in the church. It addresses families and their
commitments to one another. It speaks to ministers and teachers, calling
them to handle carefully the Word of God (2 Tim 2:15). James Boice contends that biblical preaching and teaching "that is patterned on the preaching of the apostles and other early witnesses will always be biblical in the
sense that the very words of the Bible will be the preacher's text and his
aim will be a faithful exposition and application of them," which cannot be

---

[81] M. Daniel Carroll R. and Darrell L. Bock, "The Bible and Ethics," in *The
Oxford Handbook of Evangelical Theology*, 384.
[82] Carroll R. and Bock, "The Bible and Ethics," 384.
[83] Yarnell, *Who Is the Holy Spirit?*, (see chap. 8, n. 104).

done "if the preacher is sitting in judgment on the Word rather than sitting under it."[84]

The authority of the Bible calls on us to recognize God's desire for unity, through variety, among the people of God (Eph 4:1–16; John 17; 1 Corinthians 12). It calls us to love one another (John 13:34–35) even when we disagree over the interpretation of Scripture itself.[85] We need a renewed commitment to biblical authority that enables us to relate to one another in right belief, right worship, and right practice before a watching, unbelieving world. We pray for a renewed commitment to biblical authority that will transform our performance-oriented church meetings into authentic worship and praise, rendering heartfelt service that is pleasing to God. Genuine worship must include the proclamation of the whole counsel of God's Word (Acts 20:27) grounded in its expository teaching and preaching.[86]

God's authority is vitally connected with the revelation of God. In this sense revelation and authority are two sides of the same coin. God declares his authority in his revelation, and he alone is the ultimate authority over all other lesser authorities. Thus, the greatest concern in any discussion of the Bible is its authority, its rightful role to command obedience. Any discussion of biblical authority must include an understanding of the clarity of Scripture and the sufficiency of Scripture. The doctrine of the clarity of Scripture affirms that the Bible can be understood, with the Spirit's enablement, by readers who earnestly seek to hear from and follow God. The Bible is clear enough to guide faithfully those who seek its wisdom (Ps 119:105). An affirmation of scriptural clarity should not be understood to mean that all parts are equally clear, for even the apostle Peter admitted as much when he wrote that some things in Paul's letters present challenges (1 Pet 3:16). Affirming the Bible's clarity does not mean that the Scripture must not be

---

[84] James M. Boice, "The Preacher and God's Word," in *The Foundation of Biblical Authority*, ed. J. M. Boice (Grand Rapids: Zondervan, 1978), 133–34.

[85] Rhyne Putman, *When Doctrine Divides the People of God: An Evangelical Approach to Theological Diversity* (Wheaton: Crossway, 2020); Putman, *The Method of Christian Theology: A Basic Introduction* (Nashville: B&H, 2021); Yarnell, *The Formation of Christian Doctrine*.

[86] Daniel I. Block, *For the Glory of God: Recovering a Biblical Theology of Worship* (Grand Rapids: Baker, 2016).

studied, interpreted, and taught to others (Acts 17:11; 2 Tim 3:15–16).[87] Maintaining the clarity of Scripture insists on and magnifies the role of the Holy Spirit in interpretation. As Donald Bloesch observes, "Scripture is clear when we submit to its authority and live in the light of its promises."[88]

Illumination is that work of the Holy Spirit whereby he makes the Bible understandable and applicable to believers (1 Cor 2:14). Apart from the work of the Spirit, we will not grasp the meaning, power, and significance of Scripture. Robert Plummer notes "the Spirit brings to the Christian greater cognitive understanding of the biblical text."[89] When followers of Christ approach the Scriptures with the humble desire to listen, learn, and obey, and are willing to work hard to interpret the meaning of the biblical passage, they can obtain sufficient understanding of Scripture.[90] The Spirit impresses upon the conscience of believers that the teaching of Scripture is indeed true, applicable, and incumbent on the reader. Mark Strom insightfully suggests that in and through the reading of Scripture, "the Spirit's presence and ministry assures us of our union with Jesus, of his Father's acceptance of us, and of the reality of the kingdom to which we now belong as he changes us into the image of Jesus (Rom 8:12–27; Gal 5:22)."[91]

VII. Final Conclusion

Finally, we conclude that the Bible remains the ultimate standard of authority for God's people and that the Bible's authoritative message remains imminently practical and applicable. Scripture can and does communicate across the cultural, geographical, and temporal differences between the ancient biblical world and our twenty-first-century context. Scripture is authoritative and practicable as it is rightfully and faithfully interpreted under the guidance of God the Holy Spirit who originally inspired it.[92]

---

[87] Dockery, "Special Revelation," 145–53 (see introduction, n. 24).

[88] Bloesch, *Holy Scripture*, 193 (see introduction, n. 2).

[89] Plummer, *40 Questions about Interpreting the Bible* (see introduction, n. 26).

[90] Grudem, *Systematic Theology*, 105–11 (see introduction, n. 27); Frame, *The Doctrine of the Word of God*, (see introduction, n. 27).

[91] Strom, *The Symphony of Scripture*, 212 (see introduction, n. 28).

[92] Andreas Köstenberger, *Invitation to Biblical Interpretation: Exploring the Hermeneutical Triad of History, Literature, and Theology* (Grand Rapids: Kregel,

As demonstrated in previous chapters, the Holy Spirit of God inspired the biblical writers to write the biblical text for our benefit. The Holy Spirit also leads us to recognize the authority of Scripture as the very Word of God. The Holy Spirit illumines our minds and hearts to understand the Bible's truthful and significant content. And the Holy Spirit leads us today to respond in obedience to the canonical text's message by living out the gospel with integrity in true faith.

We demonstrate our concern for biblical authority not only by careful biblical interpretation but also by careful biblical application in authentic worship, in faithful discipleship, in personal repentance, and in continual prayer. We must thus seek to understand and apply Scripture so that we may know and exalt God, so that we may think seriously and coherently about all aspects of life in order to love and serve God and others well, and so that we may take the good news of Jesus Christ to the ends of the earth for the glory of God.[93]

We pray that our book has helped you recognize that the Holy Bible is the written Word of God which affirms the great responsibility laid on all humanity through general revelation and which clearly discloses the special revelation of God to Israel and supremely in Jesus Christ. We pray you recognize the Bible is both divine and human by reason of its analogical relation to Jesus Christ, who is fully divine and fully human, and who died and rose again for the salvation of those who believe. We pray you have become convinced that Scripture was granted by the grace of the divine Trinity to us through the inspiration of the Holy Spirit. And we pray that you know that it is by the illumination of the Holy Spirit that we can understand and apply the Bible's historically grounded and eternally relevant message not only yesterday but every day. We offer it as a spiritual service to the glory of the trinitarian God, the one God who is the Father and the Son and the Holy Spirit.

2019); R. B. Jamieson and Tyler R. Wittman, *Biblical Reasoning: Christological and Trinitarian Rules for Exegesis* (Grand Rapids: Baker, 2022); Reno, *The End of Interpretation* (see introduction, 36).

[93] Matt Queen, *Recapturing Evangelism: A Biblical-Theological Approach* (Nashville: B&H, 2023); Craig Ott, *Teaching and Learning Across Cultures: A Guide to Theory and Practice* (Grand Rapids: Baker, 2021); Block, *For the Glory of God*; J. T. English, *Deep Discipleship: How the Church Can Make Whole Disciples of Jesus* (Nashville: B&H, 2020).

BIBLIOGRAPHY

Abraham, William J. *Canon and Criterion in Christian Theology*. Oxford: Oxford University Press, 1998.

———. "Intention and the Logic of Interpretation." *Asbury Theological Journal* 43, no. 1 (1988): 11–25.

Aland, Kurt, and Barbara Aland. *The Text of the New Testament: An Introduction to the Critical Editions and to the Theory and Practice of Modern Textual Criticism*. 2nd ed. Grand Rapids: Eerdmans, 1995.

Aldridge, J. W. *The Hermeneutics of Erasmus*. Richmond: John Knox, 1966.

Alexander, T. Desmond. *From Eden to the New Jerusalem*. Grand Rapids: Kregel, 2009.

Allert, Craig D. "The State of the New Testament Canon in the Second Century: Putting Tatian's Diatessaron in Perspective." *Bulletin of Biblical Research* 9 (1999): 1–18.

Allison, Gregg. *Historical Theology*. Grand Rapids: Zondervan, 2011.

Althaus, Paul. *The Theology of Martin Luther*. Translated by Robert C. Schultz. Philadelphia: Fortress, 1966.

An Orthodox Creed: Or, A Protestant Confession of Faith. London, 1679. Reprint, Fort Worth: Center for Theological Research, 2006.

Anselm of Canterbury. *The Major Works*. Edited by Brian Davies and G. R. Evans. New York: Oxford University Press, 1998.

Aquinas, Thomas. *Inaugural Lectures: Commendation and Division of Sacred Scripture*. Translated by Ralph McInerny. New York: Penguin, 1998.

———. *On Interpretation.* Translated by J. T. Oesterle. Milwaukee: Marquette University Press, 1962.

———. *Summa Theologica.* Translated by Fathers of the English Dominican Province. Westminster, MD: Christian Classics, 1981.

———. *Summa Contra Gentiles.* Translated by Anton C. Pegis. 5 vols. Notre Dame, IN: University of Notre Dame Press, 1975.

———. *The Disputed Questions on Truth.* Translated by Robert W. Mulligan, James V. McGlynn, and Robert W. Schmidt. 3 vols. Chicago: Henry Regnery, 1952–1954.

Archer, Gleason L. Jr. *A Survey of Old Testament Introduction.* Rev. ed. Chicago: Moody, 1994.

———. *The Encyclopedia of Bible Difficulties.* Grand Rapids: Zondervan, 1982.

———. "The Witness of the Bible to Its Own Inerrancy." In *The Foundation of Biblical Authority.* Edited by James Montgomery Boice. Grand Rapids: Zondervan, 1978.

Arndt, W., F. W. Danker, W. Bauer, and F. W. Gingrich. *A Greek-English Lexicon of the New Testament and Other Early Christian Literature.* 3rd ed. Chicago: University of Chicago Press, 2000.

Ashcraft, Morris. *Christian Faith and Beliefs.* Nashville: Broadman, 1984.

Atkinson, Nigel. *Richard Hooker and the Authority of Scripture, Tradition and Reason: Reformed Theologian of the Church of England?* Carlisle, Cumbria, UK: Paternoster, 1997.

Augustine, Saint. *Confessions.* Translated by R. S. Pine-Coffin. New York: Penguin, 1961.

———. *Homilies on the Gospel of John,* in *Nicene and Post-Nicene Fathers.* Edited by Philip Schaff. series I. vol. 7 New York: Christian Literature, 1888.

———. *On Christian Teaching.* Translated by R. P. H. Green. New York: Oxford University Press, 1999.

———. *The City of God.* Translated by Marcus Dods. New York: Modern Library, 1993.

———. *The Trinity.* Translated by Edmund Hill. Brooklyn, NY: New City, 1991.

Averbeck, Richard. *The Old Testament Law for the Life of the Church: Reading the Torah in Light of Christ.* Downers Grove: IVP, 2022.

Bahnsen, Greg L. "The Inerrancy of the Autographa." In *Inerrancy.* Edited by Norman L. Geisler. Grand Rapids: Zondervan, 1980.

Bailey, Justin A. *Interpreting Your World: Five Lenses for Engaging Culture.* Grand Rapids: Baker, 2022.

Baker, D. L. *Two Testaments, One Bible: The Theological Relationship Between the Old and New Testaments.* Rev. ed. 1976; Downers Grove: IVP, 1993.

Balogh, Amy, Dan Cole, and Wendy Widder. "Source Criticism." In *Social and Historical Approaches to the Bible.* Edited by Douglas Mangum and Amy Balogh. Lexham Methods Series. Bellingham, WA: Lexham, 2019.

Balogh, Amy, and Douglas Mangum. "Introducing Biblical Criticism." In *Social and Historical Approaches to the Bible.* Edited by Douglas Mangum and Amy Balogh. Lexham Methods Series. Bellingham, WA: Lexham, 2019.

Barnett, Paul. *The Second Epistle to the Corinthians.* The New International Commentary on the New Testament. Grand Rapids: Eerdmans, 1997.

Barnstone, Willis, and Marvin Meyer. *The Gnostic Bible.* Boston: Shambhala, 2003.

Barr, James. *Holy Scripture: Canon, Authority, Criticism.* New York: Oxford University Press, 1983.

———. *Old and New in Interpretation.* London: SCM, 1966.

———. "Revelation through History in the Old Testament and in Modern Theology." *Interpretation* 17, no. 2 (April 1963): 193–205.

Barrett, C. K. *The Epistle to the Romans.* Harper's New Testament Commentaries. New York: Harper & Row, 1957.

———. "The Old Testament in the New." In *Cambridge History of the Bible*. vol. 1. Cambridge: Cambridge University Press, 1970.

Barshinger, David P., and Douglas A. Sweeney, eds. *Jonathan Edwards and Scripture: Biblical Exegesis in British North America*. Oxford: Oxford University Press, 2018.

Barth, Karl. *Anselm: Fides Quarens Intellectum: Anselm's Proof of the Existence of God in the Context of His Theological Scheme*. Translated by Ian W. Robertson. London: SCM, 1960.

———. *Church Dogmatics*. Edited by Geoffrey W. Bromiley and Thomas F. Torrance. London: T&T Clark, 2004.

———. *Homiletics*. Translated by Geoffrey W. Bromiley and Donald E. Daniels. Louisville: Westminster John Knox, 1991.

———. *Rudolf Bultmann: Ein Versuch ihn zu Verstehen, Theologischen Studien und Kritiken* 34. Zürich: Evangelischer Verlag, 1952.

———. *The Word of God and the Word of Man*. Translated by Douglas Horton. Gloucester, MA: Peter Smith, 1978.

Bartholomew, Craig G. *Introducing Biblical Hermeneutics: A Comprehensive Framework for Hearing God in Scripture*. Grand Rapids: Baker, 2015.

Bartholomew, Craig G., and Heath A. Thomas, eds. *A Manifesto for Theological Interpretation*. Grand Rapids: Baker, 2016.

Bauckham, Richard. *Jesus and the Eyewitnesses: The Gospels as Eyewitness Testimony*. 2nd ed. Grand Rapids: Eerdmans, 2017.

Bauer, Walter. *A Greek-English Lexicon of the New Testament and Other Early Christian Literature*. Translated by Frederick William Danker. 3rd ed. Chicago: University of Chicago Press, 2000.

Bauerschmidt, Frederick Christian. *Thomas Aquinas: Faith, Reason, and Following Christ*. New York: Oxford University Press, 2013.

Bavinck, Herman. *Reformed Dogmatics: Prolegomena*. Edited by John Bolt. Translated by John Vriend. 4 vols. Grand Rapids: Baker, 2003.

Beale, Gregory K. *A New Testament Biblical Theology: The Unfolding of the Old Testament in the New.* Grand Rapids: Baker, 2011.

———. *Handbook on the New Testament Use of the Old Testament: Exegesis and Interpretation.* Grand Rapids: Baker, 2012.

———. *The Erosion of Inerrancy in Evangelicalism: Responding to New Challenges to Biblical Authority.* Wheaton: Crossway, 2008.

———, ed. *The Right Doctrine from the Wrong Text? Essays on the Use of the Old Testament in the New.* Grand Rapids: Baker, 1994.

Beale, G. K., and D. A. Carson. *Commentary on the New Testament Use of the Old Testament.* Grand Rapids: Baker, 2007.

Beale, G. K., and Benjamin L. Gladd. *Hidden but Now Revealed: A Biblical Theology of Mystery.* Downers Grove: IVP, 2014.

Beasley-Murray, George. R. *John.* Word Biblical Commentary. Waco: Word, 1987.

Beeke, Joel R., and Paul M. Smalley. *Reformed Systematic Theology: Revelation and God.* Wheaton: Crossway, 2019.

Behr, John. *Irenaeus of Lyons: Identifying Christianity.* New York: Oxford University Press, 2013.

Bentley, J. H. *Humanist and Holy Writ.* Princeton: Princeton University Press, 1983.

Bergen, Doris L. *The Twisted Cross: The German Christian Movement in the Third Reich.* Chapel Hill: University of North Carolina Press, 1996.

Bergen, Robert D. *1, 2 Samuel*, New American Commentary. Nashville: Broadman, 1996.

Berkouwer, G. C. *Studies in Dogmatics: Holy Scripture.* Grand Rapids: Eerdmans, 1975.

Biblia Hebraica Stuttgartensia. Edited by A. Alt, O. Eißfeldt, P. Kahle, R. Kittel et al. Stuttgart: Deutsche Bibelgesellschaft, 1984.

Biblia Sacra Utriusque Testamenti Editio Hebraica et Graeca. Stuttgart: Deutsche Bibelgesellschaft, 1994.

Bingham, D. Jeffrey. "Biblical Inspiration, Authority, and Canonicity." In *Theology, Church, and Ministry*. Edited by David S. Dockery. Nashville: B&H, 2017.

———. "One God, One Christ, One Salvation: Irenaeus 'The Peacemaker' was the Early Church's Best Warrior against the Gnostic Heresy." *Christian History and Biography* 96 (Fall 2007): 18–21.

Bird, Chad. *The Christ Key: Unlocking the Centrality of Christ in the Old Testament*. Irvine, CA: 1517 Publications, 2021.

Bird, Michael F. *What Christians Ought to Believe: An Introduction to Christian Doctrine through the Apostles' Creed*. Grand Rapids: Zondervan, 2016.

Black, C. Clifton. "Biblical Theology Revisited: An Internal Debate." *Interpretation* 70, no. 4 (October 2016): 399–416.

Black, David A., and David S. Dockery, ed. *New Testament Criticism and Interpretation*. Grand Rapids: Zondervan, 1991.

Blocher, Henri. "God and Scripture Writers: The Question of Double Authorship." In *The Enduring Authority of the Christian Scriptures*. Edited by D. A. Carson. Grand Rapids: Eerdmans, 2016.

———. "The 'Analogy of Faith' in the Study of Scripture." In *The Challenge of Evangelical Theology*. Edinburgh: Rutherford House, 1987.

Block, Daniel I. *Covenant: The Framework of God's Plan of Redemption*. Grand Rapids: Baker, 2021.

———. *For the Glory of God: Recovering a Biblical Theology of Worship*. Grand Rapids: Baker, 2016.

———. "Old Testament Theology." In *Theology, Church, and Ministry*. Edited by David S. Dockery. Nashville: B&H, 2017.

Bloesch, Donald G. *A Theology of Word and Spirit: Authority and Method in Theology*. Christian Foundations. Downers Grove: IVP, 1992.

———. *Essentials of Evangelical Theology: Volume 1: God, Authority, and Salvation*. 2 vols. San Francisco: Harper and Row, 1978.

————. *Holy Scripture: Revelation, Inspiration & Interpretation*. Downers Grove: IVP, 1994.

————. *Jesus Christ: Savior and Lord*. Downers Grove: IVP, 2005.

Blomberg, Craig L. "The Limits of Harmonization." In *Hermeneutics, Authority, and Canon*. Edited by D. A. Carson and John D. Woodbridge. Grand Rapids: Zondervan, 1986.

Boice, James Montgomery. "The Preacher and God's Word." In *The Foundation of Biblical Authority*. Edited by J. M. Boice. Grand Rapids: Zondervan, 1978.

————. *The Sovereign God*. Downers Grove: IVP, 1978.

Bokedal, Tomas. "The Rule of Faith: Tracing Its Origins." *Journal of Theological Interpretation* 7, no. 2 (Fall 2013): 233–55.

Bouwsma, William J. *John Calvin: A Sixteenth Century Portrait*. New York: Oxford University Press, 1988.

Brackney, William H. *A Genetic History of Baptist Thought*. Macon, GA: Mercer University Press, 2004.

————. "Dan Taylor." In *The Baptists*. New York: Greenwood, 1988.

Bray, Gerald L. *Biblical Interpretation: Past and Present*. Downers Grove: IVP, 1996.

————. *Creeds, Councils, and Christ: Did the Early Christians Misrepresent Jesus?* Downers Grove: IVP, 1984.

————. *Doing Theology with the Reformers*. Downers Grove: IVP, 2019.

————. *How the Church Fathers Read the Bible: A Short Introduction*. Bellingham, WA: Lexham, 2022.

————. "Tertullian." In *Shapers of Christian Orthodoxy: Engaging with Early and Medieval Theologians*. Edited by Bradley G. Green. Downers Grove: IVP, 2010.

Brown, Colin, and Craig Evans. *History of the Quests for the Historical Jesus*. 2 vols. Grand Rapids: Zondervan, 2022.

Brown, Harold O. J. *Heresies: The Image of Christ in the Mirror of Heresy and Orthodoxy from the Apostles to the Present*. New York: Doubleday, 1984.

———. "Romanticism and the Bible." In *Challenges to Inerrancy: A Theological Response*. Edited by Gordon R. Lewis and Bruce Demarest. Chicago: Moody, 1984.

———. "The Arian Connection: Presuppositions of Errancy." In *Challenges to Inerrancy: A Theological Response*. Edited by Gordon Lewis and Bruce Demarest. Chicago: Moody, 1984.

Brown, Peter. *Augustine of Hippo: A Biography*. Los Angeles: University of California Press, 1967.

Brown, Raymond. *The "Sensus Plenior" of Sacred Scripture*. Baltimore: St. Mary's University, 1955.

Bruce, F. F. *New Testament Development of Old Testament Themes*. Grand Rapids: Eerdmans, 1968.

———. *The Acts of the Apostles: The Greek Text with Introduction and Commentary*. 2nd ed. Grand Rapids: Eerdmans, 1952.

———. *The Book of the Acts*. Rev. ed. New International Commentary on the New Testament. Grand Rapids: Eerdmans, 1988.

———. *The Canon of Scripture*. Downers Grove: IVP, 1988.

———. *The Epistles to the Colossians, to Philemon, and to the Ephesians*. The New International Commentary on the New Testament. Grand Rapids: Eerdmans, 1984.

———. *The Epistle to the Hebrews*. Rev. ed. New International Commentary on the New Testament. Grand Rapids: Eerdmans, 1990.

———. *The Gospel of John*. Grand Rapids: Eerdmans, 1983.

———. "The History of New Testament Study." In *New Testament Interpretation*. Edited by I. Howard Marshall. Grand Rapids: Eerdmans, 1977.

Brueggemann, Walter. *Truth Speaks to Power: The Countercultural Nature of Scripture*. Louisville: Westminster John Knox, 2013.

Brunner, Emil. *Revelation and Reason: The Christian Doctrine of Faith and Knowledge.* Translated by Olive Wyon. Philadelphia: Westminster, 1946.

Brunner, Emil, and Karl Barth. *Natural Theology: Comprising "Nature and Grace" by Dr. Emil Brunner and the Reply "No!" by Dr. Karl Barth.* Translated by Peter Fraenkel. 1946. Reprint, Eugene, OR: Wipf and Stock, 2002.

Bryan, Christopher. *Listening to the Bible: The Art of Faithful Biblical Interpretation.* New York: Oxford University Press, 2014.

Büchsel, Friedrich. "deō." In *Theological Dictionary of the New Testament.* Edited by Gerhard Kittel, Geoffrey W. Bromiley, and Gerhard Friedrich. 10 vols. Grand Rapids: Eerdmans, 1964.

Bultmann, Rudolf. *Jesus and the Word.* Translated by Louis Pettibone Smith and Erminie Huntress Lantero. London: Collins Fontana, 1958.

———. *Kerygma and Myth.* Edited by Hans W. Bartsch. London: SPCK, 1953.

———. *New Testament Theology.* Translated by K. Grobel. New York: Scribners, 1955.

———. *The Gospel of John: A Commentary.* Translated by G. R. Beasley-Murray, R. W. N. Hoare, and J. K. Riches. Philadelphia: Westminster Press, 1971.

———. *The History of the Synoptic Tradition.* Translated by John Marsh. New York: Harper, 1968.

Bunyan, John. *Grace Abounding to the Chief of Sinners.* London: Oliphant Anderson & Ferrier, ca 1900.

Burtner, Robert W., and Robert E. Childs, eds. *John Wesley's Theology: A Collection from His Works.* Nashville: Abingdon, 1982.

Busch, Eberhard. *The Great Passion: An Introduction to Karl Barth's Theology.* Translated by Geoffrey W. Bromiley. Grand Rapids: Eerdmans, 2004.

Bush, L. Russ, and Tom J. Nettles, *Baptists and the Bible: The Baptist Doctrines of Biblical Inspiration and Religious Authority in Historical Perspective.* Chicago: Moody, 1980.

Butterfield, Herbert. *The Origins of Modern Science 1300–1800*. Rev. ed. New York: Simon & Schuster, 1957.

Cain, William E. *The Crisis in Criticism*. Baltimore: Johns Hopkins University Press, 1984.

Caird, G. B. *The Language and Imagery of the Bible*. Philadelphia: Westminster, 1980.

Calvin, John. *Institutes of the Christian Religion*. Edited by John T. McNeill. Translated by Ford Lewis Battles. Philadelphia: Westminster, 1960.

————. *The Psalmes of David and Others, with M. John Calvin's Commentaries*. Translated by Thomas East and James Middleton. London, 1571.

Campenhausen, Hans von. *The Fathers of the Church: Combined Edition of The Fathers of the Greek Church and The Fathers of the Latin Church*. Translated by W. Kohlhammer, L. A. Garrard, and Manfred Hoffmann. Peabody, MA: Hendrickson, 2000.

————. *The Formation of the Christian Bible*. Translated by J. A. Baker. Philadelphia: Fortress Press, 1972.

Candler, Peter M. Jr. "St. Thomas Aquinas." In *Christian Theologies of Scripture: A Comparative Introduction*. Edited by Justin S. Holcomb. New York: New York University Press, 2006.

Caputo, John D. *Truth: The Search for Wisdom in the Postmodern Age*. New York: Penguin, 2016.

Carey, John J. *Carlyle Marney: A Pilgrim's Progress*. Macon, GA: Mercer University Press, 1980.

Carnell, E. J. *The Case for Orthodox Theology*. Philadelphia: Fortress, 1959.

Carroll, B. H. *Inspiration of the Bible*. New York: Revell, 1930.

Carroll, M. Daniel R., and Darrell L. Bock. "The Bible and Ethics." In *The Oxford Handbook of Evangelical Theology*. Edited by Gerald R. McDermott. Oxford: Oxford University Press, 2010.

Carson, D. A., ed. *Biblical Interpretation and the Church: The Problem of Contextualization*. Nashville: Nelson, 1984.

————. "Matthew." In *The Expositor's Bible Commentary*. Edited by Frank E. Gaebelein. 12 vols. Grand Rapids: Zondervan, 1984.

————. *Collected Writings on Scripture*. Wheaton: Crossway, 2010.

————. "Mystery and Fulfillment: Toward a More Comprehensive Paradigm of Paul's Understanding of the Old and New." In *Justification and Variegated Nomism*. Edited by D. A. Carson, Peter T. O'Brien, and Mark A. Seifried. Tübingen: Mohr Siebeck, 2004.

————. "Recent Developments in the Doctrine of Scripture." In *Collected Writings on Scripture*. Wheaton: Crossway, 2010.

————. *The Gagging of God*. Grand Rapids: Zondervan, 1996.

————. *The God Who Is There: Finding Your Place in God's Story*. Grand Rapids: Baker, 2010.

————. *The Gospel According to John*. Pillar New Testament Commentary. Grand Rapids: Eerdmans, 1991.

Carson, D. A., and H. G. M. Williamson, eds. *It Is Written: Scripture Citing Scripture. Essays in Honor of Barnabas Lindars*. Cambridge: Cambridge University Press, 1988.

Cauthen, Kenneth. *The Impact of American Religious Liberalism*. New York: Harper & Row, 1962.

Chapman, Stephen B. "The Canon Debate: What It Is and Why It Matters." *Journal of Theological Interpretation* 4, no. 2 (Fall 2010): 273–94.

Cherbonnier, Edmond La Beaume. "Is There a Biblical Metaphysic?" *Theology Today* 15, no. 4 (1959): 454–69.

Childs, Brevard S. *Biblical Theology: A Proposal*. Minneapolis: Fortress, 2002.

————. *Biblical Theology of the Old and New Testaments: Theological Reflection of the Christian Bible*. Minneapolis: Fortress, 1992.

Chillingworth, William. *The Religion of Protestants a Safe Way to Salvation*. Oxford: Leonard Lichfield, 1638.

Cho, Dongsun, Yong-Su Cho, and Jeremiah Kim. *Baptist Systematic Theology*. Seoul, Korea: Jordan, 2016.

Chute, Anthony L., Nathan A. Finn, and Michael A. G. Haykin. *The Baptist Story*. Nashville: B&H, 2015.

Clapham, Andrew. *Human Rights*. New York: Oxford University Press, 2007.

Clarke, William Newton. *An Outline of Theology*. 2nd ed. London: T&T Clark, 1900.

Cole, Graham A. *Faithful Theology: An Introduction*. Wheaton: Crossway, 2020.

———. *He Who Gives Life: The Doctrine of the Holy Spirit*. Wheaton: Crossway, 2007.

———. "*Sola Scriptura:* Some Historical and Contemporary Perspectives." *Churchman* 104, no. 1 (1990): 20–34.

Colson, Charles, and Nancy Pearcey. *How Now Shall We Live?* Wheaton: Tyndale, 1999.

Compton, Bobby D. "J. Frank Norris and Southern Baptists." *Review and Expositor* 79, no. 1 (Winter 1982): 63–84.

Conn, Harvie M. "Normativity, Relevance, and Relativism." In *Inerrancy and Hermeneutic*. Edited by Harvie M. Conn. Grand Rapids: Baker, 1988.

Conner, W. T. *Christian Doctrine*. Nashville: Broadman, 1937.

———. *Revelation and God: An Introduction to Christian Doctrine*. Nashville: Broadman, 1936.

Cottret, Bernard. *Calvin: A Biography*. Translated by M. Wallace McDonald. Grand Rapids: Eerdmans, 1995.

Cranfield, C. E. B. *Romans: A Shorter Commentary*. Grand Rapids: Eerdmans, 1985.

Criswell, W. A. *Why I Preach That the Bible Is Literally True*. Nashville: Broadman, 1969.

Crocker, Lester Gilbert. "The Problem of Truth and Falsehood in the Age of the Enlightenment." *Journal of the History of Ideas* 14, no. 4 (October 1953): 575–603.

Cross, Donald A. "Augustine's Privation Account of Evil: A Defense." *Augustinian Studies* 20 (1989): 109–28.

Cullmann, Oscar. *Christ and Time: The Primitive Christian Conception of Time and History.* Translated by Floyd V. Filson. Philadelphia: Westminster, 1950.

———. *La Tradition: Problème Exégétique, Historique et Théologique.* Paris: Delachaux et Niestlé, 1953.

Culpepper, R. Alan. "Scripture." In *A Baptist's Theology.* Edited by R. Wayne Stacy. 1999; Macon, GA: Smyth and Helwys, 2021.

Cunningham, Mary Kathleen. "Karl Barth." In *Christian Theologies of Scripture: A Comparative Introduction.* Edited by Justin S. Holcomb. New York: New York University Press, 2006.

Curtis, Thomas F. *The Human Element in the Inspiration of Sacred Scripture.* New York: Appleton, 1867.

Cushman, Robert E. "Faith and Reason in the Thought of St. Augustine." *Church History* 19, no. 4 (December 1950): 271–94.

Dagg, J. L. *A Manual of Theology.* Charleston, SC: Southern Baptist Publication Society, 1858.

Dargan, E. C. *Doctrines of the Faith: A Convenient Handbook for Use in Normal Classes, Sacred Literature Courses, and Individual Study.* Nashville: Baptist Sunday School Board, 1905.

Davidson, Richard M. *Typology in Scripture: A Study of Hermeneutical TYPOS Structures.* Berrien Springs, MI: Andrews University Press, 1981.

Davies, Brian. *The Thought of Thomas Aquinas.* New York: Oxford University Press, 1992.

Davies, Brian, and G. R. Evans., eds. "Introduction." In *Anselm of Canterbury: The Major Works.* New York: Oxford University Press, 1998.

Davies, G. Henton. "Genesis." In *The Broadman Bible Commentary.* Edited by Clifton J. Allen. Nashville: Broadman, 1969.

Davis, John Jefferson. "Contextualization and the Nature of Theology." In *The Necessity of Systematic Theology*. Edited by John Jefferson Davis. Grand Rapids: Baker, 1980.

———. *Theology Primer: Resources for the Theology Student*. Grand Rapids: Baker, 1981.

Davis, Stephen T. "What Do We Mean When We Say, 'The Bible Is True'?" In *But Is It All True? The Bible and the Question of Truth*. Edited by Alan G. Padgett and Patrick R. Kiefert. Grand Rapids: Eerdmans, 2006.

Dell, William. *The Stumbling Stone*. London: Giles Calvert, 1653.

Demarest, Bruce. "The Bible in the Enlightenment Era." In *Challenges to Inerrancy*. Edited by Gordon Lewis and Bruce Demarest. Chicago: Moody, 1984.

Dever, Mark E. "John L. Dagg." In *Theologians of the Baptist Tradition*. Edited by Timothy George and David S. Dockery. Nashville: B&H, 2001.

Dibelius, Martin. *Studies in the Acts of the Apostles*. Translated by Mary Ling. New York: Scribner, 1956.

Dickinson, Travis. *Logic and the Way of Jesus*. Nashville: B&H, 2022.

Dilday, Russell. *The Doctrine of Biblical Authority*. Nashville: Convention, 1982.

Dockery, David S. "A Fresh Look at Erasmus: Foundations for Reformation Hermeneutics." In *Evangelical Hermeneutics*. Edited by Michael Bauman and David Hall. Camp Hill, PA: Christian Publications, 1995.

———. "An (Author-Oriented) Historical Model." In *Hermeneutics for Preaching*. Edited by Raymond Bailey. Nashville: Broadman, 1992.

———. "Author? Reader? Text? Toward a Hermeneutical Synthesis." *Theological Educator* 38 (Fall 1988): 7–16.

———. *Biblical Interpretation Then and Now: Contemporary Hermeneutics in the Light of the Early Church*. Grand Rapids: Baker, 1992.

———. *Christian Scripture: An Evangelical Perspective on Inspiration, Authority, and Interpretation*. Nashville: B&H, 1995.

———, ed. *Created in the Image of God: Applications and Implications for Our Cultural Confusion*. Nashville: Forefront, 2023.

———. "Introduction." In *Architect of Evangelicalism: The Collected Writings of Carl F. H. Henry*. Bellingham, WA: Lexham, 2019.

———. "Looking Back, Looking Ahead." In *Theologians of the Baptist Tradition*. Edited by Timothy George and David S. Dockery. Nashville: B&H, 2001.

———. "Martin Luther's Christological Principle: Implications for Biblical Authority and Biblical Interpretation." In *The Reformation and the Irrepressible Word of God: Interpretation, Theology, and Practice*. Edited by Scott M. Manetsch. Downers Grove: IVP, 2019.

———. "New Testament Interpretation: A Historical Survey." In *Interpreting the New Testament*. Edited by D. A. Black and David S. Dockery. Nashville: B&H, 2001.

———. "Preaching and Hermeneutics." In *A Handbook for Contemporary Preaching*. Edited by Michael Duduit. Rev. ed. Nashville: B&H, 2018.

———. *Southern Baptist Consensus and Renewal: A Biblical, Historical, and Theological Proposal*. Nashville: B&H, 2008.

———. "Southern Baptists, Evangelicalism, and the Christian Tradition." *Baptists and the Christian Tradition: Toward an Evangelical Baptist Catholicity*. Edited by Matt Y. Emerson, Christopher W. Morgan, and Lucas Stamps. Nashville: B&H, 2020.

———. "Special Revelation." In *A Theology for the Church*. Rev. ed. Edited by Daniel L. Akin. Nashville: B&H, 2014.

———. "Study and Interpretation of the Bible." In *Foundations for Biblical Interpretation*. Edited by David S. Dockery, K. A. Mathews, and Robert B. Sloan. Nashville: B&H, 1994.

———. "The Broadus-Robertson Tradition." In *Theologians of the Baptist Tradition*. Edited by Timothy George and David S. Dockery. Nashville: B&H, 2001.

————, ed. *The Challenge of Postmodernism: An Evangelical Engagement*. Rev. ed. Grand Rapids: Baker, 2001.

————. "The Crisis of Scripture in Southern Baptist Life: Reflections on the Past, Looking to the Future." *Southern Baptist Journal of Theology* 9, no. 1 (Spring 2005): 36–53.

————. "The Divine-Human Authorship of Inspired Scripture." In *Authority and Interpretation: A Baptist Perspective*. Edited by Duane Garrett and Richard R. Melick. Grand Rapids: Baker, 1987.

————. *The Doctrine of the Bible*. Nashville: Convention, 1991.

————. "The Foundation of Reformation Hermeneutics: A Fresh Look at Erasmus." In *Evangelical Hermeneutics*. Edited by Michael Bauman and David Hall. Camp Hill, PA: Christian Publications, 1995.

————. "The History of Pre-Critical Interpretation." *Faith and Mission* 10, no. 1 (Fall 1992): 3–33.

————. "The Inerrancy and Authority of Scripture: Affirmations and Clarifications." *Theological Educator* 37 (Fall 1988): 15–36.

————. "The Revelation of God." In *The Holman Illustrated Dictionary of the Bible*. Edited by Chad Brand, Charles Draper, and Archie England. Nashville: Holman Reference, 2003.

————, ed. "The Use of the Old Testament in the New Testament." *Southwestern Journal of Theology*. Entire Fall 2021 Issue.

————. "The Value of Typological Exegesis." In *Restoring the Prophetic Mantle*. Edited by George L. Klein. Nashville: Broadman, 1992.

————. "Typological Exegesis: Beyond Abuse and Neglect." In *Reclaiming the Prophetic Mantle; Preaching the Old Testament Faithfully*. Edited by George L. Klein. Nashville: Broadman Press, 1992.

Dockery, David S., and David E. Garland. *Seeking the Kingdom: The Sermon on the Mount Made Practical for Today*. Wheaton: Harold Shaw, 1992.

Dockery David S., and George H. Guthrie. *The Holman Guide to Interpreting the Bible*. Nashville: B&H, 2004.

Dockery David S., and John Stonestreet, eds. *Life, Marriage, and Religious Liberty*. Nashville: Fidelis, 2019.

Dockery, David S., and Timothy George. *The Great Tradition of Christian Thinking*. Wheaton: Crossway, 2012.

Dodd, C. H. *The Apostolic Preaching and Its Developments: Three Lectures with an Appendix on Eschatology and History*. Rev. ed. London: Hodder and Stoughton, 1963.

Dollar, George W. *A History of Fundamentalism in America*. Greenville, SC: Bob Jones University Press, 1973.

Dorrien, Gary. *The Making of American Liberal Theology: Idealism, Realism, and Modernity, 1900–1950*. Louisville: Westminster John Knox, 2003.

Downey, Glanville. *A History of Antioch of Syria from Seleucus to the Arab Conquest*. Princeton, NJ: Princeton University Press, 1961.

Drummond, Lewis. *Spurgeon: Prince of Preachers*. Grand Rapids: Kregel, 1992.

Duesing, Jason G., and Nathan A. Finn. *Historical Theology for the Church*. Nashville: B&H, 2021.

Dulles, Avery. *Models of Revelation*. New York: Doubleday, 1983.

———. *Revelation Theology: A History*. New York: Herder and Herder, 1969.

Dunn, James D. G. "The Authority of Scripture according to Scripture." *Churchman* 96, no. 3 (1982): 201–225.

———. *Unity and Diversity in the New Testament: An Inquiry into the Character of Earliest Christianity*. London: SCM, 2006.

Duvall, J. Scott, and Daniel J. Hays. *Grasping God's Word: A Hands-On Approach to Reading, Interpreting, and Applying the Bible*. Grand Rapids: Zondervan, 2020.

East, Brad. *The Doctrine of Scripture*. Eugene, OR: Cascade, 2021.

Eddy, Matthew D., and David Knight. "Introduction." In *Natural Theology: or Evidence of the Existence and Attributes of the Deity, Collected from the*

Appearances of Nature. By William Paley. Edited by Eddy and Knight. New York: Oxford University Press, 2006.

Edwards, James R. *Between the Swastika and the Sickle: The Life, Execution, and Disappearance of Ernst Lohmeyer.* Grand Rapids: Eerdmans, 2019.

Ehrman, Bart D. *Lost Christianities: The Battles for Scripture and the Faiths We Never Knew.* New York: Oxford University Press, 2003.

Eichrodt, Walther. *Theology of the Old Testament.* Translated by J. A. Baker. 2 vols. Philadelphia: Westminster Press, 1961.

Elliott, Ralph. *Message of Genesis.* Nashville: Broadman, 1961.

———. *The "Genesis Controversy" and Continuity in Southern Baptist Chaos.* Macon, GA: Mercer University Press, 1992.

Ellis, E. Earle. *The Gospel of Luke.* Rev. ed. New Century Bible. London: Marshall, Morgan, and Scott, 1974.

———. *The Old Testament in Early Christianity: Canon and Interpretation in the Light of Modern Research.* Grand Rapids: Baker, 1991.

Ellis, Gretchen. "Form Criticism." In *Social and Historical Approaches to the Bible.* Edited by Mangum and Balogh. Lexham Methods Series. Bellingham, WA: Lexham, 2019.

Ellis, William E. *A Man of Books and a Man of the People.* Macon, GA: Mercer University Press, 1985.

English, J. T. *Deep Discipleship: How the Church Can Make Whole Disciples of Jesus.* Nashville: B&H, 2020.

Enns, Peter. *Inspiration and Incarnation.* Grand Rapids: Baker, 2005.

Erasmus, Desiderius. *Christian Humanism and the Reformation: Selected Writings.* Edited by John C. Olin. New York: Harper & Row, 1965.

———. *Praise of Folly.* Translated by Betty Radice. New York: Penguin, 1994.

Erickson, Millard J. *Christian Theology.* Grand Rapids: Baker, 2013.

————. "Donald Bloesch's Doctrine of Scripture." In *Evangelical Theology in Transition: Theologians in Dialogue with Donald Bloesch*. Edited by Elmer M. Colyer. Downers Grove: IVP, 1999.

————. "Revelation." In *Foundations for Biblical Interpretation: A Complete Library of Tools and Resources*. Edited by David S. Dockery, K. A. Mathews, and Robert B. Sloan. Nashville: B&H, 1994.

Erickson, Millard J., Paul Helseth, and Justin Taylor., eds. *Reclaiming the Evangelical Center*. Wheaton: Crossway, 2004.

Erickson, Robert P. "Emanuel Hirsch: Intellectual Freedom and the Turn toward Hitler." *Kirchliche Zeitgeschichte* 24, no. 1 (2011): 74–91.

Ernest, James D. "Athanasius of Alexandria: The Scope of Scripture in Polemical and Pastoral Context." *Vigiliae Christianae* 47, no. 4 (December 1993): 341–62.

Evans, Gillian R. *The Language and Logic of the Bible: The Earlier Middle Ages*. Cambridge: Cambridge University Press, 1984.

Fee, Gordon D. *New Testament Exegesis*. Philadelphia: Westminster, 1983.

Fee, Gordon D., and Douglas Stuart. *How to Read the Bible for All Its Worth*. Grand Rapids: Zondervan, 1982.

Feinberg, John. *Light in a Dark Place: The Doctrine of Scripture*. Foundations of Evangelical Theology. Wheaton: Crossway, 2018.

Feinberg, Paul D. "The Meaning of Inerrancy." In *Inerrancy*. Edited by Norman L. Geisler. Grand Rapids: Zondervan, 1979.

Ferguson, Everett. *The Rule of Faith: A Guide*, Cascade Companions. Eugene, OR: Wipf and Stock, 2015.

Fernandéz-Armesto, Felipe. *Truth: A History and a Guide for the Perplexed*. New York: St. Martin's Press, 1997.

Finn, Nathan A. "Scripture and Authority." In *Historical Theology for the Church*. Edited by Jason G. Duesing and Nathan A. Finn. Nashville: B&H, 2021.

Folk, E. E. *Baptist Principles: Letters to My Son.* Nashville: Baptist Sunday School Board, 1909.

"For all Scripture, inspired of God." In *The Wycliffe New Testament (1388): An Edition in Modern Spelling with an Introduction, the Original Prologues and the Epistle to the Laodiceans.* Edited by W. R. Cooper. London: The British Library, 2002.

Fowl, Stephen E. "'In Many and Various Ways': Hearing the Voice of God in the Text of Scripture." In *The Voice of God in the Text of Scripture: Explorations in Constructive Dogmatics.* Edited by Oliver D. Crisp and Fred Sanders. Grand Rapids: Zondervan, 2016.

Frame, John M. "Review of Peter Enns, *Inspiration and Incarnation.*" In *The Doctrine of the Word of God.* Phillipsburg, PA: P&R, 2010.

———. *The Doctrine of the Word of God.* Phillipsburg: P&R, 2010.

France, R. T. *Jesus and the Old Testament.* Vancouver: Regent College Press, 1992.

———. "The Formula-Quotations of Matthew 2 and the Problem of Communication." *New Testament Studies* 27, no. 2 (1981): 233–51.

———. *The Gospel of Mark.* The New International Greek Text Commentary. Grand Rapids: Eerdmans, 2002.

———. *The Gospel of Matthew.* The New International Commentary of the New Testament. Grand Rapids: Eerdmans, 2007.

Freeman, Curtis. *Contesting Catholicity: Theology for Other Baptists.* Waco: Baylor University Press, 2014.

Frei, Hans W. *The Eclipse of the Biblical Narrative: A Study in Eighteenth and Nineteenth Century Hermeneutics.* New Haven, CT: Yale University Press, 1974.

Frere, Walter Howard, and C. E. Douglas., eds. *Puritan Manifestoes: A Study of the Origin of the Puritan Revolt.* London: SPCK, 1954.

Froehlich, Karlfried. "Church History and the Bible." In *Biblical Hermeneutics in Historical Perspective.* Grand Rapids: Eerdmans, 1991.

Frost, J. M., ed. *Baptist Why and Why Not*. Nashville: Baptist Sunday School Board, 1900.

Fuller, Daniel. "The Holy Spirit's Role in Biblical Interpretation." In *Scripture, Tradition, and Interpretation*. Edited by W. Ward Gasque and William Sanford LaSor. Grand Rapids: Eerdmans, 1978.

———. *The Unity of the Bible: Unfolding God's Plan for Humanity*. Grand Rapids: Zondervan, 2000.

Gallagher, Edmon L., and John D. Meade. *The Biblical Canon Lists from Early Christianity: Texts and Analysis*. New York: Oxford University Press, 2017.

Garland, David E. *Romans*. Tyndale New Testament Commentaries. Downers Grove: IVP, 2021.

Garrett, James Leo Jr. "Reappraisal of Chalcedon." *Review and Expositor* 71, no. 1 (1974): 31–42.

———. *Baptist Theology: A Four-Century Study*. Macon, GA: Mercer University Press, 2009.

———. "Biblical Authority According to Baptist Confessions of Faith." *Review and Expositor* 76, no. 1 (Winter 1979): 43–54.

———. *Systematic Theology: Biblical, Historical, and Evangelical*. 2nd ed. 2 vols. Grand Rapids: Eerdmans, 1990.

———. "The Bible at Southwestern Seminary during Its Formative Years: A Study of H. E. Dana and W. T. Conner." *Baptist History and Heritage* 21, no. 4 (October 1986): 29–43.

———. "The Theology of Walter Thomas Conner." Th.D. dissertation, Southwestern Baptist Theological Seminary, 1954.

———. *We Baptists*. Franklin, TN: Providence House, 1999.

George, Timothy. *Galatians*. New American Commentary. Nashville: Broadman, 1994.

———. *Reading Scripture with the Reformers*. Downers Grove: IVP, 2011.

———. "The Nature of God: Being, Attributes, and Acts." In *A Theology for the Church*. Rev. ed. Edited by Daniel L. Akin. Nashville: B&H, 2014.

———. *Theology of the Reformers*. Nashville: B&H, 2013.

———. "What the Reformers Thought They Were Doing." *Modern Age* 59, no. 4 (Fall 2017): 17–26.

Gerrish, B. A. *The Old Protestantism and the New: Essays on the Reformation Heritage*. Chicago: University of Chicago Press, 1982.

Gerstner, John H. "The Contributions of Charles Hodge, B. B. Warfield, and J. Gresham Machen to the Doctrine of Inspiration." In *Challenges to Inerrancy*. Edited by Gordon Lewis and Bruce Demarest. Chicago: Moody, 1984.

Gilson, Etienne. *The Christian Philosophy of St. Thomas Aquinas*. Translated by L. K. Shook. Notre Dame, IN: University of Notre Dame Press, 1956.

Goldsworthy, Graeme. *Gospel-Centered Hermeneutics: Foundations and Principles of Evangelical Biblical Interpretation*. Downers Grove: IVP, 2006.

Goppelt, Leonhard. *TYPOS: The Typological Interpretation of the Old Testament in the New*. Translated by Donald H. Madvig. Grand Rapids: Eerdmans, 1982.

Graham, Billy. *Just as I Am: The Autobiography of Billy Graham*. San Francisco: HarperCollins, 1997.

Grant, Robert M. *A Short History of the Interpretation of the Bible*. New York: Macmillan, 1963.

Grantham, Thomas. *Christianismus Primitivus*. London: Francis Smith, 1678.

Green, Michael. *The Second Epistle General of Peter and the General Epistle of Jude: An Introduction and Commentary*. Rev. ed. Tyndale New Testament Commentaries. Grand Rapids: Eerdmans, 1987.

Gregory of Nazianzus, Saint. *On God and Christ: The Five Theological Orations and Two Letters to Cledonius*. Translated by Frederick Williams and Lionel Wickham. Crestwood, NY: St. Vladimir Seminary's Press, 2002.

Gregory the Great. *Morals on the Book of Job*. Translated by John Henry Parker, J. G. F., and J. Rivington. vol. 2. London: 1844.

Grenz, Stanley J. *Theology for the Community of God*. Nashville: B&H, 1994.

Grenz, Stanley J., and John Franke. *Beyond Foundationalism: Shaping Theology in a Postmodern Culture*. Louisville: Westminster John Knox, 2001.

Greunler, Royce G. *Meaning and Understanding*. Grand Rapids: Zondervan, 1991.

Grounds, Vernon. "Scripture in Liberation Theology: An Eviscerated Authority." In *Challenges to Inerrancy: A Theological Response*. Edited by Gordon R. Lewis and Bruce Demarest. Chicago: Moody, 1984.

Grudem, Wayne. *Systematic Theology*. Grand Rapids: Zondervan, 1994.

Grudem, Wayne, John J. Collins, and Thomas R. Schreiner. eds. *Understanding the Big Picture of the Bible: A Guide to Reading the Bible Well*. Wheaton: Crossway, 2010.

Guarino, Thomas G. "Scripture." In *Evangelicals and Catholics Together at Twenty*. Grand Rapids: Brazos, 2015.

Gundlach, Bradley. *Process and Providence: The Evolution Question at Princeton, 1845–1929*. Grand Rapids: Eerdmans, 2013.

Guthrie, Donald. *The Letter to the Hebrews: An Introduction and Commentary*. Tyndale New Testament Commentary. Grand Rapids: Eerdmans, 1983.

———. *New Testament Theology*. Downers Grove: IVP, 1981.

Guthrie, George H. *Hebrews*. The NIV Application Commentary. Grand Rapids: Zondervan, 1998.

Habets, Myk. "That Was Then, This Is Now: Reading Hebrews Retroactively." In *The Voice of God in the Voice of Scripture: Explorations in Constructive Dogmatics*. Edited by Oliver D. Crisp and Fred Sanders. Grand Rapids: Zondervan, 2016.

Hagan, Kenneth. "The History of Scripture in the Church." In *The Bible in the Churches: How Various Christians Interpret the Scriptures*. Edited by Kenneth Hagan. Milwaukee: Marquette University Press, 1994.

Haines, David. *Natural Theology: A Biblical and Historical Introduction and Defense*. Landrum, SC: Davenant, 2021.

Haldane, John. "Scotland's Gift: Philosophy, Theology, and the Gifford Lectures." *Theology Today* 63, no. 4 (January 2007): 469–76.

Hall, Christopher A. *Reading Scripture with the Church Fathers*. Downers Grove: IVP, 1998.

Hamilton, James M. Jr. *Typology: Understanding the Bible's Promise-Shaped Patterns. How the Old Testament Expectations Are Fulfilled in Christ.* Grand Rapids: Zondervan, 2022.

Hamilton, Victor P. *The Book of Genesis: Chapters 1–17.* The New International Commentary on the Old Testament. Grand Rapids: Eerdmans, 1990.

Hanson, A. T. "John's Citation of Psalm LXXXII." *New Testament Studies* 11, no. 2 (January 1965): 158–62.

———. "John's Citation of Psalm LXXXII Reconsidered." *New Testament Studies* 13, no. 4 (July 1967): 363–67.

Hanson, R. P. C. *Allegory and Event: A Study of the Sources and Significance of Origen's Interpretation of Scripture*. London: SCM, 1959.

———. *The Bible as a Norm of Faith*. Durham, UK: University of Durham Press, 1963.

———. *Tradition in the Early Church*. London: SCM, 1962.

Harmon, Steven R. *Baptist Identity and the Ecumenical Future: Story, Tradition, and the Recovery of Tradition*. Waco: Baylor University Press, 2016.

Harnack, Adolf von. *The History of Dogma*. Reprint, Eugene, OR: Wipf and Stock, 2020.

———. *What Is Christianity?* 2nd ed. Translated by Thomas Bailey Saunders. New York: Putnam, 1904.

Harris, Dana M. "'Today If You Hear My Voice': The Spirit Speaking in Hebrews–Implications for Inerrancy." *Presbyterion* 45, no. 1 (2019): 108–27.

Harris, R. Laird. *Inspiration and Canonicity of the Bible: An Exegetical and Historical Study.* Grand Rapids: Zondervan, 1971.

Harrison, Carol. "Augustine." In *Dictionary for Theological Interpretation of the Bible.* Grand Rapids: Baker, 2005.

Harwood, Adam. *Christian Theology: Biblical, Historical, and Systematic.* Bellingham, WA: Lexham, 2022.

Hawkins, O. S. *In the Name of God: The Colliding Lives, Legends, and Legacies of J. Frank Norris and George W. Truett.* Nashville: B&H, 2021.

Haydon, Ron, and David Schreiner. "Canonical Criticism." In *Literary Approaches to the Bible.* Edited by Douglas Mangum and Douglas Estes. Lexham Methods Series. Bellingham, WA: Lexham, 2017.

Haykin, Michael A. G. "John Sutcliff and the Concert of Prayer." *Reformation and Revival* 1, no. 3 (1992): 65–83.

———. "'Until the Spirit be poured upon us from on High': Prayer and Revival among the English Particular Baptists in the Eighteenth Century." *Presbyterian and Reformed Journal* 12, no. 1 (January 2020): 75–95.

Hays, Richard B. *Echoes of Scripture in the Gospels.* Waco: Baylor University Press, 2016.

———. *Echoes of Scripture in the Letters of Paul.* New Haven, CT: Yale University Press, 1989.

———. *Reading Backwards: Figural Christology and the Fourfold Gospel Witness.* Waco: Baylor University Press, 2014.

———. *Reading with the Grain of Scripture.* Grand Rapids: Eerdmans, 2020.

Heen, Erik M. "Scripture." In *Dictionary of Luther and the Lutheran Tradition.* Edited by Timothy J. Wengert. Grand Rapids: Baker, 2017.

Heick, Otto W. *A History of Christian Thought*. 2 vols. Philadelphia: Muhlenberg, 1946.

Heine, Ronald E. *Origen: Scholarship in Service of the Church*. New York: Oxford University Press, 2010.

Helm, Paul. "The Idea of Inerrancy." In *Enduring Authority of the Christian Scripture*. Edited by D. A. Carson. Grand Rapids: Eerdmans, 2016.

Hendricks, William L. "Learning from Beauty." *Southwestern Journal of Theology* 29, no. 3 (1987): 19–27.

Hengel, Martin. *The Four Gospels and the One Gospel of Jesus Christ*. Translated by John Bowden. Harrisburg, PA: Trinity Press International, 2000.

Henry, Carl F. H. *God, Revelation, and Authority*. 6 vols. Waco: Word, 1976–83.

———, ed. *Jesus of Nazareth: Savior and Lord*. Grand Rapids: Eerdmans, 1966.

———. "New Dimensions in Christology." In *New Dimensions in Evangelical Thought*. Edited by David S. Dockery. Downers Grove: IVP, 1998.

———. *Personal Idealism and Strong's Theology*. Wheaton: VanKampen, 1951.

———. "The Authority and Inspiration of the Bible." *Expositor's Bible Commentary*. Edited by F. E. Gaebelein. 12 vols. Grand Rapids: Zondervan, 1979.

———. *The Identity of Jesus of Nazareth*. Nashville: Broadman, 1992.

Hensley, Jeffrey. "Friedrich Schleiermacher" In *Christian Theologies of Scripture: A Comparative Introduction*. Edited by Justin S. Holcomb. New York: New York University Press, 2006.

Hesselgrave, David. *Communicating Christ Cross-Culturally*. Grand Rapids: Zondervan, 1978.

———. "Contextualization and Revelational Epistemology." In *Hermeneutics, Inerrancy, and the Bible*. Edited by Earl D. Radmacher and Robert D. Preuss. Grand Rapids: Zondervan, 1986.

Hibbs, Pierce Taylor. "World through Word: Towards a Linguistic Ontology." *The Westminster Theological Journal* 79, no. 2 (Fall 2017): 345–64.

Higton, Mike. "Hans Frei." In *Christian Theologies of Scripture: A Comparative Introduction*. Edited by Justin S. Holcomb. New York: New York University Press, 2006.

Hillerbrand, Hans J., ed. *The Reformation: A Narrative History Related by Contemporary Observers and Participants*. Reprint, Grand Rapids: Baker, 1978.

Hinson, E. Glenn. "Eric Charles Rust: Apostle to an Age of Science and Technology." In *Science, Faith, and Revelation: An Approach to Christian Philosophy*. Edited by Robert Patterson. Nashville: Broadman, 1979.

Hirsch, E. D. Jr. *The Aims of Interpretation*. Chicago: University of Chicago Press, 1976.

———. *Validity in Interpretation*. New Haven, CT: Yale University Press, 1967.

Hitchens, Christopher. *Thomas Paine's Rights of Man: A Biography*. New York: Grove, 2006.

Hobbs, Hershel. H. *Hebrews: Challenges to Bold Discipleship*. Fincastle, VA: Scripture Truth, 2002.

———. *My Faith and Message*. Nashville: Broadman, 1993.

———. "Southern Baptists and Confessionalism: A Comparison of the Origins and Contents of the 1925 and 1963 Confessions." *Review and Expositor* 76, no. 1 (Winter 1979): 55–68.

Hodge, A. A., and B. B. Warfield. "Inspiration." *The Presbyterian Review* 2, no. 6 (1881): 225–60.

Hodge, Charles. *What Is Darwinism?: And Other Writings on Science and Religion*. New York: Scribner, 1874.

Hodges, Louis Igou. "Scripture." In *New Dimensions in Evangelical Thought*. Edited by David S. Dockery. Downers Grove: IVP, 1998.

Holmes, Stephen R. *Listening to the Past: The Place of Tradition in Theology.* Grand Rapids: Baker, 2002.

Honeycutt, Roy L. "Biblical Authority: A Treasured Heritage." *Review and Expositor* 83, no. 4 (Fall 1986): 605–622.

Hooker, Morna D. *Studying the New Testament.* Minneapolis: Augsburg, 1982.

Horton, Michael S. *Pilgrim Theology: Core Doctrines for Christian Disciples.* Grand Rapids: Zondervan, 2011.

———. "Theologies of Scripture in the Reformation and Counter-Reformation: An Introduction." In *Christian Theologies of Scripture: A Comparative Introduction.* Edited by Justin S. Holcomb. New York: New York University Press, 2006.

Horton, Susan R. *Interpreting Interpreting.* Baltimore: Johns Hopkins University Press, 1979.

Huelsman, Dale B. "The Nature and Function of Holy Scripture as Discussed in Nineteenth Century Lutheran Free Conferences: Part One." *Concordia Historical Institute Quarterly* 76, no. 3 (Fall 2003): 163–180.

Huey, F. B. Jr. *Jeremiah and Lamentations.* New American Commentary. Nashville: Broadman, 1993.

Hull, William E. "Shall We Call the Bible Infallible?" in *Perspectives in Religious Studies* 37, no. 2 (Summer 2010): 207–13.

Hunter, A. M. *The Unity of the New Testament.* London: SCM, 1957.

Hurst, John F. *History of Rationalism.* New York: Eaton and Mains, 1865.

Israel, Jonathan I. *Radical Enlightenment: Philosophy and the Making of Modernity 1650–1750.* New York: Oxford University Press, 2001.

Jacobson, Rolf A. "Psalm 8: A Natural Question." In *The Book of Psalms.* New International Commentary on the Old Testament. Edited by Nancy L. deClaissé-Walford, Rolf A. Jacobson, and Beth LaNeel Tanner. Grand Rapids: Eerdmans, 2014.

———. "Psalm 19: Tune My Heart to Sing Your Praise." In *The Book of Psalms*. New International Commentary on the Old Testament. Edited by Nancy L. deClaissé-Walford, Rolf A. Jacobson, and Beth LaNeel Tanner. Grand Rapids: Eerdmans, 2014.

James, Robison B., ed. *The Unfettered Word*. Waco: Word, 1987.

James, Robison B., and David S. Dockery, eds. *Beyond the Impasse? Scripture, Interpretation, and Theology in Baptist Life*. Nashville: B&H, 1992.

Jeffrey, David Lyle. *We Were a Peculiar People Once: Confessions of an Old-Time Baptist*. Waco: Baylor University Press, 2023.

Jamieson R. B., and Tyler R. Wittman. *Biblical Reasoning: Christological and Trinitarian Rules for Exegesis*. Grand Rapids: Baker, 2022.

Jenkins, Philip. *The Lost History of Christianity: The Thousand-Year Golden Age of the Church in the Middle East, Africa, and Asia—And How It Died*. San Francisco: HarperOne, 2009.

Jensen, Peter. *The Revelation of God*. Contours of Christian Theology. Downers Grove: IVP, 2002.

Jenson, Robert W. *A Theology in Outline: Can These Bones Live?* Oxford: Oxford University Press, 2016.

Johnson, Elliot E. *Expository Hermeneutics: An Introduction*. Grand Rapids: Zondervan, 1990.

Johnson, Gary L. W., and Ronald N. Gleason. *Reforming or Confirming? Post-Conservative Evangelical Theology and the Emerging Church*. Wheaton: Crossway, 2008.

Johnson, S. Lewis Jr. *The Old Testament in the New: An Argument for Biblical Inspiration*. Grand Rapids: Zondervan, 1980.

Jowett, Benjamin. "The Interpretation of Scripture." In *Religious Thought in the Nineteenth Century: Illustrated from Writers of the Period*. Bernard M. G. Reardon. New York: Cambridge University Press, 1966.

Juel, Donald. *Messianic Exegesis: Christological Interpretation of the Old Testament in Early Christianity*. Philadelphia: Fortress, 1988.

Kaiser, Walter C. Jr. "Hermeneutics and Evangelical Theology." In *Building on the Foundations of Evangelical Theology: Essays in Honor of John S. Feinberg*. Edited by Gregg R. Allison and Stephen J. Wellum. Wheaton: Crossway, 2015.

———. *Recovering the Unity of the Bible: One Continuous Story, Plan, and Purpose*. Grand Rapids: Zondervan, 2015.

———. *The Promise-Plan of God: A Biblical Theology of the Old and New Testaments*. Grand Rapids: Zondervan, 2008.

Kant, Immanuel. *An Answer to the Question: What Is Enlightenment?* Translated by H. B. Nisbet. New York: Penguin Books, 2009.

Kantzer, Kenneth S. "Evangelicals and the Doctrine of Inerrancy." In *The Foundation of Biblical Authority*. Grand Rapids: Zondervan, 1978.

———. "Systematic Theology as a Practical Discipline" In *Doing Theology for the People of God: Studies of J. I. Packer*. Edited by Donald Lewis and Alister McGrath. Downers Grove: IVP, 1996.

Kavin, Rowe C. "What If It Were True? Why Study the New Testament." *New Testament Studies* 68, no. 2 (April 2022): 144–55.

Keener, Craig S. *Spirit Hermeneutics: Reading Scripture in Light of Pentecost*. Grand Rapids: Eerdmans, 2016.

Kelly, J. N. D. *Early Christian Doctrines*. Rev. ed. New York: HarperCollins, 1960.

———. *Jerome: His Life, Writings, and Controversies*. Peabody, MA: Hendrickson, 1996.

Kim, Brittany and Charlie Trimm. *Understanding Old Testament Theology: Mapping the Terrain of Recent Approaches*. Grand Rapids: Zondervan, 2020.

Kim, Whan. "The Reliability and Authority of the Bible." In *ESV Global Study Bible*. Edited by J. I. Packer, Wayne Grudem, and Ajith Fernando. Wheaton: Crossway, 2012.

King, Martin Luther Jr. "Letter from Birmingham City Jail (1963)." In *A Testament of Hope: The Essential Writings and Speeches of Martin Luther*

King Jr. Edited by James Melvin Washington. New York: HarperCollins, 1991.

Kirk, Kenneth E. *The Epistle to the Romans in the Revised Version with Introduction and Commentary.* The Clarendon Bible. Oxford: Oxford University Press, 1937.

Klein, William W., Craig L. Blomberg, and Robert L. Hubbard Jr. *Introduction to Biblical Interpretation.* Dallas: Word, 1993.

Klooster, Fred H. "The Role of the Holy Spirit in the Hermeneutic Process: The Relationship of the Spirit's Illumination to Biblical Interpretation." In *Hermeneutics, Inerrancy, and the Bible.* Edited by Earl D. Radmacher and Robert D. Preus. Grand Rapids: Academie Books, 1984.

Knight, George III. *The Pastoral Epistles.* The New International Greek Testament Commentary. Grand Rapids: Eerdmans, 1992.

Kolb, Robert, and Timothy J. Wengert, eds. *The Book of Concord: The Confessions of the Evangelical Lutheran Church.* Translated by Charles Arand, Eric Gritsch, Robert Kolb, William Russell, James Schaaf, Jane Strohl, and Timothy J. Wengert. Minneapolis: Fortress, 2000.

Köstenberger, Andreas. "Editorial." *Journal of the Evangelical Theological Society* 55, no. 1 (March 2012): 1–5.

———. *Invitation to Biblical Interpretation: Exploring the Hermeneutical Triad of History, Literature, and Theology.* Grand Rapids: Kregel, 2019.

Kreider, Glenn R., and Michael J. Svigel. *A Practical Primer on Theological Method: Table Manners for Discussing God, His Works, and His Ways.* Grand Rapids: Zondervan, 2019.

Kruger, Michael J. *The Question of Canon: Challenging the Status Quo in the New Testament Debate.* Downers Grove: IVP, 2013.

Kruse, Colin G. *John: An Introduction and Commentary.* Tyndale New Testament Commentary. Downers Grove: IVP, 2003.

Kynes, William, and Greg Strand. *Evangelical Convictions.* Minneapolis: Free Church Publications, 2011.

Kyrtatis, Dimitris J. "Historical Aspects of the Formation of the New Testament Canon." In *Canon and Canonicity: The Formation and Use of Scripture*. Edited by Einar Thomassen. Copenhagen: Museum Tusculanum Press, 2010.

Ladd, George Eldon. "Biblical Theology, History of." In *The International Standard Bible Encyclopedia*. Edited by Geoffrey W. Bromiley. 4 vols. Grand Rapids: Eerdmans, 1979.

———. *Theology of the New Testament*. Grand Rapids: Eerdmans, 1974.

Langsdorf, Lenore. "Current Paths Toward an Objective Hermeneutic." *Criswell Theological Review* 2 (1987): 145–54.

LaSor, William Sanford. "The *Sensus Plenior* and Biblical Interpretation." In *Scripture, Tradition, and Interpretation*. Edited by W. Ward Gasque and William Sanford LaSor. Grand Rapids: Eerdmans, 1978.

LaSor, William Sanford, David Allan Hubbard, and Frederic William Bush. *Old Testament Survey: The Message, Form, and Background of the Old Testament*. Grand Rapids: Eerdmans, 1982.

Latourette, Kenneth Scott. *A History of Christianity*. Rev. ed. Peabody, MA: Prince Press, 2007.

Lawrence, J. B. "The Bible, Our Creed." Southern Baptist Home Missions. Nashville: Convention, 1957.

———. "The Word and Words of God." Southern Baptist Home Missions. Nashville: Convention, 1952.

Lawrence, Michael. *Biblical Theology in the Life of the Church*. Wheaton: Crossway, 2010.

Lea, Thomas D., and Hayne P. Griffin Jr. *1, 2 Timothy, Titus*. The New American Commentary. Nashville: B&H, 1992.

Lee, Gregory W. *Today When You Hear His Voice: Scripture, the Covenants, and the People of God*. Grand Rapids: Eerdmans, 2016.

Lee, R. G. *The Word of God: Not Broken and Not Bound*. Orlando: Christ for the World, 1930.

Legaspi, Michael C. *The Death of Scripture and the Rise of Biblical Studies.* New York: Oxford University Press, 2011.

Leith, John H. "John Calvin: Theologian of the Bible." *Interpretation* 25, no. 3 (July 1971): 329–44.

Leithart, Peter J. "That Eminent Pagan: Calvin's Use of Cicero in Institutes 1.1–5." *The Westminster Theological Journal* 52 (1990): 1–12.

Leonard, Bill J. *God's Last and Only Hope.* Grand Rapids: Eerdmans, 1990.

Leonard, Jeffery. "Redaction Criticism." In *Social and Historical Approaches to the Bible.* Edited by Mangum and Balogh. Lexham Methods Series. Bellingham, WA: Lexham, 2019.

Levering, Matthew. *Participatory Biblical Exegesis: A Theology of Biblical Interpretation.* Notre Dame, IN: University of Notre Dame Press, 2008.

Lewis, Jack P. "Jamnia after Forty Years." *Hebrew Union College Annual* 70–71 (1999–2000): 233–59.

Lindbeck, George. *The Nature of Doctrine: Religion and Theology in a Postliberal Age.* Philadelphia: Westminster John Knox, 1985.

Lindsell, Harold. *Battle for the Bible.* Grand Rapids: Zondervan, 1976.

Linnemann, Eta. *Historical Criticism of the Bible: Methodology or Ideology: Reflections of a Bultmannian Turned Evangelical.* Translated by Robert W. Yarbrough. Grand Rapids: Baker, 1990.

———. *Is There a Synoptic Problem? Rethinking the Literary Dependence of the First Three Gospels.* Translated by Robert W. Yarbrough. Grand Rapids: Baker, 1992.

Locke, John. *Two Treatises of Government.* 2nd ed. New York: Cambridge University Press, 1967.

Lohse, Bernard. *Martin Luther's Theology: Its Historical and Systematic Development.* Translated by Roy A. Harrisville. Minneapolis: Augsburg, 1999.

Longenecker, Richard N. *Biblical Exegesis in the Apostolic Period.* Grand Rapids: Eerdmans, 1975.

———. *Contours of Christology in the New Testament*. Grand Rapids: Eerdmans, 2005.

———. *The Christology of Early Jewish Christianity*. London: SCM, 1970.

———. *The Epistle to the Romans: A Commentary on the Greek Text*. Grand Rapids: Eerdmans, 2016.

Lovelace, Richard. "Inerrancy: Some Historical Perspectives." In *Inerrancy and Common Sense*. Edited by Roger Nicole and J. Ramsey Michaels. Grand Rapids: Baker, 1980.

Lubac, Henri de. *Medieval Exegesis: The Four Senses of Scripture*. vol. 1. Translated by Mark Sebanc. Grand Rapids: Eerdmans, 1998.

Luhrmann, D. *An Itinerary for New Testament Study*. Translated by I. Bowdon. Philadelphia: Trinity, 1989.

Lumpkin, William L., and Bill J. Leonard., eds. *Baptist Confessions of Faith*. 2nd ed. Valley Forge, PA: Judson, 2011.

Luther, Martin. "Der Brief des Paulus an die Römer." In *Luther Testament: Neues Testament und Psalmen mit Sonderseiten zu Luthers Leben und den Stätten seines Wirkens*. Stuttgart: Deutsche Bibelgesellschaft, 1995.

———. *Luther's Works*. Edited by Jaroslav Pelikan. 55 vols. St. Louis: Concordia; Philadelphia: Fortress, 1955–1986.

MacArthur, John. "The Sufficiency of the Written Word." In *Sola Scriptura: The Protestant Position on the Bible*. Edited by Don Kistler. Morgan, PA: Soli Deo Gloria, 1995.

MacCulloch, Diarmaid. *The Later Reformation in England 1547–1603*. London: Macmillan, 1990.

Machen, J. Gresham. *Christianity and Liberalism*. New York: Macmillan, 1923.

Macleod, Donald. "Jesus and Scripture." In *The Trustworthiness of God: Perspectives on the Nature of Scripture*. Edited by Paul Helm and Carl R. Trueman. Grand Rapids: Eerdmans, 2002.

Maier, Gerhard. *The End of the Historical-Critical Method.* Translated by Edwin W. Leverenz and Rudolph F. Norden. St. Louis: Concordia, 1977.

Maier, Paul L. "Fanaticism as a Theological Category in the Lutheran Confessions." *Concordia Theological Quarterly* 44, no. 2–3 (July 1980): 173–81.

Mandelbrote, Scott. "The Uses of Natural Theology in Seventeenth-Century England." *Science in Context* 20, no. 3 (September 2007): 451–80.

Manly, Basil Jr. *The Bible Doctrine of Inspiration: Explained and Vindicated.* New York: A. C. Armstrong and Sons, 1888.

Manson, T. W. "The Failure of Liberalism to Interpret the Bible as the Word of God." In *The Interpretation of the Bible.* Edited by C. W. Dugmore. London: SPCK, 1944.

Marsden, George. *Fuller Seminary and the New Evangelicalism.* Grand Rapids: Eerdmans, 1987.

Marsh, William M. "Scripture and Tradition." In *Historical Theology for the Church.* Edited by Jason G. Duesing and Nathan A. Finn. Nashville: B&H, 2021.

Marshall, Bruce D. *Trinity and Truth.* New York: Cambridge University Press, 2000.

Marshall, I. Howard. *Biblical Inspiration.* Grand Rapids: Eerdmans, 1982.

———. *I Believe in the Historical Jesus.* Grand Rapids: Eerdmans, 1977.

———. *The Acts of the Apostles: An Introduction and Commentary.* Tyndale New Testament Commentaries. Grand Rapids: Eerdmans, 1980.

Martinez, Enrique. "God as Highest Truth According to Aquinas." *Religions* 12, no. 6 (2021): 1–8.

Mathews, Kenneth A. *Genesis 11:27–50:26.* New American Commentary. Nashville: B&H, 2005.

McBeth, H. Leon. *The Baptist Heritage: Four Centuries of Baptist Witness.* Nashville: Broadman, 1987.

McCaulley, Esau. *Reading Scripture While Black.* Downers Grove: IVP, 2020.

McDermott, Gerald R., ed. *The Oxford Handbook of Evangelical Theology.* Oxford: Oxford University Press, 2010.

McDonald, H. D. *Jesus: Human and Divine: An Introduction to Christology.* Grand Rapids: Zondervan, 1968.

———. "The Bible in Twentieth-Century British Theology." In *Challenges to Inerrancy: A Theological Response.* Edited by Gordon Lewis and Bruce Demarest. Chicago: Moody, 1984.

McDonald, Lee Martin. *The Origin of the Bible: A Guide for the Perplexed.* New York: T&T Clark, 2011.

McGowan, A. T. B. *The Divine Spiration of Scripture: Challenging Evangelical Perspectives.* Downers Grove: IVP, 2009.

McGrath, Alister E. "A Blast from the Past? The Boyle Lectures and Natural Theology." *Science and Christian Belief* 17, no. 1 (April 2005): 25–33.

———. *Emil Brunner: A Reappraisal.* Malden, MA: Wiley Blackwell, 2014.

———. *Luther's Theology of the Cross: Martin Luther's Theological Breakthrough.* New York: Basil Blackwell, 1985.

———. *Reformation Thought: An Introduction.* 3rd ed. Malden, MA: Blackwell, 1999.

McKellar, Matthew, and David S. Dockery. "The Authority and Sufficiency of Scripture for Pastoral Ministry and Preaching." In *The Authority and Sufficiency of Scripture.* Edited by Adam Greenway and David S. Dockery. Fort Worth: Seminary Hill, 2022.

McNally, Robert E. "Medieval Exegesis." *Theological Studies* 22, no. 3 (September 1961): 445–54.

Metzger, Bruce M., and Bart D. Ehrman. *The Text of the New Testament: Its Transmission, Corruption, and Restoration.* 4th ed. New York: Oxford University Press, 2005.

Mikolaski, Samuel J. "Jesus Christ: Prophet, Priest, and King." In *Basics of the Faith: An Evangelical Doctrine to Christian Doctrine.* Edited by Carl F. H. Henry. Bellingham, WA: Lexham, 2019.

Mohler, R. Albert Jr. "When the Bible Speaks, God Speaks: The Classic Doctrine of Biblical Inerrancy." In *Five Views on Biblical Inerrancy*. Edited by J. Merrick and S. M. Garrett. Grand Rapids: Zondervan, 2013.

Moo, Douglas J. *The Epistle to the Romans*. The New International Commentary on the New Testament. Grand Rapids: Eerdmans, 1996.

———. "The Problems of Sensus Plenior." In *Hermeneutics, Authority, and Canon*. Edited by D. A. Carson and John D. Woodbridge. Grand Rapids: Zondervan, 1986.

Moody, Dale. *The Word of Truth*. Grand Rapids: Eerdmans, 1981.

Moody, Dwight. "The Bible." In *Has Our Theology Changed: Southern Baptist Thought Since 1845*. Edited by Paul A. Basden. Nashville: B&H, 1994.

Moore, Russell D. "Natural Revelation." In *A Theology for the Church*. Rev. ed. Edited by Daniel L. Akin. Nashville: B&H, 2014.

———. *The Kingdom of Christ*. Wheaton: Crossway, 2004.

More, Henry. *An Antidote against Atheism*. London: Roger Daniel, 1653.

Morgan, Christopher W. *Christian Theology: The Biblical Story and Our Faith*. Nashville: B&H, 2020.

Morgan, Robert. "New Testament Theology as Implicit Theological Interpretation of Christian Scripture." *Interpretation* 70, no. 4 (2016): 383–98.

Morris, Leon. *The Gospel According to John*. Rev. ed. New International Commentary on the New Testament. Grand Rapids: Eerdmans, 1995.

Morrison, John D. *Has God Said? Scripture, the Word of God, and the Crisis of Theological Authority*. Eugene, OR: Pickwick, 2006.

Moule, C. F. D. "Fulfillment Words in the New Testament: Use and Abuse." *New Testament Studies* 14, no. 3 (April 1968): 293–320.

———. *The Birth of the New Testament*. London: SCM, 1981.

———. *The Origin of Christology*. Cambridge: Cambridge University Press, 1977.

Mounce, Robert H. *The Book of Revelation*. Rev. ed. The New International Commentary on the New Testament. Grand Rapids: Eerdmans, 1977.

Mounce, William D. *The Pastoral Epistles*. Word Biblical Commentary. Nashville: Word, 2000.

———. *Why I Trust the Bible: Answers to Real Questions and Doubts People Have about the Bible*. Grand Rapids: Zondervan, 2021.

Mueller, J. Theodore. "The Holy Spirit and the Scriptures." In *Revelation and the Bible*. Edited by Carl F. H. Henry. Grand Rapids: Baker, 1958.

Muller, Richard. *The Study of Theology: From Biblical Interpretation to Contemporary Formation*. Grand Rapids: Zondervan, 1991.

Mullins, E. Y. "Baptists and Creeds." In *The Axioms of Religion*. Compiled by R. Albert Mohler Jr. Edited by Timothy George and Denise George. Nashville: B&H, 1997.

———. *Christianity at the Crossroads*. Nashville: Baptist Sunday School Board, 1924.

———. "Duties and Dangers of this Present Hour." Southern Baptist Convention, 1923.

———. *The Christian Religion in Its Doctrinal Expression*. Philadelphia: Judson, 1917.

Murray, Stuart. *Biblical Interpretation in the Anabaptist Tradition*. Scottdale, PA: Herald Press, 2000.

Nadler, Steven. *A Book Forged in Hell: Spinoza's Scandalous Treatise and the Birth of the Secular Age*. Princeton, NJ: Princeton University Press, 2011.

———. "Scripture and Truth: A Problem in Spinoza's *Tractatus Theologico-Politicus*." *History of Ideas* 74, no. 4 (October 2013): 623–42.

———. *Spinoza: A Life*. 2nd ed. New York: Cambridge University Press, 2018.

Neibuhr, Reinhold. "The Concept of 'Order of Creation' in Emil Brunner's Social Ethic." In *The Theology of Emil Brunner*. Edited by Charles W. Kegley. New York: Macmillan, 1962.

Nettles, Thomas J. "Creedalism, Confessionalism, and the Baptist Faith and Message." In *The Unfettered Word: Southern Baptists Confront the Authority-Inerrancy Question*. Edited by Robison B. James. Waco: Word, 1987.

Newman, Robert C. "The Council of Jamnia and the Old Testament Canon." *The Westminster Theological Journal* 38, no. 3 (Spring 1976): 319–49.

Newman, Stewart Albert. *W. T. Conner: Theologian of the Southwest*. Nashville: Broadman, 1964.

Nicholson, Graeme. *Seeing and Reading*. Atlantic Highlands: Humanities, 1984.

Nicole, Roger. "James I. Packer's Contribution to the Doctrine of Inerrancy." In *Doing Theology for the People of God: Studies in Honor of J. I. Packer*. Edited by Donald Lewis and Alister McGrath. Downers Grove: IVP, 1996.

———. "The Neo-Orthodox Reduction." In *Challenges to Inerrancy: A Theological Response*. Edited by Gordon R. Lewis and Bruce Demarest. Chicago: Moody, 1984.

Nihinlola, Emiola. *Theology Under the Mango Tree: A Handbook of African Christian Theology*. Logos, Nigeria: Fine Print and Manufacturing, 2013.

Nineham, D. E. "Schweitzer Revisited." In *Explorations in Theology 1*. London: SCM, 1977.

Noll, Mark A. *America's Book: The Rise and Decline of a Bible Civilization, 1794–1911*. Oxford: Oxford University Press, 2022.

———, ed. *The Princeton Theology 1812–1921: Scripture, Science, and Theological Method from Archibald Alexander to Benjamin Breckinridge Warfield*. Grand Rapids: Baker, 1983.

Nowlin, William Dudley. *Fundamentals of the Faith*. Nashville: Baptist Sunday School Board, 1922.

Novum Testamentum Graece. Stuttgart: Deutsche Bibelgesellschaft, 2017.

Numbers, Ronald L. "Charles Hodge and the Beauties and Deformities of Science." In *Charles Hodge Revisited: A Critical Appraisal of His Life and Work.* Edited by John W. Stewart and James H. Moorhead. Grand Rapids: Eerdmans, 2002.

Oberman, Heiko A. *Forerunners of the Reformation: The Shape of Late Medieval Thought.* Translated by Paul L. Nybus. New York: Holt, Rinehart, and Winston, 1966.

———. *The Dawn of the Reformation: Essays in Late Medieval and Early Reformation.* Edinburgh: T&T Clark, 1992.

O'Collins, Gerald. *Inspiration: Towards a Christian Interpretation of Biblical Inspiration.* Oxford: Oxford University Press, 2018.

———. *Revelation: Towards a Christian Interpretation of God's Self-Revelation in Jesus Christ.* New York: Oxford University Press, 2016.

Oden, Thomas C. *The Rebirth of Orthodoxy.* San Francisco: HarperCollins, 2003.

Oliver, Alexander D. "Abstract Entities" In *The Oxford Companion to Philosophy.* Edited by Ted Honderich. Oxford: Oxford University Press, 1995.

Olson, Roger. *Against Liberal Theology: Putting the Brakes on Progressive Christianity.* Grand Rapids: Zondervan, 2022.

"Omnis scriptura divinitus inspirata." *Biblia Sacra Vulgatae Editionis, Sixti V et Clementis VIII.* London: Bagster, [n.d.].

O'Neill, J. C. "Adolf von Harnack and the Entry of the German State into Ware, July-August 1914." *Scottish Journal of Theology* 55 (2002): 1–18.

Orwell, George. *Orwell on Truth.* London: Harvill Secker, 2017.

Osborn, Eric. "Reason and the Rule of Faith in the Second Century." In *The Making of Orthodoxy: Essays in Honour of Henry Chadwick.* Edited by Rowan Williams. New York: Cambridge University Press, 1989.

———. "Tertullian." In *The First Christian Theologians: An Introduction to Theology in the Early Church.* Edited by G. R. Evans. Oxford: Blackwell, 2004.

Osborne, Grant R. *Matthew*. Exegetical Commentary on the New Testament. Grand Rapids: Zondervan, 2010.

————. *The Hermeneutical Spiral: A Comprehensive Introduction to Biblical Interpretation*. Downers Grove: IVP, 2006.

Osborne, Grant R., and Philip W. Comfort. *John and 1, 2, and 3 John*. Cornerstone Bible Commentary. Carol Stream, IL: Tyndale, 2007.

Ott, Craig. *Teaching and Learning Across Cultures: A Guide to Theory and Practice*. Grand Rapids: Baker, 2021.

Otten, Willemien. "Nature and Scripture: Demise of a Medieval Analogy." *Harvard Theological Review* 88, no. 2 (April 1995): 257–84.

Packer, J. I. "Calvin's View of Scripture." In *God's Inerrant Word: An International Symposium on the Trustworthiness of Scripture*. Edited by John W. Montgomery. Minneapolis: Bethany, 1974.

————. "Infallible Scripture and the Role of Hermeneutics." In *Scripture and Truth*. Edited by D. A. Carson and John D. Woodbridge. Grand Rapids: Baker, 1983.

————. "Infallibility and Inerrancy." In *New Dictionary of Theology*. Edited by D. Wright, S. Ferguson, and J. I. Packer. Downers Grove: IVP, 1988.

————. "Notes on Biblical Inerrancy." Lecture 12. Regent College, Fall 1978.

————. "The Adequacy of Human Language." In *Inerrancy*. Edited by Norman L. Geisler. Grand Rapids: Zondervan, 1980.

————. "Reading the Bible Theologically." In *ESV Systematic Theology Study Bible*. Edited by Christopher W. Morgan and Stephen J. Wellum. Wheaton: Crossway, 2017.

————. *Truth and Power: The Place of Scripture in the Christian Life*. Wheaton: Harold Shaw, 1996.

Packer, J. I., and Thomas C. Oden. *One Faith*. Downers Grove: IVP, 2004.

Padilla, Osvaldo. "Postconservative Theologians and Scriptural Authority." In *The Enduring Authority of the Christian Scriptures*. Edited by D. A. Carson. Grand Rapids: Eerdmans, 2016.

Paine, Thomas. "The Age of Reason (1794)." In *The Thomas Paine Reader*. Edited by Michael Foot and Isaac Kramnick. New York: Penguin, 1987.

Pao, David W. *Colossians and Philemon*. Exegetical Commentary on the New Testament. Grand Rapids: Zondervan, 2012.

Parker, D. C. "Review Article: The Text of the New Testament." *Journal of Theological Studies* NS, 57 (2006): 551–67.

Parsons, Mikael C. *Crawford Howell Toy: The Man, the Scholar, the Teacher*. Macon, GA: Mercer University Press, 2019.

Payne, Jesse M. *Carl F. H. Henry on the Holy Spirit*. Bellingham, WA: Lexham, 2021.

Peckham, John C. *Canonical Theology: The Biblical Canon, Sola Scriptura, and Theological Method*. Grand Rapids: Eerdmans, 2016.

Pelikan, Jaroslav. *Christianity and Classical Culture: The Metamorphosis of Natural Theology in the Christian Tradition with Hellenism*. New Haven, CT: Yale University Press, 1993.

———. *The Christian Tradition: A History of the Development of Doctrine*. 5 vols. Chicago: University of Chicago Press, 1984.

Pennington, Jonathan. *Heaven and Earth in the Gospel of Matthew*. Grand Rapids: Baker, 2007.

Peterson, David G. *Romans*. Biblical Theology for Christian Proclamation. Nashville: B&H, 2017.

Peterson, Eugene. "Eat This Book: The Holy Community at Table with the Holy Scriptures." *Theology Today* 56, no. 1 (1999): 5–17.

Pierard, R. V. "Theological Liberalism." In *Evangelical Dictionary of Theology*. Edited by Daniel J. Treier and Walter A. Elwell. 3rd ed. Grand Rapids: Baker, 2017.

Pierce, Madison N. *Divine Discourse in the Epistle to the Hebrews: The Recontextualization of Spoken Quotations of Scripture*. New York: Cambridge University Press, 2020.

Pinnock, Clark. *Scripture Principle*. San Francisco: Harper and Row, 1984.

Pinson, J. Mathew. *Arminian and Baptist: Explorations in a Theological Tradition.* Nashville: Randall, 2015.

Piotrowski, Nicholas. *In All the Scriptures: The Three Contexts of Biblical Hermeneutics.* Downers Grove: IVP, 2021.

Piper, John. *A Peculiar Glory: How the Christian Scriptures Reveal Their Complete Truthfulness.* Wheaton: Crossway, 2016.

———. *Reading the Bible Supernaturally: Seeing and Savoring the Glory of God in Scripture.* Wheaton: Crossway, 2017.

Playoust, Marc R. "Oscar Cullmann and Salvation History." *Heythrop Journal* 12, no.1 (1971): 29–43.

Plummer, Robert. *40 Questions about Interpreting the Bible.* Grand Rapids: Kregel, 2010.

Polman, A. D. R. *The Word of God According to St. Augustine.* Translated by A. J. Pomerans. Grand Rapids: Eerdmans, 1961.

Porter, Calvin L. "Paul as Theologian: Romans." *Encounter* 65, no. 2 (Spring 2004): 109–36.

Potterie, Ignace de la. *La Vérité dans Saint Jean.* vol. 1. *Le Christ et la vérité, L'Esprit et la vérité.* Rome: Biblical Institute, 1977.

Poythress, Vern S. "Adequacy of Human Language and Accommodation." In *Hermeneutics, Inerrancy, and the Bible.* Edited by Earl D. Radmacher and Robert D. Preus. Grand Rapids: Zondervan, 1984.

———. "Divine Meaning of Scripture." *The Westminster Theological Journal* 48, no. 2 (Fall 1986): 241–79.

———. "Understanding an Alleged 'Contradiction.'" In *Inerrancy and Worldview: Answering Modern Challenges to the Bible.* Wheaton: Crossway, 2012.

Presley, Stephen. "Scripture and Tradition." In *Historical Theology for the Church.* Edited by Jason G. Duesing and Nathan A. Finn. Nashville: B&H, 2021.

Putman, Rhyne. "Baptists, *Sola Scriptura,* and the Place of Christian Tradition." In *Baptists and the Christian Tradition.* Edited by Matt Y. Emerson, Christopher W. Morgan, and Lucas Stamps. Nashville: B&H, 2020.

———. *In Defense of Doctrine: Evangelicalism, Theology, and Scripture.* Minneapolis: Fortress, 2015.

———. *The Method of Christian Theology: An Introduction.* Nashville: B&H, 2021.

———. *When Doctrine Divides the People of God: An Evangelical Approach to Theological Diversity.* Wheaton: Crossway, 2020.

Queen, Matt. *Recapturing Evangelism: A Biblical-Theological Approach.* Nashville: B&H, 2023.

Rack, Henry D. *Reasonable Enthusiast: John Wesley and the Rise of Methodism.* 3rd ed. London: Epworth, 2002.

Radmacher, E. D., and R. D. Preus., eds. *Hermeneutics, Inerrancy, and the Bible.* Grand Rapids: Zondervan, 1984.

Rae, Michael C. "Authority and Truth." In *The Enduring Authority of the Christian Scriptures.* Edited by D. A. Carson. Grand Rapids: Eerdmans, 2016.

Ramm, Bernard. *After Fundamentalism: The Future of Evangelical Theology.* San Francisco: Harper & Row, 1983.

———. *Protestant Biblical Interpretation: A Textbook of Hermeneutics.* 3rd ed. Grand Rapids: Baker, 1970.

———. *Special Revelation and the Word of God.* Grand Rapids: Eerdmans, 1961.

Rashkover, Randi. "Liberalism, Post-Liberalism, and the Fact-Value Divide." *Modern Theology* 33, no. 1 (2017): 140–62.

Ravel, Suresh. *Metacriticsm.* Athens, GA: University of Georgia Press, 1981.

Reeve, J. J. "My Personal Experience with Higher Criticism." In *The Fundamentals: A Testimony to the Truth*. Edited by A. C. Dixon and R. A. Torrey. 1917; Grand Rapids: Baker, 1980.

Reid, J. K. S. *The Authority of Scripture: A Study of the Reformation and Post-Reformation Understanding of the Bible*. London: Methuen, 1957.

Reno, R. R. *The End of Interpretation: Reclaiming the Priority of Ecclesial Exegesis*. Grand Rapids: Baker, 2022.

Reventlow, Henning Graf. *Problems of Biblical Theology in the Twentieth Century*. London: SCM, 1986.

———. *The Authority of the Bible and the Rise of the Modern World*. Translated by John Bowden. London: SCM, 1984.

Reymond, Robert L. *A New Systematic Theology of the Christian Faith*. Nashville: Thomas Nelson, 1998.

Rice, John R. *Our God-Breathed Book*. Murfreesboro, TN: Sword of the Lord, 1969.

Richards, E. Randolph, and Brandon J. O'Brien. *Misreading Scripture with Western Eyes*. Downers Grove: IVP, 2012.

Richards, W. Wiley. *Winds of Doctrine: The Origin and Development of Southern Baptist Theology*. Lanham, MD: University Press of America, 1991.

Ricoeur, Paul. *Essays on Biblical Interpretation*. Edited by L. S. Mudge. Philadelphia: Fortress, 1980.

———. *Hermeneutics and the Human Sciences: Essays on Language, Action, and Interpretation*. Edited and Translated by John B. Thompson. Cambridge: Cambridge University Press, 1980.

———. *Interpretation Theory: Discourse and the Surplus of Meaning*. Fort Worth: Texas Christian University Press, 1976.

———. *The Conflict of Interpretations: Essays in Hermeneutics*. Edited by Don Ihde. Evanston: Northwestern University Press, 1974.

Ridderbos, Herman. *Paul: An Outline of His Theology.* Translated by John Richard De Witt. Grand Rapids: Eerdmans, 1975.

Ridenour, Autumn Alcott. *Sabbath Rest as Vocation: Aging Toward Death.* London: T&T Clark, 2018.

Rist, James M. "Christian Theology and Secular Philosophy." In *The First Christian Theologians: An Introduction to Theology in the Early Church.* Edited by G. R. Evans. Malden, MA: Blackwell, 2004.

Ritschl, Dietrich. *The Logic of Theology: A Brief Account of the Relationship between Basic Concepts in Theology.* Translated by John Bowden. Philadelphia: Fortress, 1987.

Roberts, Alexander, and James Donaldson, eds. *The Apostolic Fathers, Justin Martyr, Irenaeus.* Ante-Nicene Fathers. 10 vols. 1885. Reprint, Peabody, MA: Hendrickson, 1994.

Roberts, Vaughn. *God's Big Picture: Tracing the Storyline of the Bible.* Downers Grove: IVP, 2003.

Rogers, Jack, and Donald McKim. *The Authority and Interpretation of the Bible.* San Francisco: HarperCollins, 1979.

Rogerson, John, Christopher Rowland, and Barnabas Lindars. *The Study and Use of the Bible.* Edited by Paul Avis. 3 vols. Grand Rapids: Eerdmans, 1988.

Rosner, Brian S. "'Written for Us': Paul's View of Scripture." In *A Pathway into the Holy Scripture.* Edited by Philip E. Satterthwaite and David F. Wright. Grand Rapids: Eerdmans, 1994.

Russell, D. S. *The Method and Message of Jewish Apocalyptic: 200BC–AD100.* London: SCM, 1964.

Rust, Eric. *Nature and Man.* London: Lutterworth, 1953.

———. *Salvation History: A Biblical Understanding.* Richmond: John Knox, 1962.

Sanday, William. *The Oracles of God: Nine Lectures on the Doctrine of Biblical Inspiration.* New York: Longmans, 1894.

Sandeen, Ernest. *The Roots of Fundamentalism: British and American Millenarianism, 1800–1930.* Chicago: University of Chicago Press, 1970.

Sandys-Wunsch, John, and Laurence Eldredge. "J. P. Gabler and the Distinction between Biblical and Dogmatic Theology: Translation, Commentary, and Discussion of His Originality." *Scottish Journal of Theology* 33, no. 2 (April 1980): 133–58.

Sasse, Hermann. *Luther and the Word of God,* in *Accents in Luther's Theology: Essays in Commemoration of the 450th Anniversary of the Reformation.* Edited by Heino O. Kadal. St. Louis: Concordia, 1967.

Saucy, Robert. *Scripture.* Nashville: W Publishing Group, 2011.

———. *Scripture: Its Power, Authority, and Relevance.* Nashville: Thomas Nelson, 2001.

Schaff, Philip. *The Principle of Protestantism as related to the Present State of the Church.* Translated by John W. Nevin. Chambersburg, PA: Publication Office of the German Reformed Church, 1845.

———, ed. *Augustin: The Writings against the Manichaens, and against the Donatists.* Nicene and Post-Nicene Fathers. First Series. 14 vols. 1887. Reprint, Peabody, MA: Hendrickson, 1994.

Schaff, Philip, and Henry Wace, eds. *Eusebius: Church History, Life of Constantine the Great, and Oration in Praise of Constantine.* Nicene and Post-Nicene Fathers. Second Series. 14 vols. 1890. Reprint, Peabody, MA: Hendrickson, 1994.

Schenck, Ken. "God Has Spoken: Hebrews' Theology of the Scriptures." In *The Epistle to the Hebrews and Christian Theology.* Edited by Richard Bauckham et al. Grand Rapids: Eerdmans, 2009.

Schlatter, Adolf. "The Theology of the New Testament and Dogmatics." In *The Nature of New Testament Theology: The Contribution of William Wrede and Adolf Schlatter.* Edited by Robert Morgan. Studies in Biblical Theology. 2nd series. vol. 25. London: SCM, 1973.

Schleiermacher, Friedrich. *Hermeneutics and Criticism and Other Writings.* Translated by Andrew Bowie. New York: Cambridge University Press, 1998.

———. *Hermeneutics: The Handwritten Manuscripts.* Edited by H. Kimmerle. Translated by James Duke and H. J. Forsman. Missoula, MT: Scholars, 1977.

———. *The Christian Faith.* Edited by H. R. Mackintosh and J. S. Stewart. Reprint, Edinburgh: T&T Clark, 1960.

Schnackenburg, Rudolf. *The Johannine Epistles: Introduction and Commentary.* Translated by Reginald H. Fuller. Tunbridge Wells, UK: Burns & Oates, 1992.

Schnittjer, Gary Edward. *Old Testament Use of Old Testament: A Book-by-Book Guide.* Grand Rapids: Zondervan, 2021.

Schökel, Luis Alonso. *The Inspired Word: Scripture in the Light of Language and Literature.* Translated by Francis Martin. New York: Herder and Herder, 1965.

Schreiner, Thomas R. *Hebrews.* Biblical Theology for Proclamation. Nashville: B&H, 2015.

———. *1, 2 Peter and Jude.* Christian Standard Commentary. Nashville: B&H, 2020.

Schweitzer, Albert. *The Quest of the Historical Jesus: A Critical Study of Its Progress from Reimarus to Wrede.* Translated by W. Montgomery. London: Black, 1911.

Scruton, Roger. *Kant.* Rev. ed. New York: Oxford University Press, 2000.

Seifrid, Mark A. "Natural Law and the Purpose of the Law in Romans." *Tyndale Bulletin* 49, no. 1 (May 1998): 115–29.

Sigmund, Paul E. "Law and Politics." In *The Cambridge Companion to Aquinas.* Edited by Norman Kretzmann and Eleonore Stump. New York: Cambridge University Press, 1993.

Silva, Moisés. "κράτος." In *New International Dictionary of New Testament Theology and Exegesis.* 2nd ed. 5 vols. Grand Rapids: Zondervan, 2014.

———, ed. *New International Dictionary of New Testament Theology and Exegisis*. 2nd ed. 5 vols. Grand Rapids: Zondervan, 2014.

———. "Old Princeton, Westminster, and Inerrancy." In *Inerrancy and Hermeneutic*. Edited by Harvie M. Conn. Grand Rapids: Baker, 1988.

Slade, Darren M. "Patristic Exegesis: The Myth of the Alexandrian-Antiochene Schools of Interpretation." *Socio-Historical Examination of Religion and Ministry* 1, no. 2 (2019): 155–76.

Sloan, Robert B. "Canonical Theology of the New Testament." In *Foundations for Biblical Interpretation: A Complete Library of Tools and Resources*. Edited by David S. Dockery, Kenneth A. Mathews, and Robert B. Sloan. Nashville: B&H, 1994.

———. "Frank Stagg." In *Baptist Theologians*. Edited by Timothy George and David S. Dockery. Nashville: Broadman, 1990.

———. *The Favorable Year of the Lord: A Study of Jubilary Theology in the Gospel of Luke*. Austin, TX: Schola, 1977.

———. "Use of the Old Testament in the New Testament." In *Reclaiming the Prophetic Mantle: Preaching the Old Testament Faithfully*. Edited by George L. Klein. Nashville: Broadman, 1992.

Smalley, Beryl. *The Study of the Bible in the Middle Ages*. Oxford: Blackwell, 1952.

Smith, Christian. *The Bible Made Impossible: Why Biblicism Is Not a Truly Evangelical Reading of Scripture*. Grand Rapids: Brazos, 2011.

Smith, R. Scott. "Non-Foundational Epistemologies and the Truth of Scripture." *The Enduring Authority of the Christian Scriptures*. Edited by D. A. Carson. Grand Rapids: Eerdmans, 2016.

Smith, Randall B. "Thomas Aquinas's Principium at Paris." In *Towards a Biblical Thomism: Thomas Aquinas and the Renewal of Biblical Theology*. Edited by Piotr Roszak and Jörgen Vijgen. Pamplona, Espana: Ediciones Universidad de Navarra, 2018.

Smith, Robert Jr. *Doctrine that Dances: Bringing Doctrinal Preaching and Teaching to Life*. Nashville: B&H, 2008.

Smither, Edward L. *Christian Mission: A Concise Global History.* Bellingham, WA: Lexham, 2019.

Snodgrass, Klyne. "The Use of the Old Testament in the New Testament." In *New Testament Criticism and Interpretation.* Edited by D. A. Black and David S. Dockery. Grand Rapids: Zondervan, 1991.

Sorell, Tom. *Descartes.* New York: Oxford University Press, 1996.

Soskice, Janet Martin. *Metaphor and Religious Language.* Oxford: Clarendon, 1985.

Southern, R. W. *Anselm: A Portrait in a Landscape.* New York: Cambridge University Press, 1990.

Spinoza, Baruch. "*Theological-Political Treatise* (1670)." In *The Collected Works of Spinoza.* Edited by Edwin Curley. vol. 2. Princeton, NJ: Princeton University Press, 2016.

Spivey, James. "Benajah Harvey Carroll." In *Theologians of the Baptist Tradition.* Edited by Timothy George and David S. Dockery. Nashville: B&H, 2001.

Stagg, Frank. *New Testament Theology.* Nashville: Broadman, 1962.

Stein, Stephen J. "The Quest for the Spiritual Sense: The Biblical Hermeneutics of Jonathan Edwards." *Harvard Theological Review* 70, no. 1–2 (January–April 1977): 99–113.

Steinmetz, David C. *Calvin in Context.* New York: Oxford University Press, 1995.

———. *Taking the Longview: Christian Theology in Historical Perspective.* Oxford: Oxford University Press, 2011.

———. "The Superiority of Pre-Critical Exegesis." *Theology Today* 37, no. 1 (April 1980): 27–38.

Stephens, W. P. *The Theology of Huldrych Zwingli.* New York: Oxford University Press, 1986.

Stott, John R. W. *Between Two Worlds.* Grand Rapids: Eerdmans, 1982.

———. *The Incomparable Christ.* Downers Grove: IVP, 2004.

————. "Theology: A Multidimensional Discipline." In *Doing Theology for the People of God: Studies in Honor of J. I. Packer*. Edited by Donald Lewis and Alister McGrath. Downers Grove: IVP, 1996.

Streeter, Burnett Hillman. *The Four Gospels, A Study of Origins: Treating of the Manuscript Tradition, Sources, Authorship, and Dates*. London: Macmillan, 1924.

Strickland, Michael. "The Integration of Oral Jesus Tradition in the Early Church." *Early Church Studies* 5, no. 1 (2015): 132–43.

Strivens, Robert. *Philip Doddridge and the Shaping of Evangelical Dissent*. New York: Routledge, 2015.

Strom, Mark. *The Symphony of Scripture: Making Sense of the Bible's Many Themes*. Downers Grove: IVP, 1990.

Strong, Augustus Hopkins. *A Tour of the Missions: Observations and Conclusions*. Philadelphia: Griffith and Rowland, 1918.

Stuhlmacher, Peter. *Biblical Theology of the New Testament*. Translated by Daniel P. Bailey. Grand Rapids: Eerdmans, 2018.

————. *How to Do Biblical Theology*. Princeton Theological Monographs. Eugene, OR: Pickwick, 1995.

Swain, Scott. "The Bible and the Trinity in Recent Thought: Review, Analysis, and Constructive Proposal." *Journal of the Evangelical Theological Society* 60, no. 1 (March 2017): 35–48.

Sweeney, Douglas A. *Edwards the Exegete: Biblical Interpretation and Anglo-Protestant Culture on the Edge of the Enlightenment*. Oxford: Oxford University Press, 2016.

Swinburne, Richard. *Revelation: From Metaphor to Analogy*. New York: Oxford University Press, 1992.

Tanner, Norman P., ed. *Decrees of the Ecumenical Councils*. 2 vols. Washington, DC: Georgetown University Press, 1990.

Tasker, R. V. G. *The Old Testament in the New Testament*. London: Hodder & Stoughton, 1962.

Tavard, George H. *The Starting Point of Calvin's Theology*. Grand Rapids: Eerdmans, 2000.

Taylor, Justin. "Luther's Saying: 'Justification Is the Article by Which the Church Stands or Falls.'" The Gospel Coalition. August 2011; https://www.thegospelcoalition.org/blogs/justin-taylor/luthers-saying/.

Taylor, Mark. *1 Corinthians*. The New American Commentary. Nashville: B&H, 2014.

TeSelle, Eugene. *Augustine*. Abingdon Pillars of Theology. Nashville: Abingdon, 2006.

———. *Augustine the Theologian*. 1970. Reprint, Eugene, OR: Wipf and Stock, 2002.

The Book of Common Prayer. New York: Oxford University Press, 1969.

The Enchiridion of Erasmus. Translated by Raymond Himelick. Bloomington, IN: Indiana University Press, 1964.

"The First Epistle of Clement to the Corinthians." In *The Apostolic Fathers with Justin Martyr and Irenaeus*. Edited by Alexander Roberts, James Donaldson, and A. Cleveland Cox, Ante-Nicene Fathers. 10 vols. 1885. Reprint, Peabody, MA: Hendrickson Publishers, 1994.

The New Testament: The Text of the Worms Edition of 1526 in Original Spelling. Edited by W. R. Cooper. Translated by William Tyndale. London: The British Library, 2000.

The Second London Baptist Confession of Faith. London, 1689. Reprint, Pensacola, FL: Chapel Library.

The Oxford Dictionary of the Christian Church. 2nd ed. Edited by F. L. Cross and E. A. Livingstone. New York: Oxford University Press, 1974.

Thiselton, Anthony C. "Canon." In *The Thiselton Companion to Christian Theology*. Grand Rapids: Eerdmans, 2015.

———. "Speech-Act Theory and the Claim that God Speaks: Nicholas Wolterstorff's *Divine Discourse*." *Scottish Journal of Theology* 50, no. 1 (1997): 97–110.

————. *The Thiselton Companion to Christian Theology*. Grand Rapids: Eerdmans, 2015.

————. *The Two Horizons*. Grand Rapids: Eerdmans, 1980.

————. "Truth." In *Dictionary of New Testament Theology*. Edited by Colin Brown. 3 vols. Grand Rapids: Zondervan, 1979.

Thomassen, Einer. "Some Notes on the Development of Christian Ideas about a Canon." In *Canon and Canonicity: The Formation and Use of Scripture*. Edited by Einer Thomassen. Copenhagen: Museum Tusculanum Press, 2010.

Thompson, Mark D. *A Sure Word on Which to Stand: The Relation of Authority and Interpretive Method in Luther's Approach to Scripture*. Eugene, OR: Wipf & Stock, 2007.

————. *The Doctrine of Scripture: An Introduction*. Wheaton: Crossway, 2022.

————. "The Sufficient Word." In *Tend My Sheep: The Word of God and Pastoral Ministry*. Edited by Keith G. Condie. London: Latimer Trust, 2016.

Tidwell, J. B. *Thinking Straight about the Bible or Is the Bible the Word of God*. Nashville: Broadman, 1936.

Torrance, Thomas F. *Theological Science*. New York: Oxford University Press, 1969.

Torrey, R. A., ed. *The Fundamentals*. 12 vols. Reprint, Los Angeles: Bible Institute of Los Angeles, 2017.

Towner, Philip H. *The Letters to Timothy and Titus*. The New International Commentary on the New Testament. Grand Rapids: Eerdmans, 2006.

Tran, Huong Thi. "Martin Luther's Views on and Use of Aristotle: A Theological-Philosophical Assessment." *Constantine's Letters* 13, no. 2 (2020): 124–36.

Treier, Daniel J. "Contemporary Theological Hermeneutics." In *Dictionary for Theological Interpretation of the Bible*. Grand Rapids: Baker, 2005.

Trueman, Carl R. *Luther's Legacy: Salvation and English Reformers 1525–1556.* New York: Oxford University Press, 1994.

———. "The God of Unconditional Promise." In *The Trustworthiness of God: Perspectives on the Nature of Scripture.* Edited by Paul Helm and Carl Trueman. Grand Rapids: Eerdmans, 2002.

Tseng, Shao Kai. *Immanuel Kant.* Great Thinkers. Phillipsburg, NJ: P&R, 2020.

Tull, James E. *Shapers of Baptist Thought.* Valley Forge, PA: Judson, 1972.

Tully, Eric *Reading the Prophets as Christian Scripture: A Literary, Canonical, and Theological Interpretation.* Grand Rapids: Baker, 2022.

Turner, H. E. W. *The Pattern of Christian Truth: A Study in the Relations between Orthodoxy and Heresy in the Early Church.* London: Mowbray, 1954.

Turner, J. Clyde. "That Wonderful Book." In *Things We Believe.* Nashville: Convention, 1956.

Vang, Preben. *The Bible Story: From Genesis to Revelation.* Nashville: B&H, 2019.

VanGemeren, Willem A. "Psalms." In *The Expositor's Bible Commentary.* Edited by Frank E. Gaebelein. 12 vols. Grand Rapids: Zondervan, 1991.

Vanhoozer, Kevin J. "Augustinian Inerrancy: Literal Meaning, Literary Truth, and Literate Interpretation in the Economy of Biblical Discourse." In *Five Views on Biblical Inerrancy.* Edited by J. Merrick and Stephen M. Garrett. Grand Rapids: Zondervan, 2013.

———. *Biblical Authority after Babel: Retrieving the Solas in the Spirit of Mere Christianity.* Grand Rapids: Brazos, 2016.

———. *Biblical Narrative in the Philosophy of Paul Ricoeur.* Cambridge: Cambridge University Press, 1990.

———, ed. *Dictionary for Theological Interpretation of the Bible.* Grand Rapids: Baker, 2005.

———. *First Theology: God, Scripture, and Hermeneutics.* Downers Grove: IVP, 2002.

———. "From Bible to Theology." In *Theology, Church, and Ministry.* Edited by David S. Dockery. Nashville: B&H, 2017.

———. "Holy Scripture." In *Christian Dogmatics: Reformed Theology for the Church Catholic.* Edited by Michael Allen and Scott R. Swain. Grand Rapids: Baker, 2016.

———. *Is There Meaning in This Text? The Bible, the Reader, and the Morality of Literary Knowledge.* Grand Rapids: Zondervan, 2009.

———. "Lost in Interpretation? Truth, Scripture, and Hermeneutics." *Journal of the Evangelical Theological Society* 48, no. 1 (March 2005): 89–114.

———. "May We Go Beyond What Is Written After All? The Pattern of Theological Authority and the Problem of Doctrinal Development." In *The Enduring Authority of the Christian Scriptures.* Edited by D. A. Carson. Grand Rapids: Eerdmans, 2016.

———. *The Drama of Doctrine: A Canonical-Linguistic Approach to Christian Theology.* Louisville: Westminster John Knox, 2005.

———. "The Semantics of Biblical Language." In *Hermeneutics, Authority, and Canon.* Edited by D. A. Carson and John D. Woodbridge. Grand Rapids: Zondervan, 1986.

———. "What Is Theological Interpretation of the Bible?" In *Dictionary for Theological Interpretation of the Bible.* Grand Rapids: Baker, 2005.

———. "Word of God." In *Dictionary for Theological Interpretation of the Bible.* Edited by K. J. Vanhoozer. Grand Rapids: Eerdmans, 2005.

Vanhoozer, Kevin J., and Daniel J. Treier. *Theology and the Mirror of Scripture: A Mere Evangelical Account.* Downers Grove: IVP, 2015.

Verhoef, P. A. "Luther and Calvin's Exegetical Library." In *Calvin Theological Journal* 3, no. 1 (April 1968): 5–20.

Visser, Sandra, and Thomas Williams. *Anselm.* New York: Oxford University Press, 2009.

Vos, Geerhardus. "The Idea of Biblical Theology as a Science and as a Theological Discipline: Inaugural Address." In *Inauguration of the Rev. Geerhardus Vos, Ph.D., D.D., as Professor of Biblical Theology*. New York: Anson D. F. Randolph and Company, 1894.

Wacker, Grant. *Augustus H. Strong and the Dilemma of Historical Consciousness*. Macon, GA: Mercer University Press, 1985.

Walker, Andrew T. "Religious Liberty and the Public Square." In *First Freedom: The Beginning and End of Religious Liberty*. Edited by Jason G. Duesing, Thomas White, and Malcolm B. Yarnell III. 2nd ed. Nashville: B&H, 2016.

Wallace, O. C. S. *What Baptists Believe*. Nashville: Baptist Sunday School Board, 1934.

Waltke, Bruce K. *The Dance between God and Humanity: Reading the Bible Today as the People of God*. Grand Rapids: Eerdmans, 2013.

Ward, Matthew. *Pure Worship: The Early English Baptist Distinctive*. Eugene, OR: Pickwick, 2014.

Ward, Ronald A. *The Pattern of Our Salvation: A Study of New Testament Unity*. Waco: Word, 1978.

Ward, Wayne E. *The Holy Spirit*. Layman's Library of Christian Doctrine. Nashville: Broadman, 1987.

Warfield, Benjamin Breckinridge. *Revelation and Inspiration*. New York: Oxford University Press, 1932.

Watkin, Christopher. *Biblical Critical Theory: How the Bible's Unfolding Story Makes Sense of Modern Life and Culture*. Grand Rapids: Zondervan, 2022.

Webster, John. *Barth*. New York: Continuum, 2000.

———. "Barth, Karl." In *Dictionary for Theological Interpretation of the Bible*. Edited by Kevin J. Vanhoozer. Grand Rapids: Baker, 2005.

———. "Hermeneutics in Modern Theology: Some Doctrinal Reflections." *Scottish Journal of Theology* 51, no. 3 (1998): 307–41.

————. *Holy Scripture: A Dogmatic Sketch.* New York: Cambridge University Press, 2003.

————. *The Domain of the Word: Scripture and Theological Reason.* New York: T&T Clark, 2012.

Weiss, Konrad. *"pherō,* etc." In *Theological Dictionary of the New Testament.* Edited by Gerhard Kittel, Geoffrey W. Bromiley, and Gerhard Friedrich. 10 vols. Grand Rapids: Eerdmans, 1964.

Wells, David F. *The Person of Christ: A Biblical and Historical Analysis of the Incarnation.* Westchester, IL: Crossway, 1984.

Wells, David F., and John D. Woodbridge, eds. *The Evangelicals: Who They Are, What They Believe, and Where They Are Changing.* Nashville: Abingdon, 1975.

Wenham, John. *Christ and the Bible.* Eugene, OR: Wipf & Stock, 2009.

Werner, Martin. *The Formation of Christian Dogma: An Historical Study of Its Problem,* trans. S. G. F. Brandon. German ed. 1941, ET. New York: Harper & Brothers, 1957.

Wesley, John. *Works of John Wesley: Journal from September 13, 1773 to October 24, 1790.* vol. 4. Grand Rapids: Zondervan, 1958.

Westcott, Brooke Foss, and Fenton John Anthony Hort. *The New Testament in the Original Greek: The Text Revised.* New York: Harper and Brothers, 1881.

White, James Emery. "Inspiration and Authority of Scripture." In *Foundations for Biblical Interpretation.* Edited by David S. Dockery, Kenneth A. Mathews, and Robert B. Sloan. Nashville: B&H, 1994.

White, Thomas Joseph. *Wisdom in the Face of Modernity: A Study in Thomistic Natural Theology.* 2nd ed. Ave Maria, FL: Sapientia, 2016.

White, W. R. "The Authoritative Criterion." *Baptist Distinctives.* Nashville: Convention, 1946.

Williams, Anna N. *The Divine Sense: Intellect in Christian Theology.* New York: Cambridge University Press, 2007.

Williamson, Colwyn. "Proposition" In *The Oxford Companion to Philosophy*. Edited by Ted Honderich. New York: Oxford University Press, 1995.

Wills, Gregory A. *Southern Baptist Theological Seminary, 1859–2009*. Oxford: Oxford University Press, 2009.

Wilson, Mark R. *William Owen Carver's Controversies in the Baptist South*. Macon, GA: Mercer University Press, 2010.

Wink, Walter. *The Bible in Human Transformation*. 2nd ed. Minneapolis: Fortress, 2010.

———. *The Human Being: Jesus and the Enigma of the Son of the Man*. Minneapolis: Fortress, 2002.

Winter, Sean. "God Revealed and Hidden: Barth's Exegesis of Romans 11:33–36." *Colloquium* 50, no. 1 (2018): 46–58.

Witham, Larry. *The Measure of God: Our Century-Long Struggle to Reconcile Science and Religion*. New York: HarperCollins, 2005.

Witherington, Ben III. *The Living Word of God: Rethinking the Theology of the Bible*. Waco: Baylor University Press, 2009.

Witherspoon, J. B. *The Book We Teach*. Nashville: Baptist Sunday School Board, 1934.

Wolterstorff, Nicholas. *Divine Discourse: Philosophical Reflections on the Claim that God Speaks*. New York: Cambridge University Press, 1995.

Wood, A. Skevington. *Captive to the Word: Martin Luther, Doctor of Sacred Scripture*. Grand Rapids: Eerdmans, 1969.

Wood, Charles M. *The Formation of Christian Understanding*. Philadelphia: Westminster, 1981.

Woodbridge, John D. *Biblical Authority: Infallibility and Inerrancy in the Christian Tradition*. Grand Rapids: Zondervan, 2015.

———. "The Authority of Holy Scripture: Commitments for Christian Higher Education in the Evangelical Tradition." In *Christian Higher Education: Faith, Teaching, and Learning in the Evangelical Tradition*. Wheaton: Crossway, 2018.

———. "The International Council on Biblical Inerrancy." *Presbyterian* 48, no. 1 (Spring 2022): 37–59

Wooddell, Joseph D. "The Scripture." In *Baptist Faith and Message 2000: Critical Issues in America's Largest Protestant Denomination.* Edited by Douglas K. Blount and Joseph D. Wooddell. Lanham, MD: Rowman & Littlefield, 2007.

Wrede, William. "The Task and Methods of 'New Testament Theology.'" In *The Nature of New Testament Theology: The Contribution of William Wrede and Adolf Schlatter.* Edited by Robert Morgan, Studies in Biblical Theology. 2nd series. vol. 25. London: SCM, 1973.

Wright, N. T. *Colossians and Philemon: An Introduction and Commentary.* Tyndale New Testament Commentaries. Downers Grove: IVP, 1986.

———. *Jesus and the Victory of God.* London: SPCK, 1996.

Yarbrough, Robert. "Adolf Schlatter's, 'The Significance of Method for Theological Work: Translation and Commentary.'" *Southern Baptist Journal of Theology* 1, no. 2 (Summer 1997): 64–76.

———. *The Letters to Timothy and Titus.* The Pillar New Testament Commentary. Grand Rapids: Eerdmans, 2018.

Yarnell, Malcolm B. III. "Christian Justification: A Reformation Baptist View." *Criswell Theological Review,* New Series 2 (Spring 2005): 71–89.

———. "Eschatology." In *Historical Theology for the Church.* Edited by Jason G. Duesing and Nathan Finn. Nashville: B&H, 2021.

———. "Introduction and Notes to Hebrews." In *CSB Study Bible.* Nashville: Holman, 2017.

———. "John Locke and the Baptists." In *Baptist Political Theology.* Edited by Thomas S. Kidd, Paul D. Miller, and Andrew T. Walker. Nashville: B&H, 2023.

———. *John Locke's 'Letters of Gold'.* Oxford: Centre for Baptist History and Heritage, 2017.

———. *God the Trinity: Biblical Portraits.* Nashville: B&H, 2016.

————. *Royal Priesthood in the English Reformation*. New York: Oxford University Press, 2013.

————. "Shall We 'Build Bridges' or 'Pull Down Strongholds?'" *Southwestern Journal of Theology* 49, no. 2 (Spring 2007): 200–219.

————. *The Formation of Christian Doctrine*. Nashville: B&H, 2007.

————. "The Potential Impact of Calvinist Tendencies upon Local Baptist Churches." In *Whosoever Will: A Biblical-Theological Critique of Five-Point Calvinism*. Edited by David L. Allen and Steve W. Lemke. Nashville: B&H, 2010.

————. *Who Is the Holy Spirit? Biblical Insights into His Divine Person*. Nashville: B&H, 2019.

————. "Whose Jesus? Which Revelation?" *Midwestern Journal of Theology* 1, no. 1–2 (2003): 33–53.

Yarnell, Malcolm B. III, and David S. Dockery. "The Authority and Sufficiency of Scripture: An Introduction." In *The Authority and Sufficiency of Scripture*. Edited by Adam W. Greenway and David S. Dockery. Fort Worth: Seminary Hill Press, 2022.

Young, E. J. *Thy Word Is Truth*. Grand Rapids: Eerdmans, 1963.

Zachhuber, Johannes. "Religion vs. Revelation? A Deceptive Alternative in Twentieth-Century German Theology." In *Religious Experience and Contemporary Theological Epistemology*. Edited by L. Boeve, Y. De Maeseneer, and S. Van Den Bossche. Leuven: Leuven University Press, 2005.

Zachman, Randall C. "John Calvin." In *Christian Theologies of Scripture: A Comparative Introduction*. Edited by Justin S. Holcomb. New York: New York University Press, 2006.

Zaspel, Fred G. *The Theology of B. B. Warfield: A Systematic Summary*. Wheaton: Crossway, 2010.

Zemek, George J. *The Word of God in the Child of God: Exegetical, Theological, and Homiletical Reflections from the 119th Psalm*. Eugene, OR: Wipf & Stock, 2005.

Ziegler, Roland F. "Luther and Lutheran Orthodoxy: *Claritas* and *Perspicuitas Scripturae*." *Concordia Theological Quarterly* 81, no. 1–2 (January–April 2017): 119–36.

Zwingli, Ulrich. "*Of the Clarity and Certainty of the Word of God (1522).*" In *Zwingli and Bullinger*. Translated by Geoffrey W. Bromiley. Library of Christian Classics. Philadelphia: Fortress Press, 1953.

Zuck, Roy B. "The Role of the Holy Spirit in Hermeneutics." *Bibliotheca Sacra* 141, no. 562 (April-June 1984): 120–30.

NAME INDEX

SUBJECT INDEX

image of God, 9, 54, 73, 85, 208, 237, 261, 271
immanence, 175
inerrancy, 9, 39–40, 148, 211, 216, 221–23, 227–35, 238, 253, 344–45, 351, 359–61, 369
infallibility, 39, 148, 221–23, 226–27, 341–42, 344–45, 359, 369
inspiration, 2, 6–9, 39, 113–14, 147–48, 152, 158–64, 177, 183, 190–91, 196, 210, 220, 224, 226, 228, 230, 236–37, 253–54, 263, 306, 336, 341–42, 344, 354, 369, 403
   concursive, 8–10, 36, 149, 237
   definition, 149–50
   dictation theories, 153
   dynamic theories, 154–55
   history, 167–71
   Jesus's role, 166–67
   partial theories, 154
   verbal plenary, 155–57, 362
interpretation, 230–31, 264, 275, 282, 290, 326, 347, 359, 370–72, 384, 394
   Alexandrian school, 284
   Antiochene school, 284
   Christological, 128, 197, 297, 370, 375, 395–96
   fourfold method, 288–90, 373
   humility in approach, 264–68, 387
   literal, 284, 293, 296, 377
   Origen's threefold method, 285–86
   practice, 386–89
   proposed model, 390–96
   Reformation, 296–303
interpretive pluralism, 231–32

Israel, 3, 5, 22, 28, 38, 48, 51, 56, 59, 67, 91, 119, 123–24, 129–32, 134, 166, 173, 185, 198, 270, 273, 275, 285, 301, 317–18, 395, 403

J

Jesus Christ
   authority, 141–42, 248–50
   deity, 103, 139–40, 142, 282
   fulfillment, 121–22, 124–25, 127–28, 131, 133, 140, 166, 272–73, 370
   humanity, 22–23, 53, 138–40, 283
   incarnation, 72
   Lord and Savior, 6, 140
   message, 119–20
   New Testament, 134–41
   Old Testament, 128–34, 141
   post-resurrection appearances, 270–71
   revelation, 4, 21–22, 52, 58–59, 85, 141, 250
   Son of God, 19, 24, 53, 166
   Son of Man, 272–73
   trial, 100
   truth, 101–3, 105, 113
   Word of God, 9, 12–13, 58, 102, 112, 138, 166, 176, 220, 244–46
Jews, 56, 65, 180, 198, 272, 275, 303, 380
judgment, 17, 28, 37, 40–41, 53–55, 57, 61, 64–65, 67, 78, 89, 106, 110, 115–16, 166, 175, 248, 253–54, 271–72, 279, 302, 315, 323–24, 401
justification, 27, 41, 50–51, 77, 148, 252, 292, 294, 296, 309

SCRIPTURE INDEX

2 Chronicles
12 *312*
33 *312*

Ezra
10:1–4 *198*

Nehemiah
7:73b–8:18 *198*
8:3 *270*
8:7–8 *270*

Job
41:11 *52*

Psalms
8 *61–62*
8:5–6 *62*
19 *62–63*
19:1 *4*
19:1–2 *62*
19:1–6 *62*
19:2 *63*
19:3 *63*
19:7–14 *62*
22 *130*
31:5 *92*
41–43 *130*
78:2 *132*
82 *165–66*
82:1 *166*
82:6 *165–66*
82:7 *166*
82:8 *166*
95 *38*
110 *271*
118 *130*
119 *9, 175–76, 228*
119:89–96 *175*
119:105 *11, 401*

Isaiah
6:9–10 *18, 132*
7:9 *72, 75*
7:14 *131*
8:20 *330*
11:1 *133*
11:6–8 *133*
29:13 *254*
40:8 *244*
40:13 *52*
42:1–4 *132*
43:16–21 *133*
52:13–53:12 *124, 271*
52:15 *53*
53 *320*
55:9–12 *118*
55:11 *12, 244*
56:7 *132*
61 *371*
61:1–3 *124*
65:16 *92*

Jeremiah
1:1–9 *8*
1:10 *266*
23:9–40 *270*
23:18 *52*
31 *120*
31:15 *132*
31:31–34 *38, 121, 123*
36:29–31 *255*

Ezekiel
1:26b *271*
2:1 *271*
34:1–24 *270*
40–42 *186*
46:16 *152*

3:9 *53, 275*
4:1–16 *401*
4:10 *275*
5:32 *53*
6:5 *209*
6:19 *276*

Philippians
　2:5–11 *138*

Colossians
　1:13 *248*
　1:15–16 *138, 142*
　1:17 *141*
　1:26 *53*
　1:26–27 *275*
　1:27 *53*
　2:2 *53*
　2:2–3 *275*
　2:7 *65*
　2:8 *65*
　2:9 *142*
　4:3 *53*
　4:16 *185*

1 Thessalonians
　1:5a *150*
　1:9–10 *63*
　2:13 *244, 254*
　4:13–18 *125*
　4:17 *273*
　5:23 *285*

2 Thessalonians
　1:7–10 *125*
　1:10 *124*
　2:7 *53*

1 Timothy
　1:15 *254*

2:5–6 *273*
3:9 *53*
3:16 *53*
4:13 *371*
5:18 *159*
5:23 *209*
6:20 *65*

2 Timothy
　1:13a *192*
　1:13b *192*
　2:2 *141*
　2:7 *159*
　2:8 *127*
　2:15 *11, 260, 371, 400*
　2:19 *159*
　3 *157–58, 165*
　3:8–9 *159*
　3:11 *159*
　3:15 *7, 11, 160–61, 250–51, 330*
　3:15–16 *402*
　3:15–17 *13, 158, 249–50, 372*
　3:16 *113, 147, 161, 234, 245,*
　　　251, 254, 329–30, 400
　3:16–17 *7, 236*
　3:16b *7, 250*
　3:17 *7, 250, 330, 400*
　4:13 *185*
　4:14 *159*
　4:17–18 *159*

Titus
　1:9 *212*
　2:13 *142*

Hebrews
　1 *21*
　1:1–2 *120, 141, 166, 237*
　1:1–2a *176*
　1:1–3 *21, 44*

1:1–4 *22–23*
1:1–8 *142*
1:2 *4*
1:3 *24*
1:4 *21*
1:4–2:18 *21*
1:5–6 *37*
1:5–7 *23*
1:8 *138*
1:13 *23*
2 *21*
2:2–3 *28*
2:6 *23*
2:6–7 *37*
2:9 *28*
2:12 *23*
3 *21*
3–4 *21*
3:7 *23, 25, 255*
3:7–8 *28*
3:7–11 *38*
3:7–19 *41*
3:10 *23*
3:15 *23, 25*
4 *17, 21*
4:1 *28, 31*
4:1–2 *41*
4:3 *28, 255*
4:4 *23, 255*
4:5 *28, 31, 255*
4:7 *23, 25, 255*
4:9–11 *28*
4:11 *31*
4:12 *12, 17, 24, 118, 244, 257*
4:12–13 *111, 267*
4:13 *257*
4:15 *139*
4:16 *28*
5 *21*

5–6 *21*
5:6 *23*
5:12 *25*
6:5 *24*
6:13 *10*
7 *21*
7–10 *21*
7:11 *23*
7:21 *23*
8 *21*
8:9–11 *23*
8:13 *23*
9:6–10 *38*
9:8 *24*
9:14 *29*
9:20 *23*
9:26 *29*
10 *21*
10:7–9 *23*
10:15–16 *23*
10:15–17 *38*
10:29 *28*
10:30 *23*
11 *21, 59*
11:2 *41*
11:3 *24*
11:4–7 *41*
11:17–26 *41*
11:25 *196*
12 *21*
12:2 *41, 155*
12:19 *24*
12:21 *24*
12:26 *23, 25*
13 *21*
13:5–6 *23*
13:7 *24*
13:8 *37*
13:21 *37*